I0729554

# CATCHING THE PERFECT WAVE
## America's most important surf photographer
## of the 1960s and 1970s

At a time when surfing is more popular than ever, it's fitting to look back at the years that brought the sport into the mainstream. Developed by Hawaiian Islanders over five centuries ago, surfing began to peak on the mainland in the 1950s—becoming not just a sport, but a way of life, admired and exported across the globe. One of the key image-makers from that period is LeRoy Grannis, a surfer since 1931, who began photographing the longboard era of the early 1960s in both California and Hawaii.

This edition brings back Grannis's hair-raising, sold-out Collector's Edition, curated from the photographer's personal archives, to showcase his most vibrant work in a compact and affordable format—from the bliss of catching the perfect wave at San Onofre to dramatic wipeouts at Oahu's famed North Shore.

An innovator in the field, Grannis suction-cupped a waterproof box to his board, enabling him to change film in the water and stay closer to the action than any other photographer of the time. He also covered the emerging surf lifestyle, from "surfer stomps" and hordes of fans at surf contests to board-laden woody station wagons along the Pacific Coast Highway. It is in these iconic images that a sport still in its adolescence embodied the free-spirited nature of an era—a time before shortboards and celebrity endorsements, when surfing was at its bronzed best.

Cover
**Duke Classic Finalists, Sunset Beach, 1969**

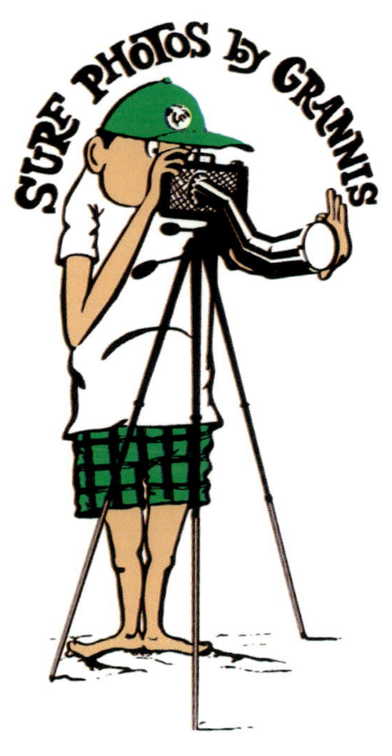

SURF PHOTOS by GRANNIS

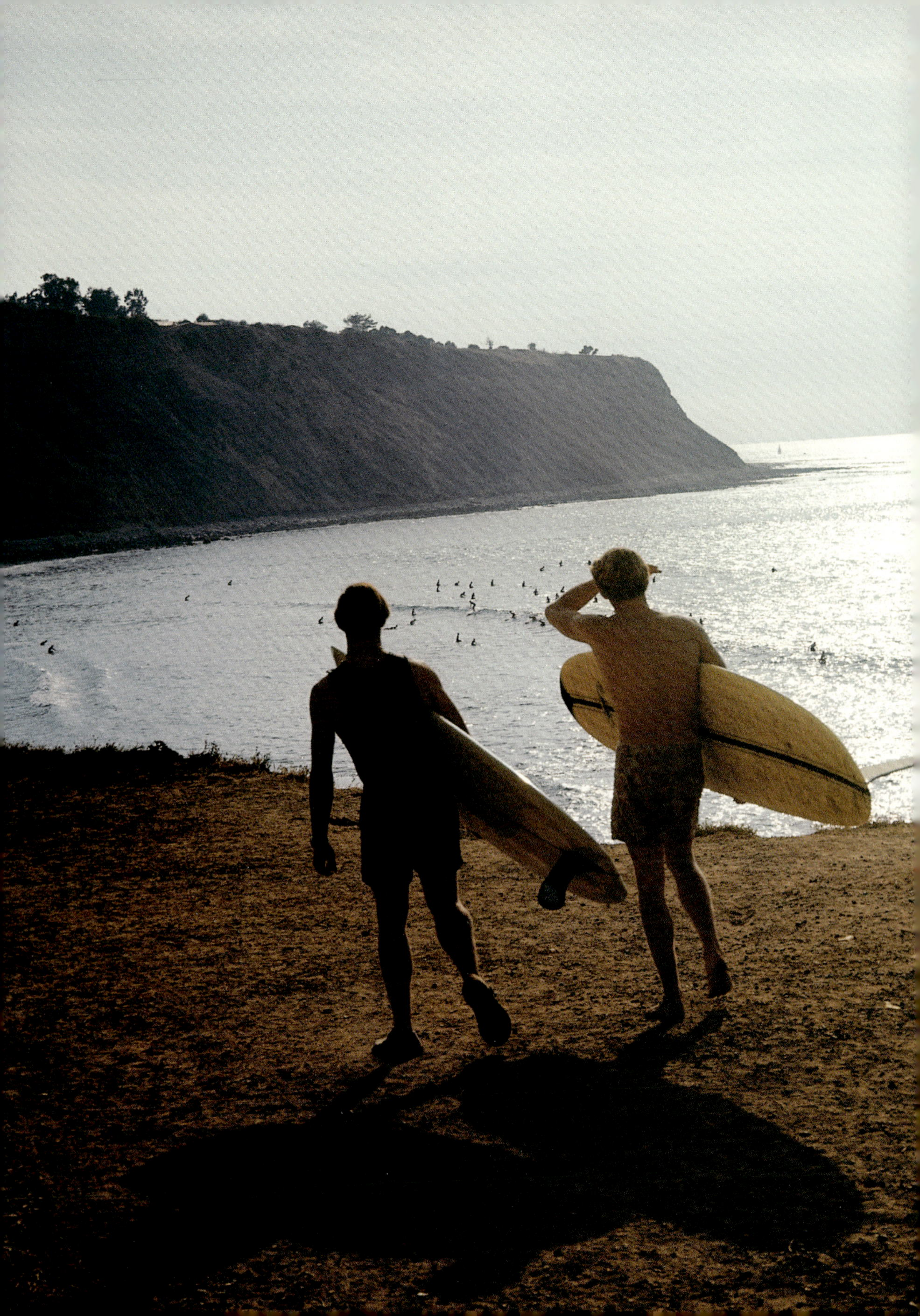

# LEROY GRANNIS

# SURF PHOTOGRAPHY

## OF THE 1960s AND 1970s

Jim Heimann (Ed.)
Steve Barilotti (Essay)

TASCHEN

# Contents



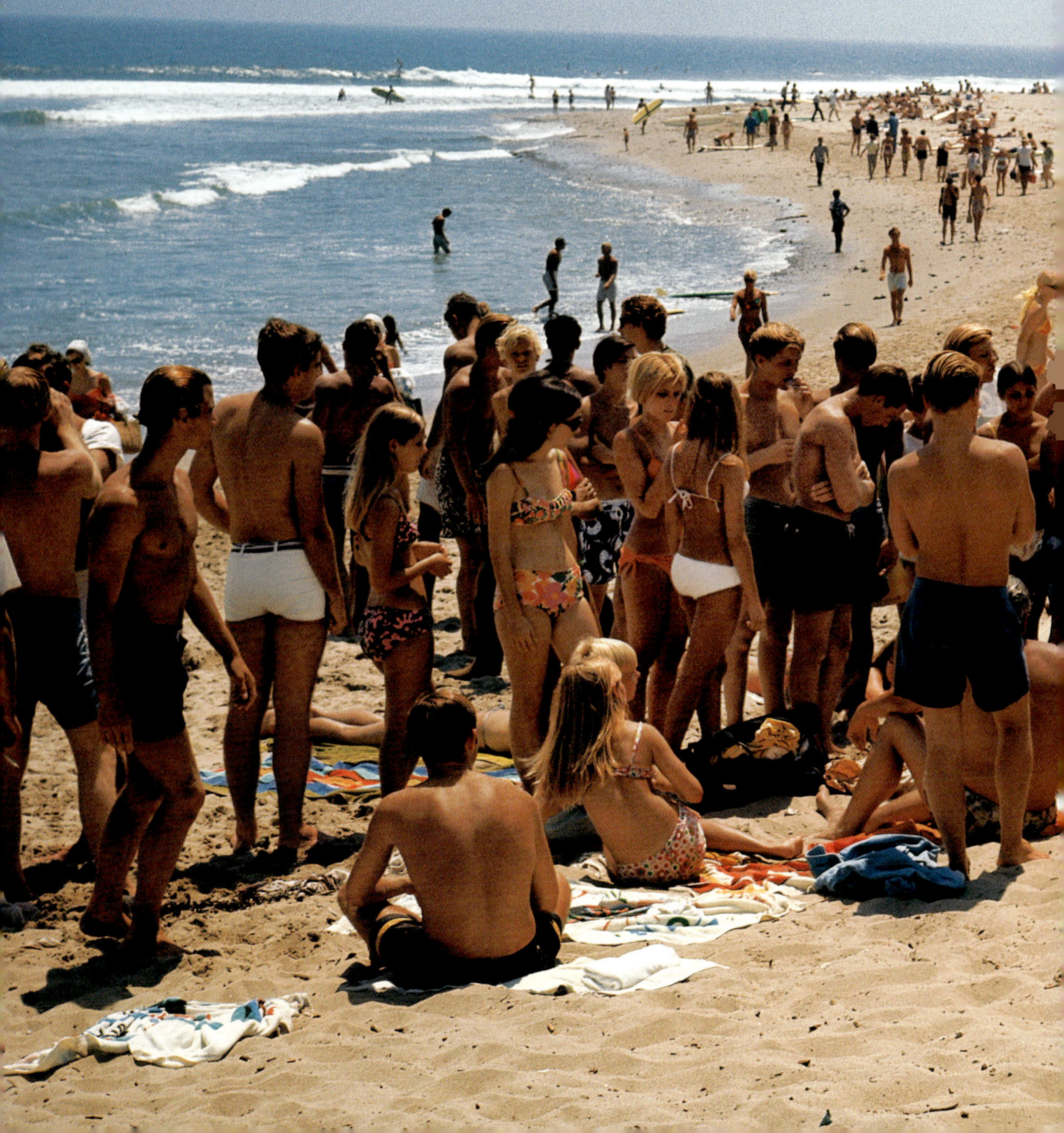

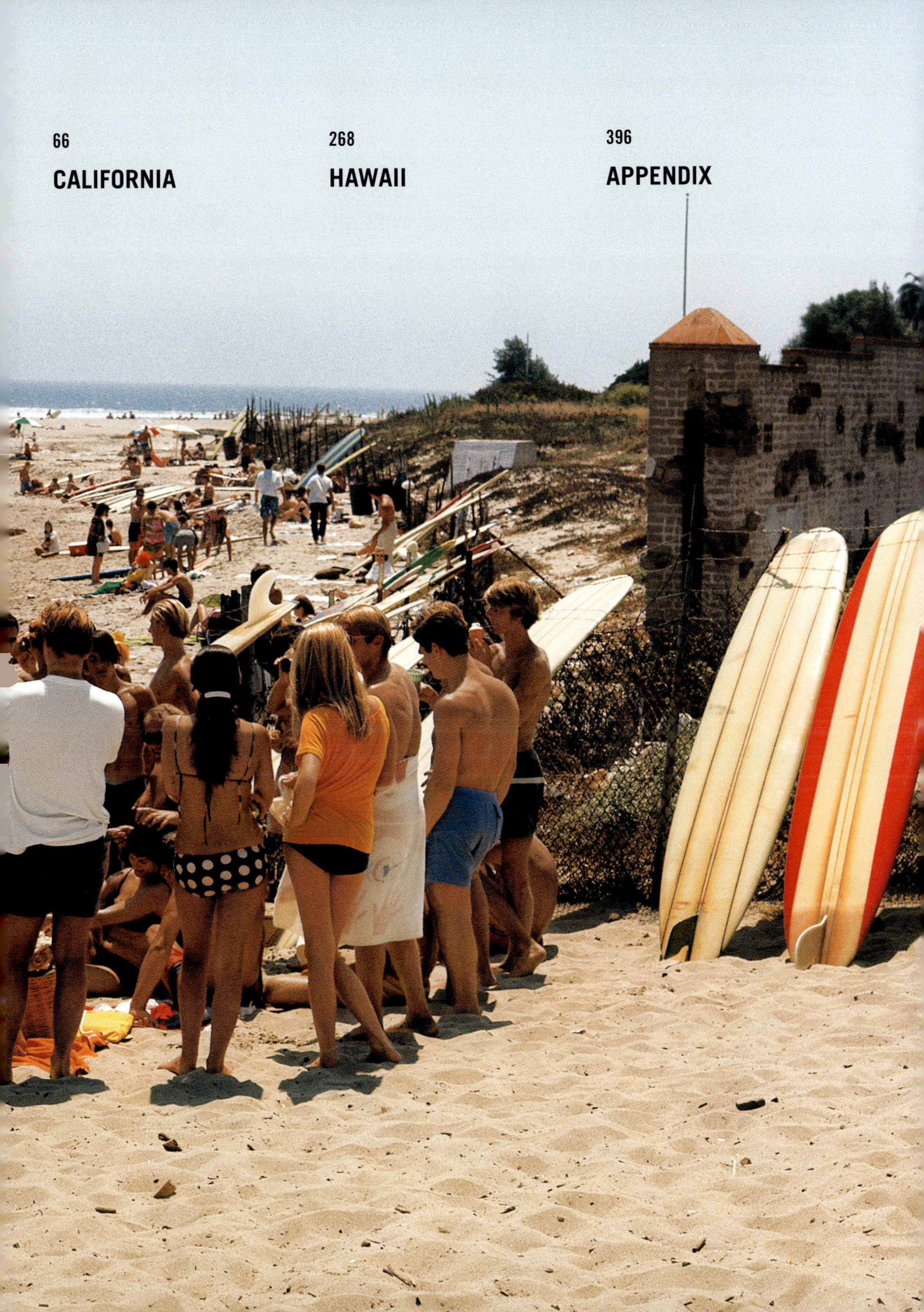
66
CALIFORNIA
268
HAWAII
396
APPENDIX

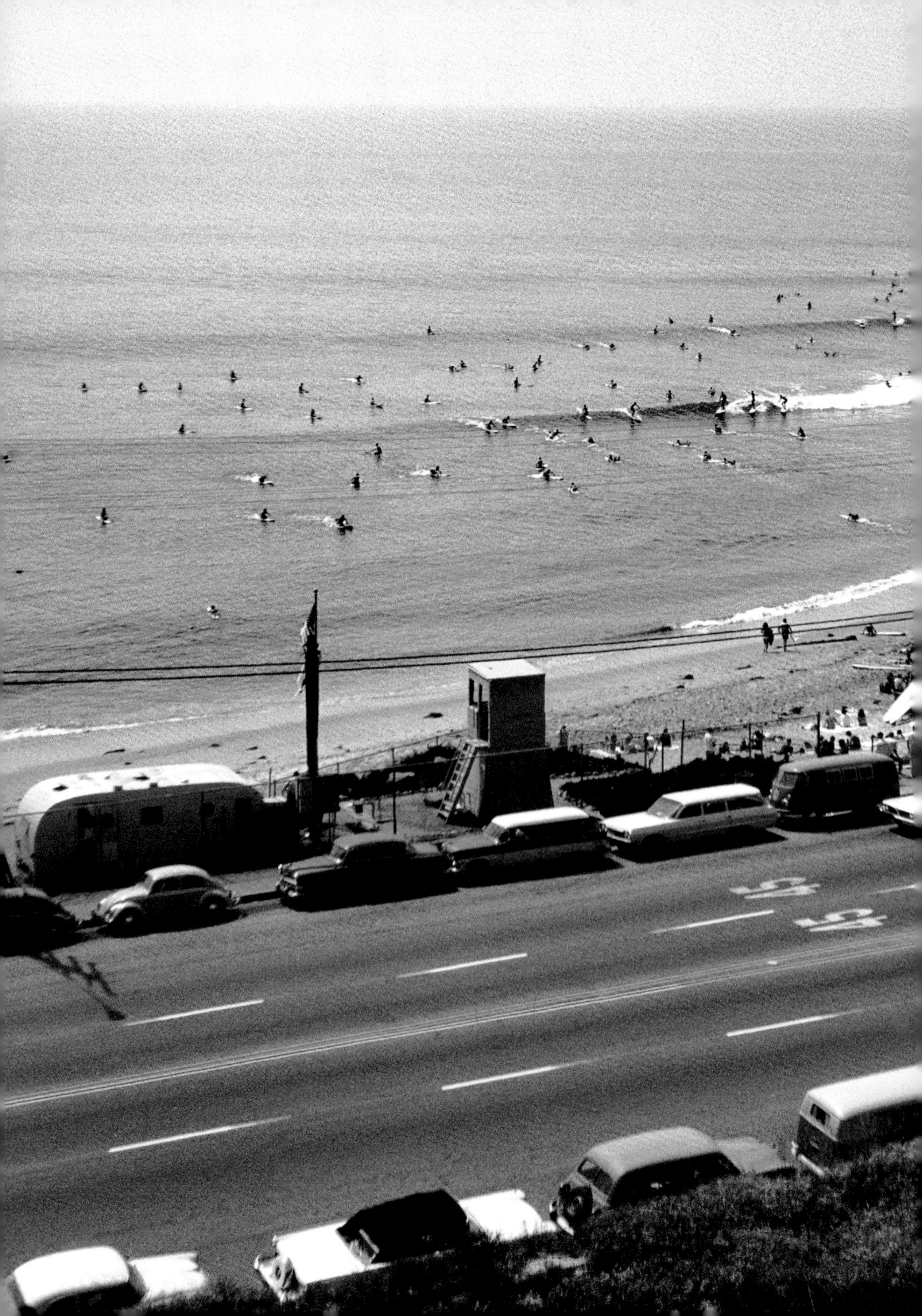

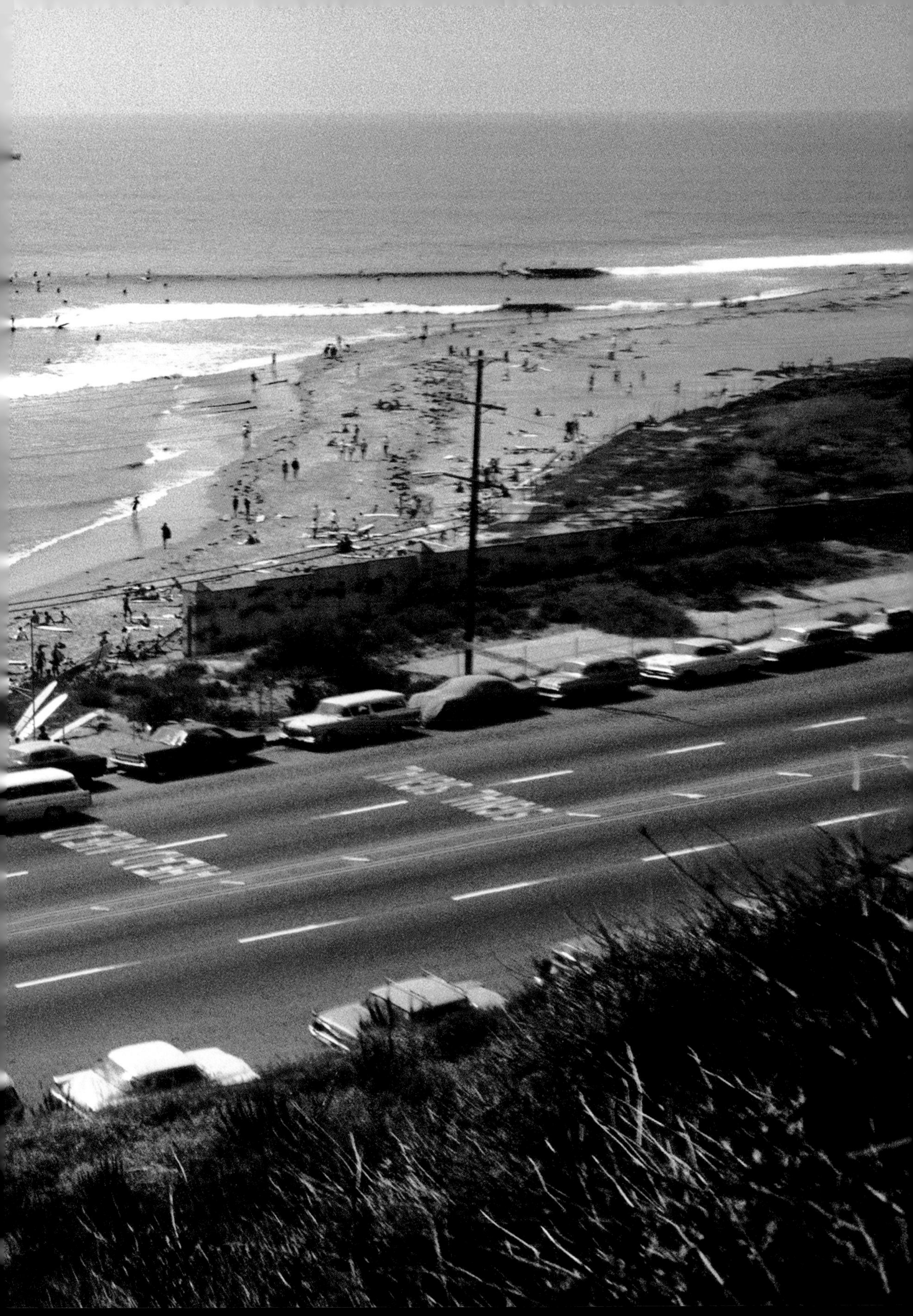

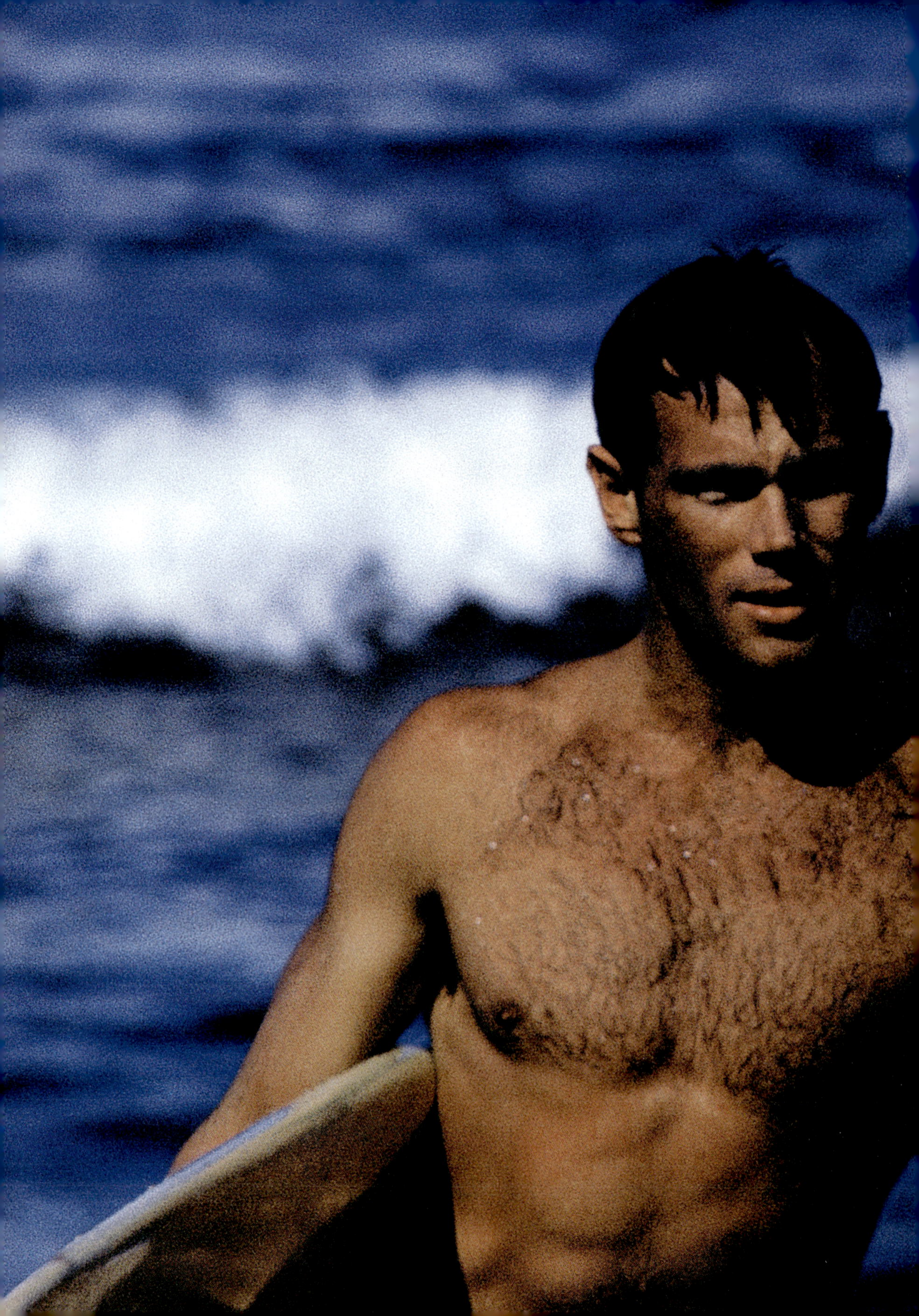

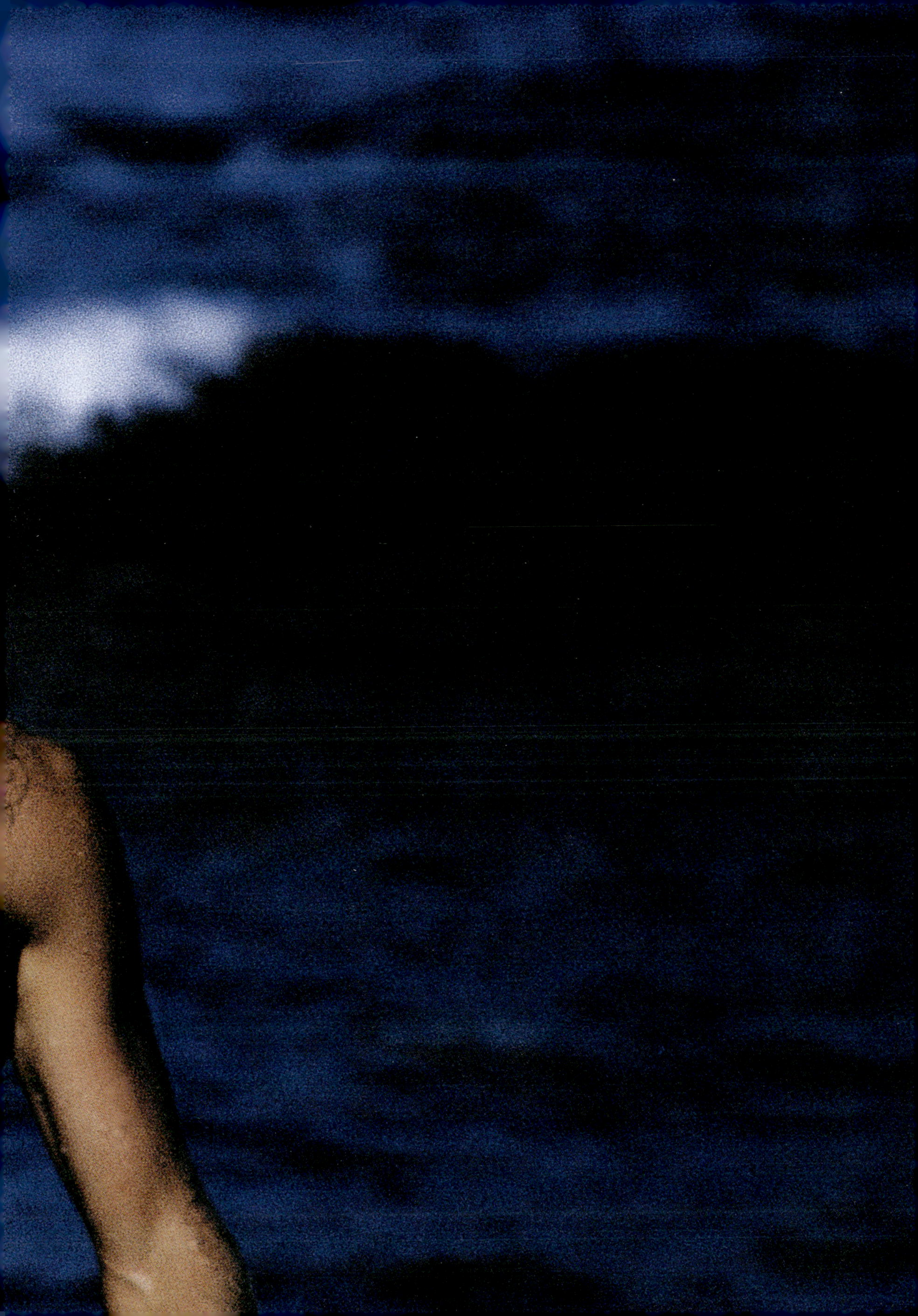

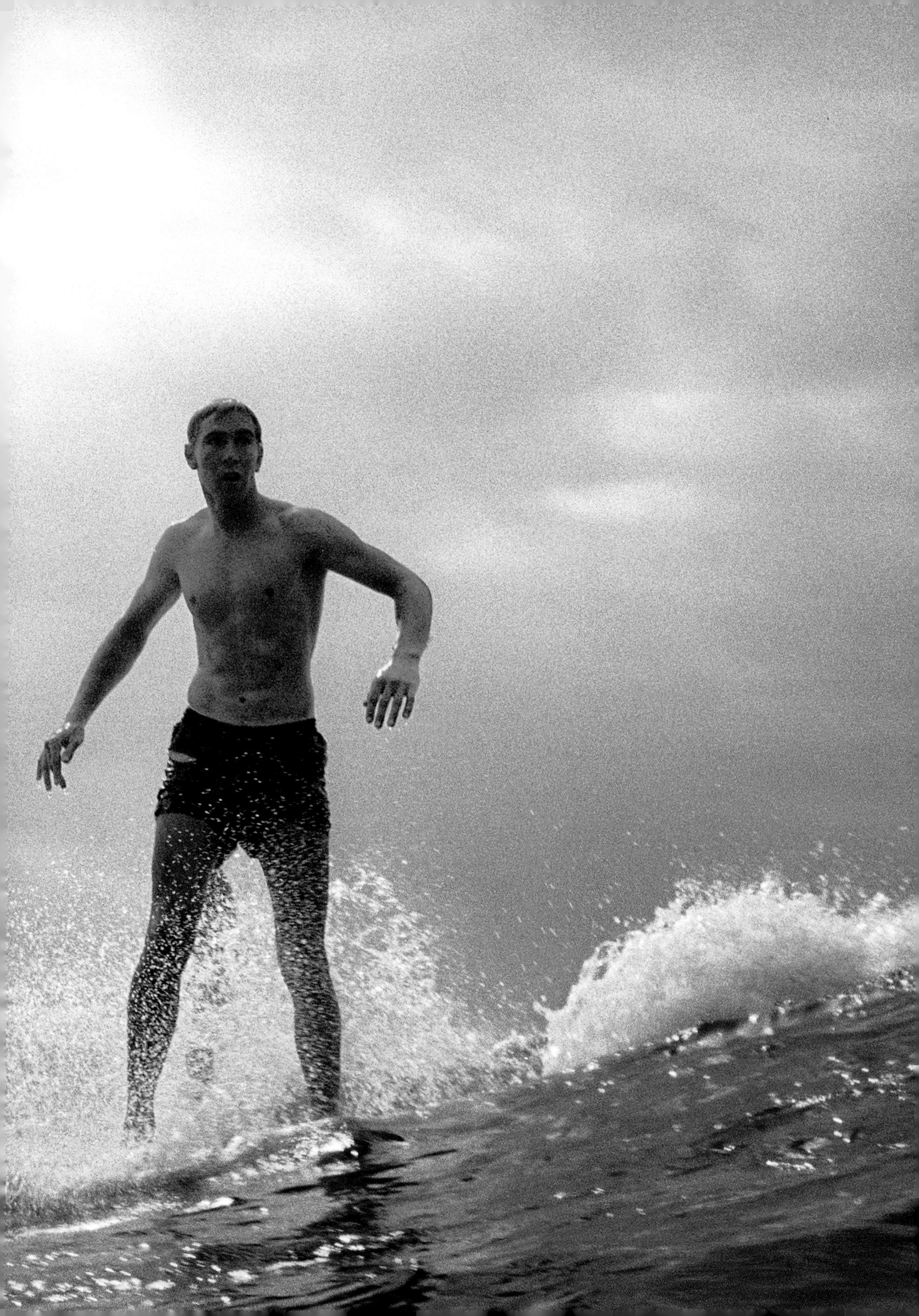

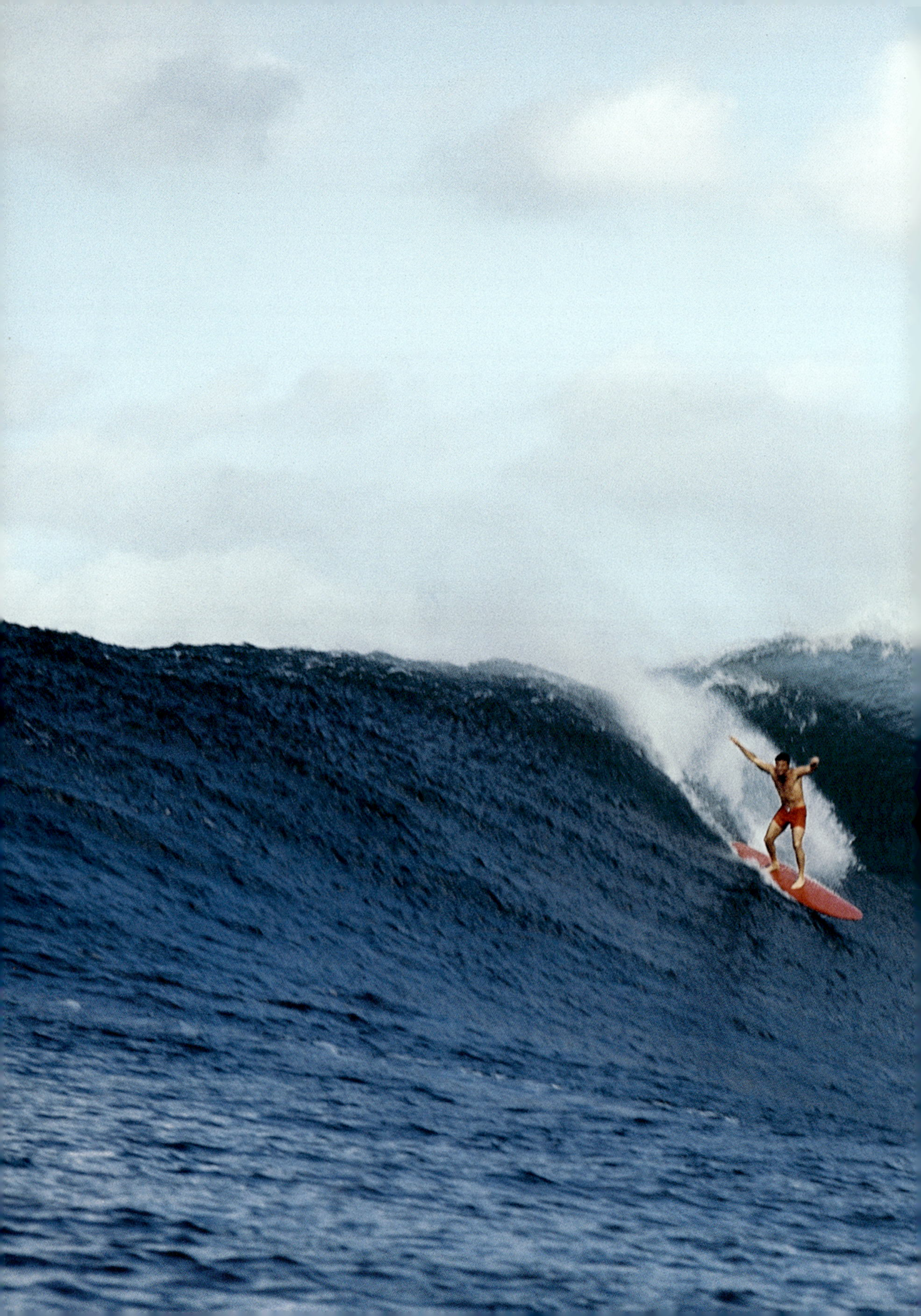

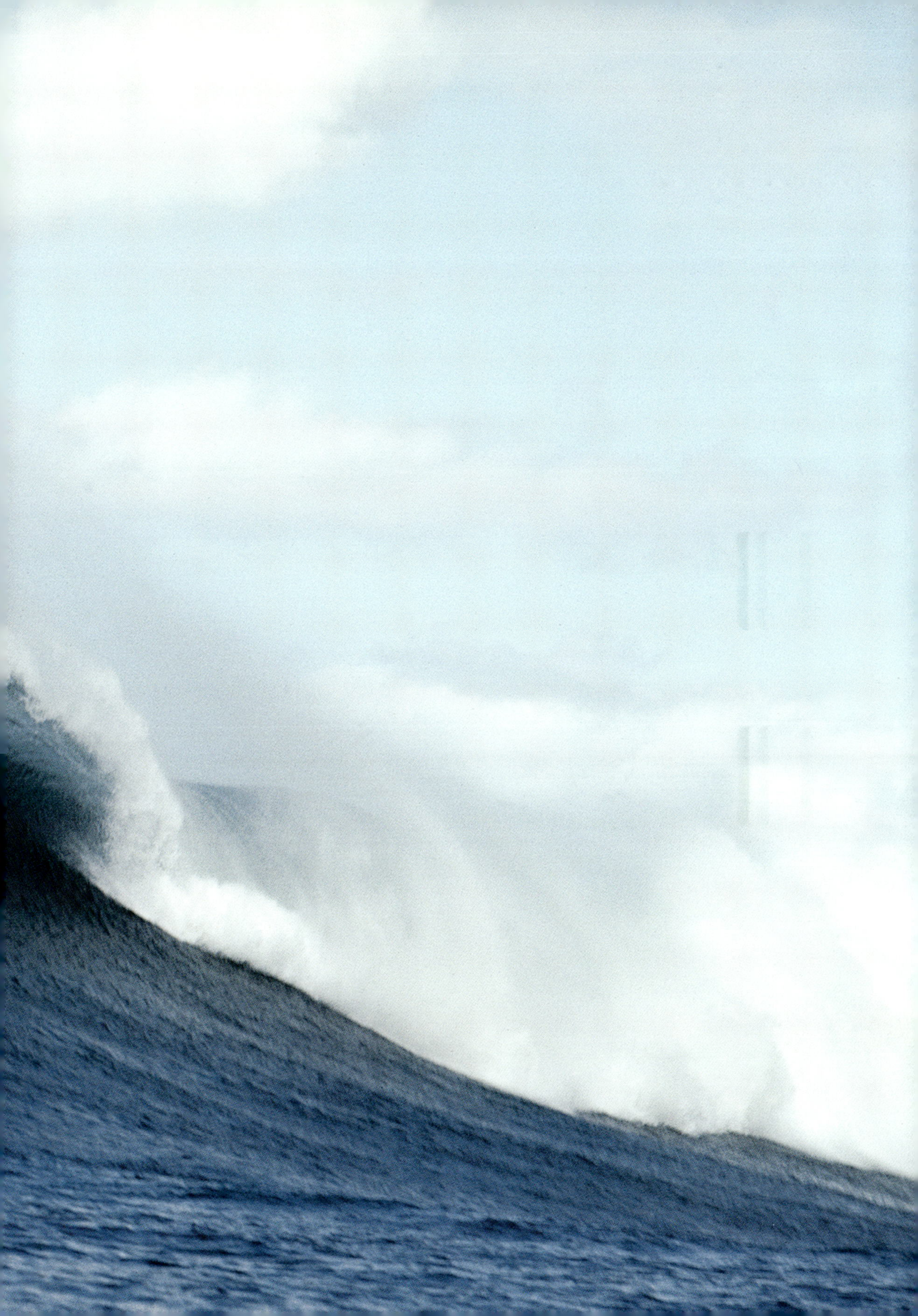

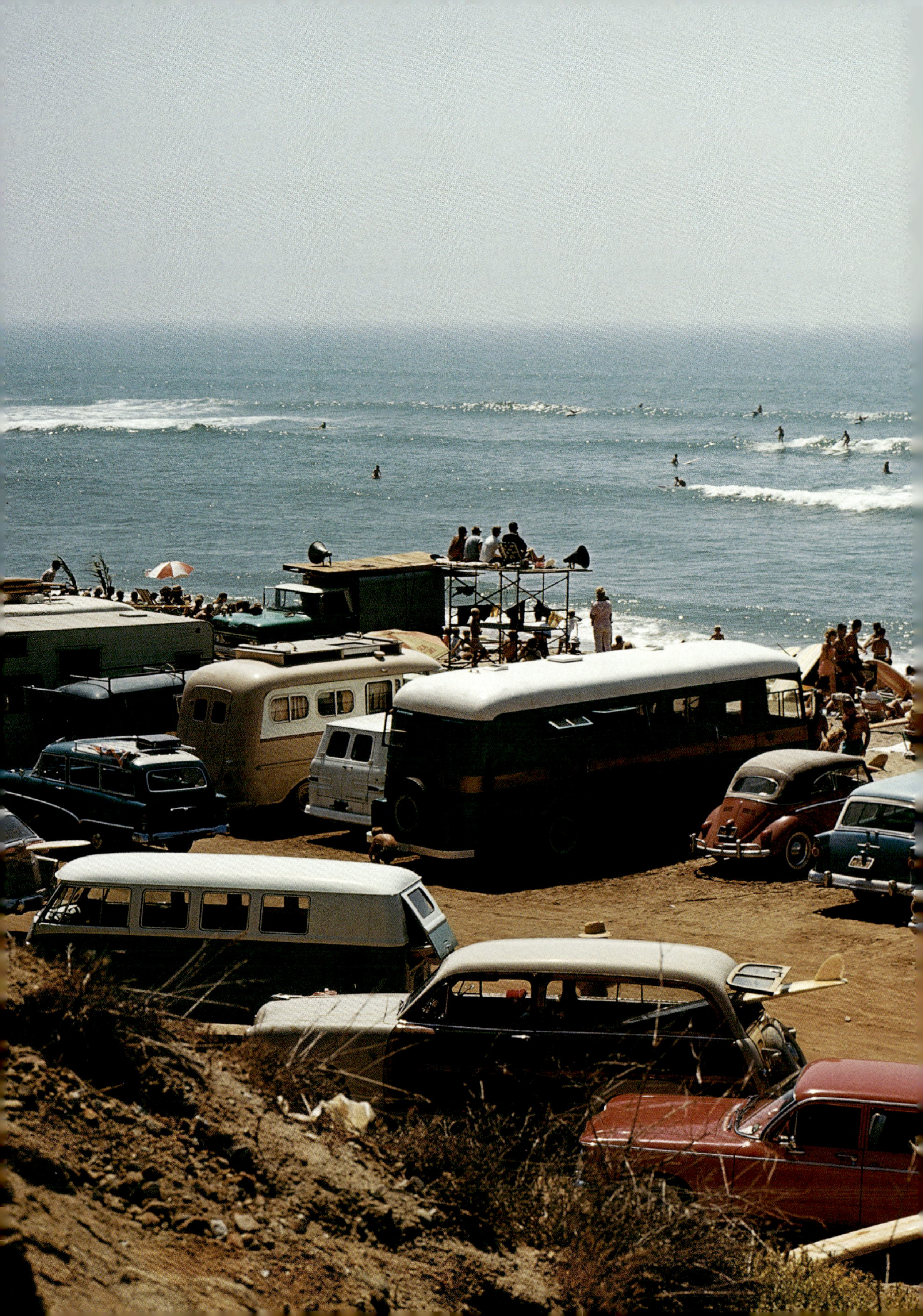

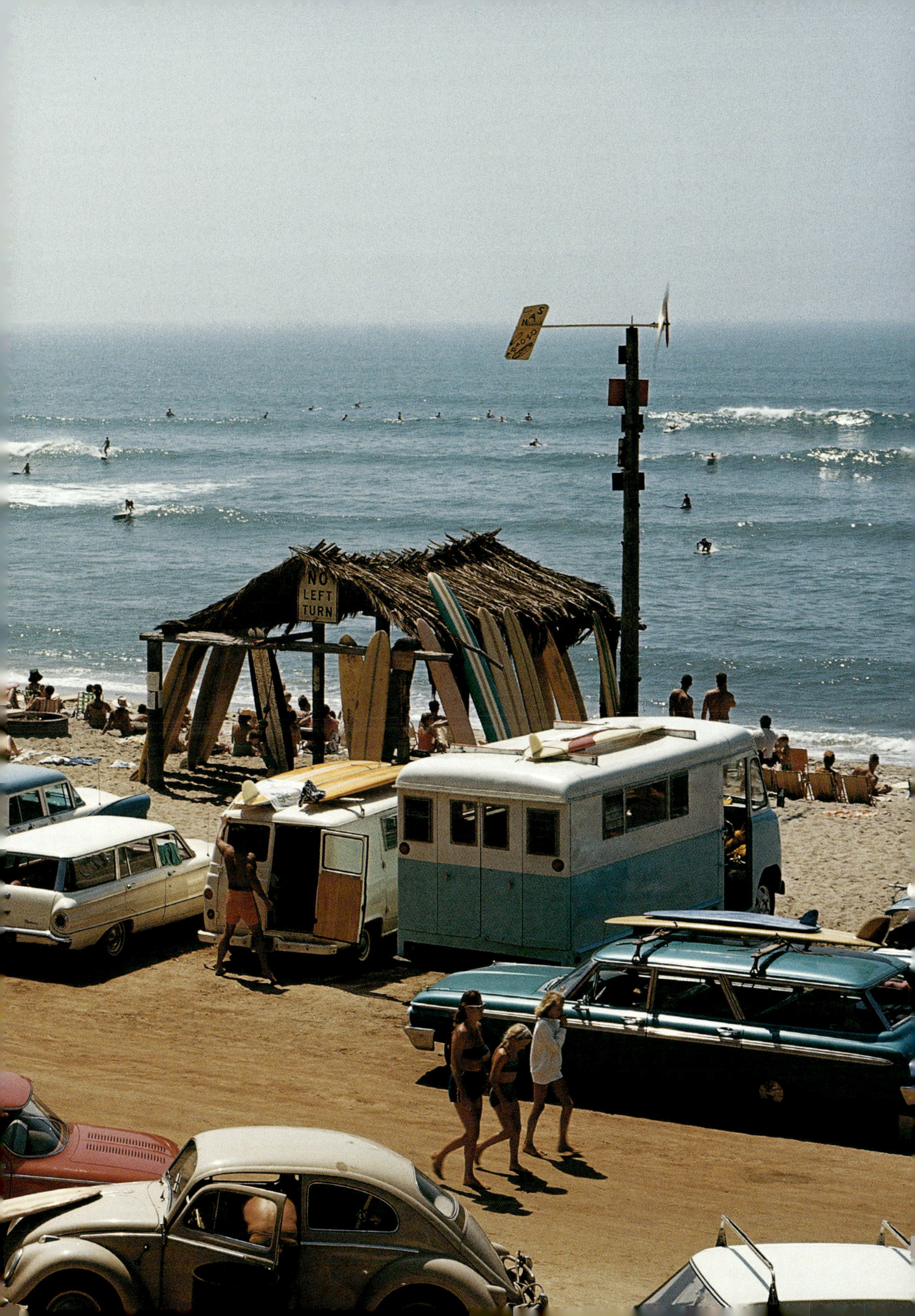

NO
LEFT
TURN

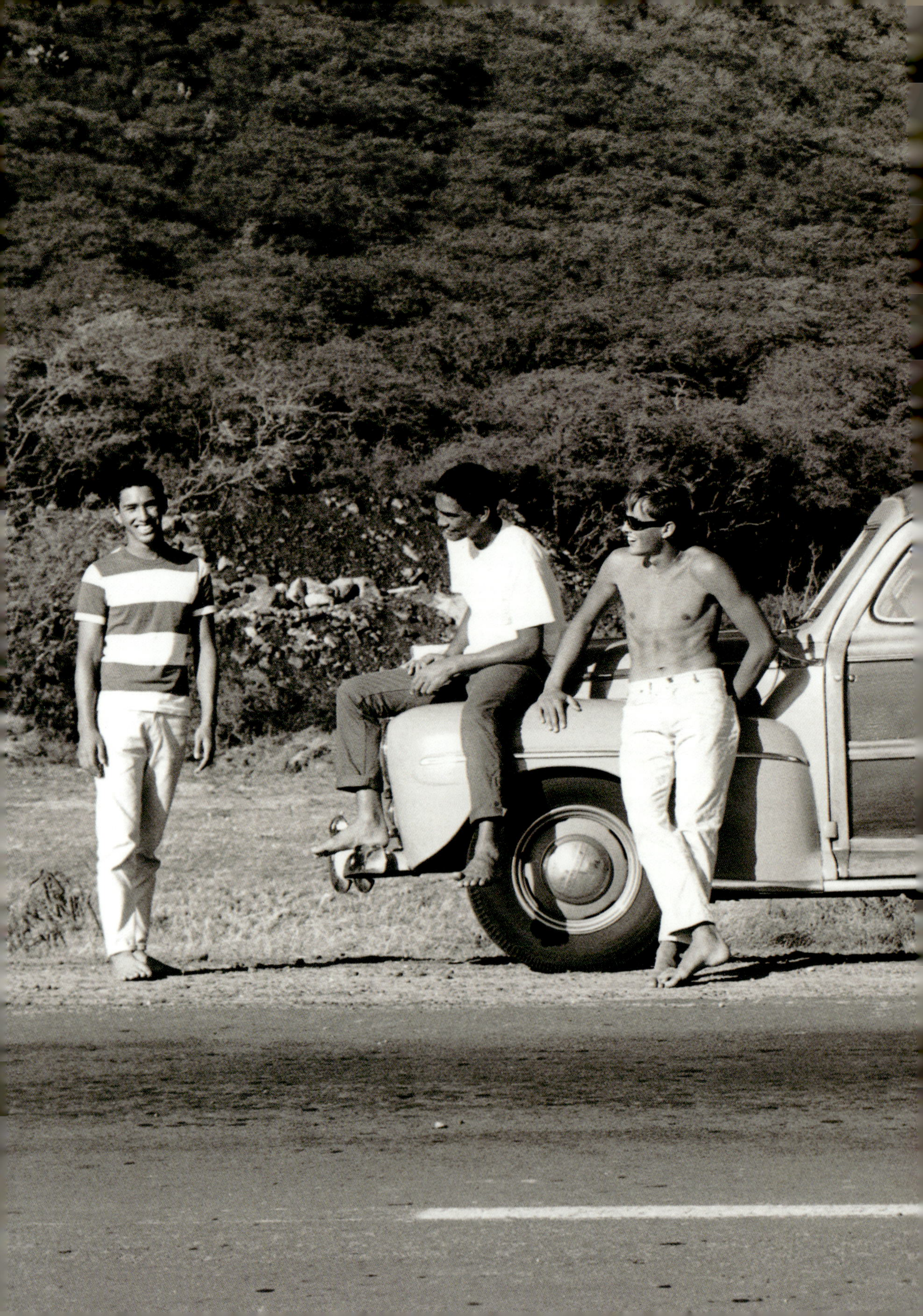

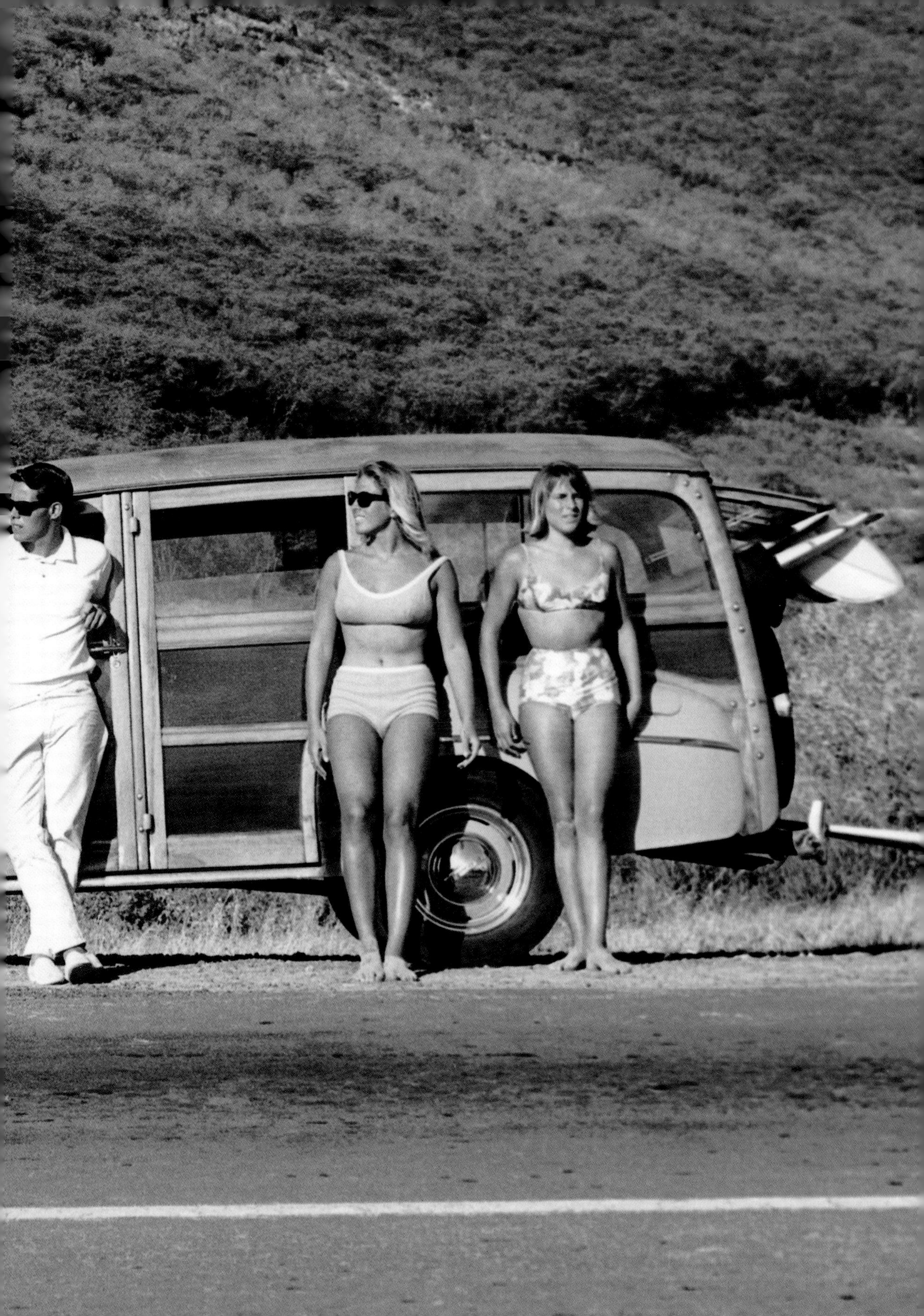

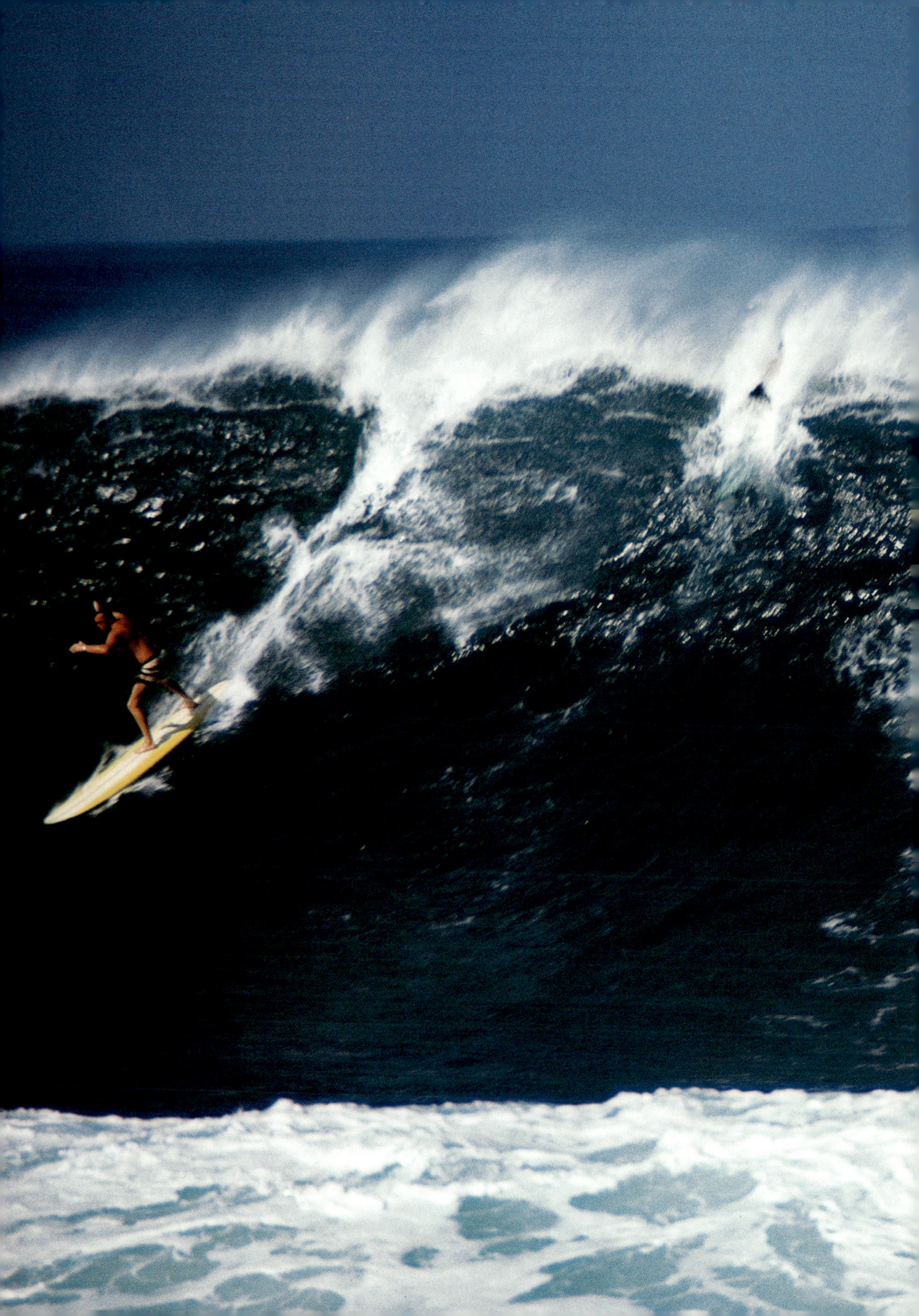

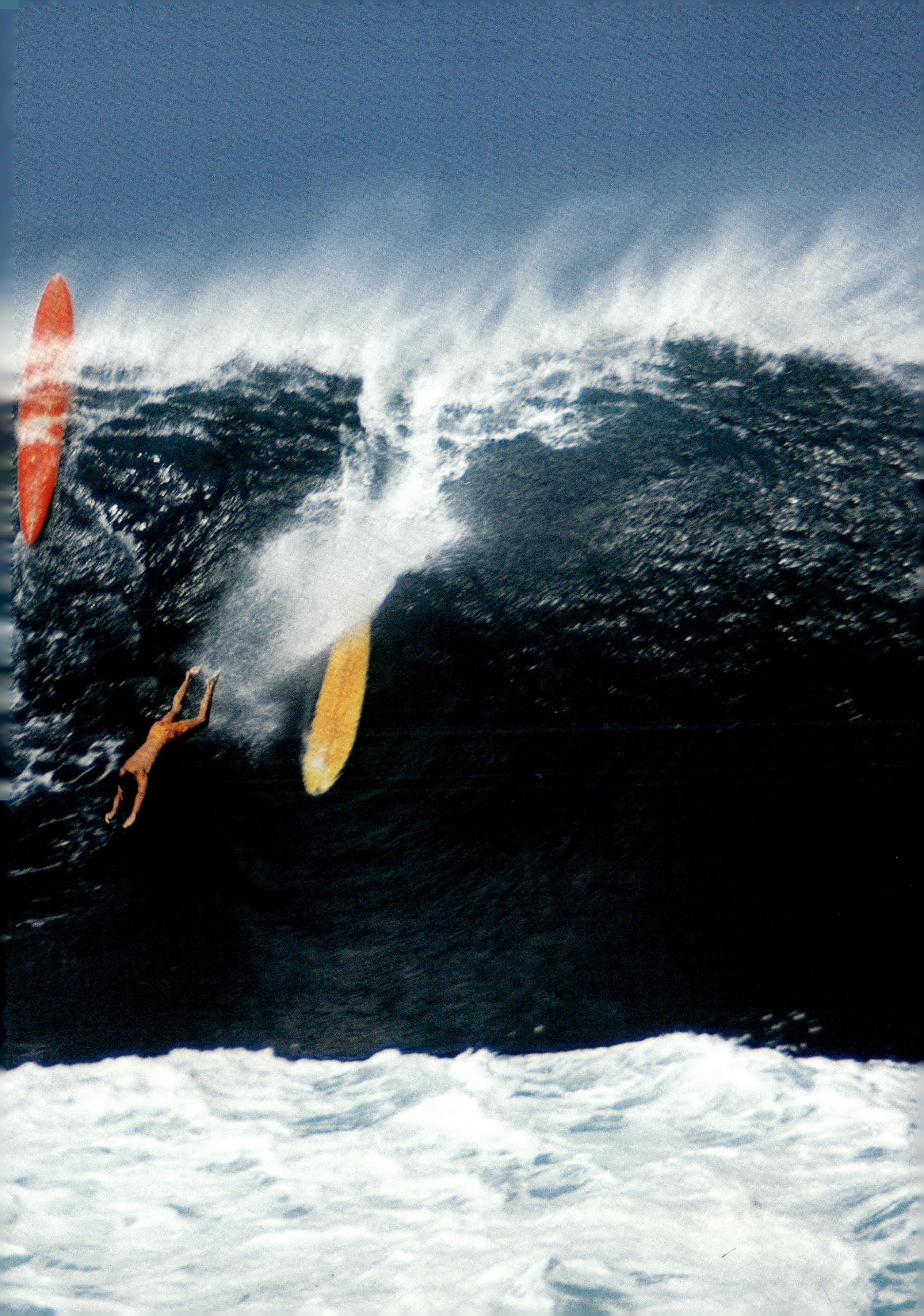

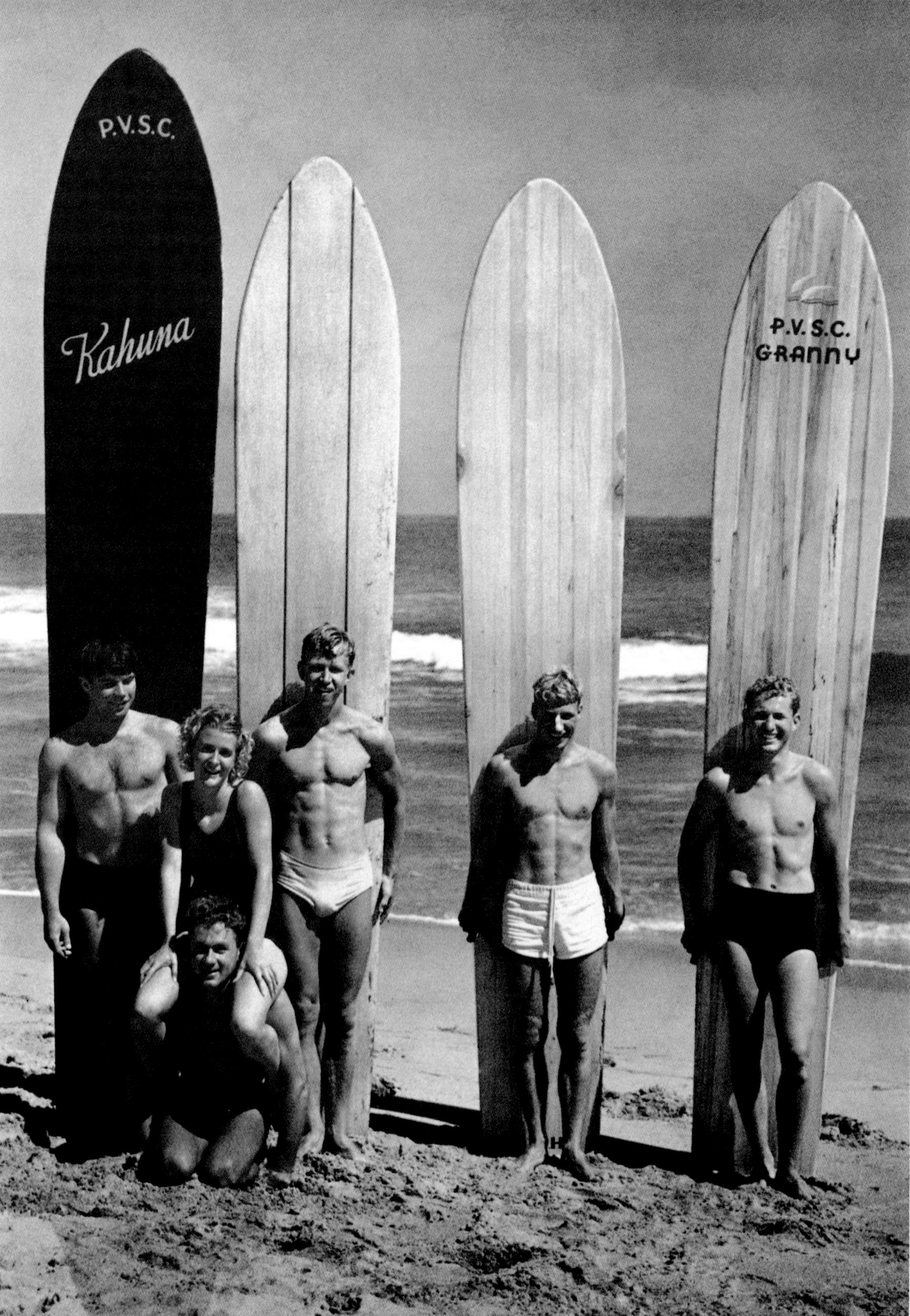

P.V.S.C.
Kahuna
P.V.S.C.
GRANNY

# CAPTURING THE PERFECT WAVE:
## The Surf Photography of LeRoy Grannis

*By Steve Barilotti*

The revolution was shot in black-and-white, on a Sunday afternoon, at 250th of a second. October 2, 1966. World Surfing Championships, Ocean Beach, San Diego. Forty thousand spectators jammed the beach and the newly opened Ocean Beach pier. At the exact moment that eighteen-year-old Robert "Nat" Young hoisted an awkward California-shaped trophy over his head, there were more than three hundred and forty thousand U.S. troops in Vietnam, Brian Wilson was on the verge of releasing his masterpiece, "Good Vibrations," and LSD would remain legal for three more months. Surfboards averaged ten and a half feet in length and weighed thirty pounds. Nat Young was now world champion. And the surfing world had quietly tilted ninety degrees off its axis.

A tall, brash Australian, Young was flanked on the victory dais by the soft-spoken Hawaiian Jock Sutherland and California small-wave whiz kid Corky Carroll. A small group of local and national media, among them *Newsweek* and *The New York Times*, jostled to get close to the winners. LeRoy Grannis, *International Surfing Magazine's* sole staff photographer, roamed the fringes of the crowd, methodically snapping off trophy shots with his salt-corroded Pentax S camera. At a key instant in the ceremony he focused and framed the jubilant Young cheering, "I feel jazzed!"

Despite the palpable buzz on the beach, Grannis remained stoically detached. For him, the event was simply the culmination of a year of weekends shooting club contests up and down the Southern California coast. Grannis, then forty-nine, was in his sixth year of surf photography and thirty-fifth as a surfer. The next weekend he would likely be back up at Malibu or Huntington Beach for another small regional contest, and the World Surfing Championships qualifying process would start anew.

**LeRoy Grannis came to surf photography in late 1959, not as a professional** or an artist, but as a middle-aged family man looking for a hobby to reduce the stress of his job. Luckily, he happened to pick up his camera at a pivotal point in surfing history. Born in Hermosa Beach, California, in 1917, Grannis was a holdover from the redwood era of West Coast surfing, when a scant two hundred California surfers rode massive eleven-foot boards on the slow rollers off San Onofre and Palos Verdes Cove with a dignified, gentlemanly esprit. They were the first generation of mainland surfers to take up the ancient sport, newly exported by Hawaiians George Freeth and Duke Kahanamoku. They were also

*Down through the ages, references to surf riding have survived; first via the chant, later in writing, and now most eloquently by the medium of the camera.*

—**Tom Blake,** pioneer surfer and surf photographer

**Palos Verdes Surfing Club, Hollywood by the Sea, California,1938**

Left to right: Tulie Clark, Mary Ann Hawkins on E. J. Oshier's shoulders, Chuck Allen, Hal Pearson, LeRoy Grannis.

Von links nach rechts: Tulie Clark, Mary Ann Hawkins auf den Schultern von E. J. Oshier, Chuck Allen, Hal Pearson, LeRoy Grannis.

De gauche à droite : Tulie Clark, Mary Ann Hawkins sur les épaules de E. J. Oshier, Chuck Allen, Hal Pearson et LeRoy Grannis.

part of surfing's renaissance, which grew from a handful of Hawaiian beach boys in Waikiki during the late nineteenth century.

Raised a block from the ocean in Hermosa Beach, Grannis began surfing at age fourteen on a borrowed redwood plank that weighed close to a hundred pounds. It was there, bobbing in the gentle swells beneath the Hermosa Beach Pier, that he met fellow surfers Lewis "Hoppy" Swarts, another Hermosa beach native, and John "Doc" Ball, an affable University of Southern California dental student who was ten years older than Grannis. The three became lifelong friends.

Ball was an expert surfer, and soon talked the teenage Grannis and Swarts into tackling the better-formed waves of Palos Verdes Cove, five miles to the south. The cove was a second home to a zealous crew of dedicated surfers, mostly jobless young men in their twenties who were waiting out the Depression in grand low-budget style. A self-reliant group, they built their own surfboards, sewed their own surf trunks, and pooled their meager cash resources to buy gasoline (and the occasional jug of cheap wine) for trips to Malibu or San Onofre. Many were also expert divers and would often harvest free feasts of lobster and abalone from the surrounding tide pools. In 1935 Ball organized the Palos Verdes Surfing Club and inducted Swarts and Grannis (by now nicknamed "Granny") in 1936.

**Surfers made for natural subjects for photographers, and the image of** bronzed Hawaiian watermen poised majestically against Diamond Head quickly became a postcard cliché. Surf imagery has always been created primarily by the surfers themselves. The surf photographers were all self-taught hobbyists; none made a living from the sales of their photos. Tom Blake, the pioneering surfer/designer, built a waterproof box for his Graflex camera in 1929 and began shooting Hawaiian beach boys from his board as they hurtled past on twelve-foot *alaia* boards in the long, rolling waves off Waikiki. He taught Doc Ball, who in turn had a big influence on Don James and, later, LeRoy Grannis. Ball was a talented photographer with a natural eye, constantly experimenting with novel angles and building prototype waterproof housings so he could take his cameras out into the waves. His candid snapshots of his buddies and their girlfriends captured the brief, halcyon era of pure surfing that vanished shortly after the Japanese attack on Pearl Harbor, Hawaii, in 1941.

With the onset of World War II, California surfing went into steep decline as most able-bodied young watermen over eighteen either enlisted or were drafted into military service. Many never returned. Although Grannis was newly married and had a baby daughter by 1941, he enlisted in the U.S. Army Air Forces two years later. By the time he graduated from flight school, however, the war had ended, and he was discharged in 1946. Back home in Hermosa Beach, Grannis became a communications engineer, and found a steady job as a switchboard installer with Pacific Bell Telephone (Grannis remained on active reserve with the U.S. Air Force, retiring as a major in 1977).

In the years following the war, Grannis surfed sporadically, but became increasingly absorbed in the demands of his job and raising four children. In late 1959 he was diagnosed with a stress-related stomach ulcer, and his doctor rec-ommended a relaxing pastime. Surf photography appeared a logical choice, as

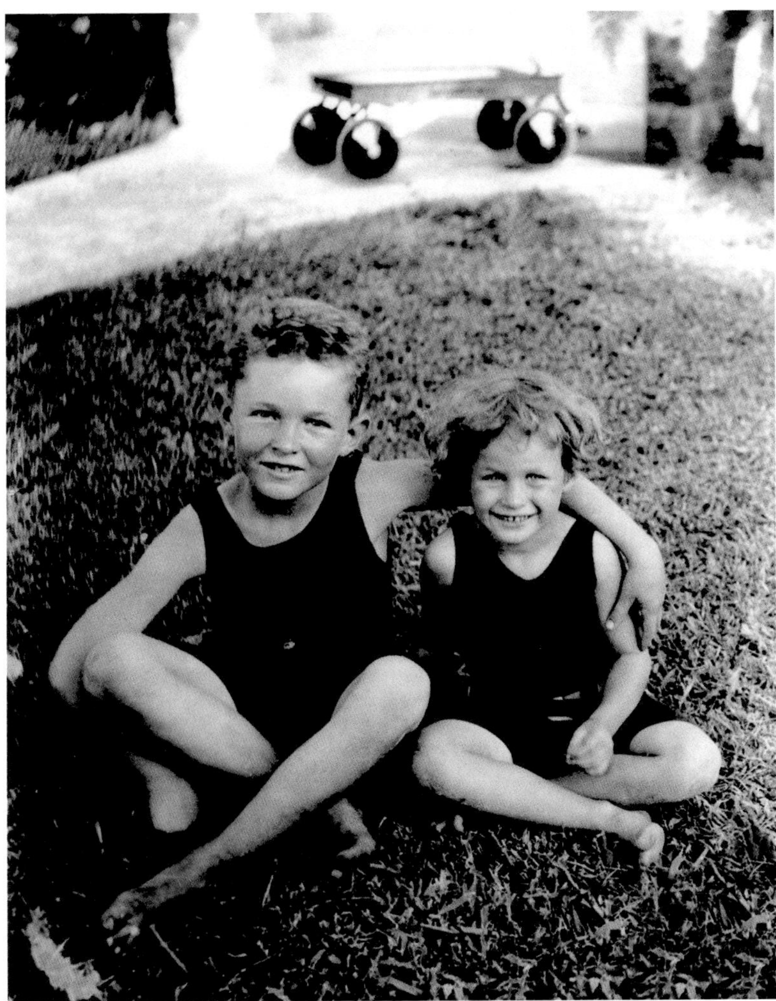

Grannis lived a few blocks from the ocean and his teenage son Frank had recently begun surfing. By June 1960 Grannis had built a darkroom in his garage and developed a few rudimentary photos, their style influenced by Doc Ball.

That summer, with an East German 35mm camera, he began shooting 22nd Street in Hermosa Beach, a stretch of undistinguished South Bay beach break that attracted a crew of young surfers eager to show off for his lens. The undisputed leader of the 22nd Street gang was Dewey Weber, who at twenty-three had already starred in several surf films and had just opened his own surfboard shop in nearby Venice Beach. The small (five-foot-three) but powerful Weber surfed aggressively and pushed the rest of the crew, which included Henry Ford, Freddie Pfahler, and Mike Zuetell, to perform their best. By the end of 1960 Grannis had shot and developed more than twenty-five hundred frames.

Grannis's darkroom was the closest thing to a one-hour photo lab in the South Bay, and at a time when surf magazines came out bimonthly, surfers were ravenous for current shots of themselves. "Sometimes I'd go right from shooting at 22nd Street to the darkroom, and before I knew it there'd be half a dozen guys

**LeRoy Grannis, Hermosa Beach, California, 1926**

LeRoy, age nine, with sister Vera, age seven, at their parents' house on Monterey Boulevard. In 1926, Hermosa's population was just 6,500. Photograph by Blanche Grannis.

LeRoy im Alter von neun Jahren mit seiner siebenjährigen Schwester Vera vor dem Haus der Eltern auf dem Monterey Boulevard. 1926 hatte Hermosa nur 6.500 Einwohner. Fotografiert von Blanche Grannis.

LeRoy à l'âge de neuf ans et sa sœur Vera, âgée de sept ans, devant la maison familiale sur Monterey Boulevard. En 1926, Hermosa ne comptait que 6 500 habitants. Photo : Blanche Grannis.

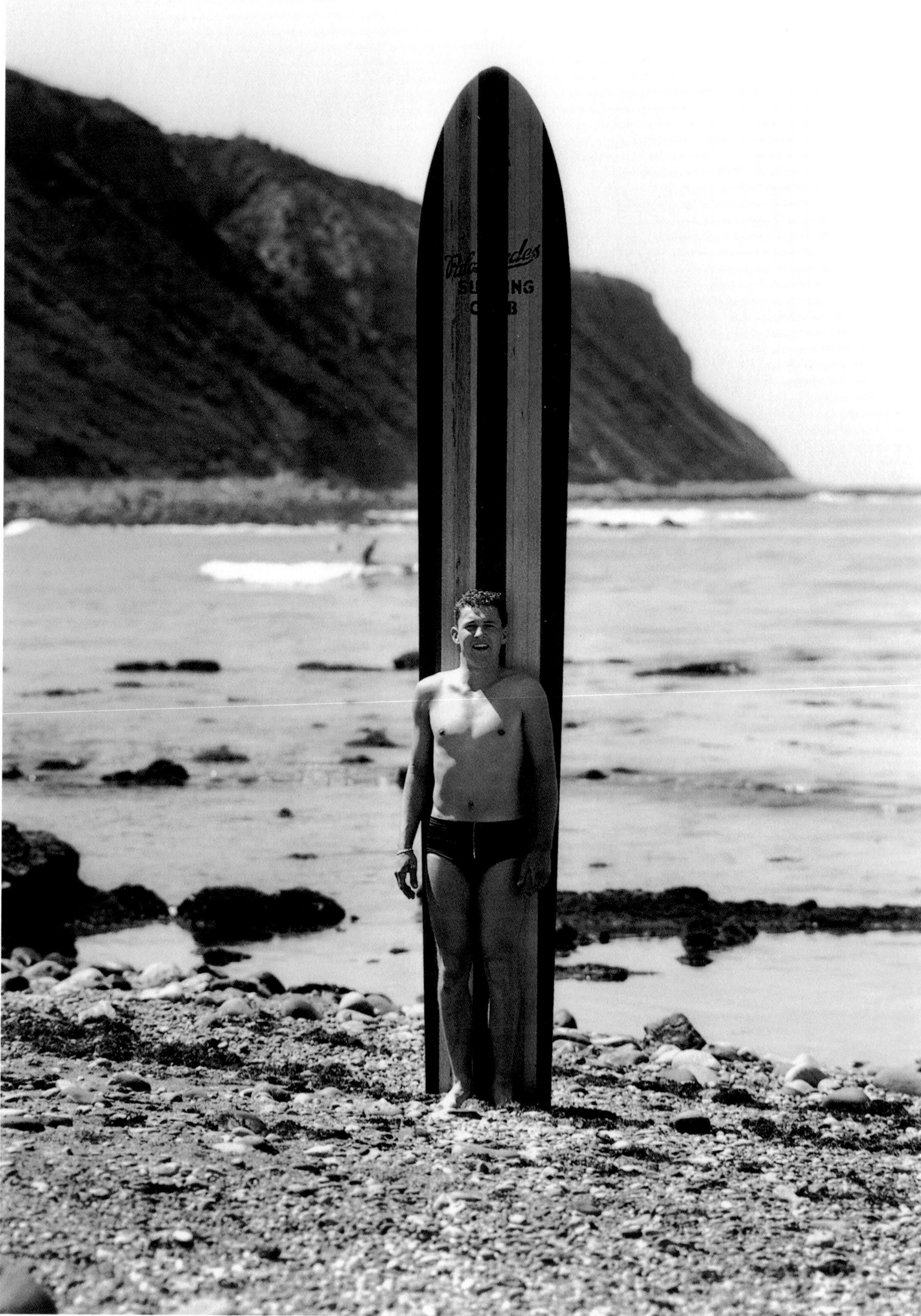
Palisades
SURFING
CLUB

waiting to see what I'd shot," Grannis recalls. "And then I'd get them in the dark-room and the body heat would become terrible. There were a couple of kids, Tom and Don Craig, who lived nearby who would go through my trash to see if I threw anything away that they wanted." From his house it was only a forty-minute drive up the then two-lane Pacific Coast Highway to Malibu, an obscure point break when Grannis surfed it in the thirties, which by 1960 was world-famous. With its perfect, tapering waves and proximity to Hollywood, "the 'Bu" had become a bona fide scene that drew surfing's elite each summer. Although extremely crowded even then, the break featured surf stars such as Lance Carson, Johnny Fain, Mike Hynson, and the legendary Miki Dora dancing across the face of the swells with a quick, theatrical style that came to be known as "hot-dogging." Grannis's photographic skills were improving, and he sold his early Malibu shots to the short-lived *Reef* magazine, initiating his career in print.

In November 1961 Grannis made his first trip to Hawaii, the epicenter of the surfing frontier at the time. After photographing small waves in Waikiki and Makaha for two weeks, he headed for the fabled North Shore of Oahu. By then a large swell had filled in, and Grannis was stunned by the sheer magnitude and power of Hawaiian waves. Using a 650mm telephoto lens, he captured the likes of Rick Grigg, Peter Cole, and Phil Edwards racing down the massive concave faces of the infamous "West Bowl" at Sunset Beach.

Grannis returned to California with renewed fervor. Over the next few years, he tripled his output and began shooting more color, lifestyle, contest, and advertising photos. Insular and budget-minded, early surf marketers looked to their own for graphic design and photos. Grannis had no experience as a commercial photographer, nonetheless he acquitted himself with simple, clever concepts. His photo of Hermosa Beach surfer Ricky Hatch deftly stepping to the tip in shoes and a spiffy business suit for Jacobs Surfboards is considered a surf-photography classic. In 1963 Grannis bought a Calypso water camera (invented by Jacques Cousteau, and the precursor to the Nikonos), and produced a touchstone shot of Henry Ford executing a perfect bottom turn at 22nd Street.

Grannis found out early on, however, that surf photography could be danger-ous for even the most experienced waterman. While shooting Hawaii's Sunset Beach with his Nikonos from the water one day, a massive "West Peak Bowl" swung unexpectedly toward the channel, breaking far outside and trapping Grannis directly in its path. He looked up to see a twenty-foot wall of white-water and three thickset eleven-foot surfboards hurtling toward his unprotected head. He dove beneath the maelstrom but managed to keep his precious camera safe. Later, with help from his old friend Doc Ball, Grannis designed and built his first rubber-lined, suction-cupped waterproof box, which allowed him to change film and shoot from the water with longer lenses and sit in the relative safety of Sunset Beach or the Waimea Bay channel for hours without returning to shore.

On land, Grannis loved the clean, cool remove provided by the Century 1000 telephoto lens. Viewed from a half-mile away, artfully framed surfers appeared as heroic figures within a vast arena such as Sunset Beach. But it was his dedica-tion to the rest of the beach scene that fills a large gap in surfing's collective



**LeRoy Grannis, Palos Verdes Cove, California, 1946**

Grannis showing off his twelve-foot hand-shaped redwood-and-balsa square-tail plank. The rare Ecuadorean balsa had been stored for the duration of World War II. Photograph by Doc Ball.

Grannis präsentiert stolz sein selbst gefertigtes zwölf Fuß langes Square-Tail-Brett aus Redwood und Balsa. Das seltene Balsaholz aus Ecuador war während des gesamten Zweiten Weltkrieges eingelagert gewesen. Fotografiert von Doc Ball.

LeRoy Grannis posant fièrement devant son *square tail* de douze pieds taillé à la main dans le séquoia et le balsa. Les stocks du précieux balsa équatorien avaient été mis à l'abri pendant la Seconde Guerre mondiale. Photo: Doc Ball.

memory today. Grannis's photography, especially from 1960 to 1965, caught surfing at a critical juncture between cult and culture. Upon first glance, his photos may evoke nostalgia for a simpler, more naive era, but closer inspection reveals that he was documenting surfing's rapid evolution into an iconic lifestyle. His photos captured the real thing, providing a bridge between the world of Beach Boy lyrics and the reality of the Southern California beach scene. Surf language, surf music, surf art, surf media, surf fashion—all the basic elements of what are now considered essential to modern surf culture were either conceived or codified within this brief window of time. Grannis was one of the few surf photographers to swing his camera off the wave action and record it all.

In 1964, after a highly successful winter trip to Hawaii, Grannis teamed with future surfwear tycoon Dick Graham to start *International Surfing Magazine* (later shortened to *Surfing,* and still the second oldest surf magazine in the world). Grannis became its founding photo editor, associate editor, and primary photographer, in addition to his full-time job with Pacific Bell Telephone. Each weekend, he dutifully covered the endless series of amateur and club contests. In doing so he caught a generation of now legendary surfers in their gawky adolescence. As many were the same age as his teenage son, he turned an often paternal lens on his subjects, capturing candid portraits that belie the reticence of a middle-aged man approaching strangers to pose for pictures. Among his photographic mentors and peers, Grannis struck a clear middle note between art and photojournalism. His photos were well framed, focused, and gifted with a generous depth of field that allowed a viewer time to pore over the ecology of the moment. His use of slow, fine-grained film, exposed by the book and painstakingly processed, allowed for highly detailed enlargements. "There was a texture about Grannis's shots that for me took them into another realm," says Brad Barrett, a staff photographer and photo editor at *Surfer* magazine from 1968 to 1973.

**In the early sixties there were fewer than half a dozen published surf** photographers in the U.S., and with the exception of John Severson, all shot purely as a sideline hobby. Each, however, had a clearly defined style and agenda. Severson, a former art teacher, brought a raw, bebop aesthetic to his shots. Ron Stoner favored warm, burnished tones and a lush, romanticized view. Ron Church was a professional industrial photographer with advanced technical expertise and state-of-the-art underwater cameras. His black-and-white photographs were heroic but often cold renderings of the reigning surf gods. As a surfer and coastal native, Grannis, on the other hand, shot the local scene with an unfiltered sense of verité.

Surf filmmaker and publisher John Severson was one of the first to expand surf photography into surf media. In 1960 he published *The Surfer,* a thirty-six-page booklet of his photography and art to be sold for extra cash at screenings of his documentary *Surf Fever.* The booklet was hugely popular, and the first printing of 5,000 sold out quickly. He followed up in 1961 with a quarterly, and a year later went bimonthly. Severson hired a small staff and became a full-time editor and publisher. Soon Grannis was contributing to *Surfer* magazine, as well as the short-lived *Surfing Illustrated.*

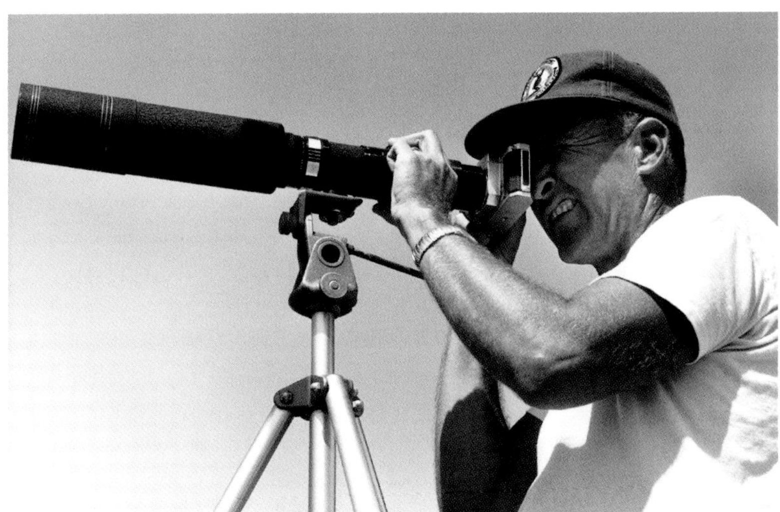

The early surf 'zines had been kitchen-table projects, created and distributed by the sport's devotees. When *Surfer* emerged, print as a mass medium was becoming accessible to low-budget publishers such as Severson, and media leaders had begun to exploit this niche sport in movies such as *Gidget* (1959) and *Ride the Wild Surf* (1964). In Southern California, action shots and colorful graphics of surfing had become eye candy for Hollywood's film and television industries. "Suddenly there was an opportunity to get unprecedented distribution for an image that you hand made," says John Van Hamersveld, a one-time *Surfer* magazine art director and creator of the legendary Day-Glo *The Endless Summer* poster. "It was the taking of this small isolated culture by the media, through the magazines or through the surf movies, up to the producers of mass culture."

By 1966 the surfing "fad" of five years earlier had become an authentic youth culture, complete with its own language, music, fashion, media, cars, and code of honor. Mainstream interest in the scene was at an all-time high, and fortunes were being made by a small Southern California cartel of surf-related manufacturers also known as „Dana Point Mafia." The scene had gotten a huge mainstream media push in July with the 1966 coast-to-coast release of Bruce Brown's *The Endless Summer*. An inventive, easygoing documentary, it gave the non-surfing world (the "Legions of the Unjazzed," as maestro surfer Phil Edwards put it) its first legitimate view of the insular surfing culture, and the world wanted more. A new gold rush was on.

Back in San Diego, city fathers and World Surfing Championships organizers stumbled over themselves to congratulate one another on surfing's newfound respectability. With the upcoming championships, contest officials hoped to reverse a tide of "surfing hooliganism" and bad publicity that had dogged the sport during its first great boom following the release of *Gidget*. The San Diego Chamber of Commerce saw a huge increase in tourism as the sexy, fast-growing beach sport captivated the nation's free-spending youth, seemingly overnight.

A surge of conservatism was encroaching upon the once bohemian lifestyle as well. An ongoing campaign conducted primarily by John Severson's *Surfer*

**LeRoy Grannis, Ocean Beach, California, 1963**

A salt-crusted tripod and a hundred-yard squint—the hallmarks of a die-hard surf photographer. Grannis shooting the Western Surfing Association contest. Photograph by Frank Grannis.

Ein salzverkrustetes Stativ und ein zugekniffenes Auge – die Markenzeichen eines passionierten Surffotografen. Grannis bei Aufnahmen während des Wettbewerbs der Western Surfing Association. Fotografiert von Frank Grannis.

L'apanage du photographe de surf invétéré : un trépied rongé par le sel et … des yeux de lynx. LeRoy Grannis en pleine séance photo lors du championnat de la Western Surfing Association. Photo : Frank Grannis.

Pioneering surf fashion at "Sano"
in the halcyon years just before
World War II. Grannis and Tracy
were married a month after this
photo was taken. Photograph by
Dorothy Hacket.

Die Vorreiter der Surfmode in
„Sano" in den unbeschwerten
Jahren vor Ausbruch des Zweiten
Weltkrieges. Grannis und Tracy
heirateten einen Monat, nachdem
dieses Foto aufgenommen wurde.
Fotografiert von Dorothy Hacket.

Les débuts de la mode du surf à
San Onofre dans les années dorées
qui ont précédé la Seconde Guerre
mondiale. Grannis et Tracy se
marient un mois après cette prise
de vue. Photo : Dorothy Hacket.

magazine was attempting to purge the surfing scene of "undesirable" elements. The magazine's editorial tone skewed toward self-righteousness, as guest editors and carefully selected reader letters gloated over organized surfing's defeat of the surf punks, or "hodads," who had blackened surfing's name with lowbrow pranks and a generally rotten attitude toward authority figures. "[Surfing] no longer just appeals to the oddball type," declared John Hannon, a leading East Coast surfboard manufacturer, in an interview with *Newsweek*. "These kids have haircuts and their fingernails are clean; they won't tolerate the troublemakers."

**The opening volley of the "Shortboard Revolution"—and the disintegration** of the simpler years of the early sixties surf scene—was served on October 2, 1966, in Ocean Beach, San Diego. It was there, under overcast skies in small, soft surf, that Nat Young won the World Surfing Championships with a radical, hard-turning approach that stunned the ruling elite. When David Nuuhiwa, the lithe Hawaiian favorite famed for long, elegant noserides, insisted, "You must try to blend into the wave," the cocky Young retorted, "I don't want to blend in with anything!" Young's rhetoric was as inflammatory as his equipment. He won the contest on "Magic Sam," a self-made surfboard, measuring nine feet four inches—a full foot shorter than the standard of the day. Designed with fellow Aussie Bob McTavish, it featured a tall, scimitar-like fin created by the eccentric American surf savant George Greenough. Virtually overnight a generation of powerful, state-of-the-art surfboards were pushed to the edge of the scrap heap by a drastic, forced evolution in technology, maneuvers, and mind-set. With Nat Young's victory, surfing veered away from mainstreaming for more than a decade. Big Nat, nicknamed "the Animal" for his gutsy approach to wave riding, had shown the surfing world the future. Before 1966 the gold-standard maneuver was to "hang ten" (balance stylishly on the end of the board with ten toes hanging over the nose). Now, anything was possible. It was called "mind surfing." And it was, as *Surfer* magazine journalist Paul Gross wrote, "a mass desertion from everything that had gone on before." Yet, at the time, nobody seemed to notice.

Simultaneously, psychedelic drugs raged through the surf culture like a wildfire, expanding some minds, blowing others. Surfing became introverted and underground as former Jantzen-wearing hotdoggers morphed into bearded Zen-spouting mystics. Contests were no longer cool; nobody cared who came in first. Nobody cared, period. Suddenly, surfing wasn't about tricks and trophies, but about balancing one's karmic flow within "crystalline cathedrals of molten glass," in the words of a *Surfer* magazine reader. As early as 1966, Rick Griffin was slipping sly drug references into his cartoons for *Surfer*, which enraged many of the magazine's prominent advertisers. The adventurous, free-ranging lifestyle also led many surfers into part-time careers as international drug smugglers. "You were on the bus or you were off the bus," wrote Drew Kampion, *Surfer* magazine's editor from 1968 to 1972. "You got it or you didn't. You believed in gravity or you believed in space. You were rigid or you flowed, and there was a whole lot of flowin' goin' on."

After a brief fling with mainstream respectability the culture was reclaiming its antiestablishment roots, a move that did not go unnoticed by the outside world.

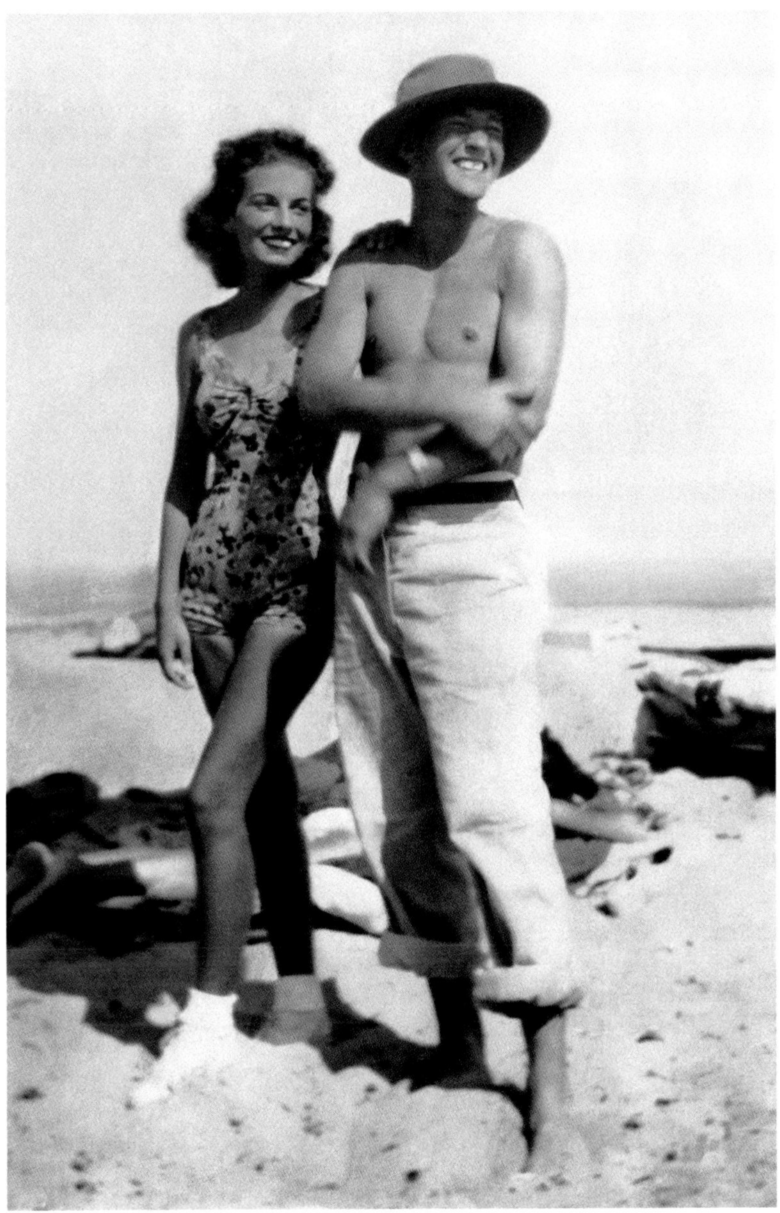

In his widely published 1966 essay "The Pump House Gang," pop culture critic Tom Wolfe reported that many surfers "were shifting from the surfing life to the advance guard of something else—the psychedelic head world of California." Where corporate America once saw a generation of compliant young consumers, they now saw long hair, pot smoke, and a defiant middle finger extended toward unchecked materialism.

The economic fallout was profound. Over the next few years most of the major board shops downsized or went out of business. At *Surfer,* advertising revenues plunged, the magazine shrank, and the editorial gestalt shifted markedly left of center. Under Kampion's new, radicalized regime, *Surfer* became a vector

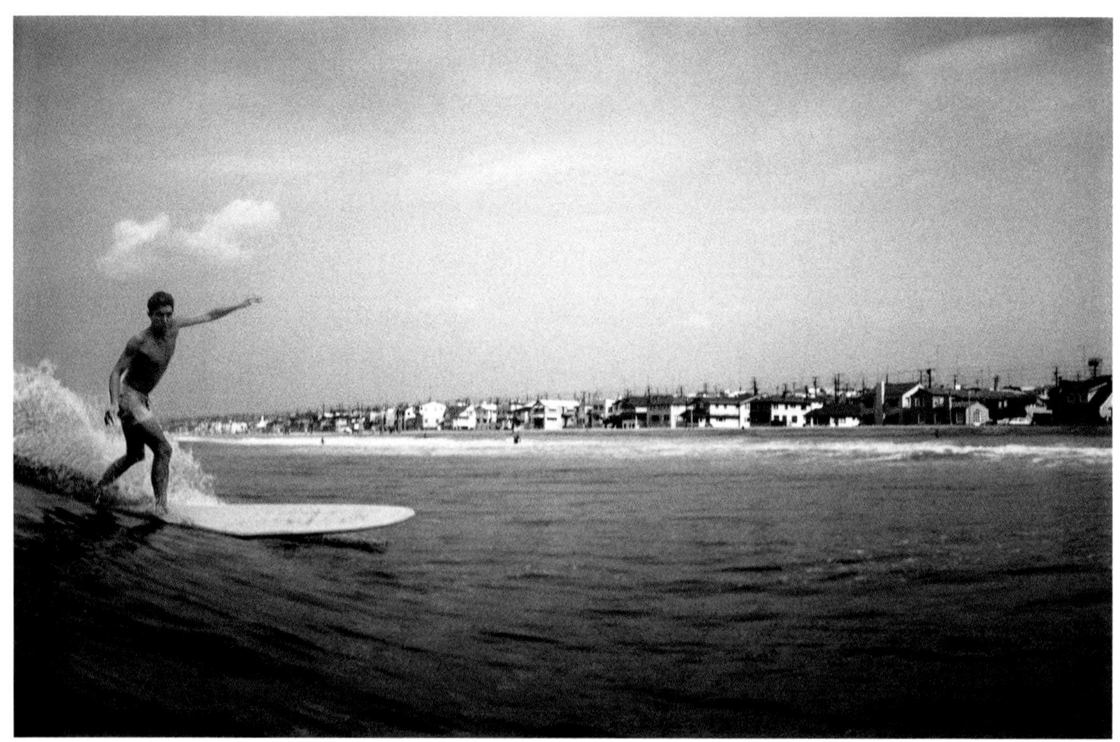

of the burgeoning counterculture, celebrating peace, free love, tuberides, and every surfer's right to drop out and get really, really stoned. Kampion, who publicly railed against most organized competitive surfing with articles such as "Bad Karma at Huntington Beach" and "The Death of All Contests," sought to promote surfing as a metaphor for cosmic balance rather than a crass marketing ego trip. He was also openly critical of the escalation of the Vietnam War, which was snatching surfers off the beach at an alarming rate, and declared open season on incoming U.S. president Richard Nixon for moving next door to Trestles Beach in San Clemente and closing off the premier surf break whenever he visited the "Western White House."

Grannis was, by virtue of his generational bias, out of step with surfing's new antiestablishment establishment, and frankly, he could not have cared less. A World War II veteran who had helped his good friend Hop Swarts run contests for his newly formed United States Surfing Association, Grannis held steadfast to the idea that competitive surfing advanced the sport and promoted its more socially acceptable side. In 1968 Grannis published an editorial in defense of good, clean surfing competition, dismissing the critics as "bellyachers" who had no right to complain. "The last few years have seen a rash of sick articles knocking competition by surfing has-beens, nonsurfing Hawaiian columnists, trunk salesmen, and frustrated would-be editors," he wrote. "The reason they are all downgrading competition is that they can't meet the competition themselves."

By the end of the sixties, however, most contests, and even *Surfer* magazine's once prestigious Surfer Poll Awards, were passé. The nearest thing to professional-

## Hermosa Beach, 1963

In 1963, the average Hermosa Beach bungalow sold for $22,000. Today, it would go for several million dollars.

1963 kostete ein durchschnittlicher Bungalow in Hermosa Beach 22.000 Dollar. Heute würde man dafür mehrere Millionen Dollar zahlen.

En 1963, un bungalow de Hermosa Beach se vendait en moyenne 22 000 dollars. Aujourd'hui, il faut compter plusieurs millions de dollars.

level competitive surfing was a groovy anti-contest contest called an "Expression Session," in which the top surfers showcased their prowess free of judges, points, and trophies. "This has been the year of the development, if not the invention, of many things: shortboards, V-bottoms, baby guns, flexible fins, short fins, radical board design in general," wrote Kampion in 1968. "It is the rare surfer who surfs in the same style that he did last year." Nevertheless, Grannis wrote a follow-up editorial accurately predicting a return to longboards and noseriding one day. Through it all, Grannis continued to aim his camera at a sport he was devoted to, recording image after image of both longboarders and shortboarders, in spite of surf-world politics.

**In early December 1969, Hawaii and California were rocked by what was** called "the swell of the century." Mountainous thirty-foot waves lashed the North Shore of Oahu, destroying sixty homes and tossing large boats one hundred yards inland. Although the entire North Shore proved too huge to ride, Greg Noll and a small crew of surfers tackled the slightly diminished waves at Makaha on the island's west side. It was there that Noll caught what was arguably the largest wave ever ridden up to that date. He barely survived the resulting wipeout. "In a sport racked by change, hype, and revolution, a no-bullshit fifties-dinosaur caught the last great wave of 1969," reported Drew Kampion.

The Swell of 1969 has come to be viewed by the surfing world as a geophysical finale to surfing's most divisive and turbulent decade. "What we went through in December '69," sixties legend Skip Frye recalled many years later, "… in a way marked the transition from the whole sixties longboard thing to the shortboard era. It was kind of a wash-through, and we were playing a whole different ball game afterward." Grannis felt that board size was merely a logistic and was able to bridge the divide between the two generations with his photography. "I was shooting surfers, not boards," he says. "The way of life didn't change that much for me."

LeRoy Grannis's last surf photo for *International Surfing* was published in 1971. By the end of the seventies, he had retired from Pacific Bell Telephone and moved from Hermosa Beach to Carlsbad, California. Continuing to surf and shoot images, his prints and negatives remained neatly filed in three-ring binders in his home for more than twenty years. While a small, fringe culture of passionate surfers developed their lifestyle into a global industry, a primal decade of surfing's history was nearly forgotten.

A pioneer in the sport and its photography, Grannis captured surfing history at the brink of its evolution and iconography. This retrospective of his photographs—from the classics of the catalog to never-before-published material unearthed from his archive—grants viewers access to a lifestyle that has transitioned from a handful of practitioners to a $4 billion-a-year industry. Today, as endless images from professional surf photographers flood the market, the elegant simplicity of Grannis's photos and the period he captured provide a critical window into the birth of a culture. "I was a surfer and I shot what I liked to see," Grannis shrugs modestly. "I suppose you could say I was lucky."


**Dewey Weber, 22nd Street, Hermosa Beach, California, 1964**

Weber, "the Little Man on Wheels," was considered the archetypal sixties "hotdogger" for his speedy footwork and flashy style.

Weber, „Der kleine Mann auf Rädern", galt dank seiner schnellen Beinarbeit und seines auffälligen Stils als einer der archetypischen „Hotdogger" der Sechziger.

Dewey Weber, dit « Le Petit Bonhomme à roulettes », est considéré comme le modèle des « hotdoggers » des années 1960 en raison de la vivacité de son jeu de jambes et de son style exubérant.

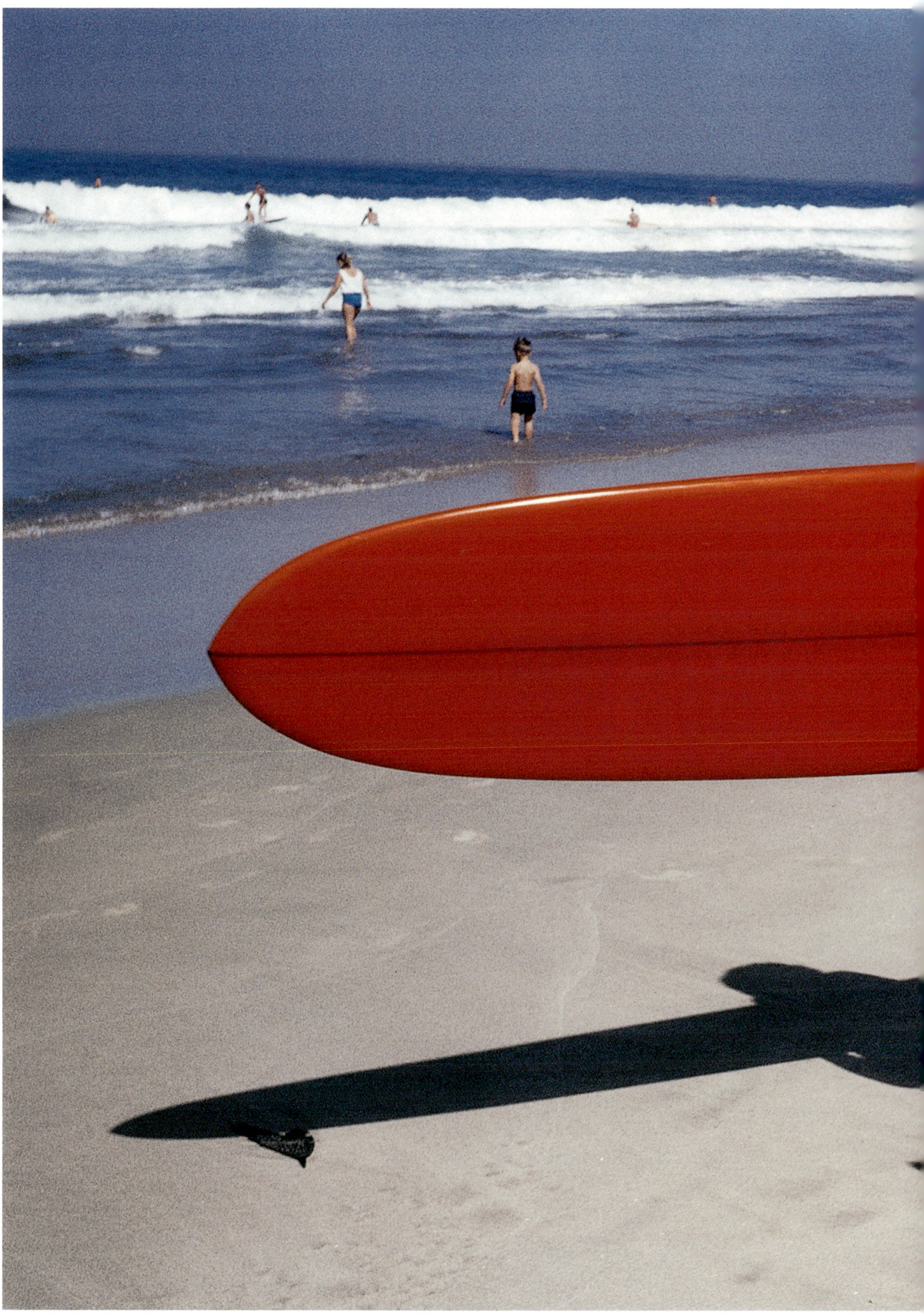

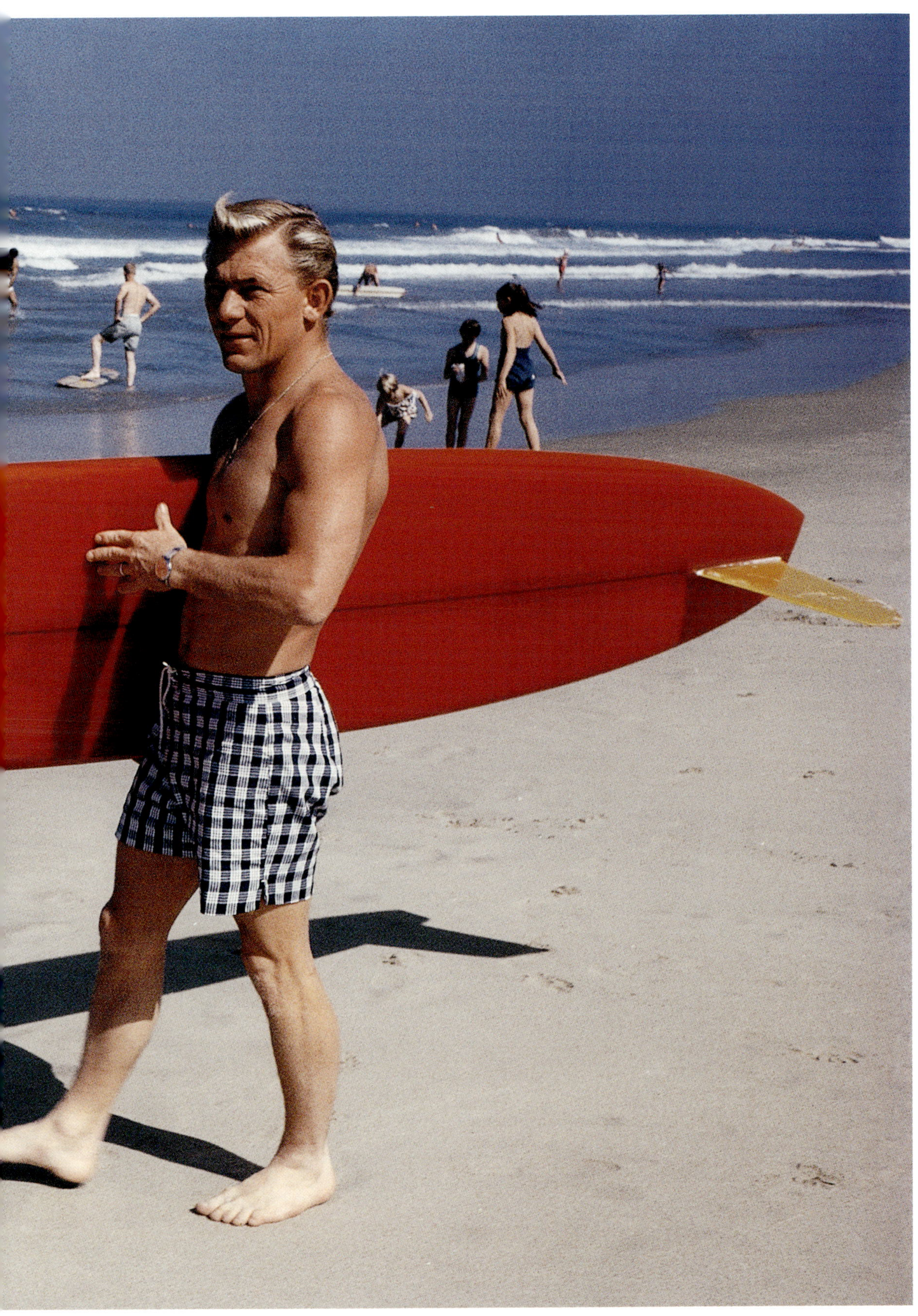

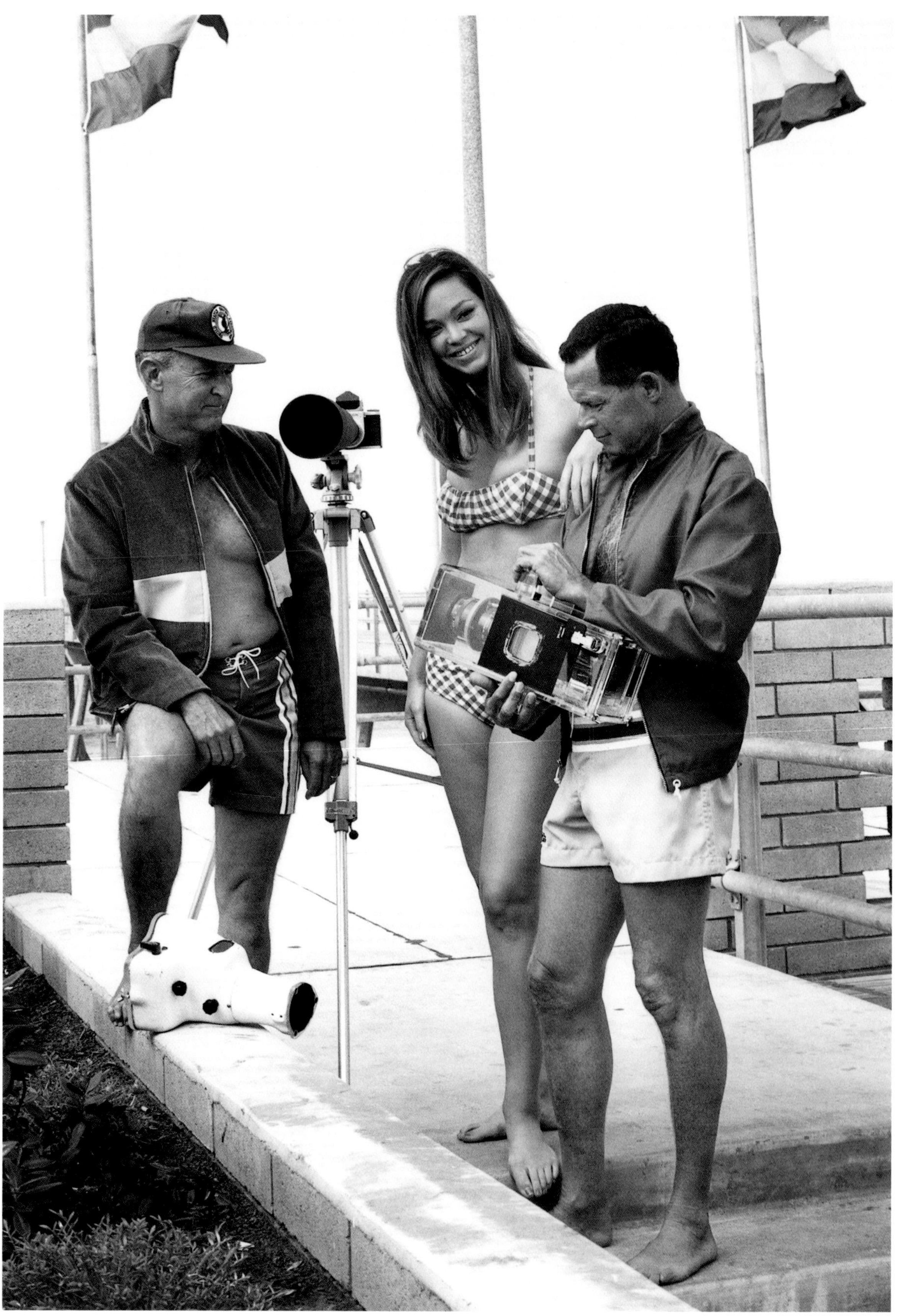

# AUF DER JAGD NACH DER PERFEKTEN WELLE:
## Die Surffotografie von LeRoy Grannis

*Von Steve Barilotti*

Die Revolution fand an einem Sonntagnachmittag statt, fotografiert in Schwarz-Weiß mit einem Zweihundertfünfzigstel. Es war am 2. Oktober 1966. Weltmeisterschaft im Wellenreiten, Ocean Beach, San Diego. Vierzigtausend Zuschauer standen wie die Heringe am Strand und auf dem neuen Ocean-Beach-Pier. In genau dem Augenblick, in dem der achtzehnjährige Robert „Nat" Young eine merkwürdige Trophäe in der Form des Staates Kalifornien in die Luft stemmte, befanden sich über 340.000 US-Soldaten in Vietnam, Brian Wilson stand kurz vor der Veröffentlichung seines Meisterwerks *Good Vibrations* und LSD sollte noch drei Monate lang legal bleiben. Surfbretter waren durchschnittlich zehneinhalb Fuß lang und wogen fünfzehn Kilo. Nat Young war jetzt Weltmeister. Und die Welt des Wellenreitens war gerade unbemerkt komplett aus ihrer Achse gekippt. Young, ein großer, vorlauter Australier, wurde auf dem Siegertreppchen von dem stillen Hawaiianer Jock Sutherland und dem kalifornischen Wunderkind der kleinen Welle Corky Carroll flankiert. Ein Kontingent von Journalisten der regionalen und überregionalen Presse, darunter *Newsweek* und *The New York Times*, kämpfte um die besten Plätze bei den Siegern. LeRoy Grannis, einziger fester Fotograf des Magazins *International Surfing*, trieb sich an den Rändern der Menschenmenge herum und machte Schnappschüsse mit seiner rostigen Pentax-S-Kamera. Im entscheidenden Augenblick der Feierlichkeiten stellte er auf den jubelnden Young scharf, als der brüllte: „Ich fühle mich spitze!"

Trotz der spürbaren Aufregung am Strand blieb Grannis stoisch und hielt sich abseits. Für ihn war es nichts weiter als der Endpunkt eines Jahres, in dem er jedes Wochenende landauf, landab an der südkalifornischen Küste Clubwettbewerbe fotografiert hatte. Grannis war damals neunundvierzig, seit sechs Jahren Surffotograf und seit fünfunddreißig Jahren Surfer. Am nächsten Wochenende würde er wahrscheinlich schon wieder in Malibu oder Huntington Beach bei einem kleinen Regionalwettbewerb sein, wo der Qualifizierungswettkampf für die World Surfing Championships wieder von vorne anfing.

**LeRoy Grannis kam Ende 1959 weder mit professionellem noch künstle**rischem Anspruch zur Surffotografie, sondern als Familienvater in den besten Jahren, der nach einem Hobby suchte, um den Stress in seinem Berufsleben auszugleichen. Glücklicherweise griff er an einem Wendepunkt der Surfgeschichte zur Kamera. Der 1917 in Hermosa Beach, Kalifornien, geborene Grannis war ein Überbleibsel der Redwoodplanken-Ära des West Coast Surfing, als gerade mal



LeRoy Grannis, Bettina Brenna, Don James, Hermosa Beach, California, 1965

Thanks to Jacques Cousteau's innovations, surf photographers were now able to paddle out to the action with lightweight waterproof camera housings. Photograph by Frank Grannis.

Dank der Neuentwicklungen von Jacques Cousteau konnten Surffotografen jetzt mit leichten, wasserfesten Kameragehäusen rauspaddeln und das Geschehen direkt verfolgen. Fotografiert von Frank Grannis.

Grâce aux innovations de Jacques-Yves Cousteau, les photographes de surf peuvent aujourd'hui s'approcher au plus près de l'action équipés d'appareils photos logés dans des boîtiers étanches et légers. Photo : Frank Grannis.

**LeRoy Grannis, Hermosa Beach,
California, 1969**

Grannis in trim with another
Cousteau invention—the Calypso
amphibious camera. Photograph
by John Grannis.

Grannis in Aktion mit einer
weiteren Erfindung von Cousteau –
der Calypso-Amphibienkamera.
Fotografiert von John Grannis.

Grannis se familiarisant avec
une autre invention de Cousteau,
l'appareil photo amphibie Calypso.
Photo : John Grannis.

zweihundert kalifornische Surfer auf massiven Elf-Fuß-Brettern die langsamen Wellen von San Onofre und Palos Verdes Cove mit der Würde wahrer Gentlemen ritten. Sie waren die erste Generation amerikanischer Surfer, die den uralten, gerade von den Hawaiianern George Freeth und Duke Kahanamoku eingeführten Sport dort ausübten. Sie waren Teil der Wiedergeburt des Wellenreitens, die von einer Handvoll hawaiianischer Beach Boys in Waikiki am Ende des neunzehnten Jahrhunderts eingeleitet worden war.

Einen Steinwurf vom Meer entfernt in Hermosa Beach aufgewachsen, begann Grannis als Vierzehnjähriger mit dem Surfen, auf einer geborgten Redwoodplanke, die fast hundert Pfund wog. Dort, in den sanften Wellen unter dem Hermosa-Beach-Pier, lernte er zwei andere Surfer kennen, Lewis „Hoppy" Swarts, ebenfalls aus Hermosa Beach stammend, und John „Doc" Ball, einen leutseligen Zahnmedizinstudenten der University of Southern California, der zehn Jahre älter war als Grannis. Die drei blieben für den Rest ihres Lebens Freunde. Ball war ein hervorragender Surfer und überredete die Teenager Grannis und Swarts bald dazu, es mit den sauberer laufenden Wellen im Palos Verdes Cove acht Kilometer weiter südlich aufzunehmen. Die Bucht war einer begeisterten Crew ernsthafter Surfer bereits ein zweites Zuhause geworden, die meisten davon arbeitslose junge Männer um die zwanzig, die sich bis zum Ende der Weltwirtschaftskrise in großartigem, aber billigem Stil die Zeit vertrieben. Die Männer brauchten nicht viel, bauten ihre eigenen Surfbretter, nähten ihre Surfshorts selbst und warfen ihre knappen Barschaften zusammen, um den Sprit für Ausflüge nach Malibu oder San Onofre bezahlen zu können (und gelegentlich eine billige Flasche Wein). Etliche waren gleichzeitig erfahrene Taucher und fingen sich kostenlose Hummer-Festmahle und Seeohren in den Gezeitenpools. 1935 rief Ball den Palos Verdes Surfing Club ins Leben, in den Swarts und Grannis (jetzt bereits unter seinem Spitznamen „Granny") 1936 aufgenommen wurden.

**Wellenreiter boten sich als Motive für Fotografen an, und das Bild vom**
hawaiianischen Wellenbezwinger, der majestätisch vor Diamond Head stand, wurde schnell zum Postkartenklischee. Surfbilder wurden immer in erster Linie von Surfern selbst gemacht. Sämtliche Surffotografen hatten sich das Fotografieren selbst beigebracht und betrieben es als Hobby, nicht um ihren Lebensunterhalt damit zu verdienen. Tom Blake, der große Surfpionier und Erfinder, baute 1929 eine wasserdichte Box für seine Graflex-Kamera und begann, die hawaiianischen Wasserratten abzulichten, die auf zwölf Fuß langen Alaia-Brettern durch die lang laufenden Wellen vor Waikiki glitten. Er brachte Doc Ball das Handwerk bei, und Ball hatte wiederum großen Einfluss auf Don James und später auf LeRoy Grannis. Ball war ein echtes Fototalent mit gutem Blick, probierte ständig neue Blickwinkel aus und baute wasserdichte Gehäuseprototypen, in denen er seinen Apparat mit hinaus in die Wellen nehmen konnte. Die Schnappschüsse seiner Kumpels und deren Freundinnen fingen den Geist der kurzen glücklichen Tage des reinen Surfens ein, die mit dem Angriff der Japaner auf Pearl Harbor, Hawaii, 1941 endeten. Seit Kriegseintritt der Amerikaner ging es mit dem fröhlichen kalifornischen Wellenreiterleben steil bergab, da die meisten jungen, gesunden Männer über achtzehn sich entweder freiwillig zum Militär meldeten oder

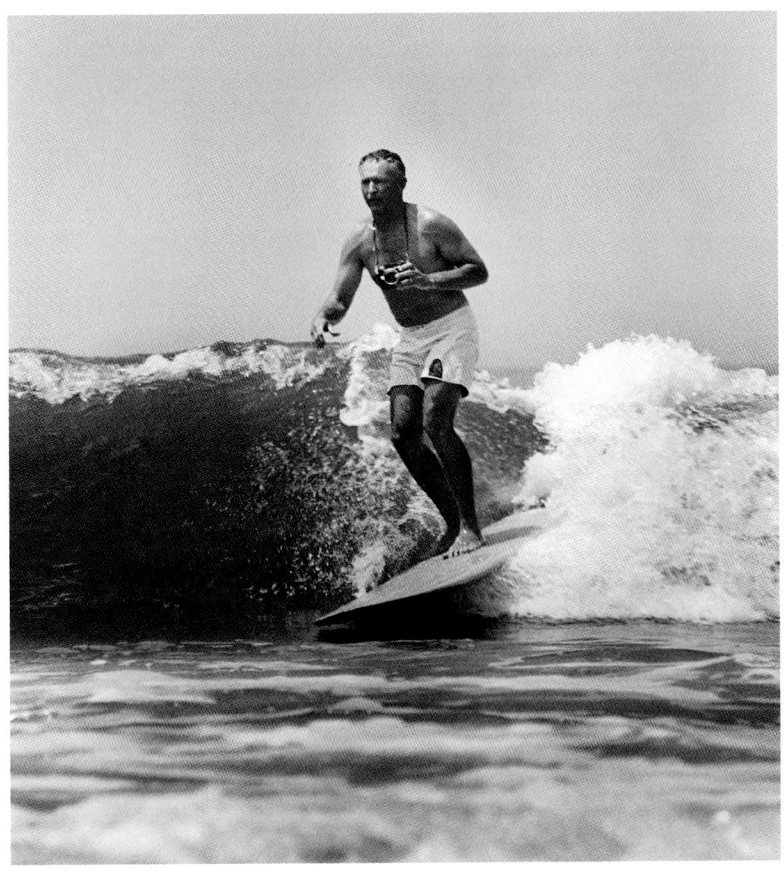

eingezogen wurden. Viele kehrten nie zurück. Obwohl Grannis gerade erst
geheiratet und 1941 eine Tochter bekommen hatte, meldete er sich zwei Jahre
später zur Luftwaffe der U.S. Army. Als er die Fliegerausbildung abgeschlossen
hatte, war der Krieg jedoch bereits vorbei, und er wurde 1946 entlassen. Nach
Hermosa Beach zurückgekehrt, wurde Grannis Fernmeldetechniker und fand eine
Anstellung als Telefonzentraleninstallateur bei Pacific Bell Telephone. (Grannis
blieb aktiver Reservist der U.S. Air Force und wurde 1977 als Major außer Dienst
gestellt.) In den Jahren nach dem Krieg surfte Grannis nur noch sporadisch, die
Arbeit und seine vier Kinder beanspruchten ihn zunehmend. Ende 1959 wurde
bei ihm ein stressbedingtes Magengeschwür festgestellt, und der Arzt empfahl ihm
ein entspannendes Hobby. Seine Wahl fiel auf die Surffotografie, da Grannis nur
ein paar Straßen vom Meer entfernt wohnte und sein halbwüchsiger Sohn Frank
gerade mit dem Wellenreiten angefangen hatte. Im Juni 1960 hatte Grannis sich
in der Garage eine Dunkelkammer eingerichtet und entwickelte erste simple
Fotos, deren Stil von Doc Ball beeinflusst war.

In jenem Sommer begann er, ausgerüstet mit einer DDR-Kleinbildkamera,
am 22nd Street Beach in Hermosa Beach zu fotografieren, einem unauffälligen
Strandabschnitt in der South Bay, an dem eine Gruppe junger Surfer aktiv war,
die ihr Können gern vor seiner Linse zeigen wollte. Unangefochtener Anführer der
22nd-Street-Gang war Dewey Weber, der mit dreiundzwanzig bereits in mehreren

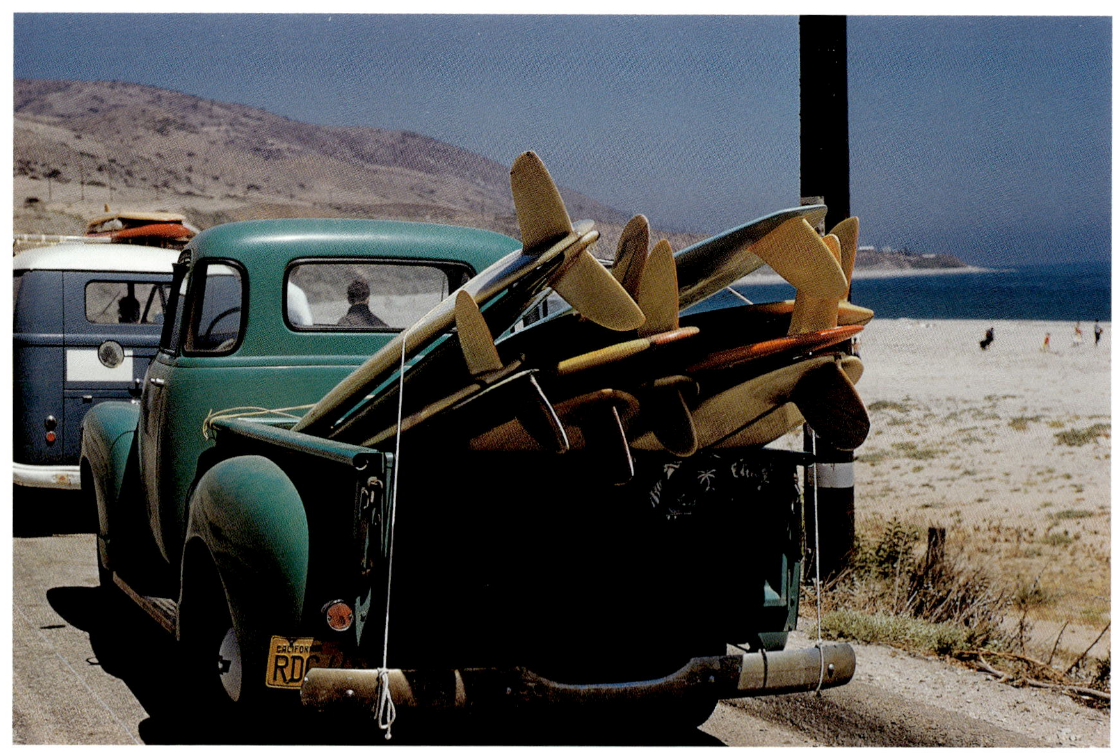



Surffilmen mitgespielt und gerade einen eigenen Surfshop im nahe gelegenen Venice Beach eröffnet hatte. Der kleine (158 cm), aber kräftige Weber surfte aggressiv und trieb den Rest der Crew (u. a. Henry Ford, Freddie Pfahler und Mike Zuetell) dazu an, ebenfalls ihr Bestes zu geben. Als das Jahr 1960 sich dem Ende zuneigte, hatte Grannis schon über 2.500 Bilder geknipst und entwickelt.

Grannis' Dunkelkammer wurde sozusagen zum Ein-Stunden-Fotoservice der South Bay; zu einer Zeit, in der die Surfmagazine nur alle zwei Monate erschienen, waren die Wellenreiter sehr interessiert an aktuellen Bildern von sich selbst. „Manchmal ging ich geradewegs vom Fotografieren an der 22nd Street in die Dunkelkammer, und ehe ich mich's versah, stand draußen ein halbes Dutzend Typen herum und wollte sehen, was ich fotografiert hatte", erinnert Grannis sich. „Und dann ließ ich sie in die Dunkelkammer rein, bis es wegen der vielen Menschen unerträglich heiß wurde. Da gab es zwei Brüder, Tom und Don Craig, die wohnten in der Nähe und durchwühlten meinen Abfall, um zu sehen, ob ich irgendetwas weggeworfen hatte, was sie vielleicht haben wollten." Von seinem Haus waren es nur vierzig Autominuten den damals zweispurigen Pacific Coast Highway hoch nach Malibu, ein ehemals unbekannter Point Break, wo Grannis in den Dreißigern gesurft hatte und der mittlerweile weltberühmt war. Mit seinen perfekt auslaufenden Wellen und der Nähe zu Hollywood war „the 'Bu" zu einem Anziehungspunkt geworden, der jeden Sommer die Surferelite anzog. Obwohl er auch damals bereits hoffnungslos überlaufen war, gab es an diesem Spot Surfstars wie Lance Carson, Johnny Fain, Mike Hynson und den legendären Miki Dora, die mit einem schnellen, theatralischen Stil an der Wellenwand entlangtanzten –

dieser Stil wurde als „hotdogging" bekannt. Grannis' fotografisches Können verbesserte sich ständig, und er verkaufte seine frühen Malibu-Bilder an das kurzlebige *Reef Magazine*, womit seine Karriere in den Printmedien begann.

Im November 1961 unternahm Grannis seine erste Reise nach Hawaii, damals die vorderste Front der Surfrevolution. Nachdem er zwei Wochen lang kleine Wellen in Waikiki und Makaha fotografiert hatte, fuhr er an den legendenumwobenen North Shore Oahus. Zu diesem Zeitpunkt erreichte ein großer Swell die Inseln, und Grannis war von der schieren Größe und Wucht der hawaiianischen Wellen zutiefst beeindruckt. Mit einem 650mm-Teleobjektiv fing er Cracks wie Rick Grigg, Peter Cole und Phil Edwards ein, die in der riesigen, hohlen „West Bowl" am Sunset Beach surften.

Grannis kehrte mit neu erwachter Begeisterung nach Kalifornien zurück. Im Laufe der nächsten Jahre verdreifachte er seinen Ausstoß an Bildern und begann zudem, auch mehr Farbbilder und Lifestyle-, Wettbewerbs- und Werbefotos zu machen. Die frühen Anbieter von Surfprodukten waren eher isoliert und sparsam und suchten in den eigenen Reihen nach ihrem Design und Fotomaterial. Als kommerzieller Fotograf hatte Grannis keinerlei Erfahrung, schlug sich jedoch mit einfachen, cleveren Konzepten wacker. Sein Bild des Hermosa-Beach-Surfers Ricky Hatch, der in Schuhen und geschniegeltem Anzug auf dem Brett steht, eine Anzeige für Jacobs Surfboards, ist ein Klassiker der Surffotografie. 1963 kaufte Grannis eine Calypso-Unterwasserkamera (entwickelt von Jacques Cousteau und Vorläufer der Nikonos) und produzierte damit eine bahnbrechende Aufnahme von Henry Ford, der an der 22nd Street einen perfekten Bottom Turn demonstrierte. Grannis musste schon früh feststellen, dass die Surffotografie selbst für den erfahrensten Ozeanschwimmer gefährlich sein konnte. Als er einmal den hawaiianischen Sunset Beach vom Wasser aus mit seiner Nikonos fotografierte, wurde er von einer riesigen Welle überrascht, die auf den Kanal der West Peak Bowl zurollte und sich weit draußen brach. Grannis saß fest, blickte auf und sah eine sieben Meter hohe Wand aus Weißwasser und drei dicke, elf Fuß lange Surfbretter, die auf seinen ungeschützten Kopf zurasten. Er schaffte es, unter den Wassermassen durchzutauchen und seine kostbare Kamera zu retten. Später entwarf und baute Grannis mithilfe seines alten Freundes Doc Ball seine erste, mit Gummi ausgekleidete und mit Saugnäpfen versehene wasserdichte Box, die es ihm ermöglichte, den Film zu wechseln, auch vom Wasser aus mit längeren Brennweiten zu fotografieren und stundenlang in der relativen Sicherheit des Sunset Beach oder Waimea-Bay-Kanals zu sitzen, ohne an Land zurückkehren zu müssen.

Auf dem Festland liebte Grannis die klare, coole Distanz, die ihm das Century-1000-Superteleobjektiv ermöglichte. Aus 800 Meter Entfernung konnte er die Surfer als heroische Gestalten vor einem riesigen Hintergrund wie dem Sunset Beach künstlerisch komponieren. Seiner tiefen Verbundenheit mit der Surfszene verdanken wir es, dass eine große Lücke im kollektiven Gedächtnis heute geschlossen werden kann. Grannis' Fotos, besonders die von 1960 bis 1965, zeigen das Wellenreiten an dem wichtigen Wendepunkt von Kult zu (Sub-)Kultur. Auf den ersten Blick mögen seine Fotos Wehmut nach einer einfacheren, naiveren Zeit auslösen, aber bei näherem Hinschauen wird deutlich, dass er die rasend schnelle

Entwicklung des Surfsports zum symbolhaften Lebensstil dokumentierte. Seine Bilder zeigen, wie es wirklich war; ihm gelang der Brückenschlag zwischen den Songtexten der Beach Boys und der Realität der südkalifornischen Strandszene. Surfjargon, Surfmusik, Surfkunst, Surfzeitschriften, Surfmode – alle Elemente, die heute als Grundlage der modernen Surfkultur gelten, wurden innerhalb dieser paar Jahre entweder erfunden oder definiert. Grannis war einer der wenigen Surffotografen, die die Kamera nicht nur auf die Action in den Wellen hielten, sondern auch das Drumherum dokumentierten.

Nach einem äußerst erfolgreichen Winteraufenthalt auf Hawaii tat Grannis sich 1964 mit dem späteren Surfbekleidungsmagnaten Dick Graham zusammen und hob das *International Surfing Magazine* aus der Taufe (es wurde später umbenannt in *Surfing* und besteht als zweitältestes Surfmagazin der Welt heute noch). Grannis wurde zum ersten Bildredakteur, Mitherausgeber und Hauptfotografen, und das alles neben seinem Vollzeitjob bei Pacific Bell Telephone. Jedes Wochenende fotografierte er pflichtbewusst die endlose Reihe der Amateur- und Clubwettbewerbe. Dabei schaffte er es, eine Generation heute legendärer Surfer als linkische Jugendliche für die Nachwelt festzuhalten. Da viele von ihnen so alt waren wie sein Sohn, betrachtete er seine Motive oft mit väterlichem Blick und erzielte so völlig natürlich wirkende Porträts, die über die Zurückhaltung des Mannes im mittleren Alter hinwegtäuschten, der Fremde bat, für seine Kamera zu posieren. Unter seinen fotografischen Vorbildern und Kollegen nahm Grannis eine klare Mittelposition zwischen Kunst und Fotojournalismus ein. Seine Bilder waren wohlkomponiert, fokussiert und mit einem großzügigen Tiefenschärfebereich ausgestattet, was dem Betrachter Zeit gab, sich in die Stimmung der Zeit hineinzuversetzen. Weil er feinkörnige Filme mit geringer Empfindlichkeit verwendete, konnte er sehr detailreiche Vergrößerungen anfertigen. „Grannis' Aufnahmen hatten das gewisse Etwas, das sie für mich zu etwas ganz Besonderem machte", sagt Brad Barrett, von 1968 bis 1973 Hausfotograf und Fotoredakteur der Zeitschrift *Surfer*.

**In den frühen Sechzigern gab es nicht mal ein halbes Dutzend Surffotografen** in den USA, die bereits etwas veröffentlicht hatten, und mit Ausnahme von John Severson betrieben alle die Fotografie nur nebenbei als Hobby. Jeder von ihnen hatte jedoch einen eindeutig definierten Stil und ein bestimmtes Anliegen. Severson, ehemaliger Kunstlehrer, vermittelte mit seinen Bildern eine ungeglättete Bebop-Ästhetik. Ron Stoner bevorzugte warme, goldbraune Töne und romantische, schöne Ansichten. Ron Church war professioneller Industriefotograf mit fortgeschrittenen technischen Kenntnissen und den neuesten Unterwasserkameras. Seine Schwarz-Weiß-Bilder waren heroische, aber oft unpersönliche Darstellungen der herrschenden Surfgötter. Als am Meer aufgewachsener Surfer fing Grannis hingegen die lokale Szene mit unmittelbarer Direktheit ein.

Der Surffilmer und Herausgeber John Severson war einer der Ersten, der die Surf-Ikonografie in andere Medien übersetzte. 1960 brachte er *The Surfer* heraus, ein sechsunddreißig Seiten starkes Heft mit Fotos und Zeichnungen von ihm selbst, mit dem er bei den Vorstellungen seines Dokumentarfilms *Surf Fever* etwas Geld hinzuzuverdienen hoffte. Das Heft war unglaublich begehrt und die erste

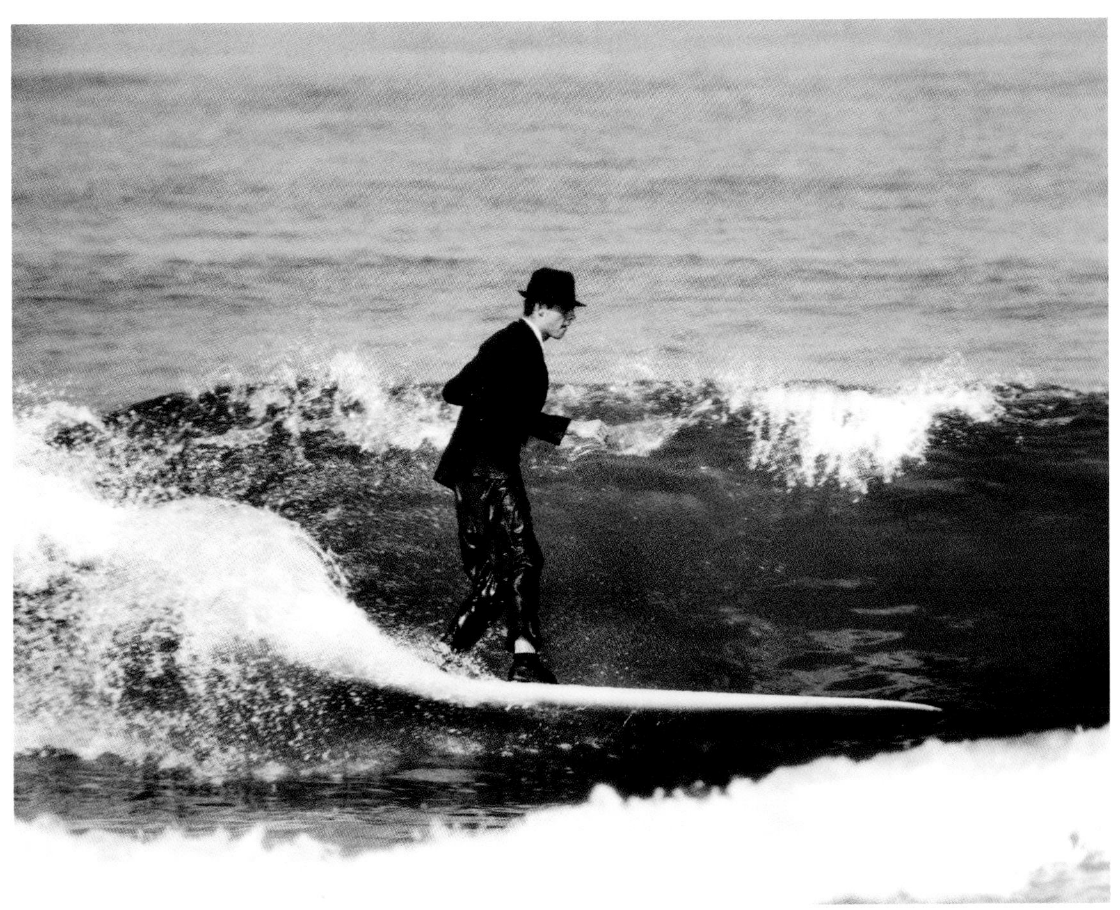

Auflage von 5.000 Stück schnell ausverkauft. 1961 folgte ein Vierteljahresblatt, das ein Jahr später dann alle zwei Monate herauskam. Severson stellte ein paar Mitarbeiter ein und wurde hauptberuflicher Chefredakteur und Herausgeber. Schon bald fotografierte Grannis für die Zeitschrift *Surfer* und für die kurzlebige *Surfing Illustrated.*

Die frühen Surfmagazine waren hausgemachte Projekte, die von den Sportbegeisterten selbst am Küchentisch geschaffen und unters Volk gebracht wurden. Als *Surfer* herauskam, wurden Druckerzeugnisse erstmals auch für Herausgeber mit niedrigen Budget wie Severson bezahlbar; außerdem hatte die Verwertung der Nischensportart in den Medien bereits begonnen, z. B. in Filmen wie *Gidget* (1959) und *Ride the Wild Surf* (1964). In Südkalifornien hatte die Film- und Fernsehindustrie von Hollywood actiongeladene, bunte Bilder vom Surfen als Blickfang entdeckt. „Plötzlich war die Möglichkeit da, ein Bild, das man gemacht hatte, auf ungeahnte Weise zu vermarkten", erzählt John Van Hamersveld, ehemaliger Artdirector bei *Surfer* und Schöpfer des legendären Leuchtfarbenplakats für *The Endless Summer.* „Diese kleine, isolierte Subkultur wurde jetzt von den Medien aufgegriffen und durch die Zeitschriften und die Surffilme hinauf zu den Produzenten der Massenkultur transportiert."

**Ricky Hatch, Hermosa Beach, 1961**

The talented 22nd Street regular in a now-famous ad for Jacobs Surfboards.

Das Multitalent von der 22nd Street in einer inzwischen berühmten Werbeanzeige für Jacobs Surfboards.

Le talentueux Ricky Hatch, un habitué de 22nd Street, dans une publicité devenue célèbre pour la marque Jacobs Surfboards.

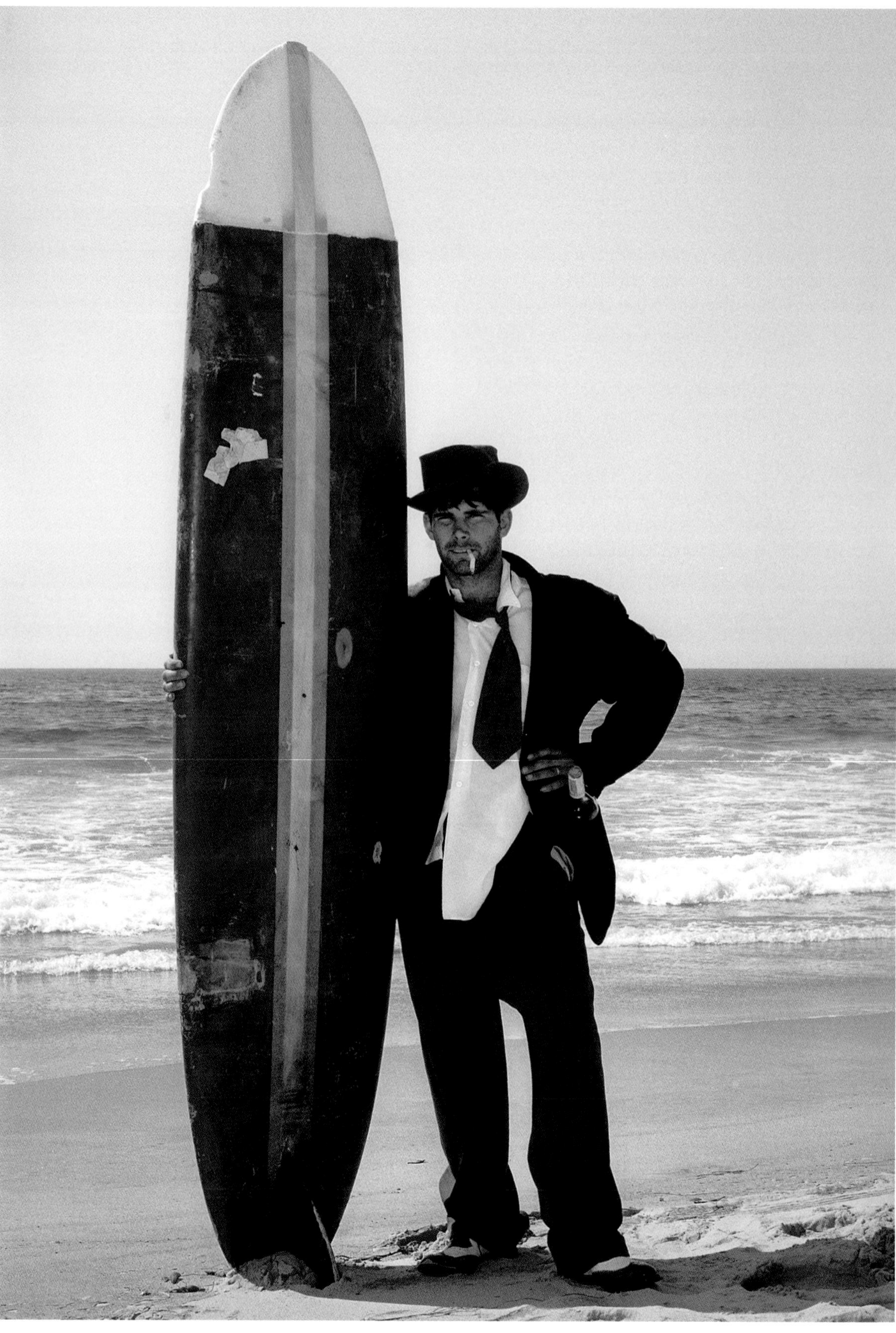

1966 hatte sich das, was fünf Jahre zuvor noch eine aufgesetzte „Surfmode" gewesen war, zu einer authentischen Jugendbewegung entwickelt, die ihre eigene Sprache, ihre Musik, Mode, Medien, Autos und Verhaltenskodizes hatte. Das Interesse des Mainstreams an dieser Szene befand sich auf dem absoluten Höhepunkt, und ein kleines südkalifornisches Herstellerkartell von Surfprodukten, auch „Dana Point Mafia" genannt, verdiente sich dumm und dämlich. Der noch in den Kinderschuhen steckende Sport – eher eine Glaubensrichtung als eine Wochenendbeschäftigung – bekam im Juli 1966 enormen Auftrieb, als im ganzen Land Bruce Browns Film *The Endless Summer* in die Kinos kam. Dieser einfallsreiche, lässige Dokumentarfilm gab der Welt der Nichtsurfer (den „Legions of the Unjazzed", wie Meistersurfer Phil Edwards es auszudrücken beliebte) den ersten realistischen Einblick in die eher abgeschlossene Surfszene, und die Welt wollte mehr davon. Eine Art Goldrauschstimmung breitete sich aus.

In San Diego beglückwünschten sich die Stadtväter und die Ausrichter der Surfweltmeisterschaft gegenseitig zum neu gewonnenen Ansehen des Wellenreitens. Die Wettbewerbsrepräsentanten hofften, bei der bevorstehenden Meisterschaft die immer zahlreicher werdenden „Surf-Hooligans" und die negativen Schlagzeilen loswerden zu können, die den Sport seit dem Kinostart von *Gidget* in der ersten großen Boomzeit verfolgt hatten. Die Handelskammer von San Diego freute sich über einen enormen Anstieg der Touristenzahlen, als diese sexy Strandsportart scheinbar über Nacht die Jugend des Landes mit ihrem lose sitzenden Geldbeutel im Sturm eroberte.

Gleichzeitig wurde das lockere Surferleben von einer konservativen Welle überrollt. John Severson führte in seiner Zeitschrift *Surfer* eine Kampagne durch, mit der die Surfszene von „unerwünschten Elementen" gereinigt werden sollte. Das Magazin schlug in seinen Beiträgen einen selbstgerechten Ton an, und in Gastbeiträgen und sorgfältig ausgewählten Leserbriefen ließ man sich hämisch über die Niederlage der Surfpunks oder „hodads" aus, die das Ansehen des Surfens angeblich mit geschmacklosen Streichen und einer allgemein negativen Einstellung gegenüber Autoritätsfiguren beschmutzt hätten. „[Das Wellenreiten] spricht nicht mehr nur Außenseiter an", verkündete John Hannon, ein führender Surfboardhersteller von der Ostküste, in einem *Newsweek*-Interview. „Diese Jungs haben einen ordentlichen Haarschnitt und saubere Fingernägel; sie werden diese Unruhestifter auf ihre Plätze verweisen."

**Die Eröffnungsrunde der „Shortboard Revolution" – und damit das Ende der** unkomplizierten frühen Sechzigerjahre – wurde am 2. Oktober 1966 in Ocean Beach, San Diego, eingeläutet. Dort, bei bedecktem Himmel mit kleinen, sanften Wellen, überraschte Nat Young die amtierende Surfelite mit einem bis dahin unbekannten radikalen Stil. Mit seinen harten und kraftvoll gefahrenen Manövern gewann er die World Surfing Championships im Handumdrehen. Als David Nuuhiwa, der geschmeidige Hawaiianer, der für seine langen, eleganten Noserides berühmt war, auf ihn einredete: „Du musst versuchen, mit der Welle eins zu werden", erwiderte Young frech: „Ich will mit gar nichts eins werden!" Youngs Ausrüstung war nicht weniger provozierend als seine Sprüche. Er gewann den Contest auf „Magic Sam", einem selbst gebauten Surfbrett, das neun Fuß, vier

Zoll lang war – einen ganzen Fuß kürzer als der damalige Standard. Er hatte es zusammen mit seinem australischen Landsmann Bob McTavish entwickelt; es besaß eine lange, krummsäbelartige Finne, die sich der exzentrische amerikanische Board-Shaper George Greenough ausgedacht hatte. Durch diesen drastischen Evolutionssprung in Technologie und Mentalität wurde praktisch über Nacht eine ganze Generation von Wettkampfboards reif für den Müllhaufen. Mit Nat Youngs Sieg sollte sich das Wellenreiten die nächsten zehn oder mehr Jahre lang vom Mainstream wegbewegen. Big Nat, wegen seines aggressiv-radikalen Stils „the Animal" genannt, hatte der Welt einen Blick in die Zukunft eröffnet. Bis 1966 war das schwierigste Manöver der Hang Ten gewesen (elegant auf dem vordersten Ende des Bretts balancieren und die Zehenspitzen beider Füße über die Nose hinaushängen lassen). Von jetzt an war alles möglich – man nannte es „mind surfing". Und es war, wie *Surfer*-Journalist Paul Gross schrieb, „eine Massenflucht weg von allem, was vorher da gewesen war". Doch niemand schien es damals so recht zu bemerken. Gleichzeitig breiteten sich die psychedelischen Drogen wie ein Steppenbrand in der Surfszene aus; bei manchen führten sie zur Erweiterung des Bewusstseins, bei anderen zum totalen Aussetzen des Denkvermögens. Das Wellenreiten wurde zu einer introvertierten, esoterischen Angelegenheit, als ehemals Jantzen-Sportswear tragende „hotdogger" zu bärtigen Zen-Anhängern mutierten. Wettbewerbe waren nicht mehr cool, niemanden interessierte es, wer Erster wurde. Es ging jetzt nicht mehr um Tricks und Trophäen, sondern um die Ausbalancierung des persönlichen Karmaflusses in „Kristallkathedralen aus geschmolzenem Glas", wie im *Surfer* nachzulesen war. Rick Griffin machte schon 1966 in seinen Cartoons für *Surfer* versteckte Anspielungen auf Drogen, was viele der Werbekunden der Zeitschriften verärgerte. Ihr nomadenhafter Lebensstil veranlasste nicht wenige Surfabenteurer zu einer Zweitkarriere als internationale Drogenschmuggler. „Man war entweder dabei oder nicht", schrieb Drew Kampion, Herausgeber des *Surfer* von 1968 bis 1972. „Man kapierte es oder man kapierte es nicht. Man glaubte an Schwerkraft oder man glaubte an Schwerelosigkeit. Man war verklemmt oder man ließ sich fallen. Alles befand sich so ziemlich im freien Fall damals."

Nach dem kurzen Liebäugeln mit der Mainstream-Respektabilität besann sich die Subkultur auf ihre Wurzeln als Protestbewegung gegen die angepasste Gesellschaft, was in der Welt draußen nicht unbemerkt blieb. In seinem weithin bekannten Essay „The Pump House Gang" berichtete Popkulturkritiker Tom Wolfe 1966, dass viele Surfer „sich vom Wellenreiten hin zu einer Vorhut ganz anderer Art entwickeln – der abgedrifteten psychedelischen Welt Kaliforniens". Wo die amerikanische Industrie einst eine Generation williger Jungkonsumenten gesehen hatte, erblickte sie jetzt nur noch lange Haare, Haschischrauch und einen ablehnend hochgestreckten Mittelfinger.

Die wirtschaftlichen Folgen waren weitreichend. Innerhalb der nächsten Jahre mussten die großen Bretthersteller sich entweder verkleinern oder dichtmachen. Beim *Surfer* gingen die Werbeeinnahmen in den Keller, die Zeitschrift wurde immer kleiner und die Redaktion immer linkslastiger. Unter der neuen, radikaleren Führung von Kampion wurde *Surfer* zum Multiplikator der immer größer werdenden Gegenkultur, die sich für Frieden, freie Liebe, Tuberides und das Recht jedes Surfers stark machte, auszusteigen und sich die Birne so richtig vollzuknallen. Kampion, der öffentlich gegen die meisten organisierten Surfwettbewerbe mit Artikeln wie „Schlechtes Karma am Huntington Beach" oder „Tod allen Wettbewerben" hetzte, wollte das Wellenreiten als Metapher für kosmische Ausgewogenheit verstanden wissen, nicht als kapitalistischen Egotrip. Auch der Eskalation des Vietnamkrieges, der die Surfer in alarmierenden Zahlen vom Strand wegriss, stand er sehr kritisch gegenüber. Er eröffnete die Jagd auf den neuen amerikanischen Präsidenten Richard Nixon, weil der es gewagt hatte, in die Nähe von Trestles Beach in San Clemente zu ziehen und dort den besten Surfspot zu blockieren, wann immer er im „Western White House" residierte.

Grannis entstammte einer ganz anderen Generation und konnte nicht viel mit dem neuen Antiestablishment-Dogma des Wellenreitens anfangen. Als jemand,

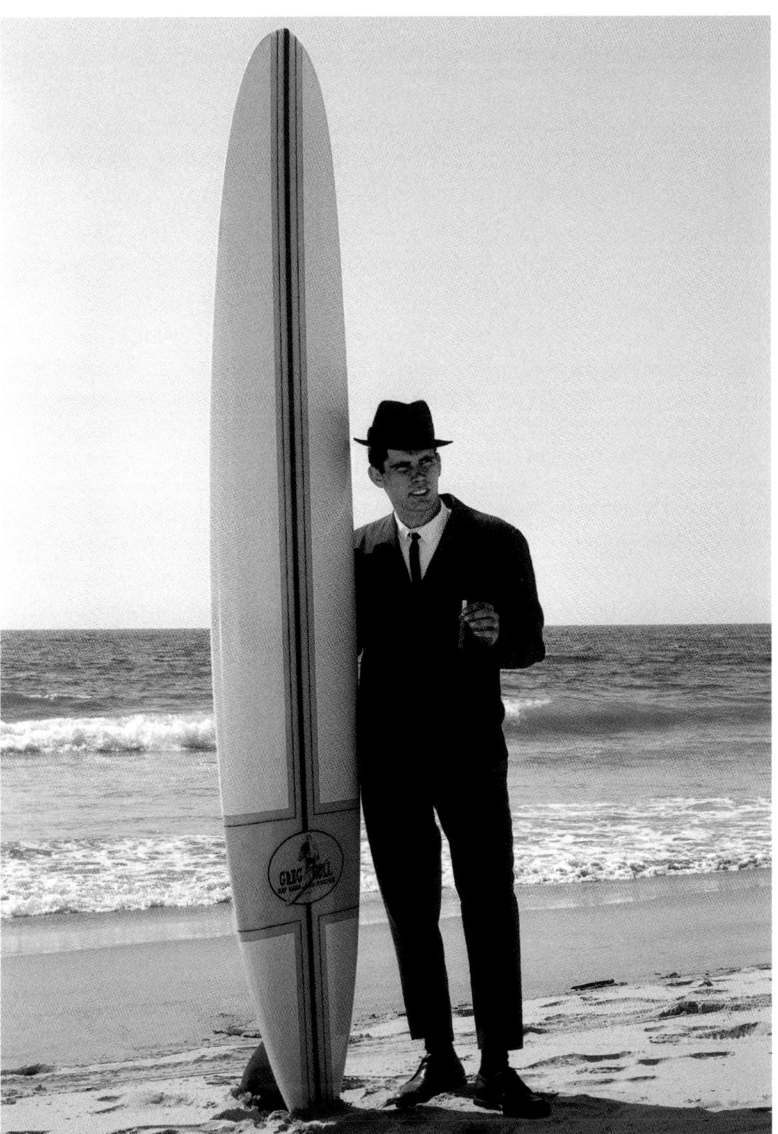


Pages 42 + 45
**Gary Dalton, Hermosa Beach, 1964**

Ad captions for Greg Noll Surfboards: "He doesn't ride Greg Noll boards" (p. 42); "He does ride Greg Noll boards" (left).

Werbeslogans für Greg Noll Surfboards: „Er surft nicht auf Greg Noll Boards" (p. 42); „Er surft auf Greg Noll Boards" (links).

Slogans publicitaires pour la marque Greg Noll Surfboards: « Sa planche n'est pas une Greg Noll » (p. 42); « Sa planche est une Greg Noll » (à gauche).

der den Zweiten Weltkrieg erlebt hatte und seinem guten Freund Hop Swarts bei der Durchführung von Wettbewerben in der neu gegründeten United States Surfing Association geholfen hatte, hielt Grannis standhaft an der Idee fest, dass das Wettbewerbswellenreiten dem Sport zugutekam und seine gesellschaftlich akzeptable Seite betonte. 1968 veröffentlichte Grannis einen Beitrag, in dem er gute, saubere Surfwettbewerbe verteidigte und ihre Kritiker als „ewige Nörgler" bezeichnete, die kein Recht hätten, sich zu beschweren. „In den letzten Jahren hat es eine Flut unsinniger Artikel gegeben, in denen die Wellenreiter von vorgestern, nicht surfende hawaiianische Journalisten, windige Handelsvertreter und frustrierte Möchtegern-Redakteure auf den Wettbewerben herumhacken", schrieb er. „Allesamt haben sie nur deswegen etwas gegen Wettbewerbe, weil sie selbst keine Chance hätten."

Dennoch gehörten Ende der Sechziger die meisten Wettbewerbe, sogar die einstmals so angesehenen Surfer Poll Awards des *Surfer*-Magazins, der Vergangenheit an. Das Ereignis, das einem professionellen Wettkampf am ehesten nahekam, war ein durchgeknallter Antiwettbewerb, der sich „Expression Session" nannte, bei dem die Topsurfer ohne alle Preisrichter, Punkte und Trophäen ihre Künste zur Schau stellten. „In diesem Jahr wurde vieles entwickelt oder sogar neu erfunden: Shortboards, V-Bottoms, Mini-Guns, flexible Finnen, kurze Finnen – insgesamt radikales Board-Design", schrieb Kampion 1968. „Es gibt nur wenige Wellenreiter, die jetzt noch so surfen wie vor einem Jahr." Nichtsdestotrotz verfasste Grannis einen weiteren Gastbeitrag, in dem er sehr richtig voraussagte, dass es eines Tages eine Rückkehr zu Longboards und zum Noseriding geben würde. Und während all dieser Umwälzungen hielt Grannis immer weiter seine Kamera auf einen Sport gerichtet, den er von ganzem Herzen liebte, und schoss unendlich viele Bilder von Longboardern wie von Shortboardern, trotz aller Grabenkämpfe zwischen den so unterschiedlichen Surfphilosophien.

**Anfang Dezember 1969 wurden Hawaii und Kalifornien von einer Jahrhundert-** flut heimgesucht. Wie Berge türmten sich die zehn Meter hohen Wellen am North Shore von Oahu auf, zerstörten sechzig Häuser und schleuderten große Boote hundert Meter weit ins Landesinnere. Auch wenn die Wellen am gesamten North Shore zu riesig waren, um sie bezwingen zu können, nahmen es Greg Noll und eine kleine Gruppe von Surfern mit den etwas kleineren Wellen in Makaha auf der Westseite der Insel auf. Dort erwischte Noll die vermutlich größte Welle, die bis zu diesem Zeitpunkt jemals gesurft worden war. Den resultierenden Wipeout überlebte er nur knapp. „In einem Sport, der mit rapiden Veränderungen, Hype und Revolution zu kämpfen hat, erwischte ein knallharter Dinosaurier aus den Fünfzigern die letzte große Welle von 1969", schrieb Drew Kampion.

Der Swell von 1969 wird in der Surfwelt allgemein als grandioses geophysikalisches Finale für die zerstrittenste und turbulenteste Dekade des Wellenreitens angesehen. „Was wir im Dezember 69 erlebten", erinnerte sich der in den Sechzigerjahren legendäre Skip Frye viel später, „war in gewisser Weise der Wechsel vom Sixties-Longboard-Ding zur Shortboard-Ära. Es war wie einmal Großreinemachen, und danach war nichts mehr wie vorher." Grannis war

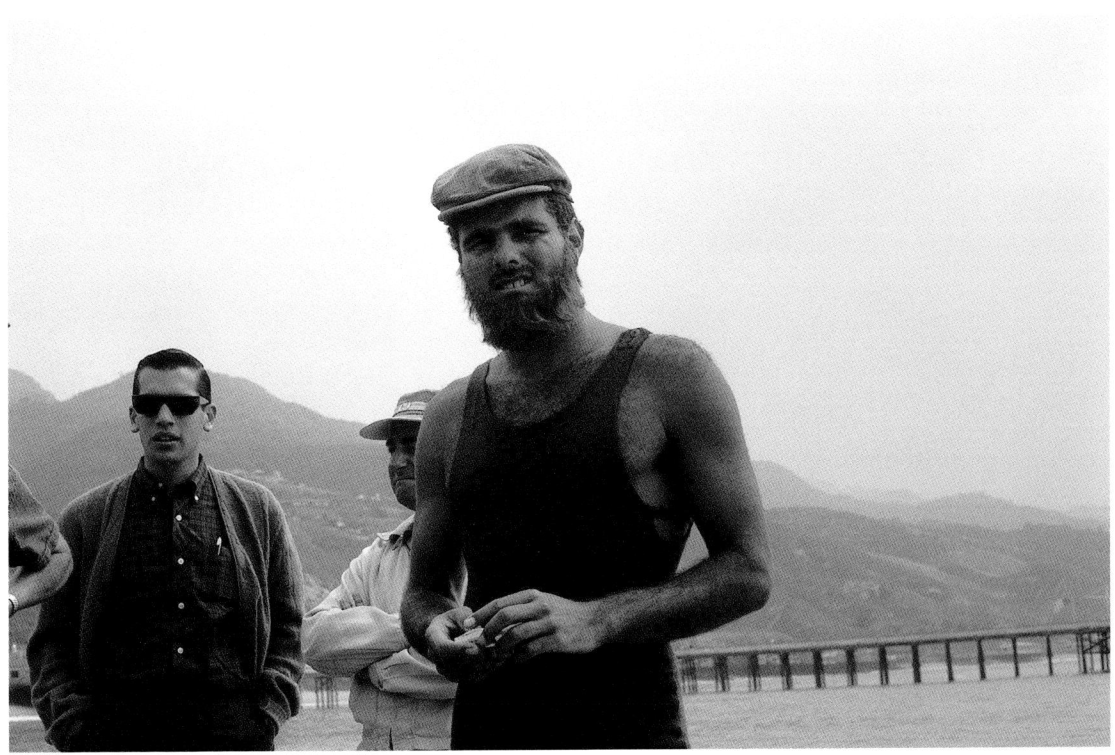

überzeugt, dass die Brettgröße nur eine Frage der Logistik war, und konnte die Kluft zwischen den beiden Generationen mit seinen Fotografien überbrücken. „Ich habe Surfer fotografiert, keine Bretter", sagt er. „Für mich veränderte sich im Grunde nicht so viel."

LeRoy Grannis' letztes Surffoto für *International Surfing* wurde 1971 veröffentlicht. Ende der Siebzigerjahre verabschiedete er sich von Pacific Bell Telephone, ging in Rente und zog von Hermosa Beach nach Carlsbad, Kalifornien. Über zwanzig Jahre lang surfte und fotografierte er dort noch weiter; seine Abzüge und Negative bewahrte er ordentlich in Ringordnern zu Hause auf. Das entscheidende Jahrzehnt in der Geschichte des Wellenreitens, als eine kleine Randgruppe passionierter Surfer aus ihrem Lebensstil eine weltumspannende Industrie machte, wäre beinahe dem Vergessen anheimgefallen.

Grannis, ein Pionier des Surfsports und dessen Fotografie, fing die Surfgeschichte am Wendepunkt ihrer Evolution ein. Diese Retrospektive seiner Bilder – von den Klassikern des Katalogs bis zu noch nie veröffentlichten, in seinem Archiv entdeckten Aufnahmen – gewährt dem Betrachter Zugang zu einem Lebensstil, der sich von einer Handvoll Begeisterter zu einem Wirtschaftszweig mit 4 Mrd. Dollar Umsatz im Jahr entwickelt hat. Heute, da zahllose Bilder professioneller Surffotografen den Markt überschwemmen, bieten Grannis' Fotos in ihrer eleganten Einfachheit und als Zeugen einer vergangenen Zeit einen wichtigen Einblick in die Entstehung einer Subkultur. „Ich war Wellenreiter und fotografierte das, was ich mir gerne ansah", wehrt Grannis bescheiden ab. „Wahrscheinlich habe ich eine Menge Glück gehabt."

**Miki Dora, Malibu, 1963**

Beat at the beach—Dora strikes at the heart of gray-flannel conformity.

Beat at the Beach – Dora protestiert gegen angepasste Flanellträger.

Sur la plage de Malibu, Miki Dora s'attaque au conformisme vestimentaire avec sa tenue beatnik.

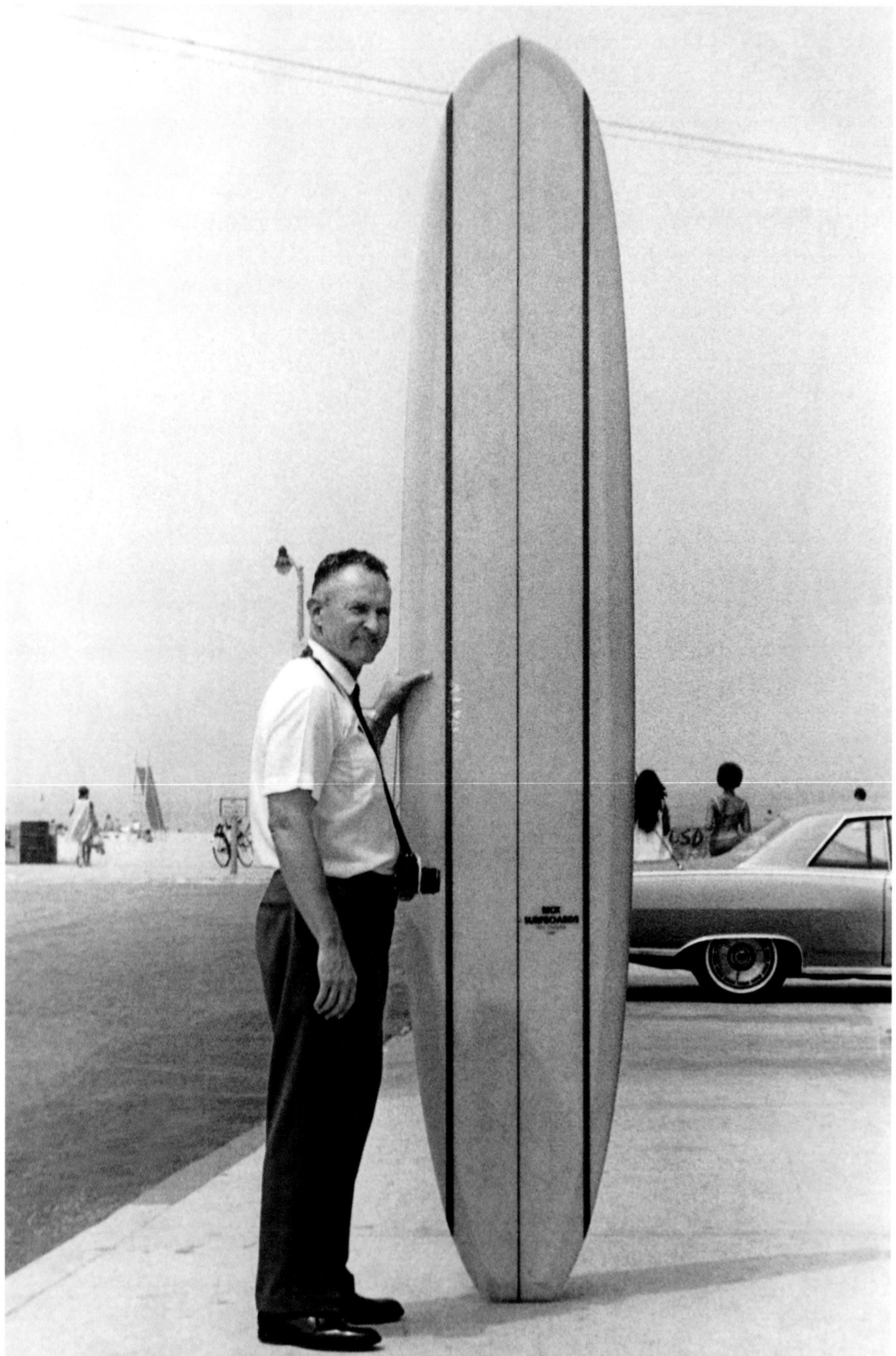

# LA VAGUE PARFAITE
## capturée par l'objectif de LeRoy Grannis

*Par Steve Barilotti*

La révolution fut immortalisée en noir et blanc par un dimanche après-midi, en l'espace de 1/250ᵉ de seconde. Ce 2 octobre 1966, Ocean Beach, près de San Diego, accueille les championnats du monde de surf. Quarante mille spectateurs sont agglutinés sur la plage et sur l'embarcadère flambant neuf. Au moment même où le jeune Robert « Nat » Young, du haut de ses dix-huit ans, soulève au-dessus de sa tête le lourd trophée en forme de Californie, quelque trois cent quarante mille G. I. s'enlisent dans les rizières du Vietnam, Brian Wilson est sur le point de sortir son album mythique *Good Vibrations* et le LSD vit ses trois derniers mois de légalité. Les planches mesurent en moyenne dix pieds et demi et pèsent plus de treize kilos. Nat Young est sacré champion du monde, et l'univers du surf vient d'opérer un virage à 180 degrés.

Sur le podium des vainqueurs, le jeune Australien – imposant par sa taille et par son tempérament fougueux – est flanqué de Jock Sutherland, un Hawaïen à la voix douce, et du Californien Corky Carroll, l'enfant prodige de la petite vague. Un petit groupe de reporters locaux et nationaux, représentant entre autres *Newsweek* et *The New York Times,* se bouscule pour être au plus près des héros du jour. LeRoy Grannis, photographe exclusif du magazine *International Surfing*, rôde dans les derniers rangs de la foule, capturant méthodiquement les images du trophée avec son Pentax S rongé par le sel. Au moment crucial de la cérémonie, il met l'image au point et cadre le jeune Young en train de jubiler : « Je suis sur un nuage ! »

Malgré l'agitation palpable qui règne sur la plage, Grannis reste stoïque et impassible. Pour lui, tout cela n'est finalement que l'apogée d'une saison passée à sillonner la Californie du Sud et à immortaliser les week-ends de compétition interclubs. Alors âgé de quarante-neuf ans, Grannis compte à son actif trente-cinq années de pratique du surf et six années de photographie consacrée à la discipline. Le week-end suivant, son boulot le conduira sans doute vers le nord, à Malibu ou à Huntington Beach, pour couvrir une nouvelle compétition locale, et les qualifications pour les prochains championnats du monde de surf reprendront bientôt.

### LeRoy Grannis s'est lancé dans la photographie de surf à la fin de l'année
1959, non pas en tant que professionnel ou artiste, mais comme un bon père de famille en quête d'un passe-temps qui lui permettrait d'évacuer le stress de la vie professionnelle. La chance a voulu qu'il ressorte son appareil photo à un



*Depuis des temps immémoriaux, les nombreux témoignages relatant la chevauchée des vagues par les hommes nous sont livrés sous des formes multiples, depuis les mélopées des anciens et les premiers écrits jusqu'aux images actuelles sublimées par l'œil du photographe.*

—**Tom Blake,** surfer de la première heure et photographe de surf

**LeRoy Grannis, Hermosa Beach, California, 1969**

On a lunch break from his day job as a supervisor with Pacific Bell Telephone.

Während einer Mittagspause des hauptberuflichen Abteilungsleiters bei Pacific Bell Telephone.

Au cours d'une pause déjeuner à l'époque où il occupait un poste de direction chez Pacific Bell Telephone.

*Grannis, qui a grandi à
quelques pas de la plage de
Hermosa Beach, a commencé
à surfer à l'âge de quatorze ans
sur une planche d'emprunt
en séquoia qui pesait près de
quarante-cinq kilos.*

**Santa Monica, 1966**

Induction into the International
Surfing Hall of Fame. Back row,
left to right: Dale Velzy (for Bob
Simmons), Buzzy Trent, Duke
Kahanamoku, Phil Edwards, Greg
Noll, Miki Dora. Front row: Pete
Peterson, George Downing, Hoppy
Swarts, Dewey Weber, Don Hansen
(for Mike Doyle).

Einführung in die International
Surfing Hall of Fame. Hintere
Reihe, von links nach rechts: Dale
Velzy (für Bob Simmons), Buzzy
Trent, Duke Kahanamoku, Phil
Edwards, Greg Noll, Miki Dora.
Vordere Reihe: Pete Peterson,
George Downing, Hoppy Swarts,
Dewey Weber, Don Hansen (für
Mike Doyle).

Visite guidée dans la galerie des
célébrités du surf international.
Debout, de gauche à droite : Dale
Velzy (représentant Bob Simmons),
Buzzy Trent, Duke Kahanamoku,
Phil Edwards, Greg Noll et Miki
Dora. Accroupis, de gauche à
droite : Pete Peterson, George
Downing, Hoppy Swarts, Dewey
Weber et Don Hansen (représentant
Mike Doyle).

tournant crucial de l'histoire du surf. Né en 1917 à Hermosa Beach en
Californie, Grannis était un rescapé de l'époque où la côte Ouest ne comptait
que quelque deux cents surfeurs californiens qui, dans un esprit de gentlemen,
flirtaient avec les vagues lentes de San Onofre et de Palos Verdes Cove sur des
planches massives de onze pieds taillées dans le séquoia. Ils incarnaient la
première génération de surfeurs californiens à avoir adopté cette vieille discipline
importée sur le continent par les Hawaïens George Freeth et Duke Kahanamoku
et ont ainsi contribué à la renaissance du surf, cette pratique introduite à la fin
du XIXe siècle par une poignée de « beach boys » hawaïens.

Grannis, qui a grandi à quelques pas de la plage de Hermosa Beach, a commencé à surfer à l'âge de quatorze ans sur une planche d'emprunt en séquoia qui
pesait près de quarante-cinq kilos. C'est là, tandis qu'il taquinait les petites vagues
qui venaient s'écraser sous la jetée, qu'il a rencontré les trois camarades de surf
qui deviendront ses amis pour la vie : le premier est Lewis « Hoppy » Swarts,
le second est un garçon natif de Hermosa beach et le troisième, John « Doc » Ball,
un sympathique gaillard de dix ans son aîné, étudiant en dentisterie à l'Université
de Californie du Sud.

Ball est un surfer confirmé et ne tarde pas à convaincre ses jeunes camarades
Grannis et Swarts d'aller se mesurer aux belles vagues de Palos Verdes Cove, à
huit kilomètres au sud. La baie de Palos Verdes était devenue la résidence secon-
daire d'une escouade de surfeurs passionnés, pour la plupart de jeunes garçons
désœuvrés d'une vingtaine d'années qui attendaient la fin de la Grande Dépression en déployant des trésors d'ingéniosité pour boucler leur budget. Ne
comptant que sur eux-mêmes, ils construisaient leurs planches de leurs propres
mains, cousaient leurs shorts de surf eux-mêmes et alimentaient de leurs maigres
économies la cagnotte commune pour acheter le carburant – et parfois une
bouteille de vin bon marché – qui leur permettait d'organiser des sorties à Malibu
ou à San Onofre. Beaucoup parmi eux étaient des plongeurs chevronnés et
régalaient la troupe de festins de homards et d'ormeaux pêchés au fond des
bassins de marée environnants. En 1935, Ball crée le Palos Verdes Surfing Club
et y introduit en 1936 ses camarades Swarts et Grannis (lequel prend dès lors
le surnom de « Granny »).

**Les photographes trouvaient dans les surfeurs des sujets naturels, à l'image**
de ces majestueux Hawaïens au teint cuivré immortalisés en équilibre sur leur
planche avec en toile de fond la silhouette impressionnante du volcan Diamond
Head – un décor de carte postale devenu mythique. L'iconographie du surf était
essentiellement due aux surfeurs eux-mêmes. Les photographes de surf étaient
tous des amateurs autodidactes ; aucun d'entre eux ne vivait de la vente de ses
photos. Tom Blake, à la fois surfer et *shaper* d'avant-garde, a fabriqué en 1929
un boîtier étanche pour son appareil photo Graflex et commencé à photographier
depuis sa planche les « beach boys » de Hawaï qui dévalaient sous l'œil de son
objectif les longues déferlantes de Waikiki sur leurs *alaia* de douze pieds. Il fut le
précepteur de Doc Ball, lequel à son tour exerça une grande influence sur Don
James et, plus tard, sur LeRoy Grannis. Ball était un photographe talentueux doté
d'un œil vif et toujours en quête d'angles nouveaux ; il a mis au point des

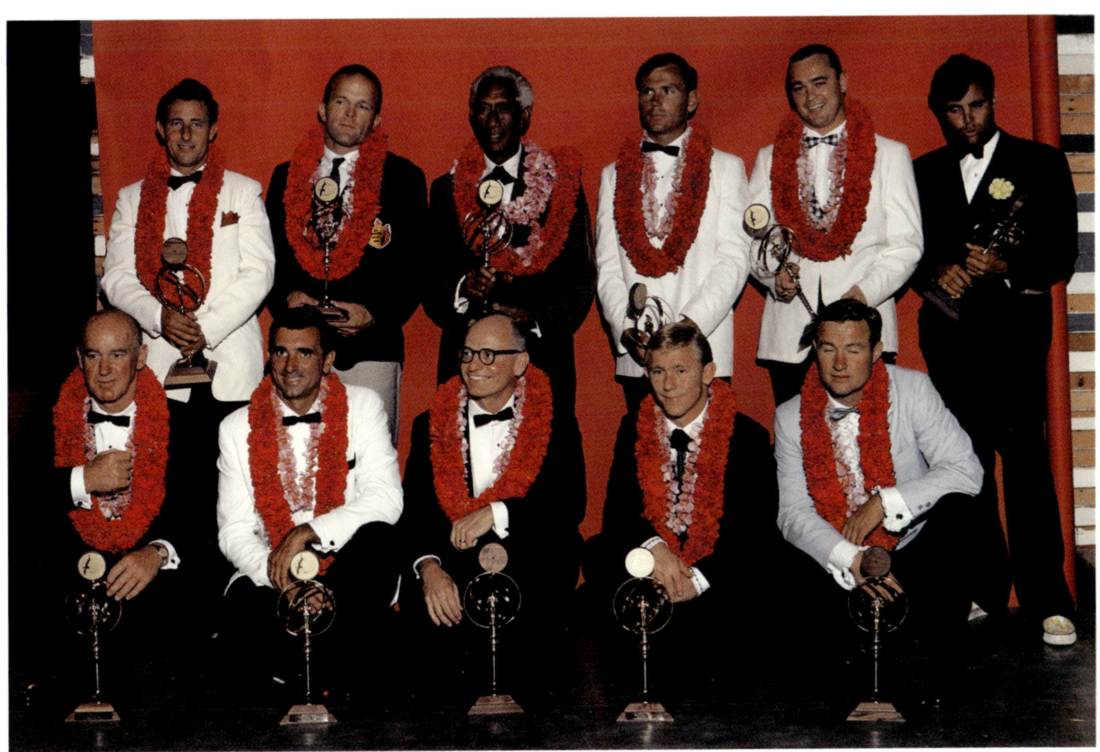

prototypes de boîtiers étanches pour pouvoir emporter son appareil photo au cœur de l'action. Ses clichés d'un naturel saisissant, avec pour modèles sa bande d'amis et leurs petites copines, ont immortalisé l'époque dorée, mais éphémère, du surf « pur » qui s'est éteinte peu après l'attaque de Pearl Harbor par les Japonais en 1941.

Avec le déclenchement de la Seconde Guerre mondiale, l'enrôlement de la plupart des jeunes surfeurs de plus de dix-huit ans aptes au service militaire marque le déclin brutal du surf californien. Beaucoup ne revirent jamais leur terre natale. Bien que jeune marié et malgré la naissance de sa fille en 1941, Grannis s'enrôle deux ans plus tard dans la U.S. Air Force. Mais lorsqu'il obtient son diplôme d'aviateur, la guerre est finie et il est libéré en 1946. De retour à Hermosa Beach, Grannis devient ingénieur en télécommunications et décroche un emploi stable d'installateur de standards téléphoniques chez Pacific Bell Telephone. (Il reste cependant en réserve active au service de la U.S. Air Force, dont il prendra sa retraite en 1977 avec le grade de commandant.)

Au cours des années qui suivent la guerre, Grannis surfe de manière sporadique, mais son travail et sa famille – il est alors père de quatre enfants – ne lui laissent que peu de répit. Vers la fin de l'année 1959, on lui diagnostique un ulcère de l'estomac dû au stress et son médecin lui recommande la pratique d'une activité de détente. Grannis s'oriente tout naturellement vers la photographie aquatique – il habite à quelques rues de l'océan et son jeune fils Franck vient de commencer à pratiquer le surf. En juin 1960, Grannis aménage une chambre

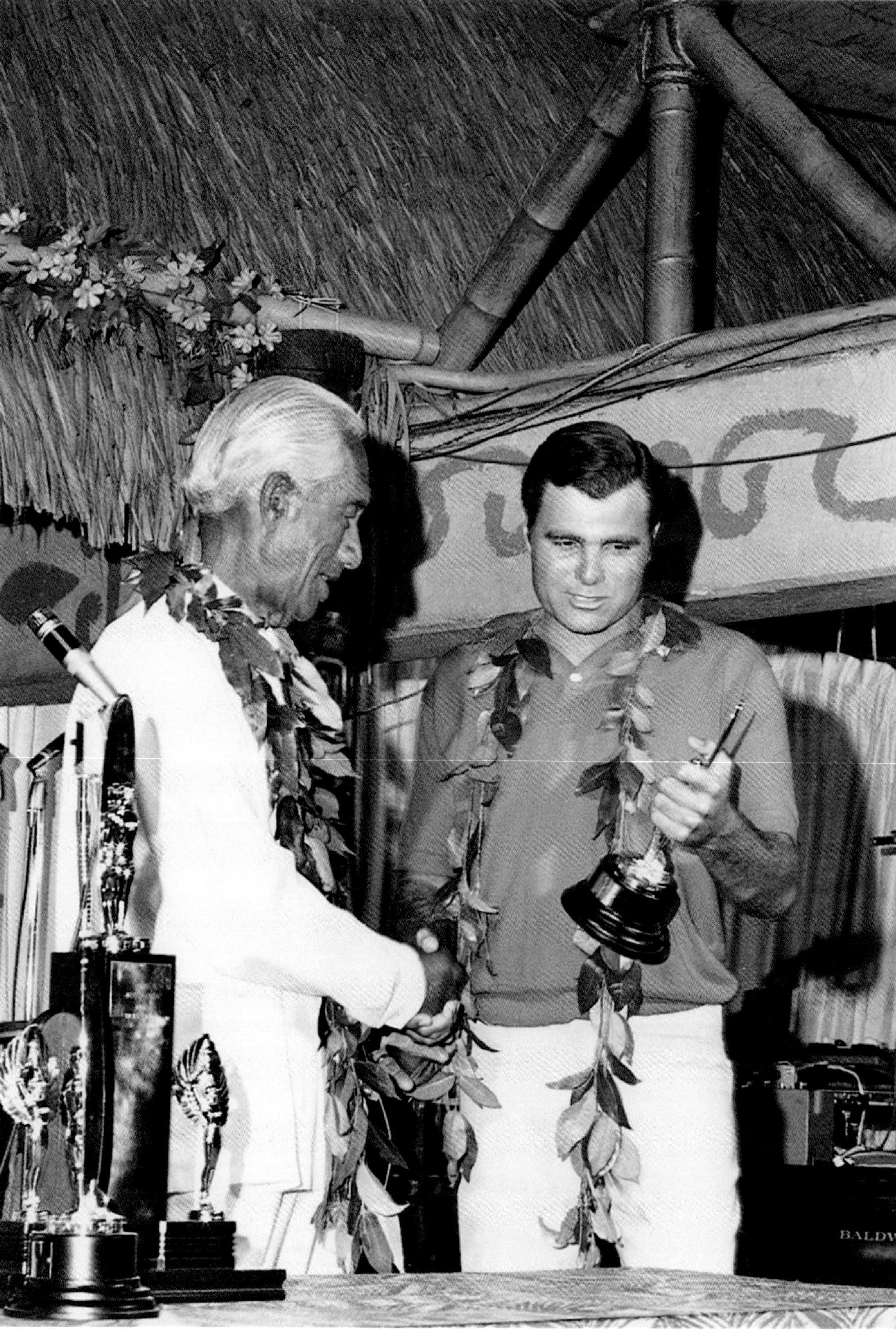

noire dans son garage et développe lui-même, de façon encore rudimentaire, quelques clichés au style fortement influencé par Doc Ball.

L'été 1960, équipé d'un appareil photo est-allemand de 35 mm, Grannis commence à photographier les surfeurs de 22nd Street sur Hermosa Beach, une portion relativement quelconque du *beach break* de Sunset Beach où une troupe de jeunes surfeurs se bousculent pour prendre la pose devant son objectif. Le leader incontesté de la bande de 22nd Street est un certain Dewey Weber, un jeune prodige de vingt-trois ans qui a déjà tourné dans plusieurs films consacrés au surf et qui vient d'ouvrir sa propre boutique de planches tout près de là, à Venice Beach. Bien que de petite taille – il ne mesure qu'un mètre soixante – Weber est un surfer puissant dont le style agressif encourage le reste de l'équipe, constituée notamment de Henry Ford, Freddie Pfahler et Mike Zuetell, à repousser les limites. À la fin de l'année 1960, Grannis a pris et développé plus de deux mille cinq cents photos.

La chambre noire de Grannis était devenue un véritable laboratoire de développement rapide à South Bay, et à une époque où les magazines de surf étaient bimensuels, les surfeurs étaient friands de clichés de leurs propres exploits sans cesse renouvelés. « Parfois, je me rendais directement de 22nd Street à ma chambre noire et, le temps de me retourner, j'avais une demi-douzaine de gars qui attendaient devant pour voir le résultat », se souvient Grannis. « Et une fois que je les avais laissés entrer, c'était la fièvre assurée dans le labo. Je me souviens de deux gamins, Tom et Don Craig, qui habitaient juste à côté ; ils n'hésitaient pas à fouiller dans mes ordures pour voir si je n'avais pas jeté des photos qu'ils voulaient récupérer à tout prix. » Sa maison n'était qu'à trois quarts d'heure de voiture de Malibu par la Pacific Coast Highway – qui n'avait alors que deux voies. À l'époque où Grannis surfait à Malibu, dans les années 1930, cet endroit n'était qu'un obscur *point break*, loin de devenir le *spot* mondialement couru des années 1960. Grâce à sa houle idéale, ses crêtes de vagues parfaitement formées et la proximité de Hollywood, « The 'Bu » devient alors un rendez-vous estival respecté de l'élite du surf. Bien que déjà extrêmement fréquenté à cette époque, le *break* accueille aussi des stars de la planche comme Lance Carson, Johnny Fain, Mike Hynson et le légendaire Miki Dora, lequel dansait sur les grosses vagues dans un style vif et théâtral qui prendrait bientôt le nom de « hotdogging ». Les talents de photographe de Grannis se confirment rapidement et la vente de ses premiers clichés de Malibu à l'éphémère magazine *Reef* marque le début de sa longue carrière de photojournaliste.

En novembre 1961, Grannis entreprend son premier voyage à Hawaï, l'avant-poste du surf de l'époque. Après deux semaines passées à photographier les petites vagues de Waikiki et de Makaha, il pousse vers le mythique North Shore, la côte nord de l'île d'Oahu. Devant le spectacle d'un *swell* de circonstance, Grannis reste captivé par la puissance et la magnitude des déferlantes de Hawaï. Équipé d'un téléobjectif de 650 mm, il fixe sur sa pellicule des surfeurs de la trempe de Rick Grigg, Peter Cole ou Phil Edwards en train de dévaler les gigantesques creux du redoutable *spot* de « West Bowl » à Sunset Beach.

Grannis rentre en Californie avec une ferveur redoublée. Au cours des années qui suivent, il développe trois fois plus de clichés et s'oriente résolument vers la couleur, le style de vie des surfeurs, la compétition et la publicité. L'industrie naissante du surf, repliée sur elle-même et soucieuse de son budget, est peu encline à se tourner vers l'extérieur et préfère réaliser elle-même ses illustrations et ses photos. Alors qu'il n'a aucune expérience de commercial, Grannis se débrouille donc pour vendre ses clichés grâce à quelques idées simples et convaincantes. C'est ainsi que la photo publicitaire qu'il réalise pour les planches Jacobs Surfboards entre dans les annales de la photographie de surf. On y voit Ricky Hatch, une figure locale de Hermosa Beach, chaussures aux pieds et affublé d'un costume noir impeccablement taillé, en train d'exécuter un habile exercice d'équilibre sur le nez de sa planche. En 1963, Grannis dégotte un appareil photo amphibie Calypso (ancêtre du Nikonos et invention de Jacques-Yves Cousteau) et réalise un cliché modèle de Henry Ford en train d'exécuter un *bottom turn* parfait à 22nd Street.

Grannis découvre bientôt que la photographie aquatique consacrée au surf est une discipline particulièrement périlleuse, y compris pour les sportifs les plus chevronnés. Un jour qu'il photographie Sunset Beach depuis le large avec son Nikonos, il est surpris par une gigantesque lame qui s'engouffre dans la passe de West Peak Bowl avant de se briser à distance du rivage et de piéger le photographe dans son sillage. Lorsqu'il relève la tête, Grannis aperçoit un mur d'écume de sept mètres de haut et trois lourdes planches de onze pieds lancées à toute vitesse en direction de sa tête dépourvue de toute protection. Dans un réflexe salutaire, il plonge sous le maelström et réussit même à sauver son précieux appareil photo. Plus tard, avec le concours de son vieil ami Doc Ball, Grannis conçoit et construit son premier boîtier étanche recouvert d'une enveloppe en caoutchouc et doté de mini-ventouses. Grâce à cet ingénieux montage, il peut rester sur l'eau pendant des heures, assis sur sa planche dans les passes relativement sûres de Sunset Beach et de Waimea Bay, à capturer les prouesses des surfeurs avec des objectifs longs, sans avoir à retourner sur le rivage pour changer de pellicule.

Sur la terre ferme, Grannis appréciait l'effet de recul, efficace et fort plaisant, que procuraient les téléobjectifs Century 1000. Cadrés de manière artistique à une distance d'environ huit cents mètres, les surfeurs ressemblaient à des figures héroïques livrant combat dans les arènes de Sunset Beach. Mais c'est d'abord son intérêt pour les coulisses du surf – les scènes de plage – qui permet aujourd'hui de combler des pans entiers de la mémoire collective des grandes heures du surf. L'objectif de Grannis, particulièrement de 1960 à 1965, a su saisir l'esprit d'un sport qui, à cette époque charnière, est passé d'une simple discipline culte à un mode de *culture* à part entière. À première vue, ses clichés peuvent évoquer une certaine nostalgie d'une époque insouciante où tout était plus simple et plus facile, mais un examen plus détaillé nous révèle un vrai travail de documentaliste sur la rapide transformation de la pratique du surf en un style de vie au statut mythique. Ses photos d'un réalisme saisissant ont contribué à jeter un pont entre le monde virtuel chanté par les Beach Boy et la réalité de la culture de plage du sud de la Californie. Le langage et la musique des surfeurs, les arts, les magazines et la mode dédiés au surf et à ses adeptes – bref tous les ingrédients de la « culture du surf » telle qu'on la connaît aujourd'hui – ont été imaginés sinon codifiés dans ce bref intervalle de temps. Et l'œil de Grannis est précisément l'un des rares

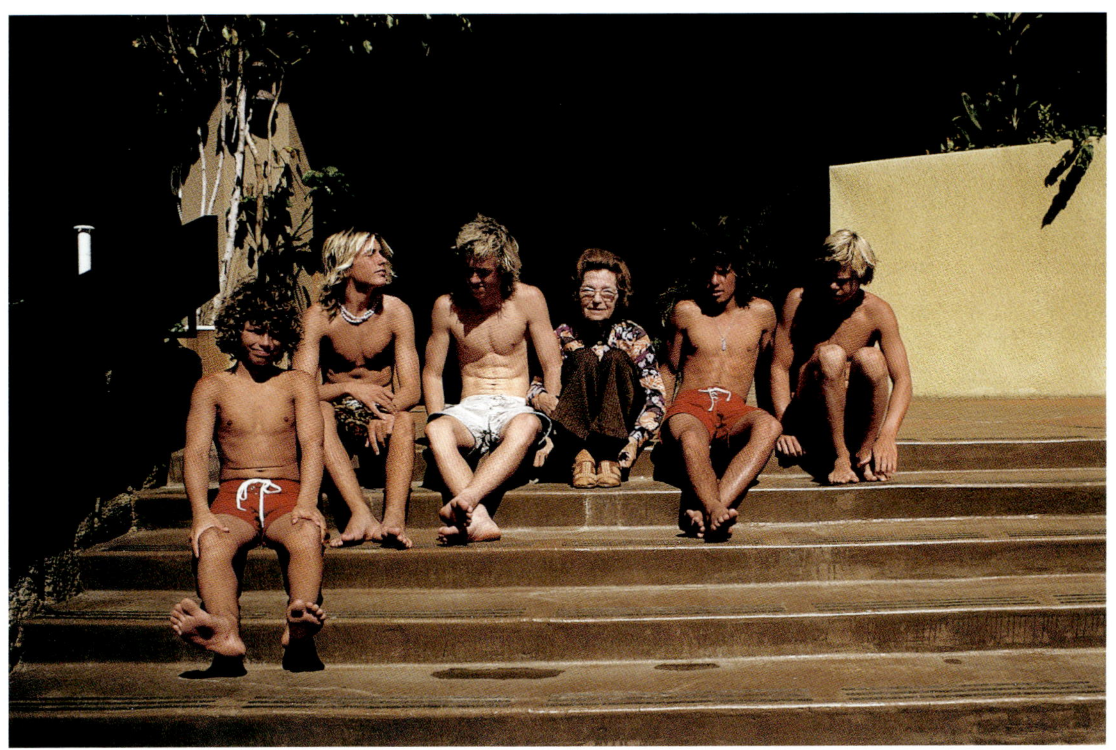

à avoir fixé sur la pellicule, dans son intégralité, la vague du changement et les témoins vivants des événements qui l'ont accompagnée.

En 1964, de retour d'un voyage à Hawaï particulièrement fructueux, Grannis s'associe au magnat du vêtement de surf Dick Graham avec lequel il lance le magazine *International Surfing* (rebaptisé « *Surfing* », c'est aujourd'hui le deuxième plus ancien magazine de surf du monde). Parallèlement à son poste à plein temps chez Pacific Bell Telephone, Grannis cumule les fonctions de premier rédacteur photo, de rédacteur en chef adjoint et de photographe en chef. Chaque week-end, en professionnel consciencieux, il couvre une pléthore de compétitions amateurs et interclubs. C'est ainsi qu'il fixe sur la pellicule les premiers pas encore hésitants d'une génération d'ados qui laisseront plus tard leur marque dans l'histoire du surf. Comme beaucoup d'entre eux avaient l'âge de son propre fils, il posait sur ces jeunes sujets un œil souvent paternel, saisissant au passage une candeur et un naturel en total contraste avec la pudeur que pouvait éprouver un homme d'âge mûr comme Grannis lorsqu'il s'agissait de demander à des inconnus de poser pour lui. Grannis se distingue de ses mentors et de ses confrères photographes par un statut à part que l'on peut situer à mi-chemin entre l'art et le photojournalisme. Ses cadrages parfaits, ses mises au point irréprochables et ses champs profonds et généreux livrent une foule de détails « naturalistes » fort instructifs, propres à titiller l'œil de tout observateur attentif. Ses films lents à grain fin, exposés dans les règles de l'art et développés avec une minutie extrême, permettent d'agrandir les détails avec une précision époustouflante. « La texture même des

**Nancy Katin, North Shore, Hawaii, 1972**

Katin (center) was the feisty grande dame of early surf fashion with her colorfully rugged Kanvas by Katin trunks. Left to right, Eddie Gay, John Grannis, Tom Witt, Katin, Mark Sosa, Scotty Houghtby.

Katin (in der Mitte) war die energische Grande Dame der frühen Surfmode. Die farbenfrohen, robusten Hosen von Kanvas by Katin waren allgegenwärtig. Von links nach rechts: Eddie Gay, John Grannis, Tom Witt, Katin, Mark Sosa, Scotty Houghtby.

La fringante Nancy Katin (au centre), grande dame des premières heures de la mode du surf. Les shorts en toile hauts en couleur de sa marque légendaire, Kanvas by Katin, étaient devenus incontournables. De gauche à droite : Eddie Gay, John Grannis, Tom Witt, Nancy Katin, Mark Sosa et Scotty Houghtby.

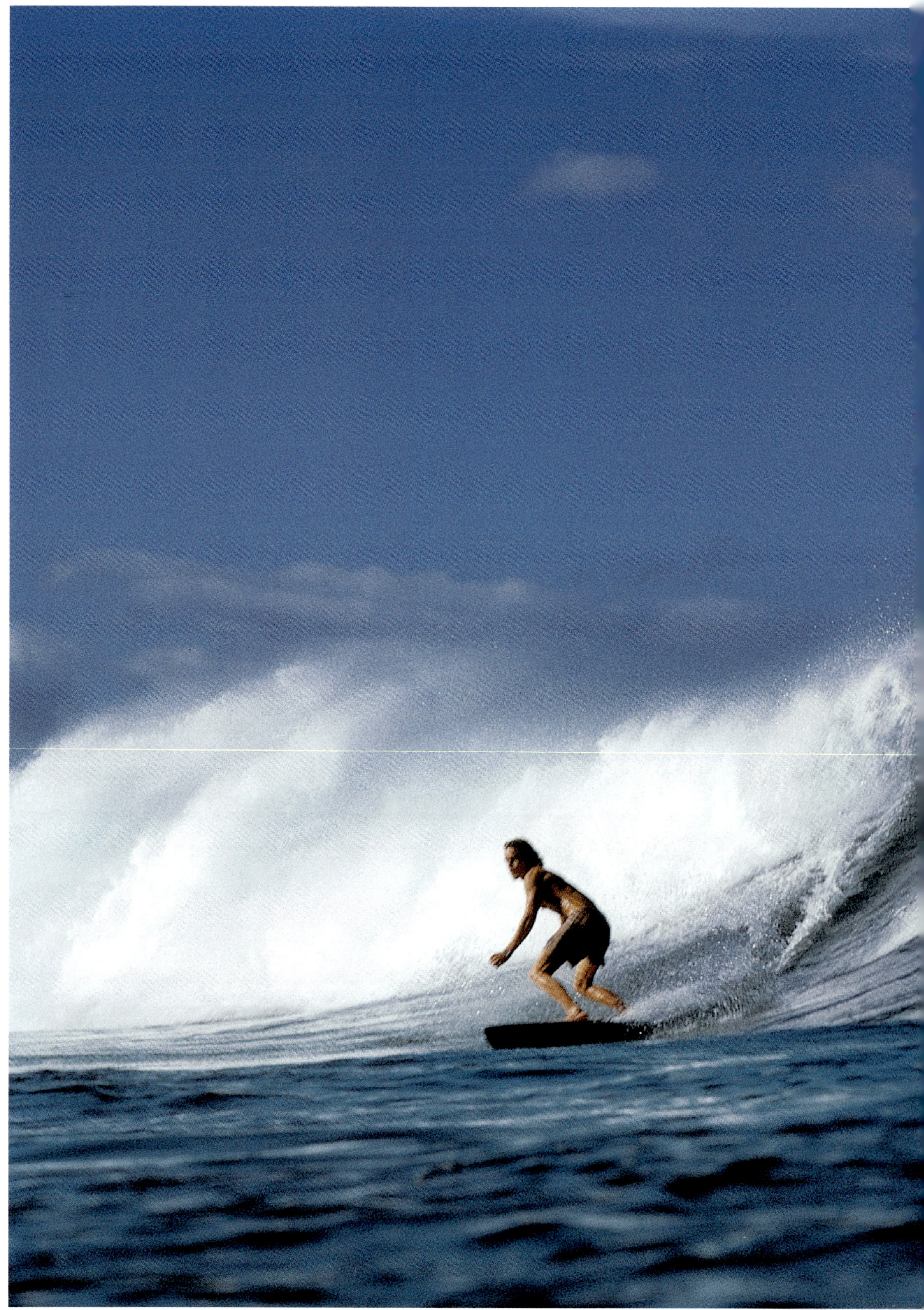

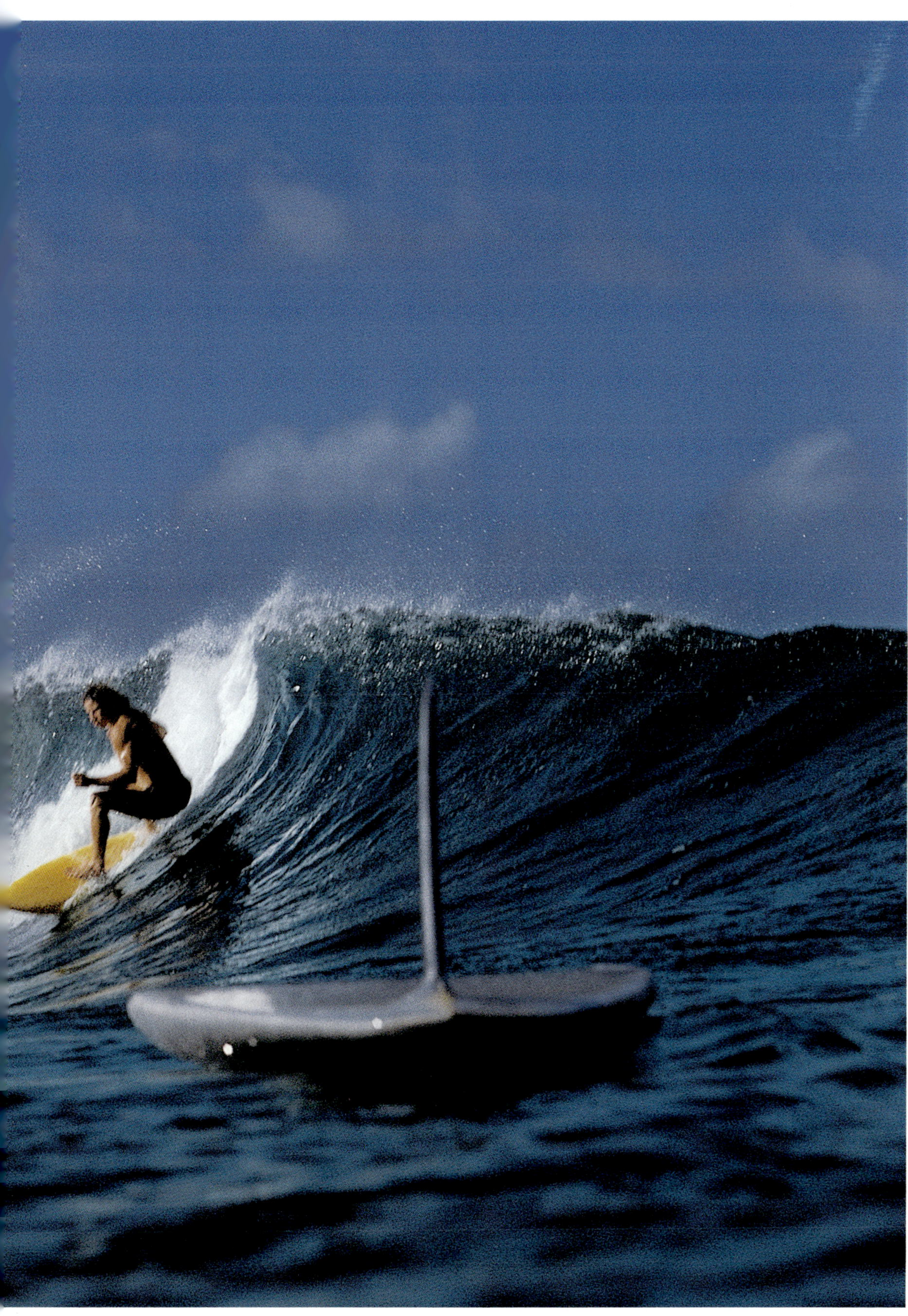

tirages de Grannis en faisait des photos d'un autre monde», confia un jour Brad Barrett, photographe attitré et rédacteur photo de *Surfer* de 1968 à 1973.

**Au début des années 1960, les États-Unis comptaient moins d'une demi-**douzaine de photographes de surf publiant leurs propres clichés et, à l'exception de John Severson, aucun d'entre eux n'en avait fait son activité principale. Mais chacun avait son style propre et ses compétitions favorites. Severson, ancien professeur d'arts graphiques, avait un faible pour l'esthétique brute et le style be-bop. Ron Stoner, quant à lui, préférait la chaleur des tons mordorés et l'exubérance des décors romantiques. Ron Church, en photographe industriel professionnel, maîtrisait à la perfection les technologiques de pointe et les appareils photos sous-marins dernier cri. Ses portraits en noir et blanc des dieux du surf mêlaient souvent héroïsme et froideur impersonnelle. Quant à Grannis, surfeur invétéré et enfant de l'océan, il capturait les scènes de la vie locale sans aucun filtre et avec un réalisme saisissant.

Éditeur et réalisateur de films consacrés au surf, John Severson fut l'un des premiers à ouvrir les portes des médias à l'iconographie du surf. En 1960, il publie *The Surfer,* un fascicule de trente-six pages consacré à son art photographique et vendu en marge des projections de son documentaire *Surf Fever.* L'ouvrage connait un succès retentissant et les 5 000 premiers exemplaires s'écoulent comme des petits pains. En 1961, il sort un trimestriel, qui devint bimensuel un an plus tard. Severson s'attache le concours d'une petite équipe et s'installe comme directeur de la publication et éditeur à temps plein. Grannis en vient bientôt à contribuer au magazine *Surfer*, ainsi qu'à l'éphémère *Surfing Illustrated.*

Les premiers magazines de surf étaient nés dans les «arrière-cuisines» d'une poignée de passionnés qui les fabriquaient et les distribuaient eux-mêmes. Lorsque *Surfer* est lancé, la presse grand public est devenue accessible aux éditeurs à petit budget comme Severson, et les grands noms des médias ont commencé à exploiter le créneau du surf en portant cette nouvelle discipline à l'écran avec *Un amour de vacances* (*Gidget*, 1959) et *Ride the Wild Surf* (1964). En Californie du Sud, les clichés et les illustrations hautes en couleur immortalisant les prouesses des surfeurs ont tôt fait de taper dans l'œil des industriels du cinéma et de la télévision hollywoodiens. «Soudain, nous avions une occasion inespérée de monnayer nos propres créations photographiques», témoigne John Van Hamersveld, ancien directeur artistique de *Surfer* et créateur de la légendaire affiche fluorescente du film *The Endless Summer.* «Au travers des magazines et du grand écran, les mass media et l'industrie de la culture se sont emparés de ce microcosme jusque-là confidentiel.»

Cette «marotte» du surf partagée par une poignée d'initiés en 1961 allait devenir cinq ans plus tard une authentique culture de la jeunesse avec ses codes linguistiques, sa musique, sa mode vestimentaire, ses médias, ses voitures et son code de l'honneur. En 1966, l'intérêt du grand public pour le surf atteint des sommets, faisant la fortune d'un petit cartel d'industriels de Californie du Sud surnommé avec humour «Dana Point Mafia». Cette nouvelle discipline à part entière – qui relevait davantage d'un système de croyance que d'un passe-temps



*Pages 56–57*
**Pipeline, 1971**

By dropping in on the surfer farther back on the wave, the one in front has forced him into a bad, even dangerous, position.

Durch Abdrängen hat der vordere Surfer den anderen in eine schlechte, wenn nicht sogar gefährliche Position gebracht.

Le second surfeur (planche jaune), gêné par le premier qui vient de lui barrer la route, se retrouve dans une position délicate, voire dangereuse.

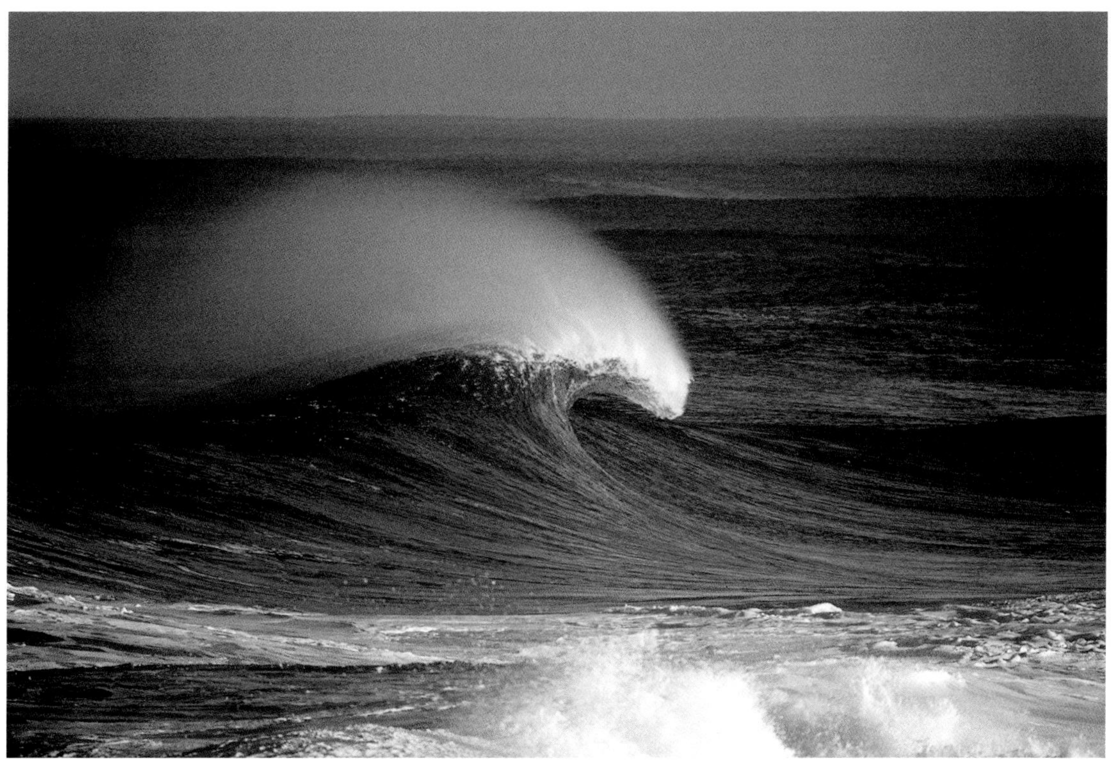

dominical – bénéficie d'une forte poussée médiatique en juillet 1966 avec
la sortie dans toutes les salles du pays de *The Endless Summer,* un film de Bruce
Brown. Ce documentaire imaginatif et décontracté accorde pour la première fois
aux masses de non-surfeurs (les «légions de frustrés», comme les qualifiait le
virtuose des vagues Phil Edwards) un ticket d'entrée dans le cercle très fermé du
surf. Le grand public réclame sa part de rêve. C'est le début d'une nouvelle ruée
vers l'or.

Lorsque San Diego se voit attribuer pour la deuxième fois la tenue des
championnats du monde du surf, les édiles locaux et les organisateurs de
l'événement, comblés par le retour de la discipline vers plus de respectabilité,
se tombent littéralement dans les bras. Les organisateurs officiels espèrent ainsi
tordre le cou au «hooliganisme du surf» et à la mauvaise presse qui avait entaché
la réputation de ce sport pendant toute la période d'euphorie qui avait suivi
la sortie de la comédie *Un amour de vacances.* En l'espace de quelques jours,
la chambre de commerce de San Diego enregistre une forte augmentation des
chiffres du tourisme, stimulés par une jeunesse consumériste captivée par ce
nouveau sport de plage à la fois sexy et symbole de liberté.

Parallèlement, une vague conservatrice s'évertue à bousculer le style de vie
bohème qui s'est installé dans le milieu du surf. À l'initiative du magazine *Surfer*
de John Severson, une inlassable campagne de respectabilité tente de redonner au
surf ses lettres de noblesses en expurgeant de la scène ses éléments «indésirables».
La ligne éditoriale du magazine adopte un ton plus péremptoire, réserve ses
colonnes à des chroniqueurs et à des courriers de lecteurs se réjouissant de la

*« La texture même des tirages
de Grannis en faisait des
photos d'un autre monde »,
confia un jour Brad Barret.*

**Backdoor Pipeline, Hawaii, 1971**

Pipeline, which pitches over a
shallow, unforgiving coral reef, has
claimed dozens of boards and a few
lives since it was first ridden in
1960.

Die Pipeline, die sich über einem
flachen, gnadenlosen Korallenriff
erhebt, hat schon vielen Brettern
und einigen Menschen das Leben
gekostet, seit sie 1960 zum ersten
Mal gesurft wurde.

Les vagues de Pipeline, qui
s'écrasent sur un impitoyable récif
de corail aux fonds plats, ont broyé
des dizaines de planches – et
quelques vies humaines – depuis
la première fois où elles ont été
surfées, en 1960.

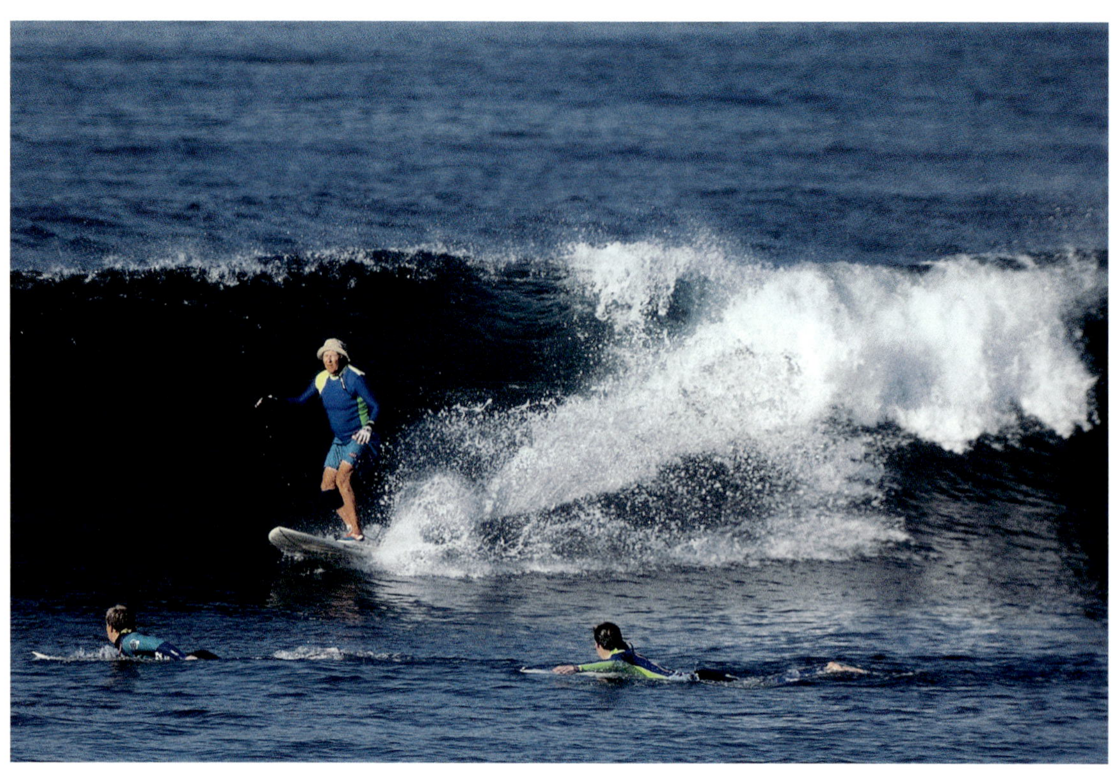

défaite organisée des « hodads », ces voyous décérébrés qui avaient entaché la réputation du surf par leurs frasques et leur attitude puante à l'égard des représentants de l'autorité. « [Le surf] n'attirait plus seulement les excentriques », a déclaré un jour John Hannon, un des principaux fabricants de planches de la Côte Est, dans une interview donnée à *Newsweek*. « La nouvelle génération est propre sur elle ; elle se coupe les cheveux et les ongles, et ne tolère pas les trublions. »

**Les premiers soubresauts de la « révolution du *shortboard* » – qui annoncent** la disparition des années d'insouciance du début des Sixties – se font sentir à Ocean Beach, près de San Diego, le 2 octobre 1966. Ce jour-là, sous un ciel couvert, le jeune Nat Young est sacré champion du monde après avoir médusé l'élite régnante du surf par son style radical et ses virages extrêmement serrés sur des vagues de faible amplitude. Lorsque David Nuuhiwa, le Hawaïen donné favori et réputé pour sa souplesse et ses longs *noserides* élégants, affirme doctement qu'il faut « se fondre dans la vague », Young lui rétorque, sûr de lui : « Pas question pour moi de me fondre dans quoi que ce soit ! » Le ton proprement iconoclaste du jeune Young est tout à l'image de sa « Magic Sam » gagnante, une planche de neuf pieds et quatre pouces – un pied plus court que la longueur standard – qu'il a fabriquée de ses propres mains. Conçue avec le concours de l'Australien Bob McTavish, la Magic Sam se distingue par un aileron proéminent en forme de cimeterre dû à un génie américain de la planche de surf, l'excentrique George Greenough. Du jour au lendemain, c'est toute une génération de planches de compétition dernier cri qui est reléguée au rang de pièces de musée.

Une révolution technologique est en marche, qui entraîne dans son sillage un bouleversement des mentalités et des techniques. Après la victoire de Nat Young, le monde du surf s'écarte des conventions pendant plus d'une décennie. Surnommé « The Animal » en raison de son style de surf impétueux, le jeune prodige vient de montrer la voie à la future génération de surfeurs. Avant 1966, la figure phare de la discipline était le « hang ten » (élégant exercice d'équilibre consistant à joindre les deux pieds à l'avant, les dix orteils retombant sur le « nez » de la planche). Désormais tout est permis. On a appelé cela le « mind surfing » ou le surf cérébral. Comme l'a fait remarquer Paul Gross, journaliste à *Surfer*, « on assistait à un abandon massif de tout ce qui avait eu cours jusque-là ». Même si, à cette époque, personne ne semblait en avoir encore pris conscience.

Pendant ce temps-là, les drogues psychédéliques faisaient rage dans le monde du surf. Avec un effet dynamisant pour certains, abrutissant pour d'autres. L'esprit du surf était à l'introversion, et le style underground de la nouvelle génération barbue explorant les bienfaits du zen dans des figures quasi mystiques avait supplanté la grâce conventionnelle des *hotdoggers* en Jantzen. Les compétitions avaient perdu leur aura. Peu importait la première place : finis les manœuvres sophistiquées et les trophées ! Seul comptait désormais l'équilibre « karmique » du surfeur glissant sur les « cathédrales de cristal en fusion », pour reprendre les termes d'un lecteur de *Surfer*. Au grand dam de certains annonceurs prestigieux, Rick Griffin glissait quant à lui quelques clins d'œil subreptices aux substances psychotropes dans les cartoons qu'il dessinait pour le même magazine. Le mode de vie vagabond et libertaire de la nouvelle génération poussa bon nombre de surfeurs vers une carrière parallèle de trafiquants de drogues. « Soit vous preniez le train en marche, soit vous restiez sur le quai », a écrit un jour Drew Kampion, directeur de la publication de *Surfer* entre 1968 et 1972. « Soit vous aviez pigé le truc, soit vous étiez en dehors du coup. Soit vous croyiez en la force gravitationnelle, soit vous croyiez en l'espace tridimensionnel. Soit vous étiez figé [sur votre planche], soit vous étiez fluide. Et y'en a un bon paquet qui préféraient la fluidité. »

À peine remis d'un flirt peu concluant avec la respectabilité et les conventions établies, la culture du surf revendique de plus belle ses racines anticonformistes, ce qui ne passe pas inaperçu. Dans son essai à succès publié en 1966, *The Pump House Gang*, le critique Tom Wolfe, spécialiste de la culture pop, constatait que de nombreux surfeurs, « auparavant simples représentants d'un style de vie lié au surf, incarnaient désormais l'avant-garde du mouvement psychédélique californien ». À la place des jeunes consommateurs dociles autrefois courtisés par l'industrie américaine, on avait désormais affaire à une génération de contestataires chevelus, fumant la marijuana et affichant, un doigt en l'air, toute leur haine pour le matérialisme débridé.

L'industrie du surf traverse alors une crise sévère. Au cours des quelques années qui suivent, la plupart des boutiques de surf doivent réduire leur activité sinon mettre la clé sous la porte. Les recettes publicitaires du magazine *Surfer* plongent, son format est réduit en conséquence et la ligne éditoriale adopte un ton franchement plus « progressiste ». La radicalisation initiée par Kampion, le directeur de la publication, transforme *Surfer* en un vecteur majeur de la

**LeRoy Grannis, Carlsbad, California, 1990**

After retirement in 1977 Grannis moved to Carlsbad, where he surfed nearly every day until well into his eighties.

Als er 1977 in Rente ging, zog Grannis nach Carlsbad, wo er fast jeden Tag surfte, bis er weit über achtzig war.

Après sa retraite en 1977, LeRoy Grannis déménage à Carlsbad où il continue à surfer son lot de vagues presque quotidiennement, même après ses quatre-vingts ans.

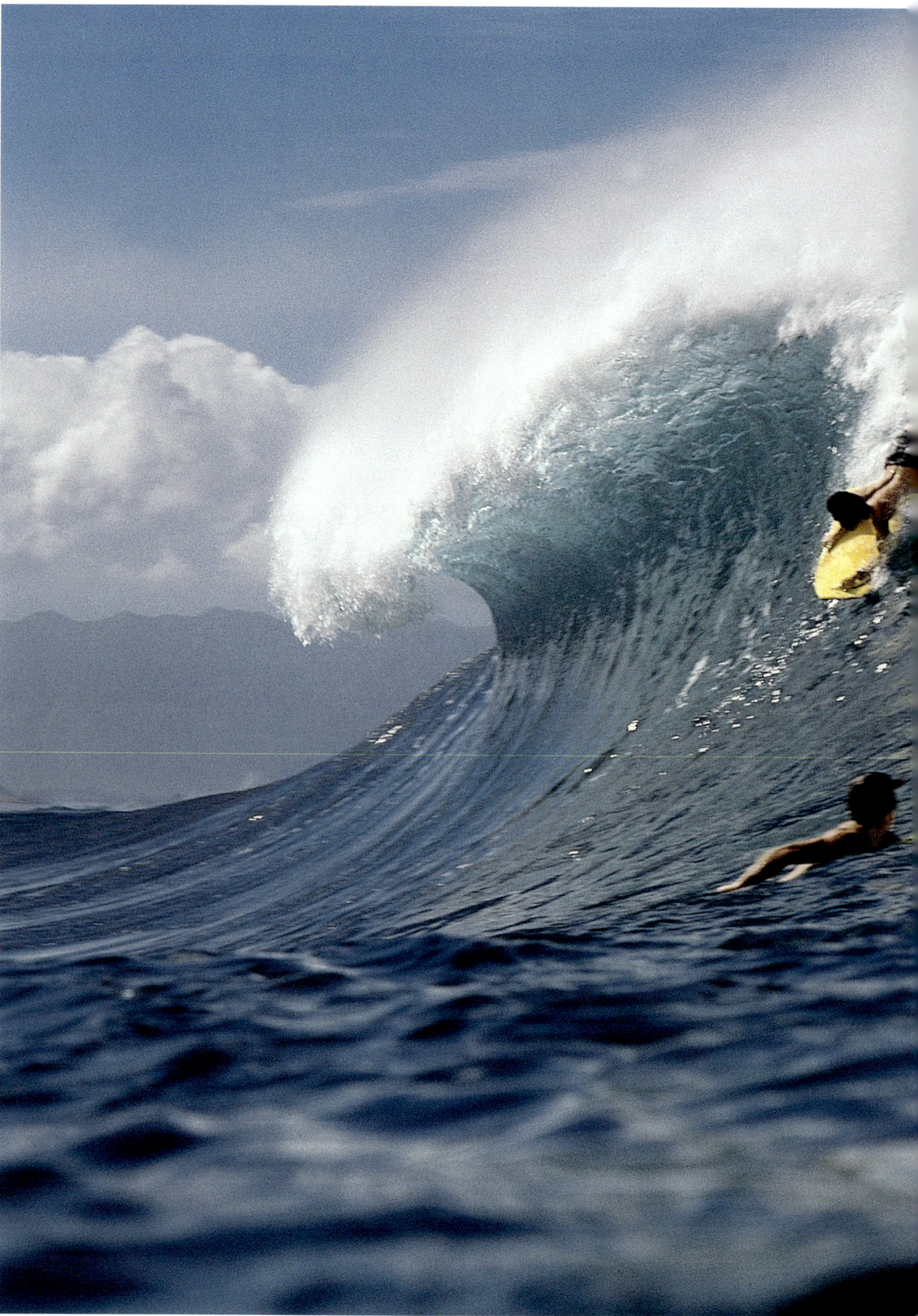

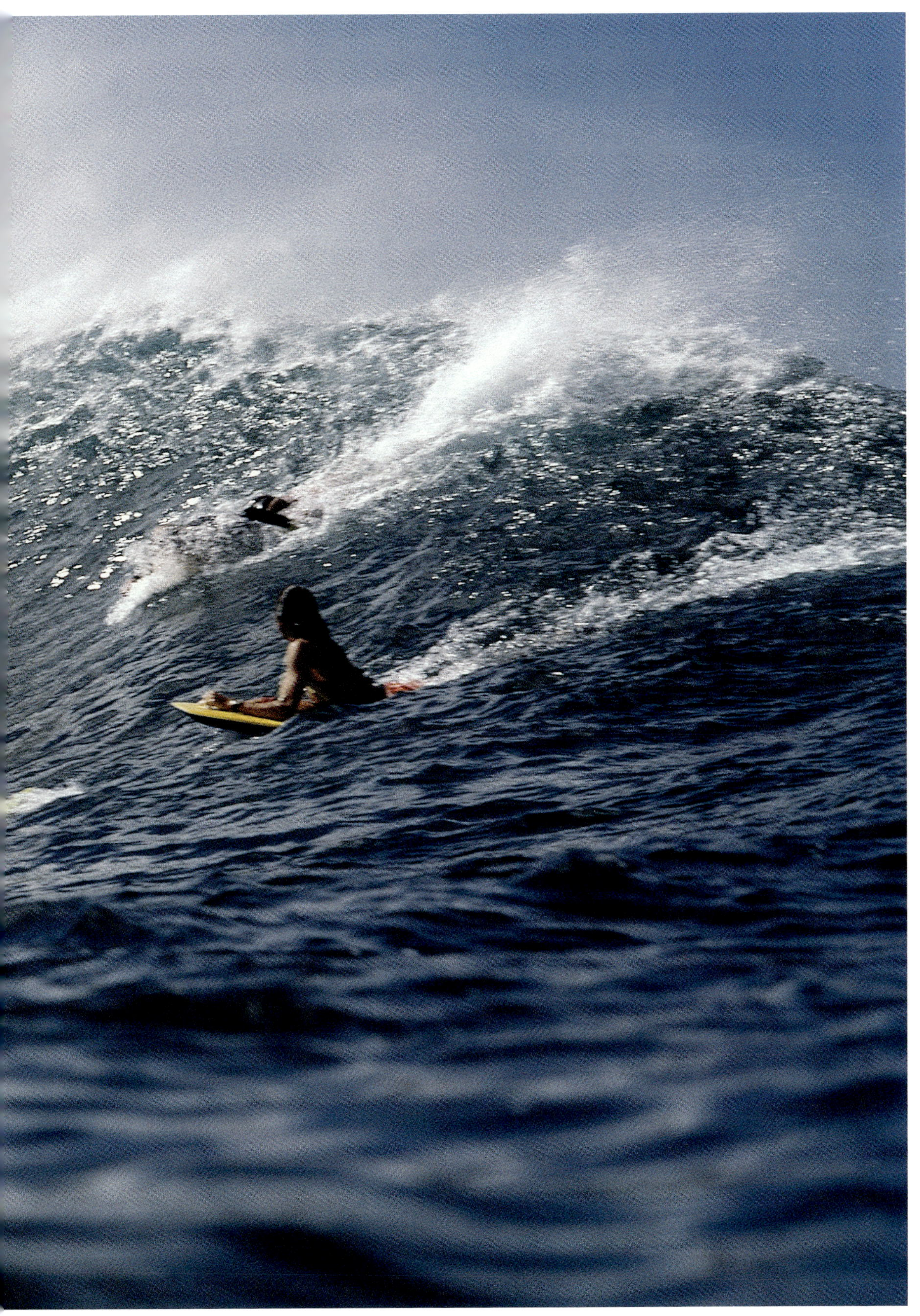

contre-culture émergente, célébrant pêle-mêle la paix, la libération sexuelle, le *tube riding* et le droit imprescriptible de tout surfeur à se mettre en marge et à se «défoncer» par *tous* les moyens à sa disposition. Kampion, qui s'insurge publiquement contre la plupart des compétitions de surf organisées, publie des articles comme «Mauvais karma à Huntington Beach» et «À bas les compétitions!», dans lesquels il cherche à promouvoir le surf comme une expérience métaphorique de l'harmonie cosmique et non comme un *ego trip* malsain vendu à une logique de marketing. Farouchement opposé à la guerre du Vietnam, qui vide les plages de leurs surfeurs à un rythme alarmant, il déclare la guerre au nouveau président Richard Nixon, qui a osé établir sa «Maison blanche de la côte Ouest», outrage suprême, à San Clemente, et plus précisément à Trestles Beach, condamnant à chacune de ses visites l'accès à l'un des *surf breaks* les plus prisés de la côte.

Grannis, qui appartient à l'ancienne génération, est en décalage avec l'anticonformisme ambiant de la nouvelle vague et se moque ouvertement des nouvelles «conventions» en vigueur dans le monde du surf. Ce vétéran de la Seconde Guerre mondiale, qui aide son fidèle ami Hop Swarts à organiser les compétitions de la United States Surfing Association que ce dernier vient de fonder, reste farouchement attaché à l'idée que les compétitions de surf contribuent à la promotion du sport, notamment sur un plan social. En 1968, Grannis publie un éditorial dans lequel il vante les valeurs éthiques des compétitions et repousse d'un revers de manche les critiques des «ronchons qui n'ont nullement le droit de se plaindre». «Ces dernières années, on a eu droit à une série d'attaques en règle de la compétition dans des articles signés par des *has been* du surf, des éditorialistes hawaïens qui n'ont jamais posé le pied sur une planche, des V.R.P. véreux et des pseudo-directeurs de rédaction frustrés», écrit-il. «S'ils dénigrent autant la compétition, c'est tout simplement parce qu'ils ne sont pas à la hauteur.»

À la fin des années 1960, pourtant, la plupart des compétitions – y compris le prestigieux Prix des lecteurs du magazine *Surfer* – appartiennent au passé. Le seul événement pouvant ressembler, et seulement de loin, à une compétition professionnelle est un anti-concours déjanté baptisé «Expression Session», au cours duquel les as du surf démontrent leurs prouesses en l'absence de tout juge, de tout score et de tout trophée. «Cette année-là fut une saison foisonnante de créations et d'inventions : le *shortboard*, le *V-bottom*, la mini-planche, l'aileron souple, l'aileron court, bref de nouvelles planches au design radical», comme le constate Kampion en 1968, qui ajoute : «Le surfeur qui n'a pas changé de style ces douze derniers mois est un oiseau rare.» Pourtant, dans un éditorial éclairé, Grannis prédit avec précision le retour du *longboard* et du *noseriding*. Année après année, Grannis continue de diriger inlassablement son objectif sur une discipline à laquelle il a consacré son talent, immortalisant image après image les exploits des *longboarders* et des *shortboarders* sans se soucier des tendances et des mouvements qui faisaient et défaisaient la culture du surf.

**Dans les premiers jours de décembre 1969, Hawaï et la Californie sont** secoués par le terrible «*swell* du siècle». Les gigantesques vagues de dix mètres qui balayent la côte nord d'Oahu détruisent soixante habitations et projettent des bateaux à cent mètres à l'intérieur des terres. Si les monstres de la côte nord se



*Pages 62–63*
**Sean Ross, Pipeline, 1980**

Ross is shown riding a paipo board, the ancient precursor to the modern bodyboard and the earliest form of board surfing.

Ross surft hier auf einem Paipo-Board, dem uralten Vorläufer des modernen Bodyboards, das auch das Brett der allerersten Surfer gewesen war.

Sean Ross chevauchant un paipo board, l'ancêtre du bodyboard moderne qui fut aussi la planche des tout premiers surfeurs de l'histoire.

révélent impossibles à dompter, Greg Noll, accompagné d'une petite équipe de surfeurs, relève le défi de surfer les vagues de Makaha sur la côte ouest de l'île, légèrement moins furieuses que sur la côte nord. Ce jour-là, Noll affirme avoir chevauché la plus grande vague de toute l'histoire du surf. Ce dont on est sûr, c'est qu'il a survécu de justesse au *wipe-out,* l'inévitable chute finale. « Dans cette discipline malmenée par le tapage publicitaire et la révolution [du *shortboard*], un pur dinosaure des années 1950 a surfé la dernière grande vague de 1969 », commenta Drew Kampion.

Le « Swell de 1969 » fut perçu dans le monde du surf comme l'ultime secousse tellurique de la décennie la plus tumultueuse et la plus controversée de son histoire. « Ce que nous avons vécu ce fameux mois de décembre 69 a signé en quelque sorte le passage de l'ère du *longboard* – emblématique des années 1960 – au sacre du *shortboard* », rappellera bien des années plus tard Skip Frye, la légende du surf des années 1960. « On a assisté à un ménage en profondeur qui a complètement bouleversé les règles du jeu par la suite. » Pour Grannis, le débat sur la taille des planches n'était qu'une question de logistique, et sa prouesse a consisté à mettre son talent de photographe au service du dialogue et de la continuité entre deux générations. « Je photographiais des surfeurs, pas des planches », confia-t-il un jour. « Les effets de mode ne changeaient pas grand-chose pour moi. »

La dernière photo de surf prise par LeRoy Grannis pour *International Surfing* fut publiée en 1971. À la fin des années 1970, il quitta Pacific Bell Telephone et Hermosa Beach pour s'installer à Carlsbad, en Californie, et profiter de sa retraite. Là-bas, il continua à s'adonner au surf et à la photo. Pendant plus de vingt ans, il conserva des centaines de clichés et de négatifs. Tandis qu'un cercle marginal de surfeurs passionnés transformait sa propre vision du surf en une industrie mondiale, c'est tout un pan de l'histoire des premières heures de ce sport qui sombrait dans un quasi-oubli.

Pionnier de la photographie sportive, Grannis a immortalisé l'histoire du surf en témoin inlassable de ses bouleversements et de son iconographie naissante. Cette rétrospective consacrée à son art – depuis les clichés classiques de son catalogue jusqu'aux témoignages inédits dénichés dans ses propres archives – invite le lecteur à découvrir un style de vie et une culture jadis réservés à une poignée d'adeptes et qui alimentent aujourd'hui une industrie rapportant chaque année quatre milliards de dollars de chiffre d'affaires. Aujourd'hui, dans l'océan de photographies professionnelles qui submerge le marché, la simplicité élégante des clichés de Grannis nous replonge avec délice dans les grands moments du surf dont il a été le témoin privilégié et nous ouvre une fenêtre sur la naissance d'une culture à part entière. « Je pratiquais le surf et j'aimais photographier ce qui plaisait à mon œil », se défend Grannis en toute modestie. « Je crois qu'on peut dire que j'ai eu beaucoup de chance. »

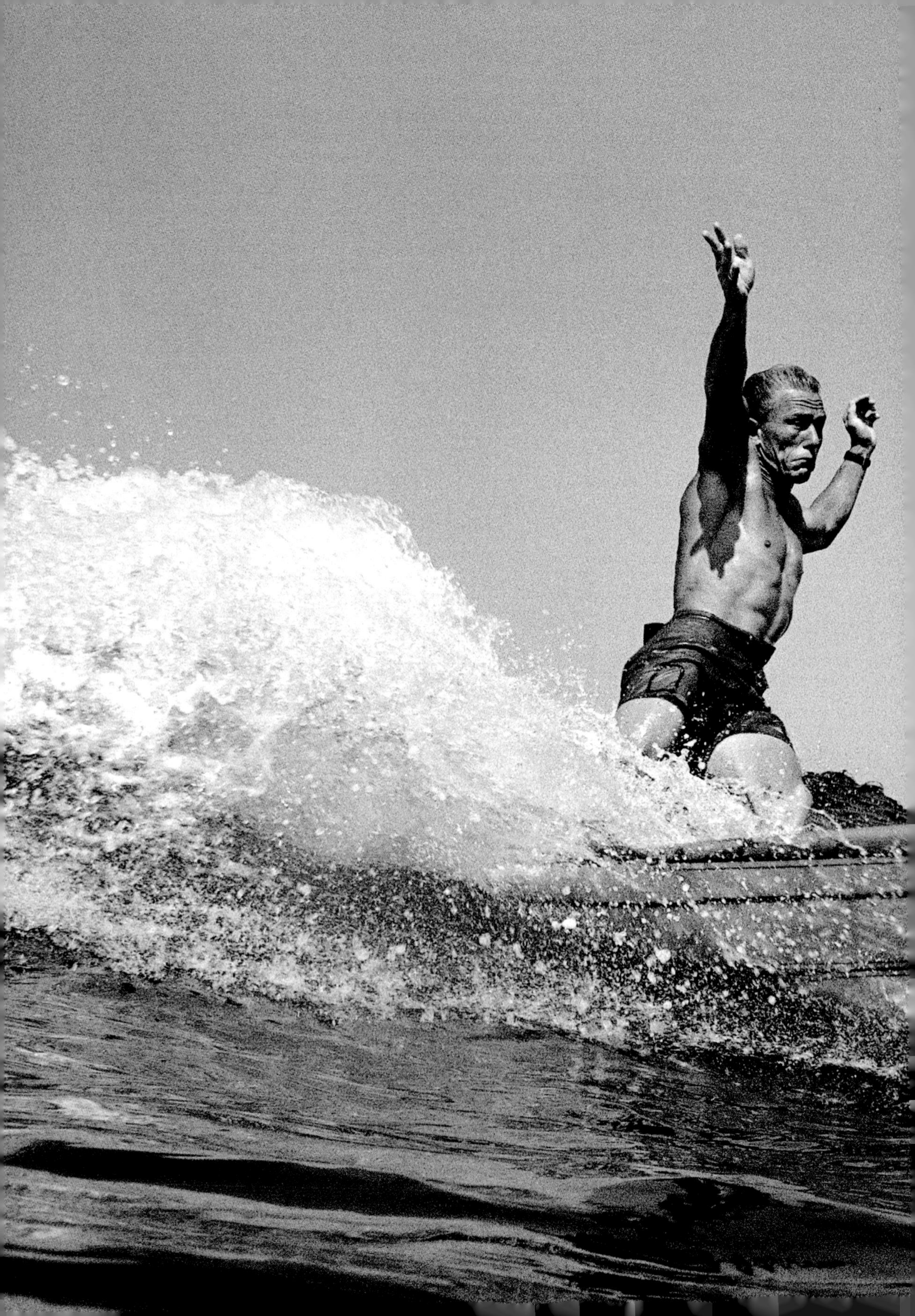

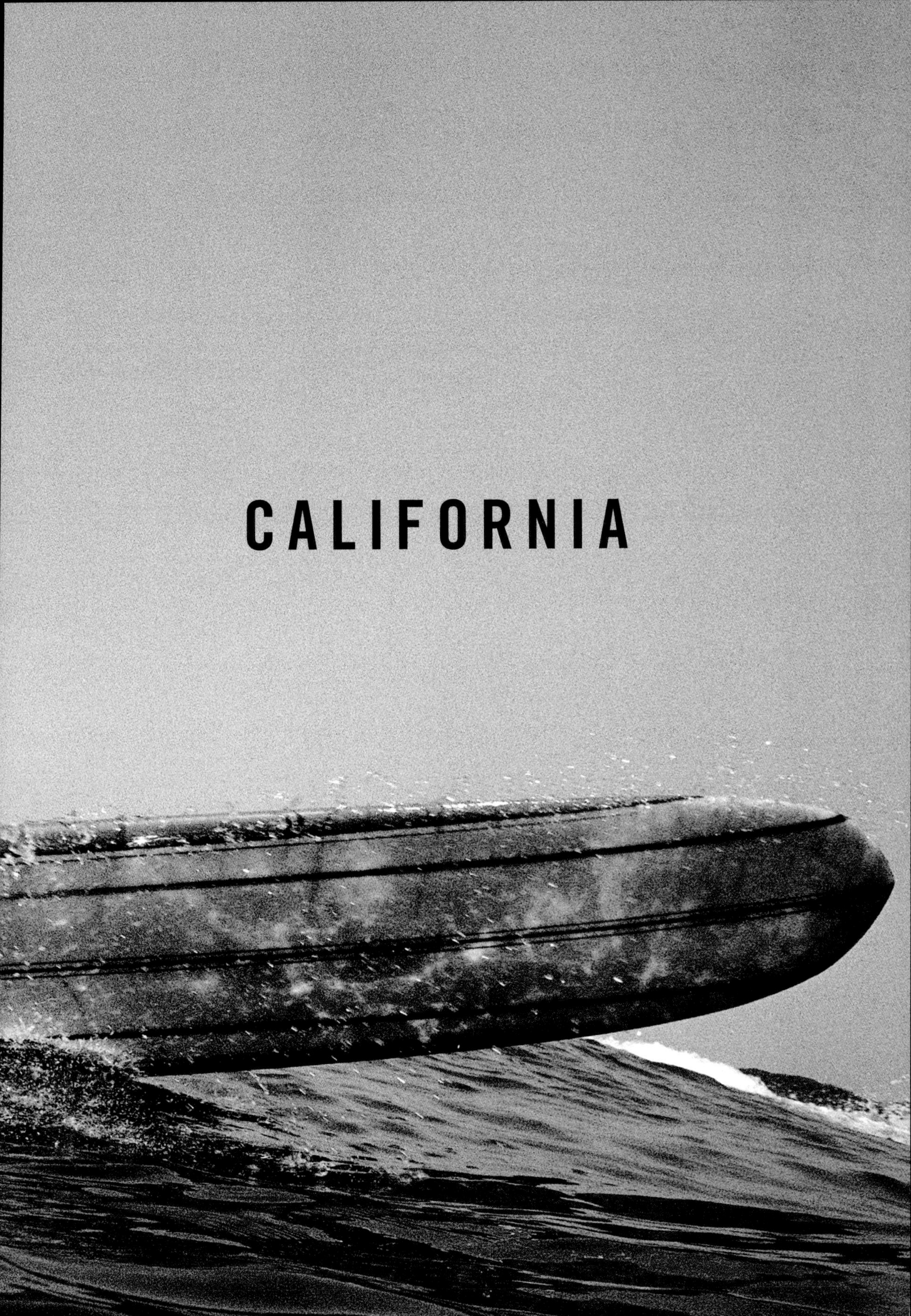

CALIFORNIA

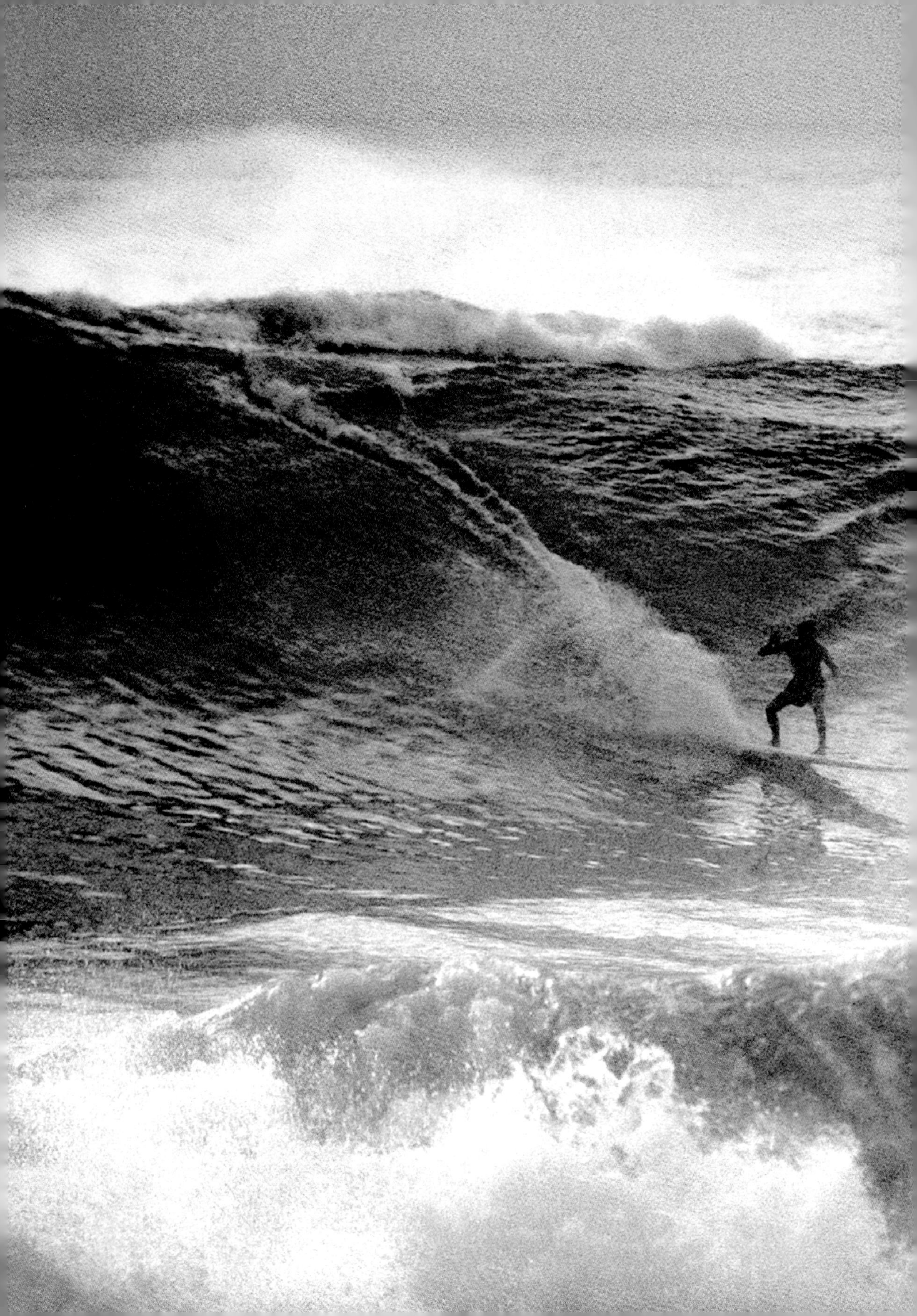

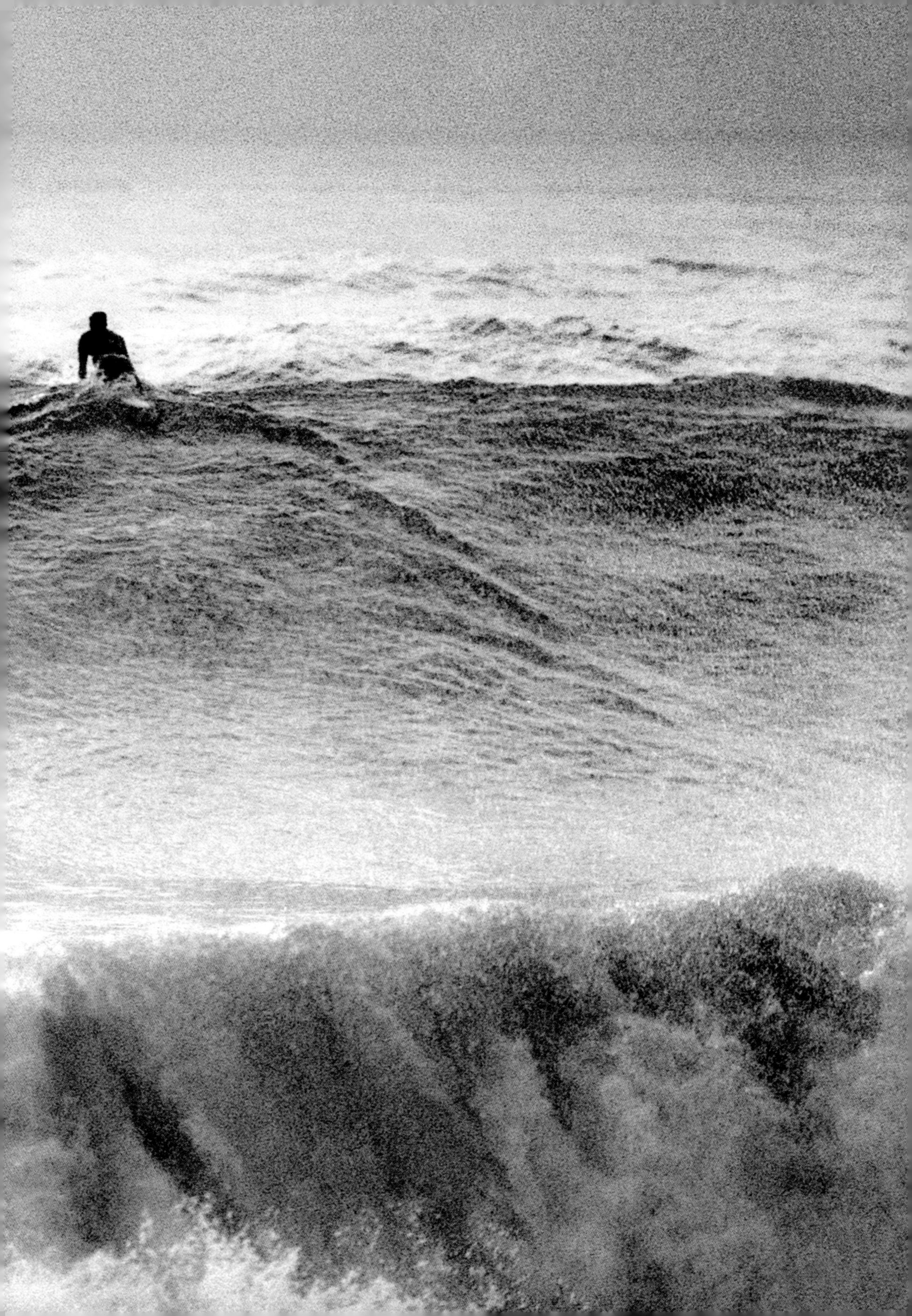

*Pages 66–67*
**Dewey Weber, 22nd Street,
Hermosa Beach, 1966**

For this one frozen moment,
surfboard tycoon Weber was
the embodiment of the mythic
California surfer.

Für diesen einen, für immer
verewigten Augenblick war der
Surfboard-Tycoon Weber die
Verkörperung des mythischen
kalifornischen Surfers.

Immortalisé par ce fameux cliché,
le magnat de la planche de surf
Dewey Weber a incarné le mythe
du surfeur californien.


*Pages 68–69*
**Jim Fox, Redondo Beach Breakwater,
1963**

A day with exceptionally large
waves at the breakwater.

Ein Tag mit außergewöhnlich hohen
Wellen an der Buhne.

Conditions exceptionnelles pour
cette session de surf au pied d'un
brise-lame.


**Chris Cattel, Huntington Beach, 1963**

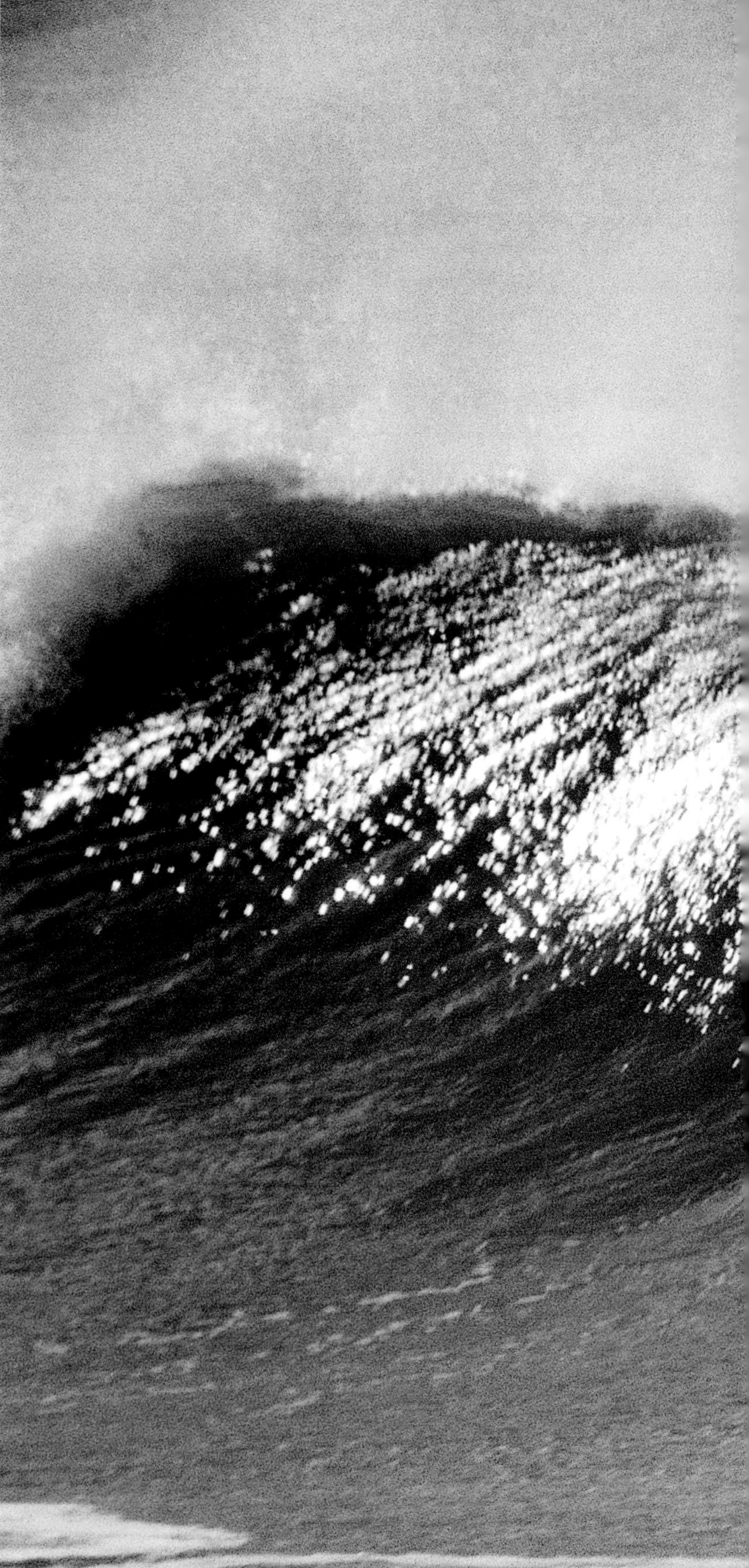

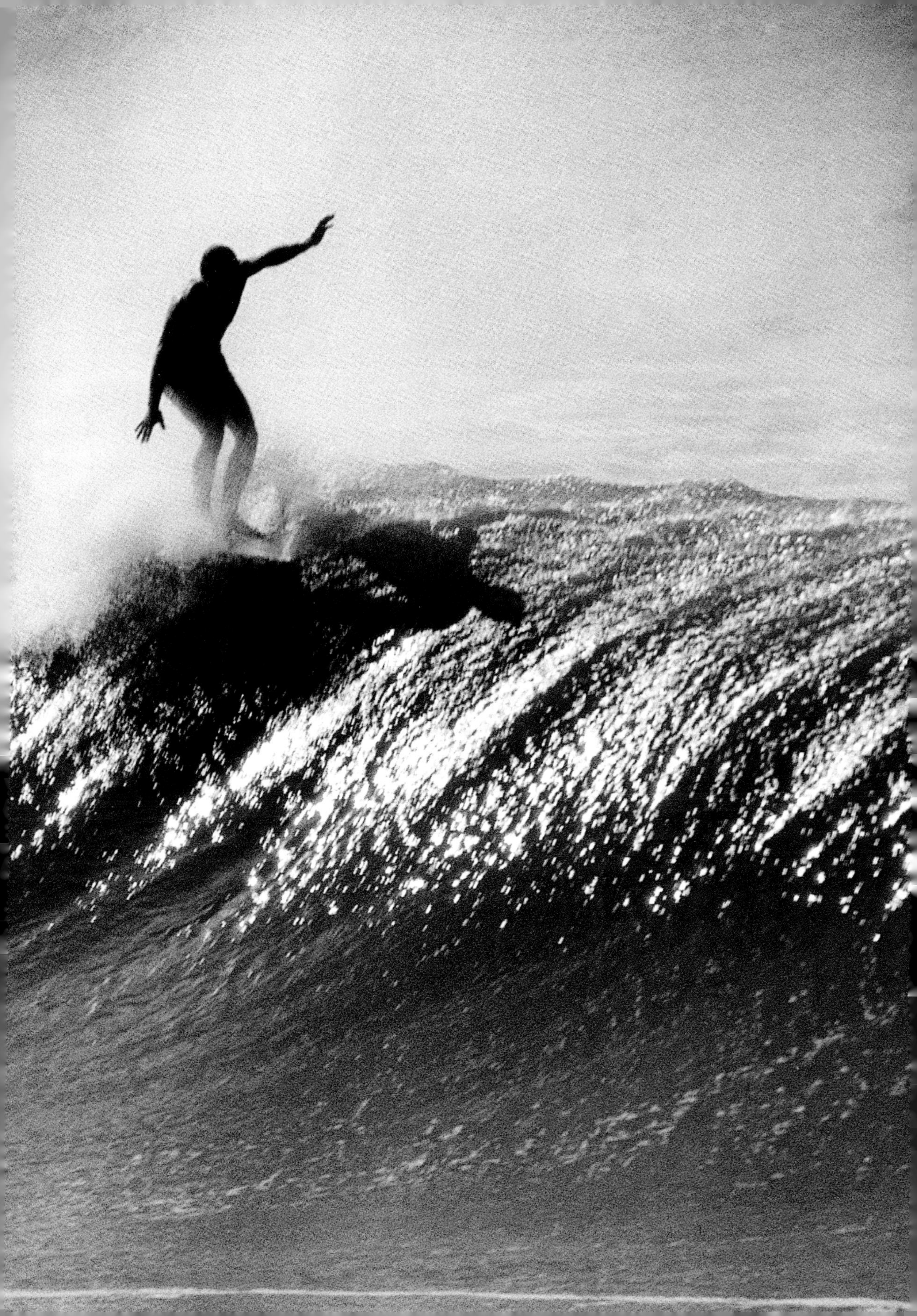

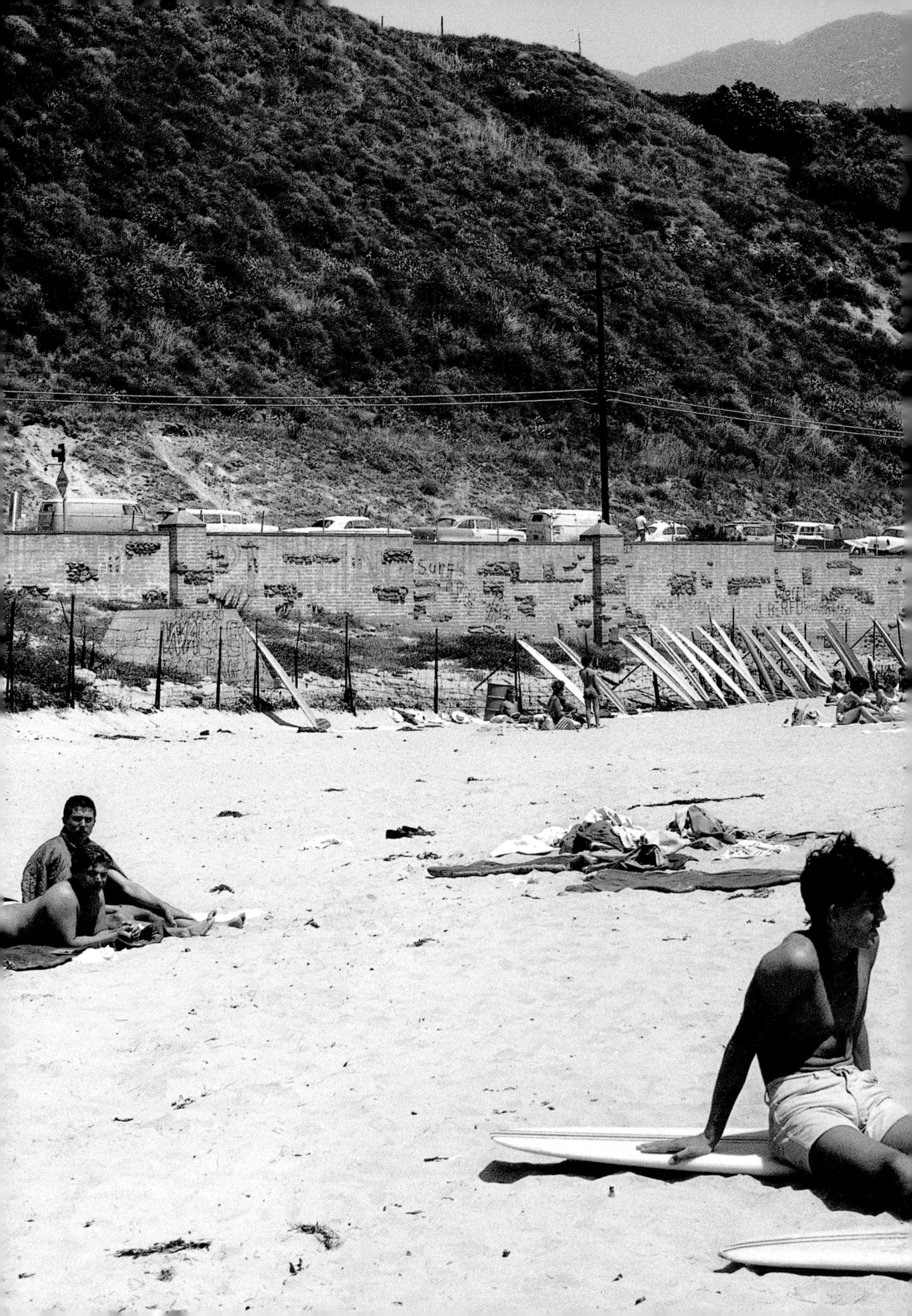

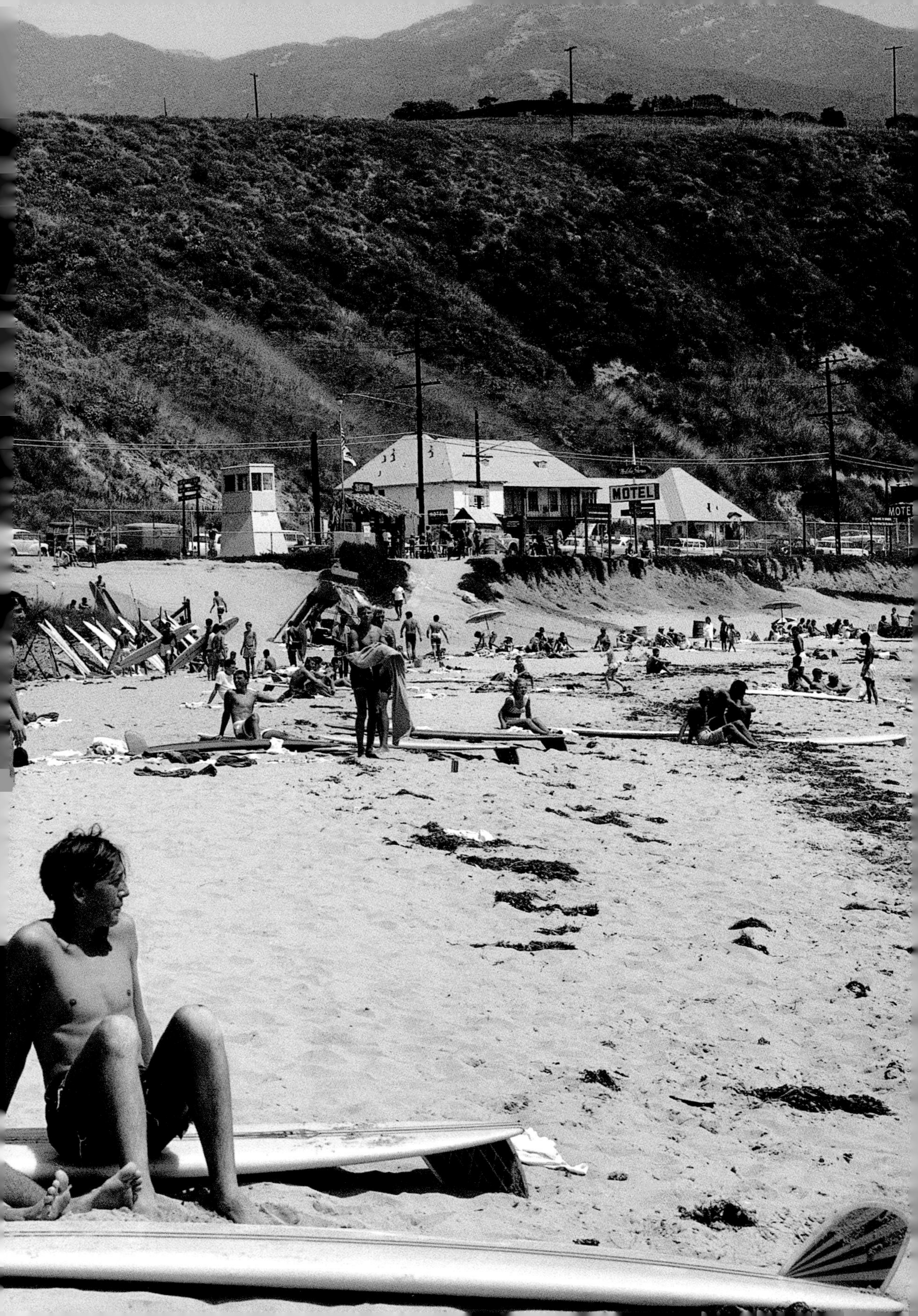

MOTEL
MOTEL

**Malibu, 1963**

Two "gremmies," or young surfers, taking a break to watch the Malibu greats. The Chumash Indians called the area Humaliwo, which means "where the surf sounds loudly."

Zwei „gremmies", oder junge Surfer, die Pause machen und den Größen von Malibu zusehen. Die Chumash-Indianer nannten die Gegend „Humaliwo" – „wo die Brandung donnert".

Deux « gremmies » – surfeurs ados – font une pause pour suivre les exploits des pointures de Malibu. Les Indiens Chumash appelaient cette zone « Humaliwo », littéralement « le lieu où gronde le ressac ».

**Lance Carson, Hermosa Beach, 1963**

Carson, nicknamed "No-Pants Lance," was renowned for wild, drunken capers and long, elegant noserides. In later years he co-founded the Surfrider Foundation.

Carsons Spitzname war „No-Pants Lance". Er war bekannt für wilde, betrunkene Kapriolen und lange, elegante Noserides. Später wurde er Mitbegründer der Surfrider Foundation.

Lance Carson, surnommé « No-Pants Lance » (Lance le sans-maillot) était réputé pour ses cabrioles extravagantes et ses longs *noserides* d'une rare élégance. Des années plus tard, il cofondera la Surfrider Foundation.



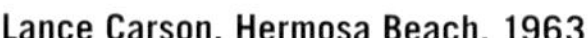

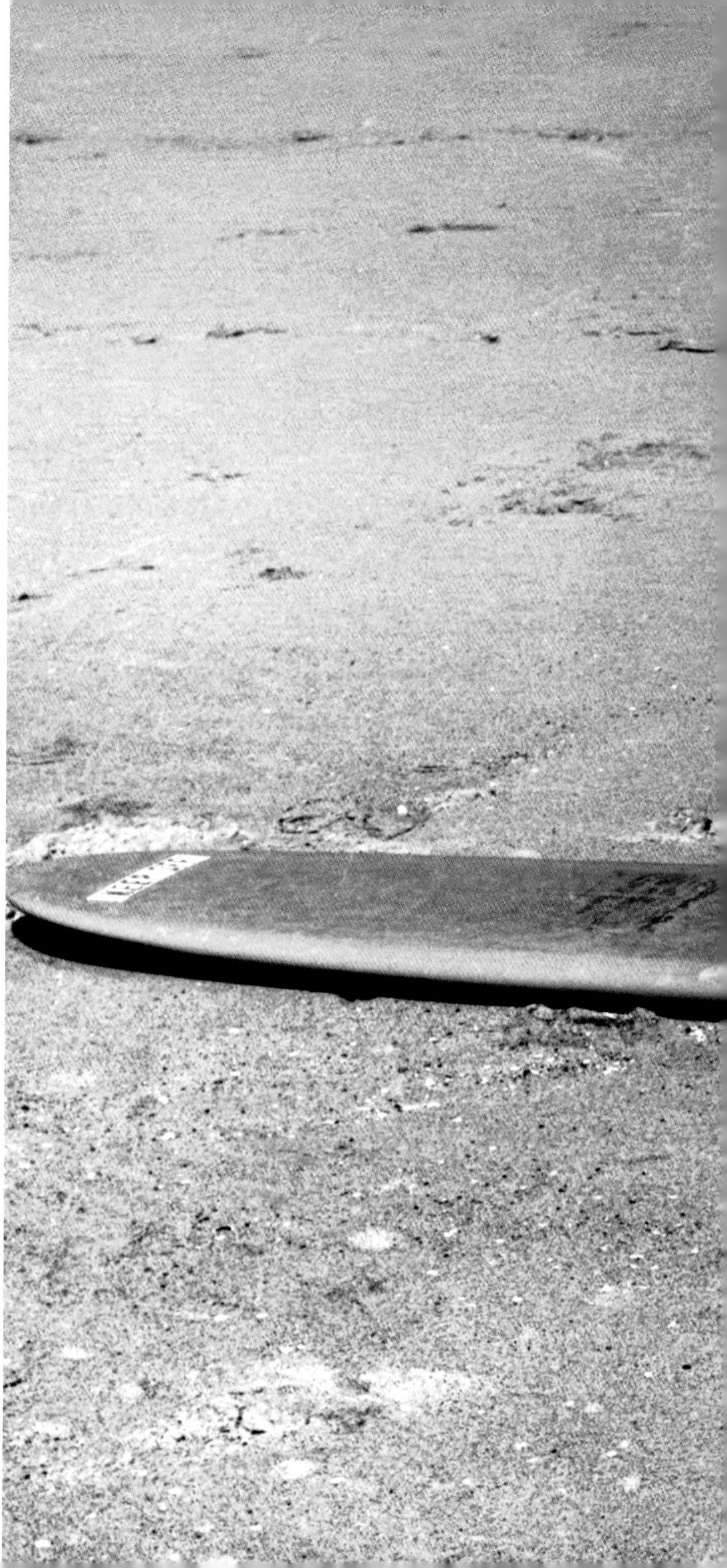

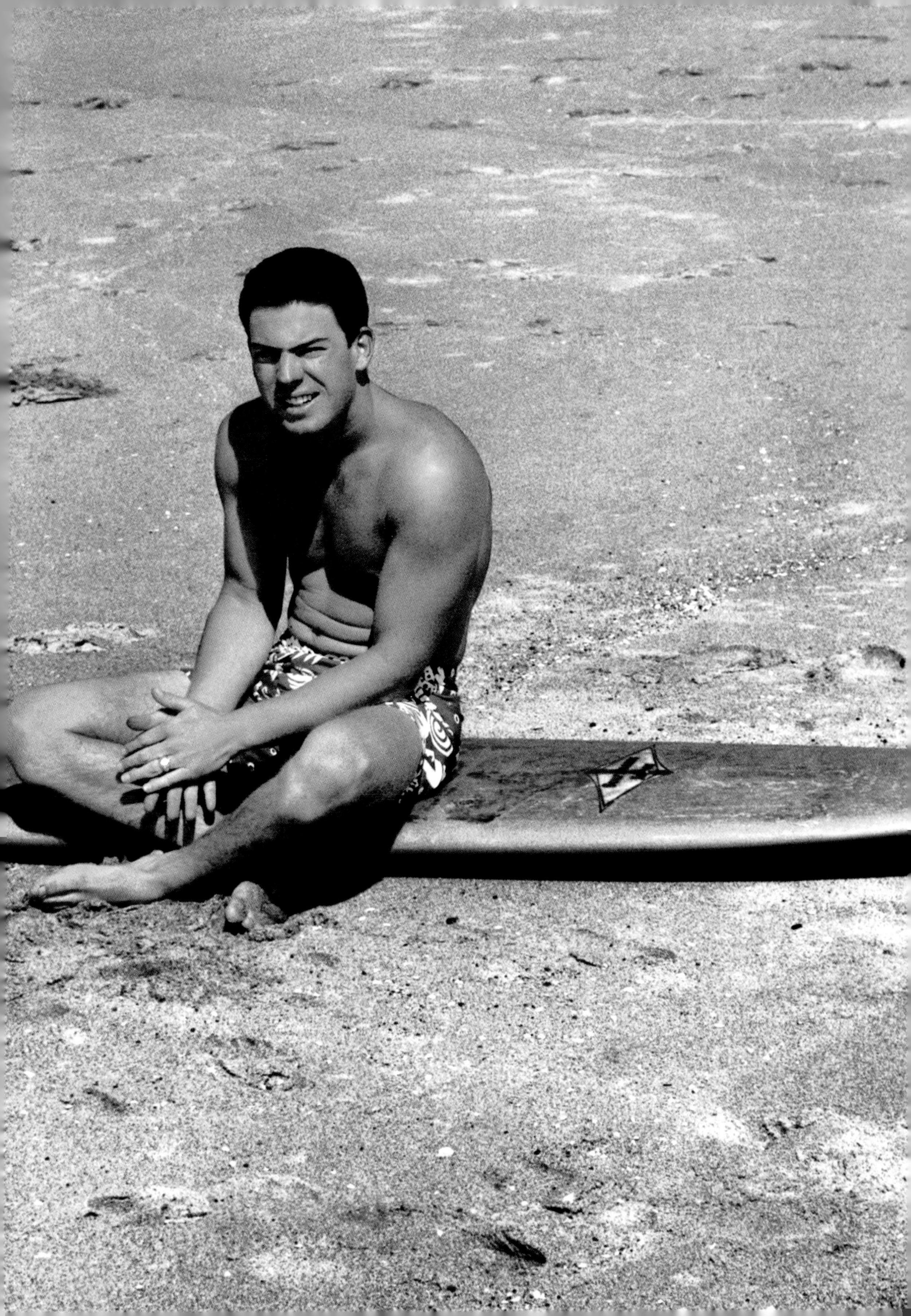

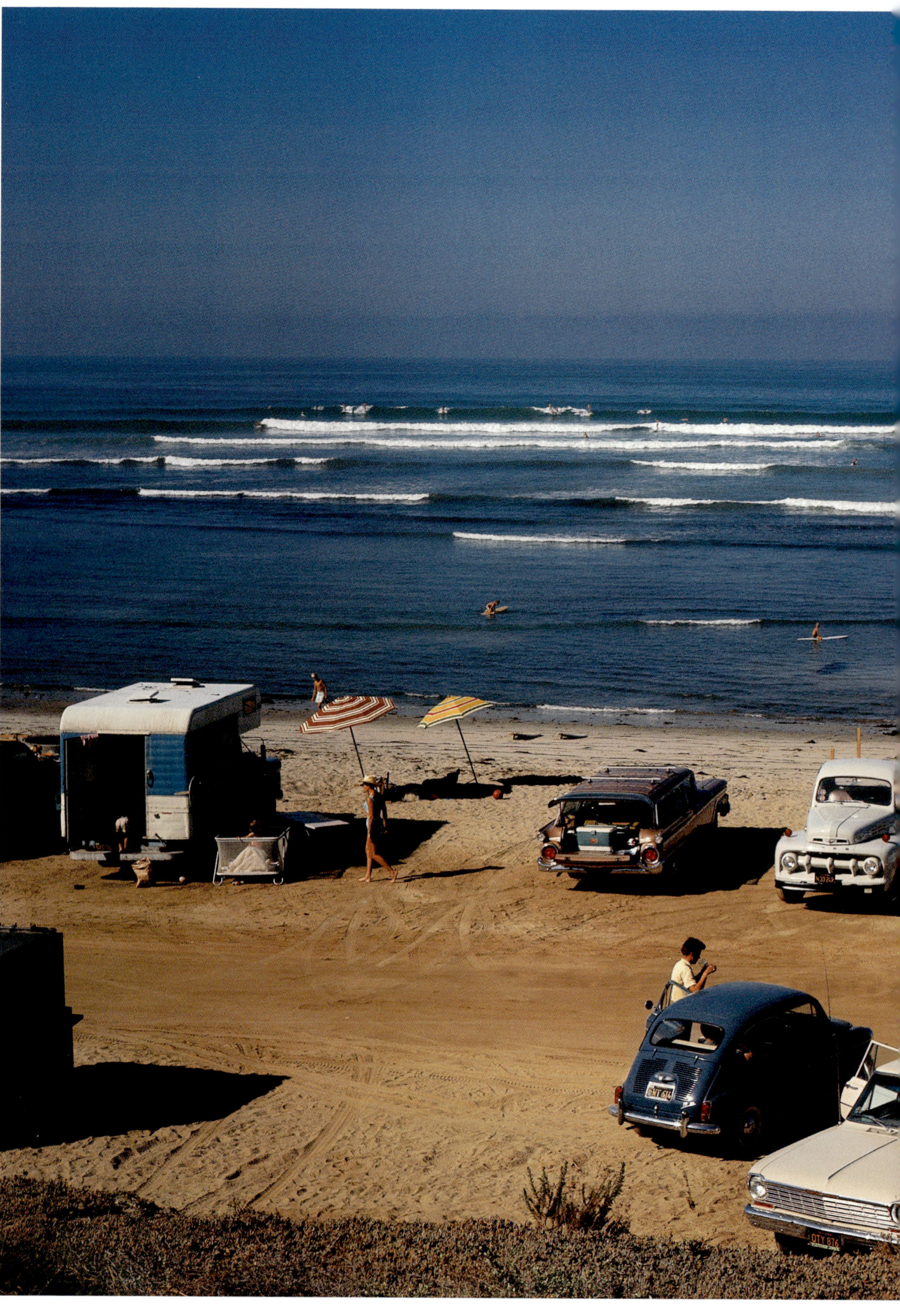

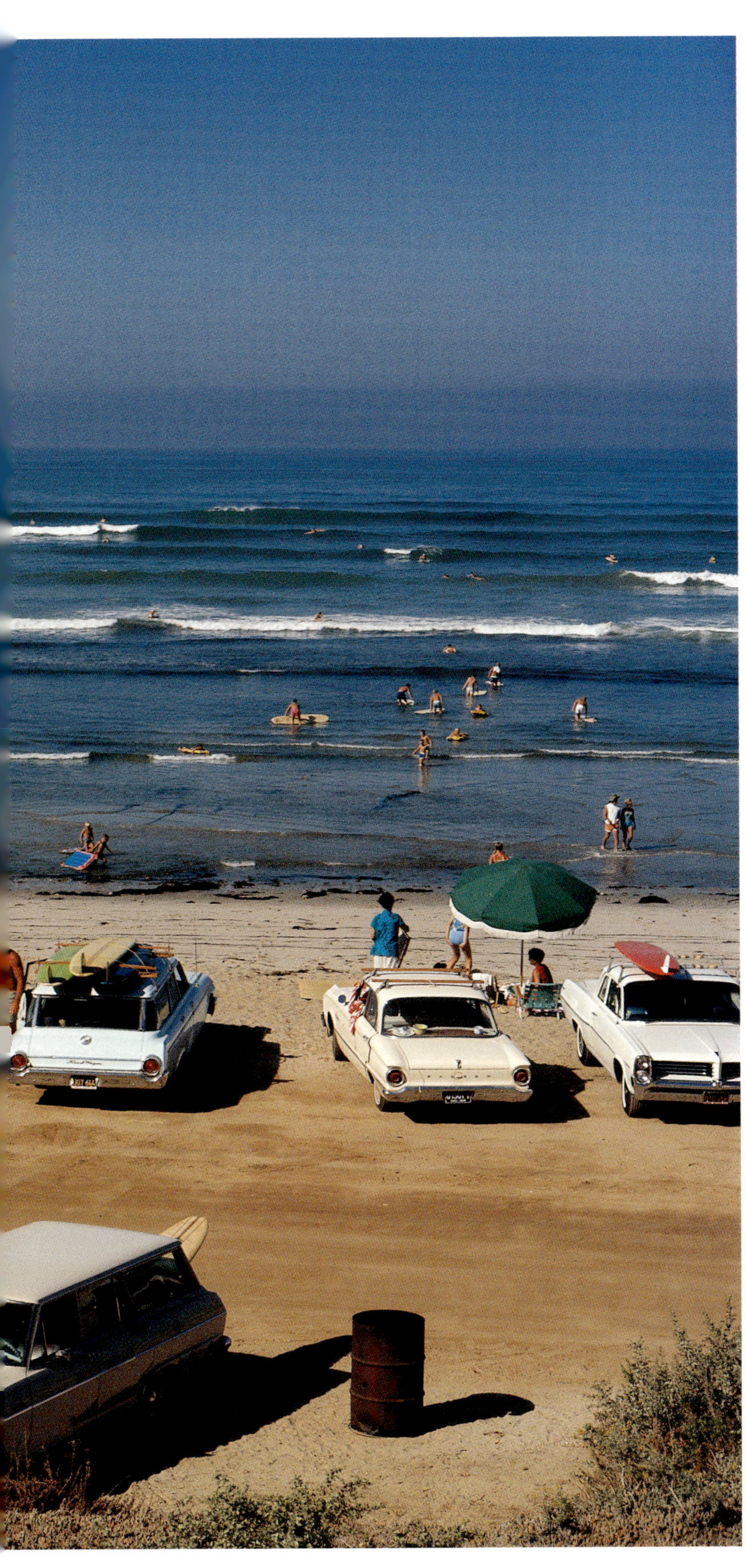

**San Onofre, 1964**

Low tide over San Onofre's long,
flat, cobblestone reef.

Ebbe auf dem langen, flachen
Kieselstein-Riff von San Onofre.

Le vaste récif de galets émergeant
sur les fonds plats de la plage de
San Onofre à marée basse.

**Lance Carson, Malibu, 1962**

The premier Malibu stylist
executing a "cheater five."

Der beste Stilist von Malibu
bei einem „Cheater Five".

Le roi de la figure de style de
Malibu exécutant un « cheater
five ».

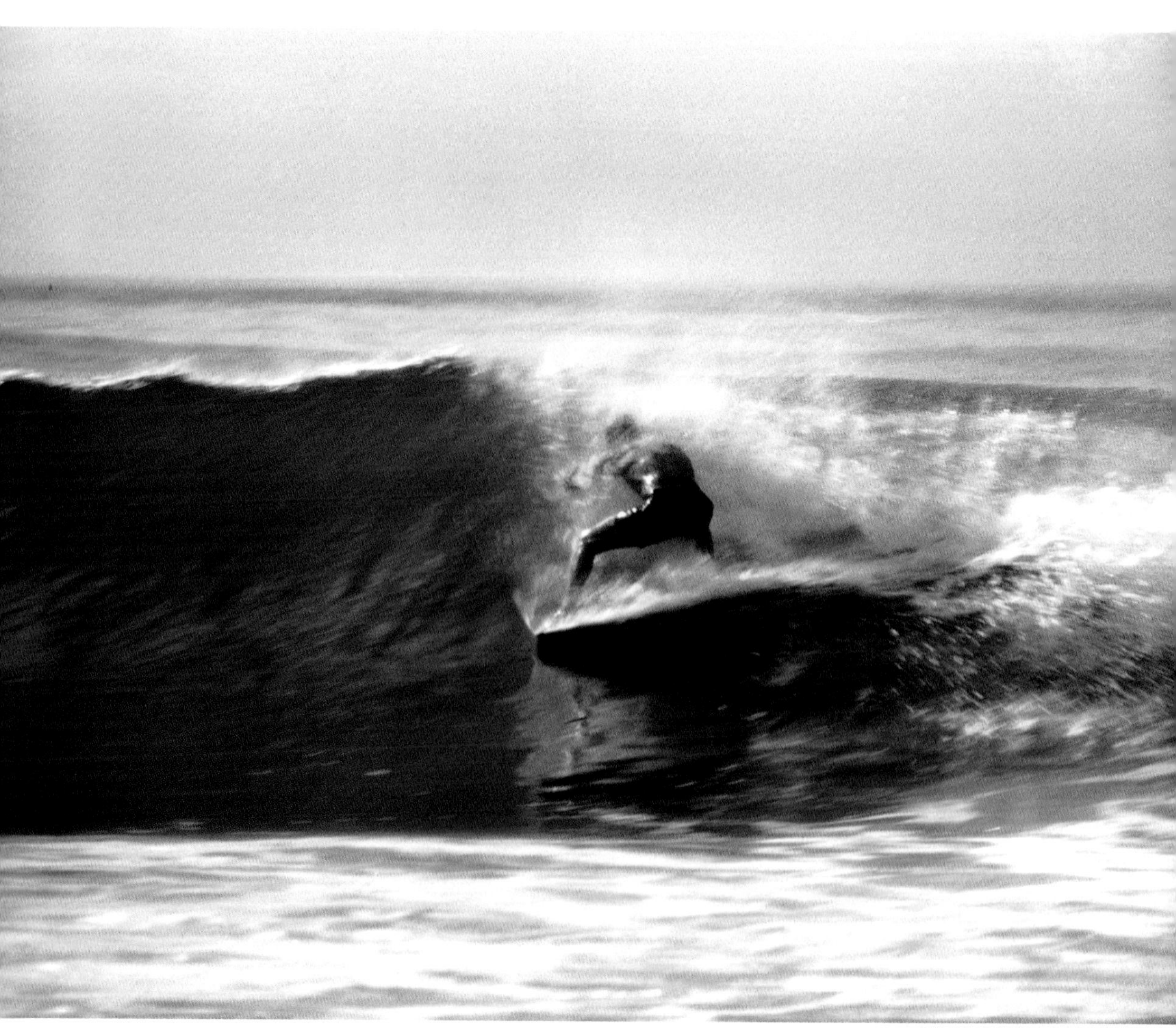

**Miki Dora, Malibu, 1960**

One of Grannis's earliest shots of "Da Cat." He trimmed with an elegant bebop style that was copied by hundreds of neophyte sixties surfers.

Einer von Grannis' frühen Schnappschüssen von „Da Cat". Sein eleganter Bebop-Style wurde in den Sechzigern von Hunderten von Neophyten nachgeahmt.

Un des premiers clichés de « Da Cat » signés Grannis. Il maîtrisait sa planche avec élégance et dans un style be-bop qui fut copié par des centaines de néophytes dans les années 1960.

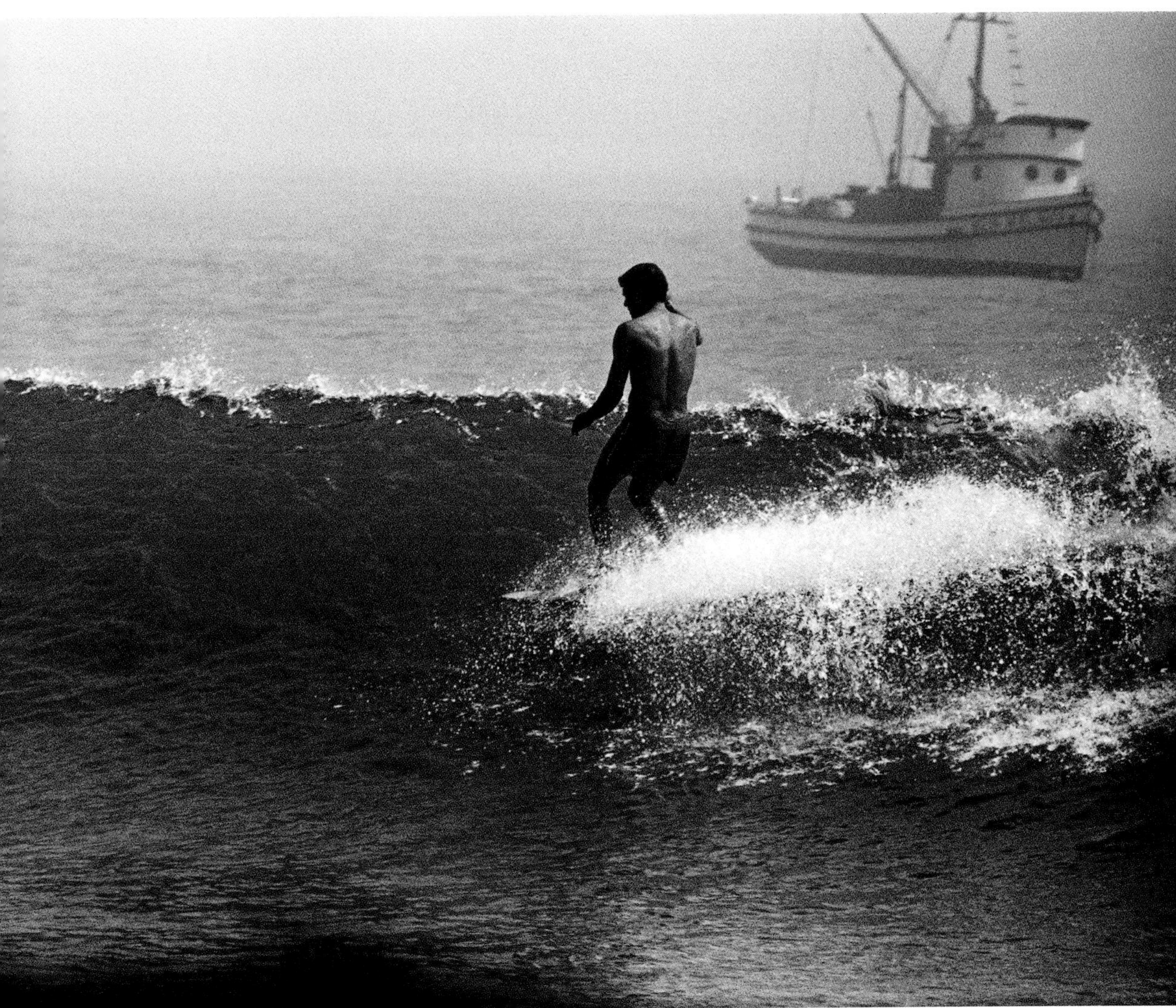

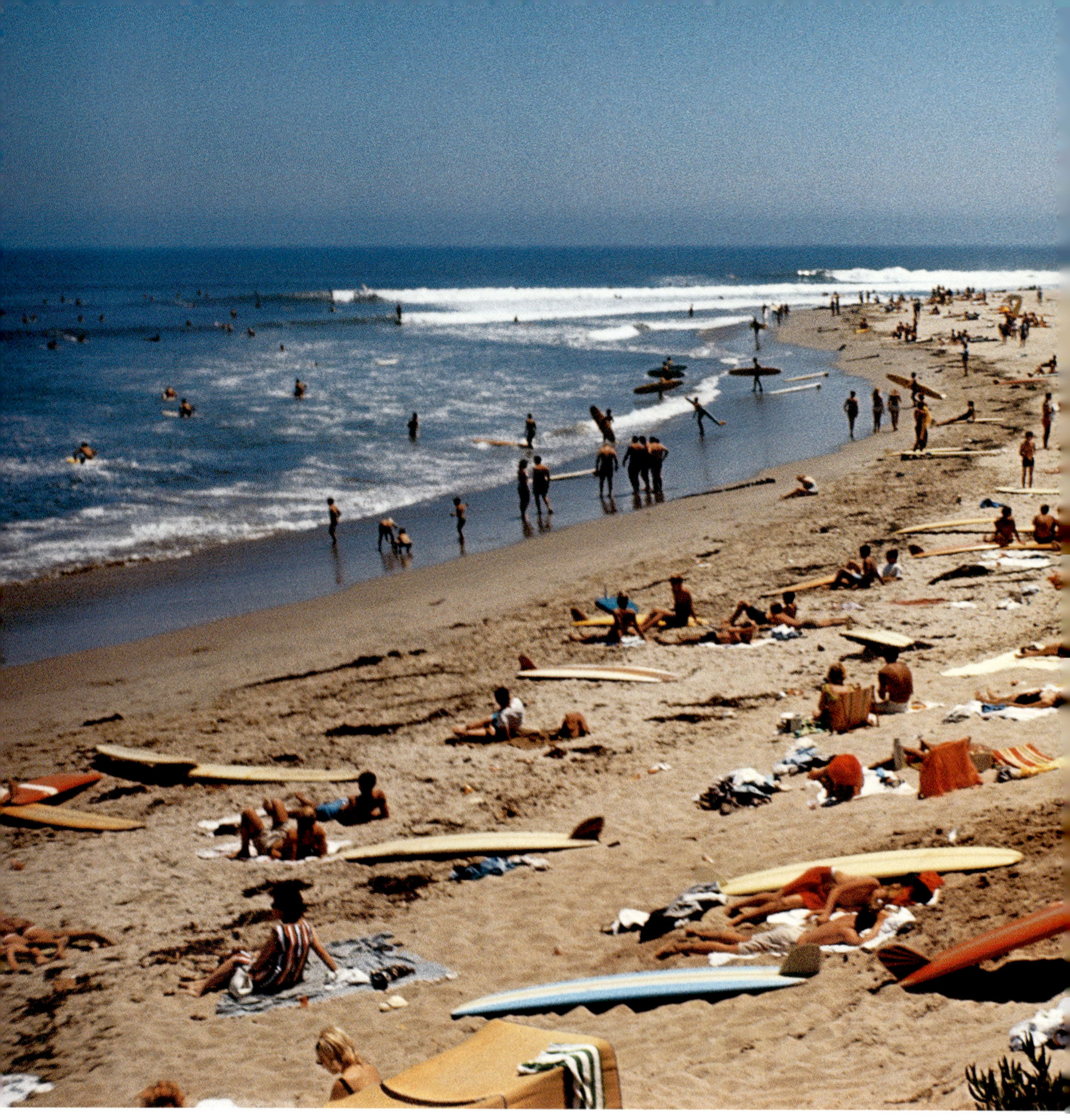

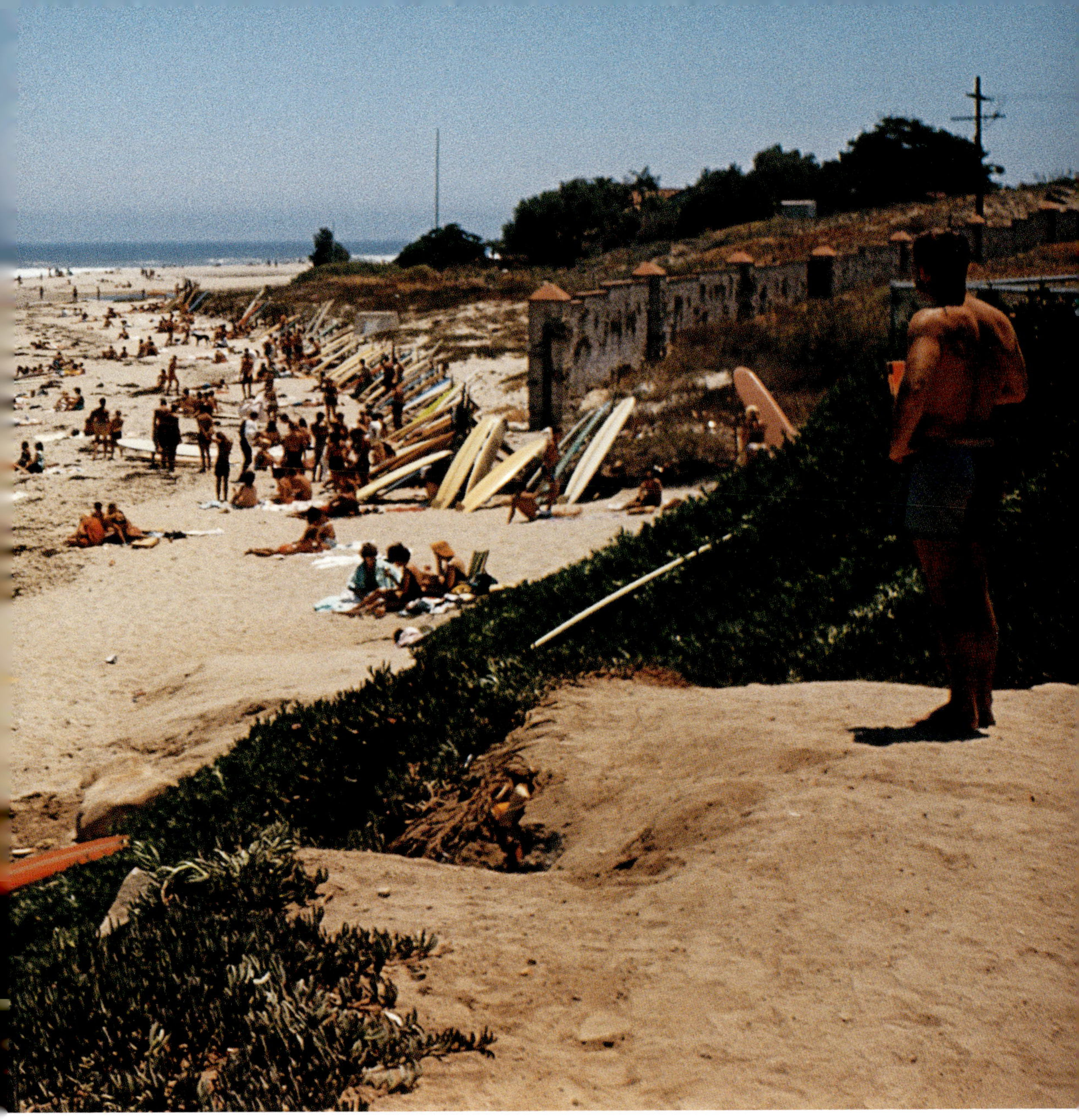

**Malibu, circa 1965**

Malibu Point, inhabited by the
Chumash Indians in ancient times,
has been called "the cradle of
modern surfing."

Malibu Point, einst von den
Chumash-Indianern bewohnt,
wurde als die „Wiege des modernen
Surfens" bezeichnet.

Malibu Point, autrefois peuplé par
les Indiens Chumash, a été baptisé
le « Berceau du surf moderne ».

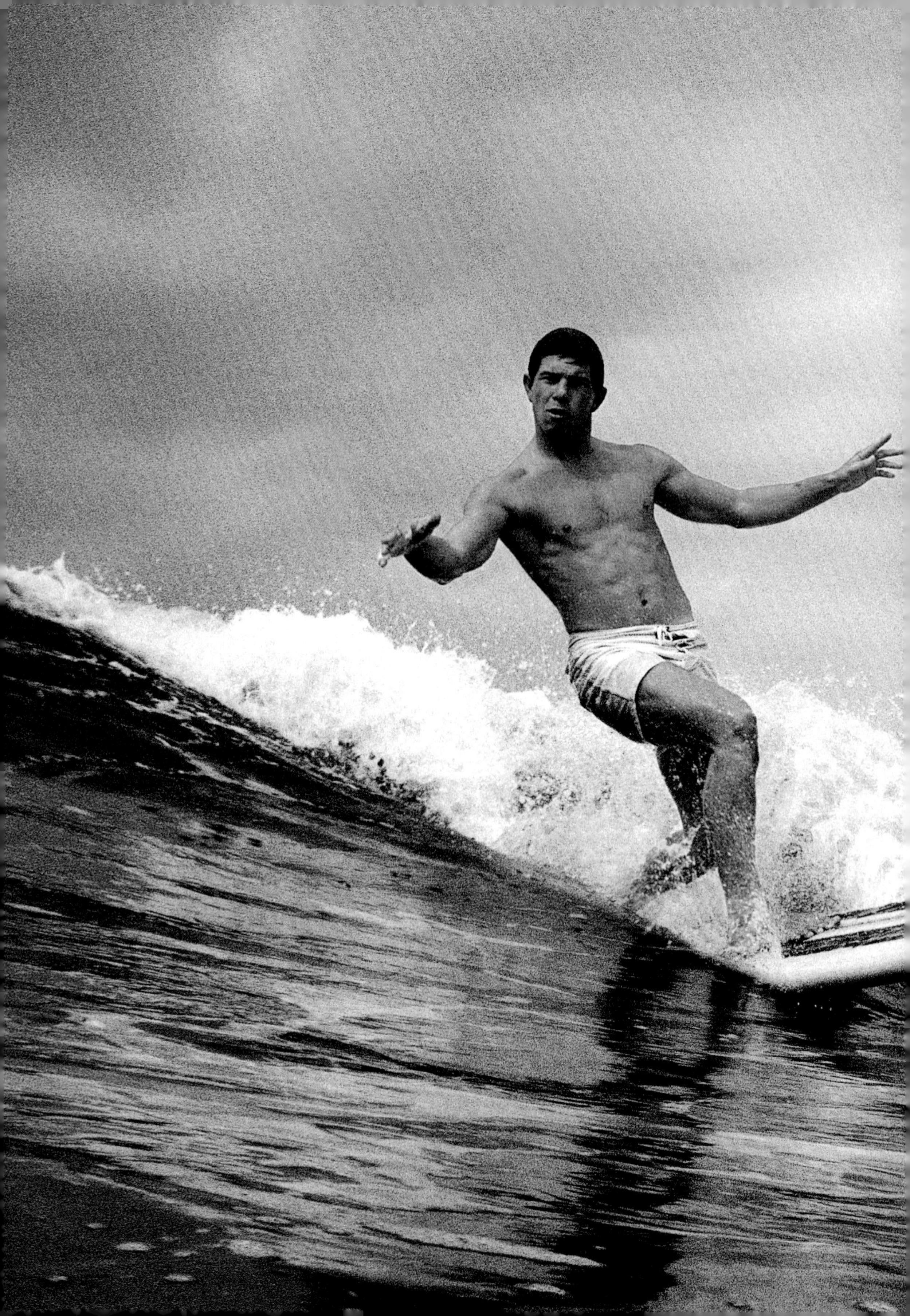

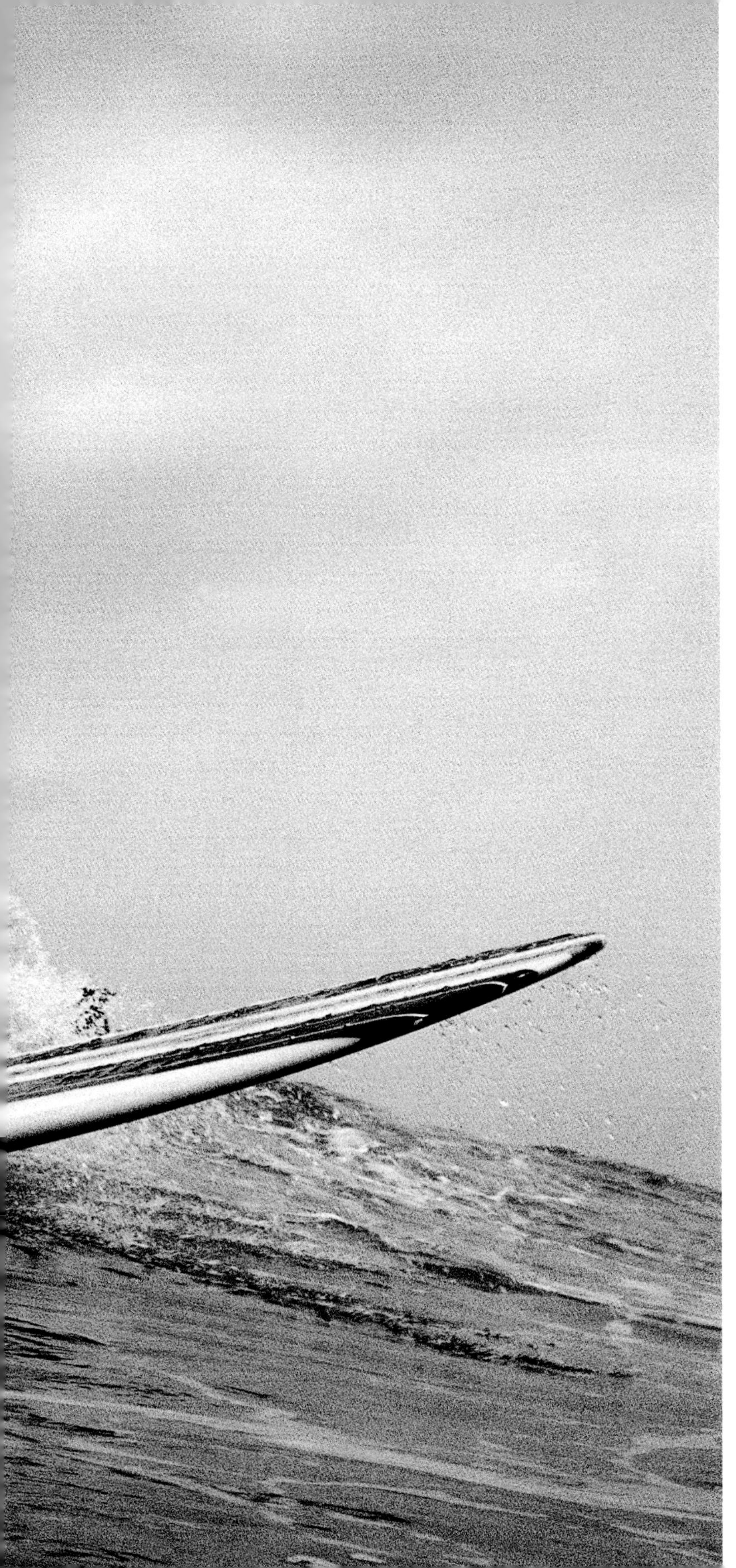

**Henry Ford, Hermosa Beach, 1963**

Ford was a talented 22nd Street local who starred in many of Bruce Brown's early surf films, such as *Slippery When Wet.*

Ford war ein talentierter Surfer vom 22nd Street Beach, der in vielen frühen Surffilmen von Bruce Brown mitspielte, z. B. in *Slippery When Wet.*

Le talentueux Henry Ford, originaire de 22nd Street, fut la vedette de nombreux films de surf réalisés par Bruce Brown, dont *Slippery When Wet.*

**Dewey Weber, Malibu, 1965**

Weber, a one-time Duncan yo-yo
champ and university wrestling
all-star, was also a champion surf
competitor. He's shown here
in the finals of the 1965 Malibu
Invitational.

Weber, ein ehemaliger Wrestlilng-
und Yo-Yo-Champion, nahm auch
an Surfwettkämpfen teil. Hier sieht
man ihn in der Endrunde des
Malibu Invitational 1965.

Dewey Weber, ancien champion
de yo-yo Duncan et de lutte
universitaire, fut également un
as du surf. On le voit ici lors des
épreuves finales de la Malibu
Invitational de 1965.

*Pages 86–87*
**Miki Dora, Malibu, 1961**

*Pages 88–89*
**Dave Rochlen, Malibu, 1962**

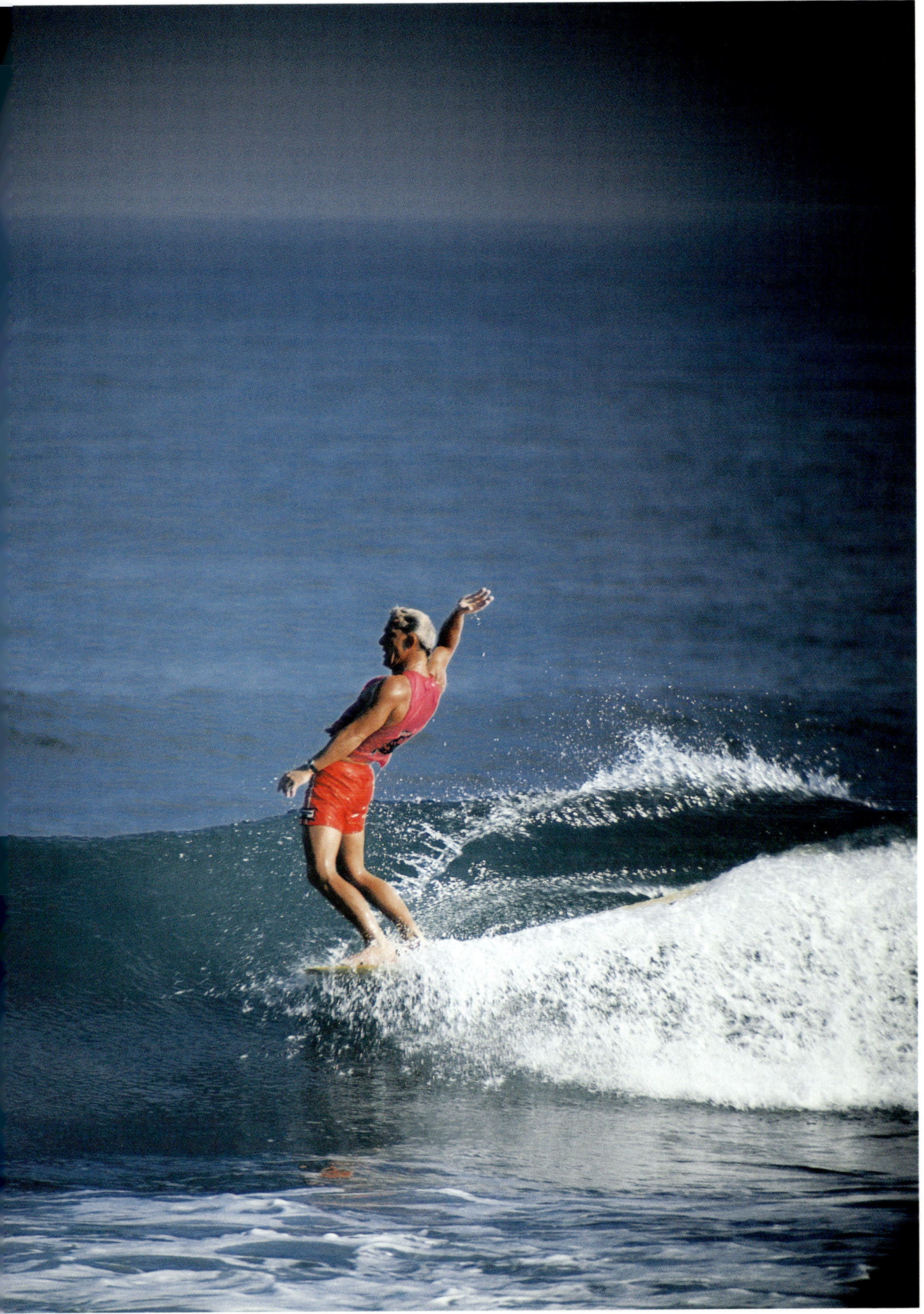

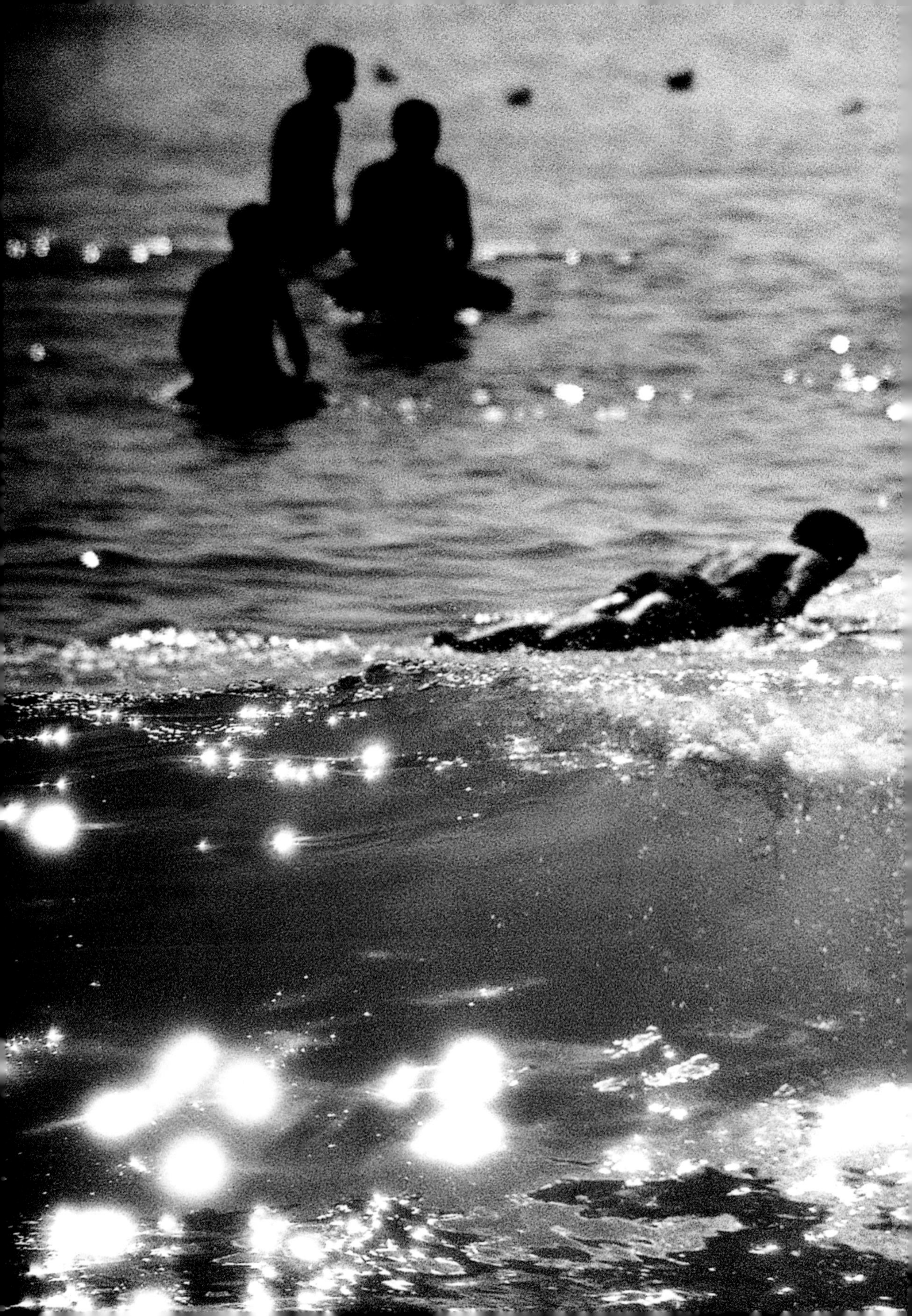

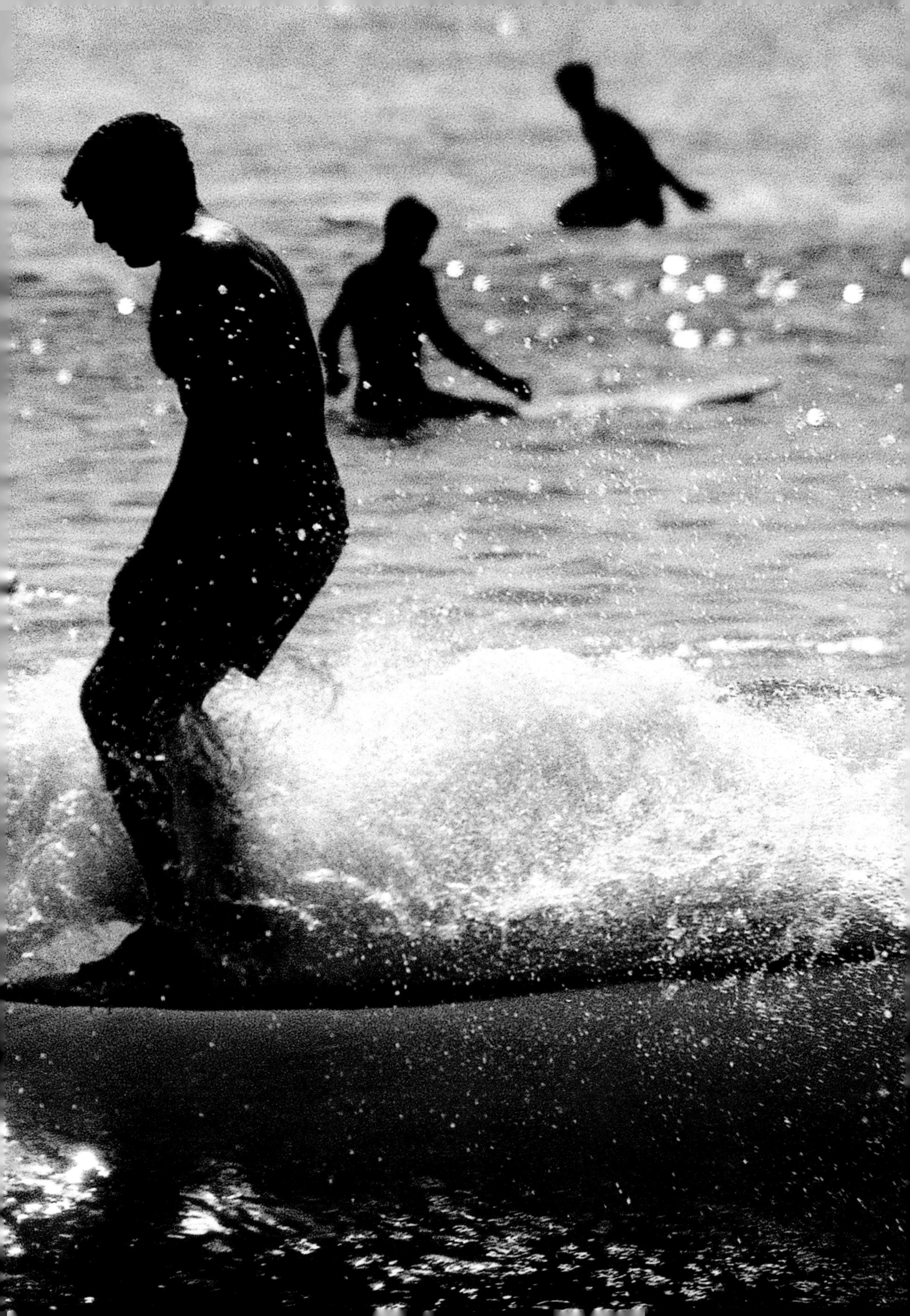

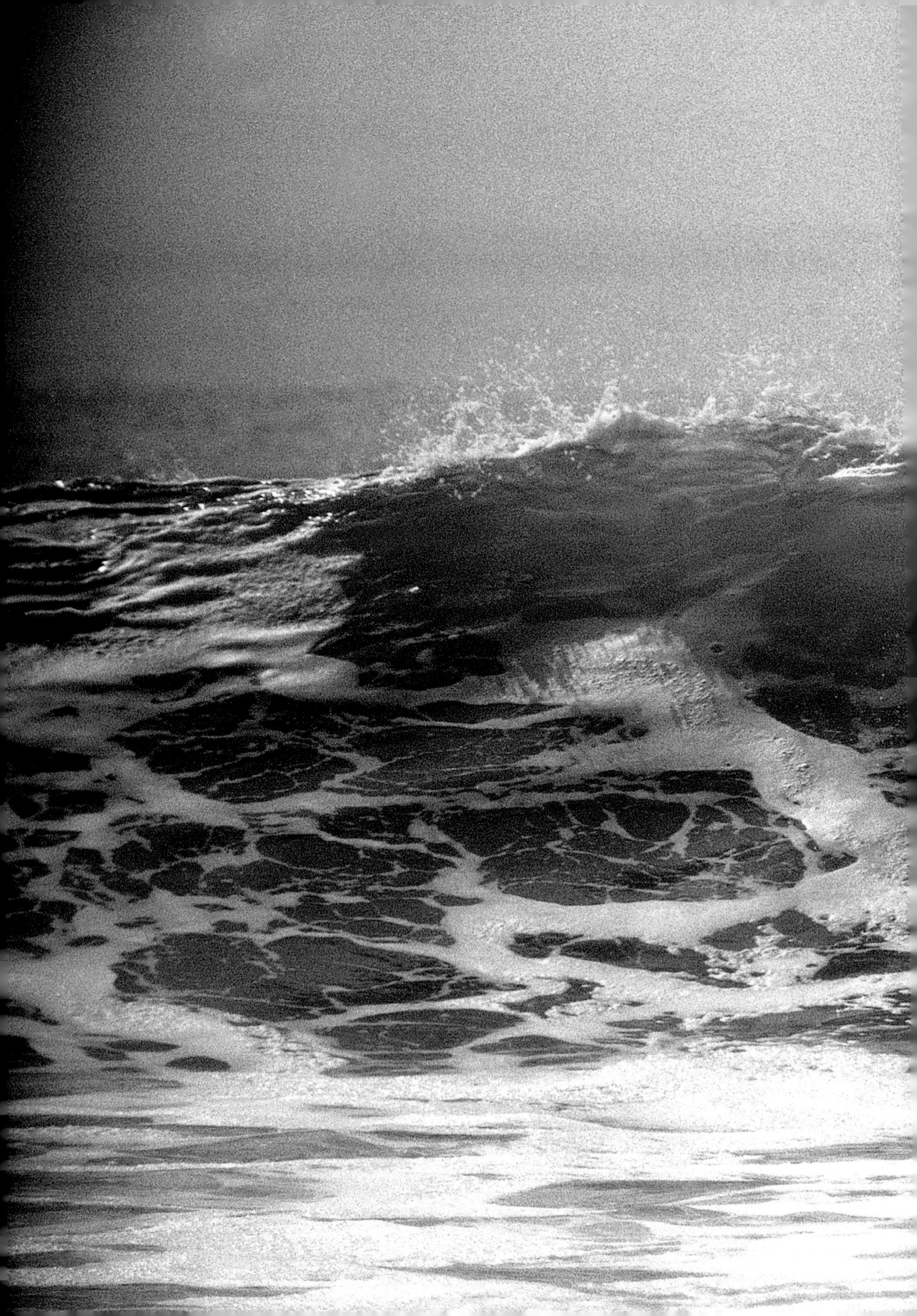

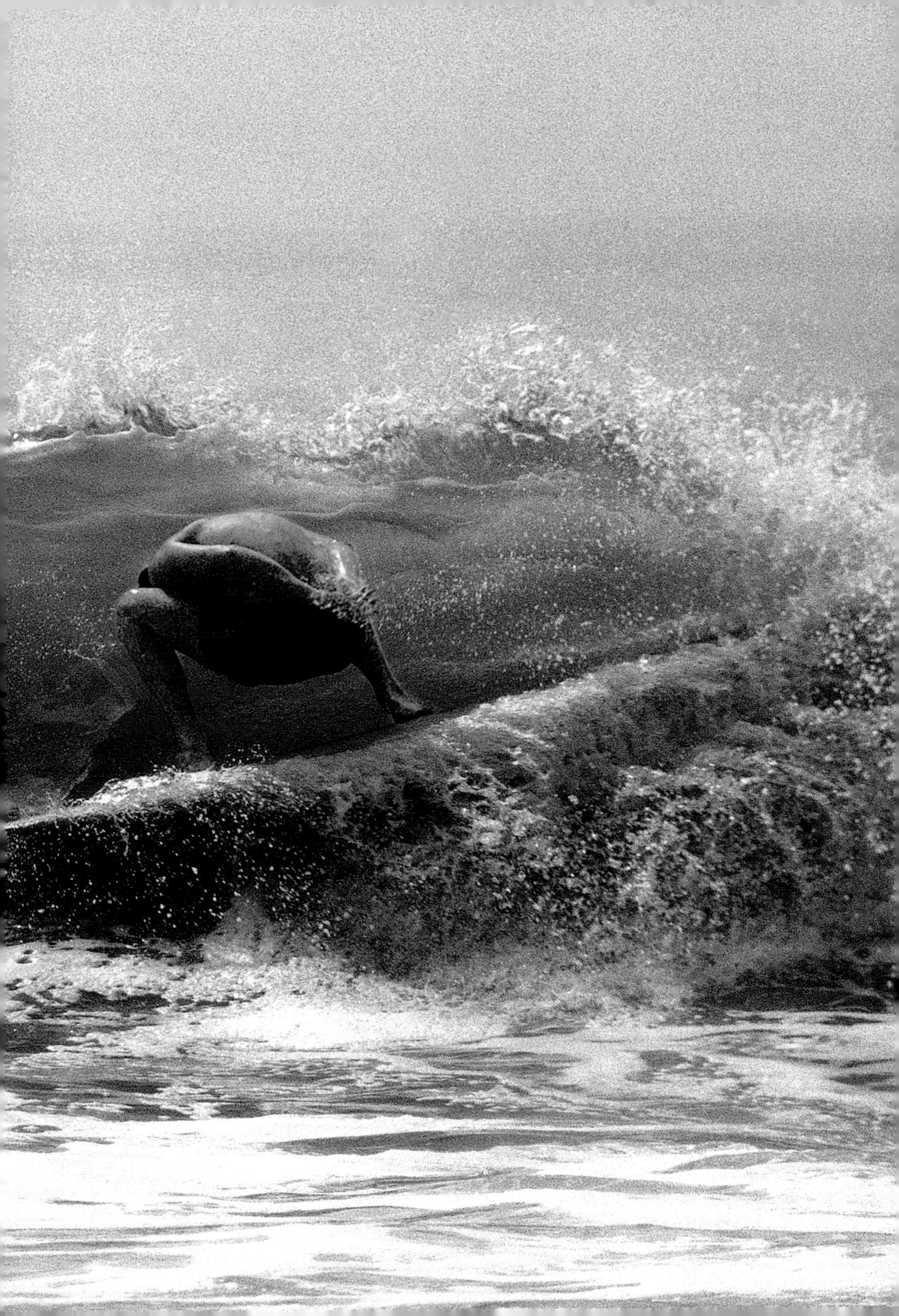

**Mike Hynson, Hermosa Beach, 1964**

The brash and stylish San Diegan
went on to costar in the 1966
documentary *The Endless Summer*.

Der elegante Draufgänger aus
San Diego spielte später in dem
Dokumentarfilm *The Endless
Summer* von 1966 mit.

Le sémillant et élégant Myke
Hynson, originaire de San Diego,
fut l'une des vedettes du célèbre
documentaire *The Endless
Summer* de 1966.

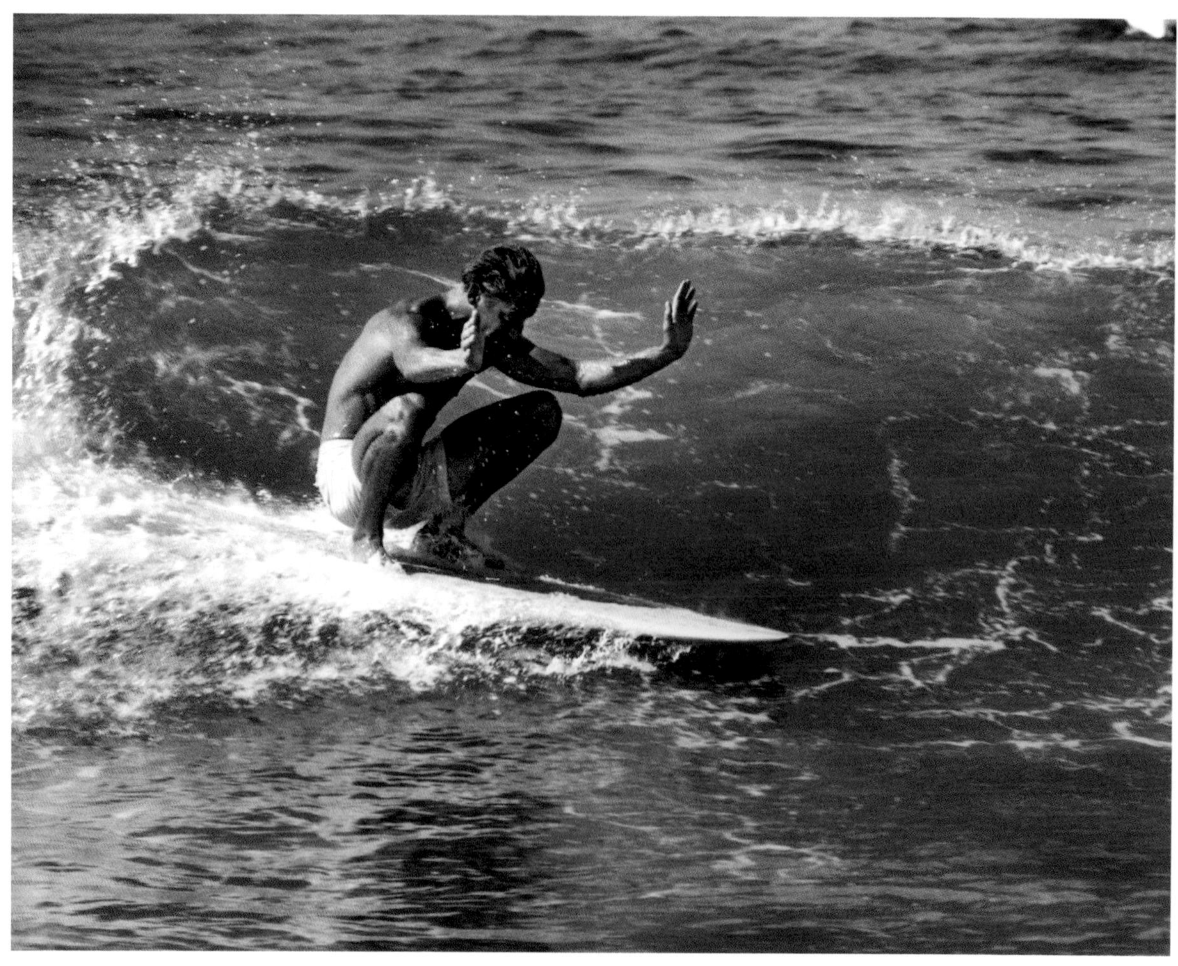

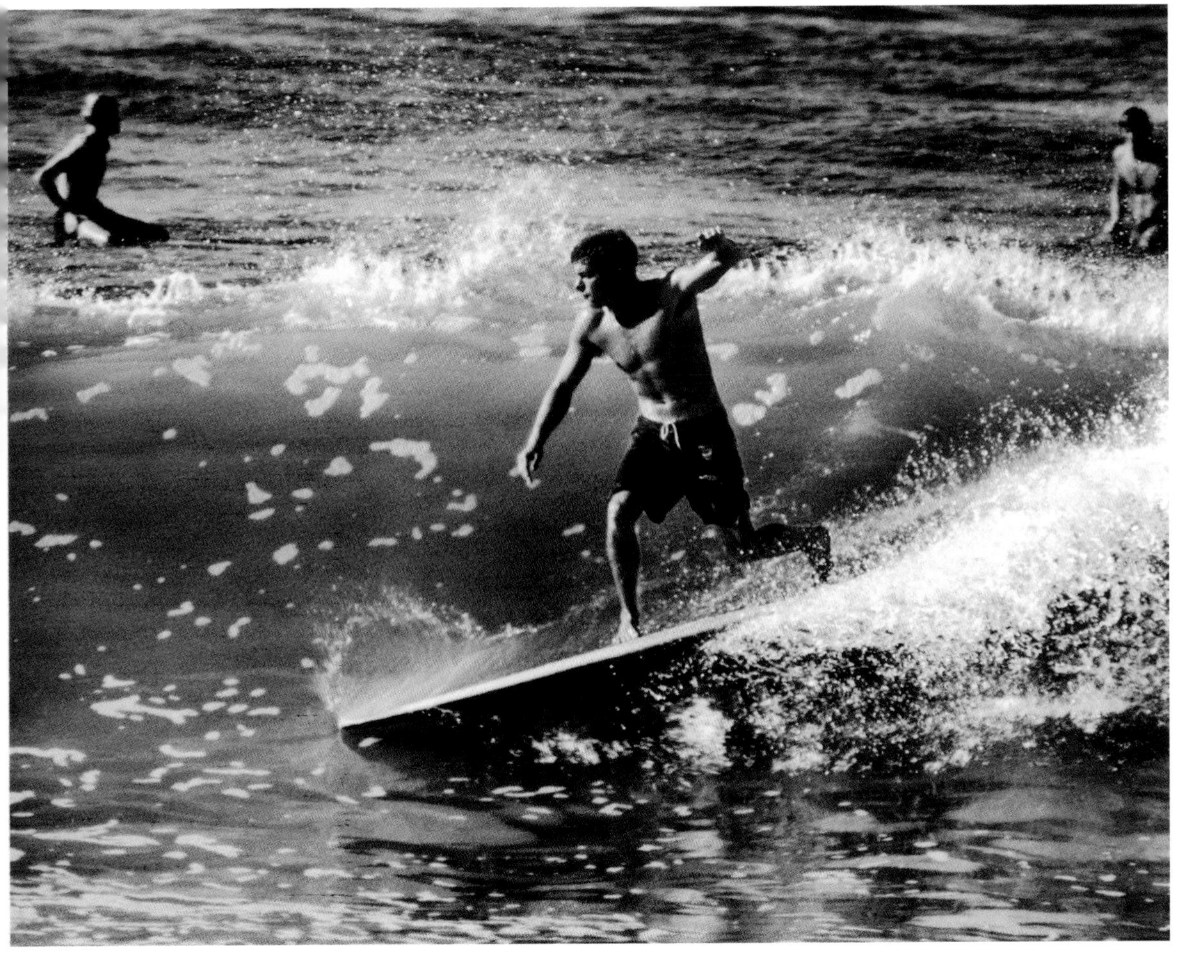

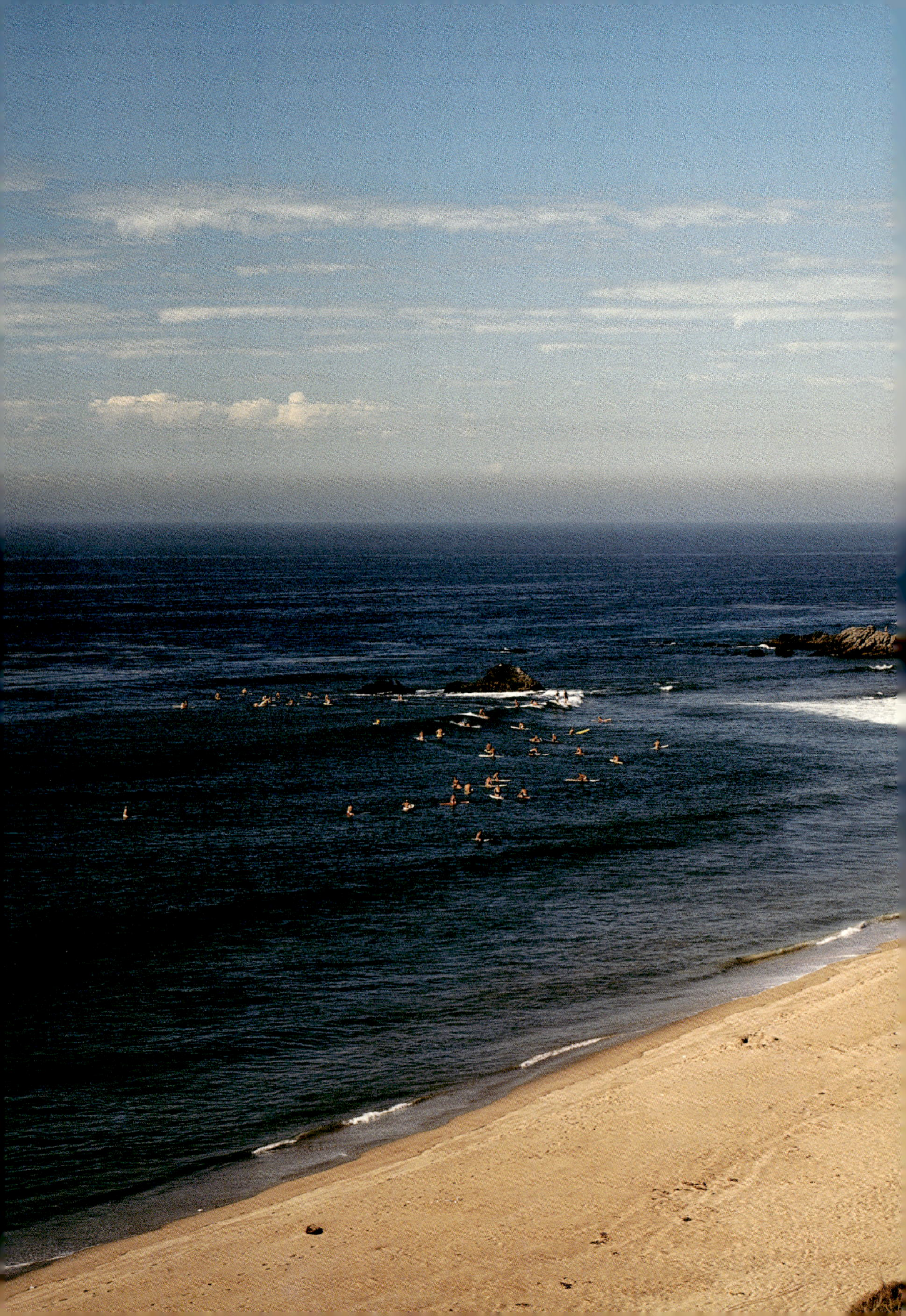

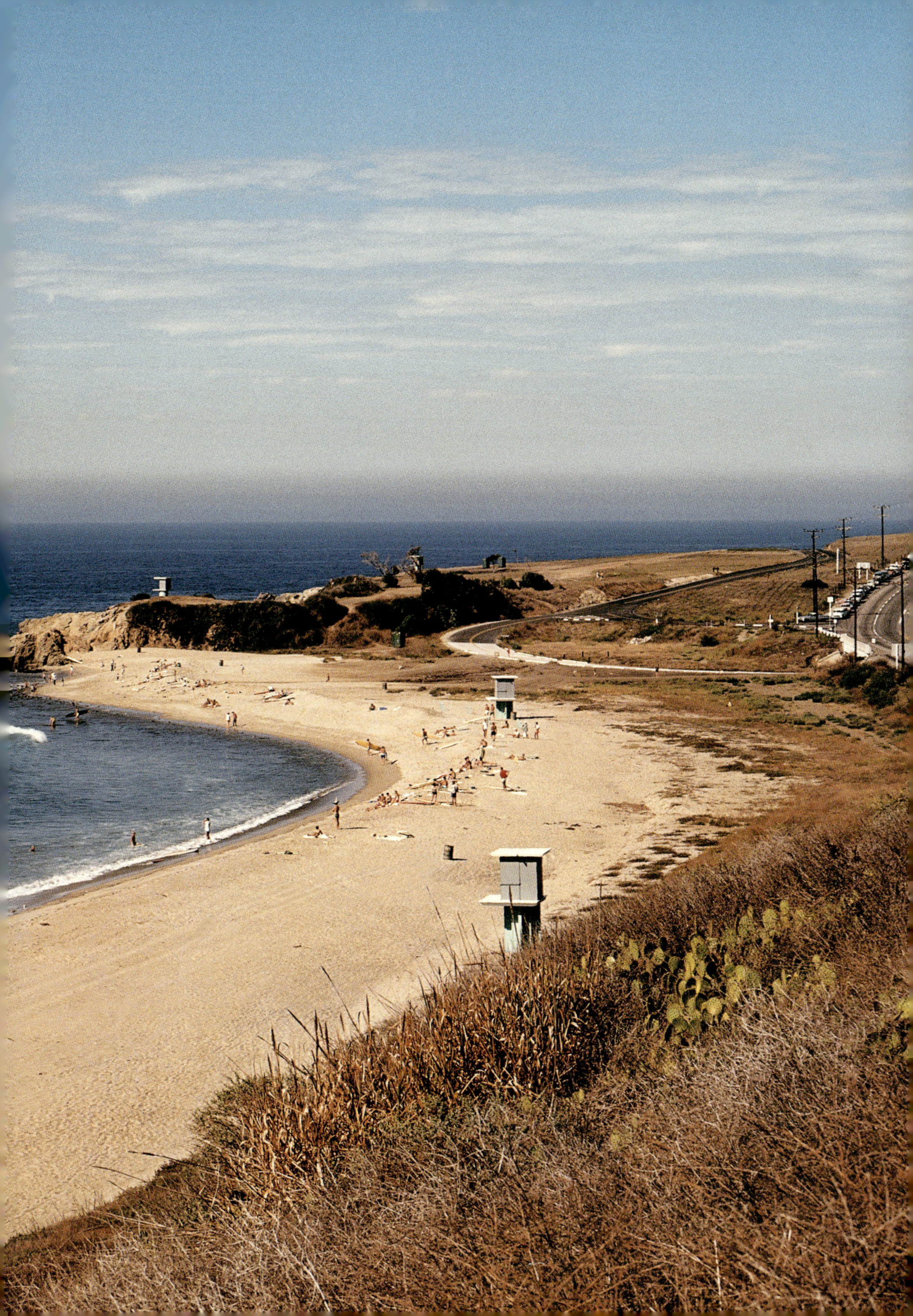

**Secos, 1963**

Arroyo Sequit, also known as
"Secos," is an archetypal California
beach that was used as a location
for the original *Gidget* movie
in 1959.

Arroyo Sequit, auch bekannt als
„Secos", ist ein typischer kali-
fornischer Strand, an dem 1959
der Film *Gidget* gedreht wurde.

Archétype de la plage californienne,
Arroyo Sequit ou « Secos » a servi
de lieu de tournage pour la
comédie originale *Un amour de
vacances* en 1959.


**Redondo Beach Breakwater, 1963**

During a big winter swell, surfers
saved themselves a brutal paddle
by timing their entry between waves
slamming the jetty's end.

Während einer starken Winterdünung sparten sich die Surfer
die gnadenlose Paddelei, indem
sie zwischen den auf das Ende des
Dammes aufschlagenden Wellen
ins Wasser gingen.

Par une forte houle hivernale, un
groupe de surfeurs attend sur la
jetée le moment opportun pour
entrer dans l'eau entre deux
déferlantes et s'épargner ainsi
un pagayage épuisant.

**Malibu Wall, 1966**

The famous Malibu Wall was
rumored to be the remains of a
ruined estate. Note the graffiti
advertisement for Miki Dora.

Die berühmte Malibu Wall ge-
hörte angeblich zur Ruine eines
Landsitzes. Ein Graffito rühmt
Miki Dora.

Le fameux mur de Malibu était
supposé être le vestige d'une
ancienne propriété. On remarquera
le graffiti vantant les mérites de
Miki Dora.

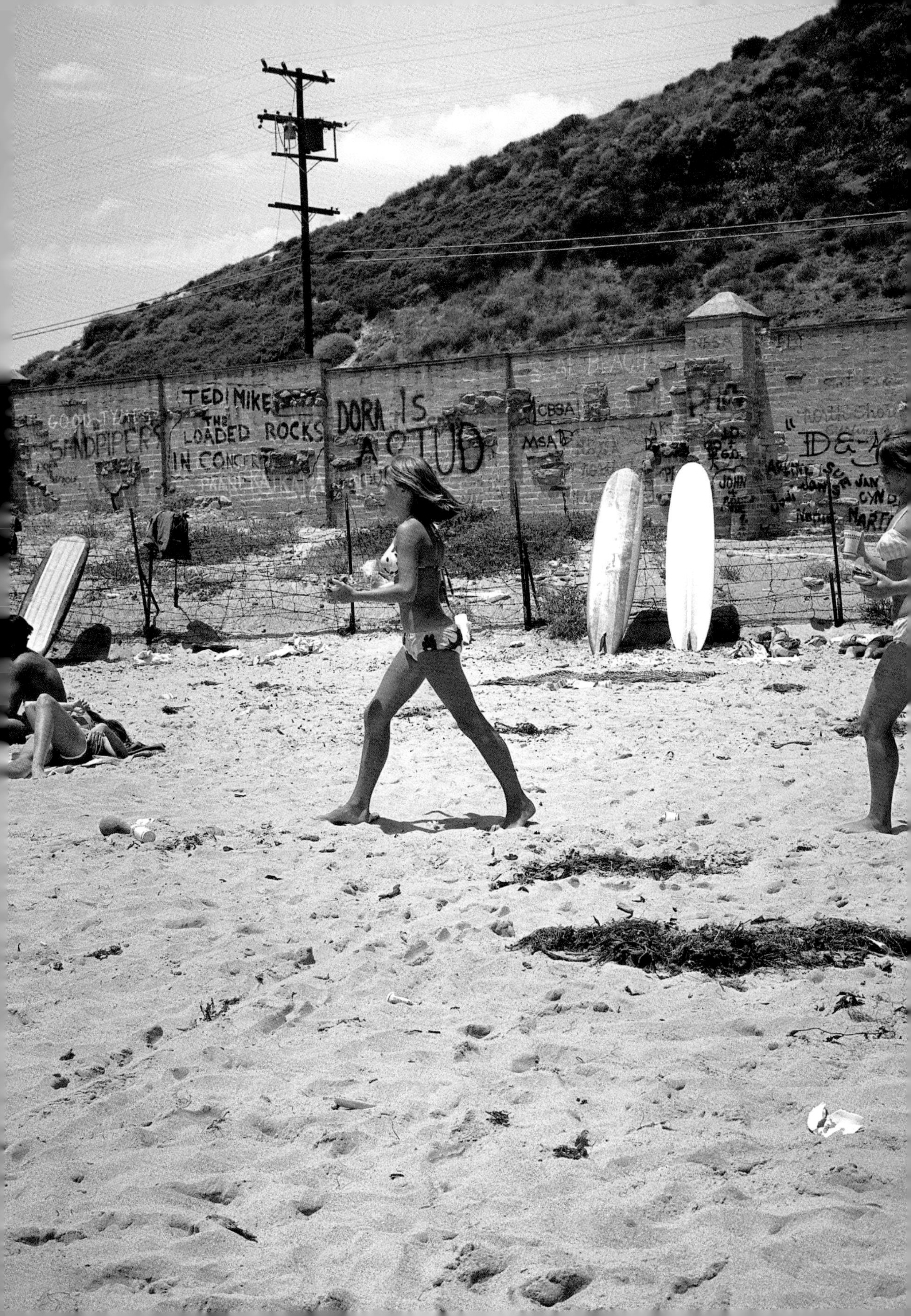

GOOD TYMES
SANDPIPERS
TED MIKE
The LOADED ROCKS
IN CONCERT
DORA IS A STUD
SEAL BEACH
CBSA
MSA
NORTH SHORE
D & A
JOHN

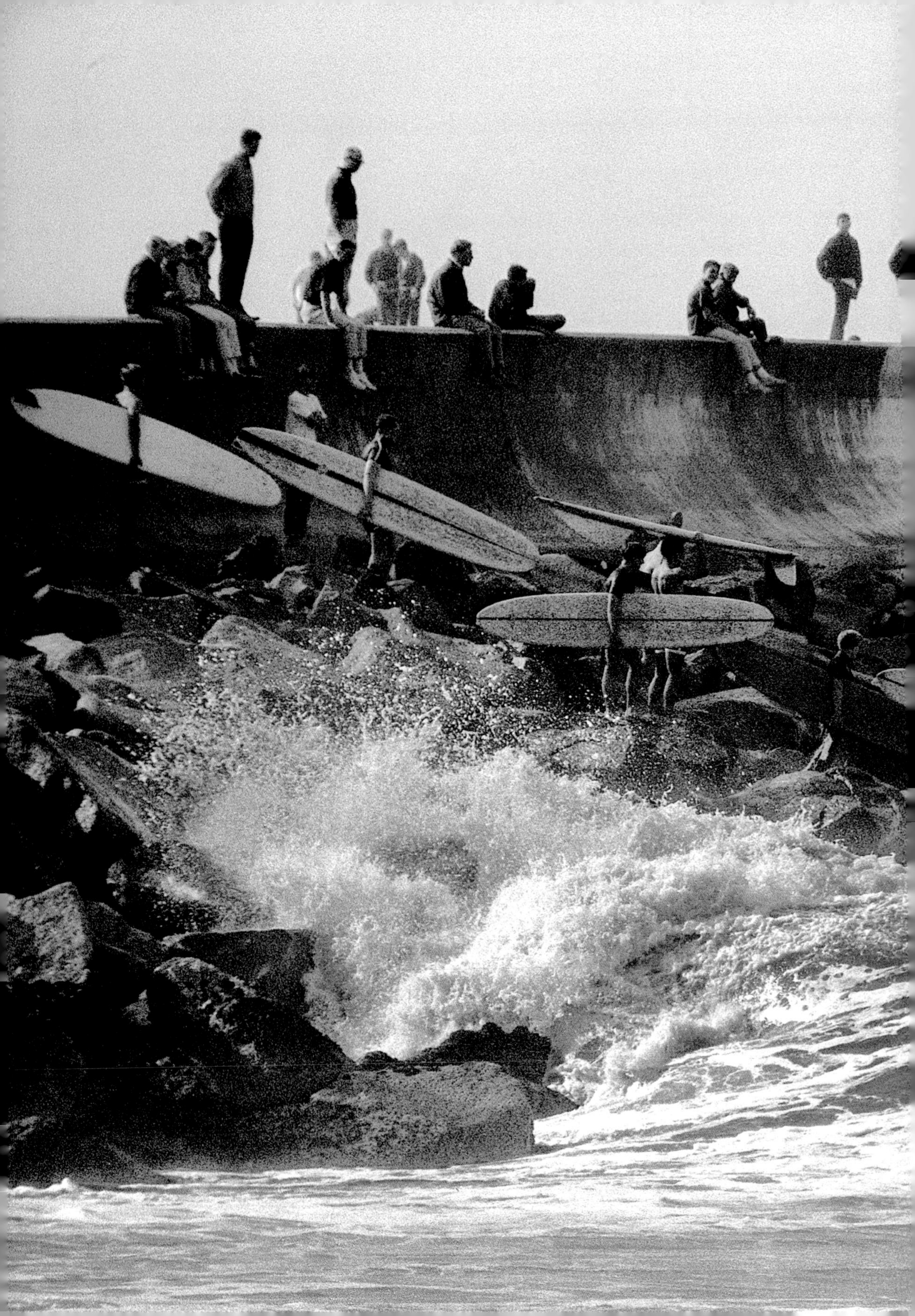

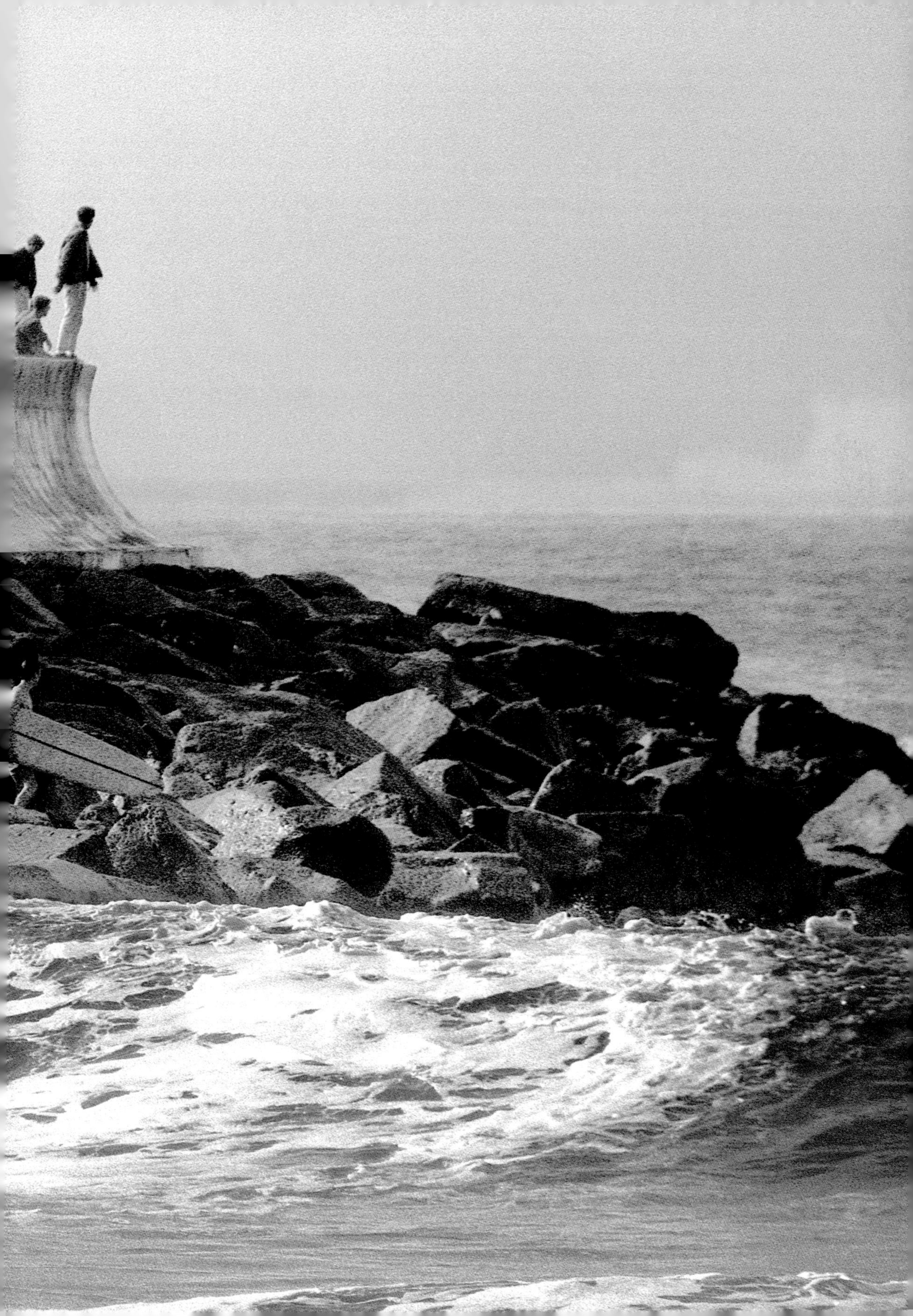

**Miki Dora, Oceanside, 1965**

Dora railed against contests as
"cheap soggy carnivals" in surf
magazines, but he craved the
attention they drew.

Dora schimpfte in Surfzeitschriften
zwar über Wettbewerbe als „bil-
ligen, nassen Karneval", genoss
aber zugleich die Aufmerksamkeit,
die sie ihm brachten.

Miki Dora dénigrait publiquement
les compétitions de surf, mais
lorsqu'il les qualifiait de « carnavals
aquatiques à deux balles » dans
les magazines spécialisés, c'était
avant tout pour attirer l'attention.


**Huntington Beach Pier, circa 1965**

"Shooting the pier" was a
cutting-edge crowd pleaser in
the sixties. If you fell, however,
you risked shredding your skin on
the razor-sharp mussels.

Mit „Shooting the pier" konnte
man in den Sechzigern bei den
Zuschauern Furore machen.
Bei einem Sturz riskierte man
jedoch, sich die Haut an den
rasiermesserscharfen Muscheln
aufzuschneiden.

Un passe-temps qui fait fureur
dans les années 1960: « Shooting
the pier » ou comment foncer sous
la jetée. Mais attention aux chutes:
les moules agglutinées sur les
piliers sont tranchantes comme
des lames de rasoir!

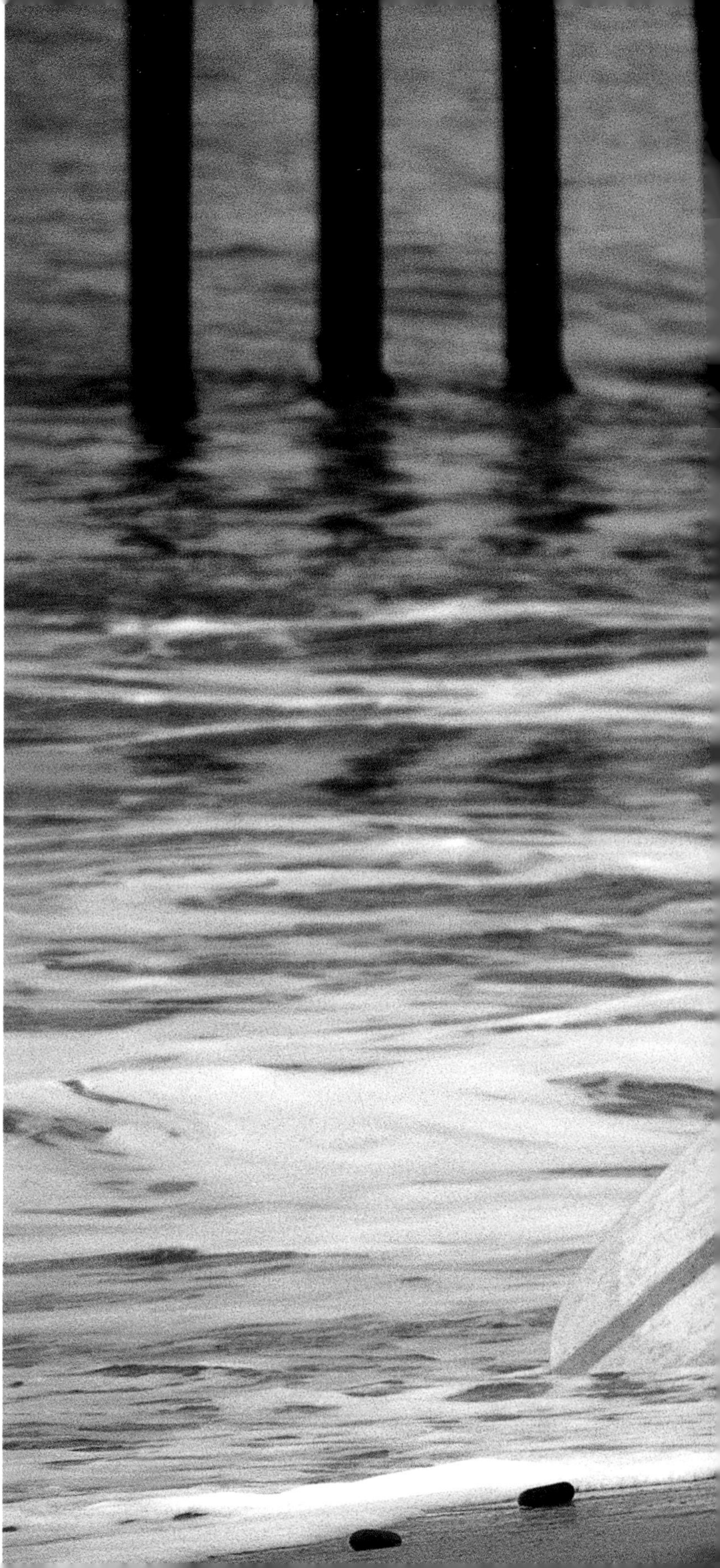

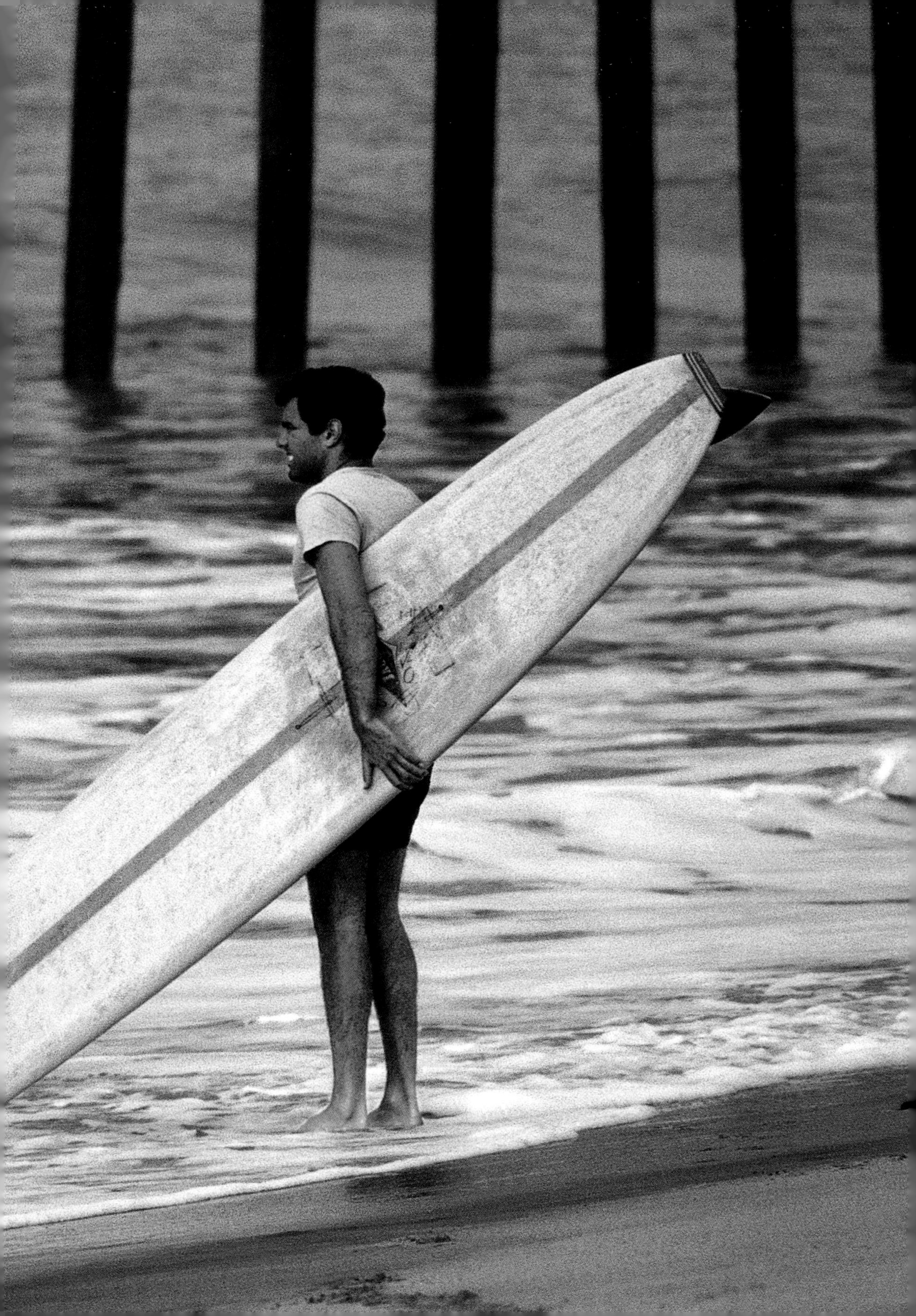

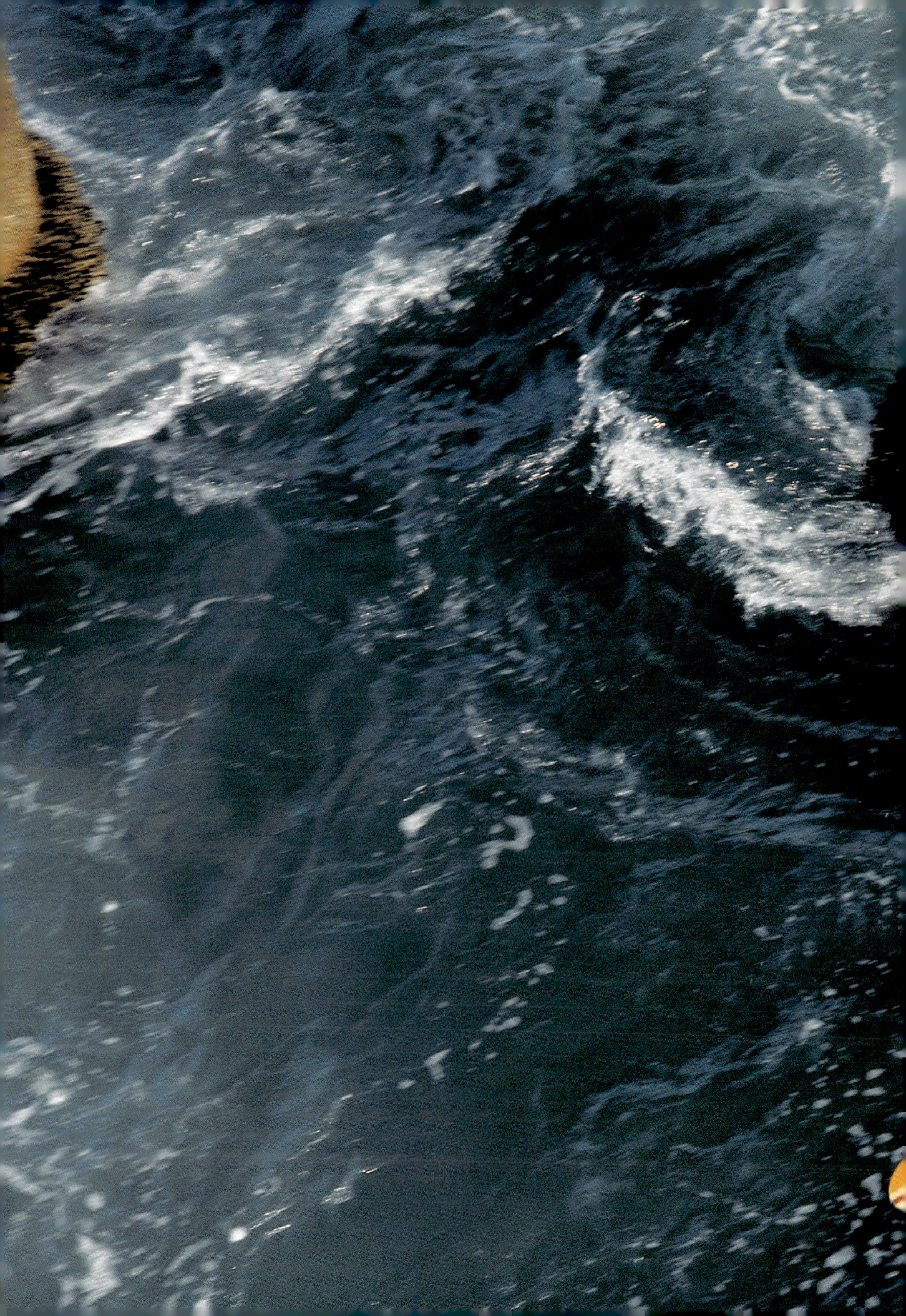

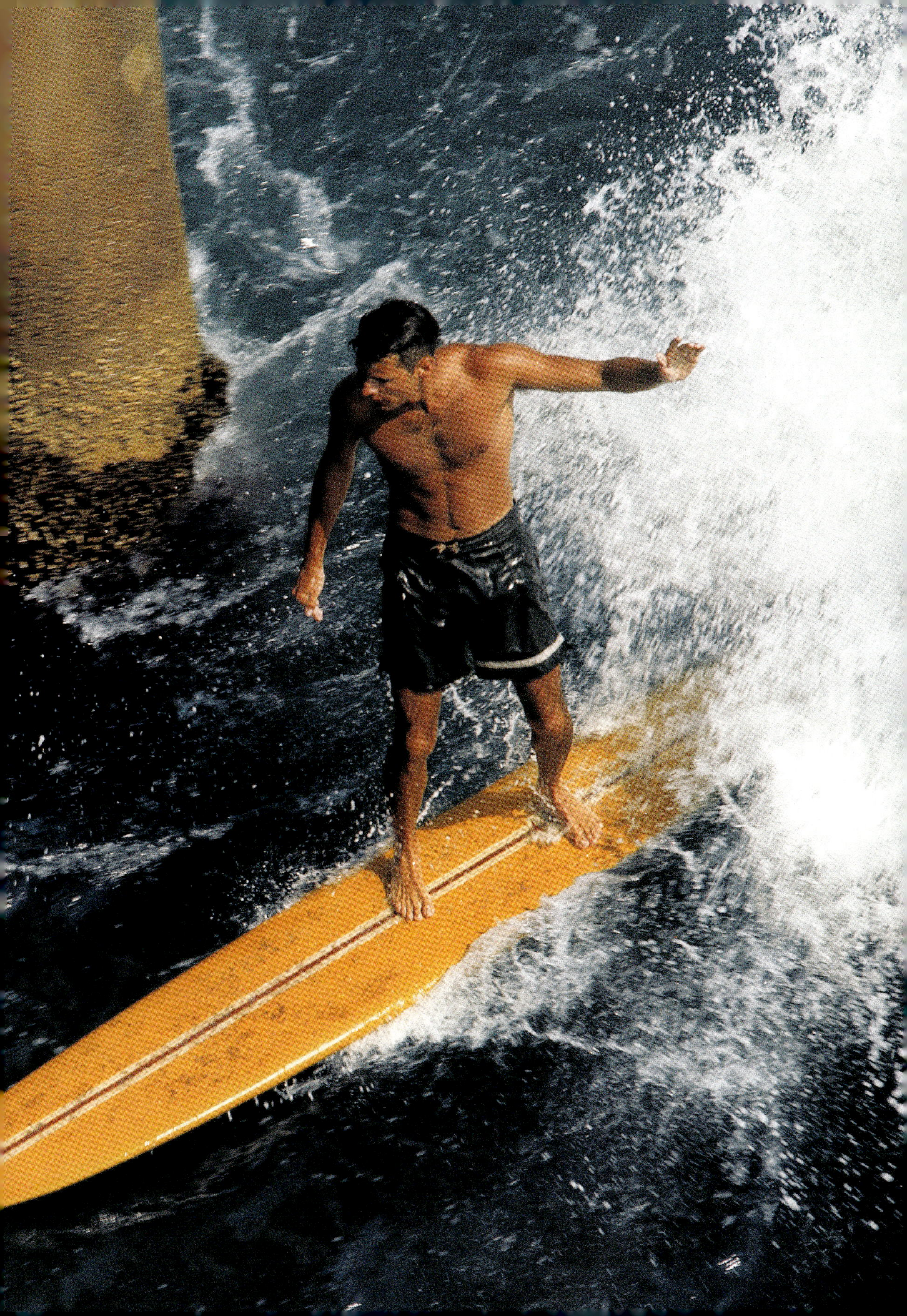

**Torrance Beach, 1964**

From this vantage you can see
the span of the South Bay, the
birthplace of the modern surf
industry.

Sicht auf die volle Länge der South
Bay, den Geburtsort der
modernen Surfindustrie.

Vue imprenable sur l'immense
bande littorale de South Bay,
berceau de l'industrie moderne
du surf.

**Torrance Beach, 1964**

"Rat's Beach," named after all the
young "surf rats" who learned on
its gentle waves before moving up
to Hermosa or Redondo.

„Rat's Beach" wurde nach den
jungen „Wasserratten" benannt, die
auf diesen sanften Wellen surfen
lernten, bevor sie nach Hermosa
oder Redondo weiterzogen.

« Rat's Beach » fut baptisée ainsi
d'après les « petits rats du surf »
qui venaient y taquiner la petite
vague avant de se lancer sur les
spots de Hermosa ou de Redondo.

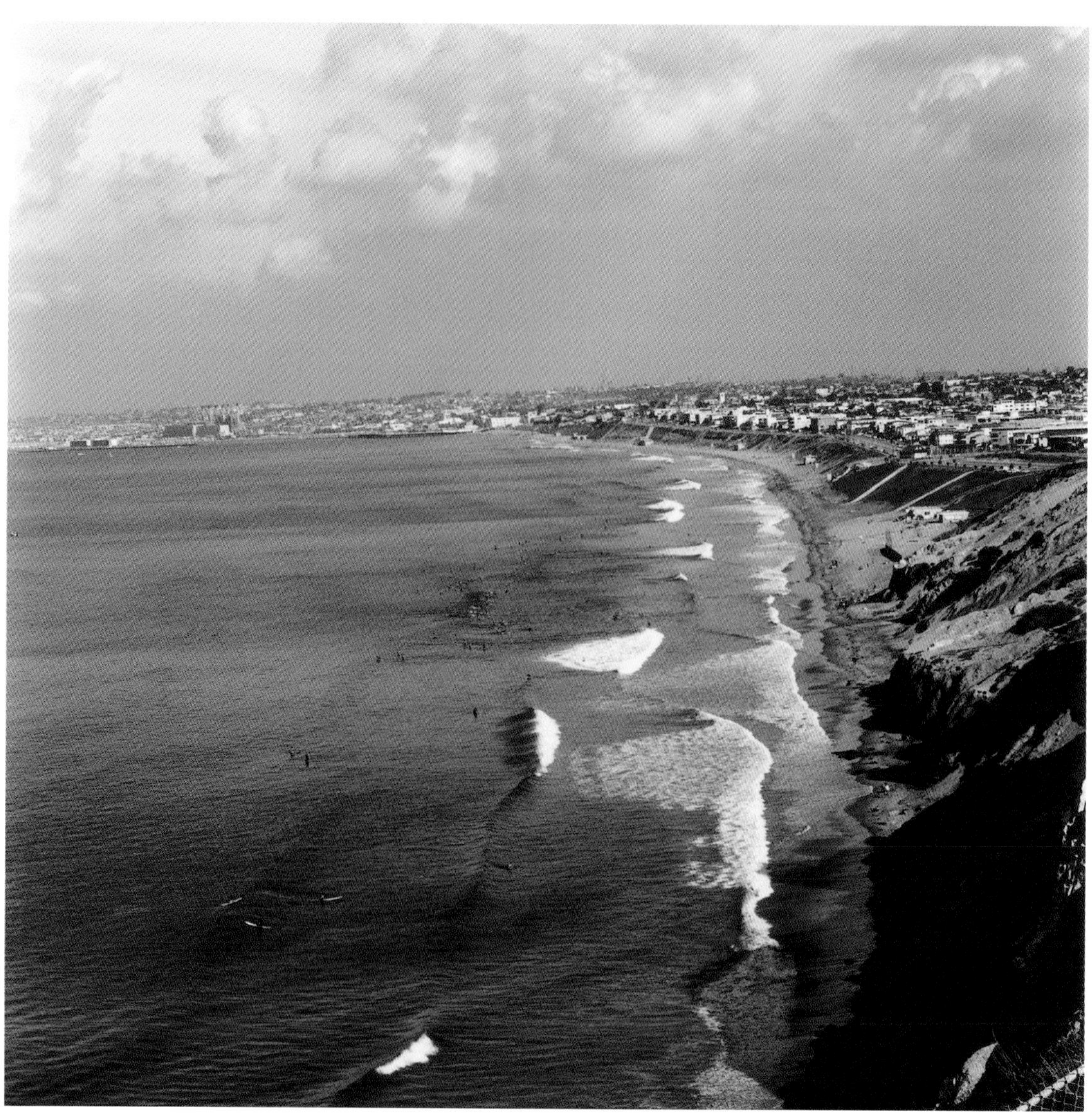

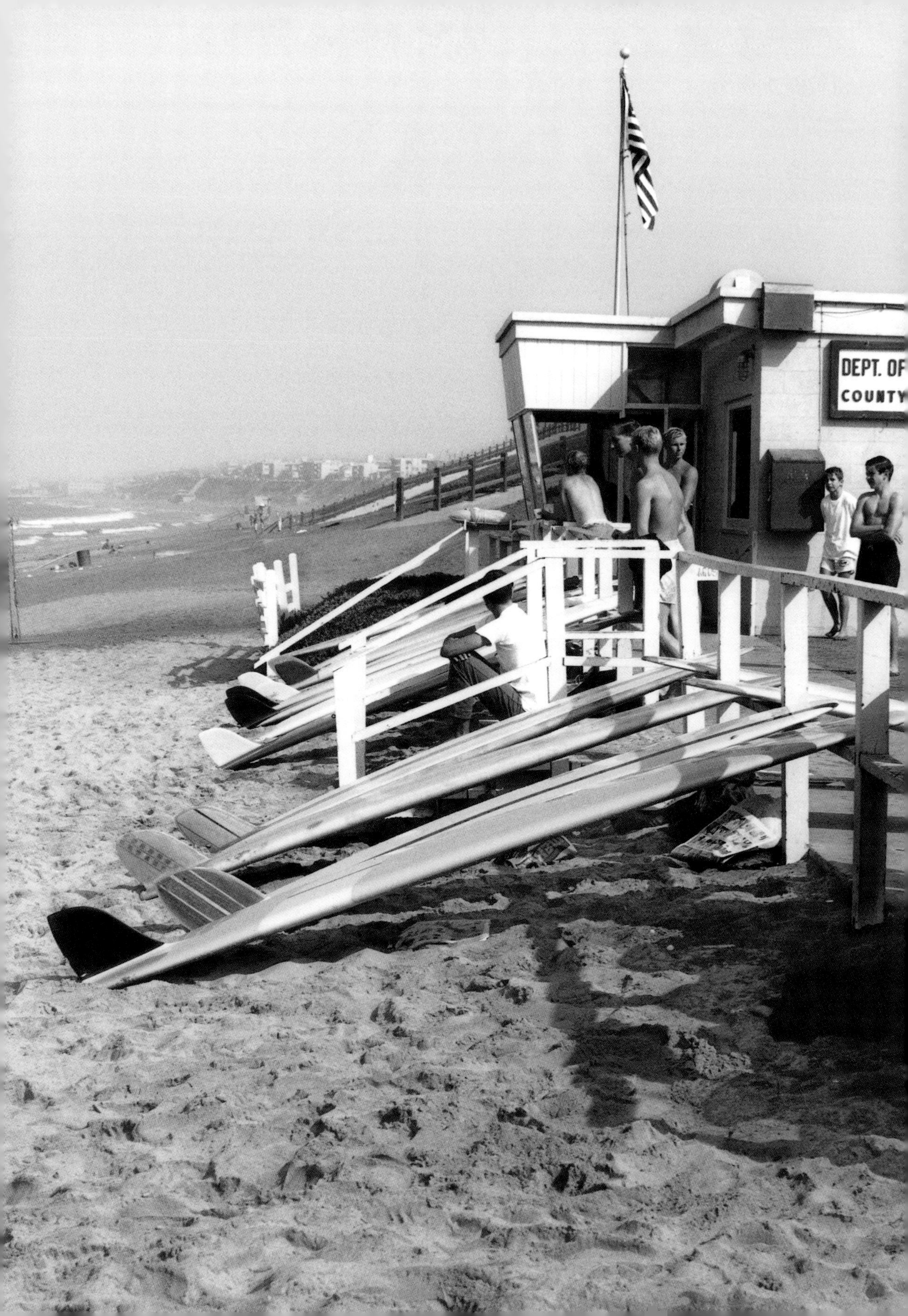

DEPT. OF
COUNTY

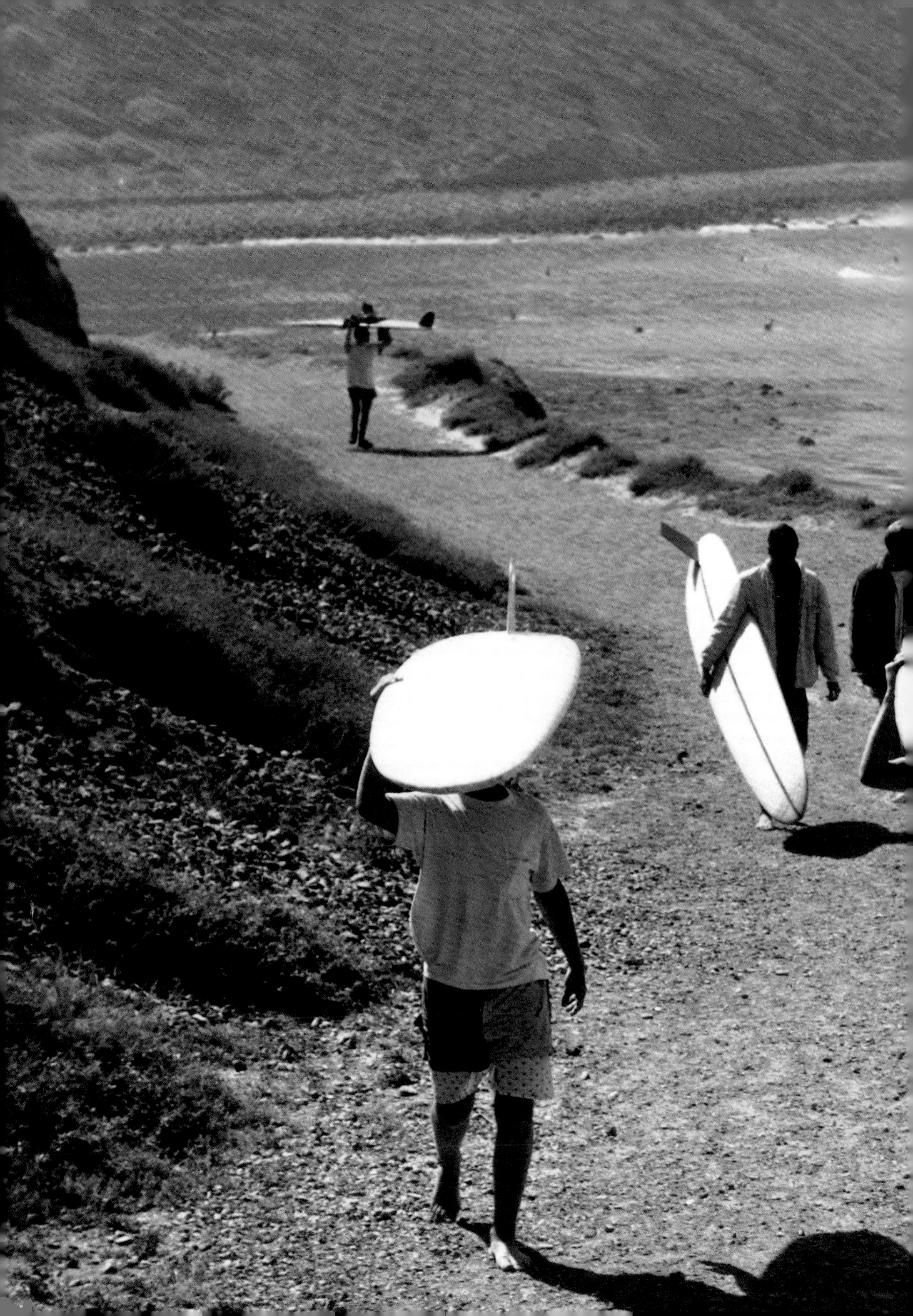

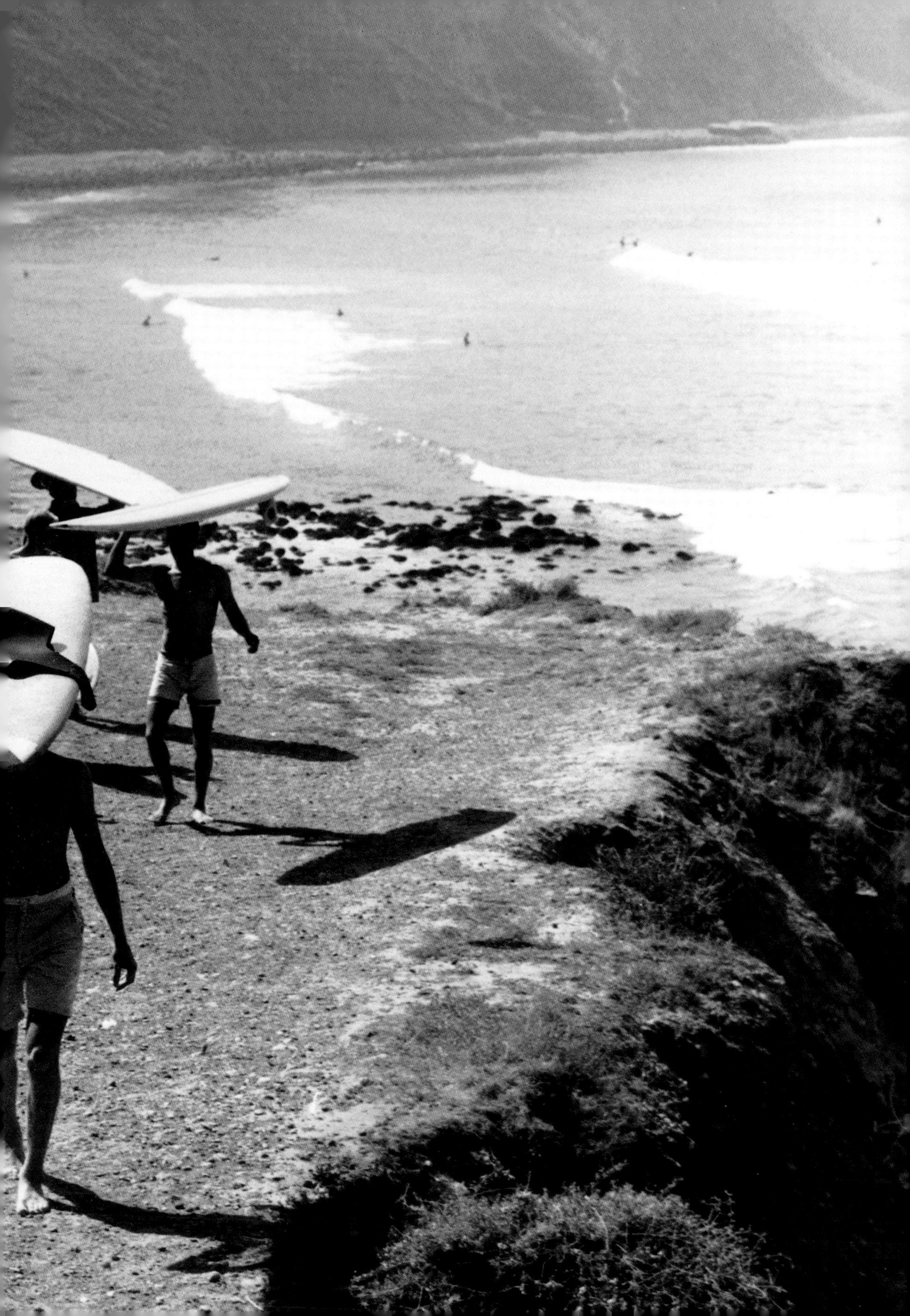

Pages 104–105
**Palos Verdes Cove, 1964**

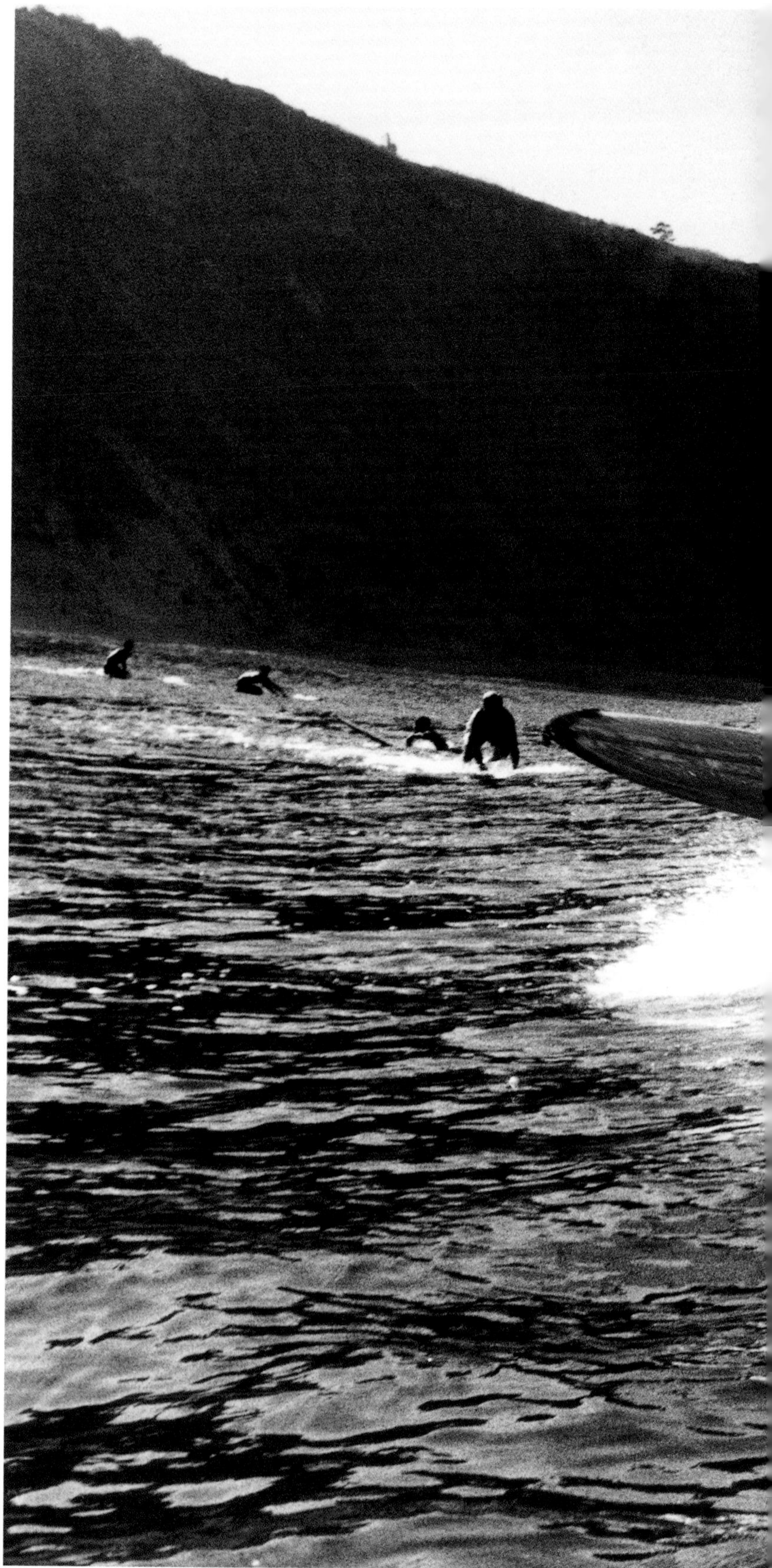

**Palos Verdes Cove, 1967**

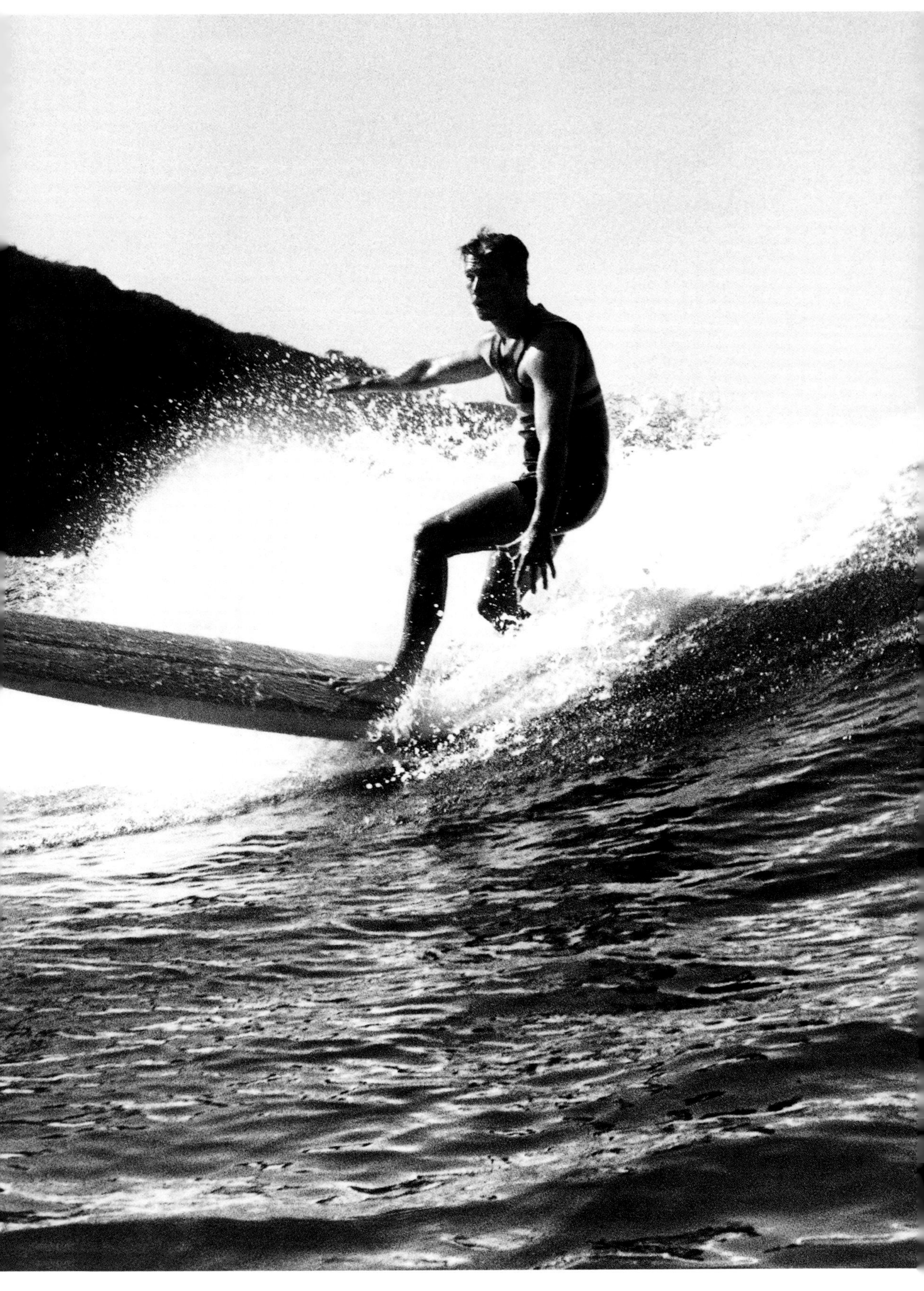

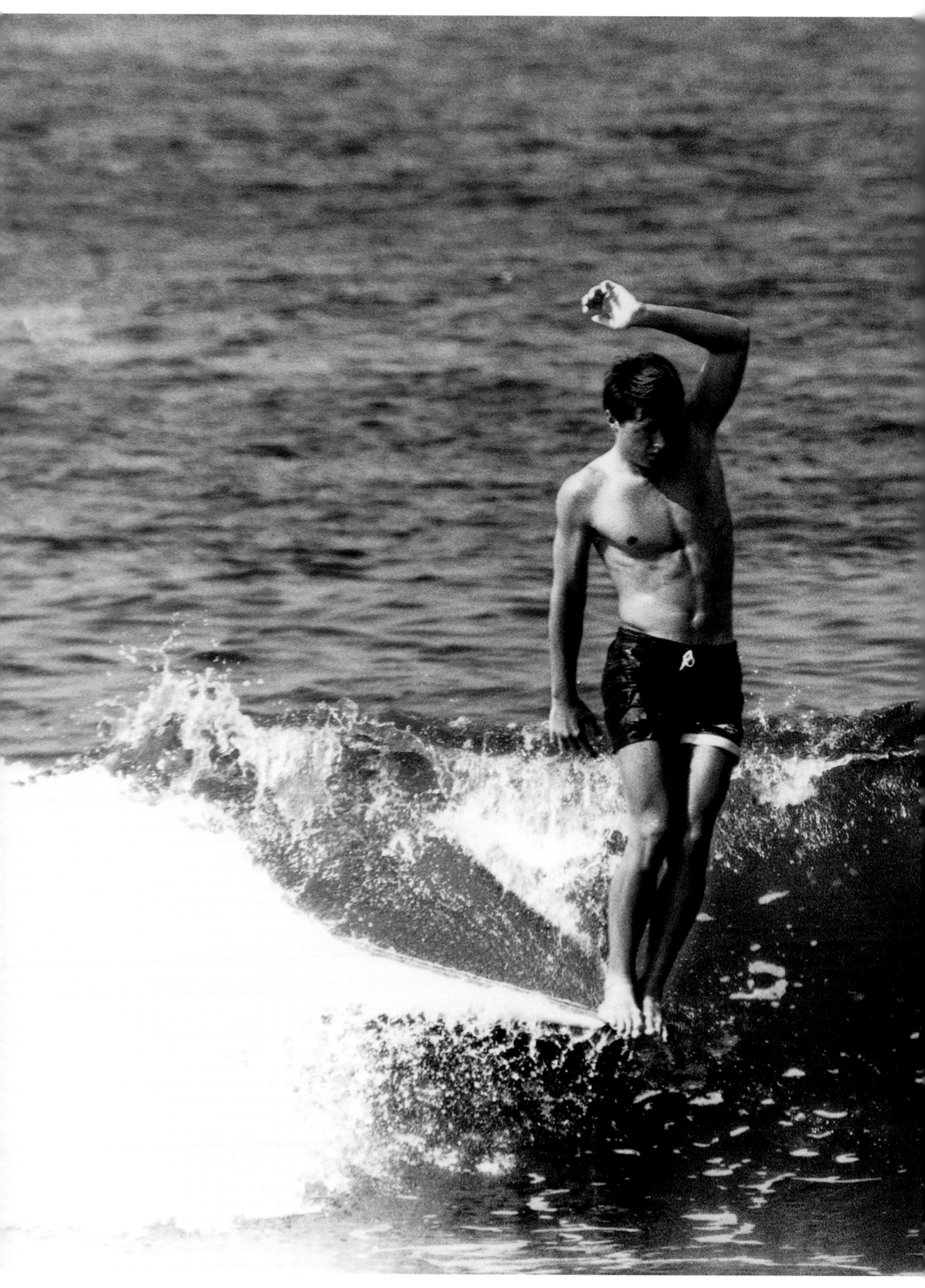

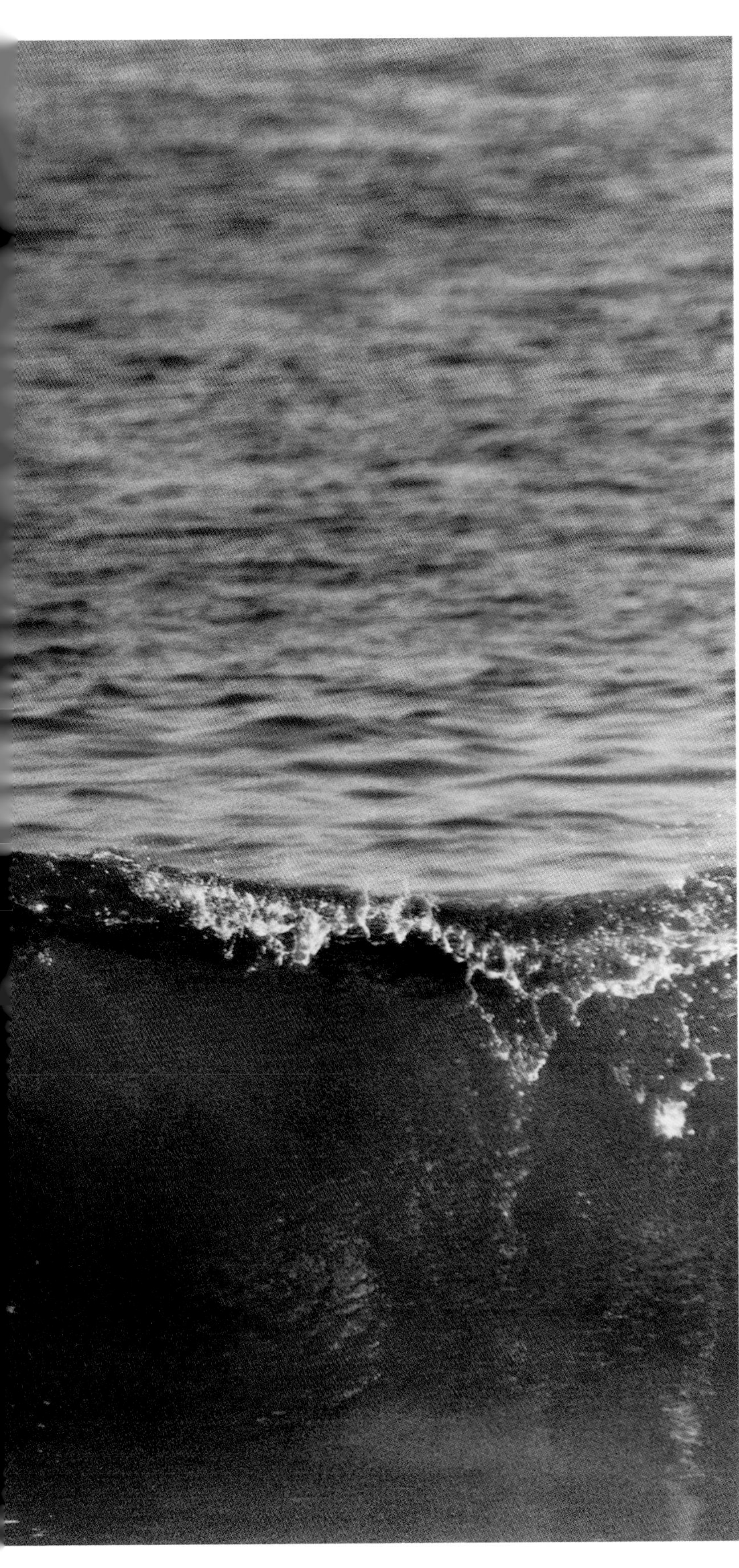

**Sparky Hudson, Hermosa Beach, 1965**

Perfectly balanced, Hudson explores the Zen of hang ten.

In perfektem Gleichgewicht erkundet Hudson das Zen des Hang Ten.

En parfait équilibre, Sparky Hudson explore les bienfaits du zen en exécutant un *hang ten*.

**Mike Hynson, Malibu, 1968**

Although Hynson was in the vanguard of the shortboard revolution, he retained an elegant style from a bygone era. Here he performs the classic "Quasimodo."

Obwohl Hynson die Shortboard-Revolution anführte, behielt er den eleganten Stil einer vergangenen Ära bei. Hier zeigt er den klassischen „Quasimodo".

Bien que Mike Hynson ait été à l'avant-garde de la révolution du shortboard, il a conservé de cette époque révolue un style élégant. On le voit ici en train d'exécuter une figure classique, un « Quasimodo ».

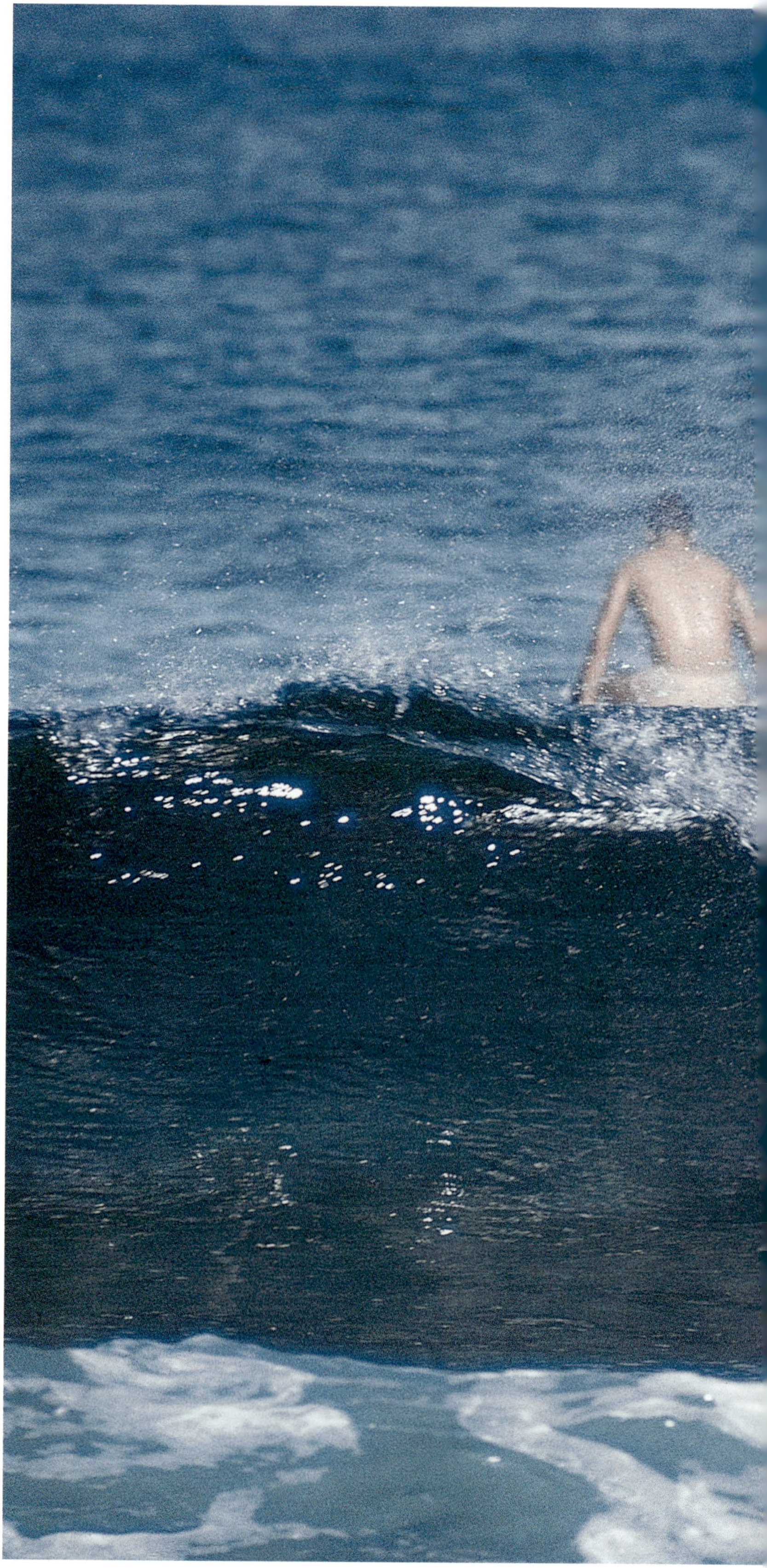

*Pages 112–113*
**Malibu, 1967**

Malibu on the verge of the shortboard revolution. Within a year, these big, beautiful boards would be dinosaurs headed for near-extinction.

Malibu unmittelbar vor der Shortboard-Revolution. Innerhalb eines Jahres wurden aus diesen großen, schönen Brettern vom Aussterben bedrohte Dinosaurier.

Malibu à l'orée de la révolution du shortboard. En l'espace d'une année, ces magnifiques planches effilées seront vouées à une quasi-disparition.

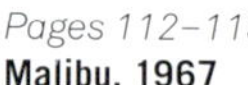

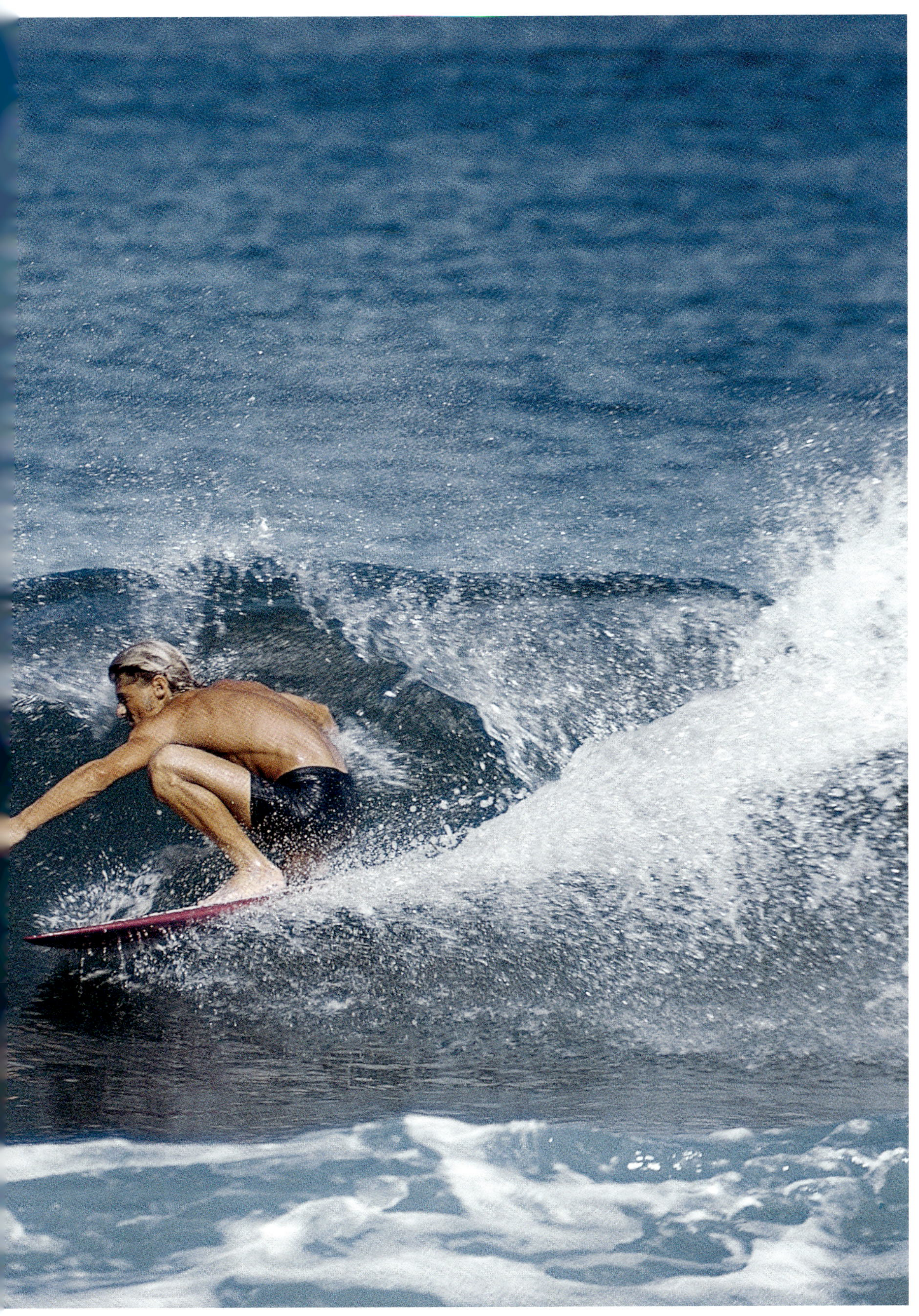

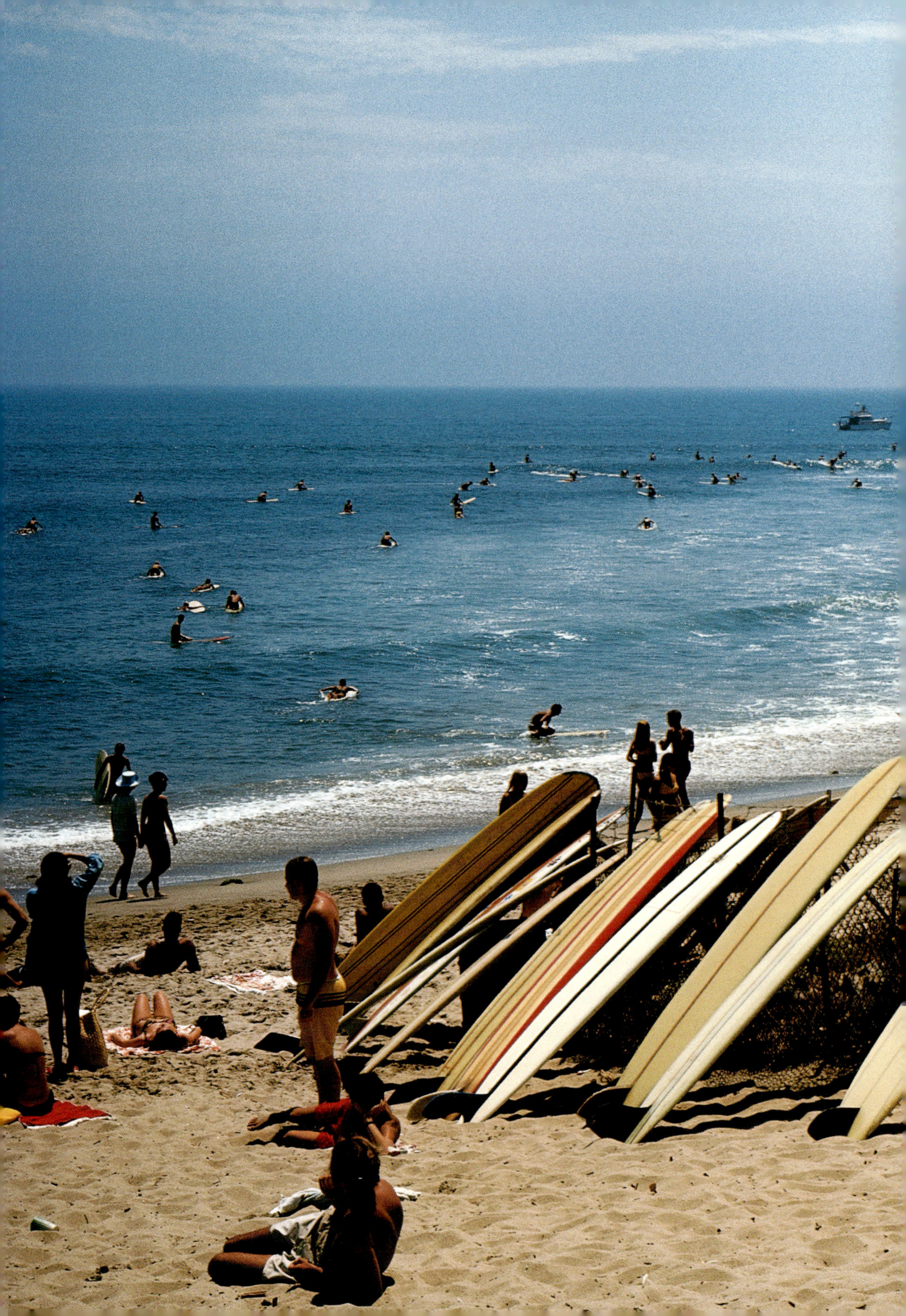

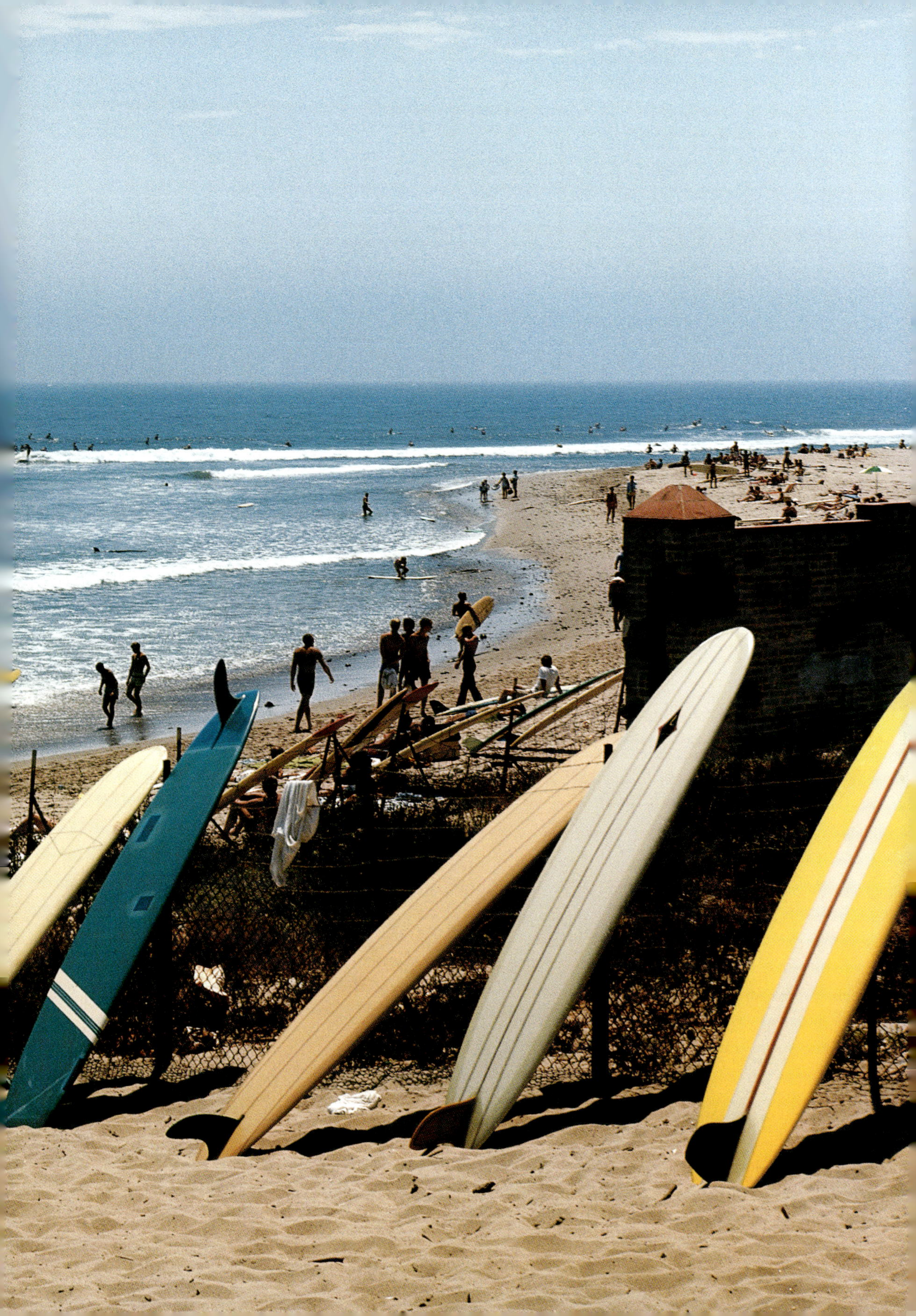

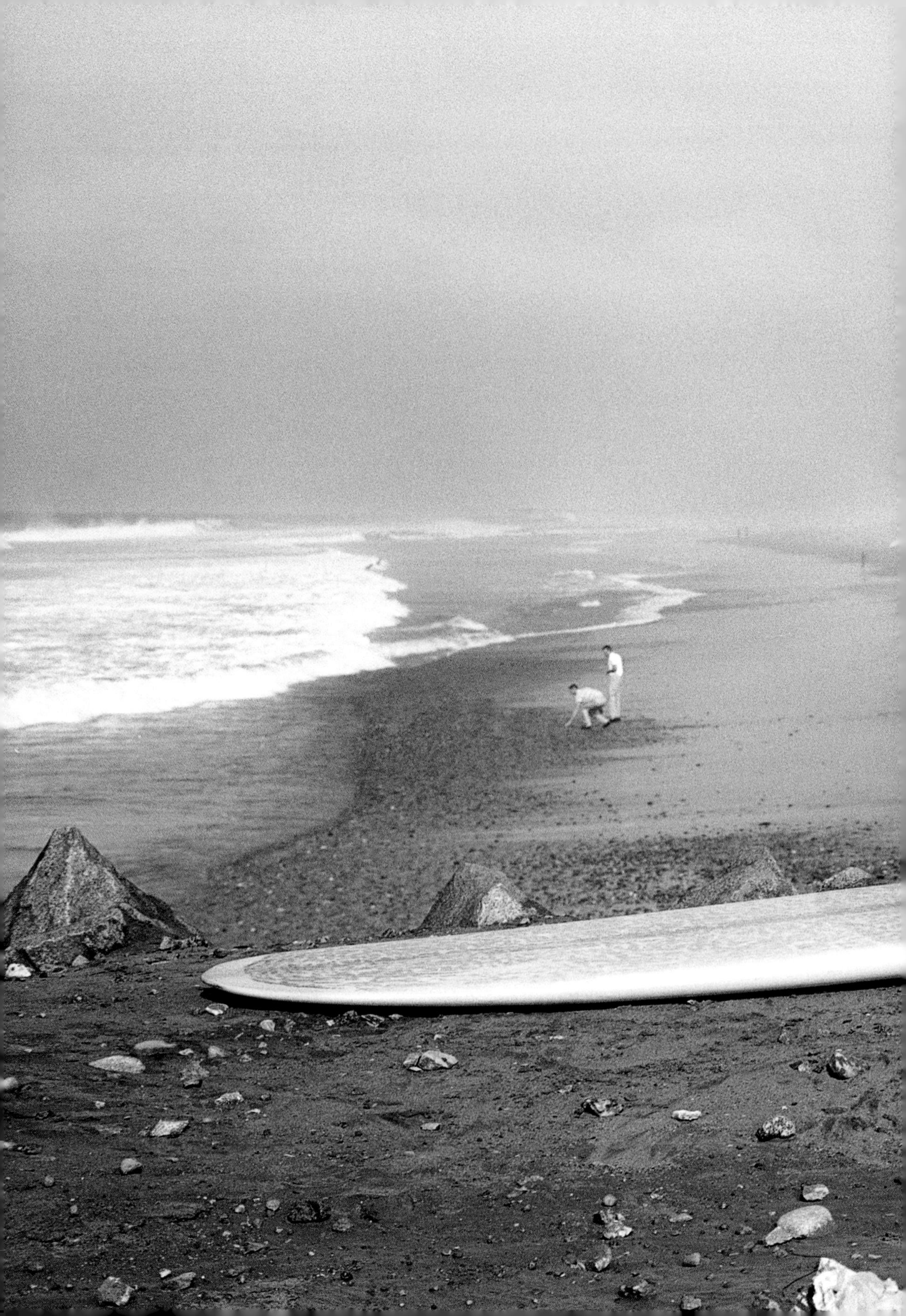

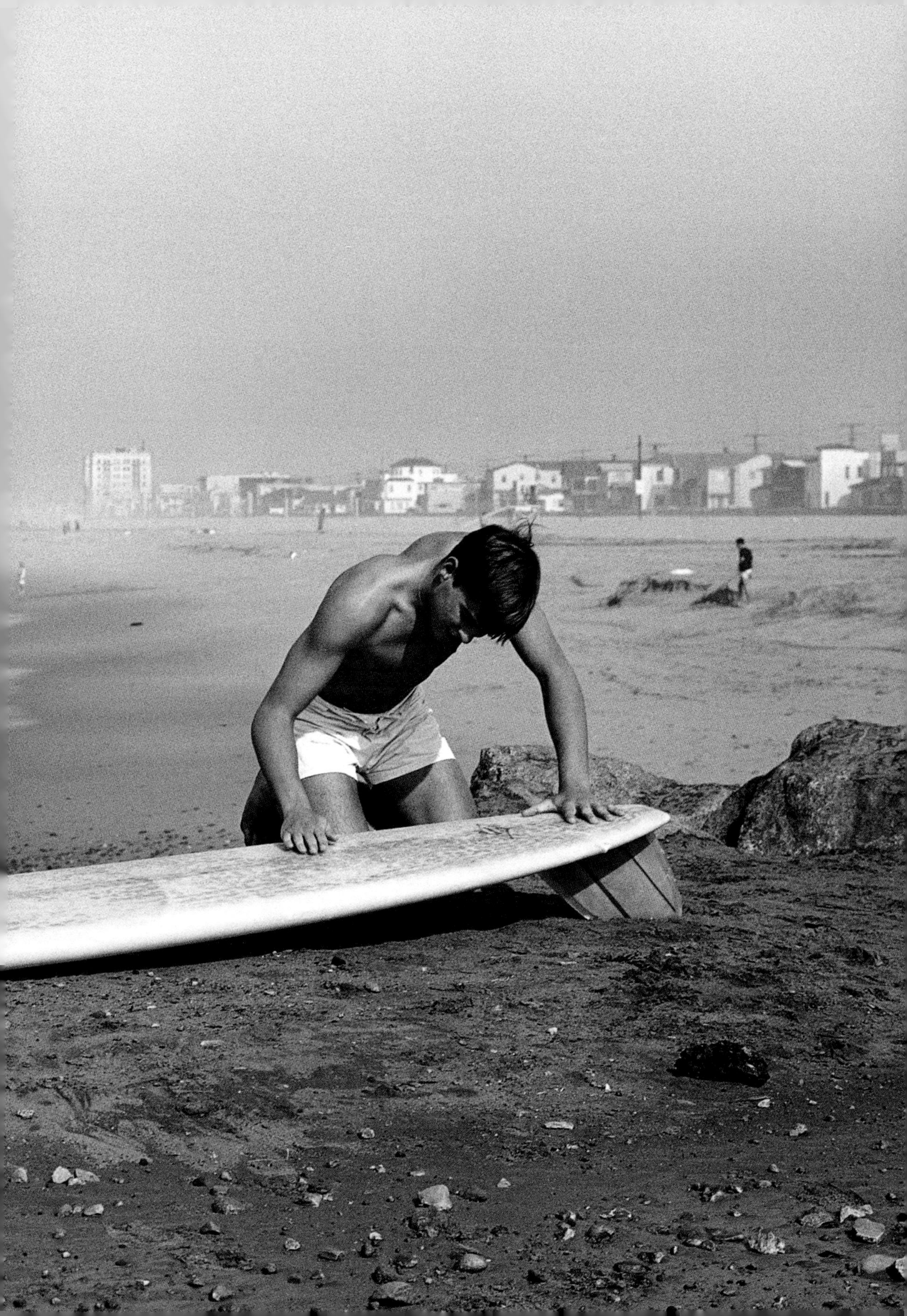

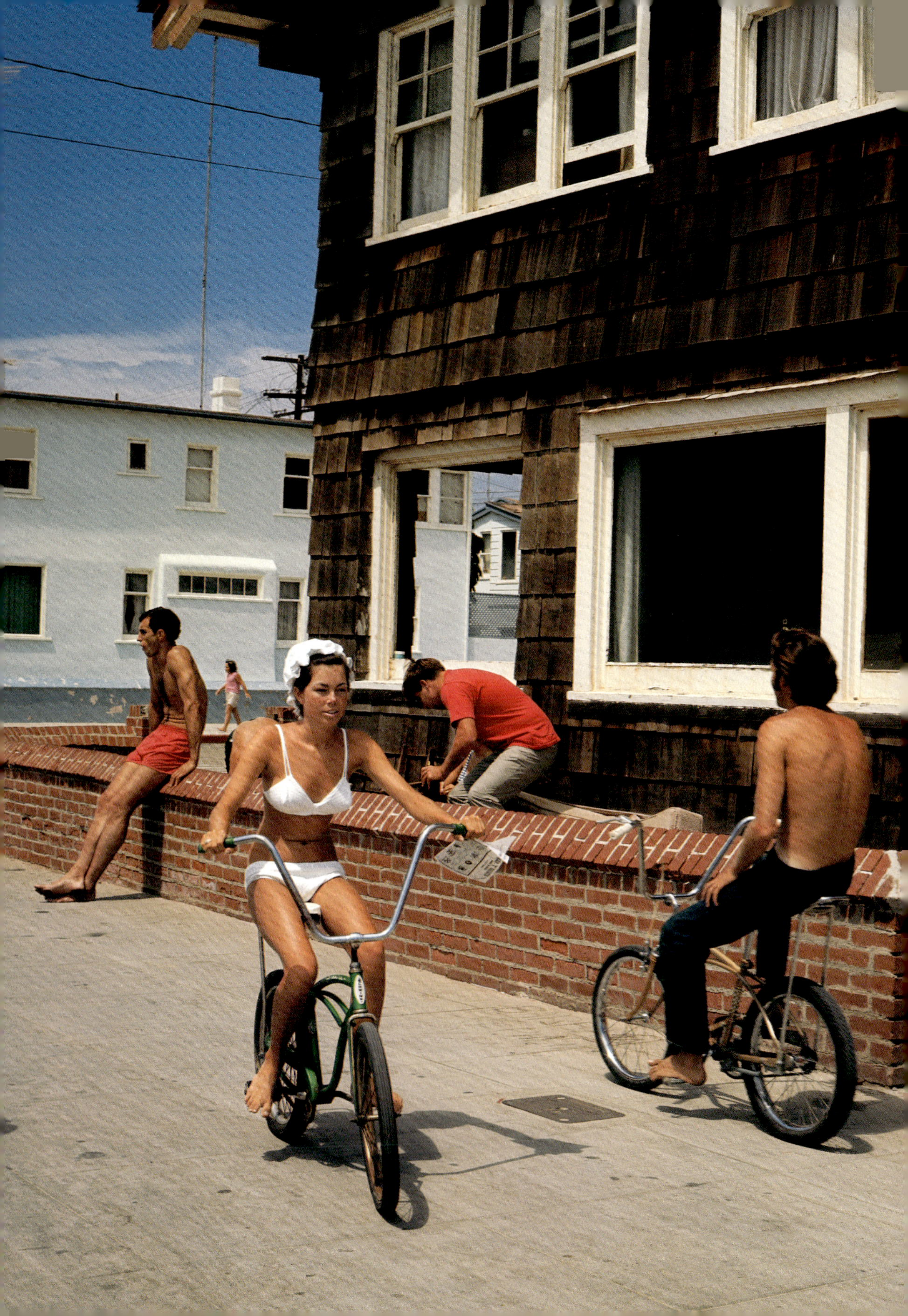

**Hermosa Beach Strand, 1967**

Then, as now, Hermosa was one long summer vacation for the young and tanned. Check out the classic stingray bicycles with butterfly handlebars.

Damals wie heute bedeutete Hermosa einen langen Sommer-urlaub für die braun gebrannte Jugend. Die Stingray-Fahrräder mit Bananensattel und Gabellenker waren ein Teil davon.

Tout comme aujourd'hui, Hermosa était à l'époque un lieu de rendez-vous estival de la jeunesse bronzée. On remarquera les bicyclettes Stingray à guidon « papillon ».

**Greg Noll Factory, Hermosa Beach, 1965**

A pair of Australian surfers drove this classic Westfalia Transporter throughout Europe before shipping it over to pay homage to surf mecca.

Ein paar australische Surfer fuhren mit diesem klassischen VW-Bus quer durch Europa, bevor sie ihn einschifften, um dem Mekka des Surfens zu huldigen.

Un couple de surfeurs australien a parcouru toute l'Europe au volant de ce combi Westfalia avant de l'expédier outre-Atlantique pour rendre hommage à la Mecque du surf.

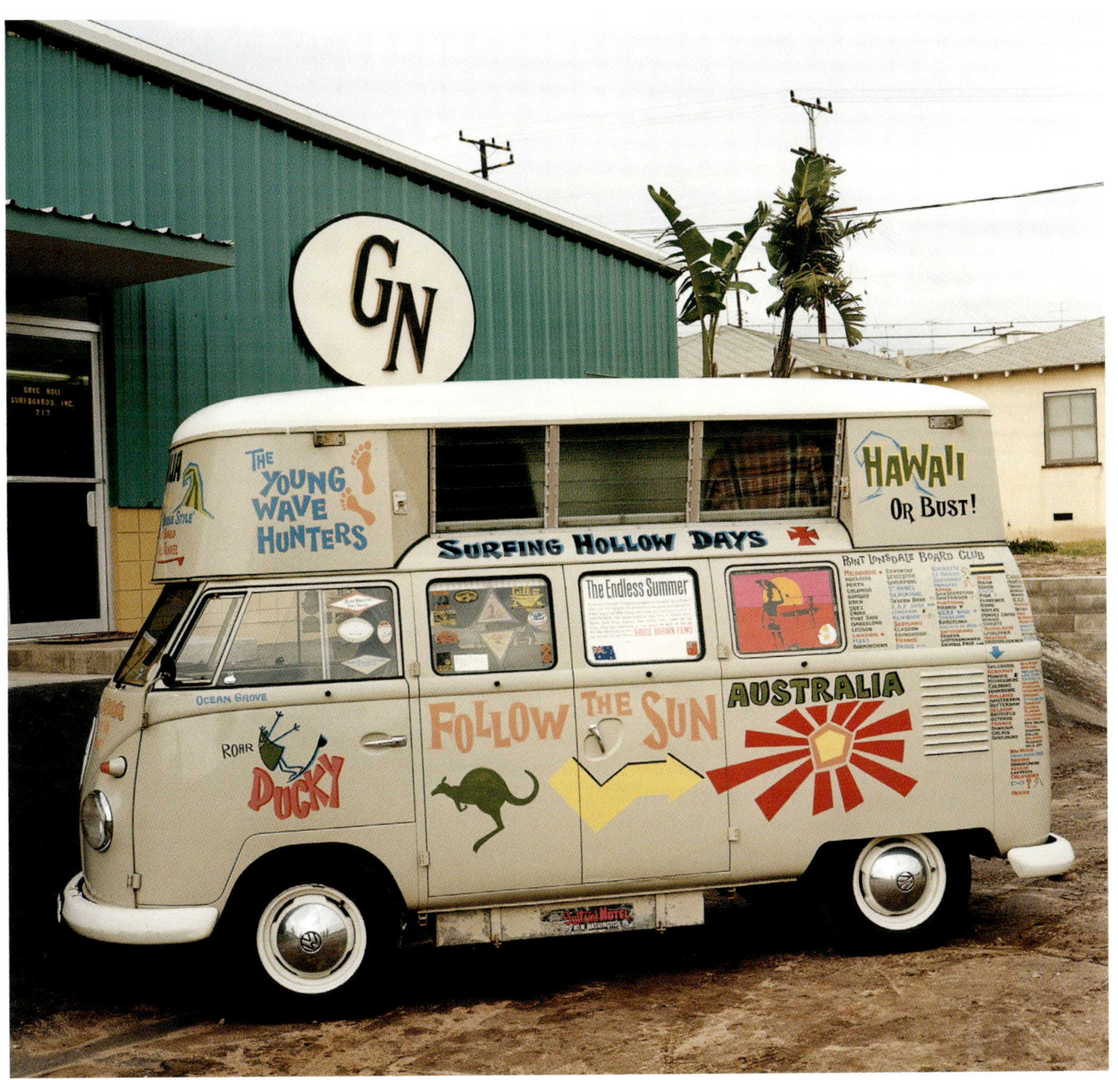

**Bing Surfboards, Hermosa Beach,
1968**

In the early sixties, a short stretch
of Pacific Coast Highway was
home to the elite of early surfboard
makers.

In den frühen Sechzigern war ein
kurzer Abschnitt des Pacific Coast
Highway von der Elite der frühen
Surfbretthersteller besiedelt.

Au début des années 1960, l'élite
des fabricants de planches de surf
avait élu domicile le long d'une
petite portion de la Pacific Coast
Highway.

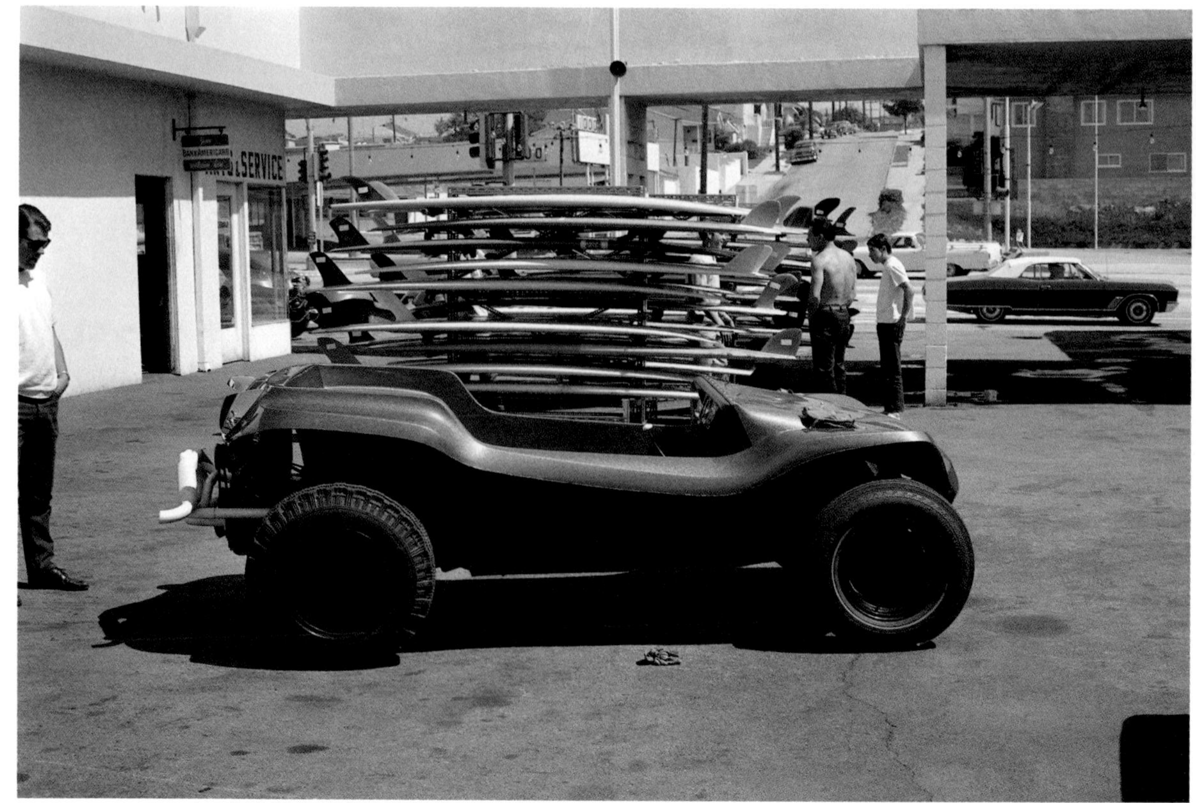

**Hermosa Beach, 1964**

On any weekend, the streets around 22nd Street would be filled with board-stuffed cars. Surfers loved station wagons because they could sleep in them.

Jedes Wochenende waren die Straßen rund um die 22nd Street mit Autos voller Surfbretter zugeparkt. Die Surfer mochten Kombis, weil sie in ihnen schlafen konnten.

Chaque week-end, les rues adjacentes à 22nd Street étaient envahies de véhicules bondés de planches de surf. Les surfeurs avaient un faible pour les breaks du type Station Wagon car ils pouvaient dormir dedans.

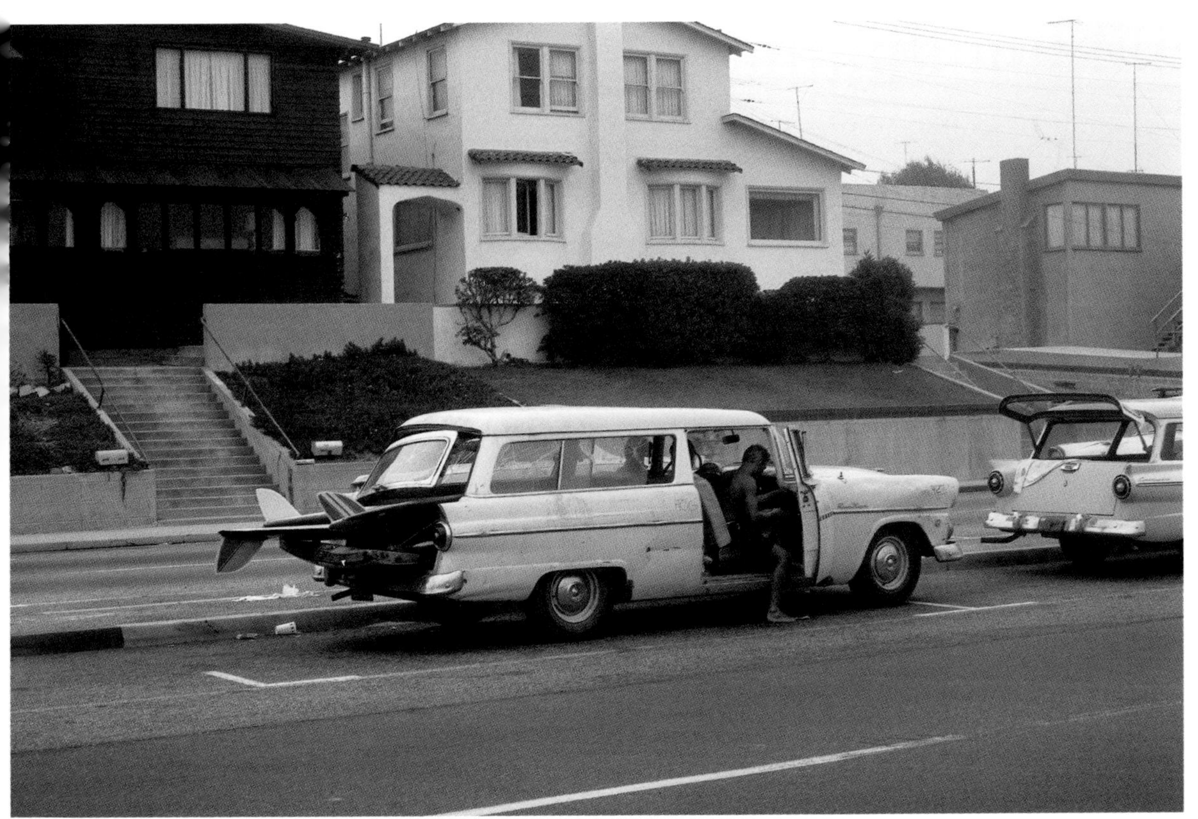

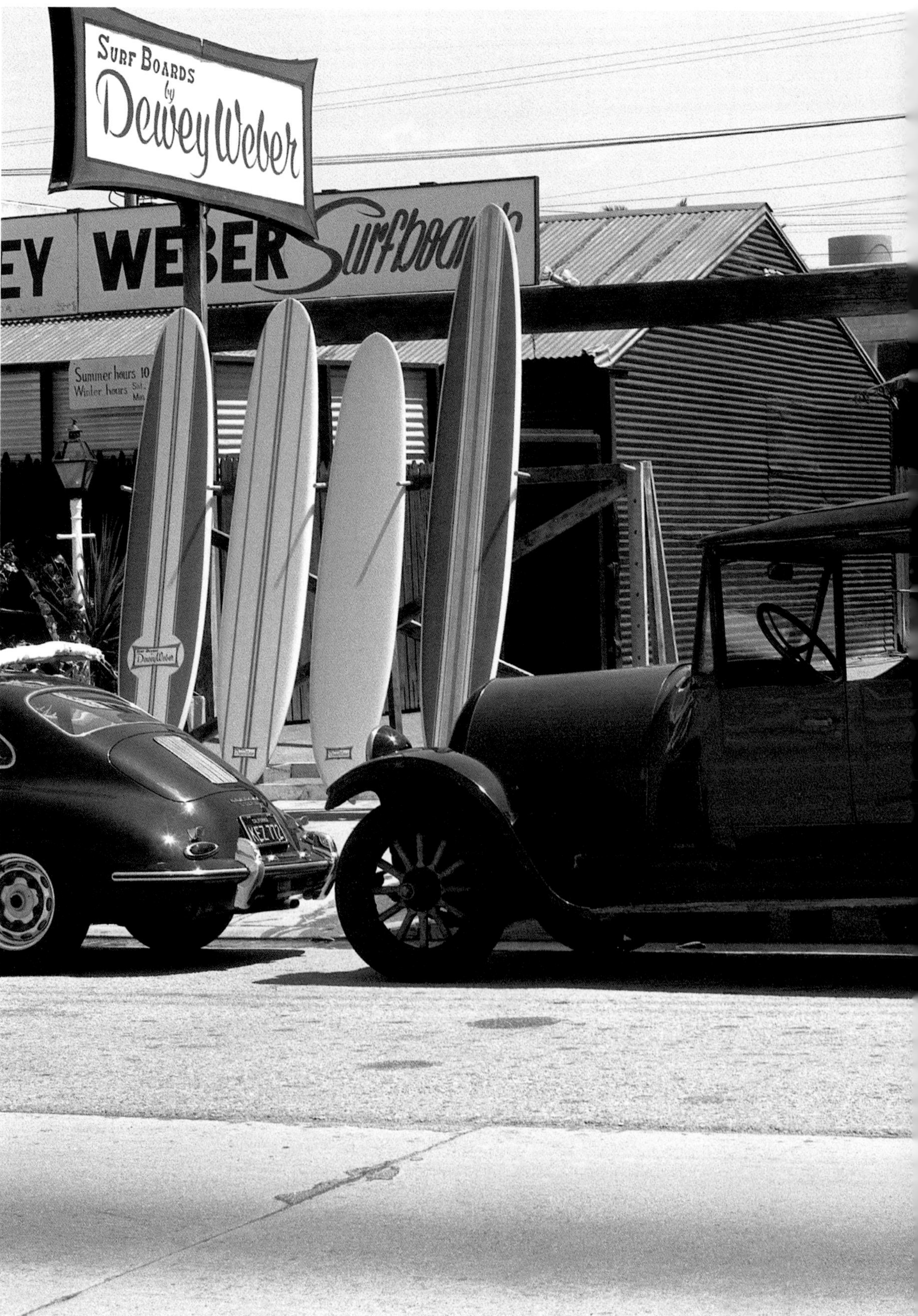

Surf Boards
by
Dewey Weber
EY WEBER Surfboards
Summer hours 10
Winter hours Sat.
Mon
Dewey Weber

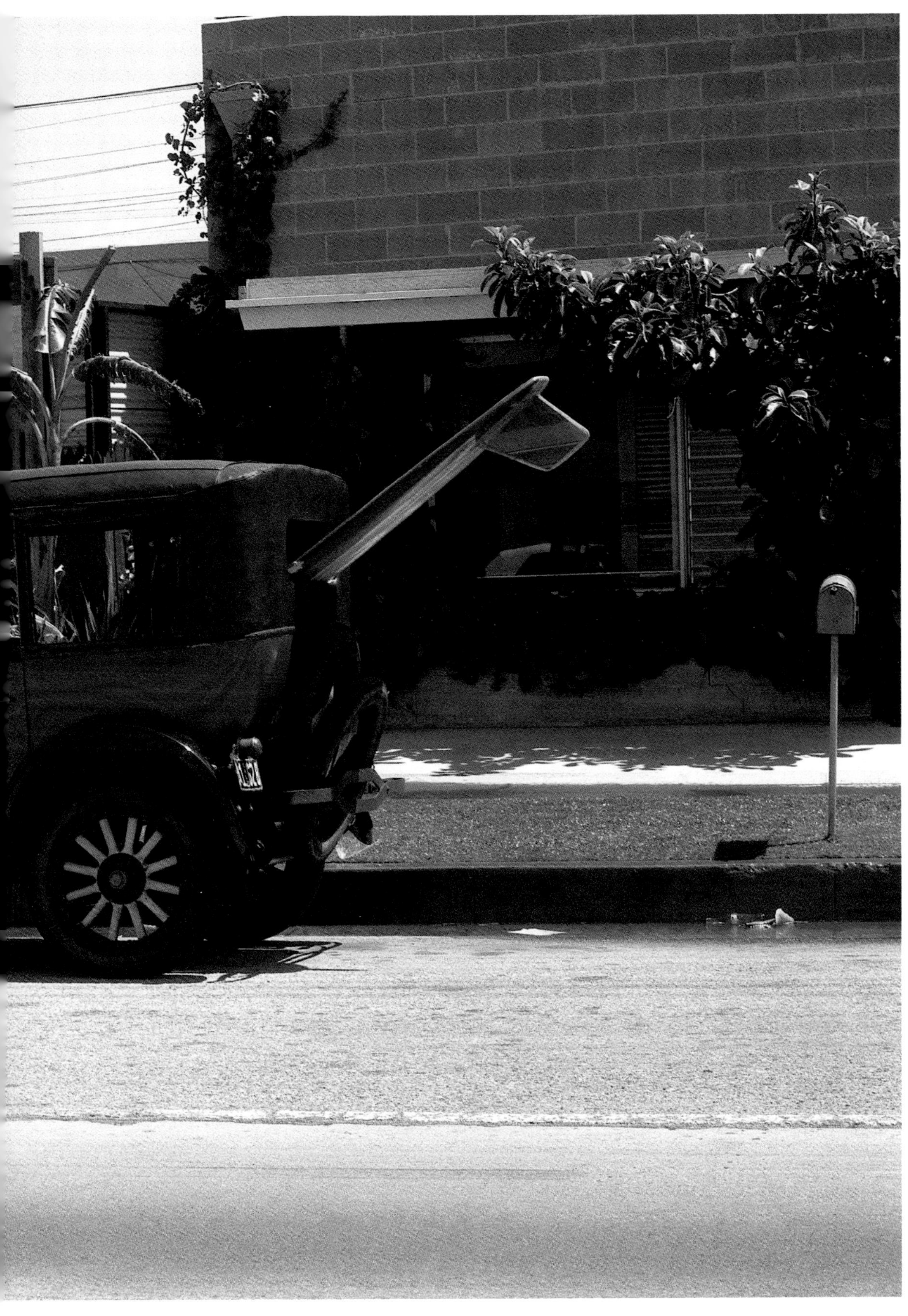

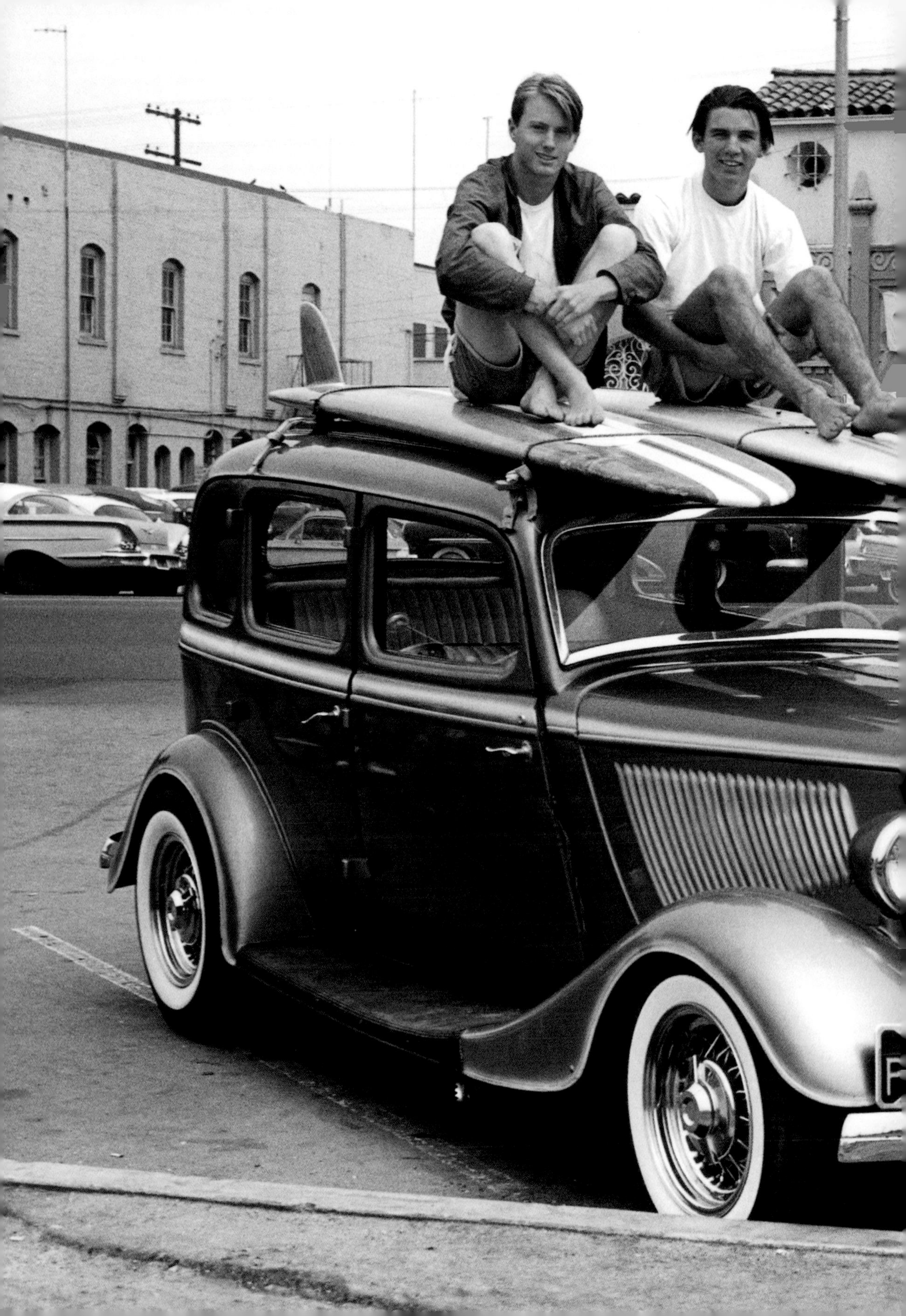

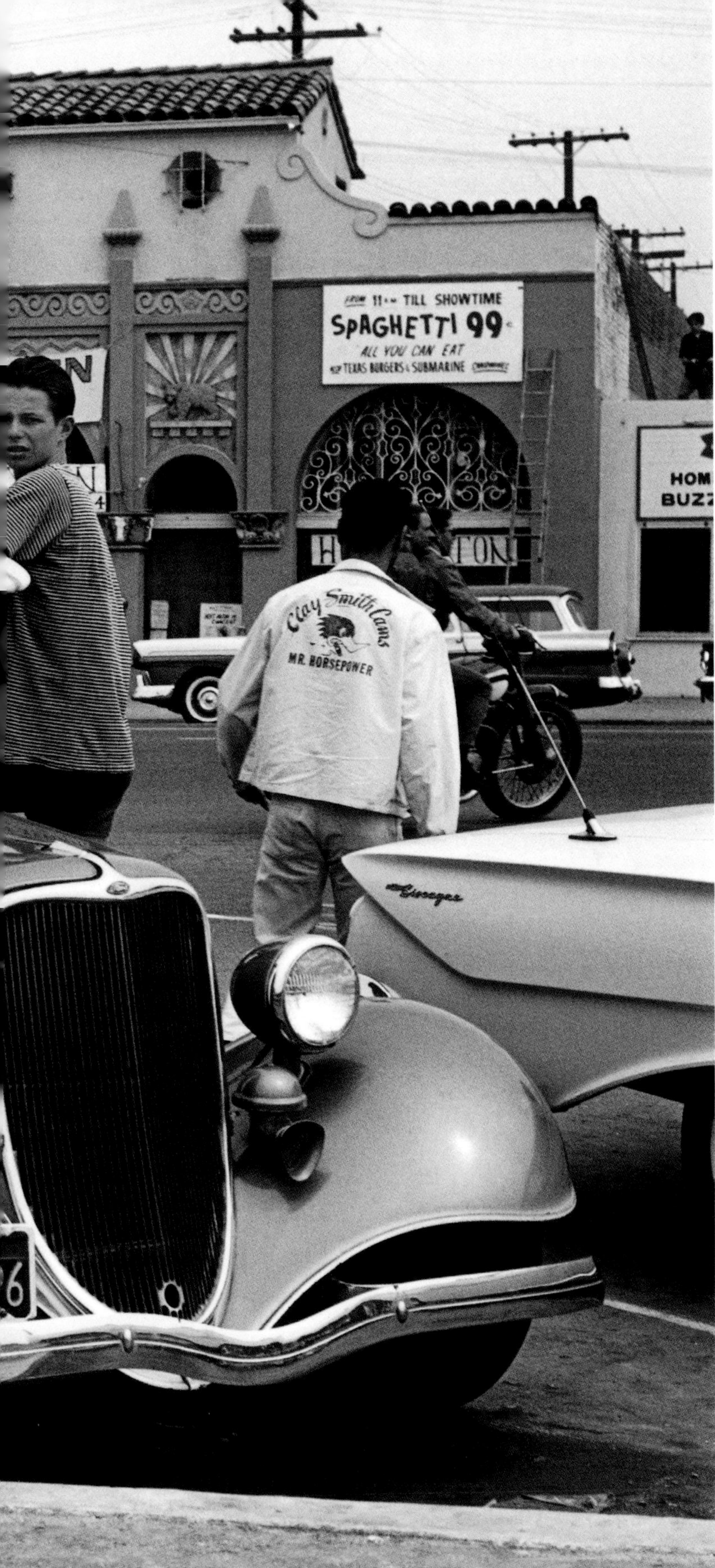





**Dewey Weber Shop, Venice, 1963**

One-of-a-kind surf wagon.

Ein einzigartiges Surfmobil.

Surf-mobile unique en son genre.

**Huntington Beach, 1964**

Gremmies checking out the 1964 U.S. Championships from a fully restored 1933 Ford Deluxe (the same model driven by outlaw John Dillinger).

„Gremmies" schauen sich die 1964er-U.S.-Championships vom Dach eines liebevoll restaurierten 1933er-Ford-Deluxe an (das gleiche Modell, das der Gangster John Dillinger fuhr).

Ados perchés sur le toit d'une Ford Deluxe de 1933 magnifiquement restaurée (le modèle conduit par le gangster John Dillinger) en train de suivre les épreuves du championnat américain de 1964.

**Redondo Beach, 1963**

Depression-era delivery truck
turned sixties surf habitat. Many
of these old cars were bought
in the fifties for under $100.

Ein Lieferwagen aus der Zeit der
großen Depression, umgewandelt
in eine Surfherberge der Sechziger.
Viele dieser alten Autos konnte
man in den Fünfzigern für weniger
als 100 Dollar kaufen.

Camionnette de livraison des
années de la Grande Dépression
transformée en camping-car
pour surfeurs dans les années
1960. De nombreux véhicules
comme celui-ci se vendaient
pour moins de 100 dollars dans
les années 1950.

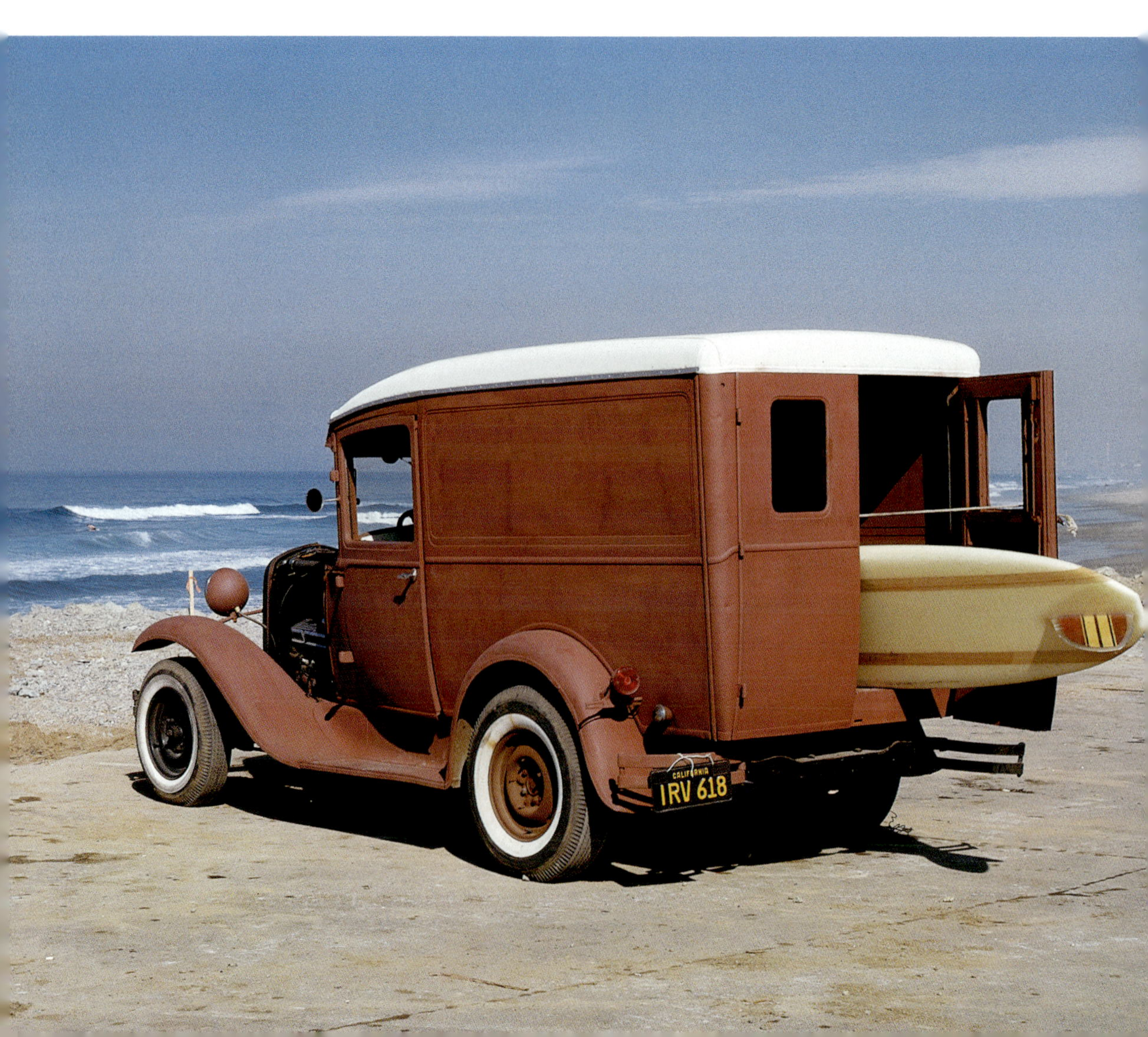

**Ford Woody, Redondo Beach, 1963**

One of Grannis's favorite subjects
was vintage "surf bombs." His surf
photos were eventually used on the
boxes of popular plastic model kits.

Zu Grannis' Lieblingsmotiven gehörten die alten Autos der Surfer.
Seine Fotos wurden später auch für
die Verpackungen von Modellbau-
autos verwendet.

LeRoy Grannis était passionné par
les « surf-mobiles » d'époque. Ses
photos de surf seront plus tard
reproduites sur les emballages de
modèles réduits.

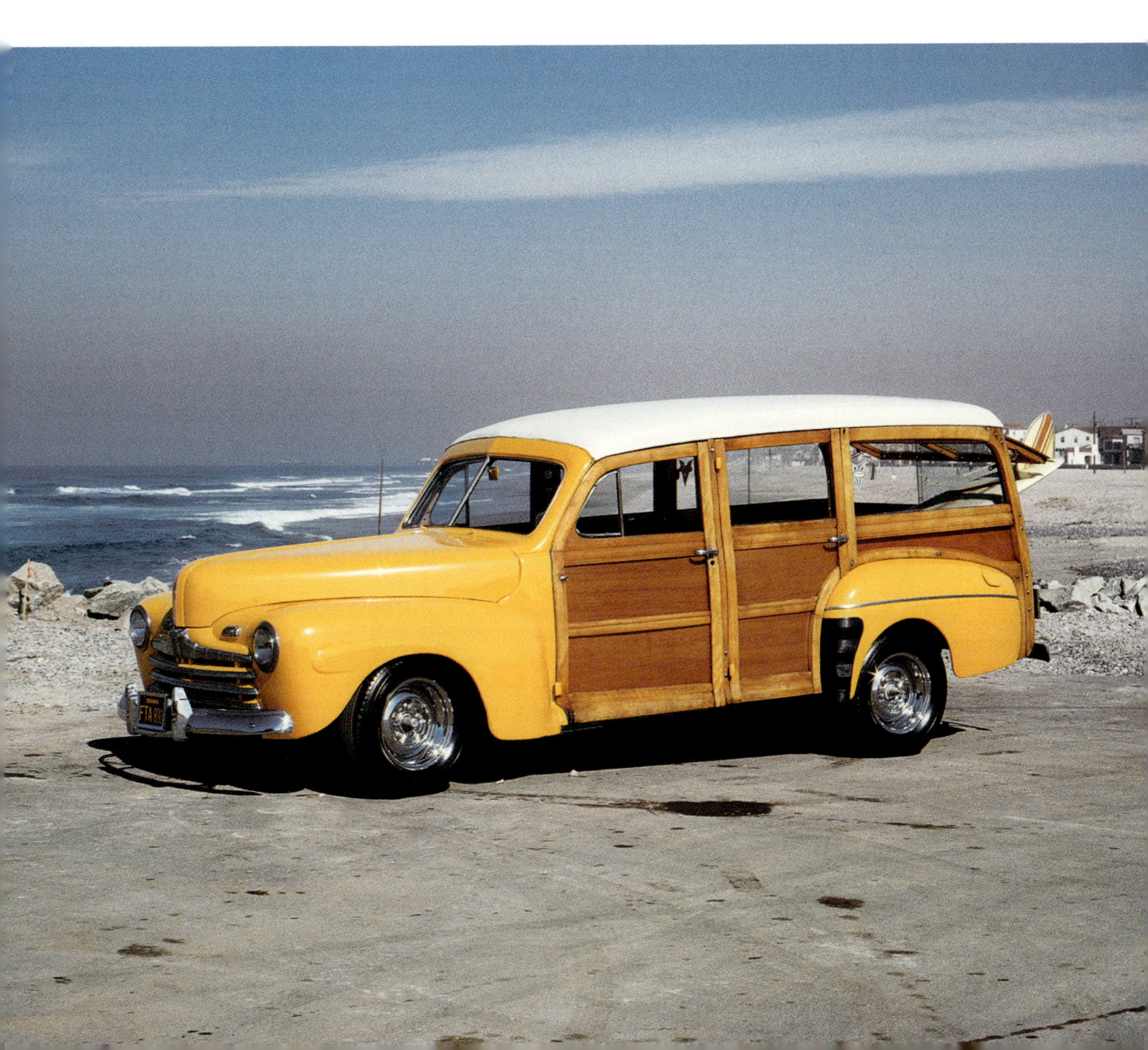

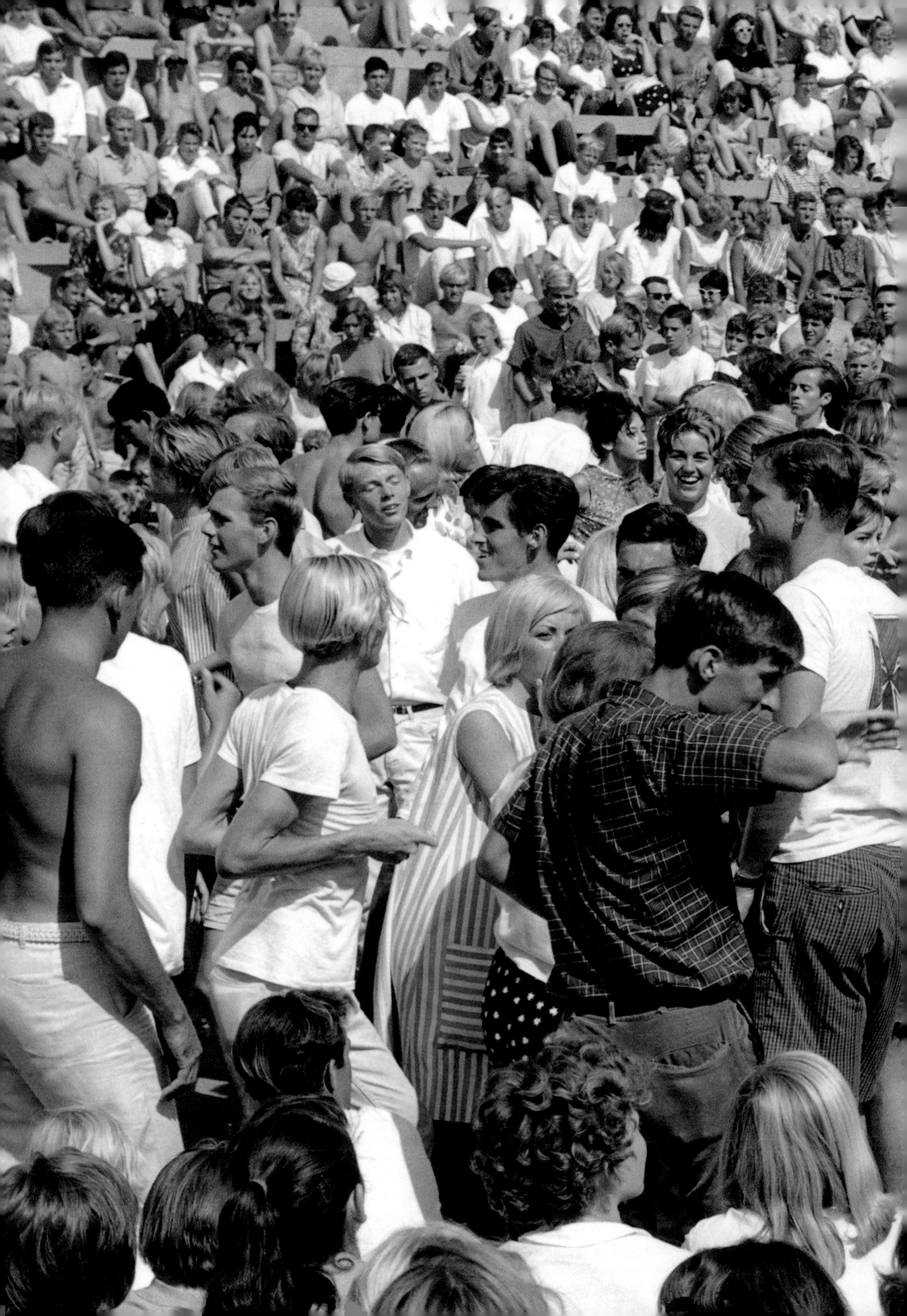

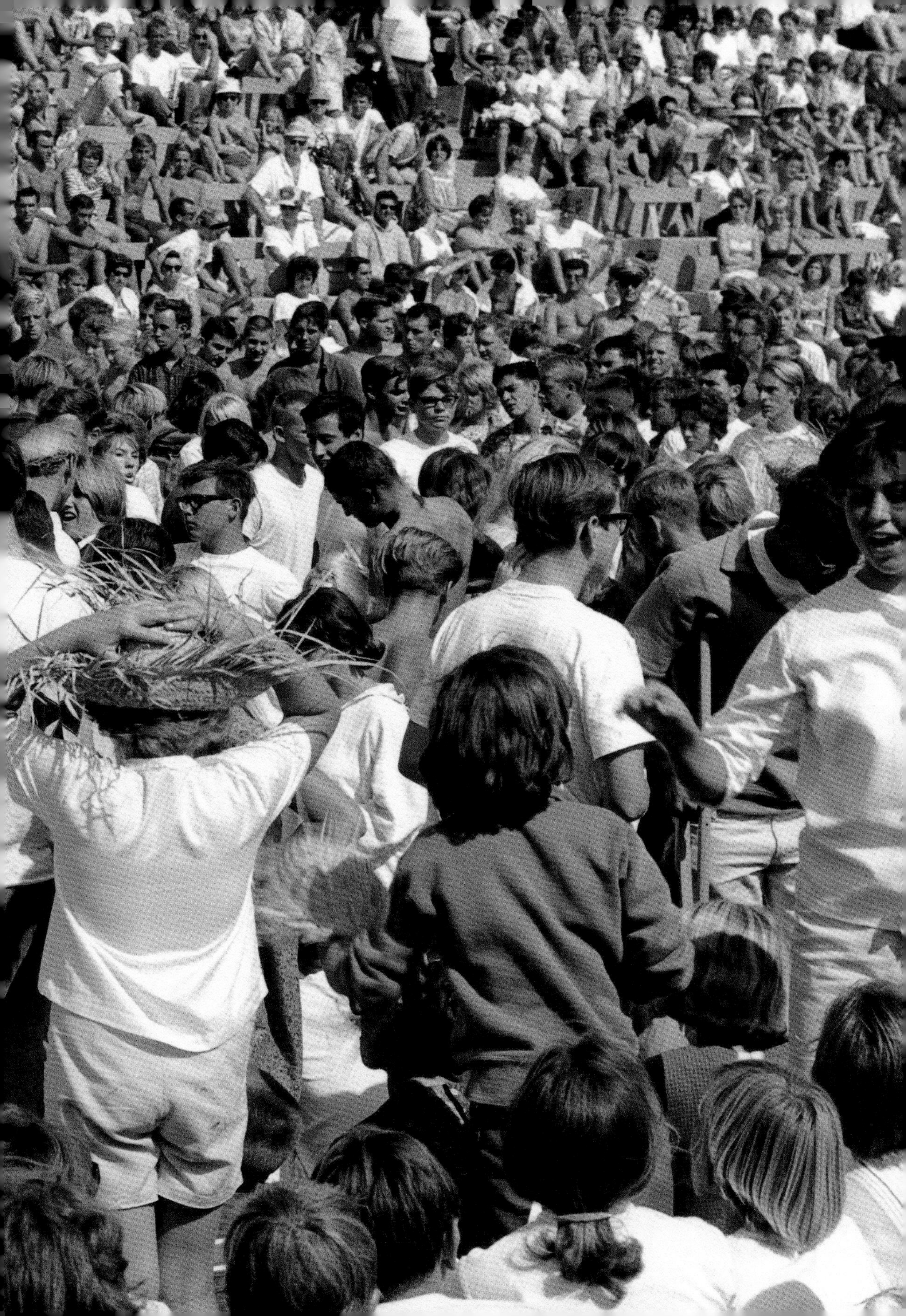

**Huntington Beach, 1962**

Just before the awards ceremony
for the West Coast Championships,
the crowd went wild dancing the
stomp to the surf sounds of The
Challengers.

Vor der Preisverleihung bei den
West Coast Championships hotteten
die Zuschauer zur Surfmusik der
Challengers ab.

Juste avant la remise des prix du
championnat de la côte Ouest, une
foule déchaînée danse le stomp
au rythme du « Surf Sound » des
Challengers.

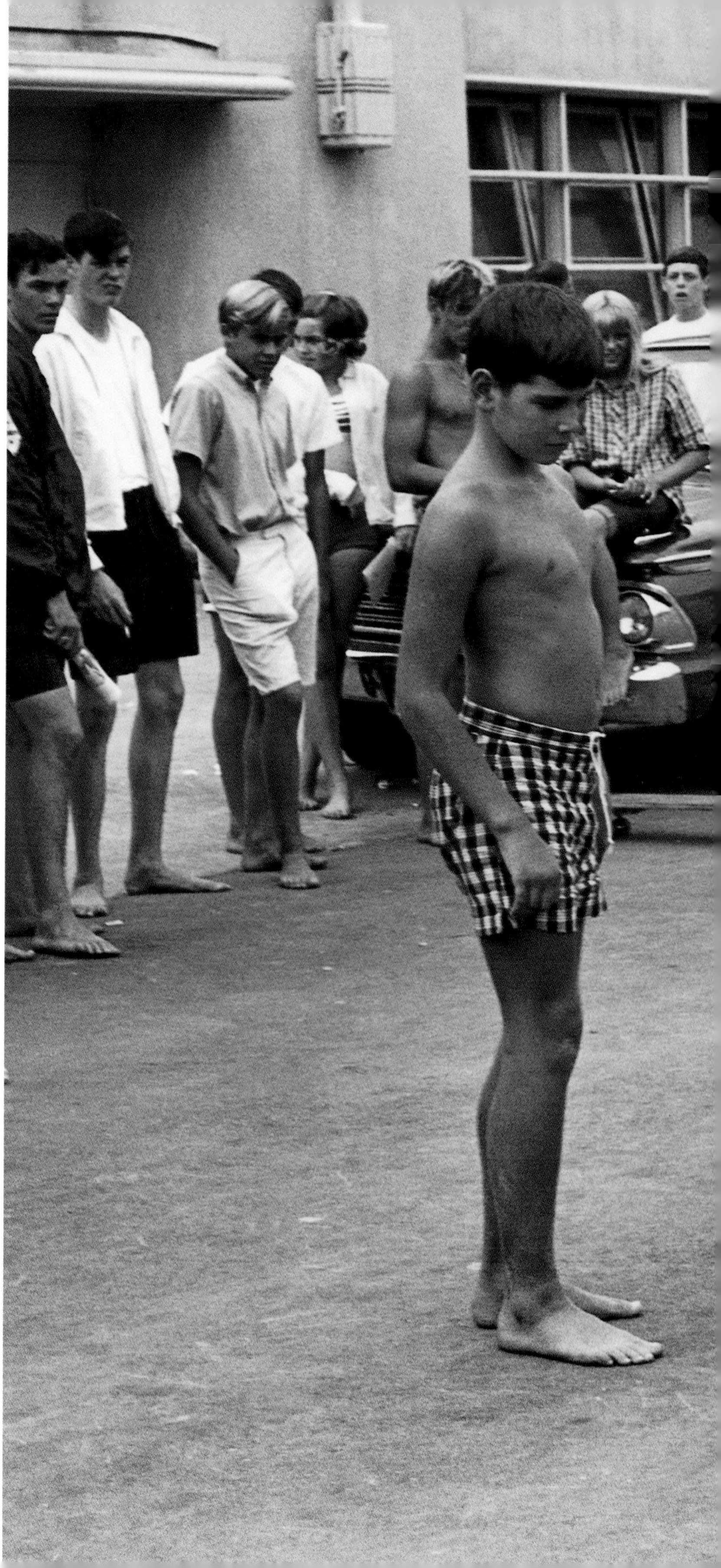

**Huntington Beach, 1964**

Skateboarding had its first big
boom in the early sixties. The
Jack's Surfboards skateboard
team put on exhibitions featuring
headstands and noserides.

Skateboarding erlebte seinen
ersten großen Boom Anfang der
Sechziger. Das Skateboardteam
von Jack's Surfboards führte
Kopfstände und Noserides vor.

Le skateboard a connu ses
premières heures de gloire au
début des années 1960. Lors
de ses exhibitions, l'équipe de
skaters de Jack's Surfboards
exécutait des figures telles que
le poirier et le *noseride*.

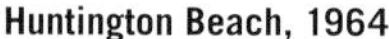

128

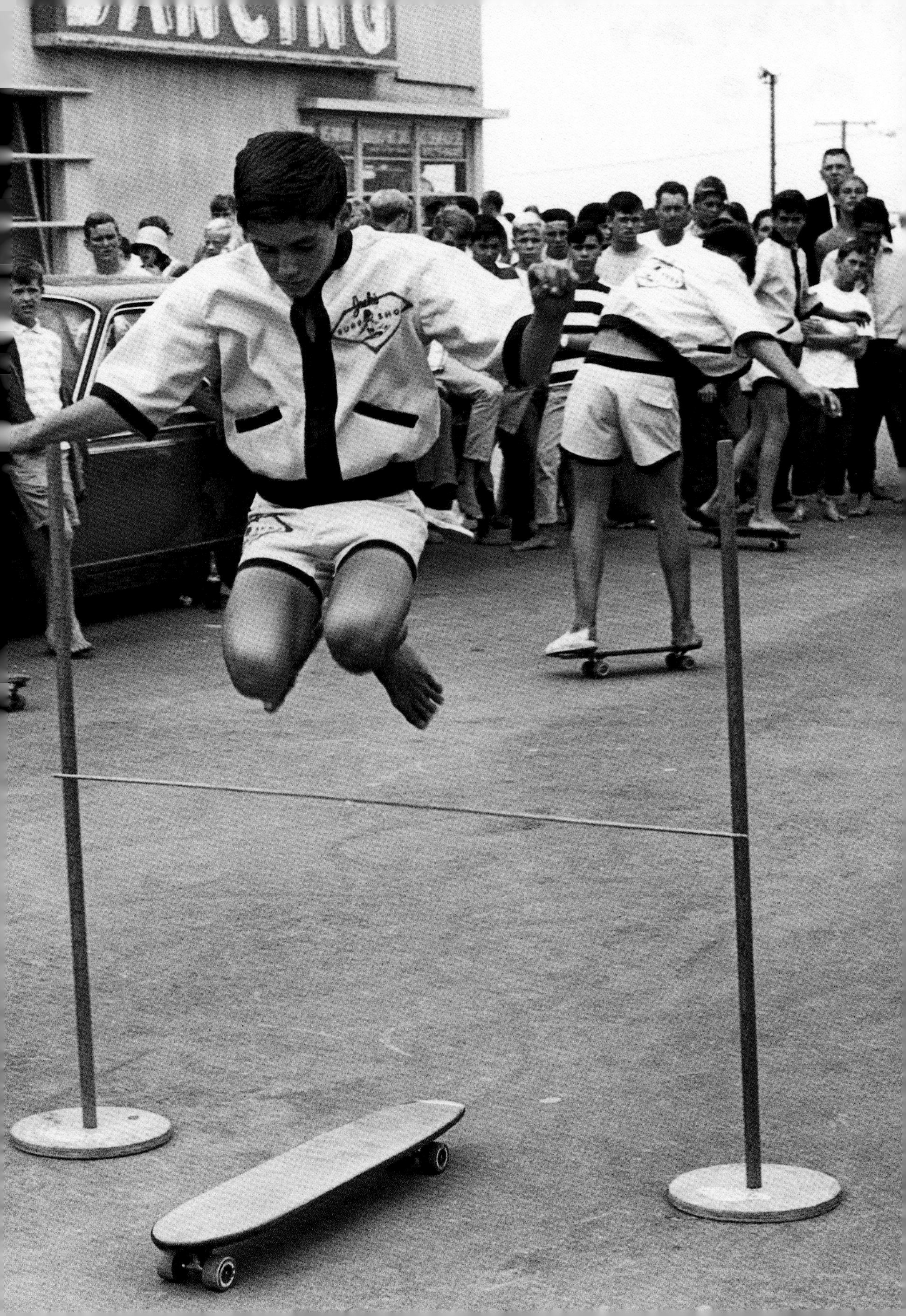
DANCING
Jack's
SURF SHOP

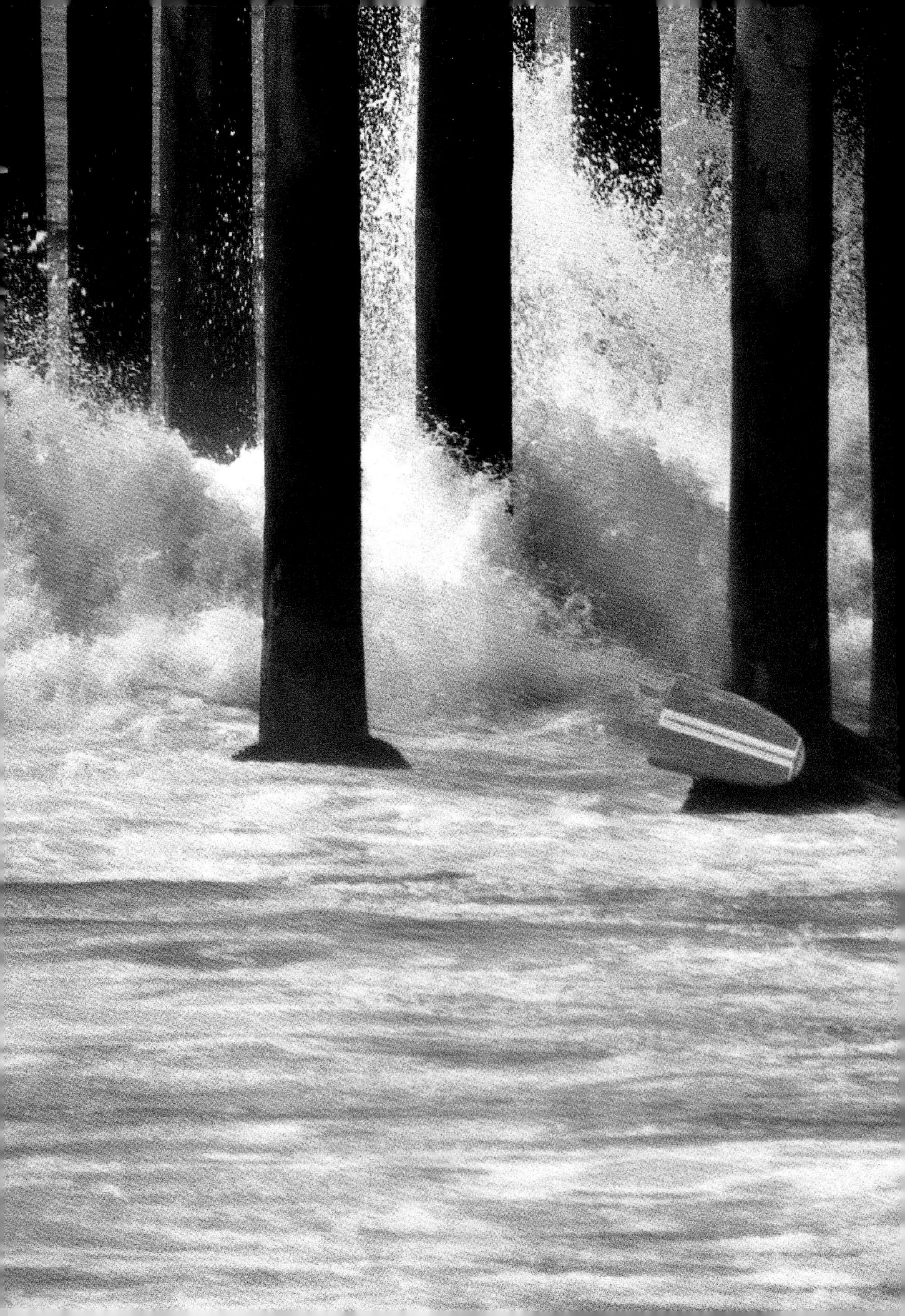

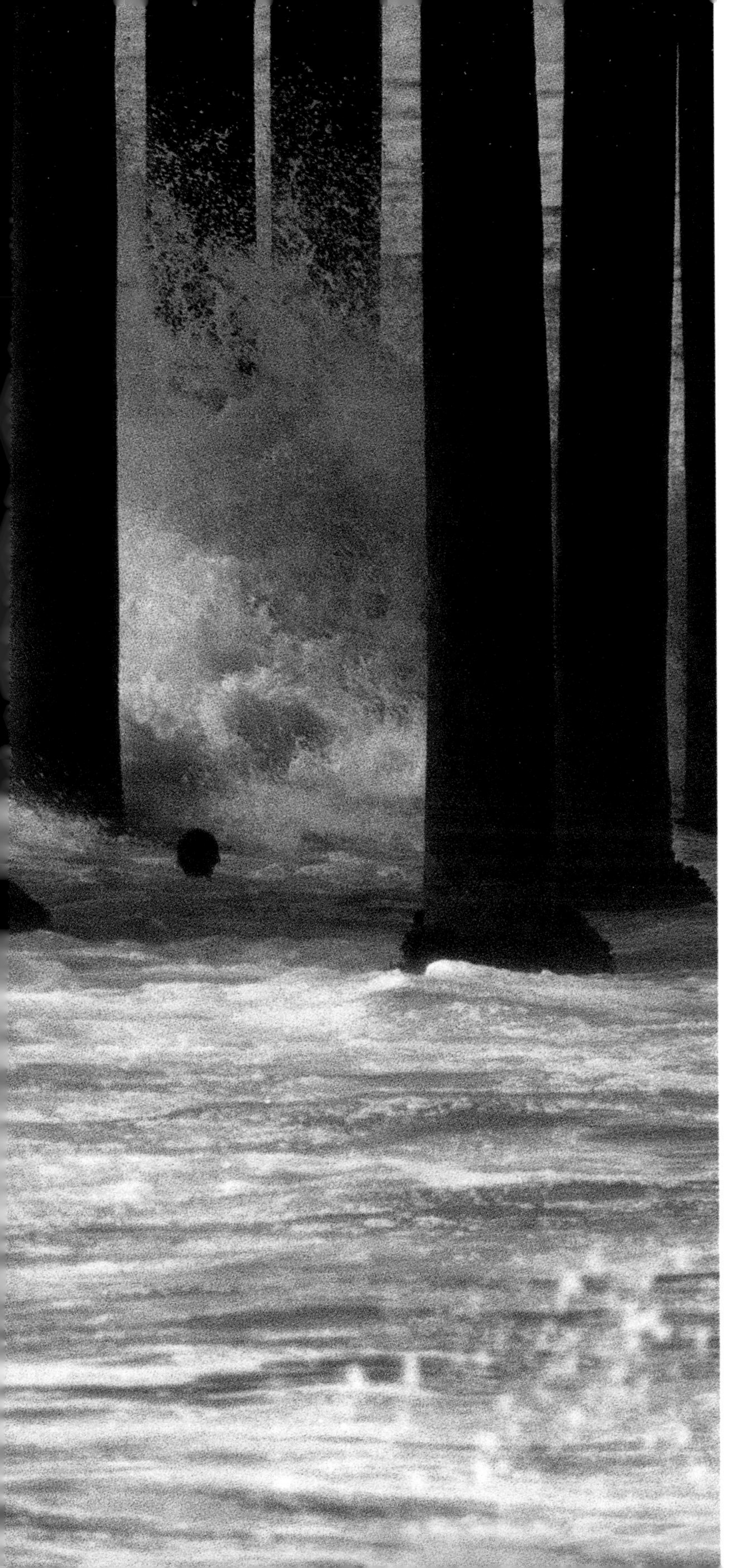

**Huntington Beach Pier, 1964**

An unlucky competitor caught
between the pilings after a wipeout
during the annual U.S. Championships. He survived—his board
didn't.

Ein Teilnehmer hatte das Pech,
nach einem Sturz bei den all-
jährlichen U.S. Championships
zwischen den Pfählen zu landen.
Er überlebte es – sein Brett nicht.

Un concurrent malchanceux projeté
par les vagues atterrit dans les
piliers d'une jetée au cours du
championnat américain. Il en
sortira sain et sauf, mais sa
planche, elle, n'a pas survécu.

## Huntington Beach, 1962

The night before the West Coast
Championships, a U.S. Navy ship
rammed an offshore oil tanker. The
oil slick drifted into the contest
area during the tandem event.
Left to right, Bob Moore, Shelly
Amarine, Hobie Alter, Laurie
Hoover, Pete Peterson.

Am Abend vor den West Coast
Championships rammte ein Schiff
der U.S. Navy einen vor der Küste
liegenden Öltanker. Der Ölteppich
trieb während des Tandem-Wett-
kampfs in den Wettbewerbsbereich.
Von links nach rechts: Bob Moore,
Shelly Amarine, Hobie Alter, Laurie
Hoover, Pete Peterson.

Dans la nuit qui précéda le
championnat de la côte Ouest, un
bâtiment de la U.S. Navy heurta
un pétrolier stationnant au large.
La nappe de pétrole a progressé
jusque dans l'aire de compétition
pendant les épreuves de tandem.
De gauche à droite : Bob Moore,
Shelly Amarine, Hobie Alter,
Laurie Hoover et Pete Peterson.

*Pages 134–135*
## Huntington Beach, 1962

Winners of the West Coast
Championships.

Die Sieger der West Coast
Championships.

Les vainqueurs du championnat
de la Côte Ouest.

*Pages 136–137*
## Huntington Beach, 1963

Beach stomp, midcontest, days
before President John F. Kennedy's
assassination. Dick Dale "King of
the Surf Guitar" in the foreground.

Beach-Disco zur Halbzeit des
Wettbewerbs, wenige Tage vor
dem Attentat auf Präsident John
F. Kennedy. Im Vordergrund
Dick Dale, der Meistergitarrist
der Surferszene.

Session de stomp sur la plage
en pleine compétition de surf,
quelques jours avant l'assassinat
de John F. Kennedy. Au premier
plan on aperçoit le guitariste Dick
Dale, considéré comme le « King »
de la scène du surf.



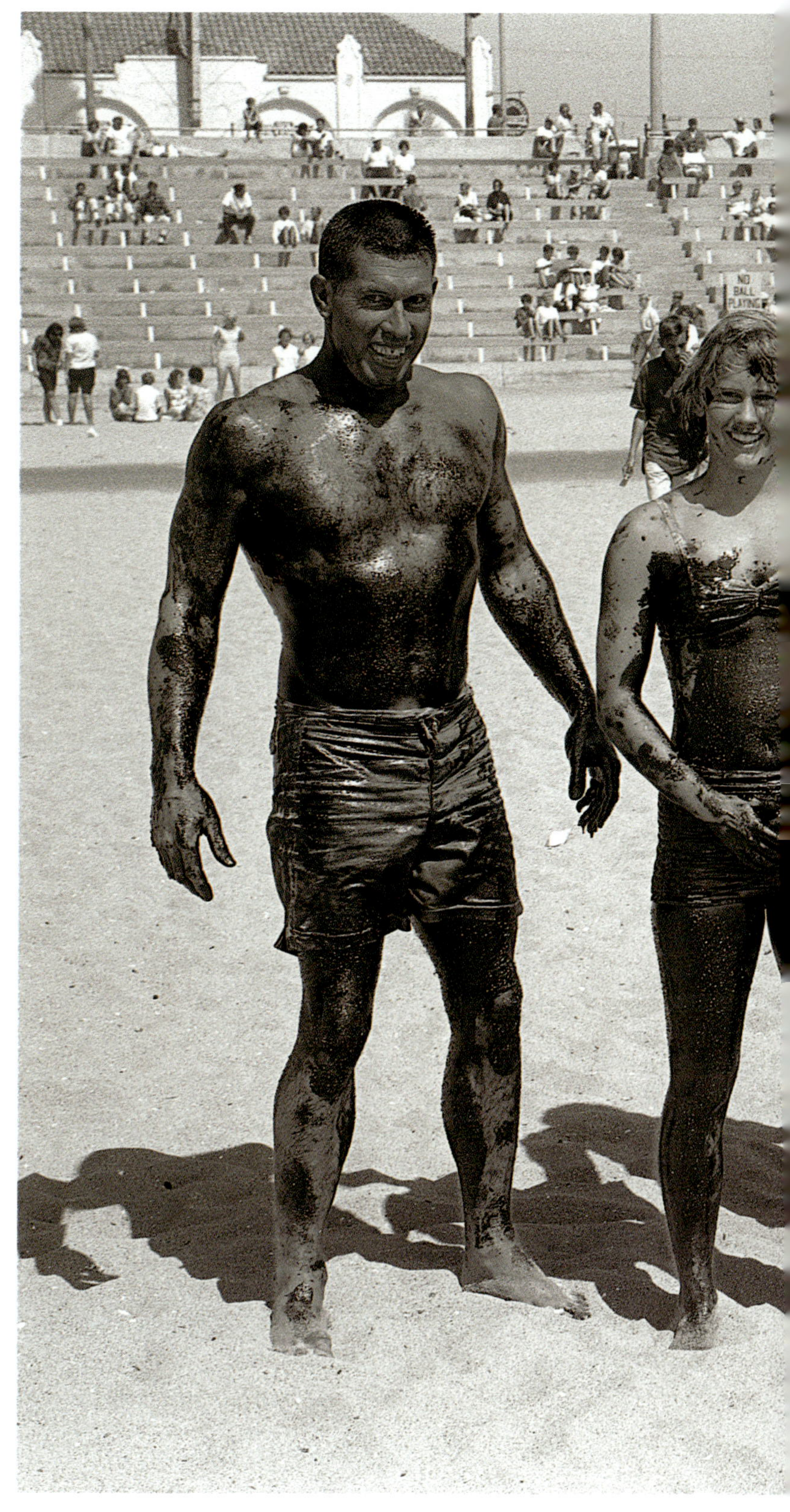

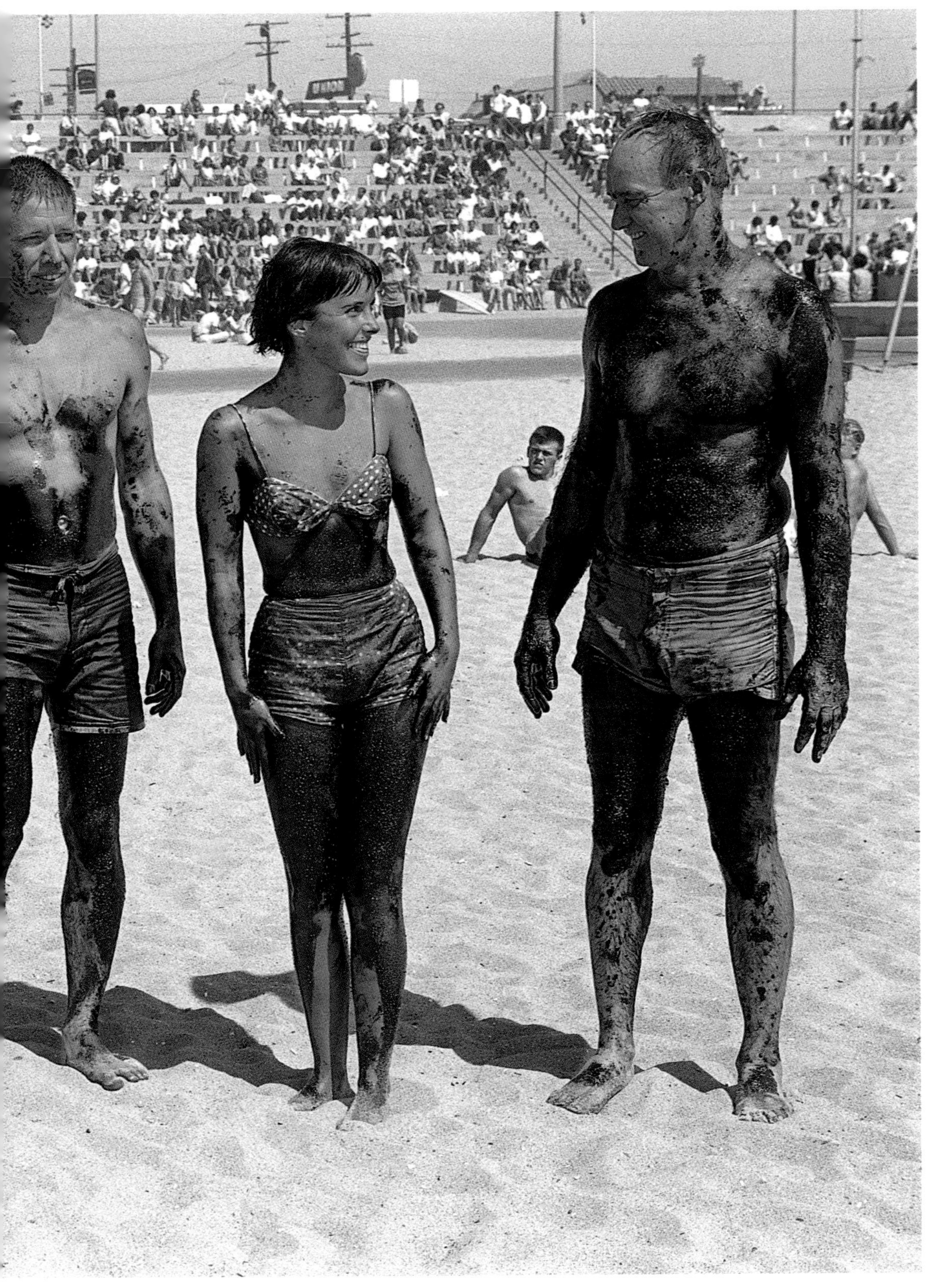

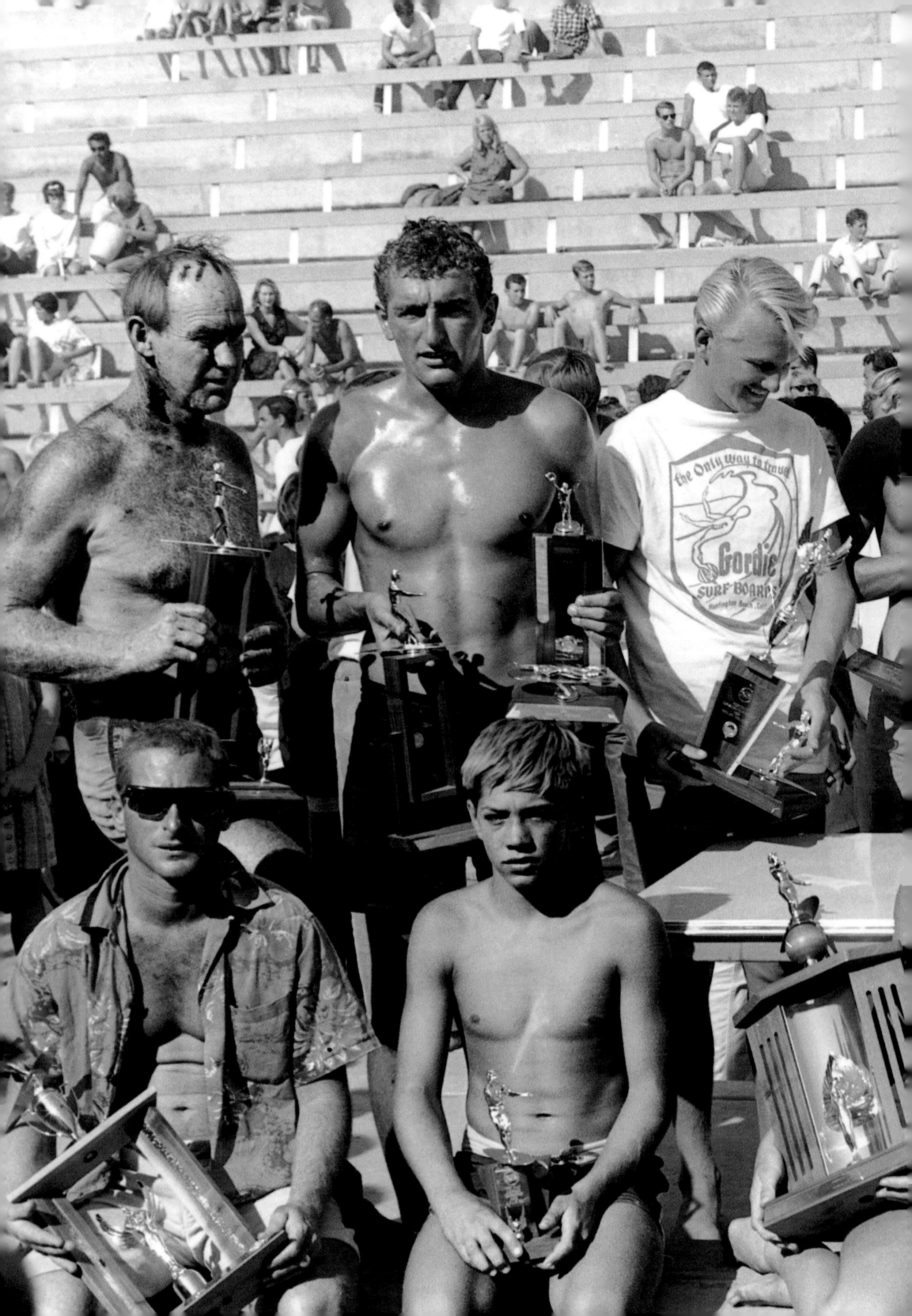

the only way to travel
Gordie
SURF BOARDS
Huntington Beach, Calif.

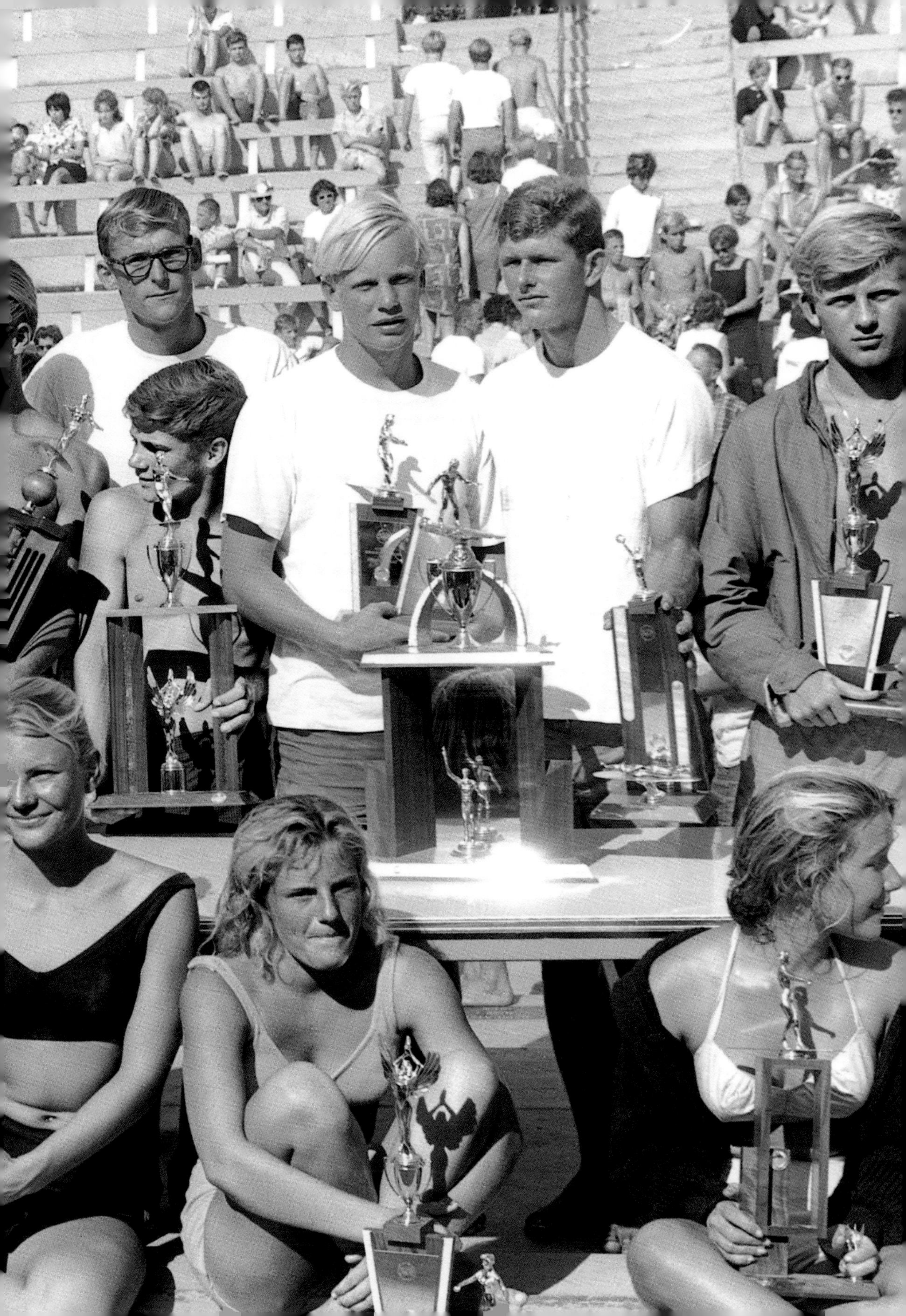

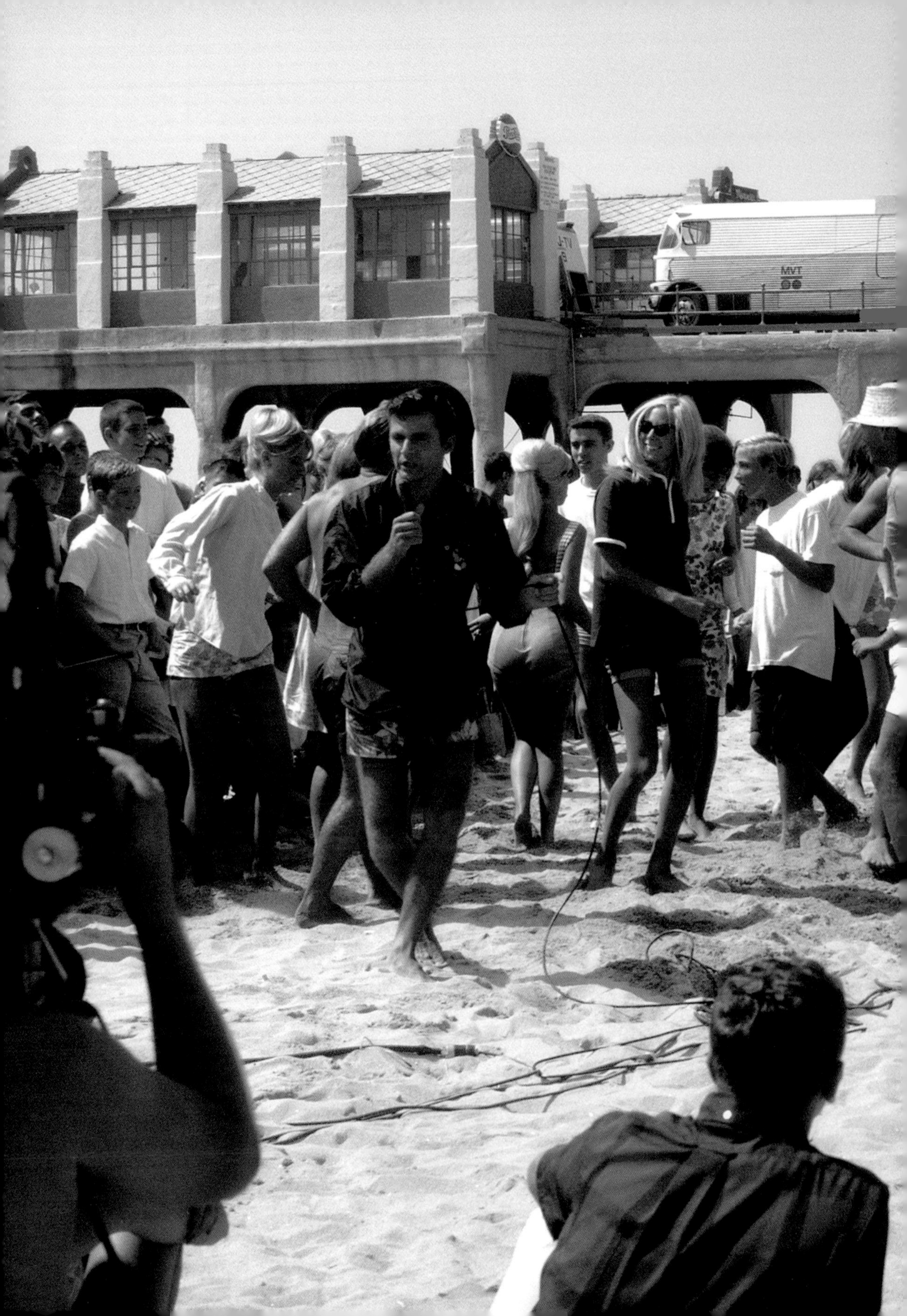

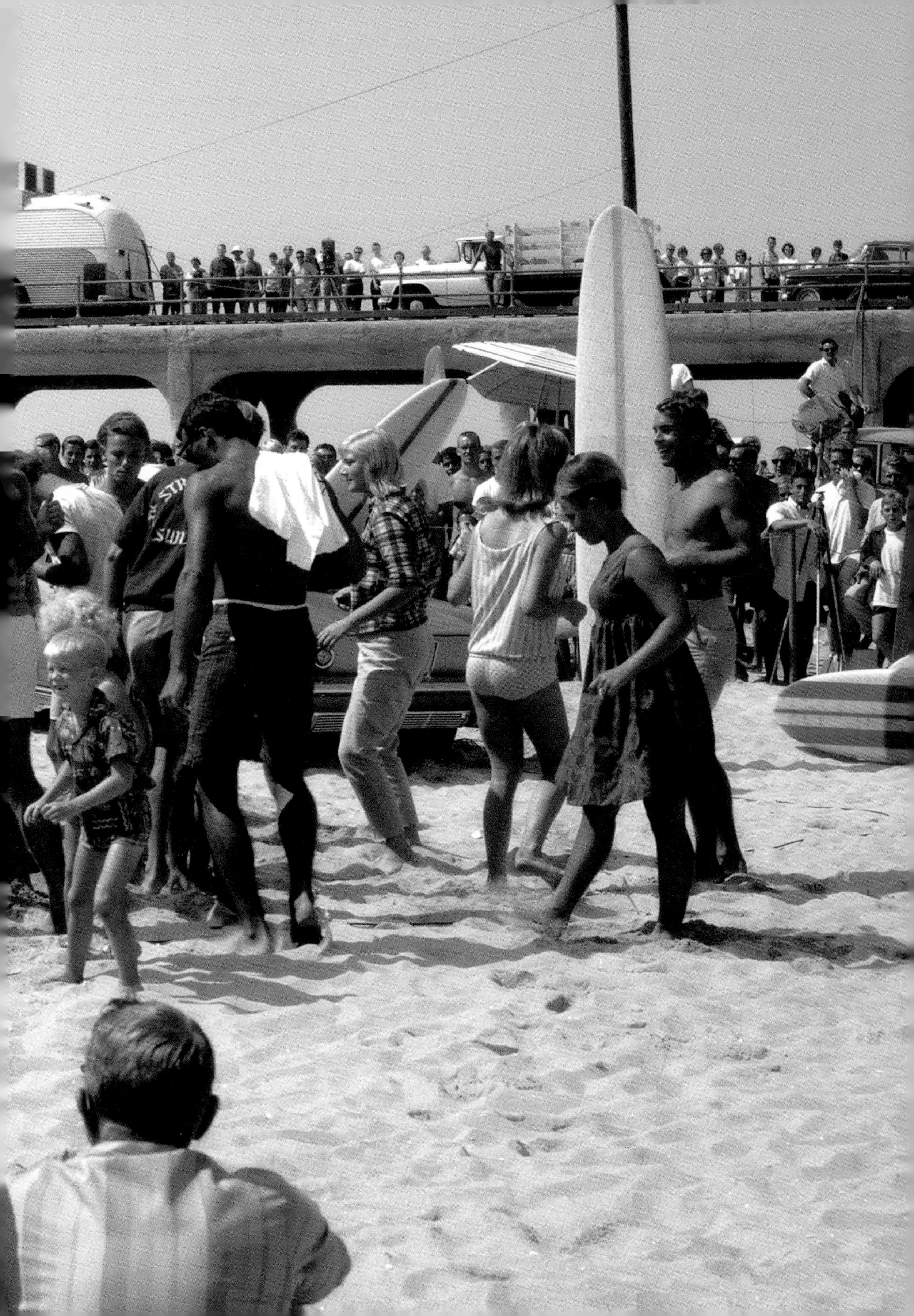

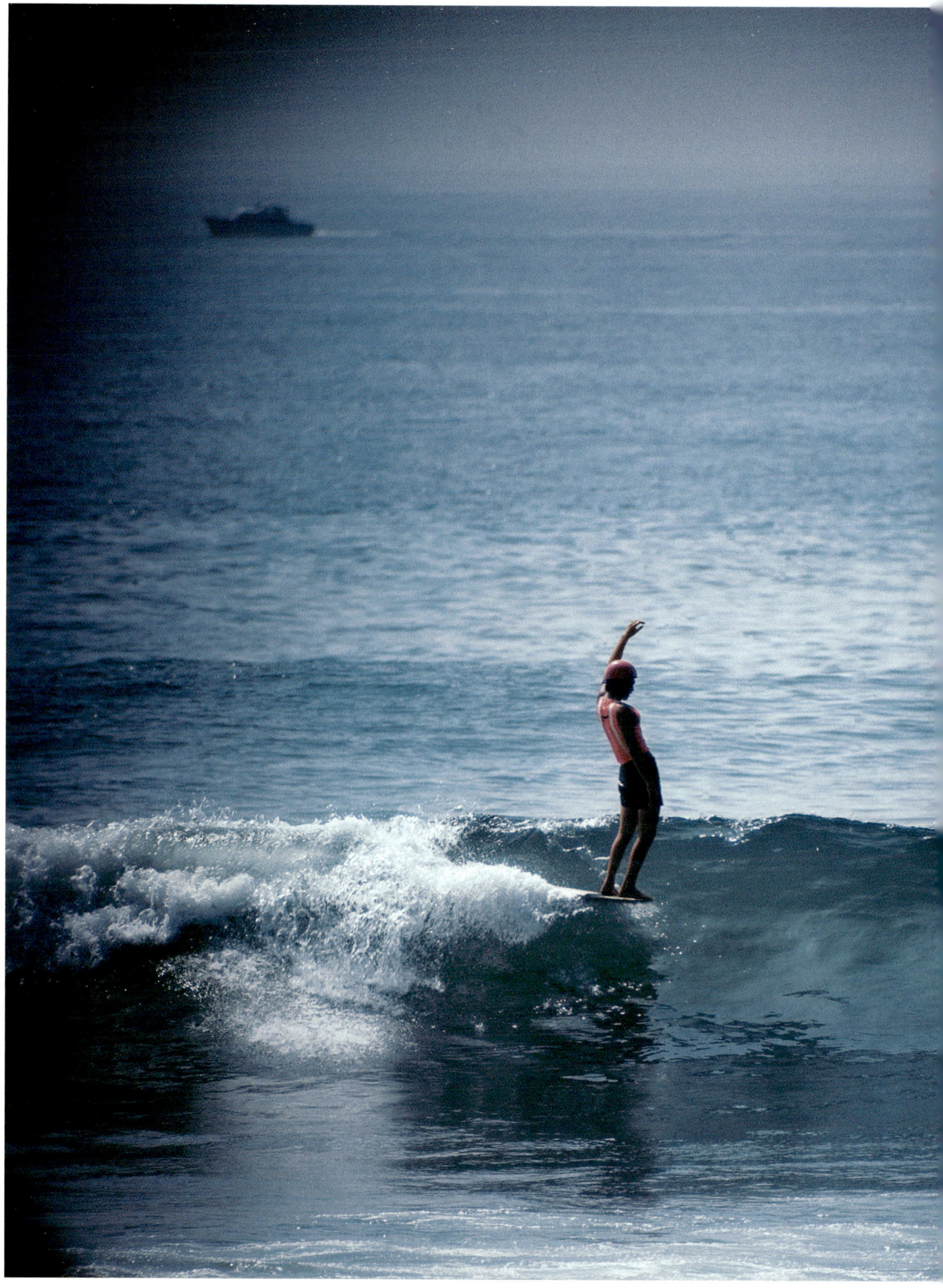

**David Nuuhiwa, Huntington Beach, 1966**

In 1966, eighteen-year-old Hawaiian–born Nuuhiwa was surfing's hottest star. That year the flashy "goofyfoot" won both the U.S. Championships and *Surfer* magazine's prestigious Surfer Poll.

1966 war der achtzehnjährige Hawaiianer Nuuhiwa der heißeste Star der Surfszene. In diesem Jahr gewann der auffallende „Goofyfoot" sowohl die U.S. Championships als auch die angesehene Leserumfrage der Zeitschrift *Surfer*.

En 1966, alors âgé de 18 ans, le Hawaïen David Nuuhiwa devient la star incontestée du surf. Cette année-là, le sémillant *goofy* remporte à la fois le championnat américain et le prestigieux Prix des lecteurs du magazine *Surfer*.

*Pages 140-141*
**Tom Morey, Malibu, 1961**

The eccentric but brilliant Morey, inventor of the hugely popular Boogie Board, has become known as "the Thomas Edison of surfing."

Der exzentrische, aber geniale Morey, Erfinder des extrem beliebten Boogie-Boards, wurde auch als „Thomas Edison des Surfens" bekannt.

L'excentrique et brillantissime Tom Morey, inventeur de la Boogie Board qui connut un succès populaire retentissant, fut baptisé le « Thomas Edison du surf ».

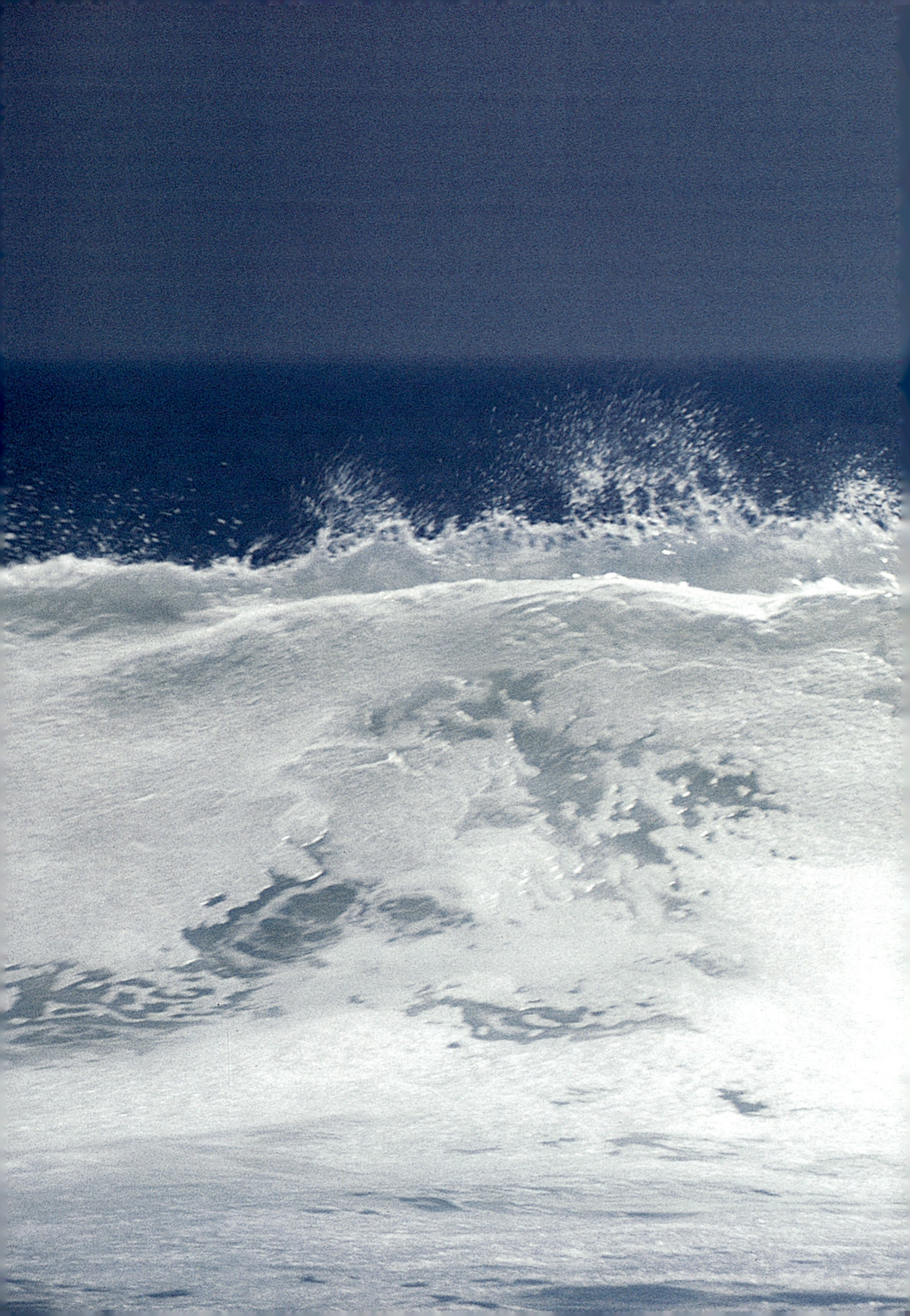

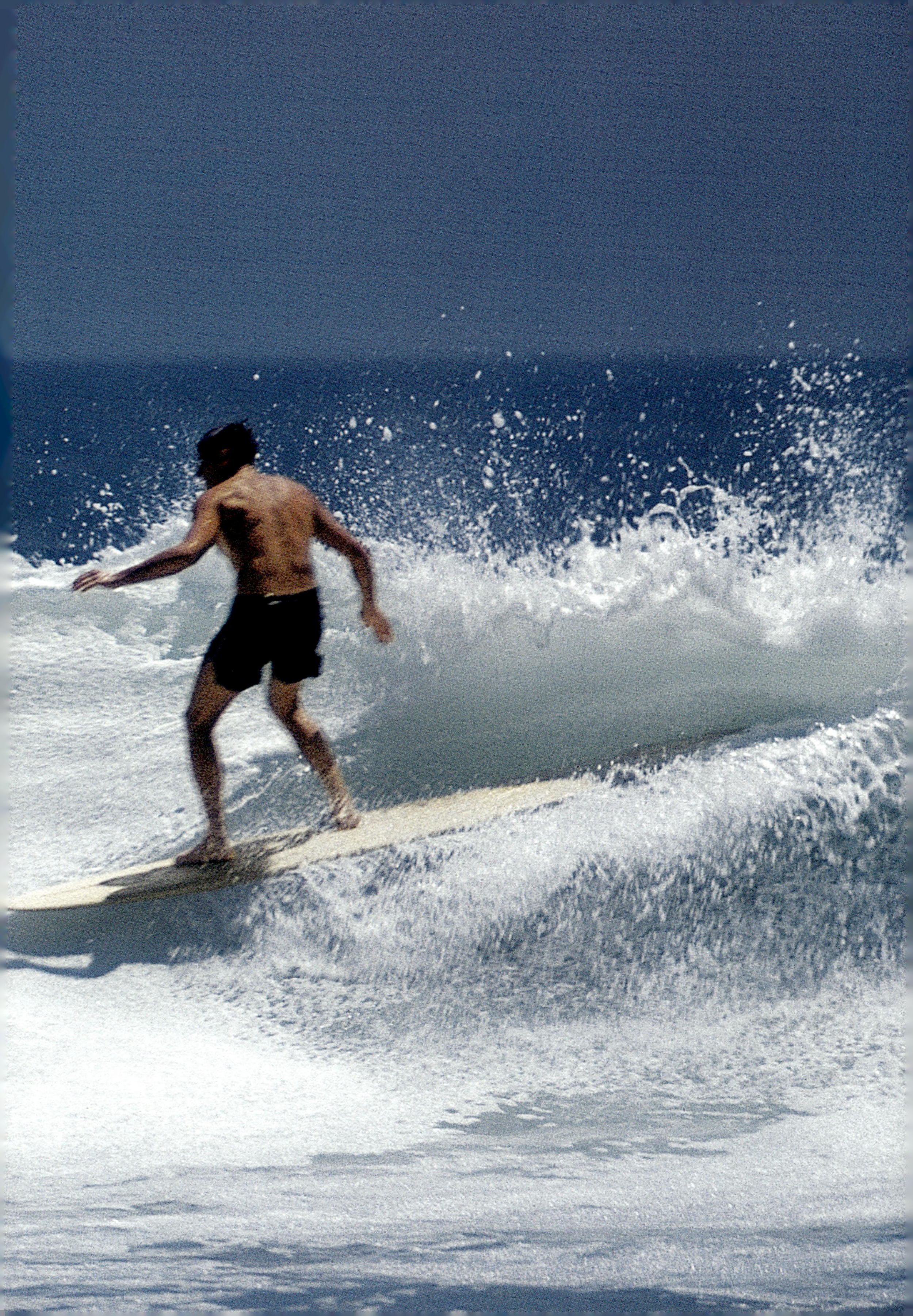

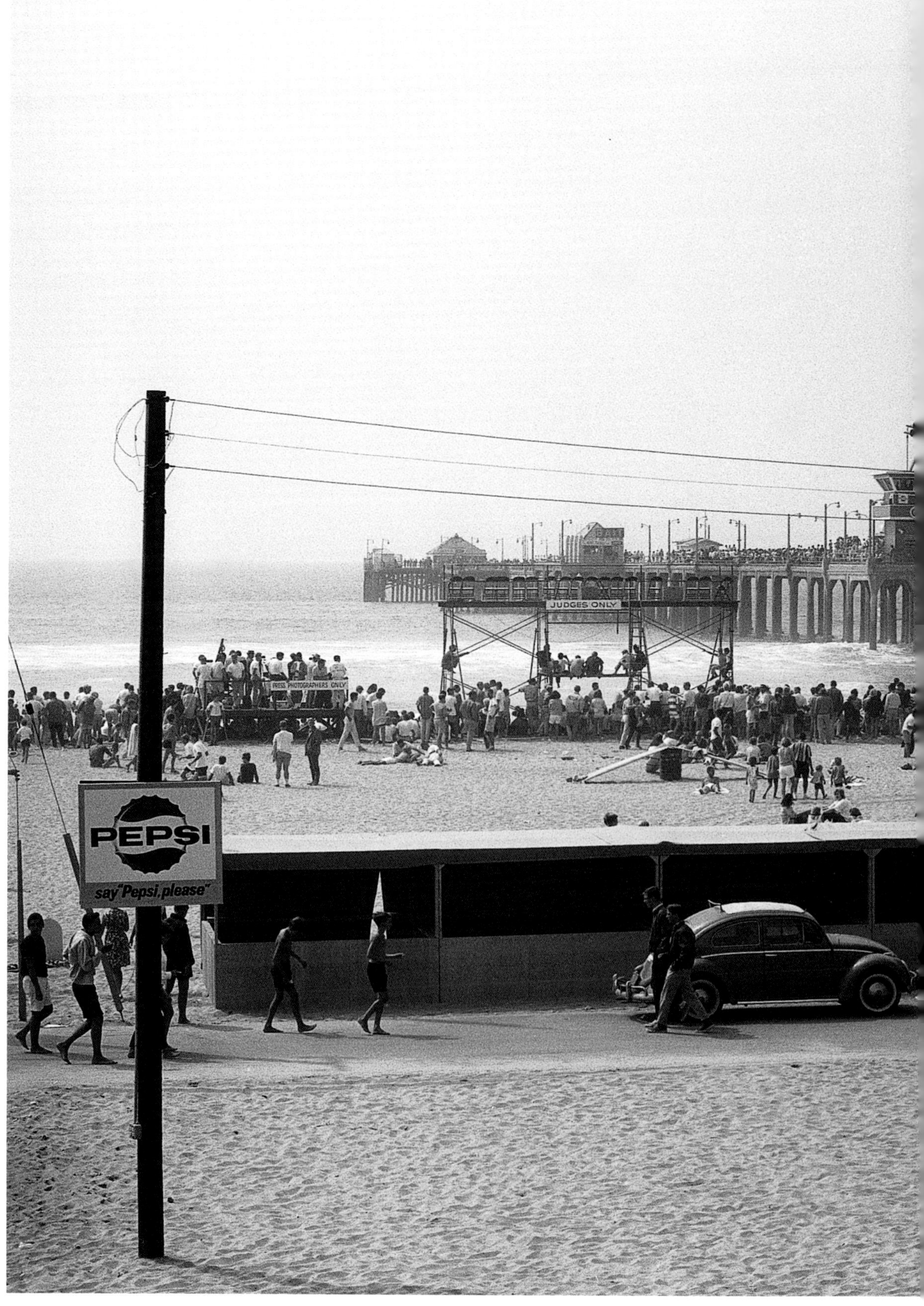
JUDGES ONLY
PRESS PHOTOGRAPHERS ONLY
PEPSI
say "Pepsi, please"

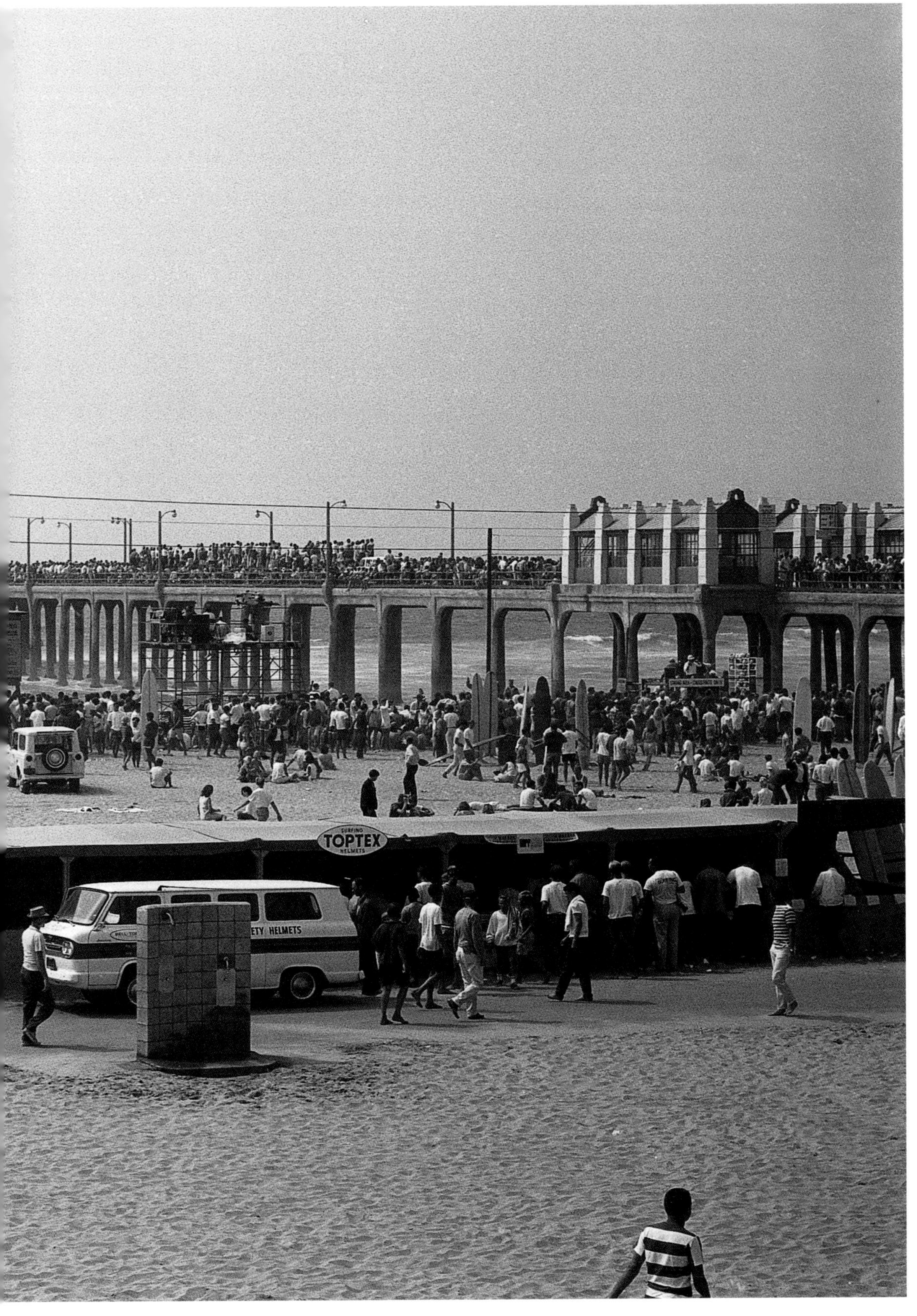
SURFING
TOPTEX
HELMETS
ETY HELMETS

*Pages 142–143*
**Huntington Beach, 1964**

The annual U.S. Championships
(now the U.S. Open) drew crowds
of up to ten thousand on a
weekend. More than fifty thousand
spectators attend today.

Die alljährlich stattfindenden U.S.
Championships (heute die U.S.
Open) zogen an einem Wochenende
bis zu 10.000 Zuschauer an.
Heutzutage sind es mehr als
50.000.

Le championnat américain annuel
(aujourd'hui U.S. Open) attire des
dizaines de milliers de spectateurs
en un seul week-end. Aujourd'hui,
il rassemble plus de 50 000
personnes.

**Ocean Beach, San Diego, 1964**

Competitors' boards at rest between
heats at the Western Surfing
Association contest.

Die Bretter der Teilnehmer machen
Pause zwischen den Heats beim
Wettbewerb der Western Surfing
Association.

Répit mérité pour ces planches de
compétition entre deux *heats* du
championnat de la Western Surfing
Association.

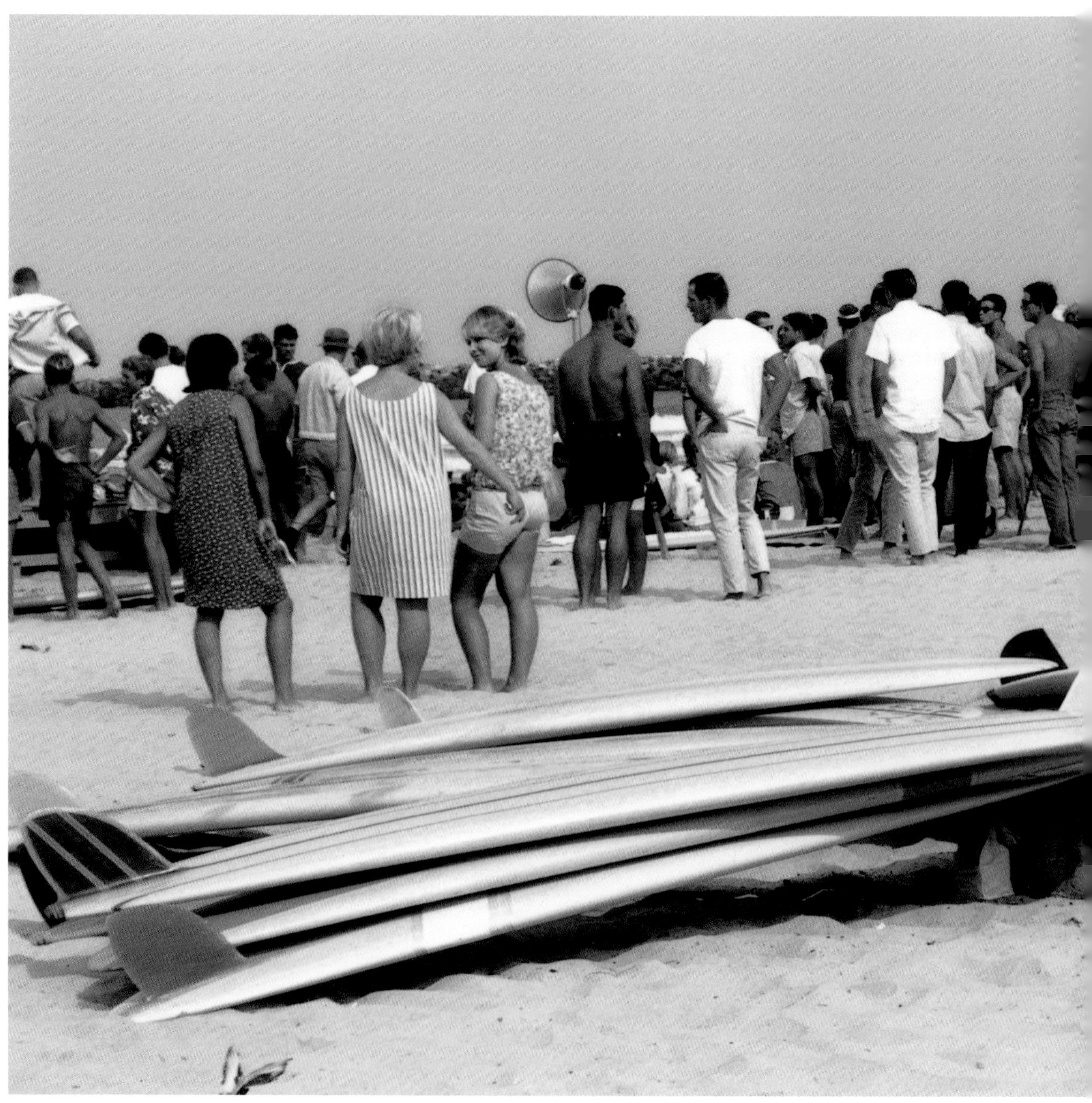

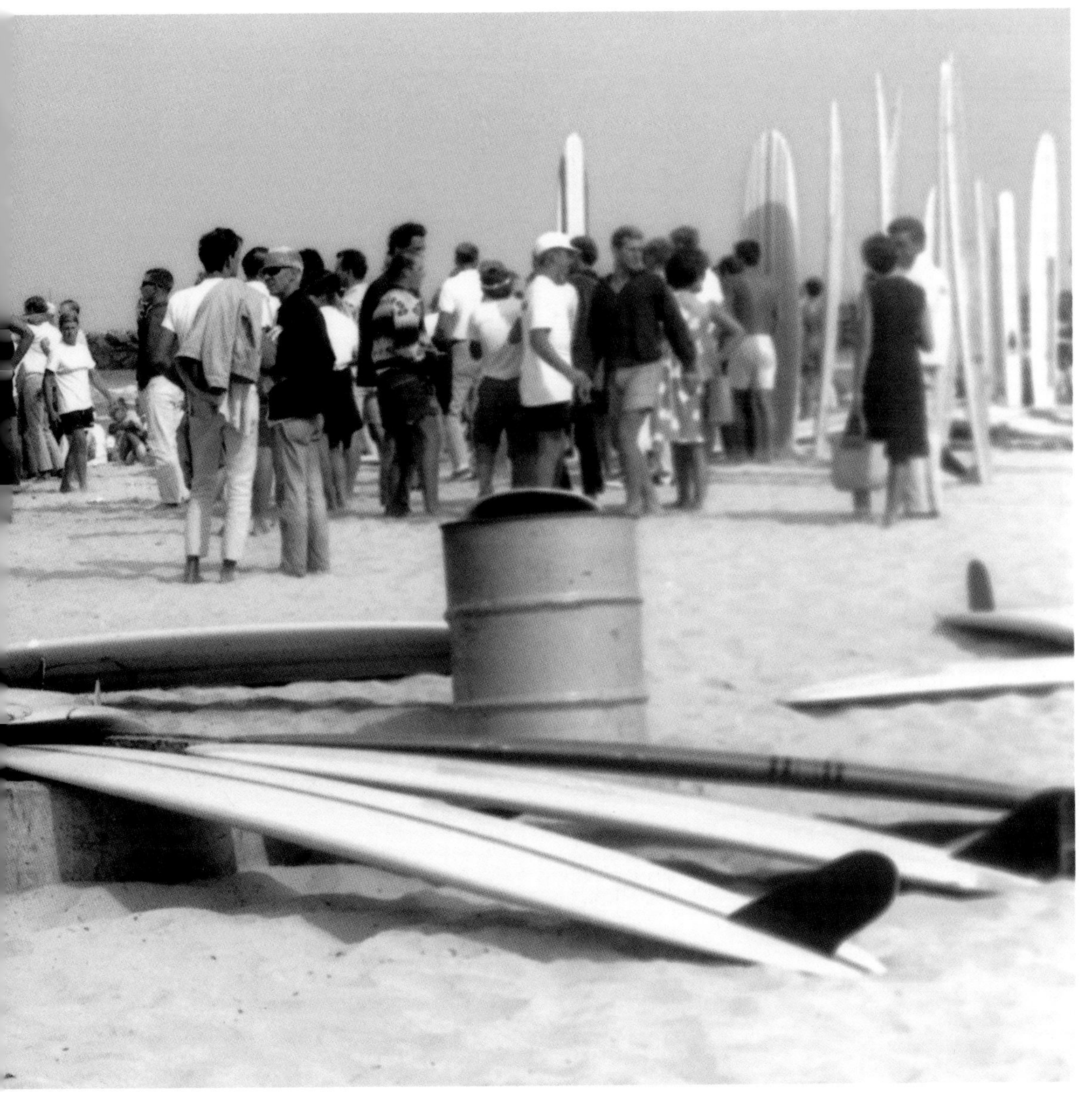

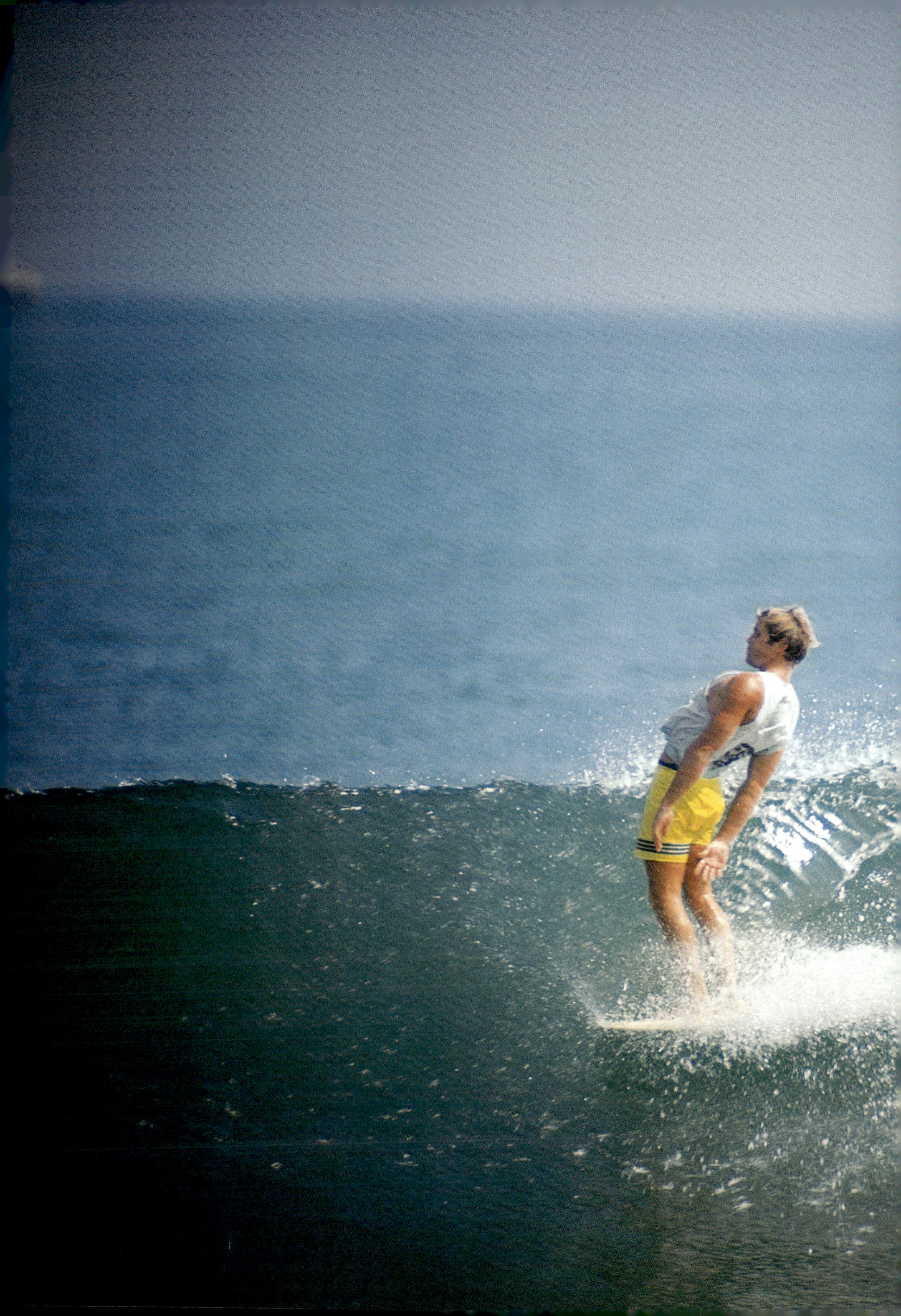

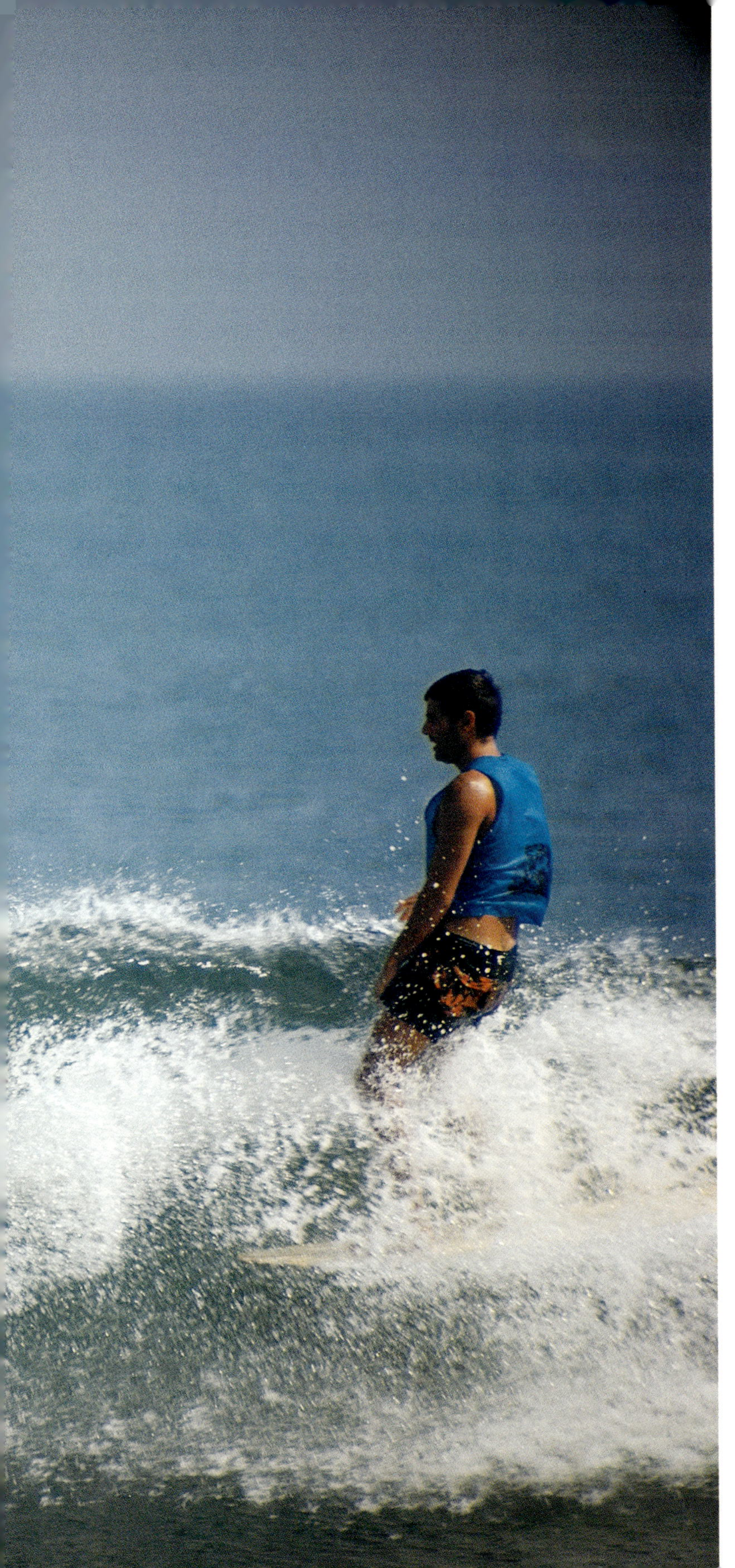

**Johnny Fain, Miki Dora, Malibu, 1965**

On what became known as "the day
war came to Malibu," superstars
Fain (left) and Dora nearly came
to blows over wave rights at the
annual club contest.

Dieser Tag ging als „Der Tag, an
dem der Krieg nach Malibu kam"
in die Surfgeschichte ein: Die
Superstars Fain (links) und Dora
gerieten beim Clubwettbewerb
wegen der Vorfahrtsregeln
aneinander.

« Guerre à Malibu » : ce jour-là,
la compétition annuelle du club
donne lieu à une violente empoi-
gnade entre les deux stars du surf
Johnny Fain (à gauche) et Miki
Dora, qui se disputent la priorité
sur les vagues.

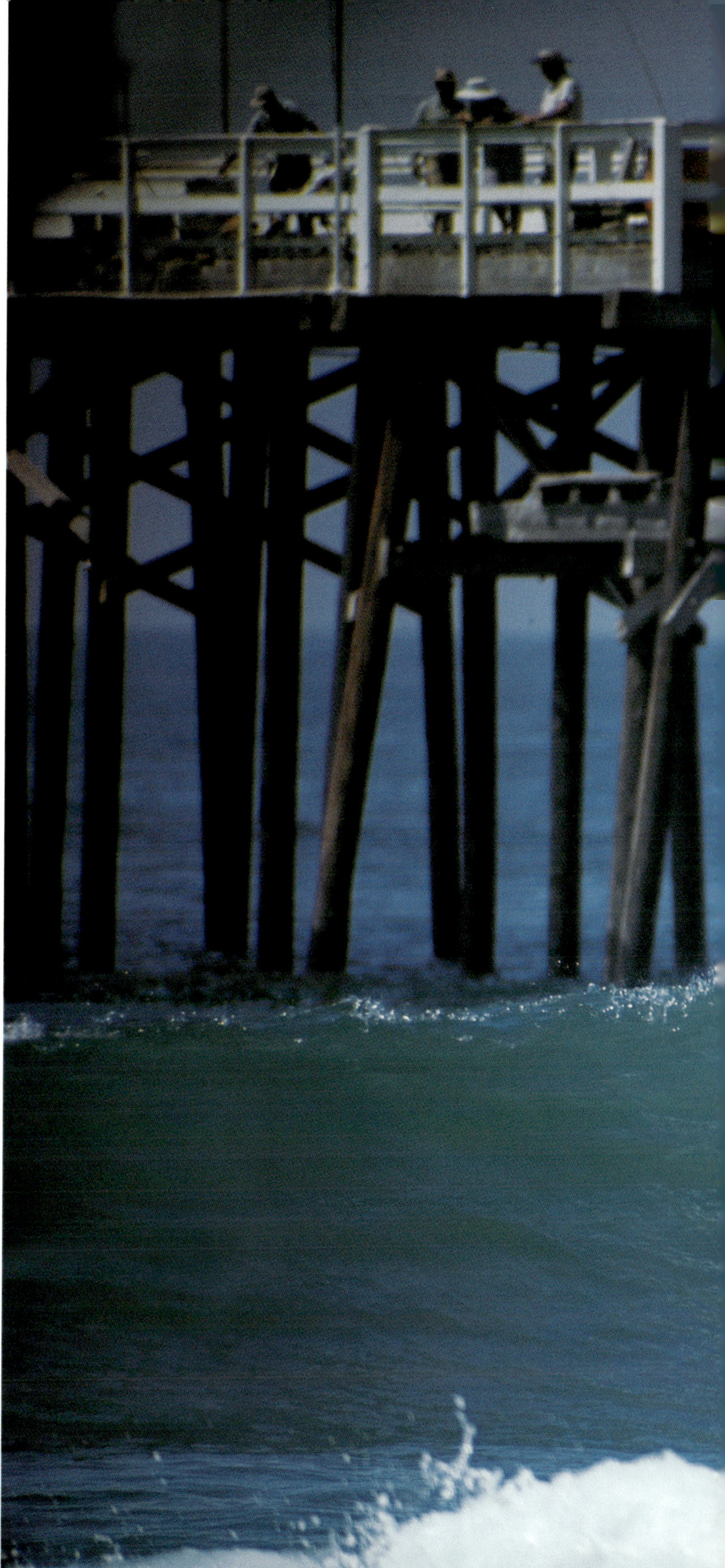

**John Peck, Oceanside, 1966**

Riding his signature Tom Morey-
designed "Penetrator" model, Peck
draws a clean line at the Western
Surfing Association contest.

Auf seinem von Tom Morey
entworfenen „Penetrator"-Brett
zieht Peck eine klare Linie beim
Wettbewerb der Western Surfing
Association.

Debout sur son inséparable
« Penetrator » conçue par Tom
Morey, John Peck exécute un
sans-faute lors du championnat
de la Western Surfing Association.

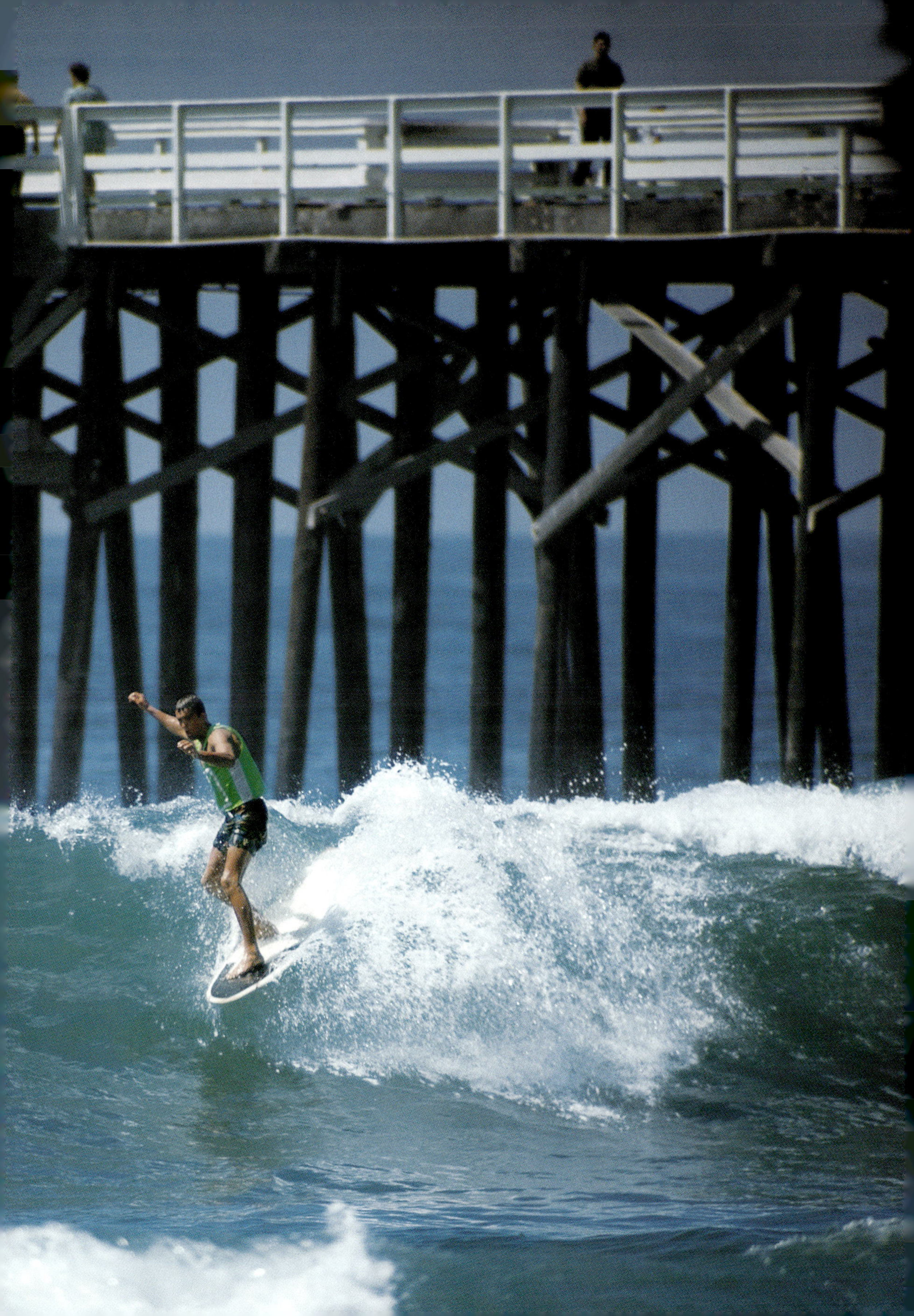

**Pacific Beach, San Diego, 1967**

Award presentations, Western
Surfing Association contest. Left to
right (with trophies): Corky Carroll,
Mark Martinson, David Nuuhiwa,
Skip Frye, Mike Purpus.

Preisverleihung beim Wettbewerb
der Western Surfing Association.
Von links nach rechts (mit
Pokalen): Corky Carroll, Mark
Martinson, David Nuuhiwa, Skip
Frye, Mike Purpus.

Remise des prix lors du champion-
nat de la Western Surfing
Association. De gauche à droite
(trophée en main): Corky Carroll,
Mark Martinson, David Nuuhiwa,
Skip Frye et Mike Purpus.

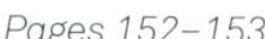

*Pages 152–153*
**Ocean Beach, San Diego, 1966**

The annual World Championships
were won by the brash, hard-turning Australian Robert "Nat" Young.
His win signaled the beginning of
the end of stately longboard era.

Die alljährliche Weltmeisterschaft
gewann der draufgängerische, harte
Turns fahrende Australier Robert
„Nat" Young. Sein Sieg markierte
den Anfang vom Ende der Ära der
stattlichen Longboards.

L'édition annuelle des championnats du monde est remportée par
l'Australien Robert « Nat » Young,
personnage fougueux et star du
virage serré. Sa victoire marque le
début de la fin des longboards, ces
longues planches au profil élégant.



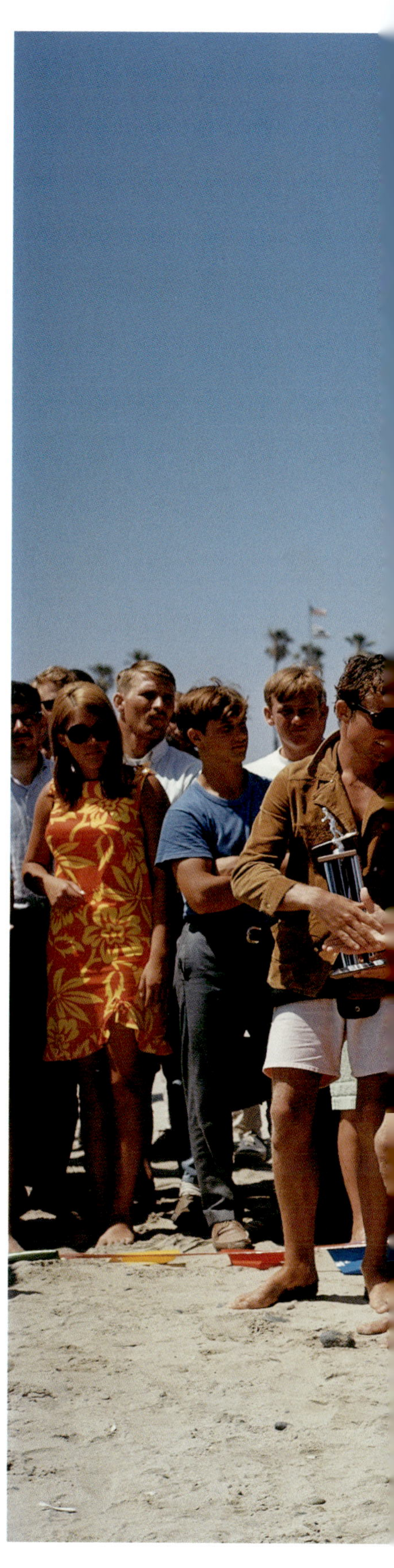

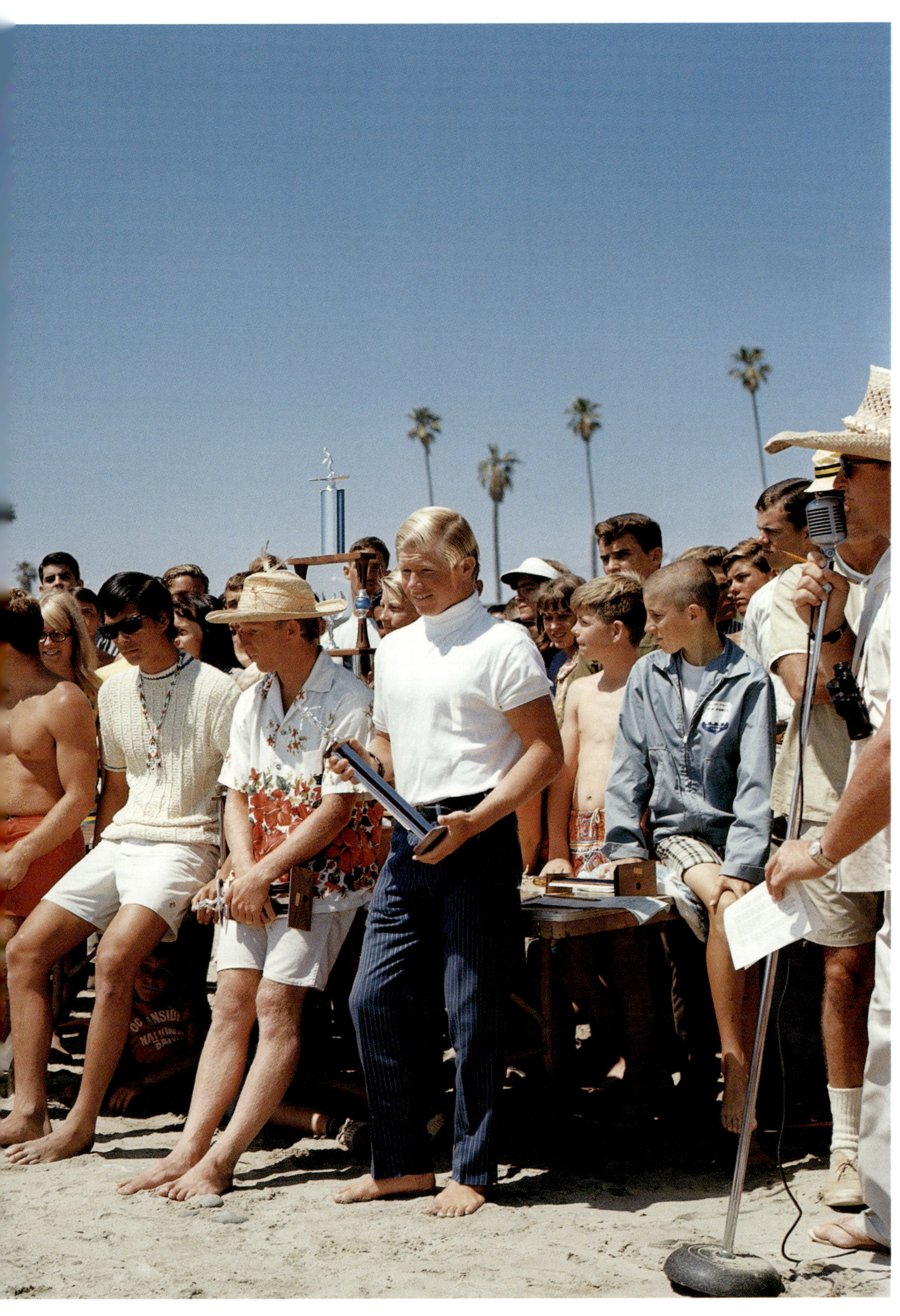

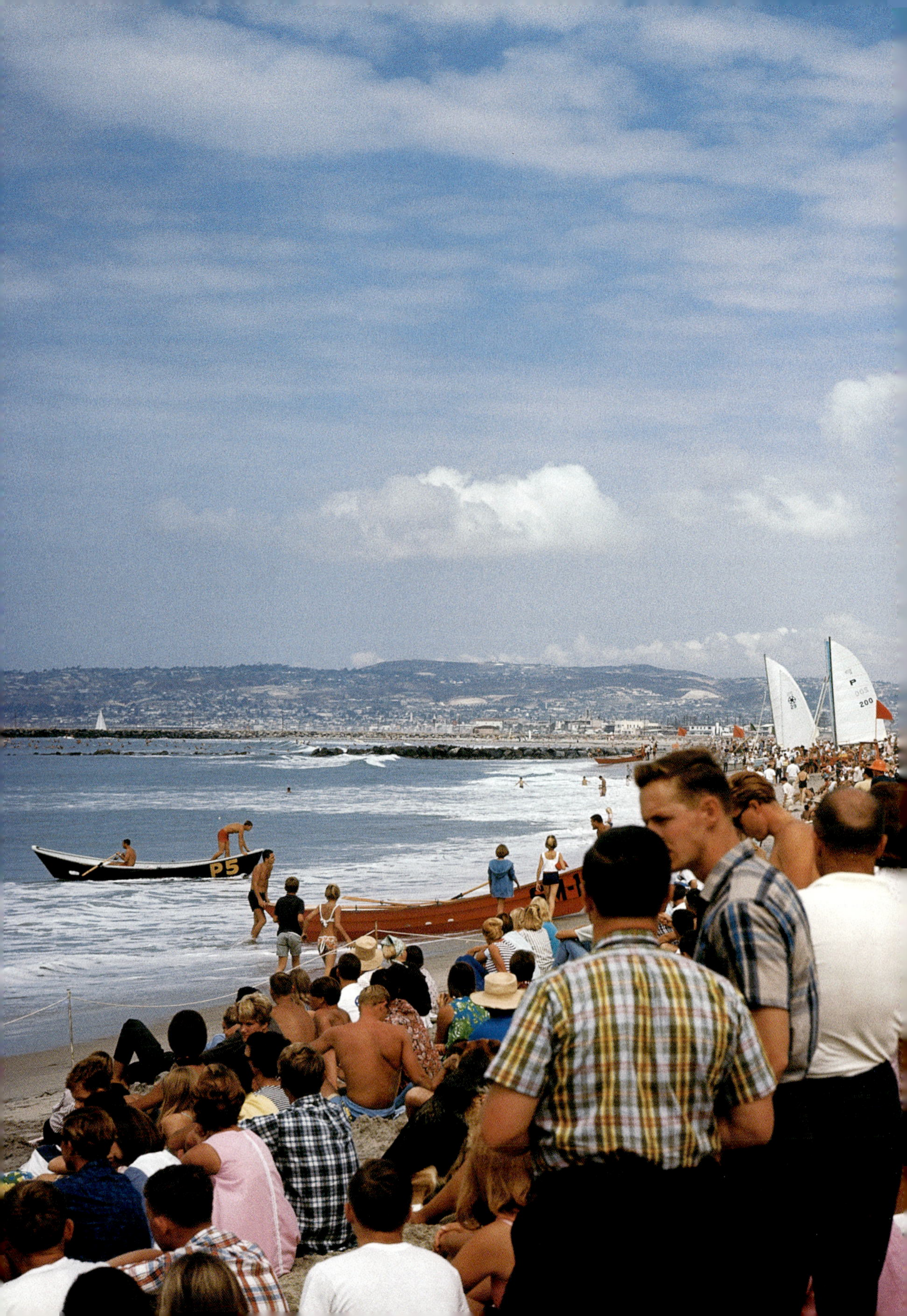

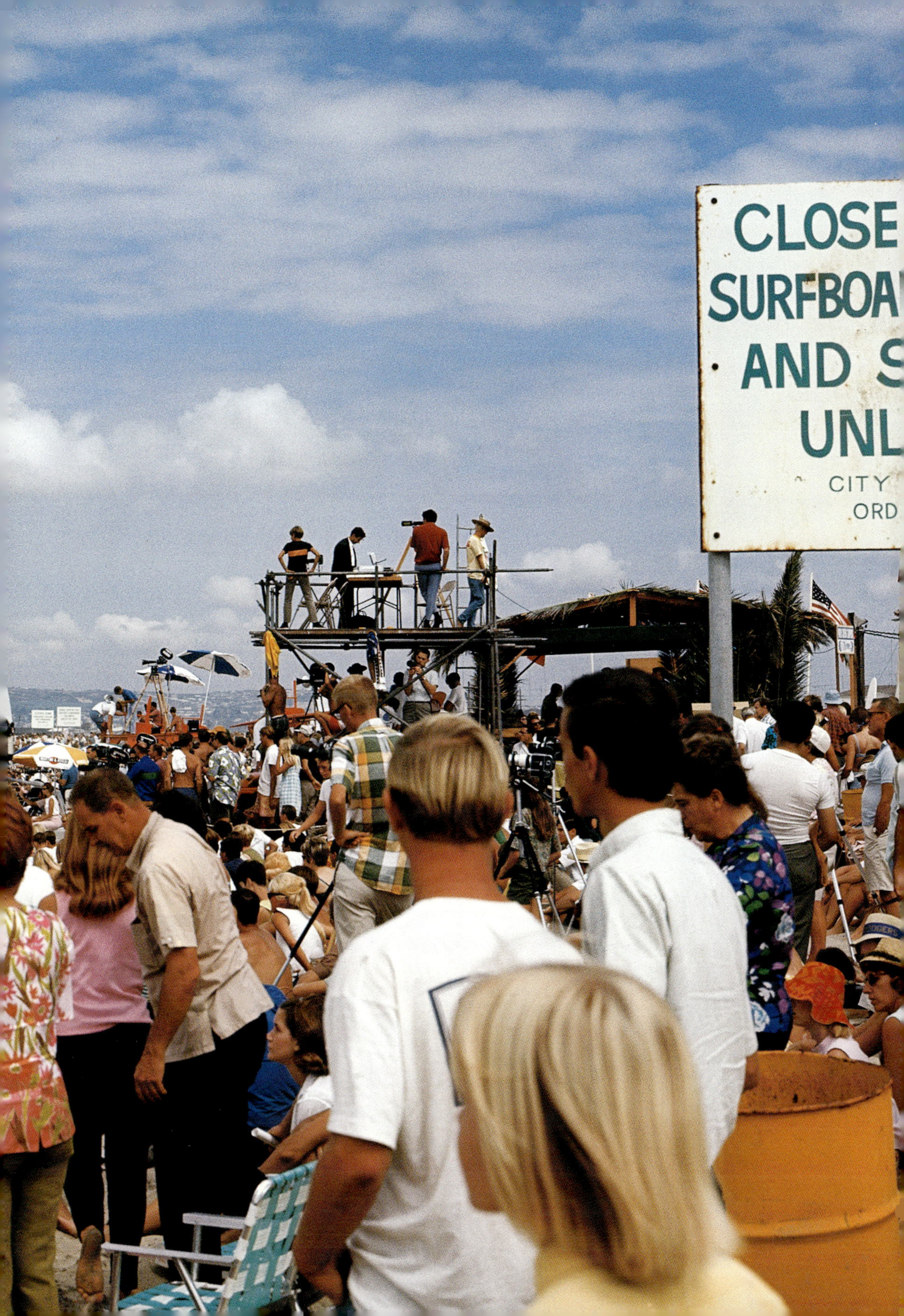

CLOSE
SURFBOA
AND S
UNL
CITY
ORD

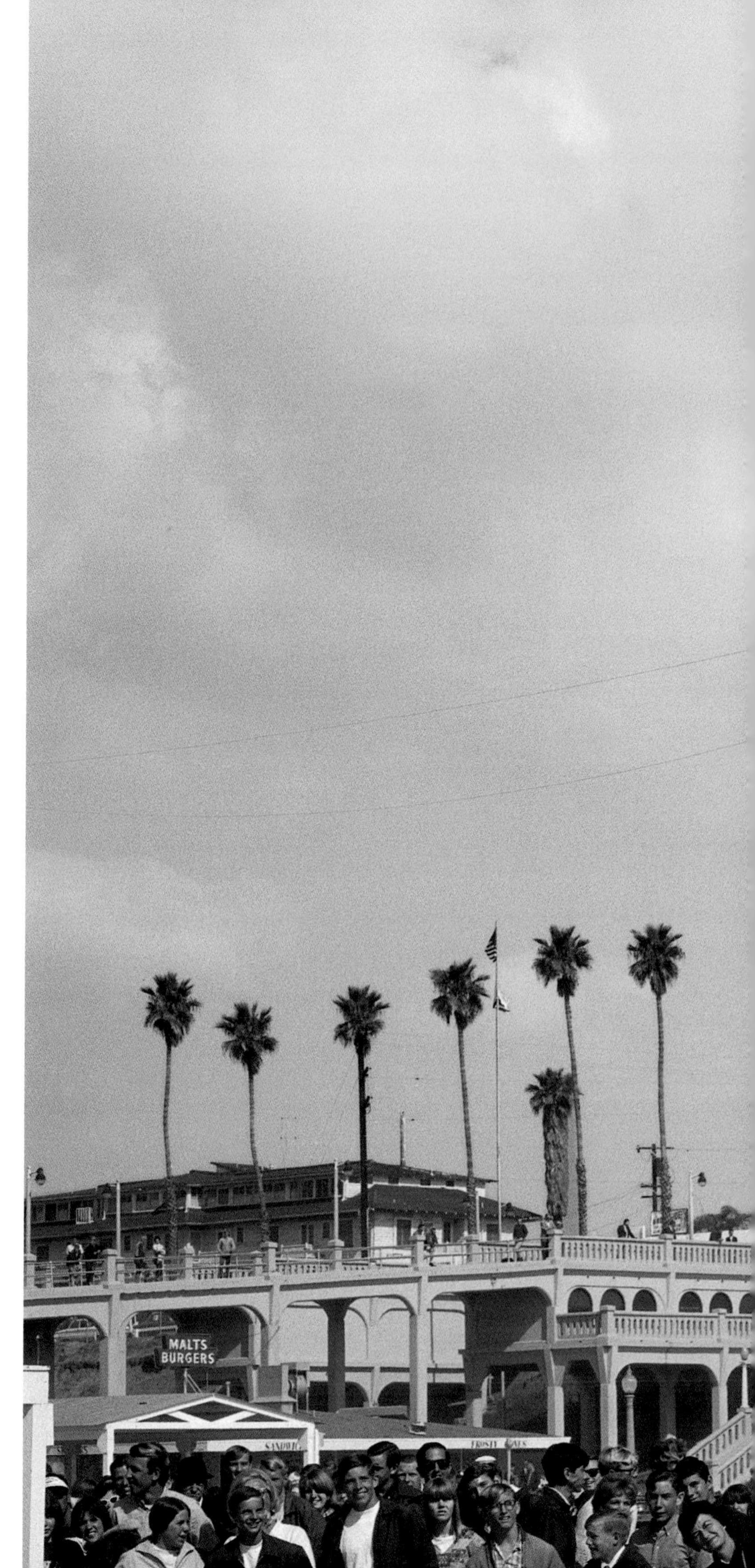

**Hevs McClelland, Oceanside, 1965**

Big Brennan "Hevs" McClelland
was the leading surf-movie
comedian throughout the sixties.
Also an early surf organizer,
he founded the U.S. Surfing
Association in 1961.

Big Brennan „Hevs" McClelland
war während der Sechziger der
führende Komiker in Surffilmen.
Er war auch bereits früh organisa-
torisch tätig und gründete 1961
die U.S. Surfing Association.

Big Brennan « Hevs » McClelland
se distingue pendant les années
1960 comme l'acteur phare des
comédies consacrées au surf.
Il devient très tôt organisateur
d'événements et fonde en 1961
la U.S. Surfing Association.

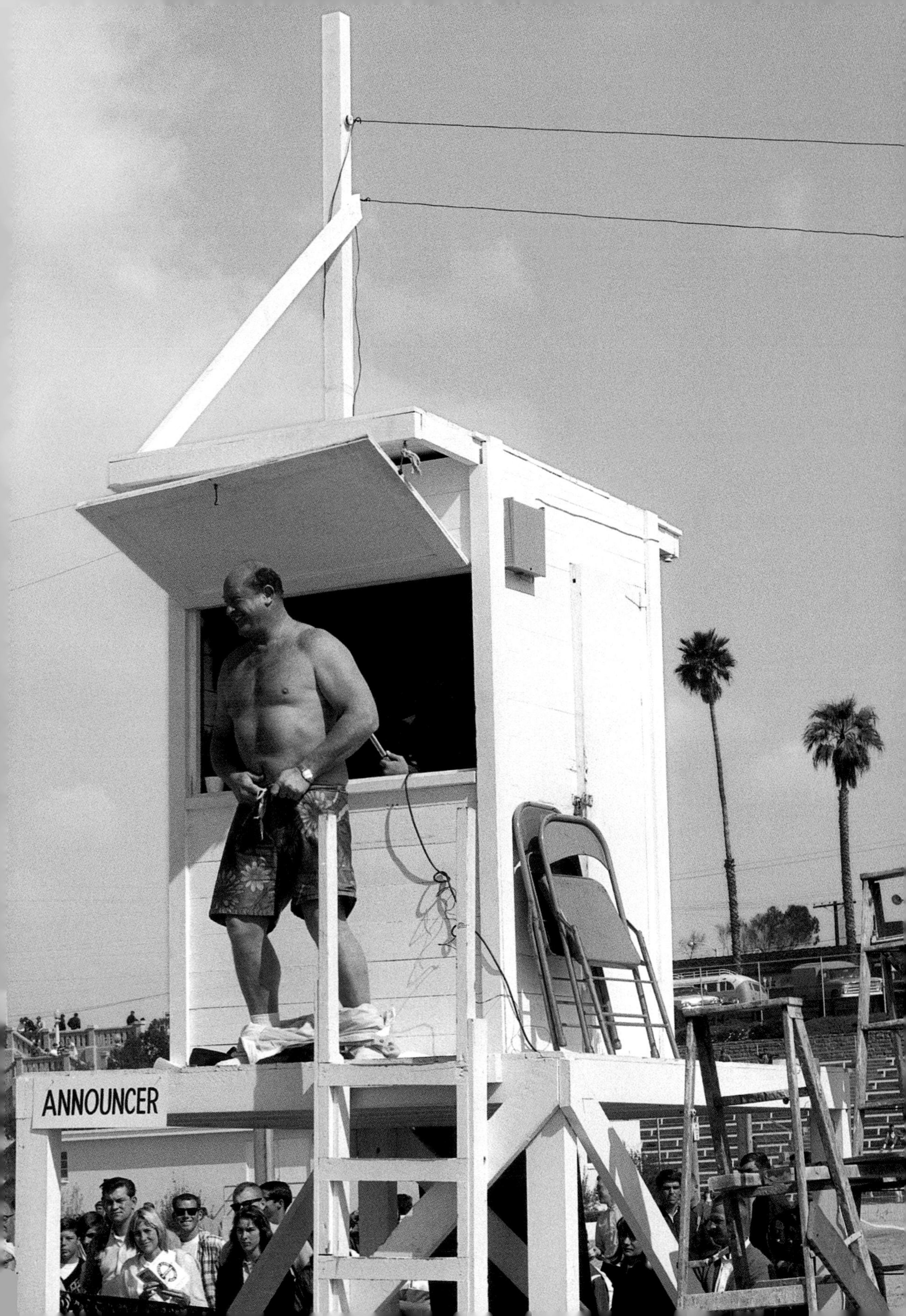
ANNOUNCER

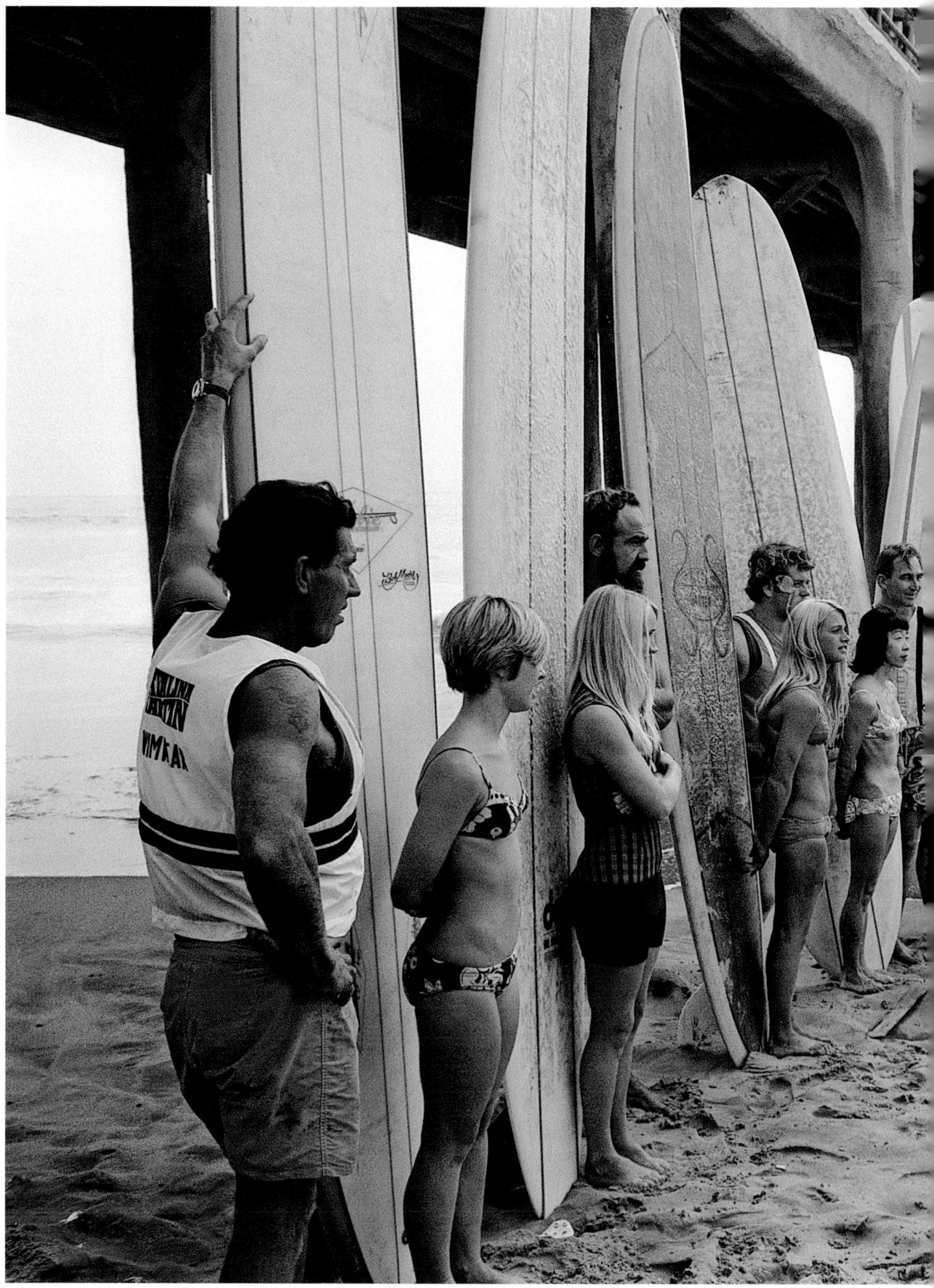

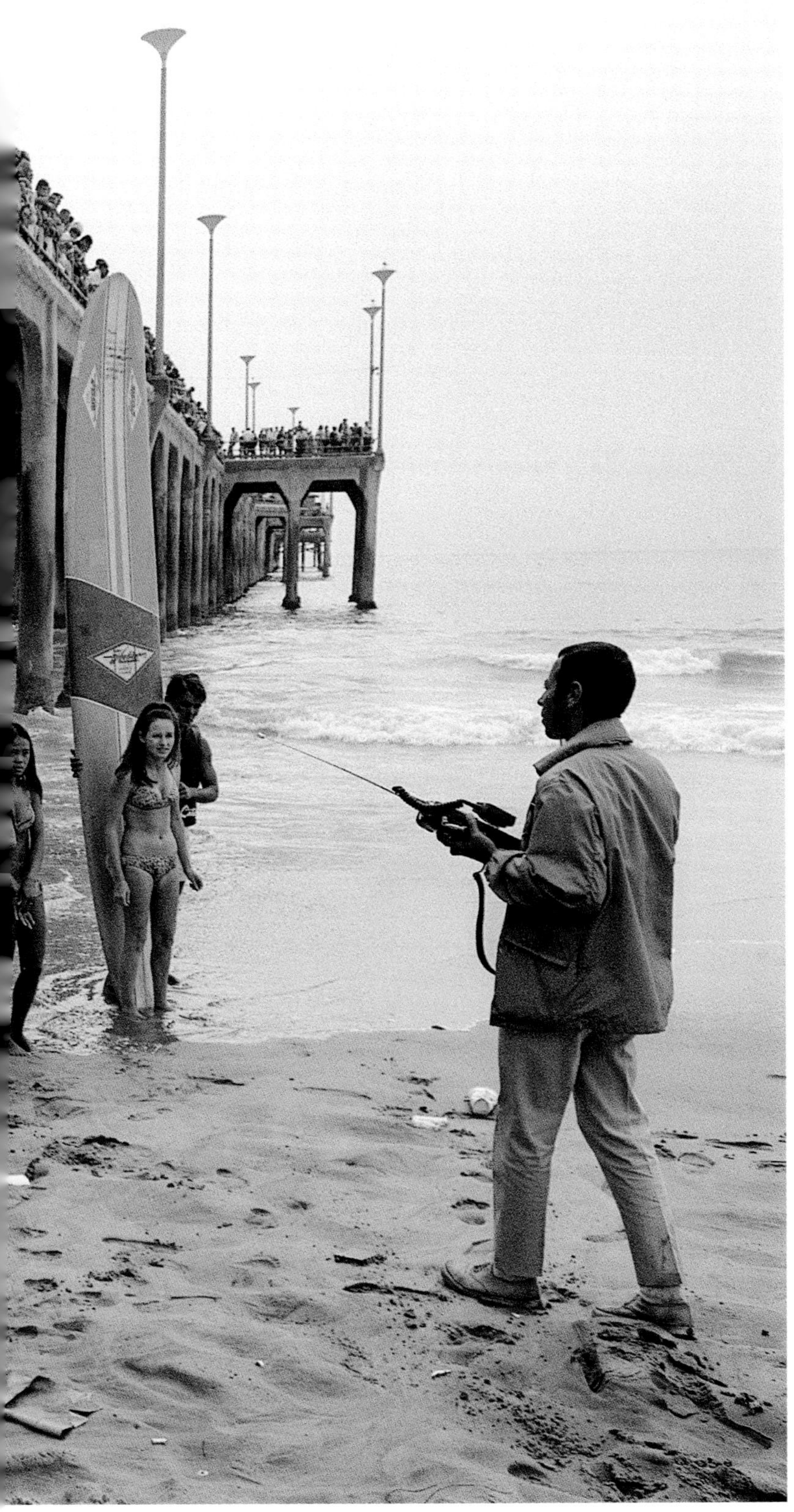



**Huntington Beach, 1968**

Tandem surfing, considered an archaic fringe sport, all but died out before experiencing a limited revival in the mid-nineties.

Tandem-Surfen galt als archaische Randsportart und war fast ausgestorben, bevor es Mitte der Neunziger ein begrenztes Comeback erlebte.

Le surf en tandem, considéré comme une épreuve obsolète et marginale, tombe en désuétude avant de connaître un fragile come-back au milieu des années 1990.

*Pages 158–159*
**Nancy Katin, Ocean Beach, San Diego, 1972**

So much had changed in the six years between World Championships at Ocean Beach. Boards got shorter, hair got longer, and minds were blown. But surfers still wore Kanvas by Katin. The designer sits next to Katie Grannis (left) and renowned surfer Dru Harrison (behind).

Es hatte sich viel verändert in den sechs Jahren seit der letzten Weltmeisterschaft in Ocean Beach. Die Boards waren kürzer, die Haare länger, das Bewusstsein erweitert. Aber die Surfer trugen immer noch Kanvas by Katin. Die Designerin sitzt neben Katie Grannis (links) und dem berühmten Surfer Dru Harrison (hinten).

Six ans après 1966, Ocean Beach accueille à nouveau les championnats du monde. Le changement est radical : les planches sont plus courtes, les cheveux plus longs et les esprits plus délurés. Mais les surfeurs arborent toujours les tenues Kanvas by Katin. La créatrice de la marque est assise à côté de Katie Grannis (à gauche) et de l'illustre surfeur Dru Harrison (derrière).

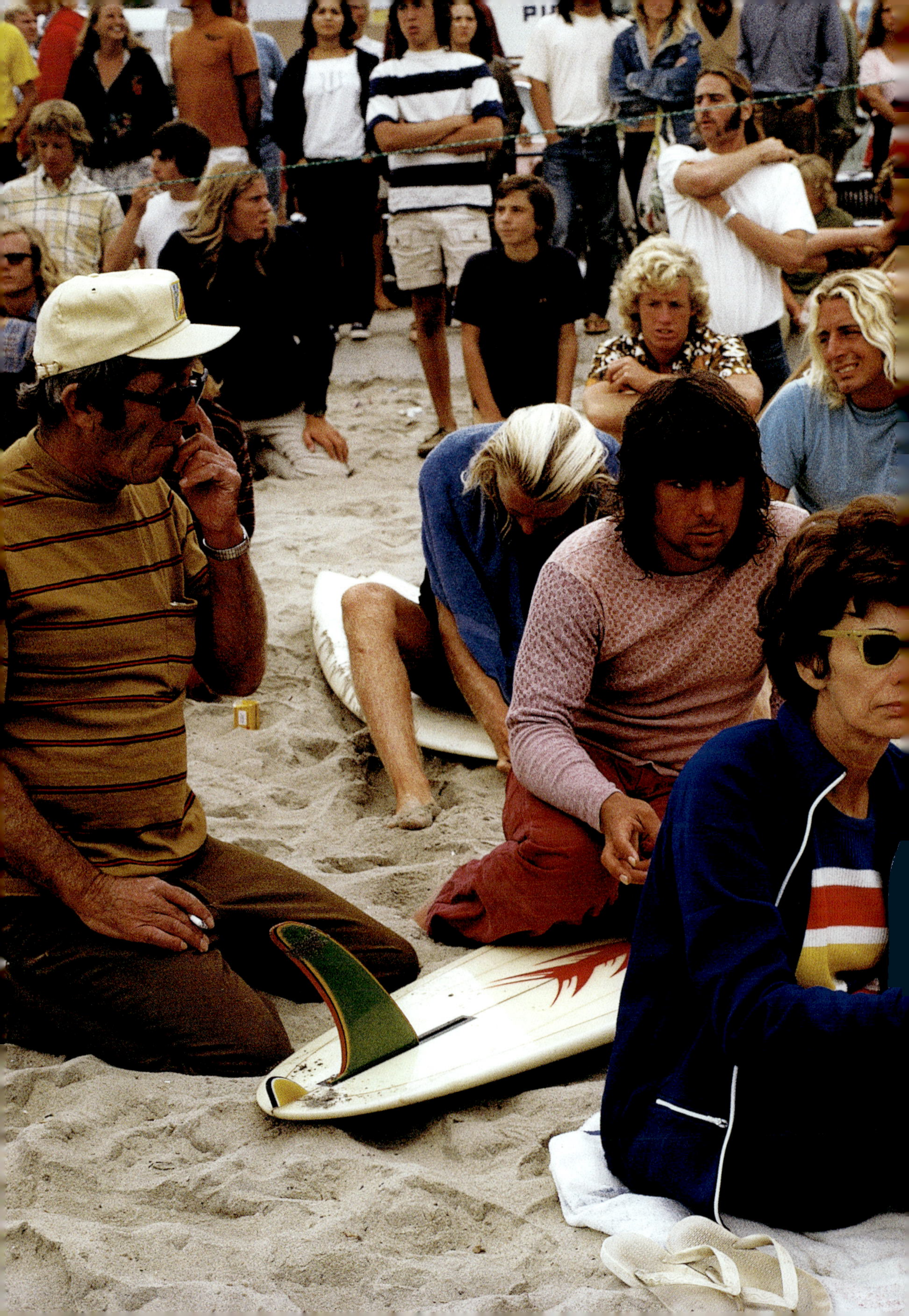

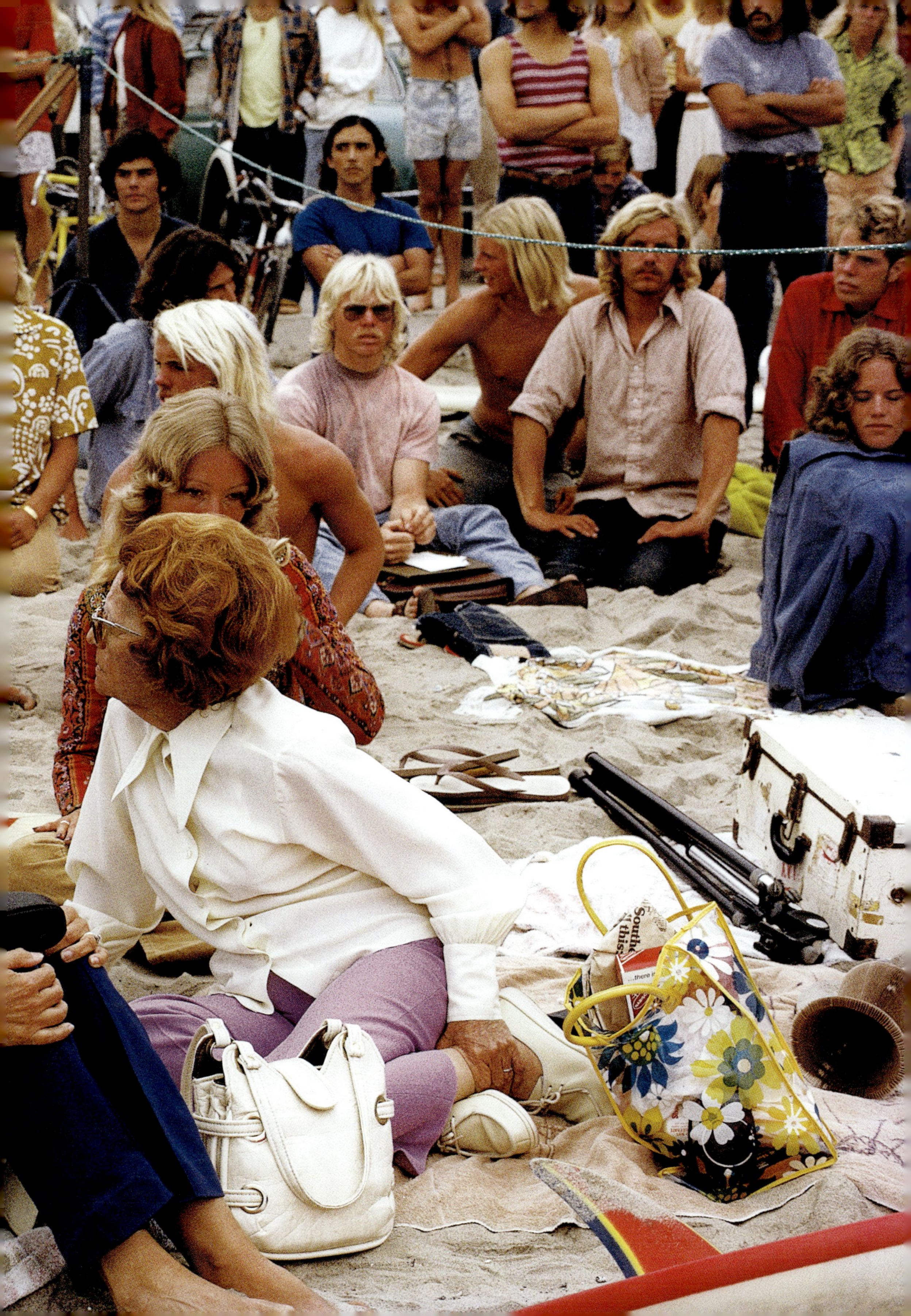

Pages 162–163

**Palos Verdes Cove, 1968**

Wetsuit ad, Lunada Bay. Left to right: Bob Nall, unidentified, Dewey Weber, Caroline Weber, JoJo Perrin, Bobby Kookin.

Werbeanzeige für Neopren-Anzüge, Lunada Bay. Von links nach rechts: Bob Nall, unbekannt, Dewey Weber, Caroline Weber, JoJo Perrin, Bobby Kookin.

Publicité pour des combinaisons en néoprène à Lunada Bay. De gauche à droite: Bob Nall, non identifié Dewey Weber, Caroline Weber, JoJo Perrin et Bobby Kookin.

**Palos Verdes Cove, circa 1965**

Ad for Hang Ten, one of the first and most successful surfwear companies. If you didn't surf, you could at least buy the pose. Left to right: Chuck Linnen, Henry Ford, Mike Doyle, Rickie Wakeland.

Anzeige für Hang Ten, einen der ersten und erfolgreichsten Hersteller von Surfbekleidung. Wer nicht surfte, konnte wenigstens so tun als ob. Von links nach rechts: Chuck Linnen, Henry Ford, Mike Doyle, Rickie Wakeland.

Publicité pour la marque Hang Ten, une des premières et des plus florissantes enseignes de vêtements de surf. Faute de savoir surfer, on pouvait au moins prendre la pose en Hang Ten. De gauche à droite: Chuck Linnen, Henry Ford, Mike Doyle et Rickie Wakeland.

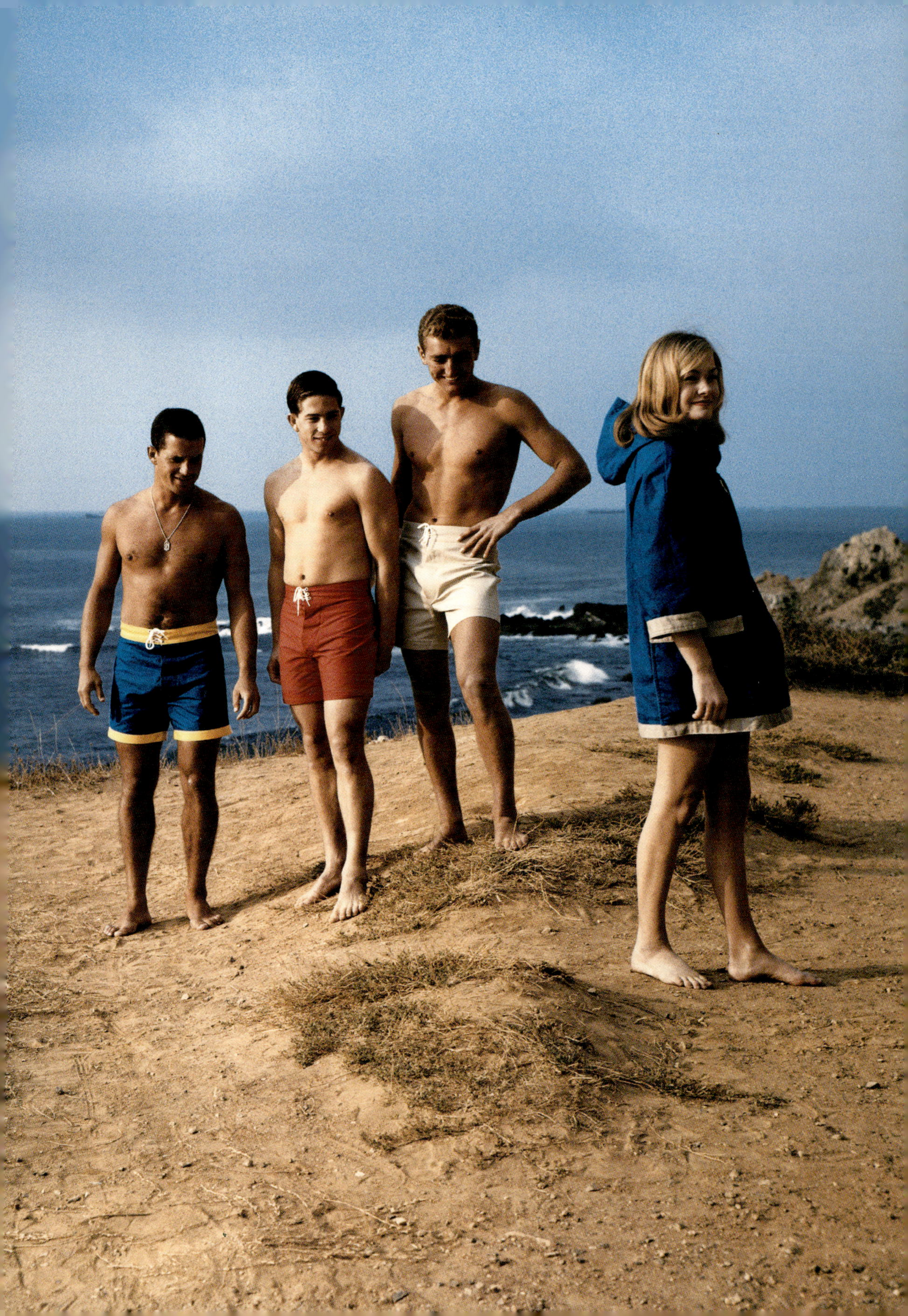

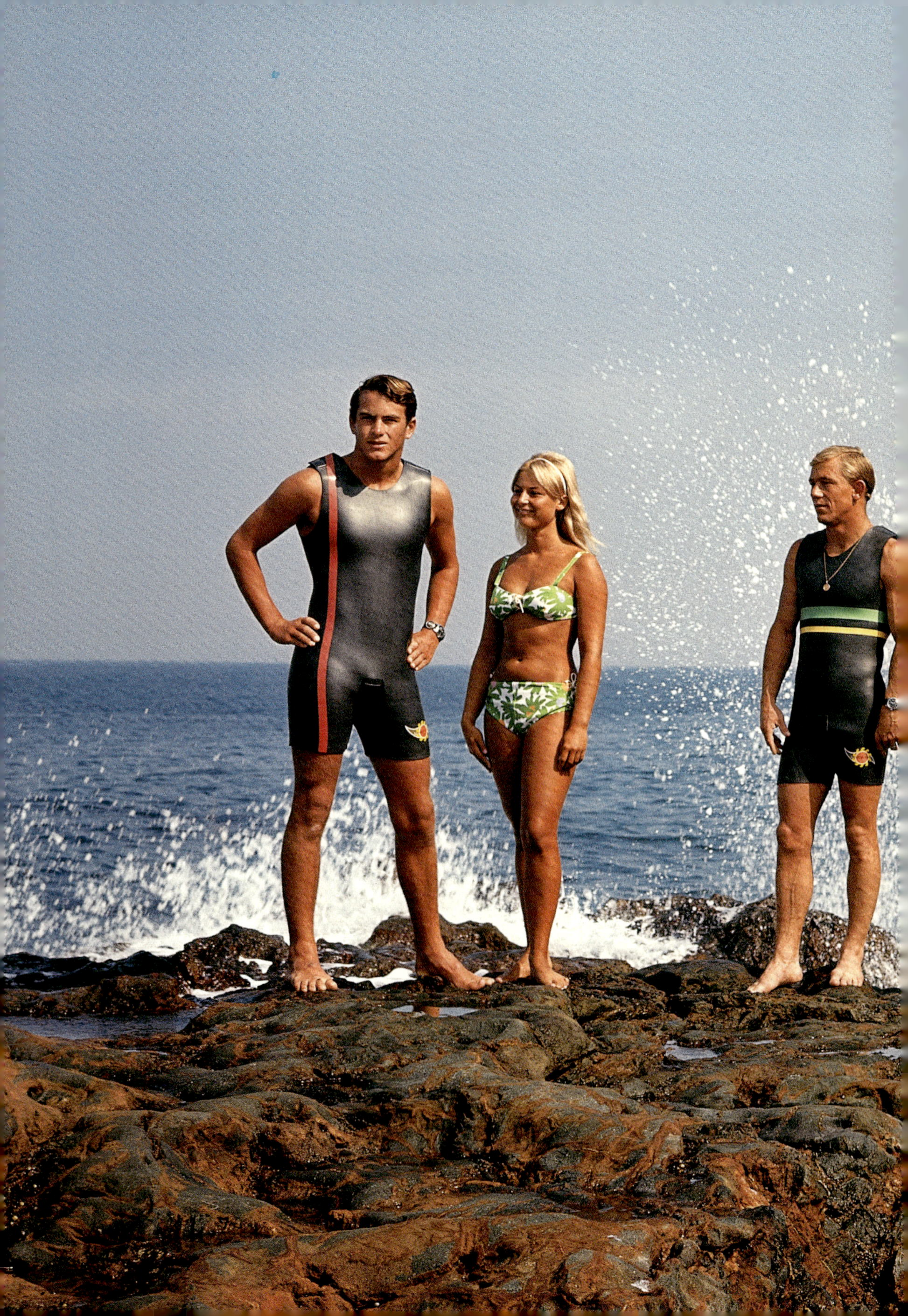

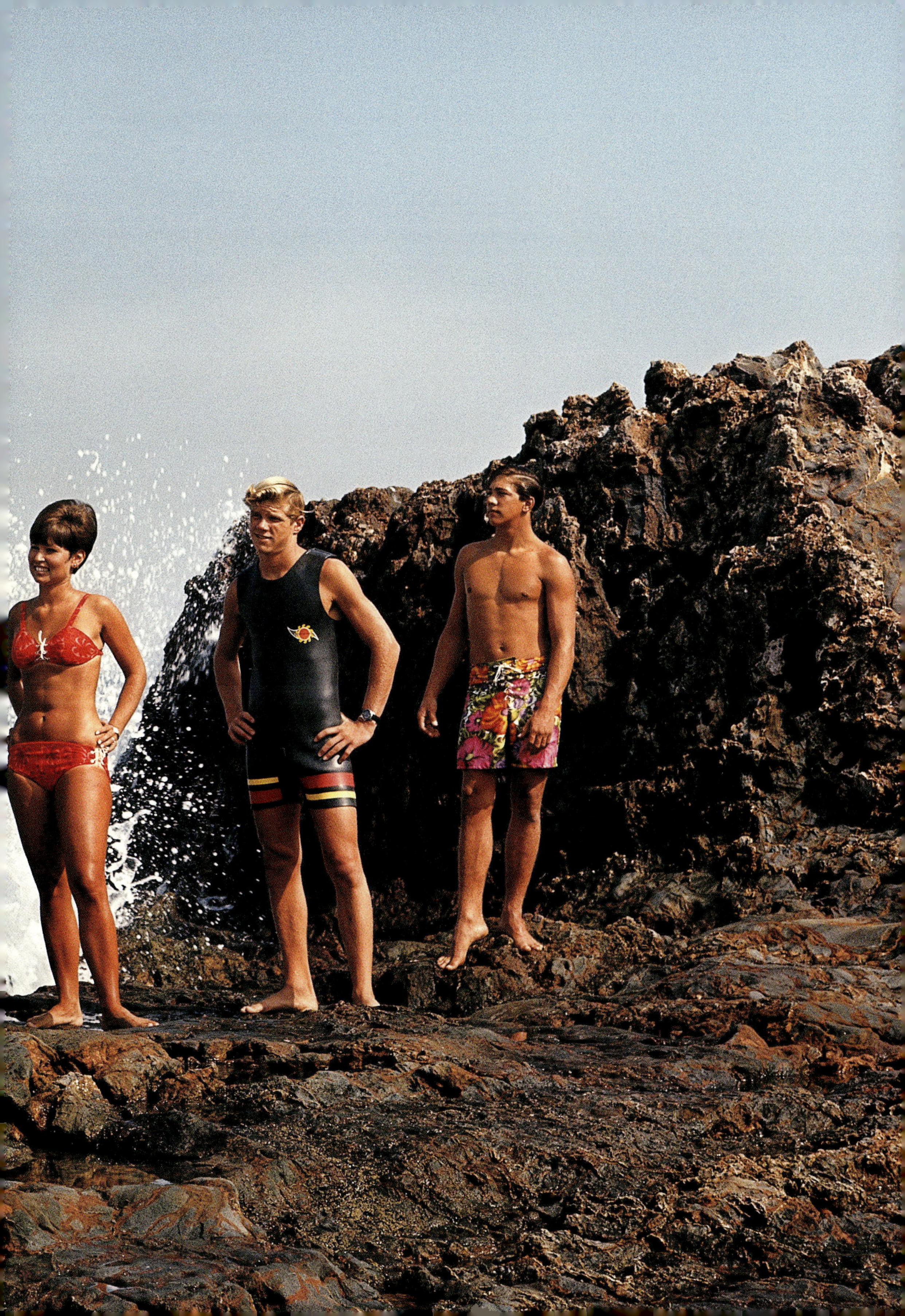

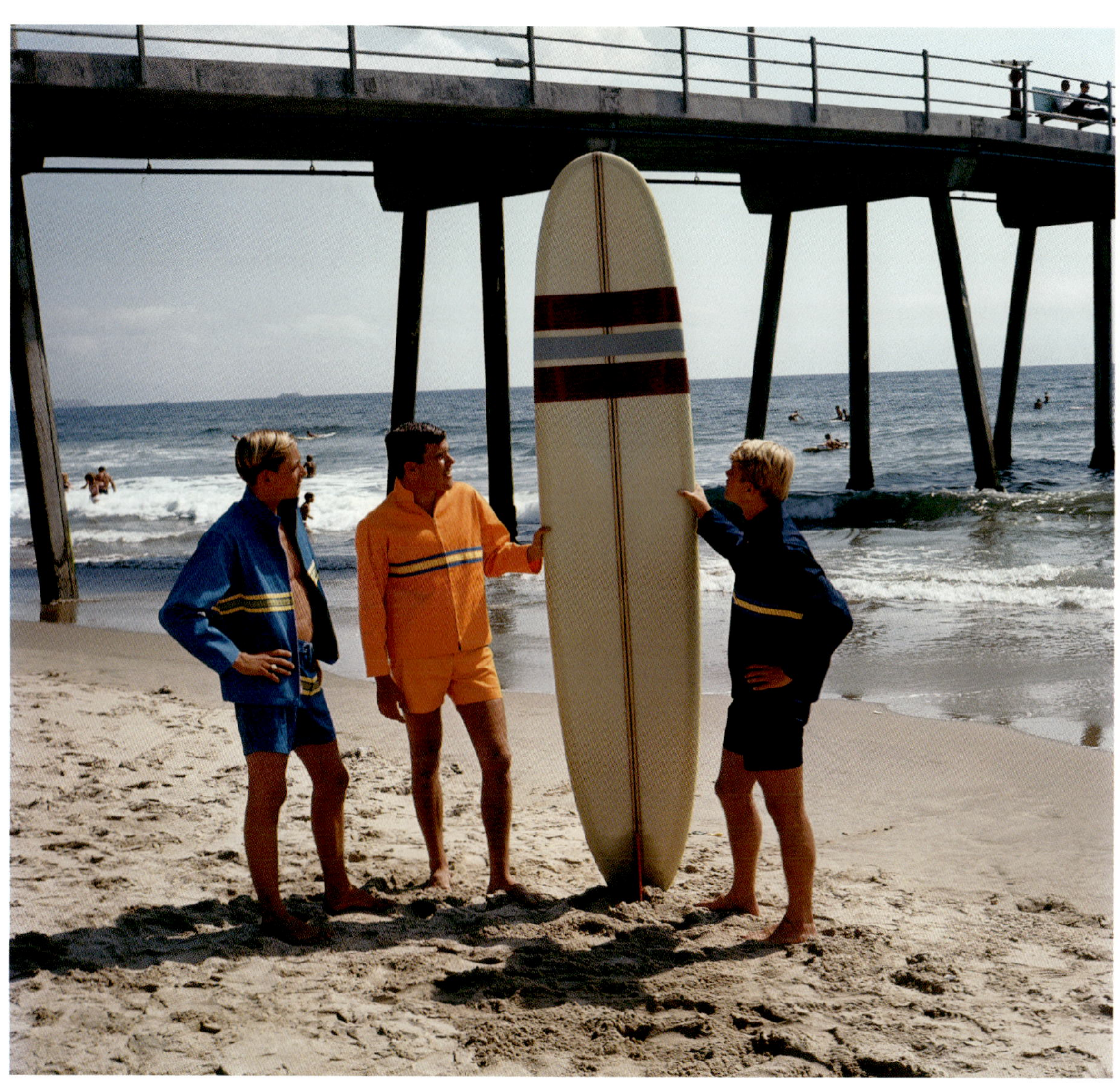

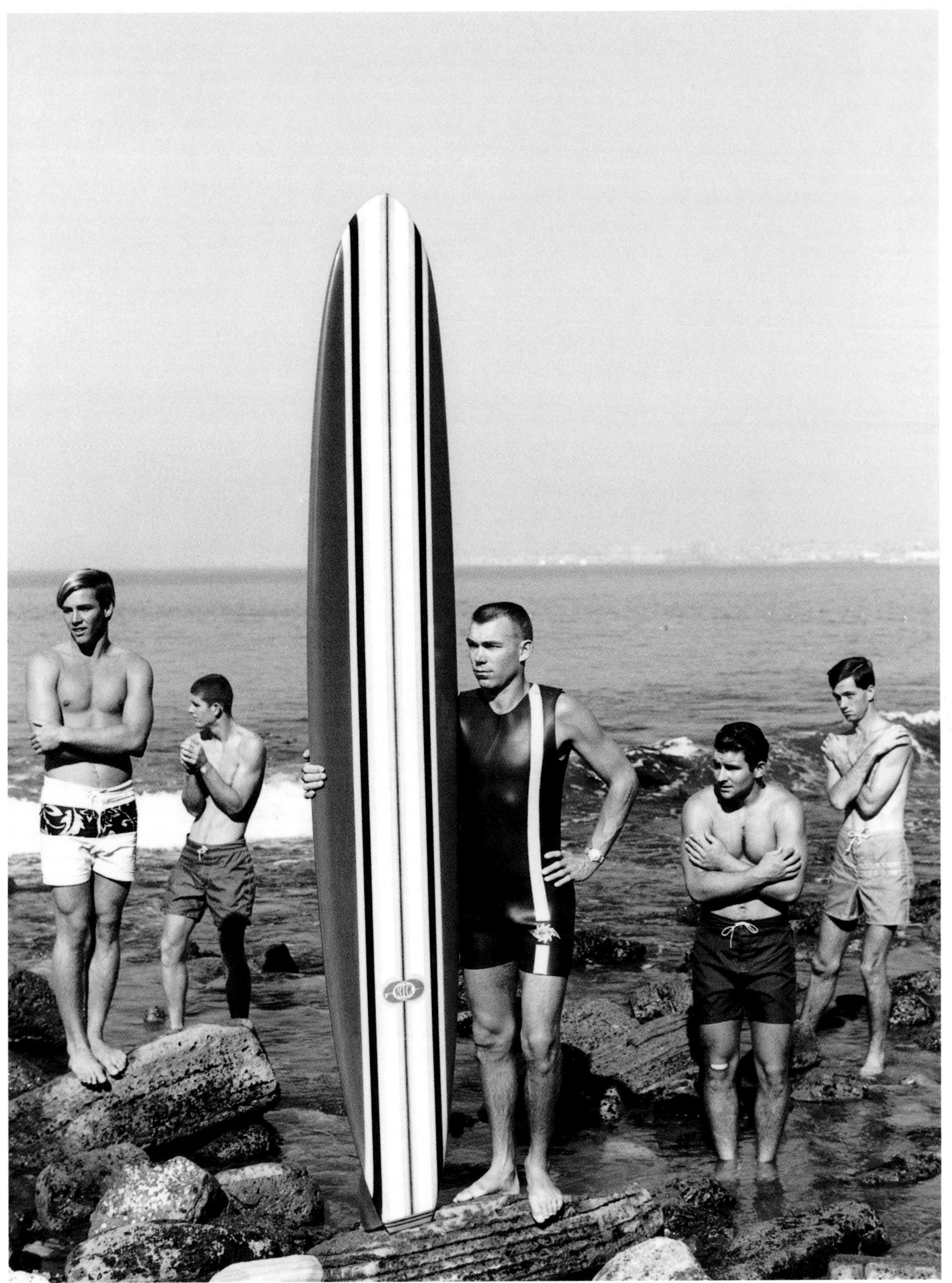

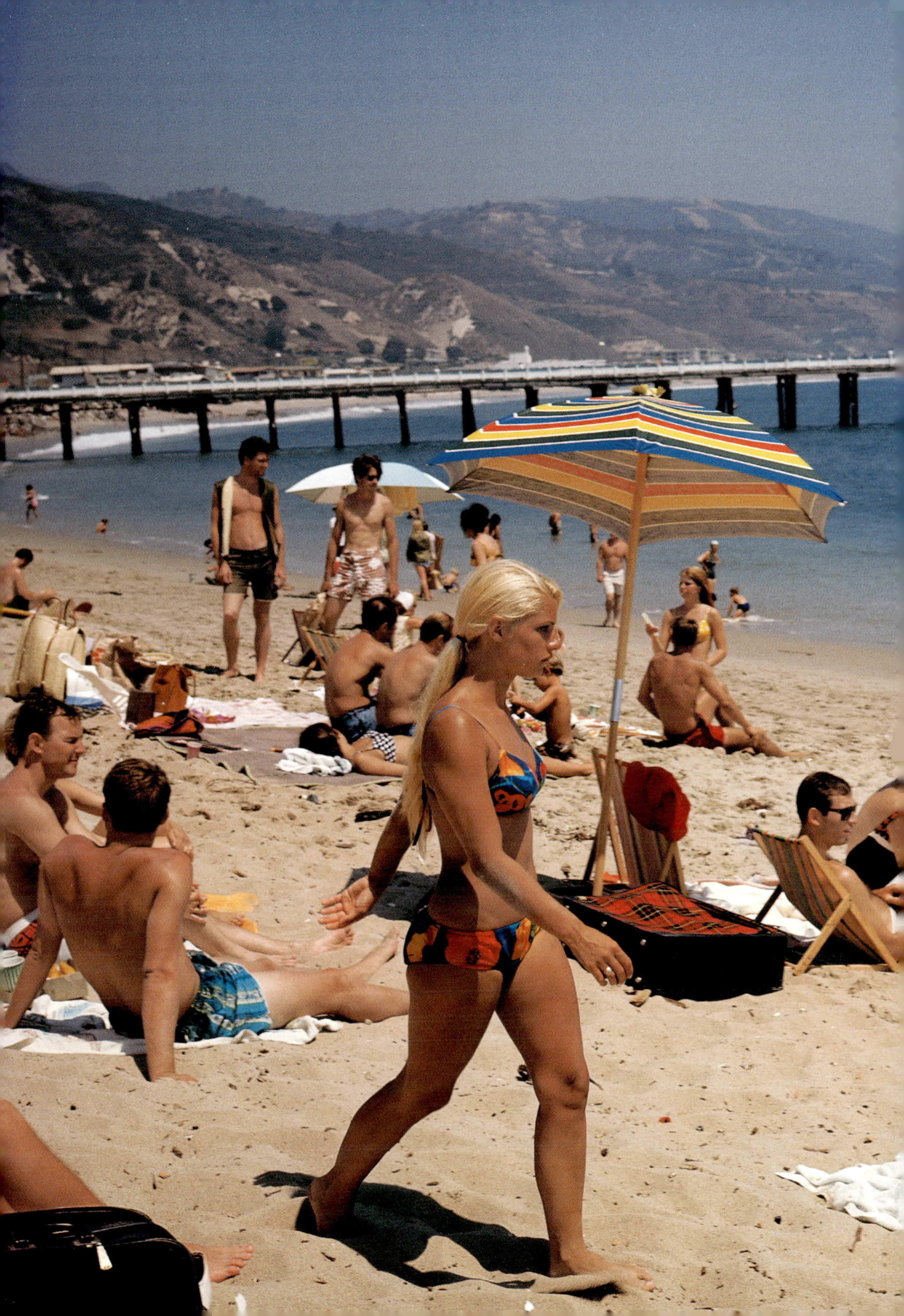

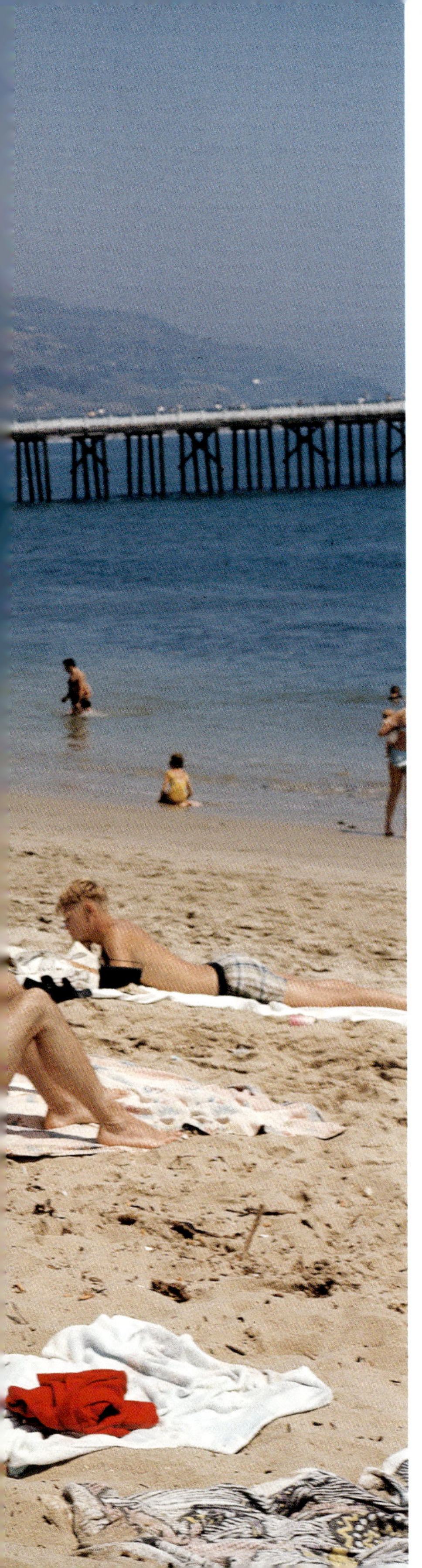

**Diane Bolton, Malibu, 1967**

Bolton was the tandem surfing
partner of Hobie Alter (of Hobie
Surfboards fame).

Bolton war Tandem-Partnerin von
Hobie Alter (bekannt durch Hobie
Surfboards).

Diane Bolton fut la partenaire de
tandem de Hobie Alter (fondateur
de la célèbre marque Hobie
Surfboards).

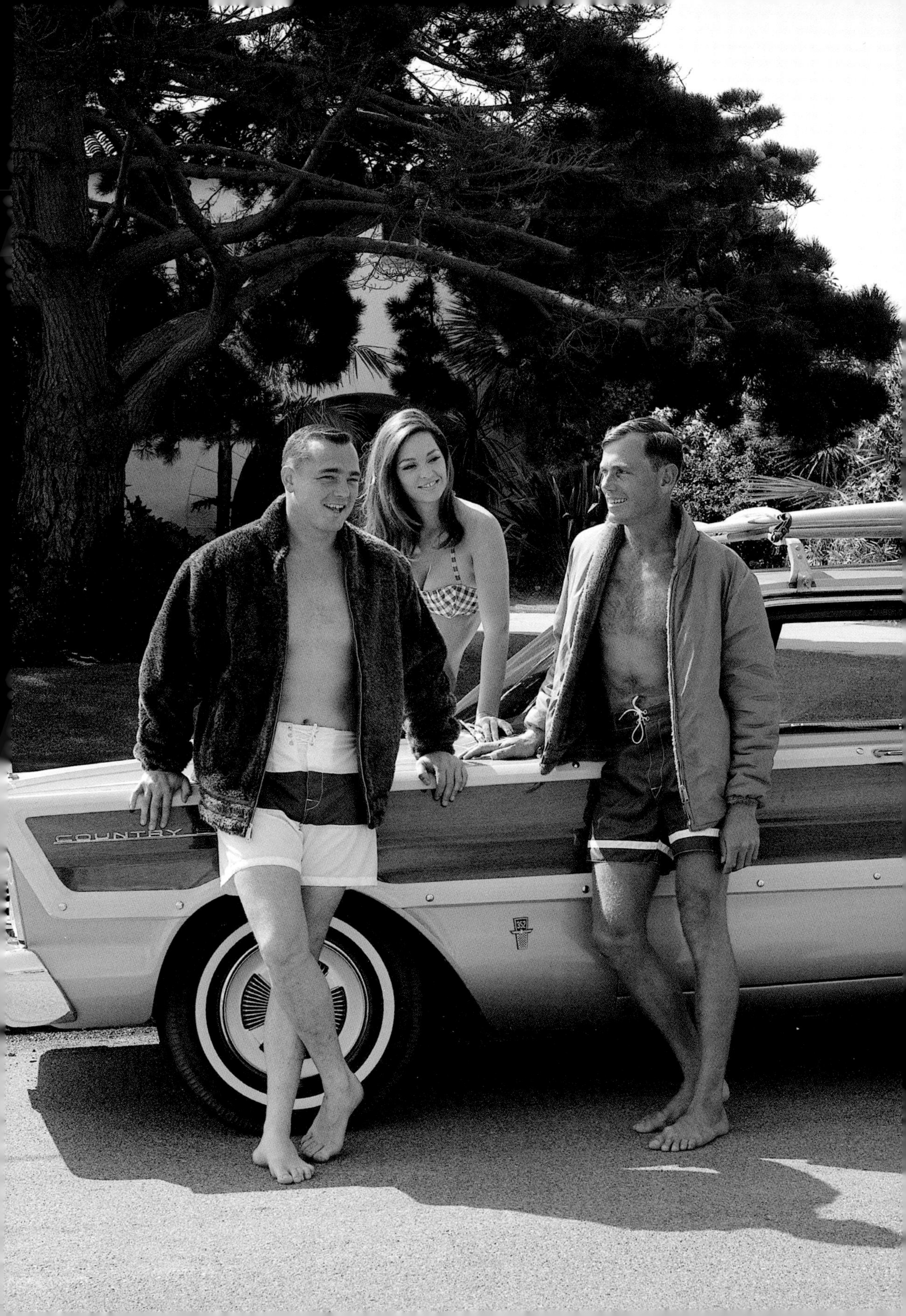

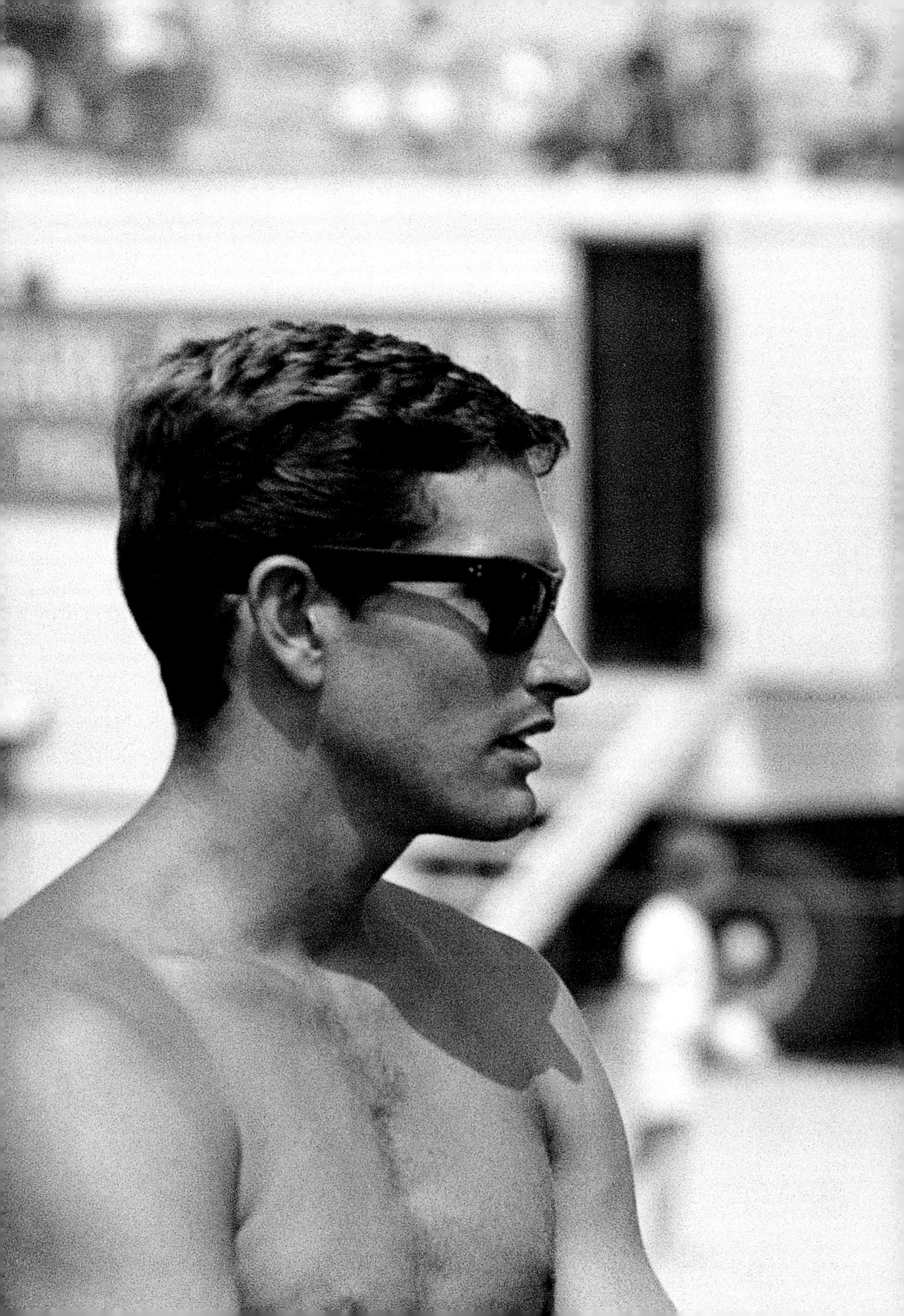

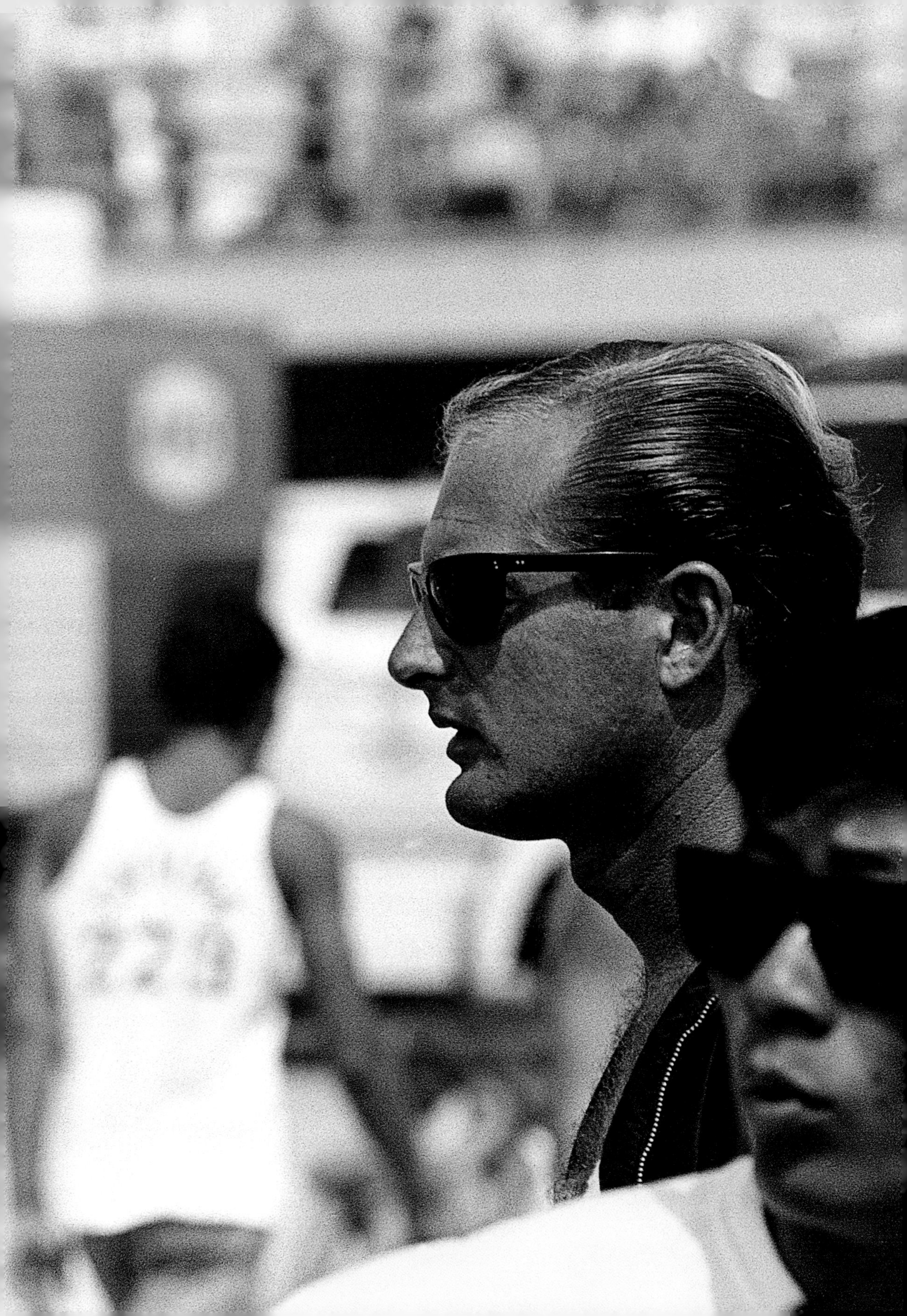

*Pages 170–171*
**Huntington Beach, 1964**

Ray-Ban battle, U.S. Championships. Joey Cabell (left) and
unidentified.

Wer hat die coolere Ray Ban?
U.S. Championships, Joey Cabell
(links) und ein Unbekannter.

« Duel » de Ray-Ban au championnat américain entre Joey Cabell
(à gauche) et son « concurrent »
(non identifié).

*Pages 174–175*
**Huntington Beach, 1964**

Mike Doyle (left) and Mickey
Muñoz represented the pinnacle of
early sixties competitive surfing.
Both would distinguish themselves
as big-wave riders at Waimea Bay.

Mike Doyle (links) und Mickey
Muñoz repräsentierten die Spitze
des Wettkampfsurfens der frühen
Sechziger. Beide glänzten später
als Big-Wave-Surfer in Waimea Bay.

Mike Doyle (à gauche) et Mickey
Muñoz incarnaient le summum de
la compétition de surf au début
des années 1960. Les deux as du
*big-wave riding* se distinguaient
par leur domptage des monstres de
Waimea Bay.

**Rick Griffin, Huntington Beach, 1964**

Rick Griffin, *Surfer* magazine's
twenty-year-old staff cartoonist,
went on to produce iconic posters
for sixties psychedelic bands. The
eye patch is from a near-fatal
accident suffered the year before.

Rick Griffin, der zwanzigjährige
Cartoon-Zeichner der Zeitschrift
*Surfer,* entwarf später Plakate für
psychedelische Sechzigerjahre-
Bands. Die Augenklappe rührt von
einem beinah tödlichen Unfall im
Vorjahr her.

Rick Griffin, le jeune dessinateur
de l'équipe du magazine *Surfer* –
il n'est alors âgé que de vingt ans
– réalise des affiches pour des
groupes psychédéliques des Sixties.
Le bandeau à l'œil rappelle
l'accident dont il a réchappé
de justesse un an plus tôt.

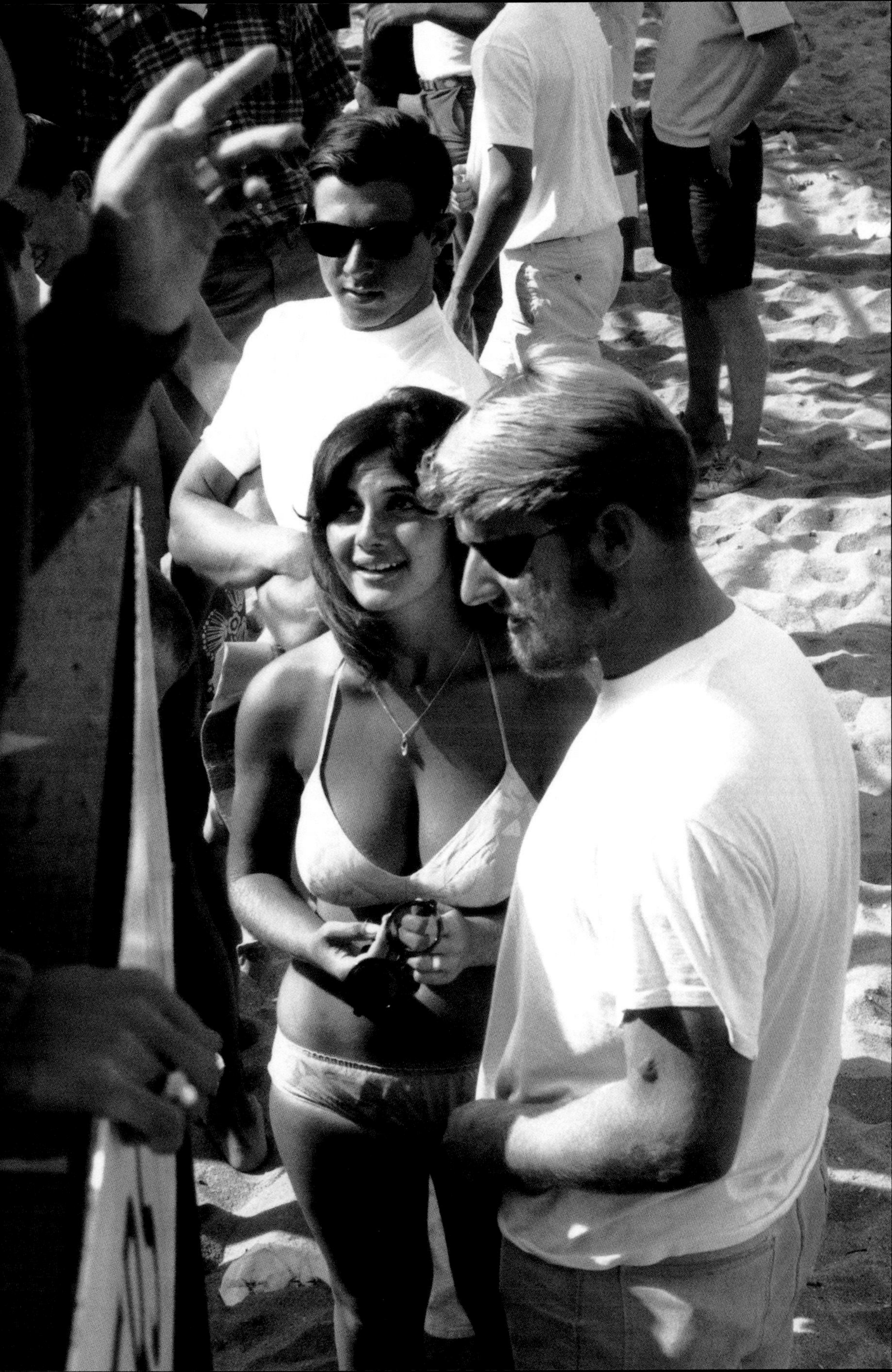

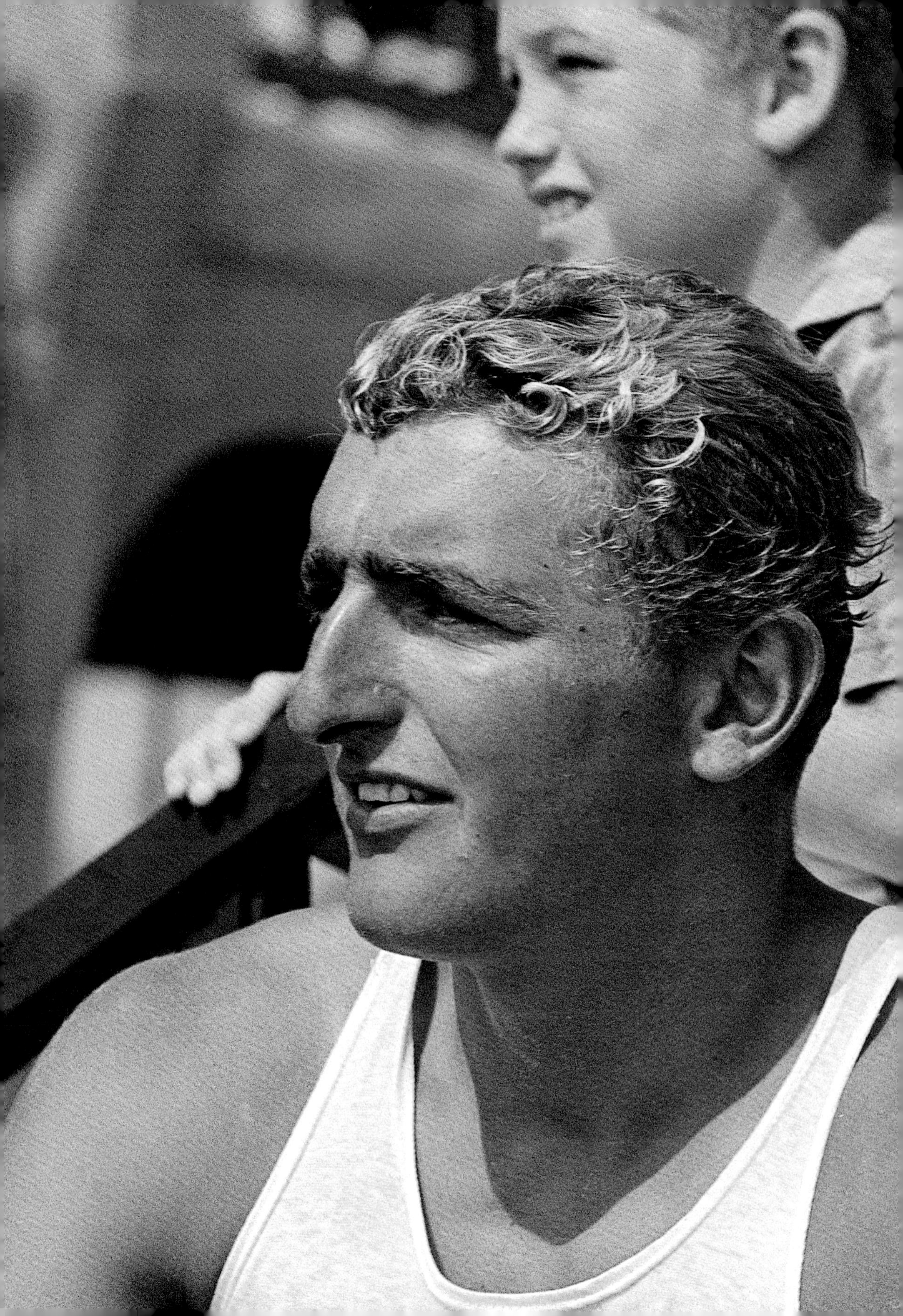

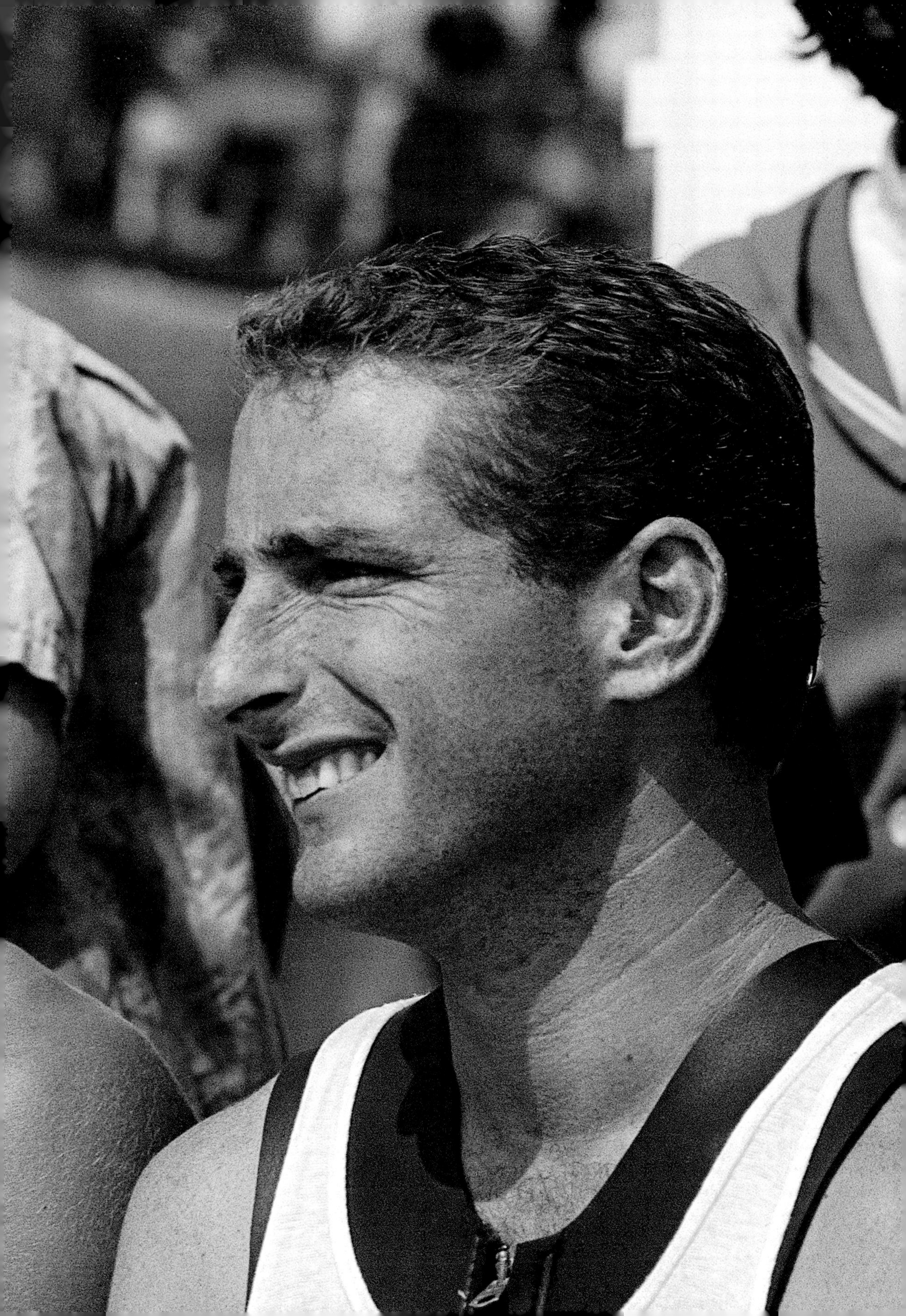

**Gail Yarbrough, Hermosa Beach,
1964**

In ancient Hawaii, women rode
alongside men and even had surf
spots named in their honor.

In Hawaii surften seit Urzeiten
Frauen genau wie Männer,
es wurden sogar Surfspots nach
ihnen benannt.

Jadis, à Hawaï, les femmes
surfaient aux côtés des hommes.
En leur honneur, certains spots
portaient même leurs noms.

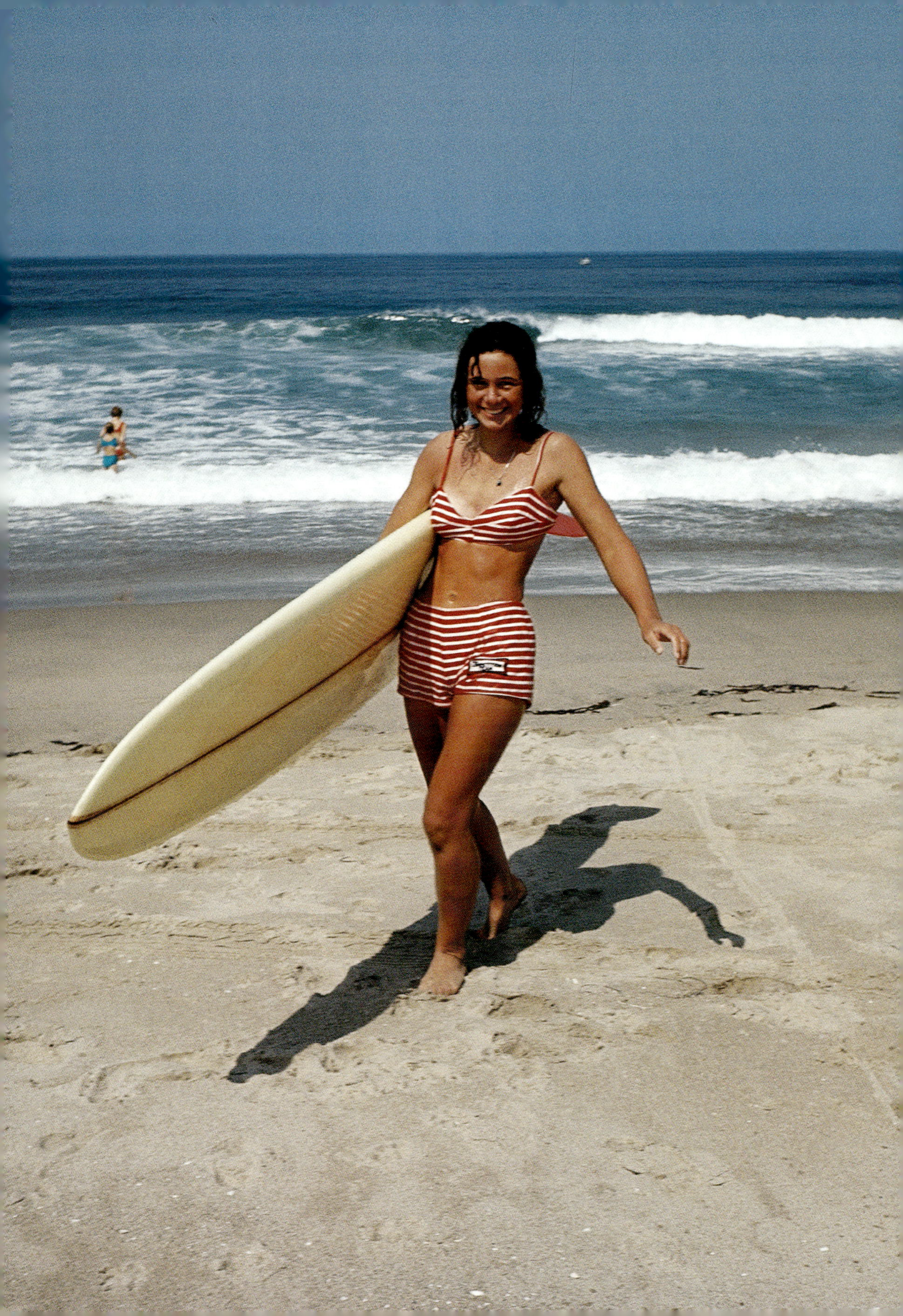

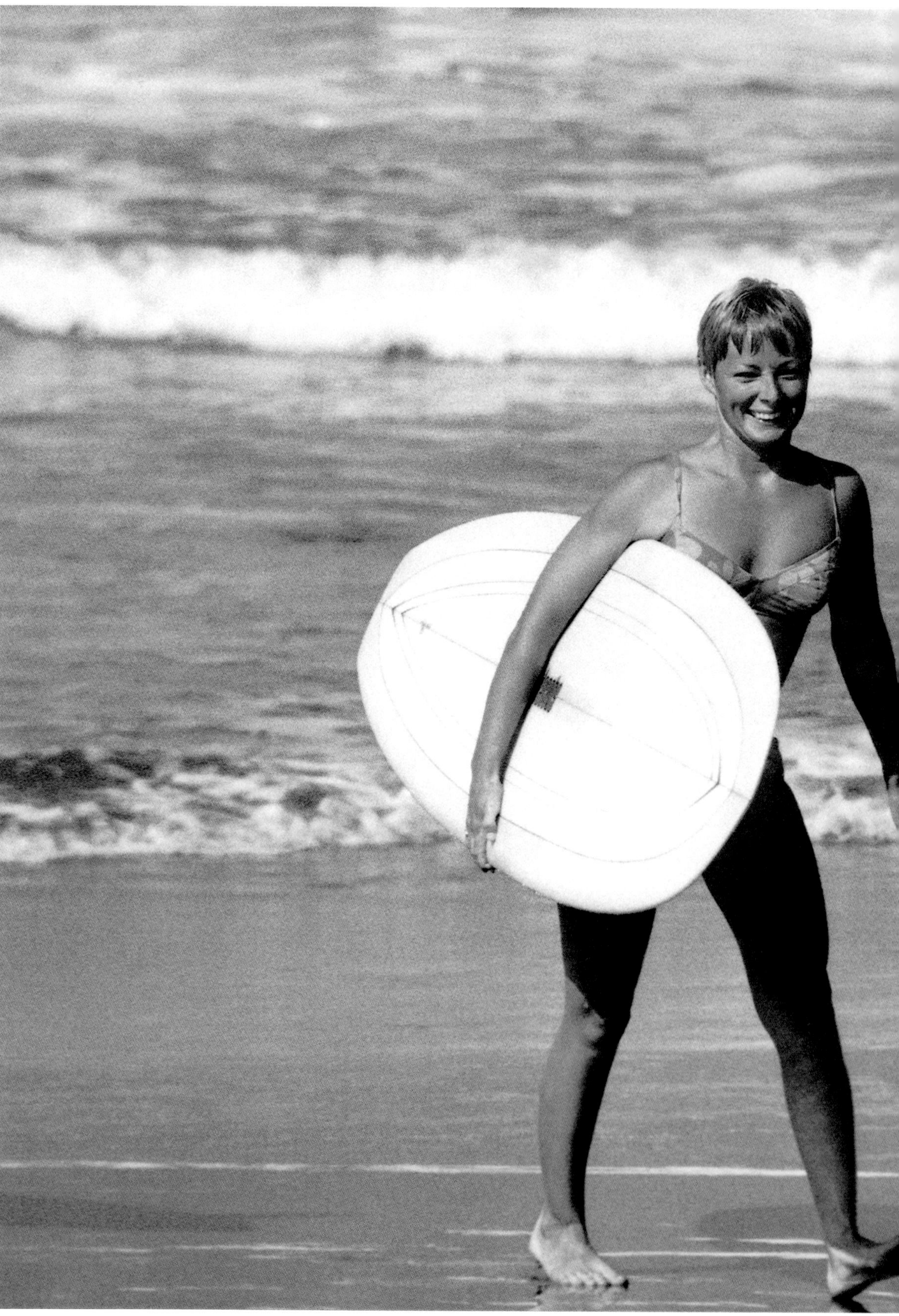

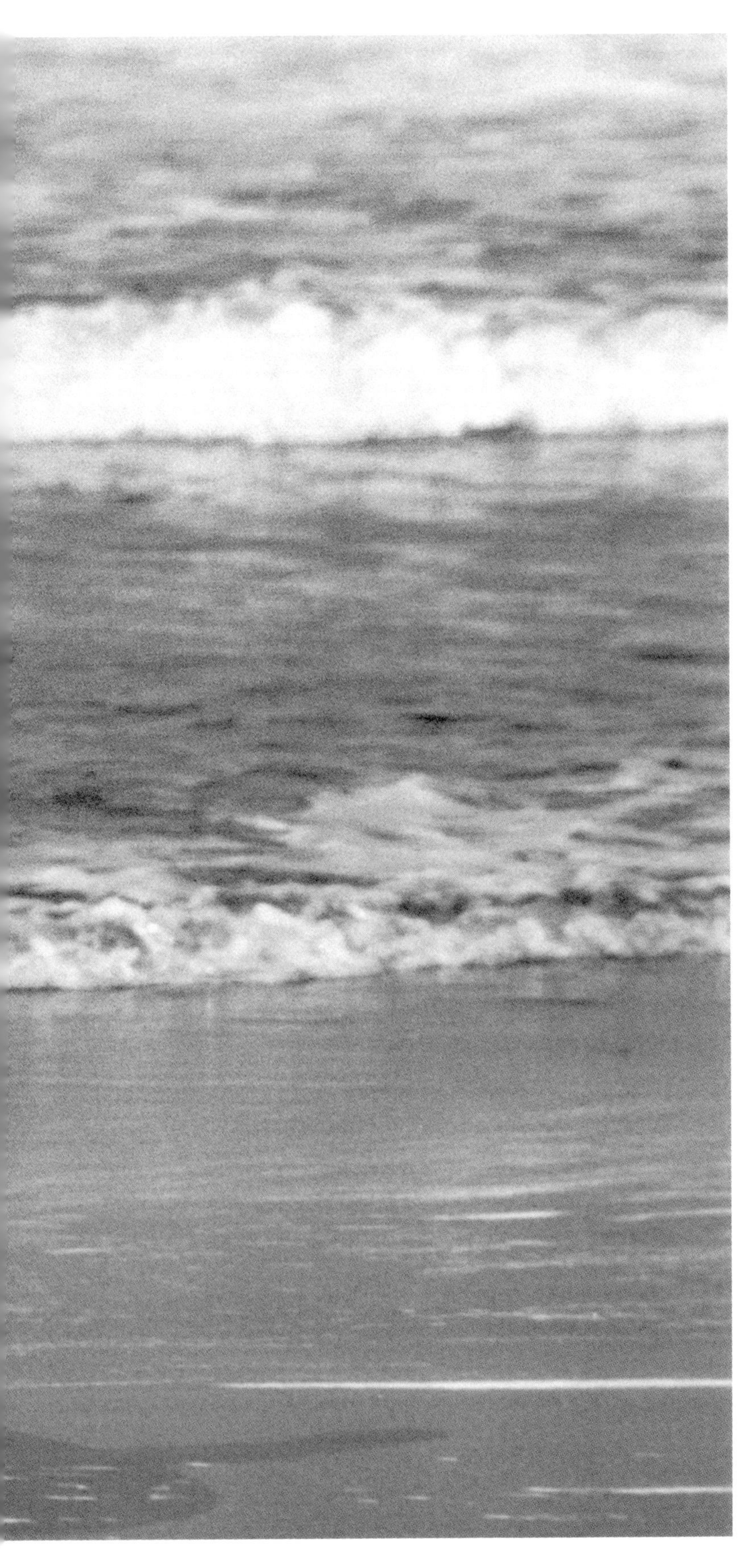

**Linda Benson, Hermosa Beach, 1968**

Powerful and scrappy, Linda Benson broke the gender barrier in 1959 when she became the first woman to ride Waimea Bay's monster waves.

Die kräftige, streitlustige Linda Benson durchbrach die Geschlechterrollen, als sie 1959 als erste Frau die gigantischen Wellen in Waimea Bay ritt.

Battante acharnée, la puissante Linda Benson s'est imposée dans le petit monde des hommes en 1959 en devenant la première femme à surfer les gigantesques vagues de Waimea Bay.

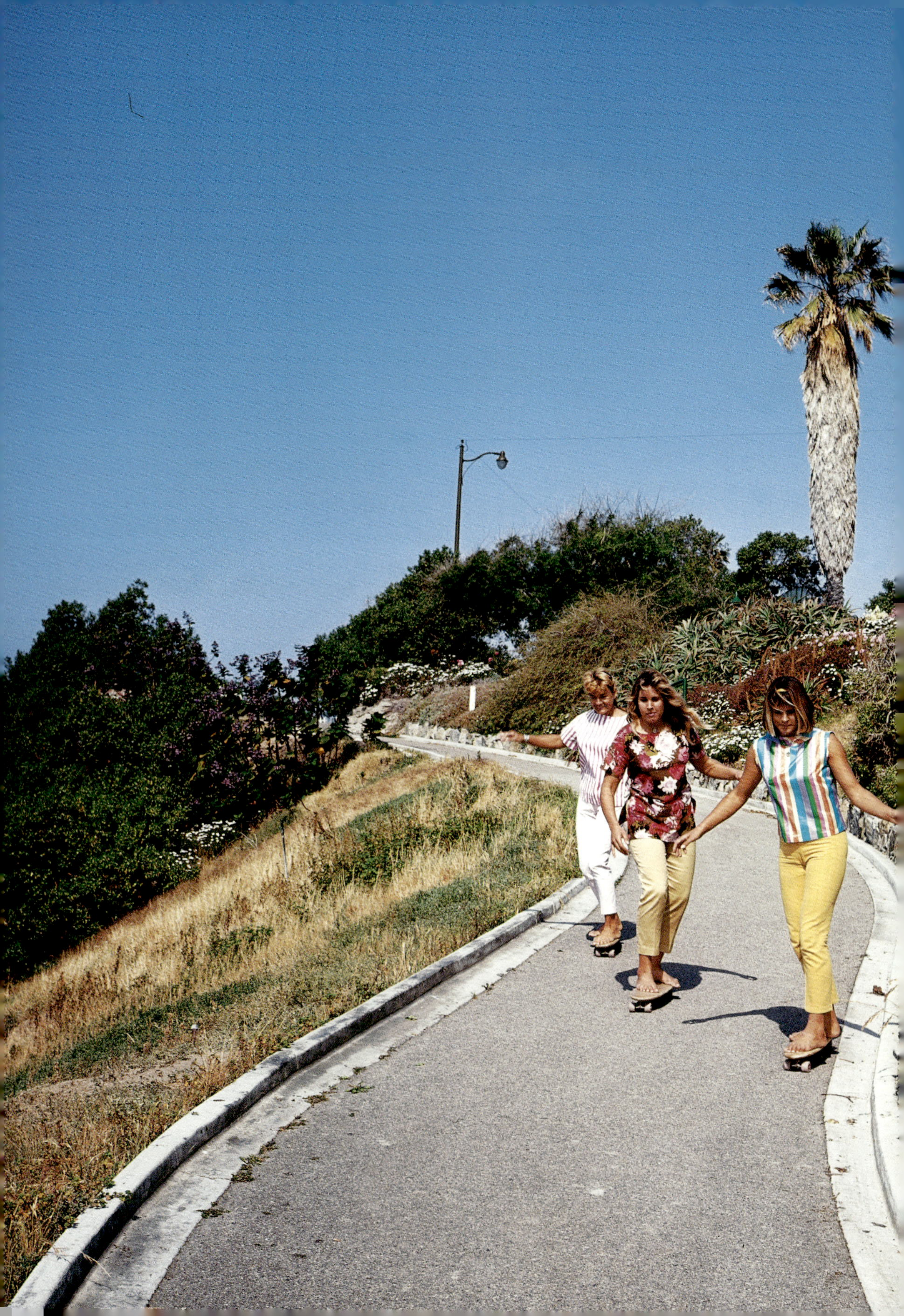

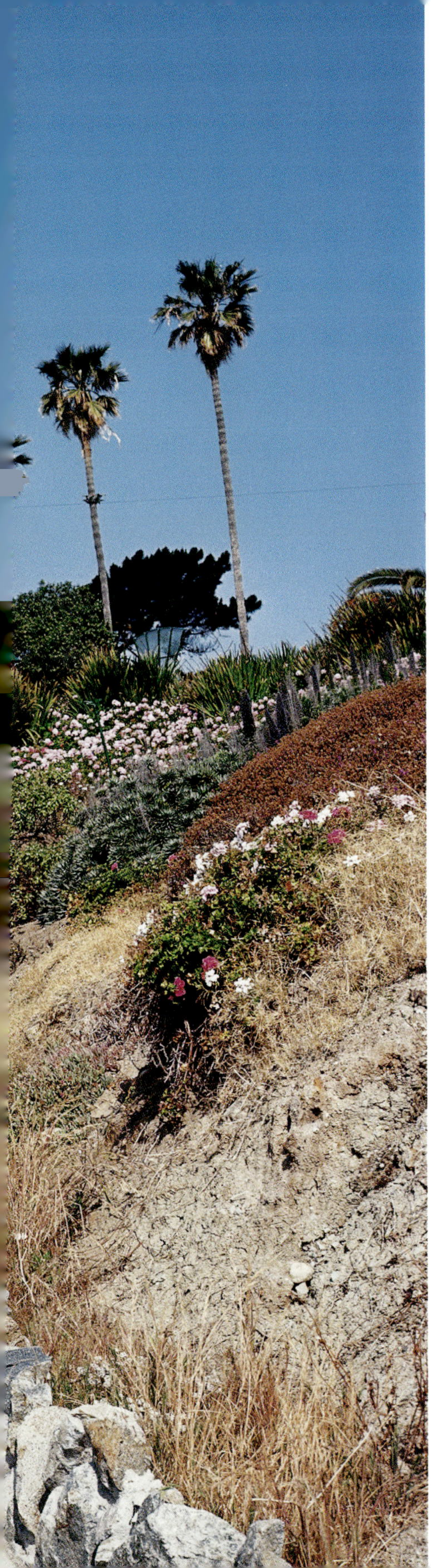



*Page 182*
**Robin Calhoun, Laguna Beach, 1964**

Robin was the youngest of the Calhouns, and an award-winning surfer.

Robin war die Jüngste der Calhouns und eine preisgekrönte Surferin.

Robin, la benjamine des sœurs Calhoun, remporta de nombreuses compétitions.

*Page 183*
**Marge Calhoun, Laguna Beach, 1964**

Marge, the matriarch, was an all-around waterwoman who learned to surf at Malibu in the late forties and later won the women's Makaha Championships.

Marge, die Matriarchin, war eine absolute Wasserfrau, die in den späten Vierzigern in Malibu surfen gelernt hatte und später die Makaha Championships für Frauen gewann.

Marge, la mère, était une athlète complète. Elle apprit le surf à Malibu à la fin des années 1940 et remporta plus tard les épreuves féminines du championnat de Makaha.

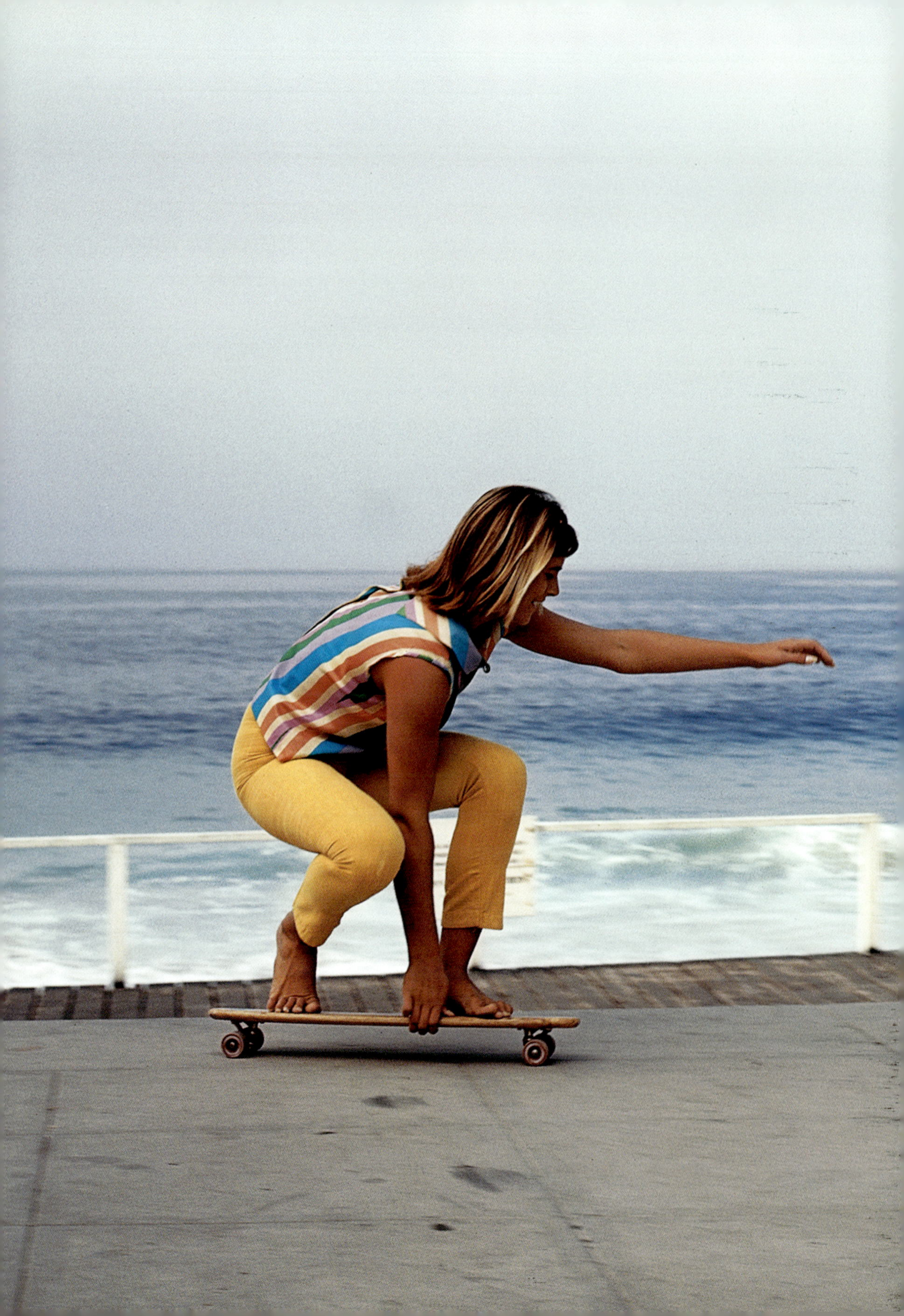

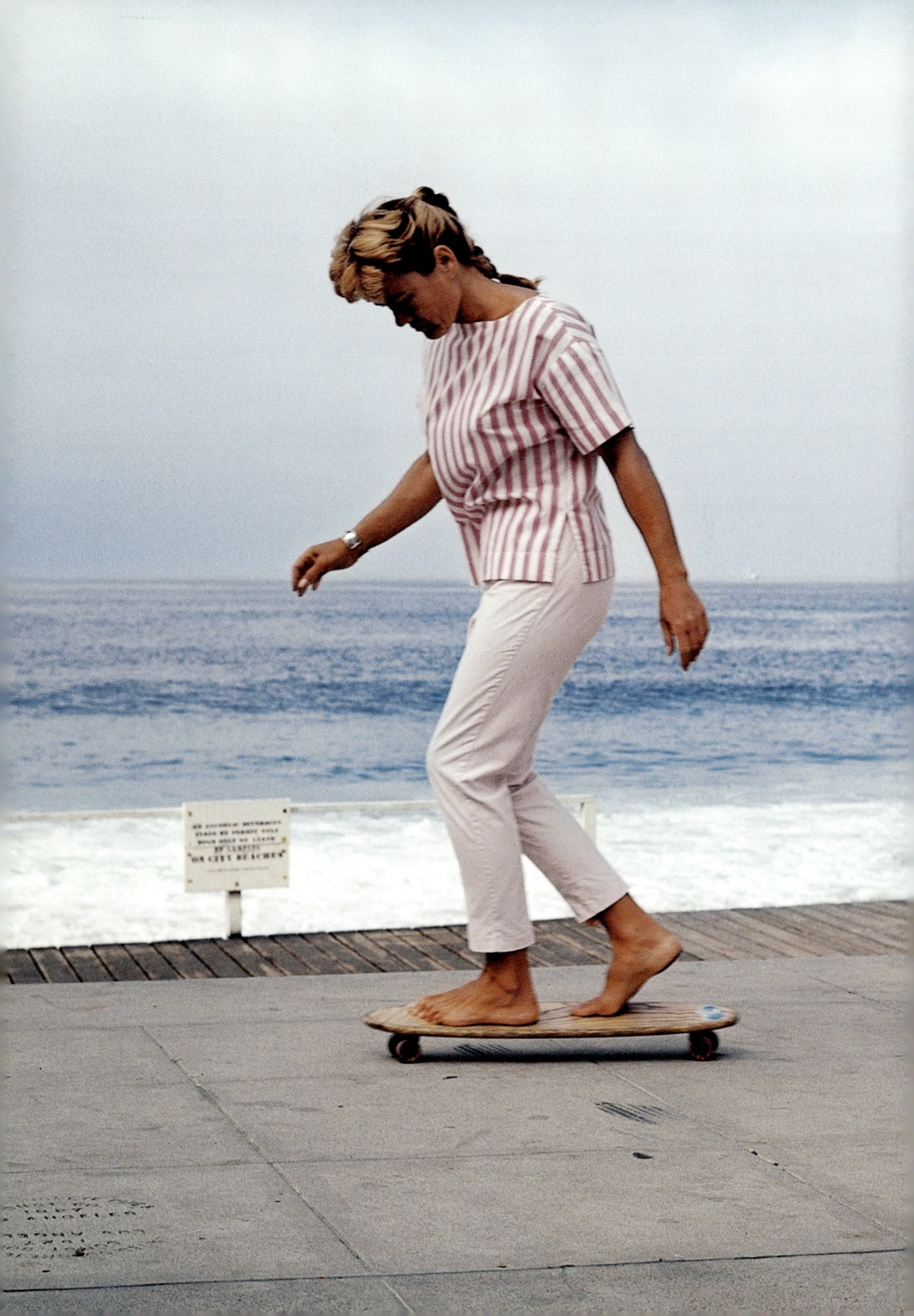

**Rickie Wakeland, Hermosa Beach,
1963**

Rickie Wakeland was one of the
statuesque blondes strategically
placed in ads to help sell
surfboards and bikinis to a fast-
growing mainstream market.

Rickie Wakeland gehörte zu den
stattlichen Blondinen, die in
Anzeigen platziert wurden, um den
Verkauf von Surfbrettern und
Bikinis auf dem schnell wachsen-
den Massenmarkt anzukurbeln.

Rickie Wakeland était une de ces
belles blondes qui prêtaient leurs
silhouettes pour des publicités
destinées à booster le marché en
plein essor des planches de surf
et des bikinis.

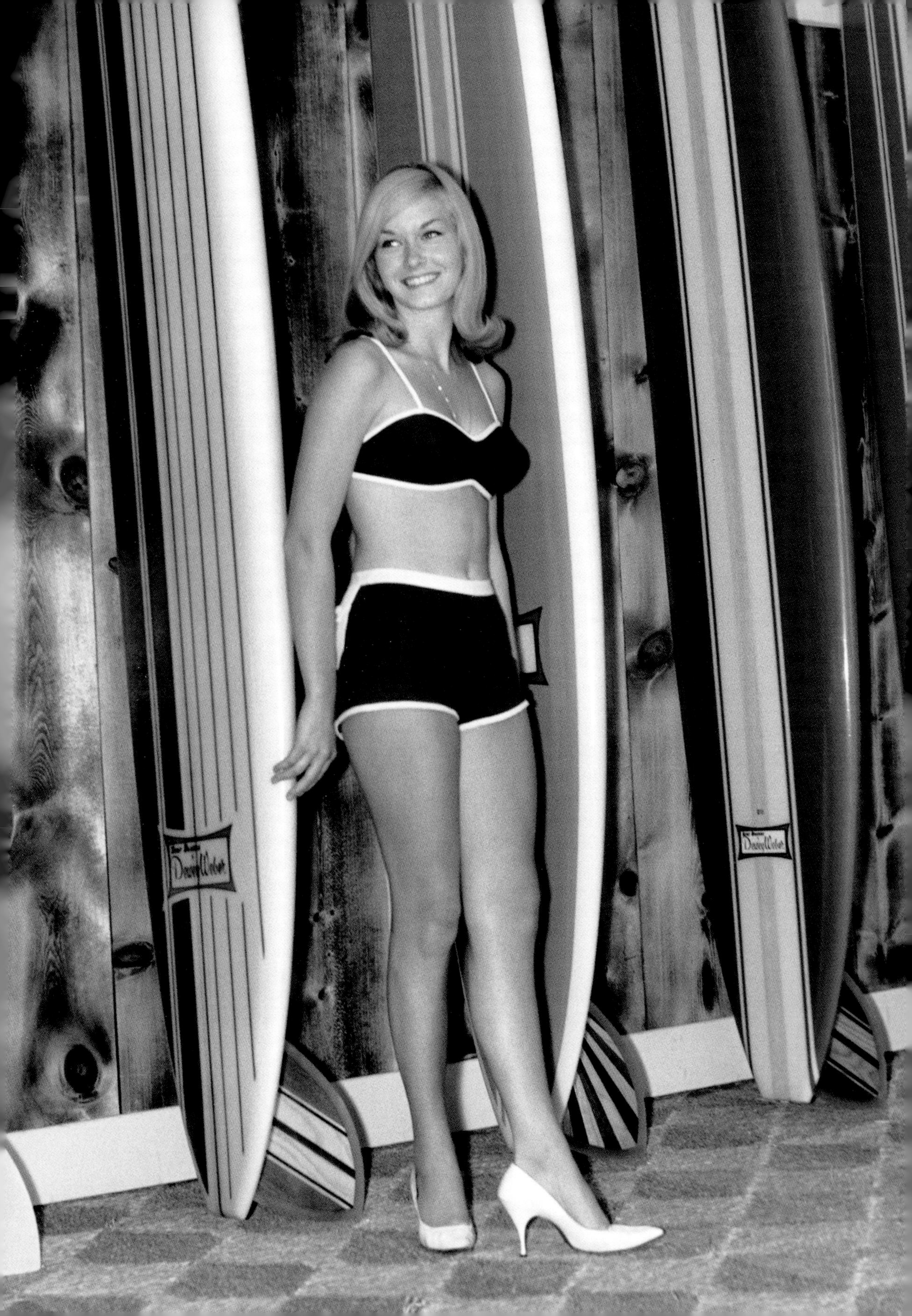

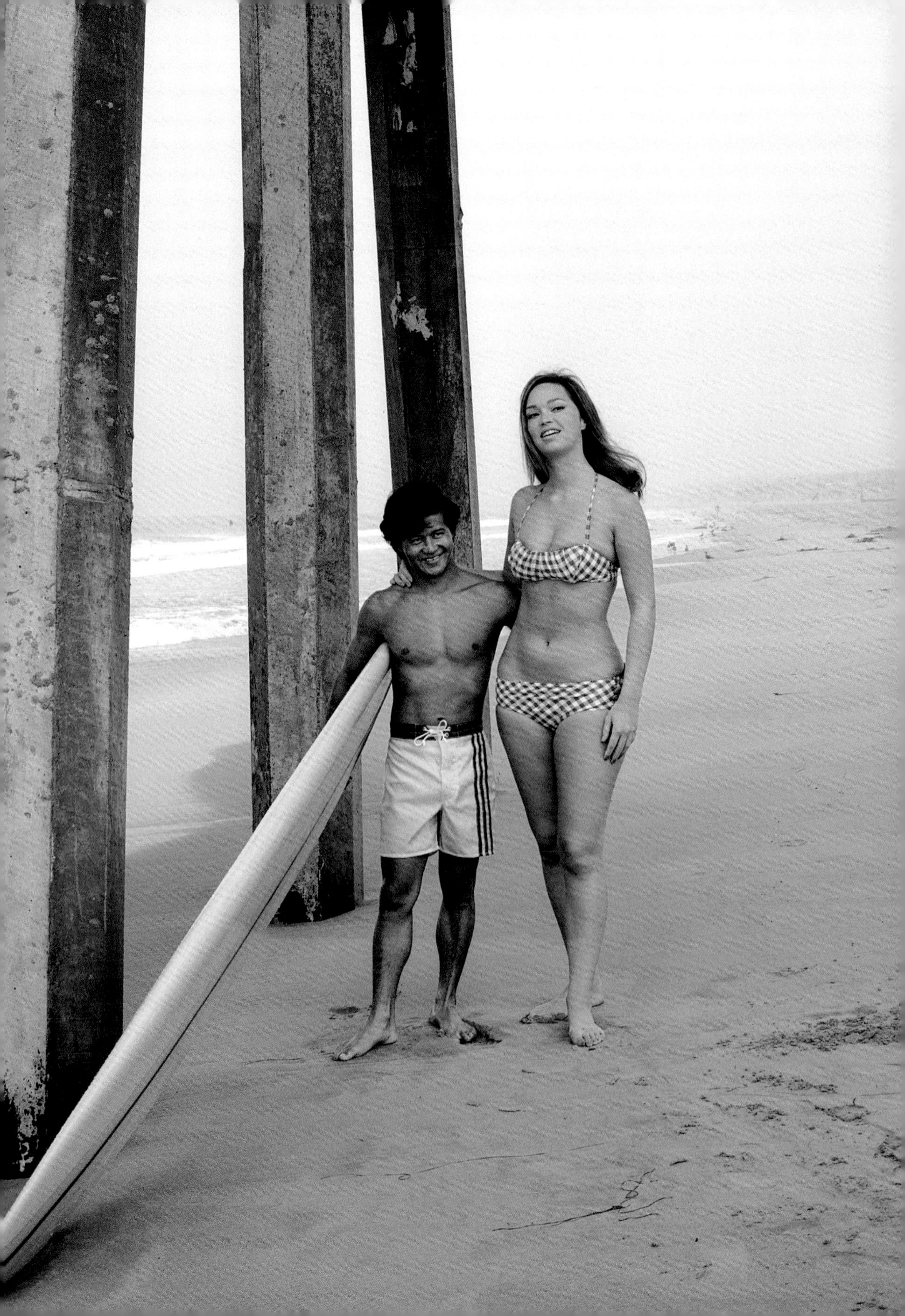

**Donald Takayama, Bettina Brenna,
Hermosa Beach, 1965**

Renowned surfer and board
shaper Takayama, shown here
clowning with Brenna, learned
to surf at age seven from the
legendary Waikiki Beach Boys.

Der berühmte Surfer und Board-
Shaper Takayama, der hier mit
Brenna herumalbert, lernte mit
sieben Jahren das Surfen von den
legendären Waikiki Beach Boys.

Surfeur et shaper de renom, Donald
Takayama, que l'on voit ici en train
de faire le pitre avec Bettina
Brenna, apprit à surfer dès l'âge
de sept ans auprès des légendaires
Waikiki Beach Boys.

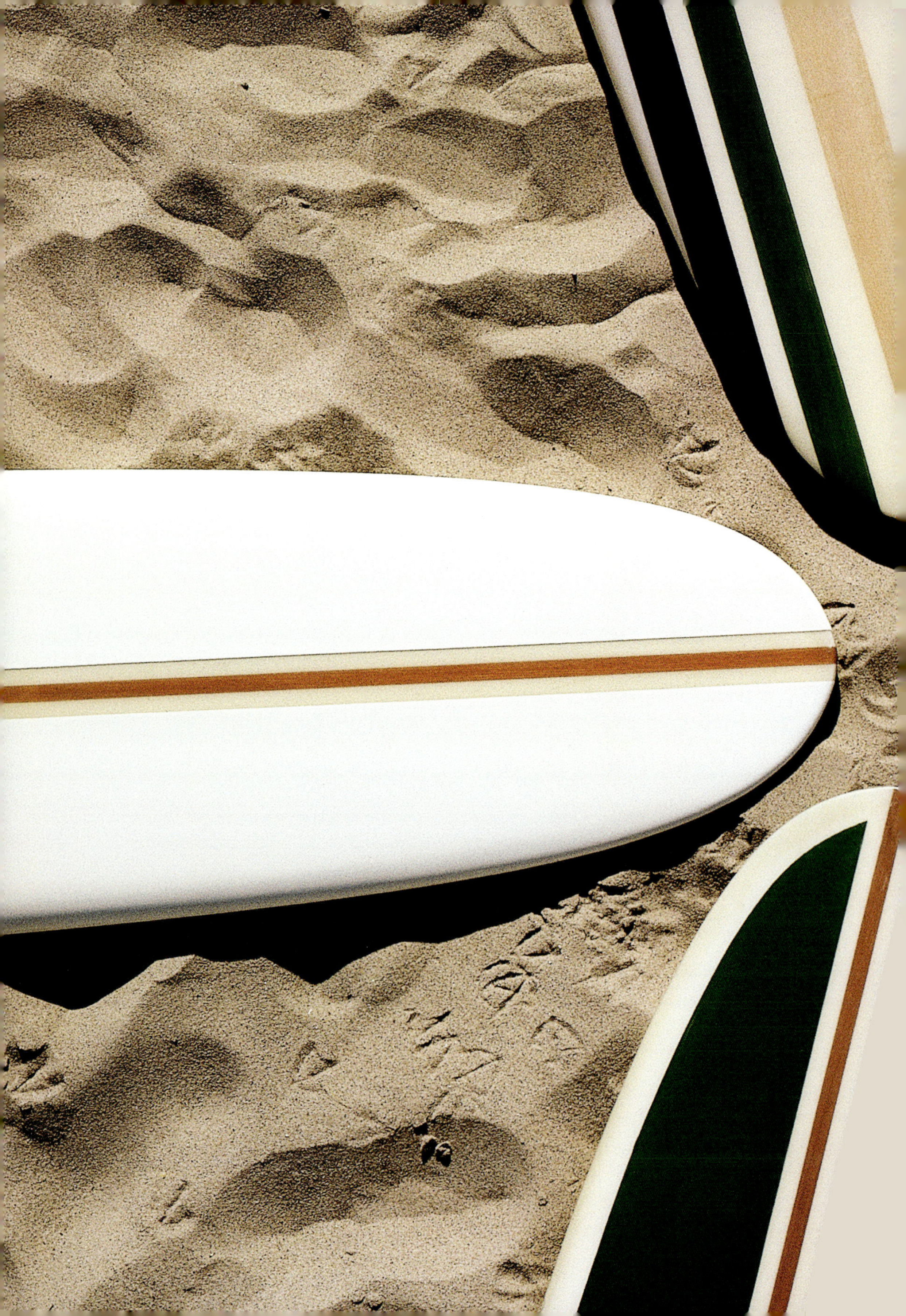

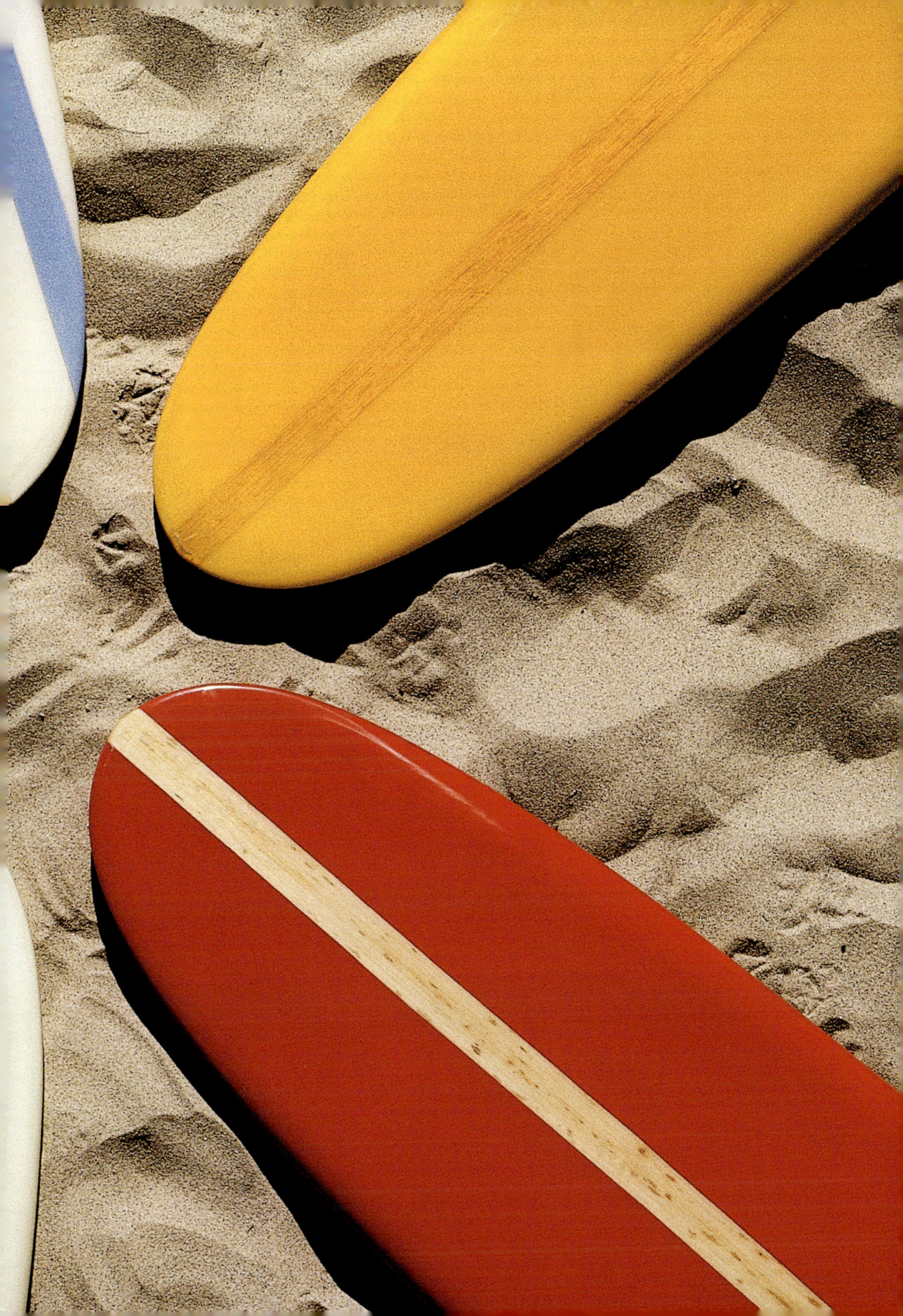

Pages 188–189
**Jacobs Surfboards Advertising Shoot,
Hermosa Beach, 1963**

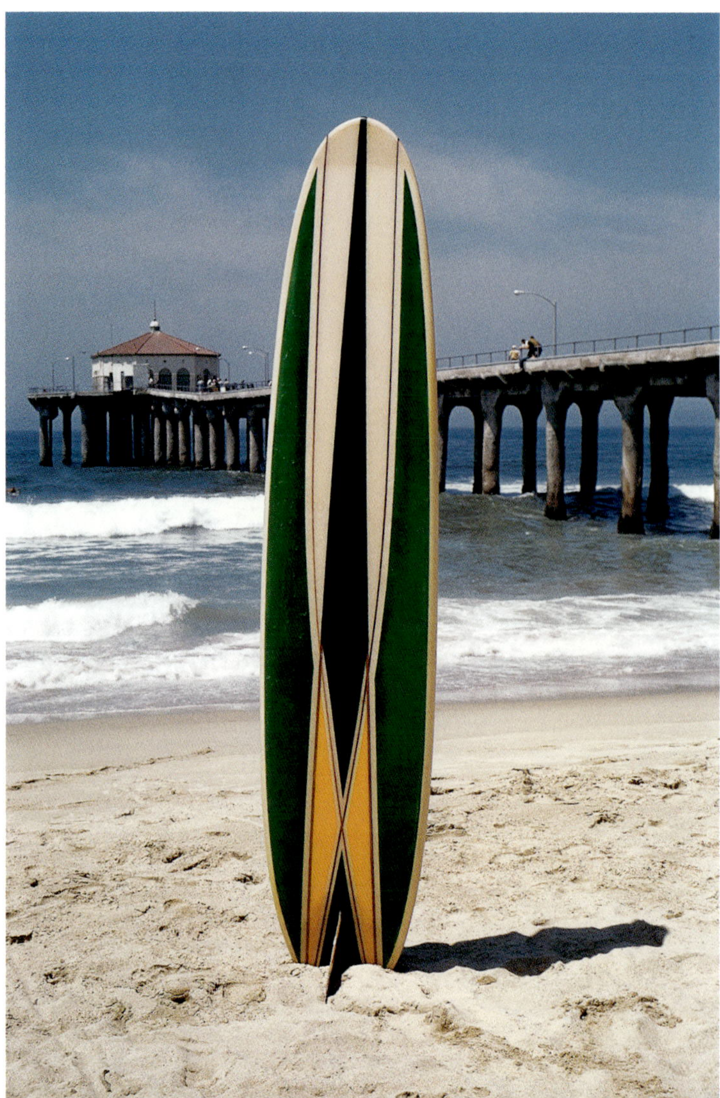

### Manhattan Beach, 1962

Using techniques borrowed from
hot rod customizers, surfers
personalized their boards with
vibrant colors and imagery.

Mit Techniken, die von den auf-
gemotzten Hot Rods abgeschaut
waren, gestalteten Surfer ihre
Bretter individuell mit leuchtenden
Farben und Bildern.

À l'aide de techniques empruntées
au tuning des *hot rods,* les surfeurs
personnalisaient leurs planches
avec des motifs expressifs et des
couleurs vibrantes.

### Mike Doyle, Hermosa Beach, 1963

Doyle was known as "Tiki Mike"
for his skill at carving wooden tikis
as a teenager. These days he's an
accomplished artist.

Doyle wurde auch „Tiki Mike"
genannt, da er als Teenager
besonders gut im Schnitzen von
hölzernen Tikis war. Heute ist er
ein anerkannter Künstler.

Mike Doyle avait reçu le sobriquet
« Tiki Mike » en raison de son talent
précoce de sculpteur de tikis.
Aujourd'hui, il est reconnu comme
un artiste accompli.

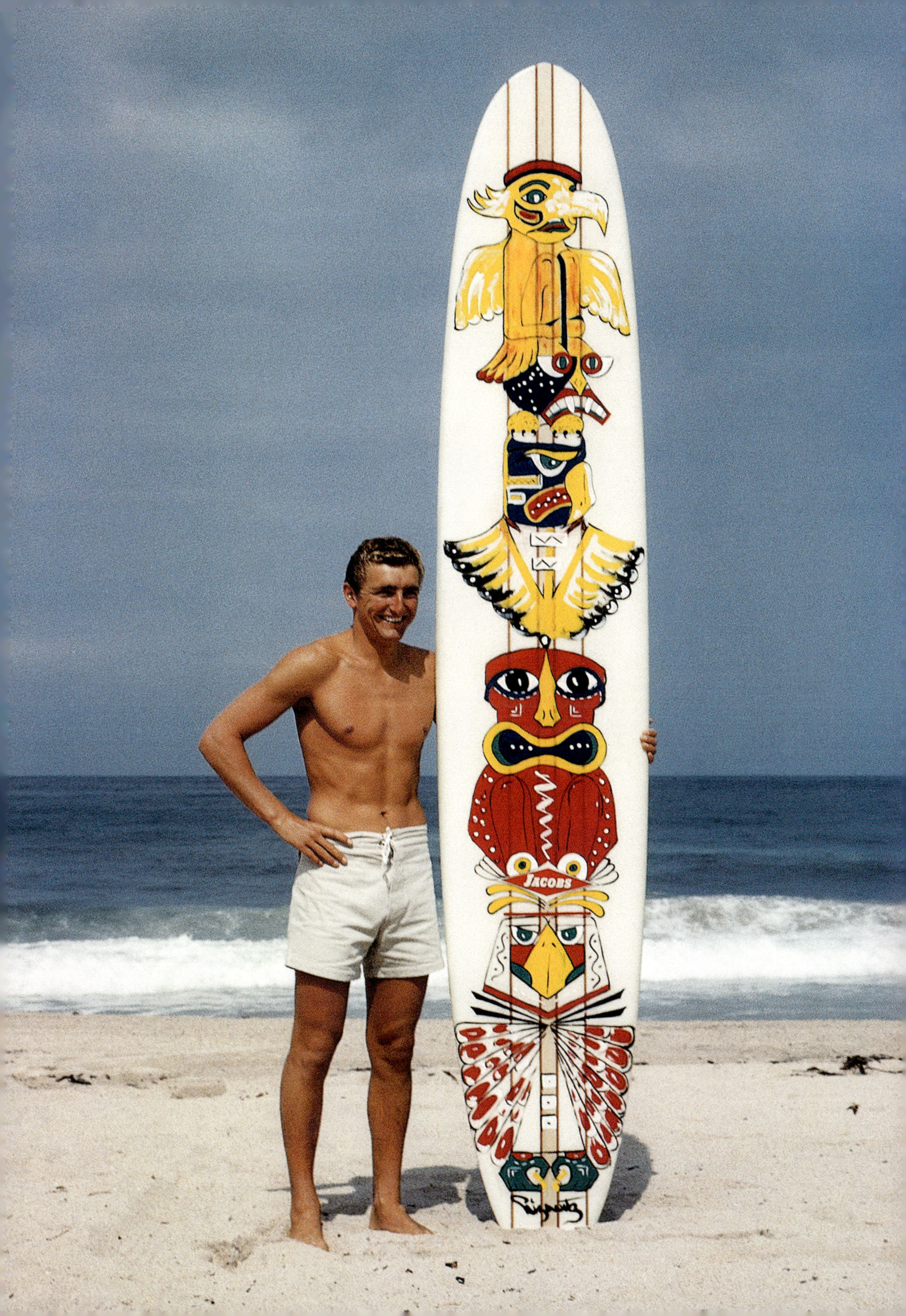
JACOBS

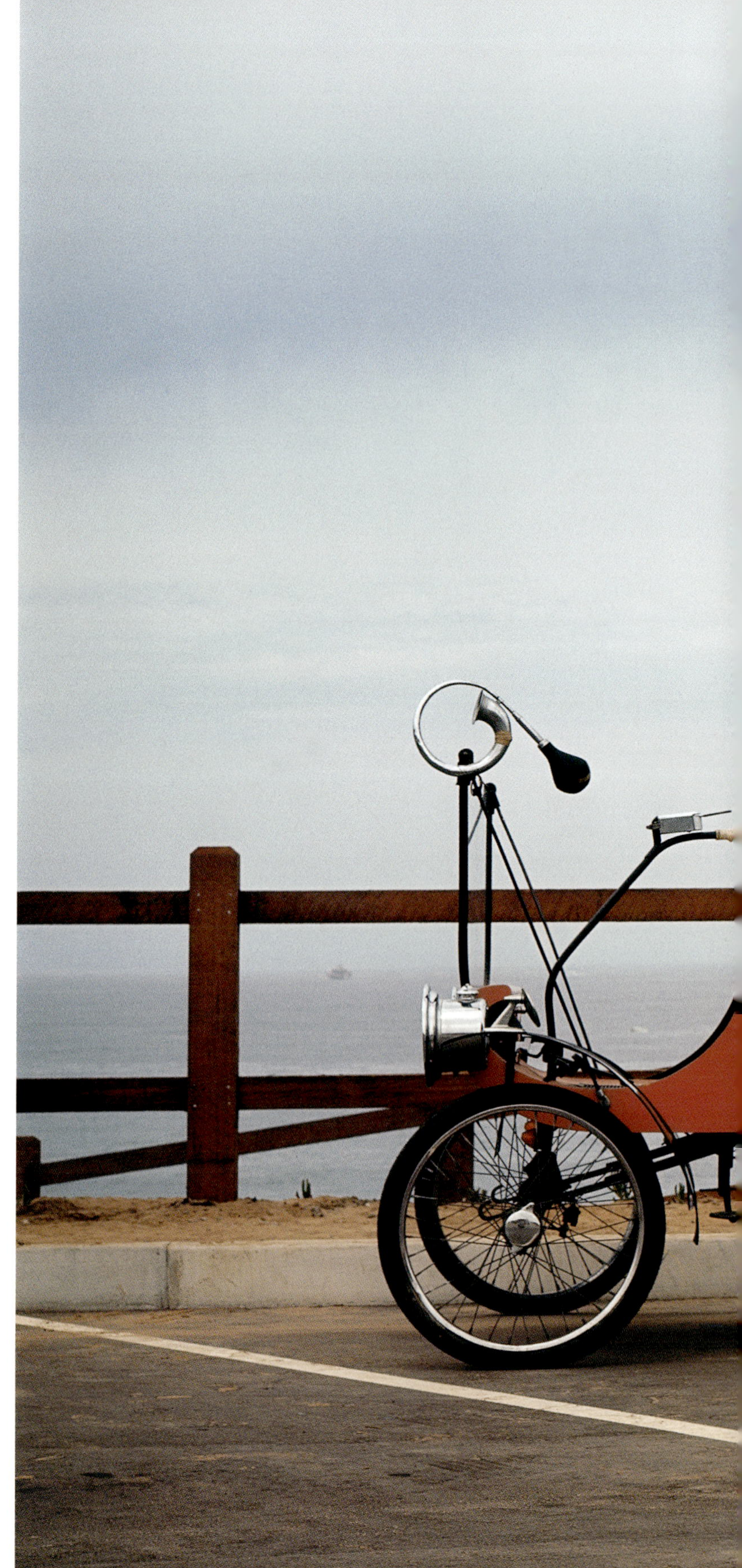

**Marsha Bainer, Torrance Beach, 1964**

Bainer was a highly popular surf model who appeared in ads for various manufacturers throughout the early to mid-sixties.

Bainer war ein sehr beliebtes Surfmodel und Anfang bis Mitte der Sechziger in Anzeigen unterschiedlicher Hersteller zu sehen.

Mannequin de surf très populaire à l'époque, Marsha Bainer a posé pour différents fabricants de planches dans la première moitié des années 1960.

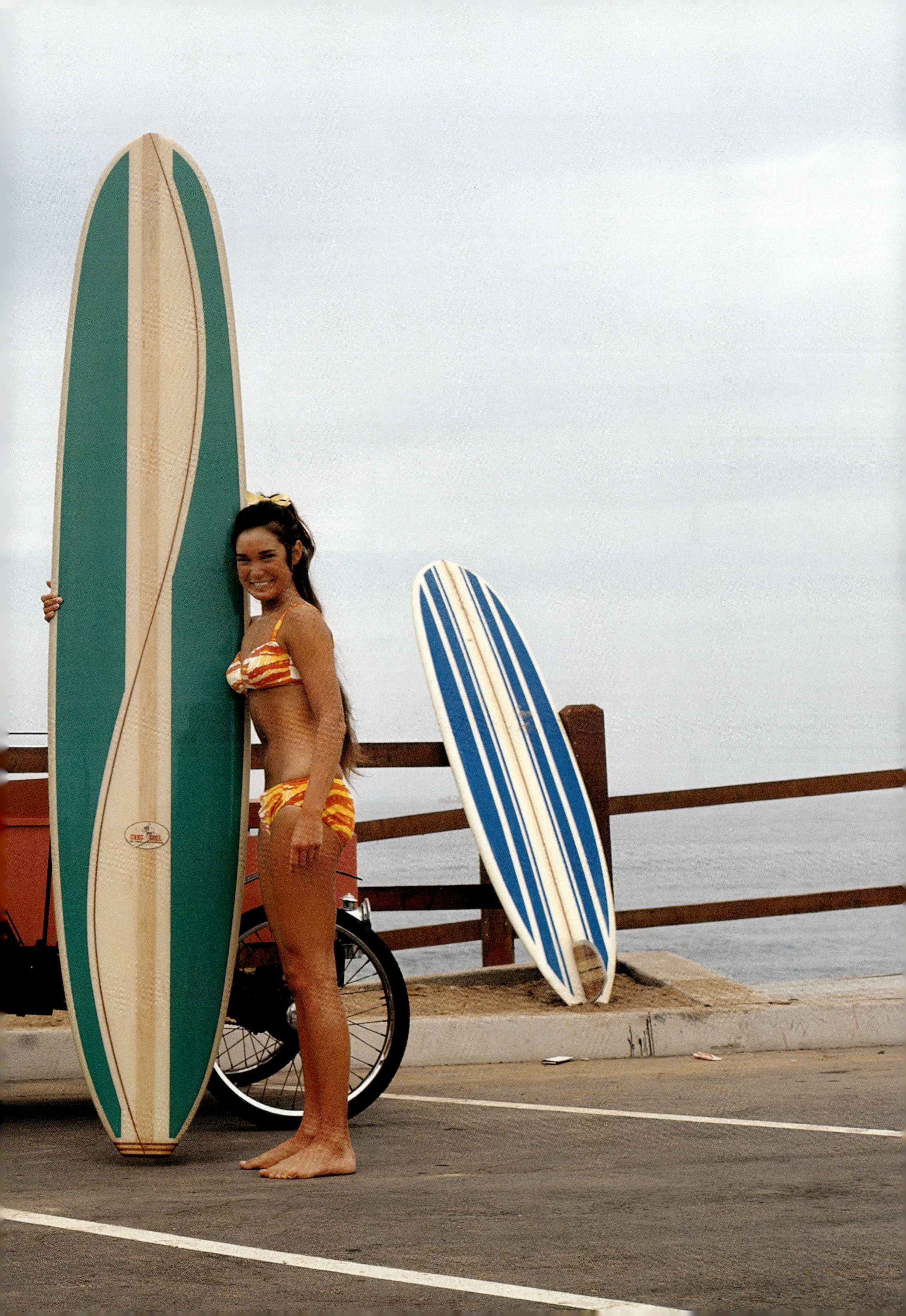

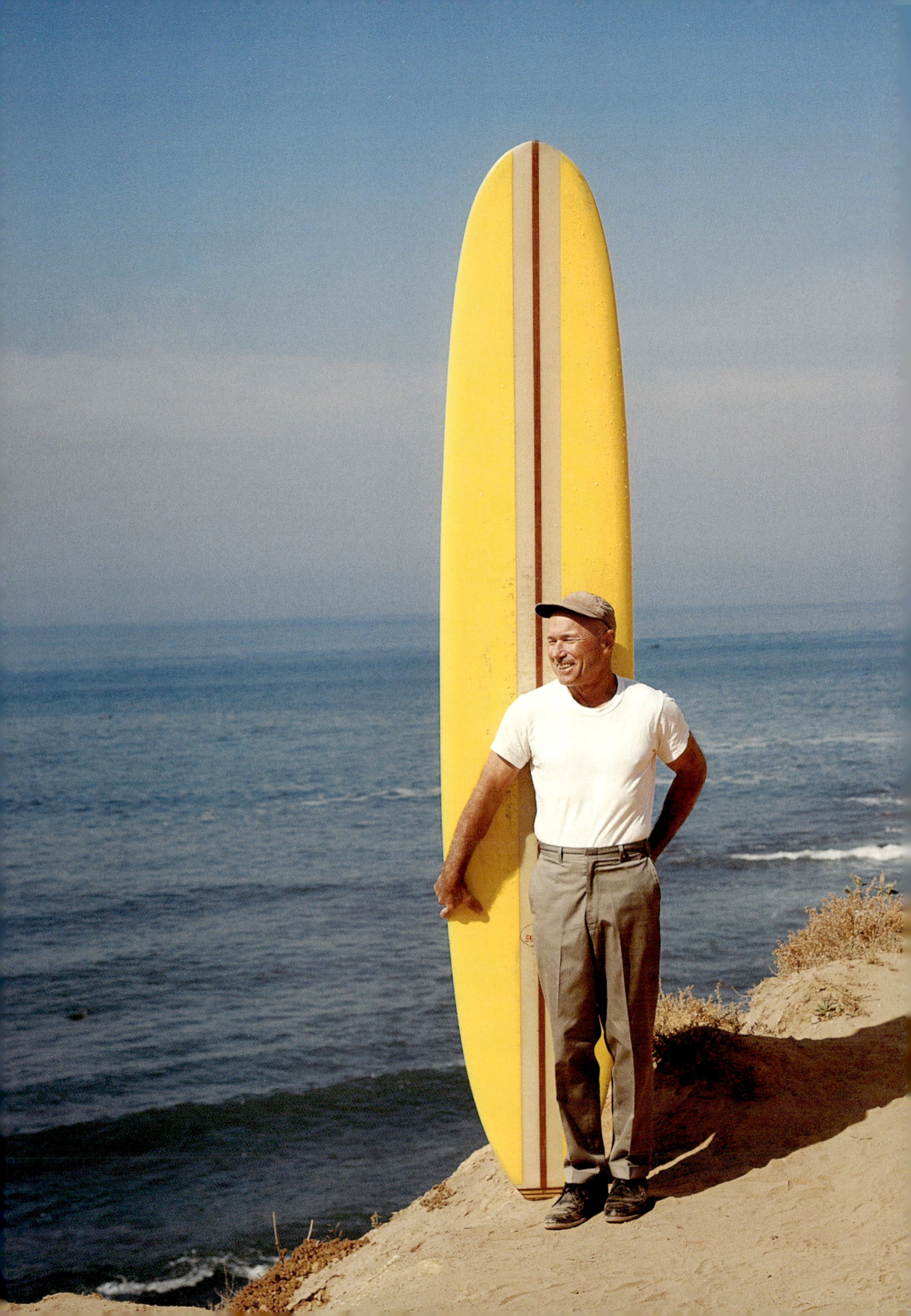

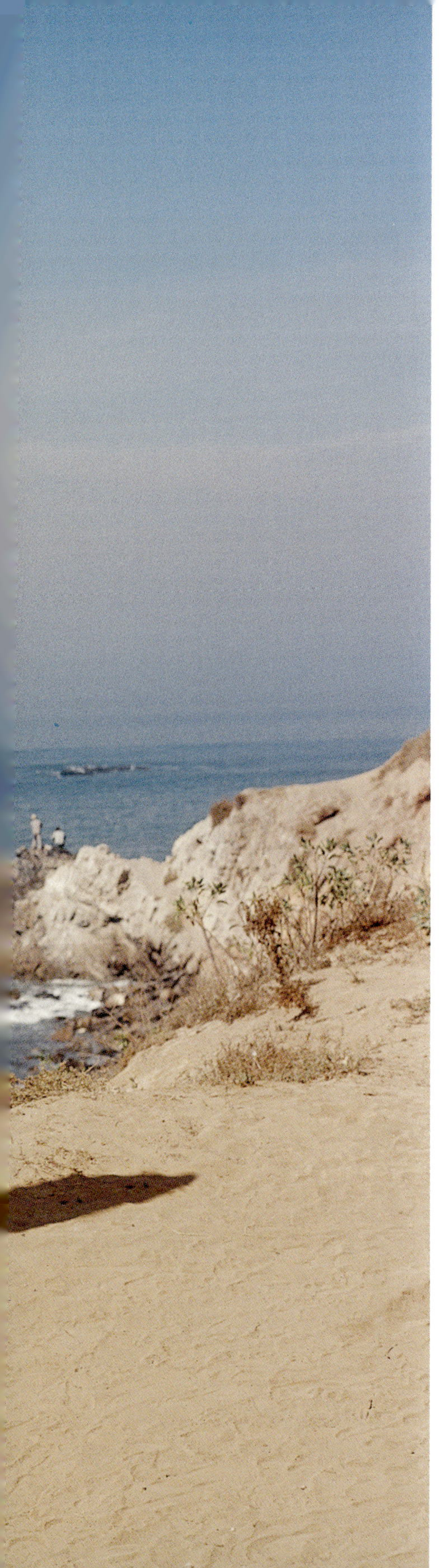

**Doc Ball, Palos Verdes Cove, 1966**

John "Doc" Ball, a pioneering
surfer and surf photographer, was
a lifelong friend and mentor to
Grannis. He passed away in 2001
at age ninety-four.

John „Doc" Ball, ein bahnbrechender Surfer und Surffotograf,
war ein lebenslanger Freund und
Mentor von Grannis. Er verstarb
2001 im Alter von vierundneunzig
Jahren.

John « Doc » Ball, photographe de
surf et un des pionniers de la
discipline, était l'ami fidèle et le
mentor de Grannis. Il est décédé
en 2001 à l'âge de 94 ans.

Pages 198–199
**Palos Verdes Cove, circa 1965**

Hang Ten ad shoot. Left to right:
Mike Doyle, Chuck Linnen, Rickie
Wakeland, Henry Ford, Robert
August.

Werbefoto für Hang Ten. Von links
nach rechts: Mike Doyle, Chuck
Linnen, Rickie Wakeland, Henry
Ford, Robert August.

Photo publicitaire pour la ligne de
vêtements Hang Ten. De gauche à
droite: Mike Doyle, Chuck Linnen,
Rickie Wakeland, Henry Ford et
Robert August.

**Donald Takayama, Peter Kahapea,
Harold Ige, Hermosa Beach, 1963**

Three transplanted Hawaiians
at 22nd Street.

Drei Exil-Hawaiianer an der
22nd Street.

Trois natifs de Hawaï sur
la plage de 22nd Street.

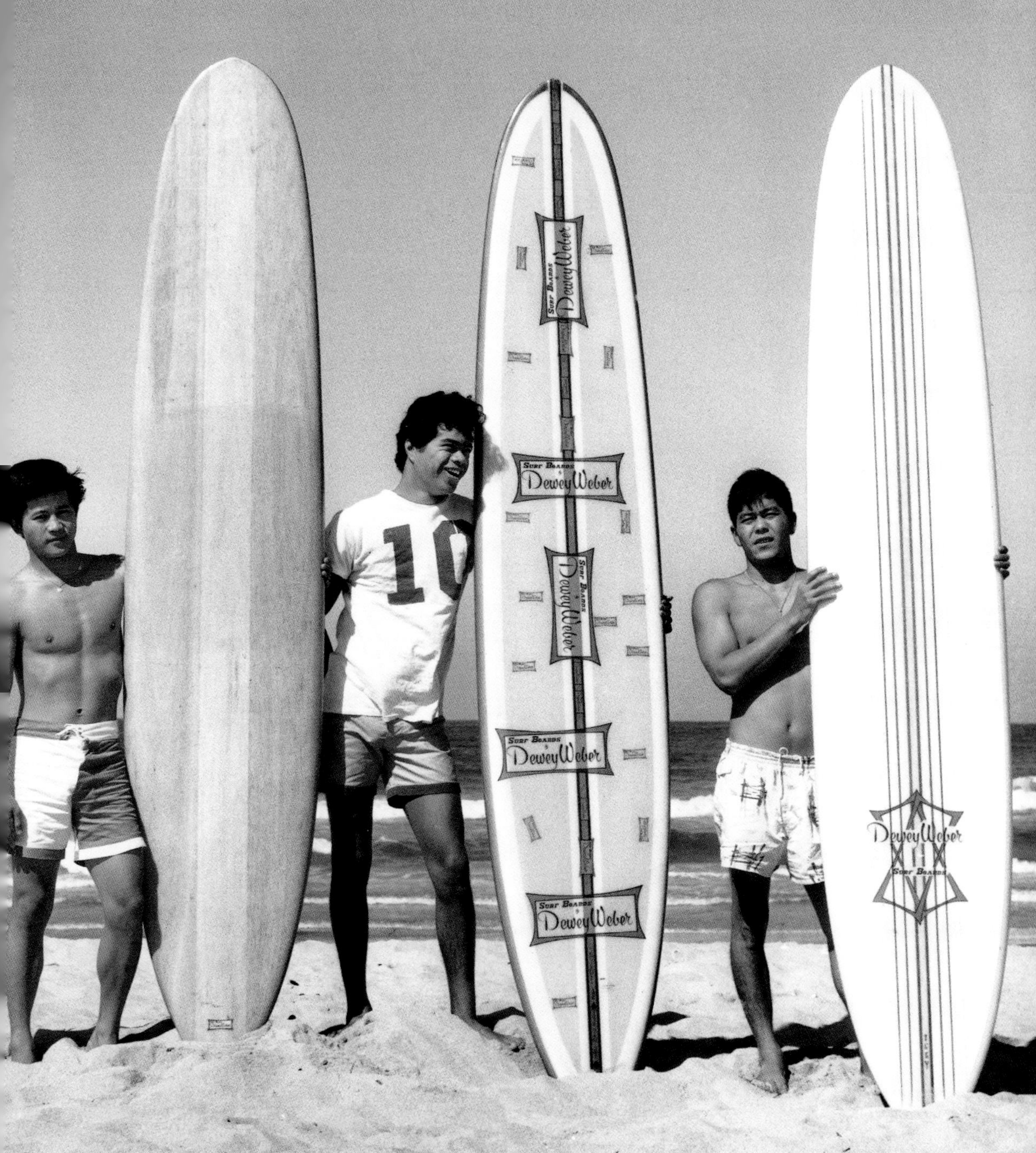

SURF BOARDS
DeweyWeber
SURF BOARDS
DeweyWeber
SURF BOARDS
DeweyWeber
SURF BOARDS
DeweyWeber
SURF BOARDS
DeweyWeber
DeweyWeber
SURF BOARDS
10

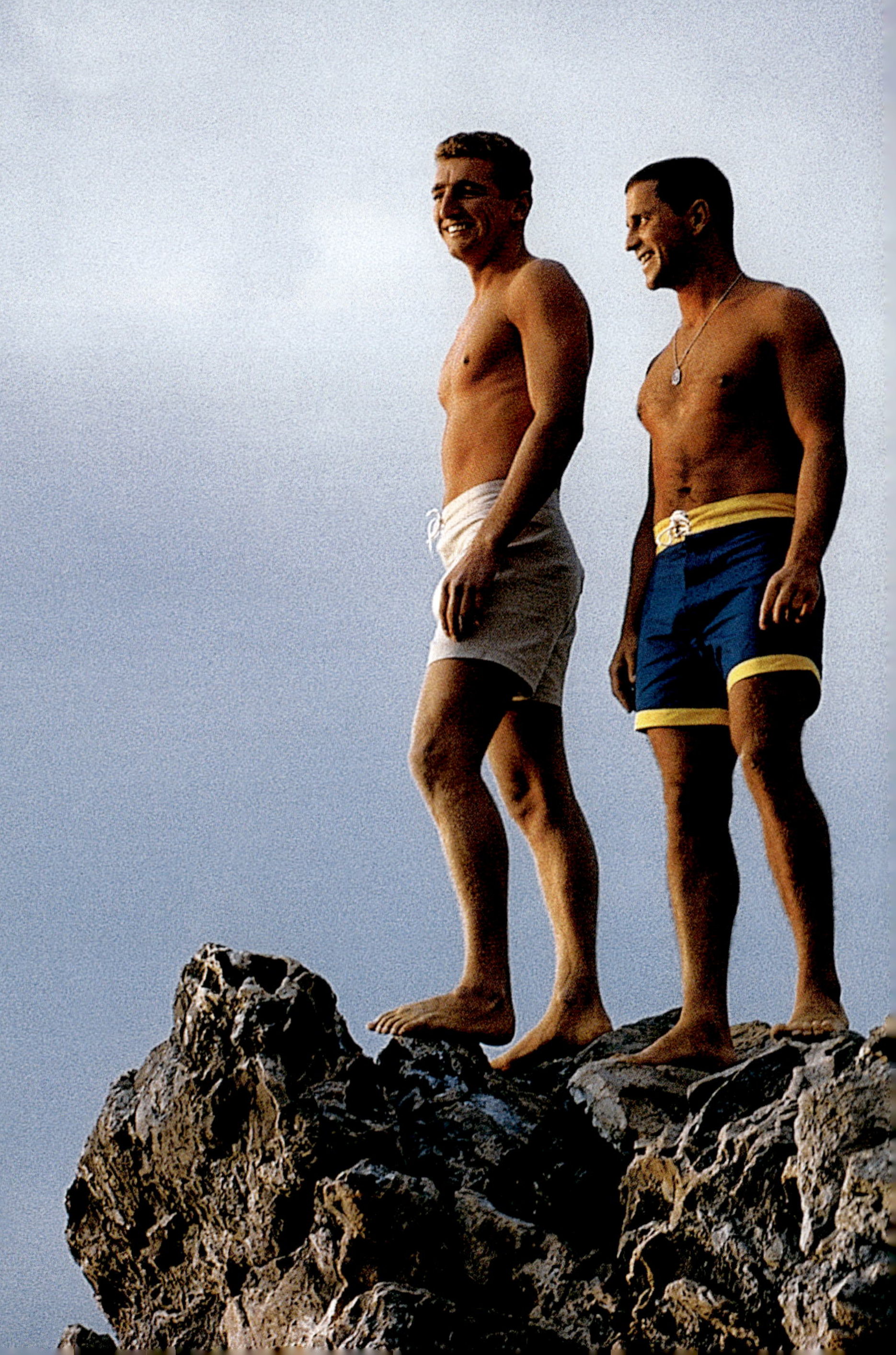

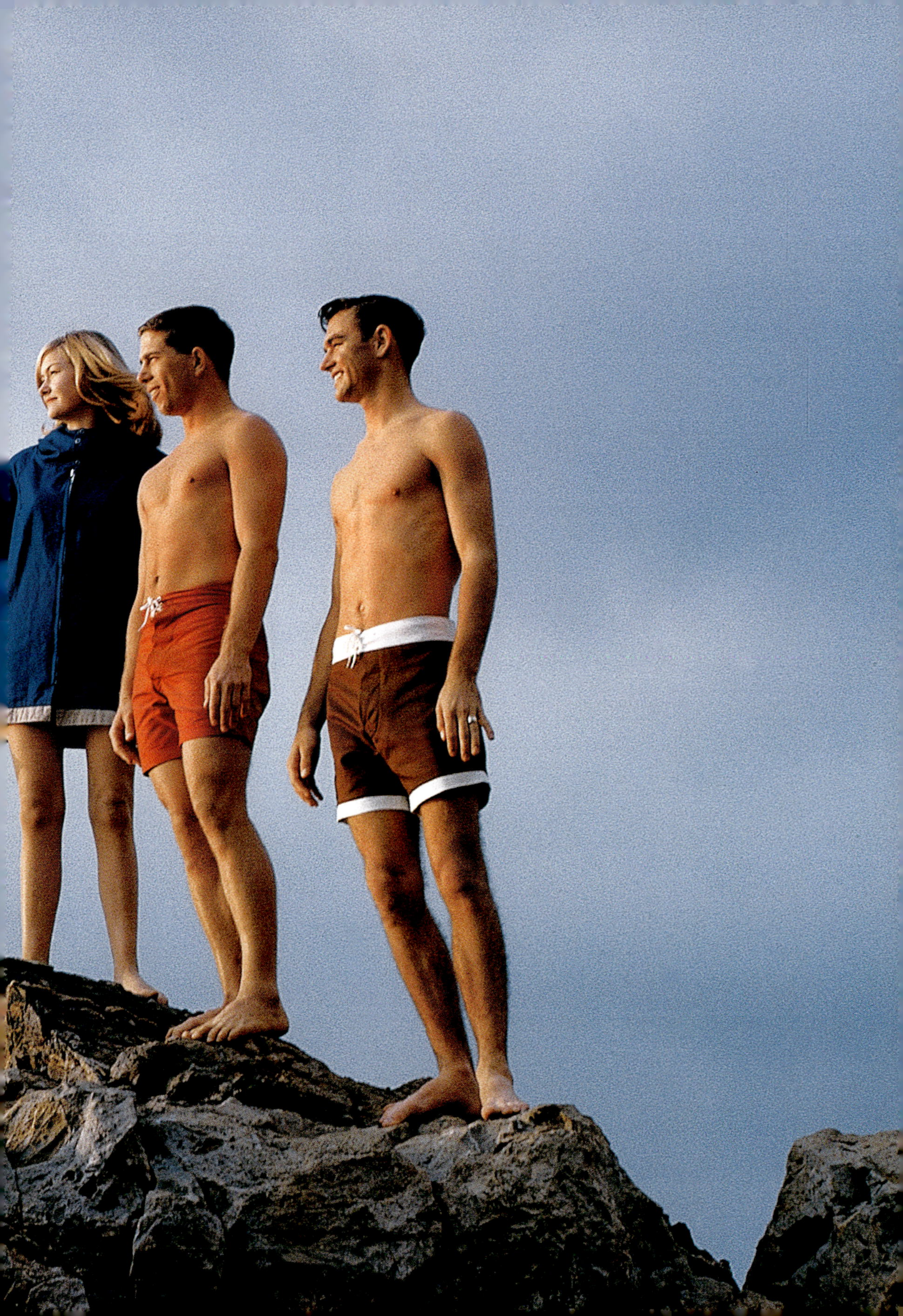

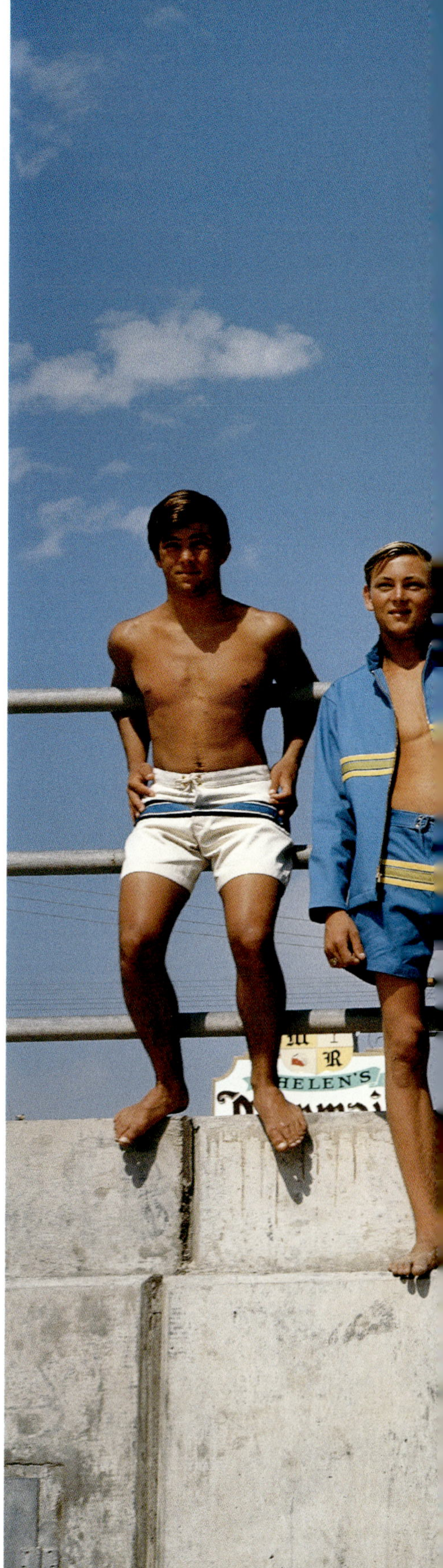


**Ocean Beach, San Diego, 1966**

Laguna swimwear ad. "… [P]retty
soon every kid in Utica, N.Y., is
buying a pair of them," wrote Tom
Wolfe in his 1968 essay "The
Pump House Gang."

Werbeanzeige für Laguna
Badebekleidung. „… Bald kaufen
sich alle Jugendlichen in Utica,
N.Y., ein Paar davon", schrieb
Tom Wolfe 1968 in seinem Essay
„The Pump House Gang".

Publicité pour les combinaisons
Laguna. « […] très rapidement,
elles devinrent incontournables
auprès des ados d'Utica, dans
l'État de New York », écrit Tom
Wolfe en 1968 dans son essai
« The Pump House Gang ».

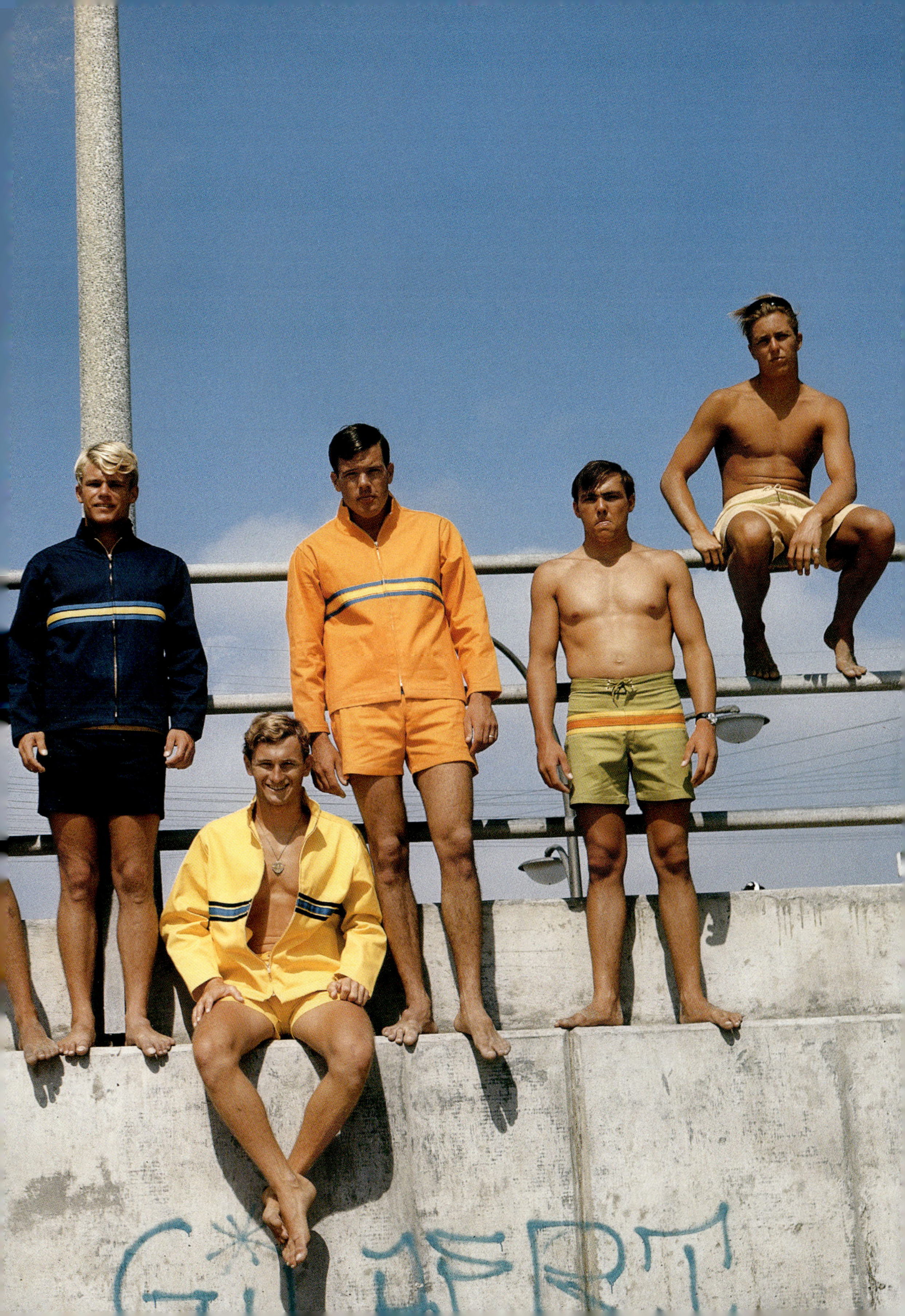
GILBERT

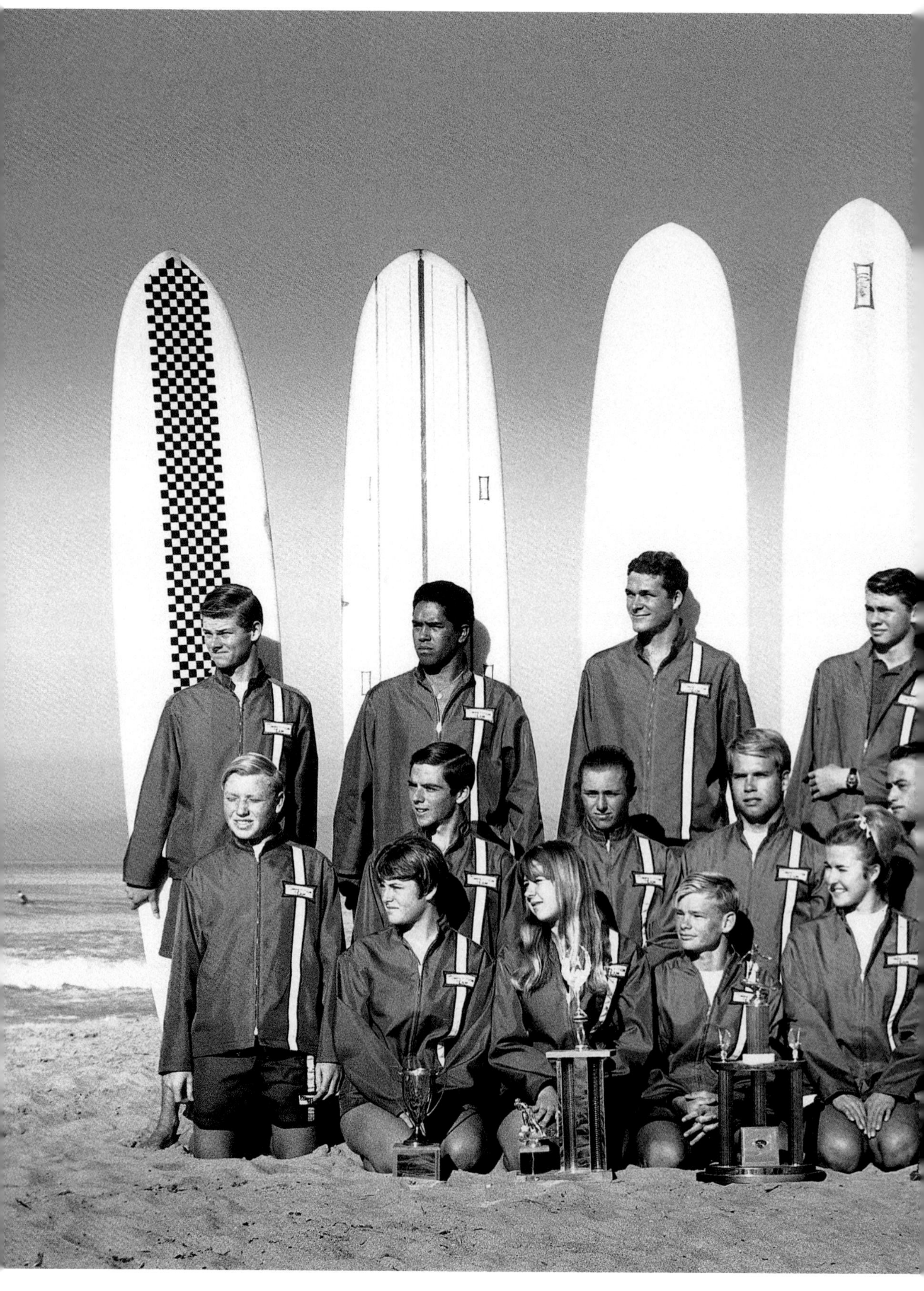

Pages 204–205
**Dewey Weber Shop, Venice, 1968**

Weber's most popular models were
the "Performer" and the "Weber
Feather." Caroline Weber in front.

Die beliebtesten Modelle von Weber
nannten sich „Performer" und
„Weber Feather". Caroline Weber
vor dem Laden.

Les modèles Performer et Weber
Feather étaient les plus prisés des
ateliers de Dewey Weber. Caroline
Weber pose devant la boutique.

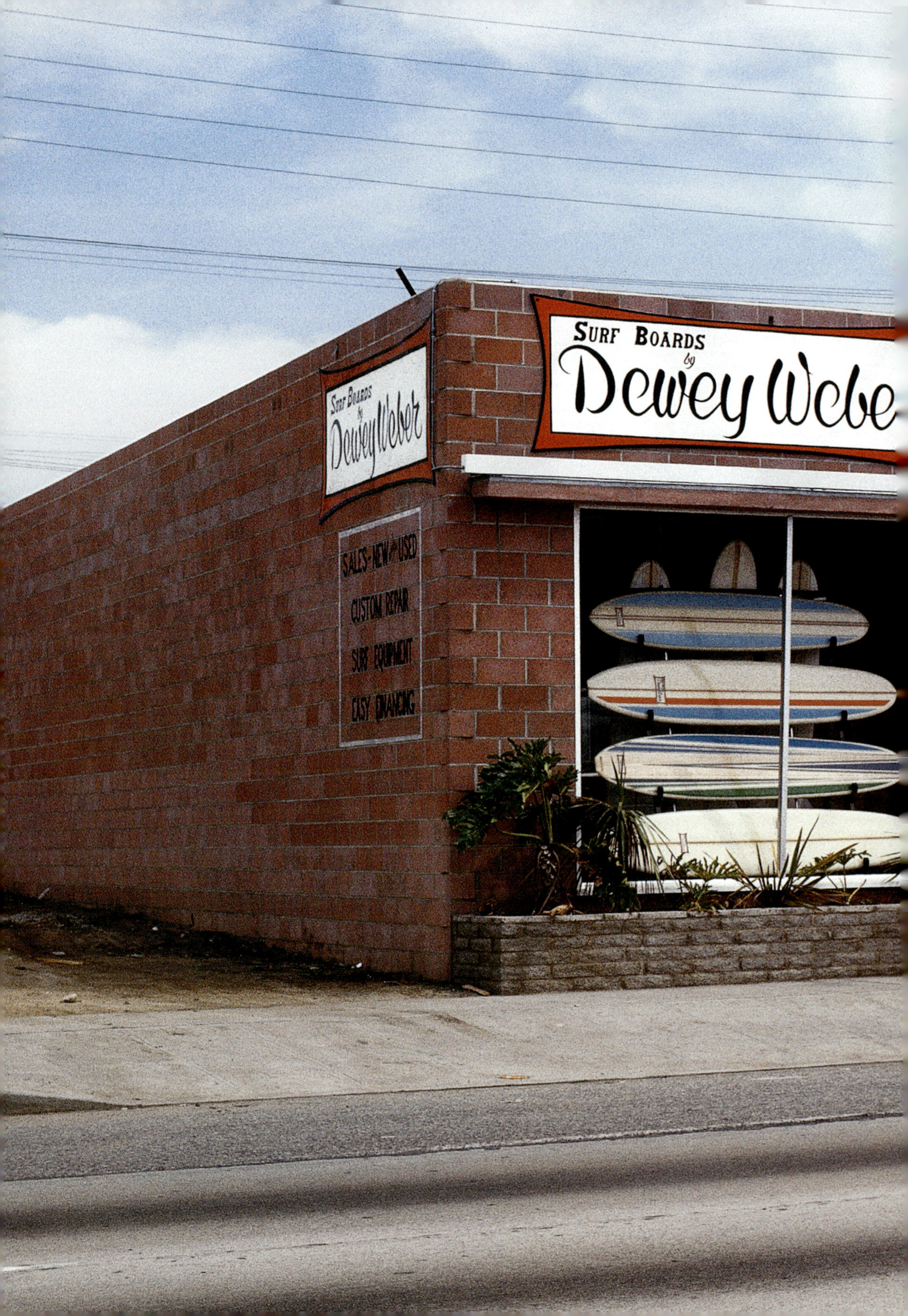

SURF BOARDS
by
Dewey Webe
SURF BOARDS
by
Dewey Weber
SALES NEW & USED
CUSTOM REPAIR
SURF EQUIPMENT
EASY FINANCING

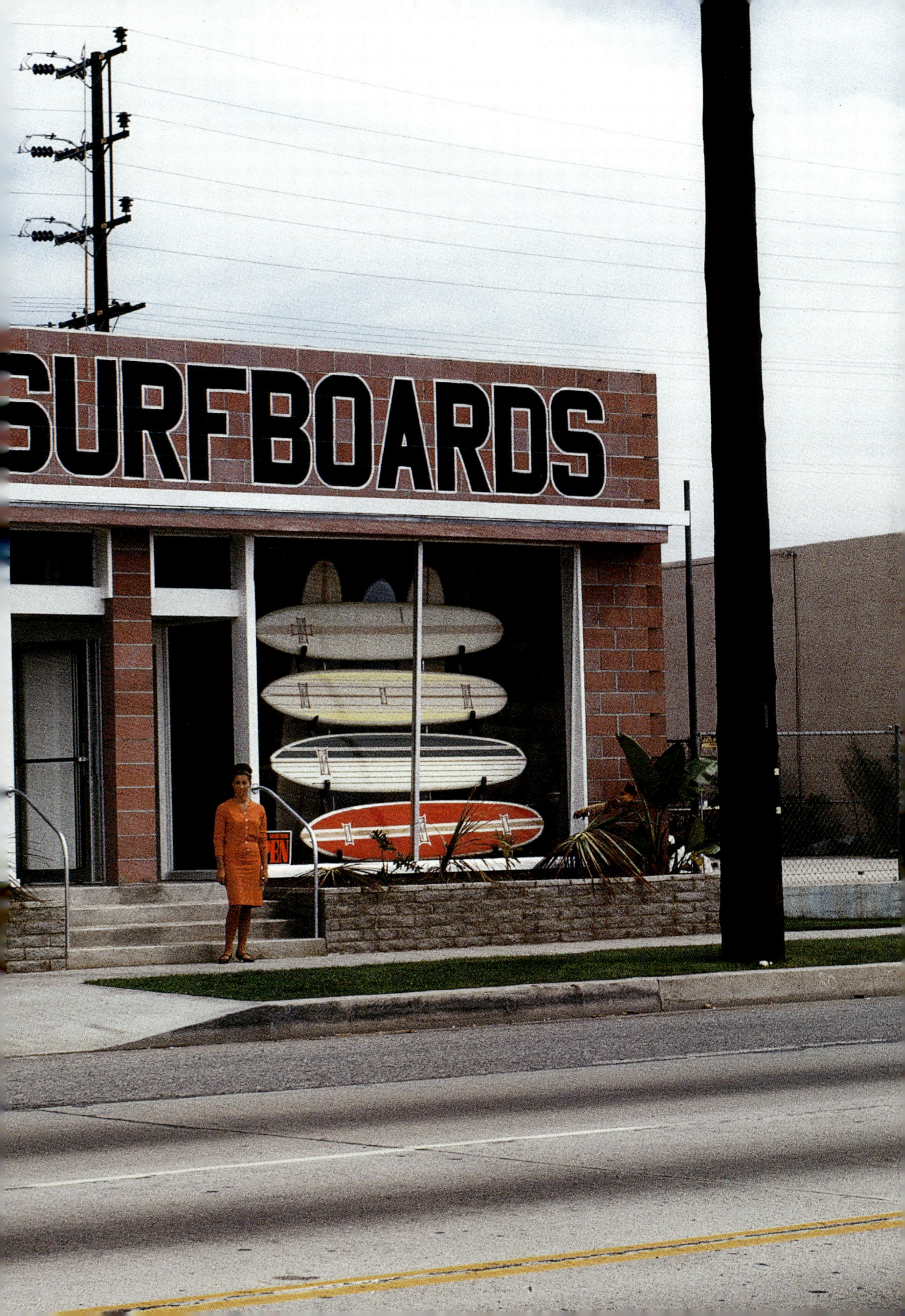
SURFBOARDS
OPEN

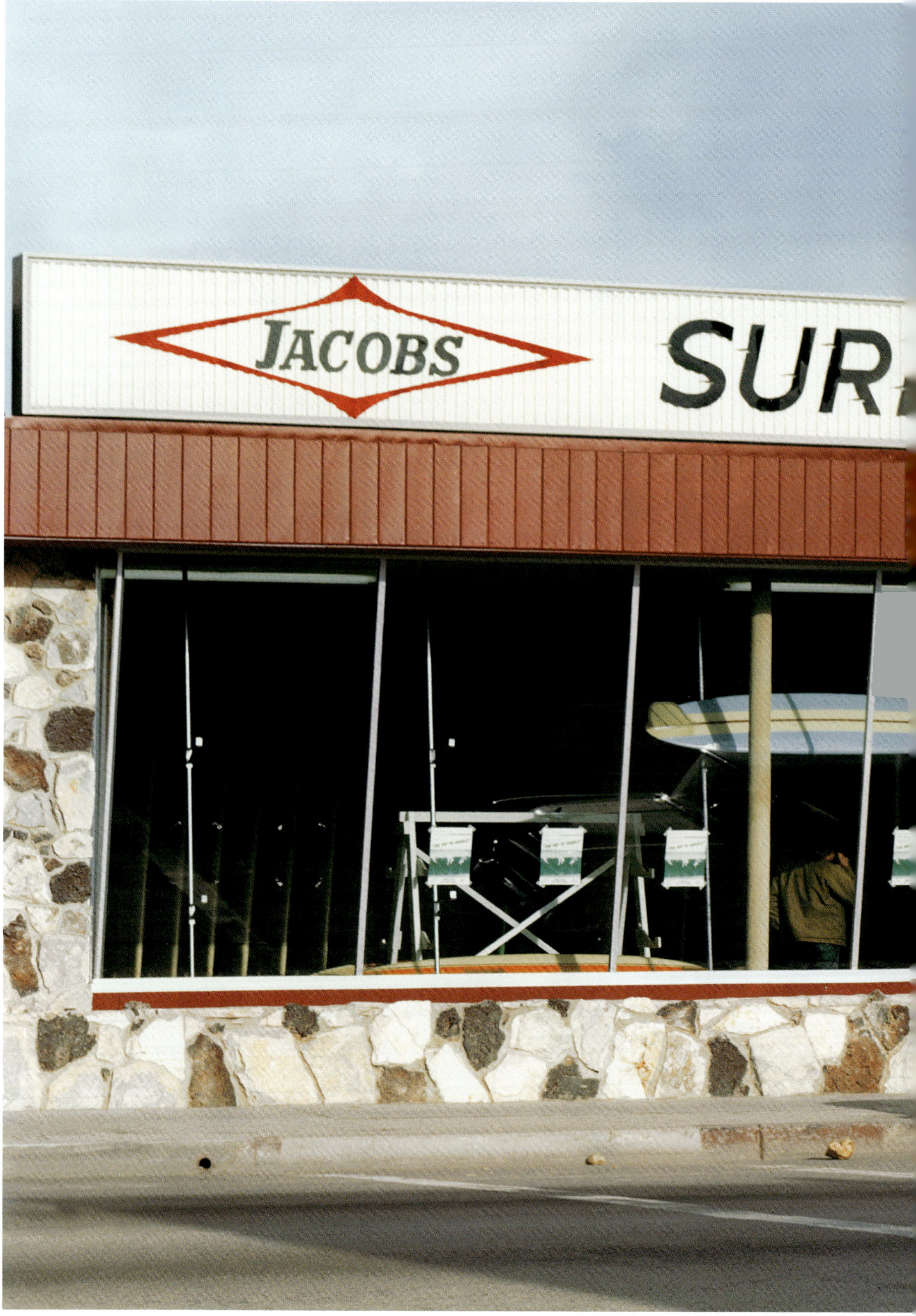

JACOBS
SUR

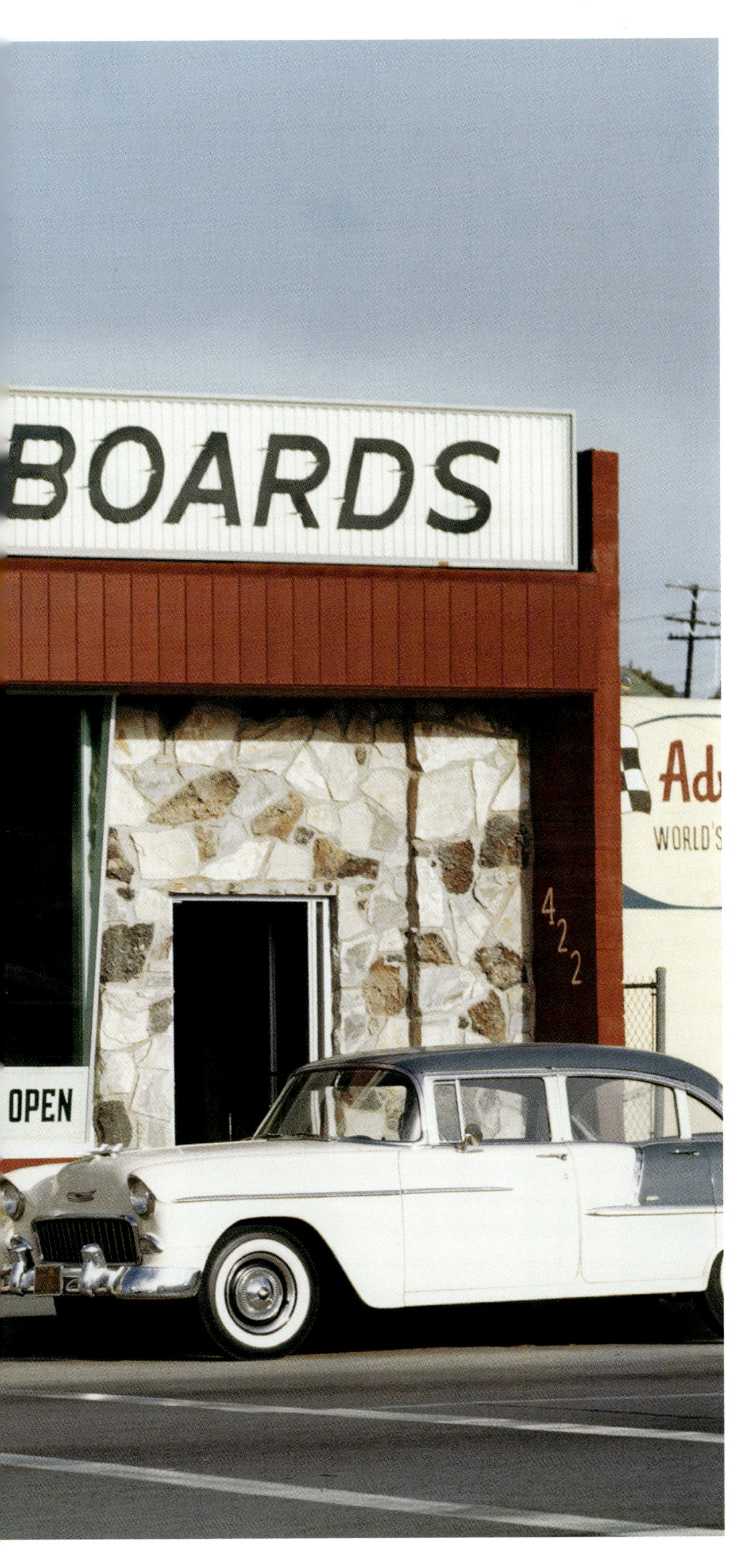



**Jacobs Shop, Hermosa Beach, 1963**

Throughout the sixties, Grannis would document most of the prominent surfboard manufacturers and their shops, including Jacobs.

Während der Sechziger porträtierte Grannis die meisten bekannten Surfbrett-Hersteller und ihre Läden, so auch Jacobs.

Pendant les anneés 1960, Grannis photographia la plupart des grands fabricants de planches et leurs magasins, comme ici Jacobs.

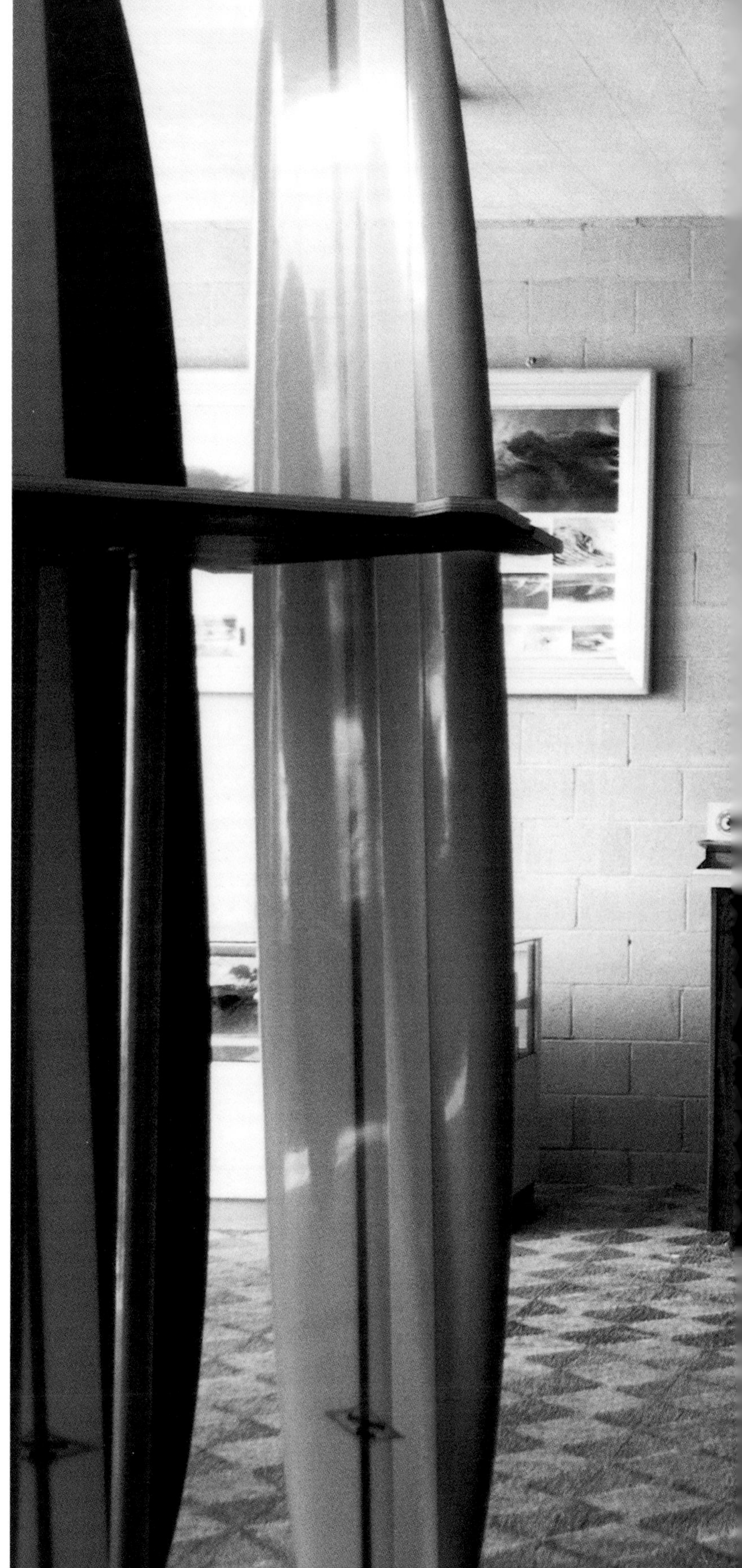

**Jacobs Shop, Hermosa Beach, 1963**

Dudley "Hap" Jacobs split from
Dale Velzy in 1959 to start his own
label. His impeccable store was
called "the Notre Dame of surf
shops."

Dudley „Hap" Jacobs stieg 1959
bei Dale Velzy aus, um seine eigene
Firma zu gründen. Sein makelloser
Laden wurde „Notre Dame unter
den Surfläden" genannt.

« Hap » Jacobs s'est séparé de
Dale Velzy en 1959 pour lancer
sa propre marque. Sa boutique
impeccablement tenue est
surnommée la « Notre-Dame
des boutiques de surf ».

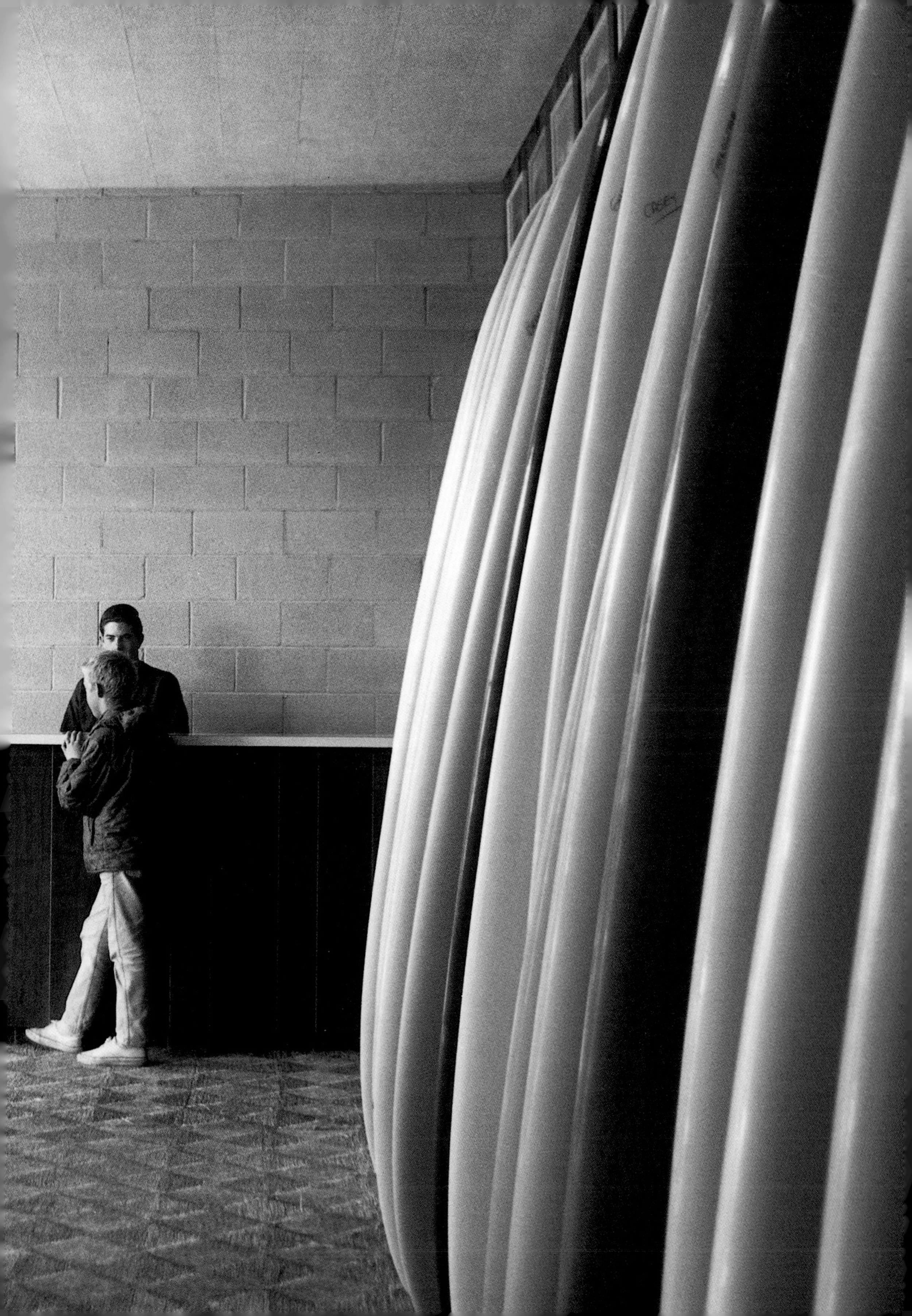

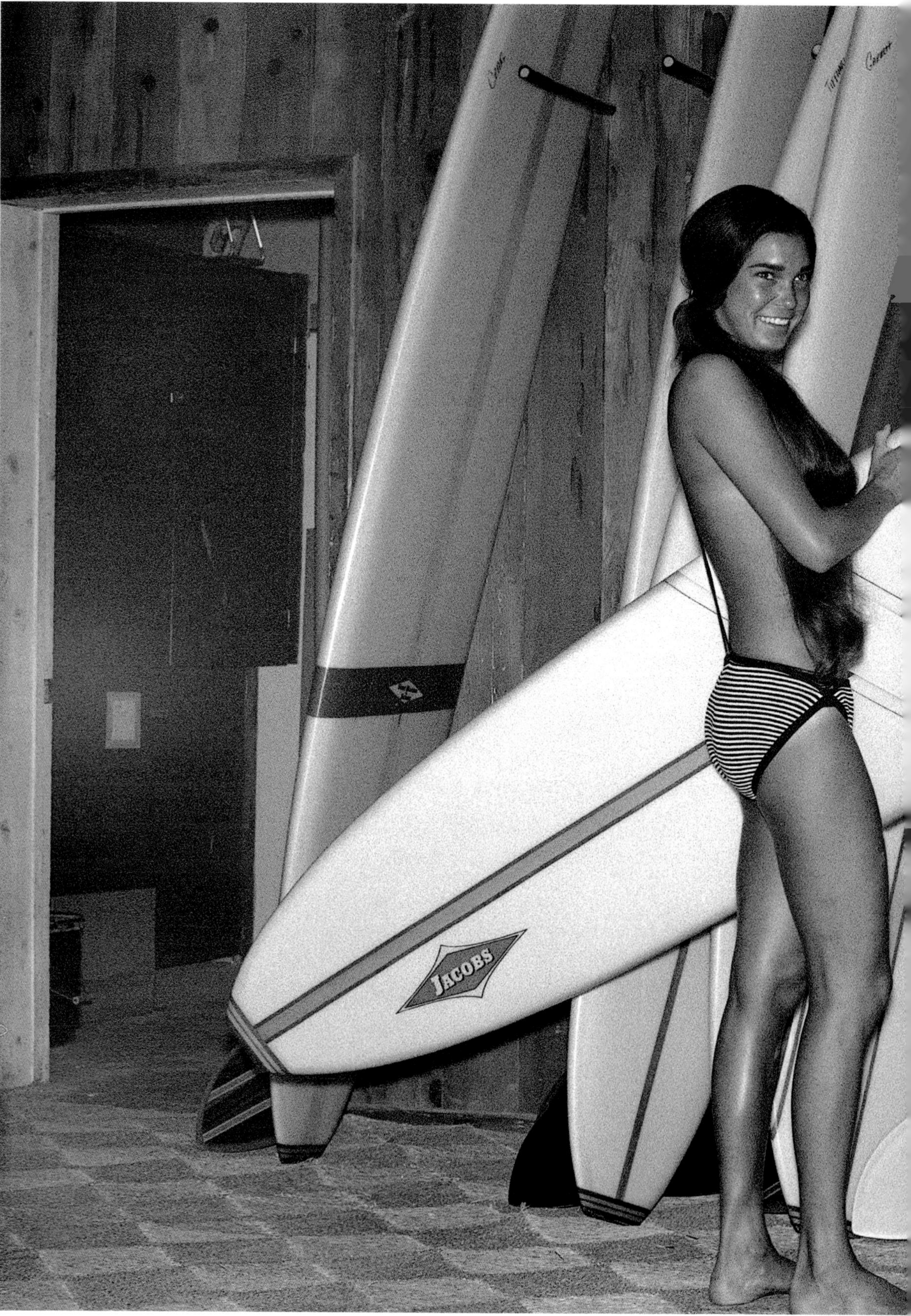

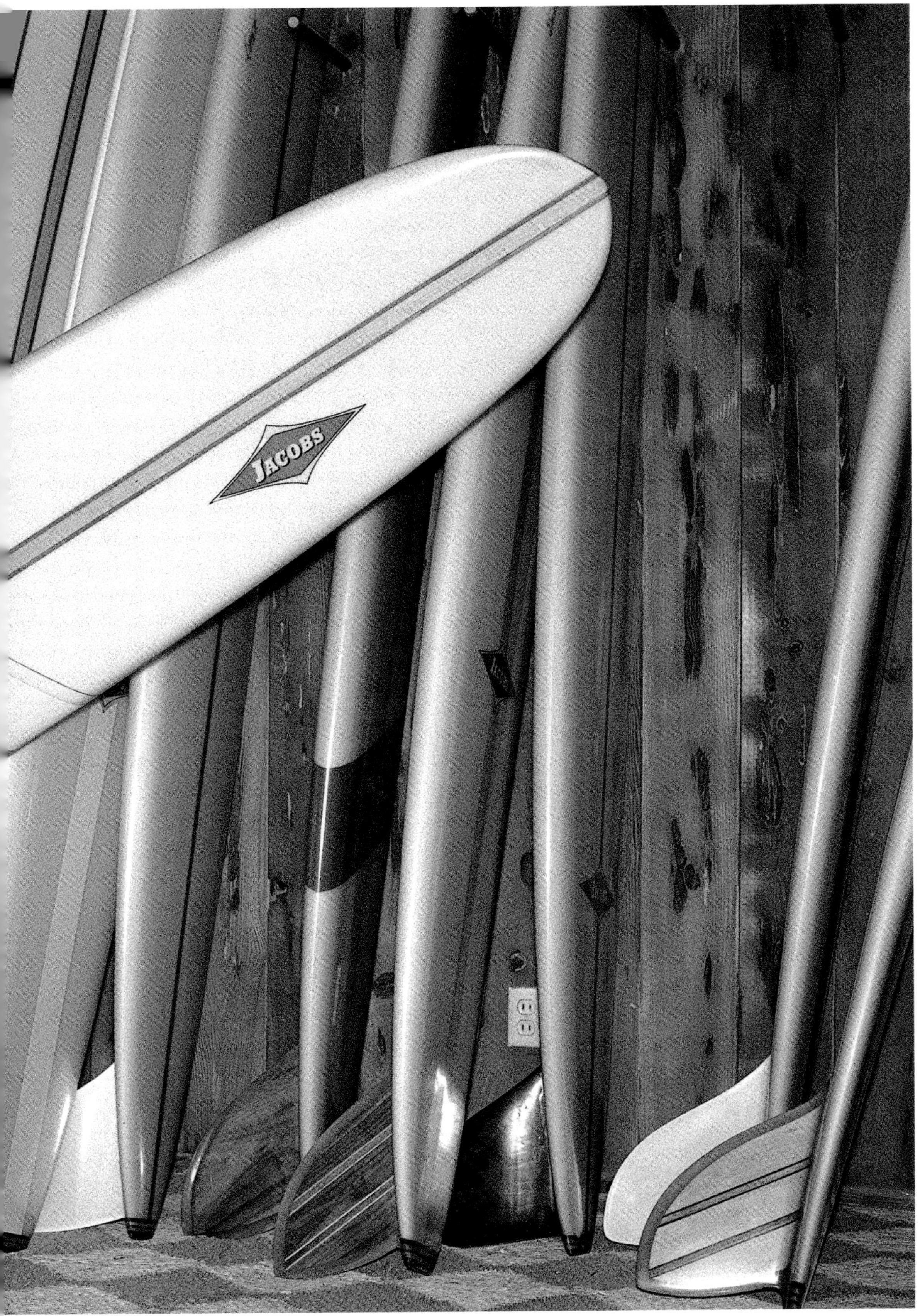
JACOBS

Pages 210–211
**Marsha Bainer, Hermosa Beach, 1964**

Seventeen-year-old Bainer posed "topless" for this Jacobs Surfboards ad.

Die siebzehnjährige Bainer posierte für die Anzeige von Jacobs Surfboards „oben ohne".

Marsha Bainer à dix-sept ans, posant sans le haut pour une publicité de Jacobs Surfboards.

**Ken Tilton, Hermosa Beach, 1962**

Tilton was Jacobs's lead shaper.

Tilton war leitender Shaper bei Jacobs.

Ken Tilton était shaper en chef chez Jacobs.

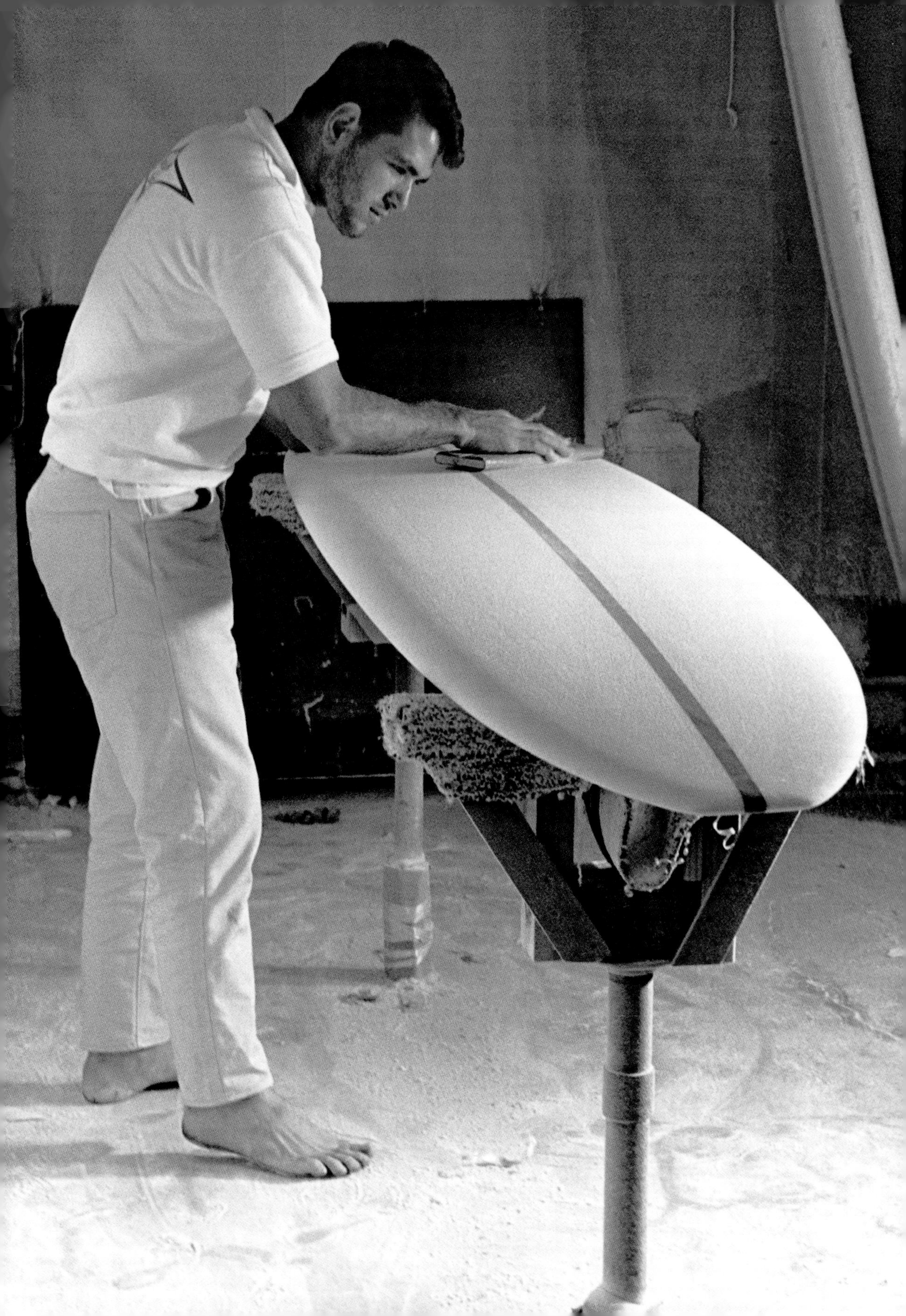

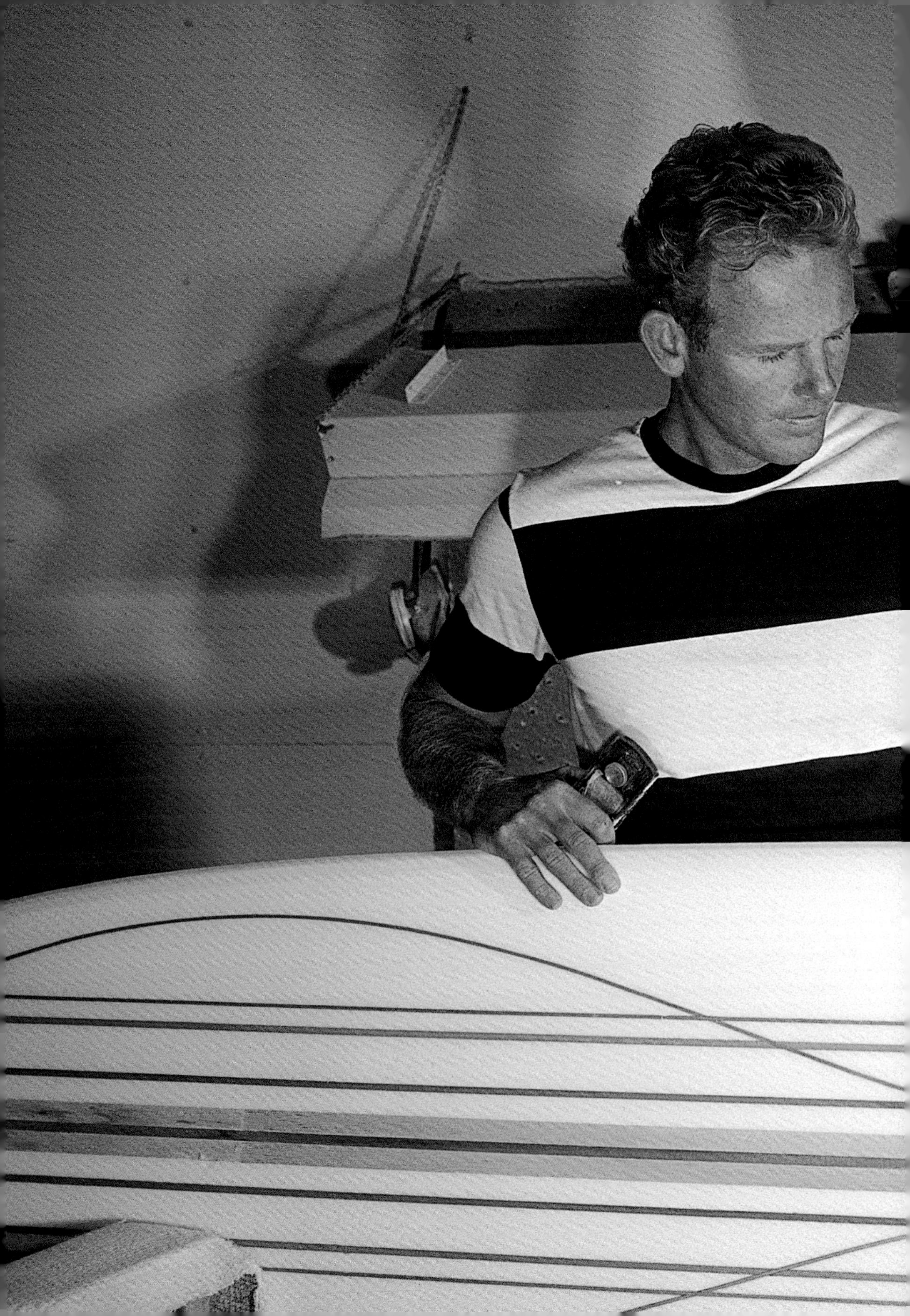

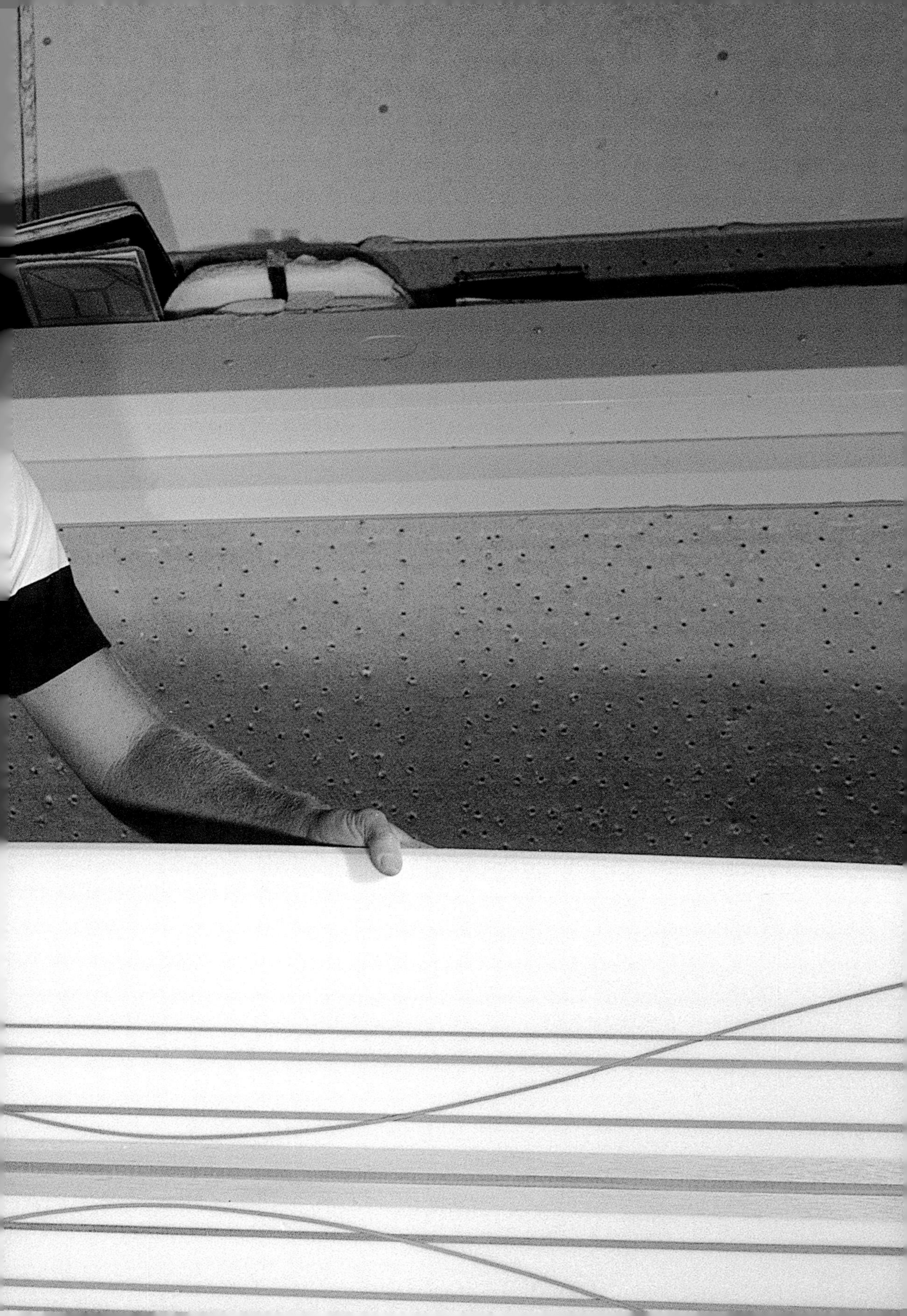

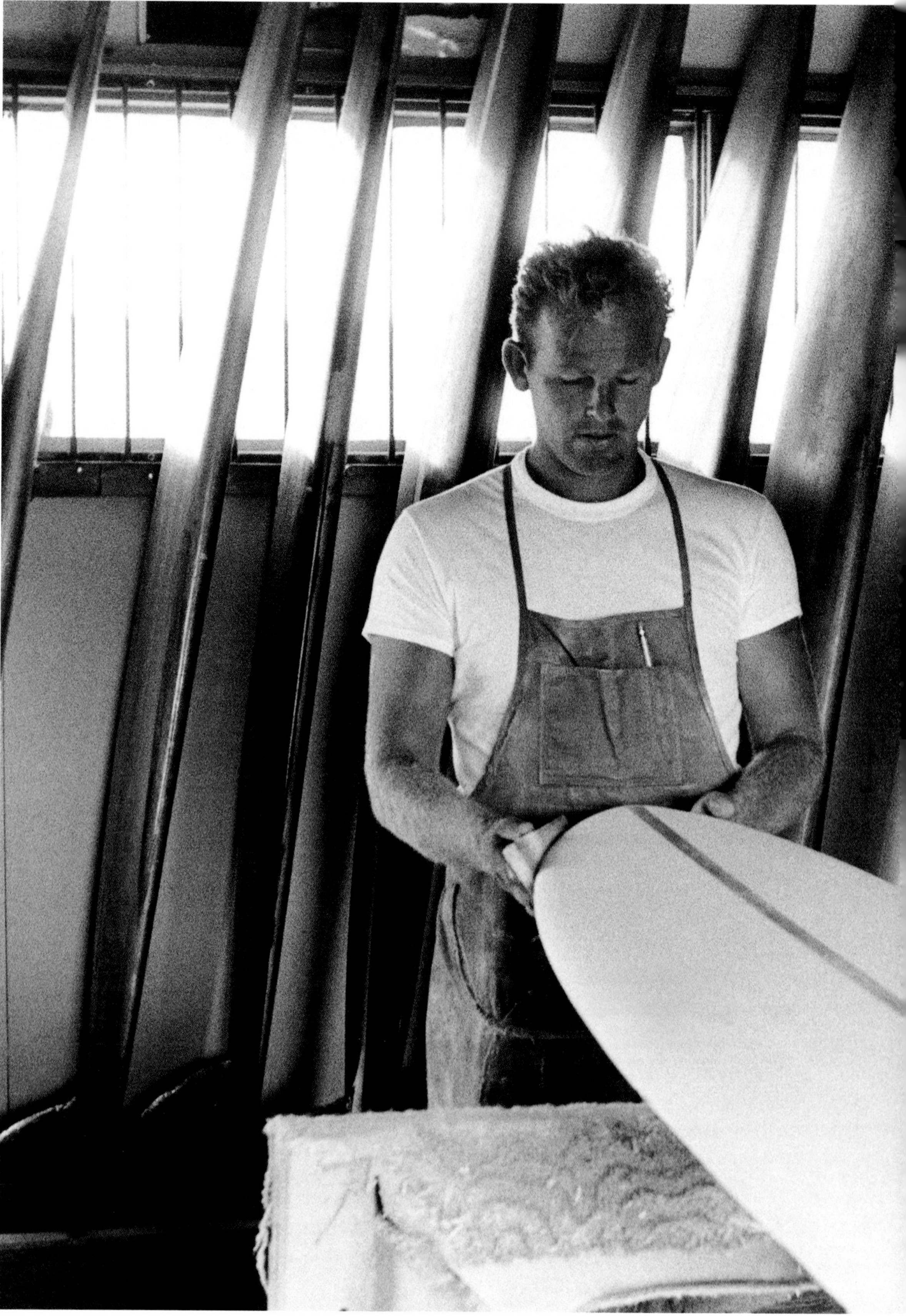

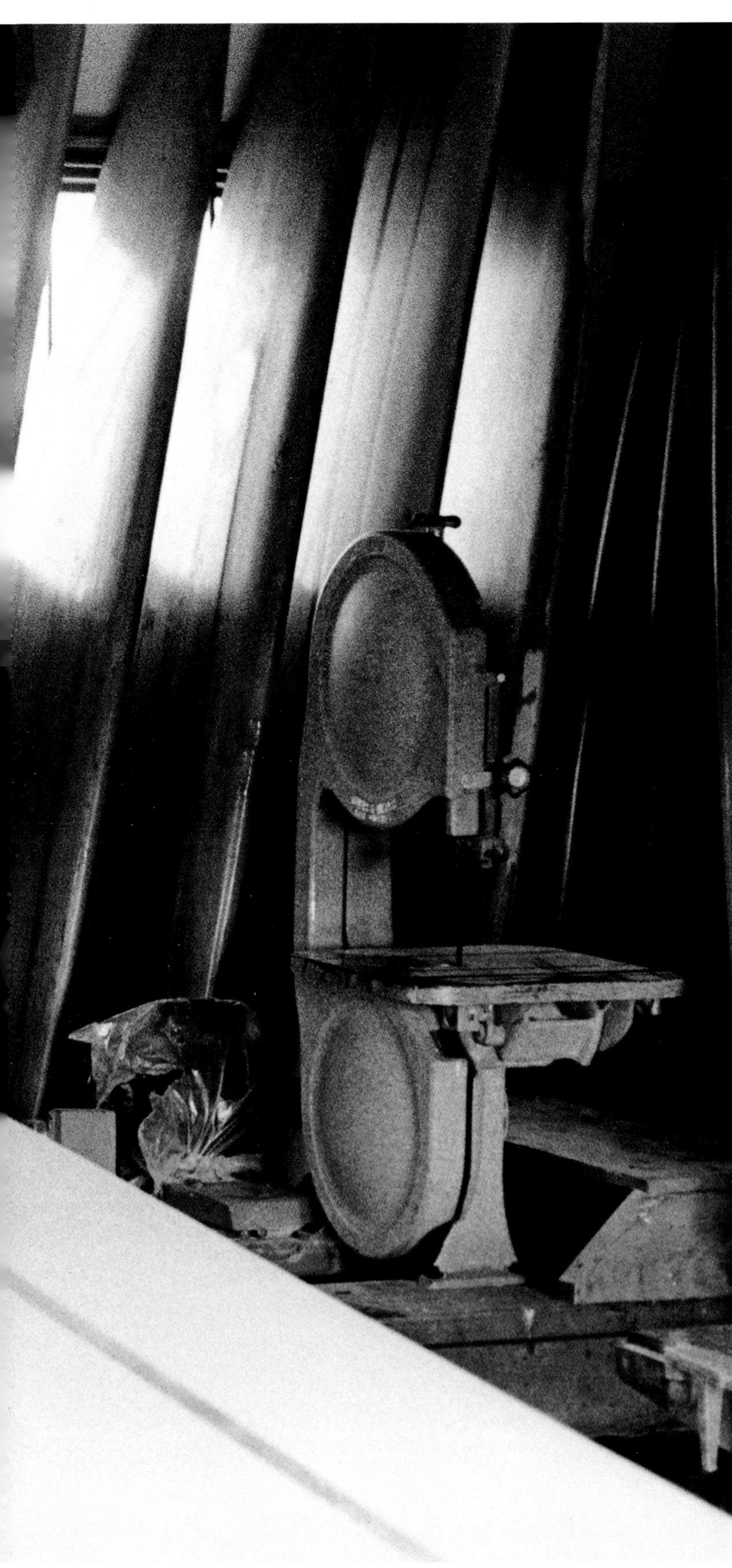



**Hap Jacobs, Hermosa Beach, 1963**

Greg Noll Shop, Hermosa Beach,
1963

If you look carefully, you can
see Noll hiding in the doorway's
shadows.

Wenn man genau hinschaut,
sieht man Noll im Schatten der
Eingangstür stehen.

L'œil attentif reconnaîtra Greg Noll
tapi dans l'ombre à l'entrée de sa
boutique.

Greg Noll Display Room, Hermosa
Beach, 1961


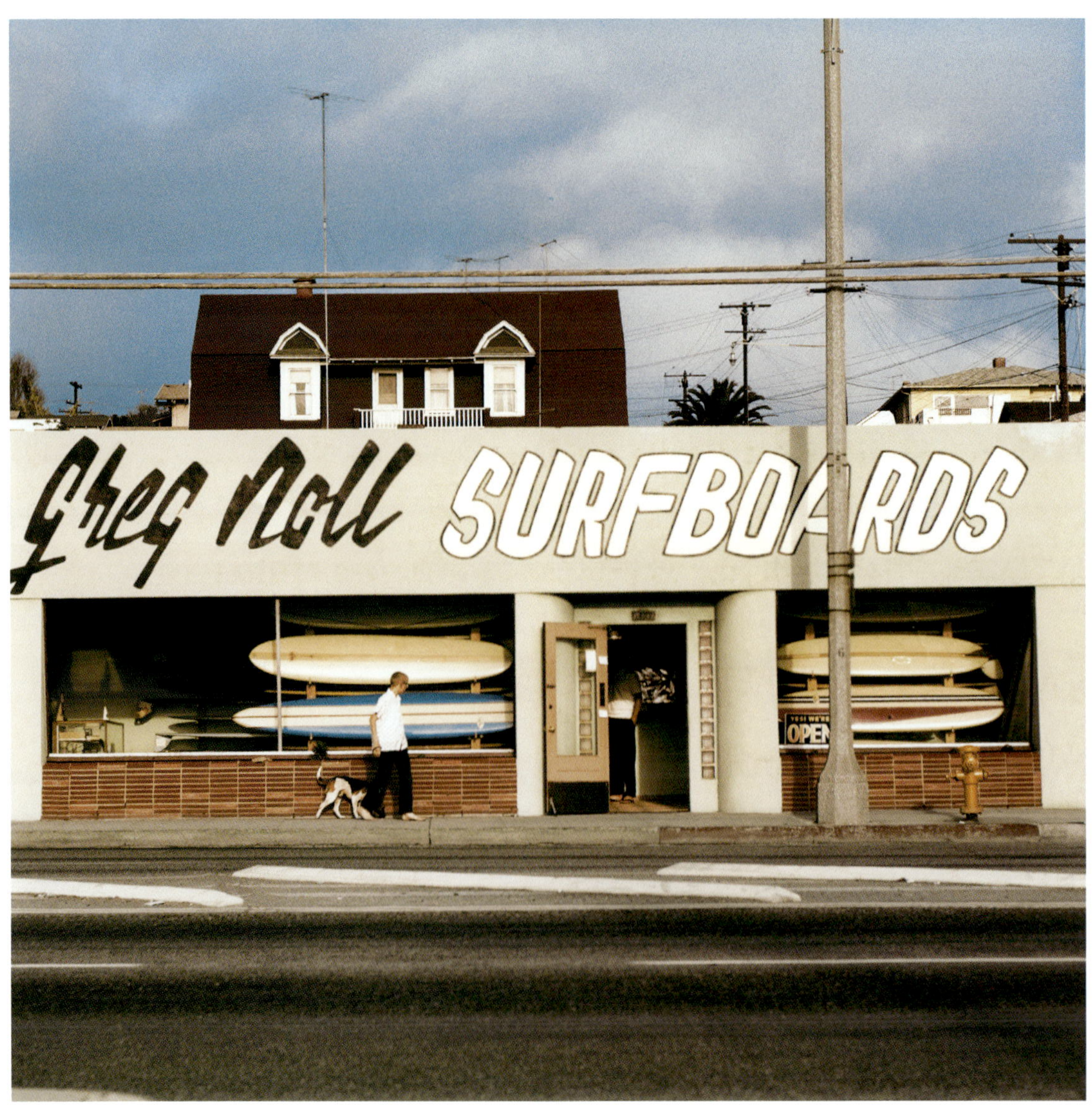


Greg Noll SURFBOARDS
OPEN

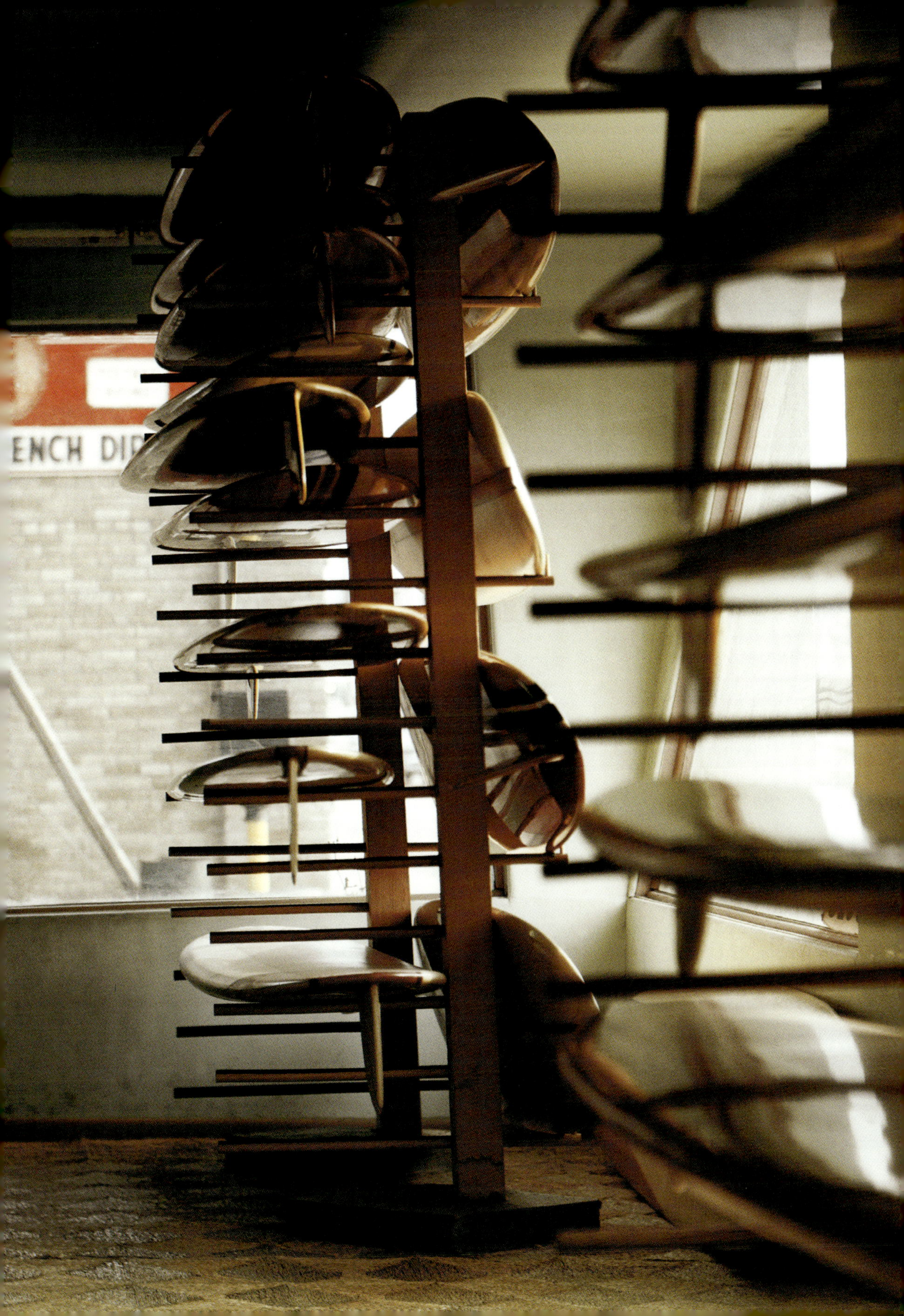
ENCH DI

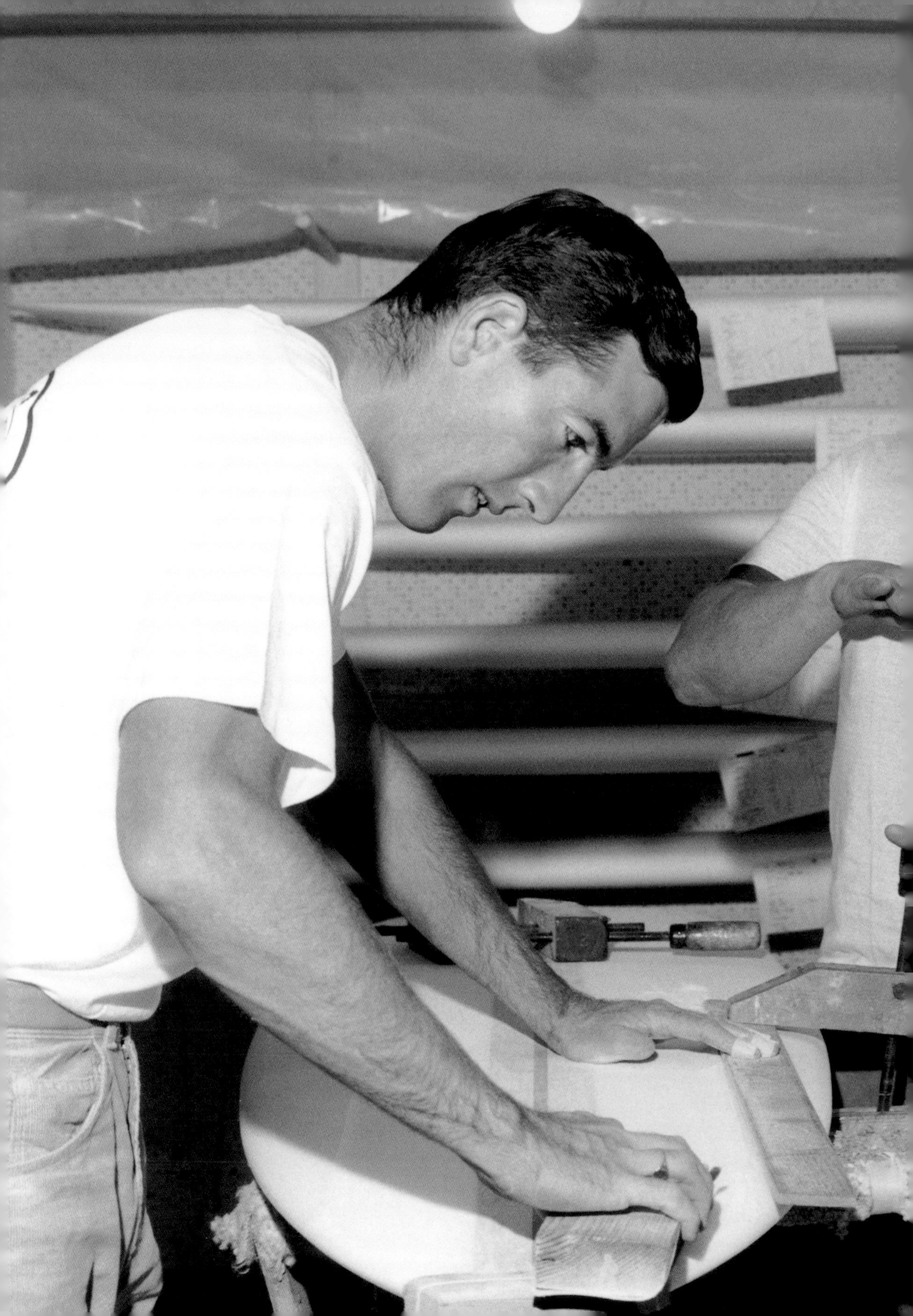

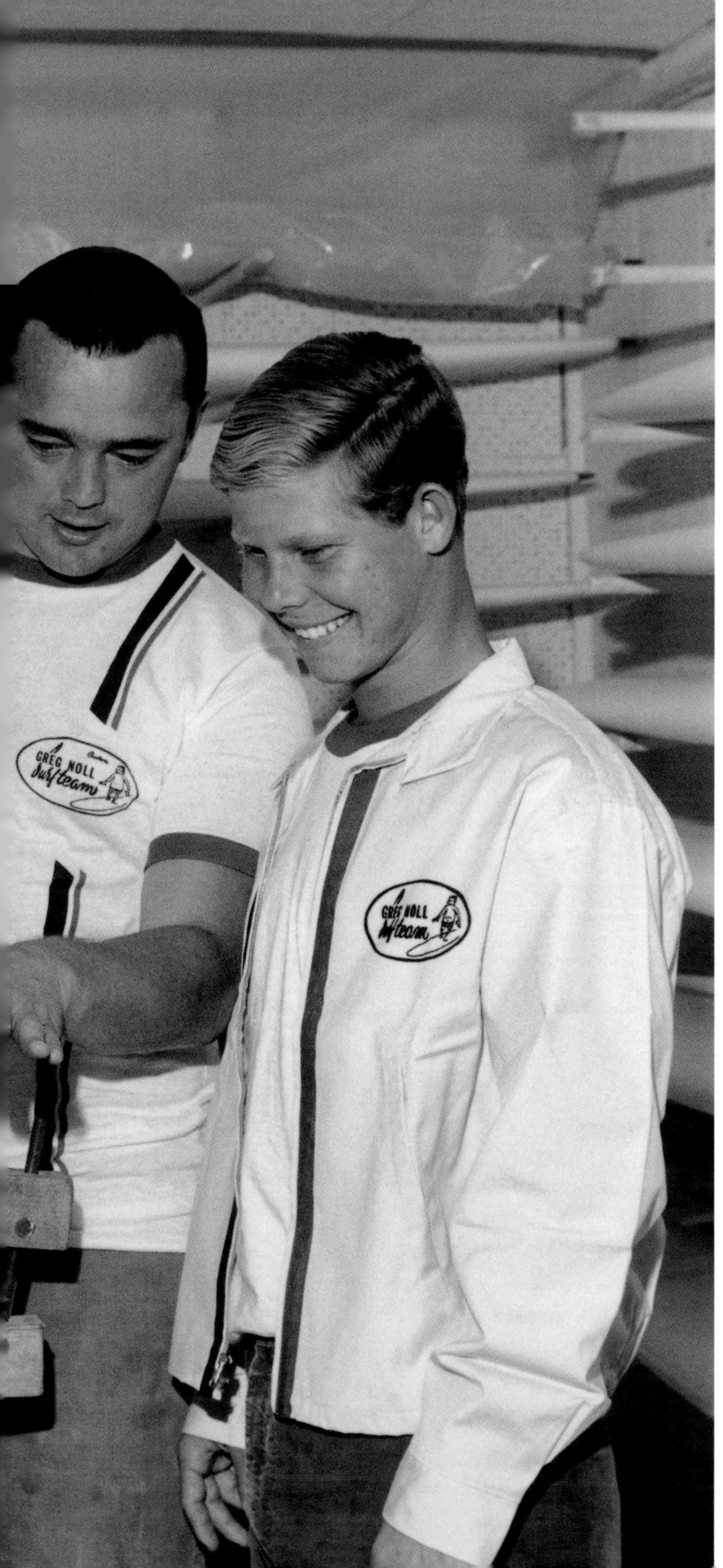

**Greg Noll Factory, Hermosa Beach,
1965**

Left to right: Rick James, Greg
Noll, Gary Propper. Propper was
an East Coast small-wave genius
renowned for his volatile style.

Von links nach rechts: Rick James,
Greg Noll, Gary Propper. Propper
war ein auf kleine Wellen
spezialisiertes Surfgenie von
der Ostküste, bekannt für seinen
unberechenbaren Stil.

De gauche à droite: Rick James,
Greg Noll et Gary Propper. Ce
dernier, véritable virtuose de la
petite vague de la côte Est, était
réputé pour son style turbulent.

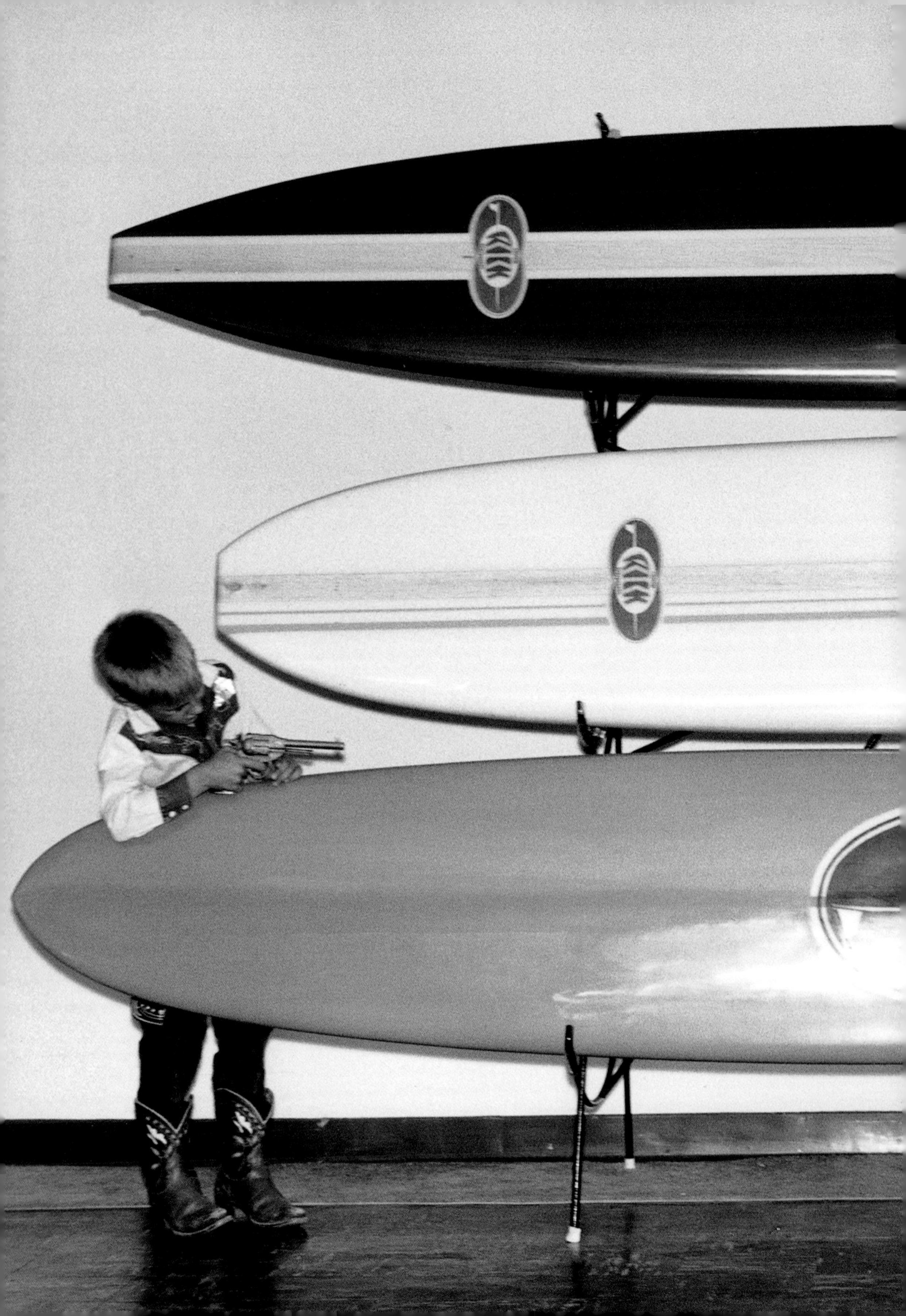

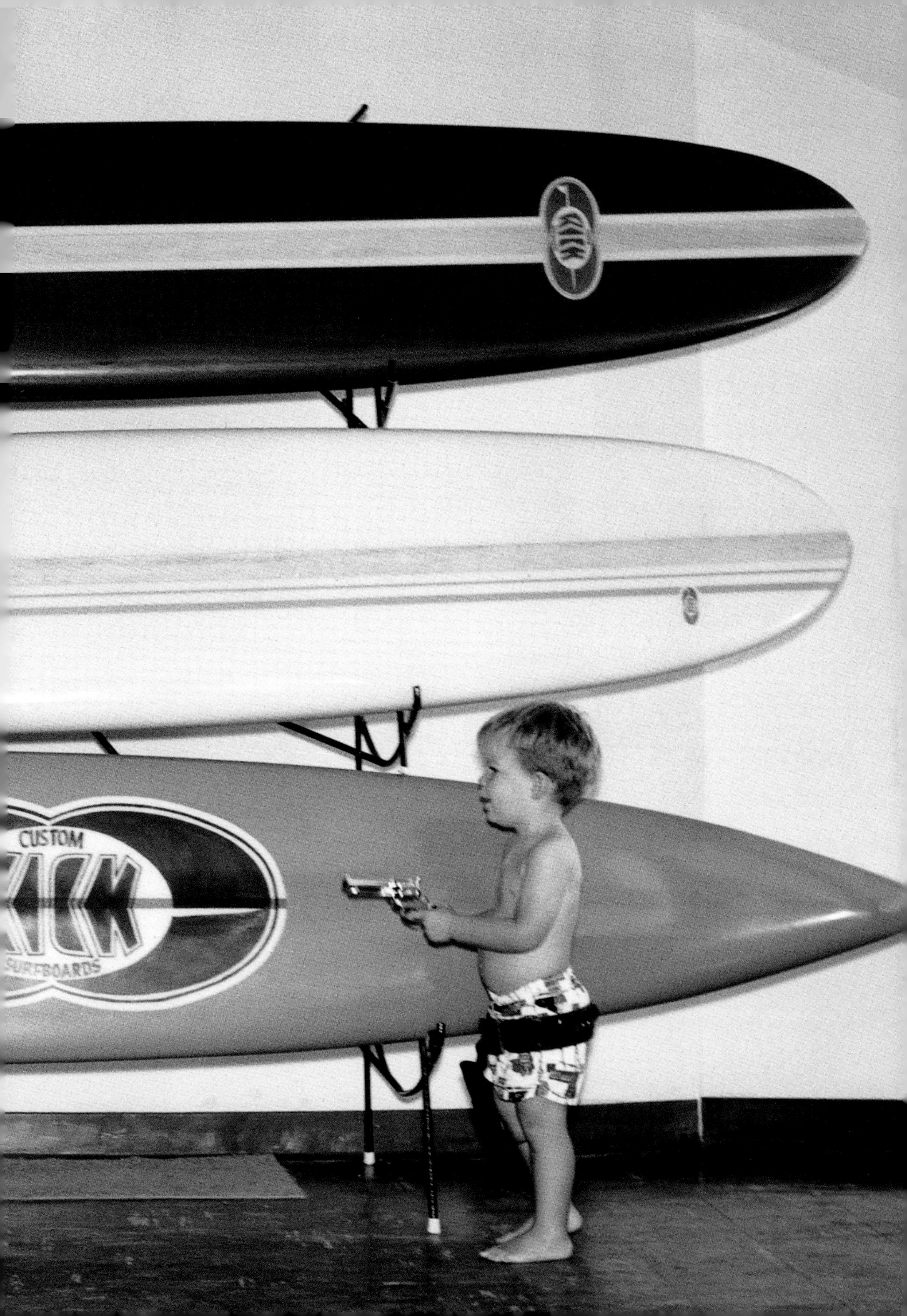

CUSTOM
KICK
SURFBOARDS

*Pages 222–223*

**Rick Surfboards, Hermosa Beach, 1963**

Young John Grannis shoots it out with the son of renowned South Bay shaper Rick Stoner at the Pacific Coast Highway shop.

Der kleine John Grannis beim Duell mit dem Sohn des berühmten South-Bay-Shaper Rick Stoner im Pacific Coast Highway Shop.

Caché derrière de «gros calibres», le petit John Grannis joue au cow-boy avec le fils de Rick Stoner, le célèbre shaper de South Bay, dans la boutique de ce dernier sur la Pacific Coast Highway.

**Bing Copeland Shop, Hermosa Beach, 1963**

Copeland's boards were some of the most prized on the West Coast. By 1974, however, he had sold the business and moved to the mountains of Idaho.

Die Bretter von Copeland gehörten zu den begehrtesten an der Westküste. 1974 verkaufte er jedoch das Geschäft und zog sich in die Berge von Idaho zurück.

Les planches de Bing Copeland comptaient parmi les plus prisées de la côte Ouest. En 1974, après avoir cédé sa boutique, il s'est retiré dans les montagnes de l'Idaho.

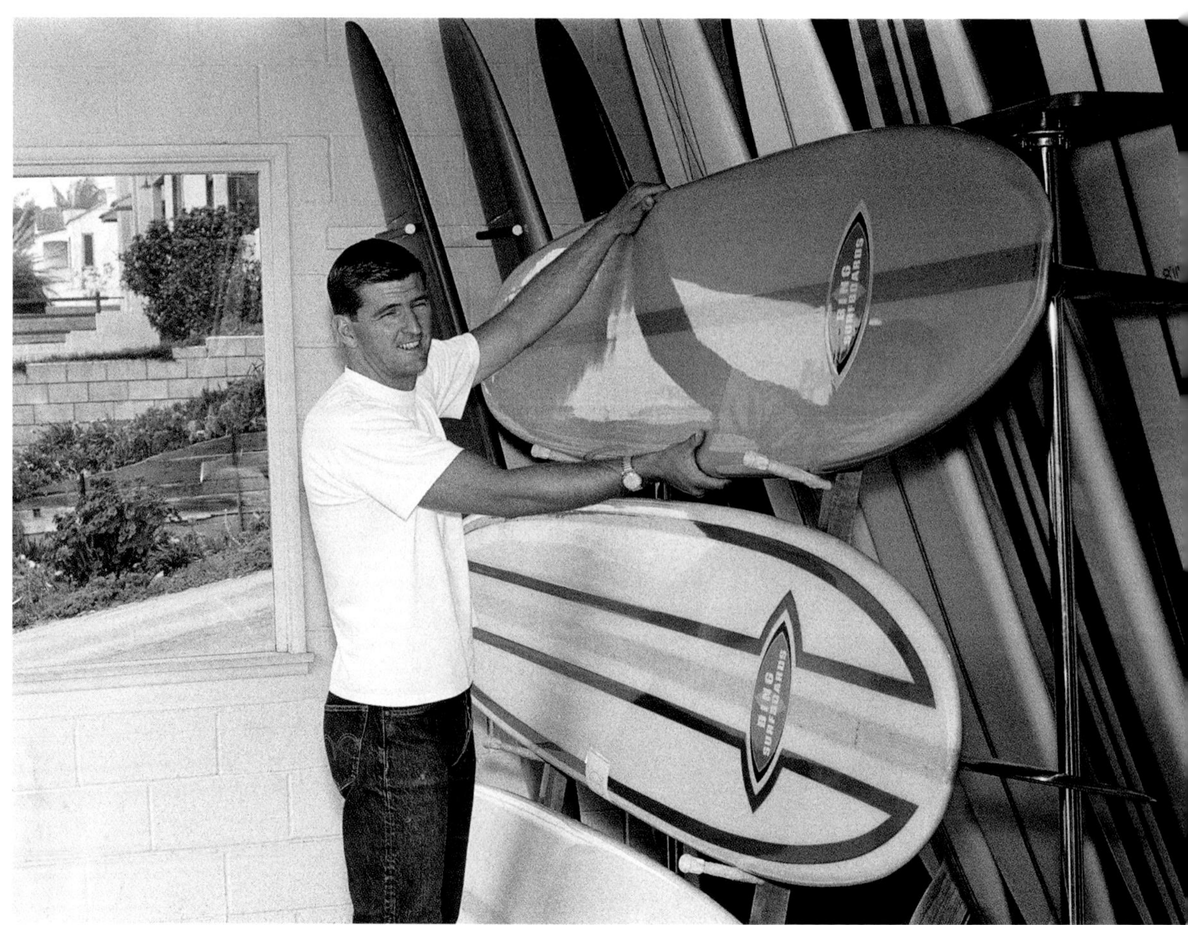

**Joe Quigg, Orange County, 1963**

Quigg, a visionary surfboard
designer, is credited with making
the first shortboard prototype,
the "Darrylin" board.

Quigg, ein Visionär der Surfbrett-
entwicklung, stellte den ersten
Prototyp eines Shortboards her,
das „Darrylin"-Board.

C'est au créateur visionnaire Joe
Quigg que l'on doit la « Darrylin
Board », le tout premier prototype
de shortboard.


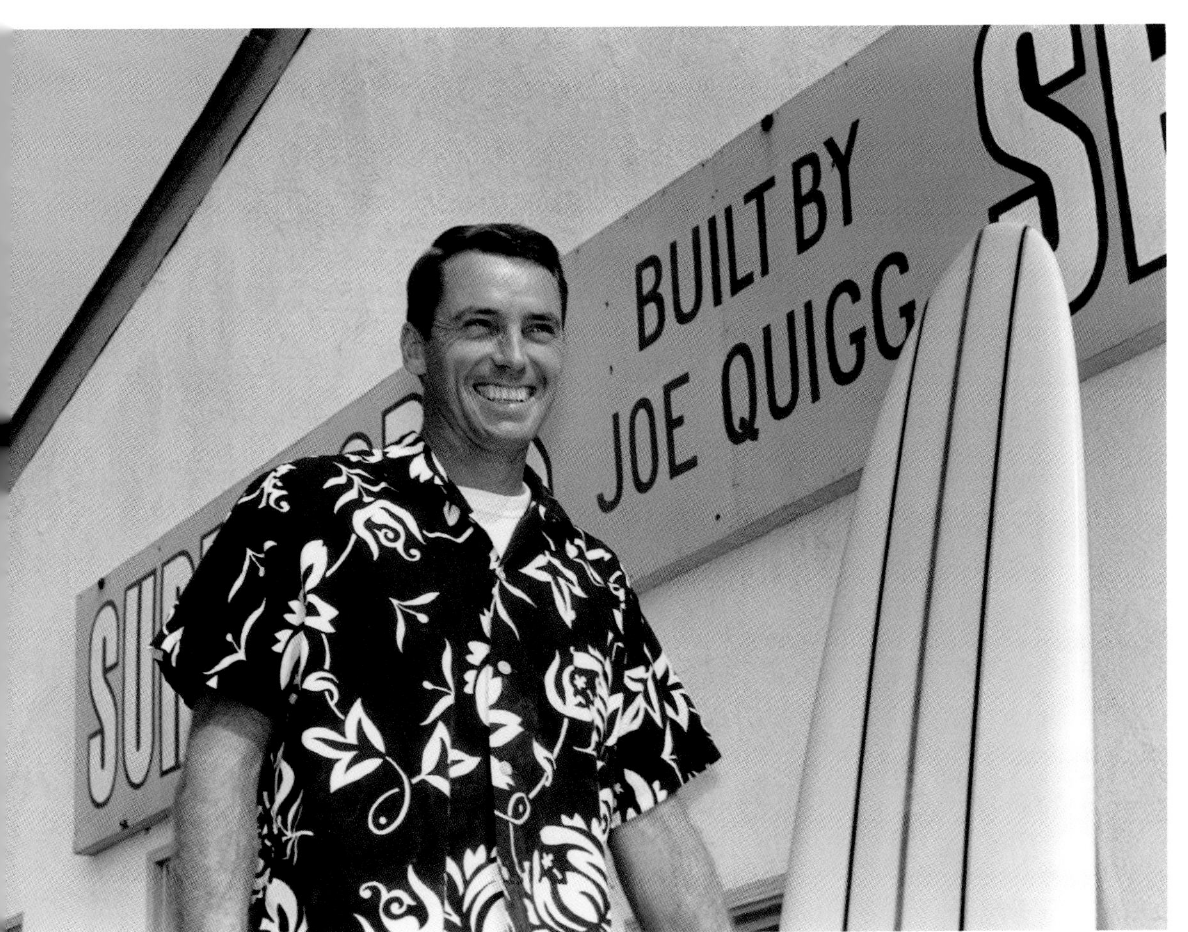

BUILT BY
JOE QUIGG
SURF

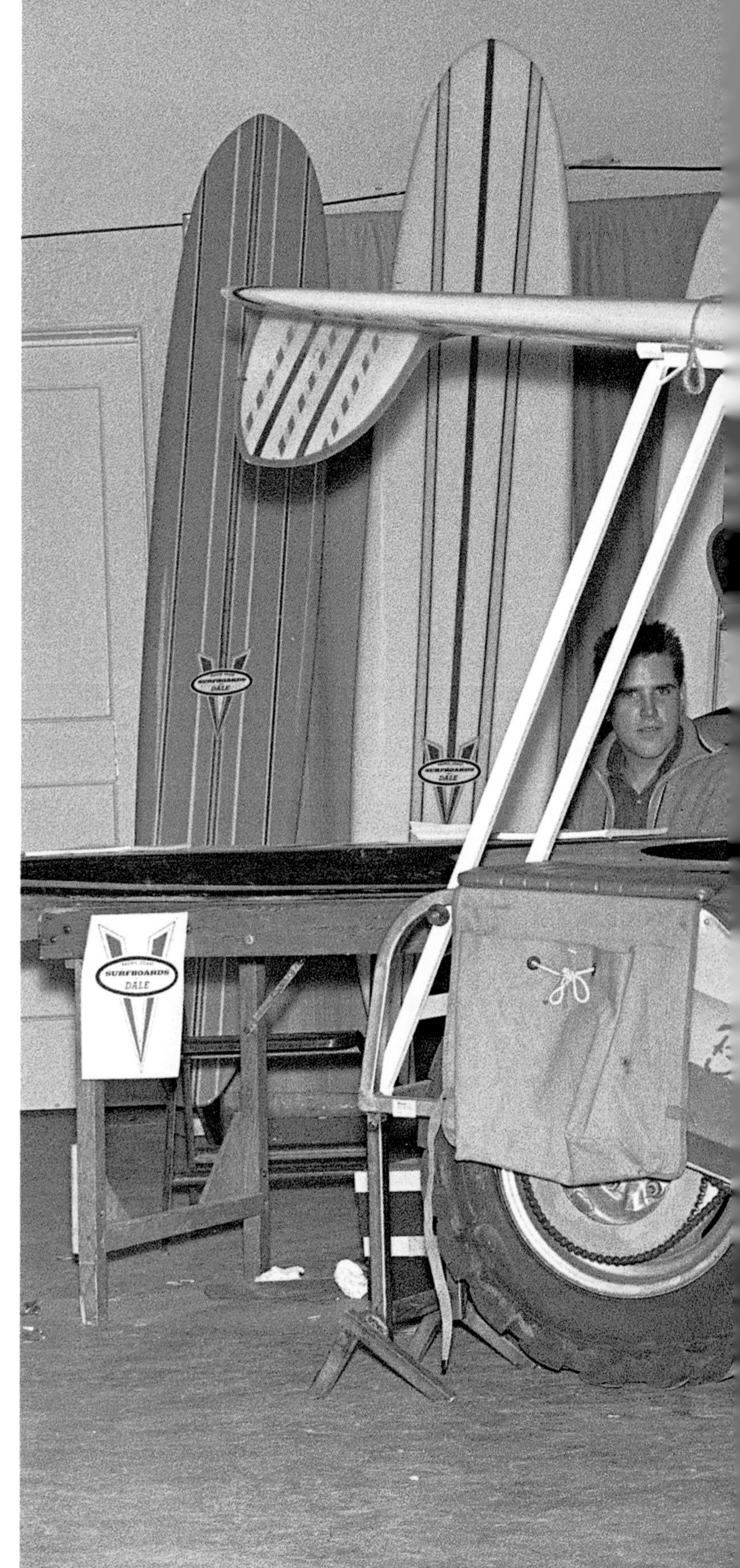


**Dale Velzy, Santa Monica, 1963**

Velzy, a charismatic entrepreneur
who split his passions equally
between surfing, hot rods, and
horses, was always on the lookout
for the next big thing. This beach
buggy wasn't it.

Velzy, ein charismatischer
Geschäftsmann, dessen Leiden-
schaften Surfen, Hot Rods und
Pferde waren, war immer auf der
Suche nach dem nächsten großen
Ding. Dieser Beach Buggy war
es nicht.

L'homme d'affaires charismatique
Dale Velzy avait trois passions : le
surf, les *hot rods* et les chevaux.
Il était constamment à l'affût d'un
bon coup. Ce buggy de plage ne
fera pas son affaire.

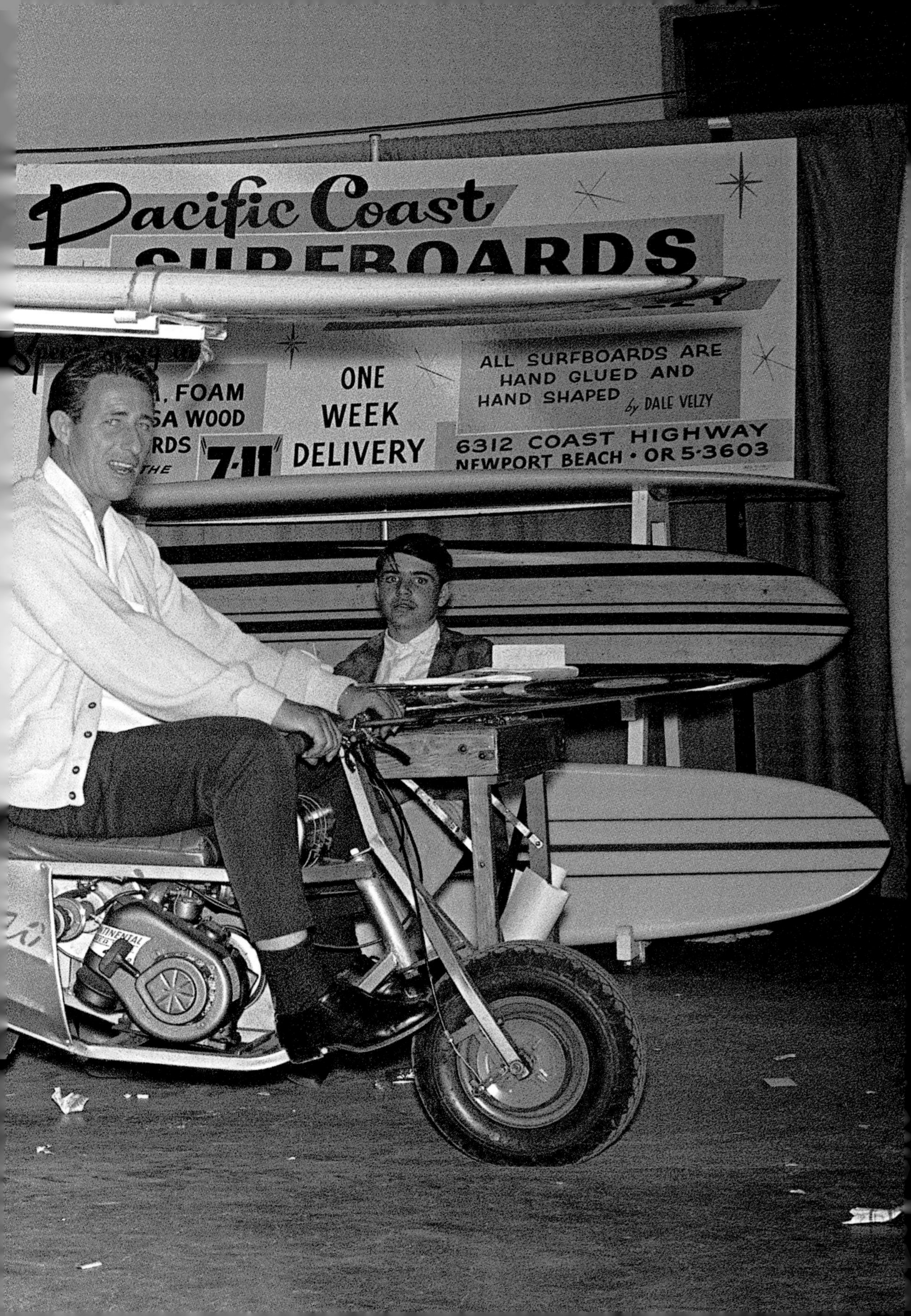

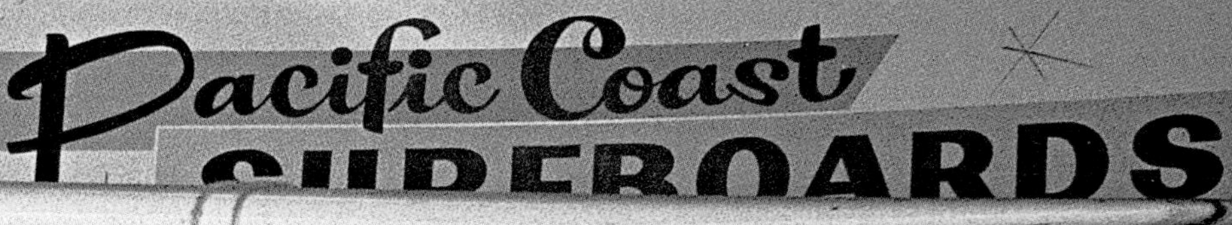
Pacific Coast
SURFBOARDS
ONE WEEK DELIVERY
ALL SURFBOARDS ARE HAND GLUED AND HAND SHAPED by DALE VELZY
FOAM
SA WOOD
RDS
7-11
6312 COAST HIGHWAY
NEWPORT BEACH • OR 5-3603

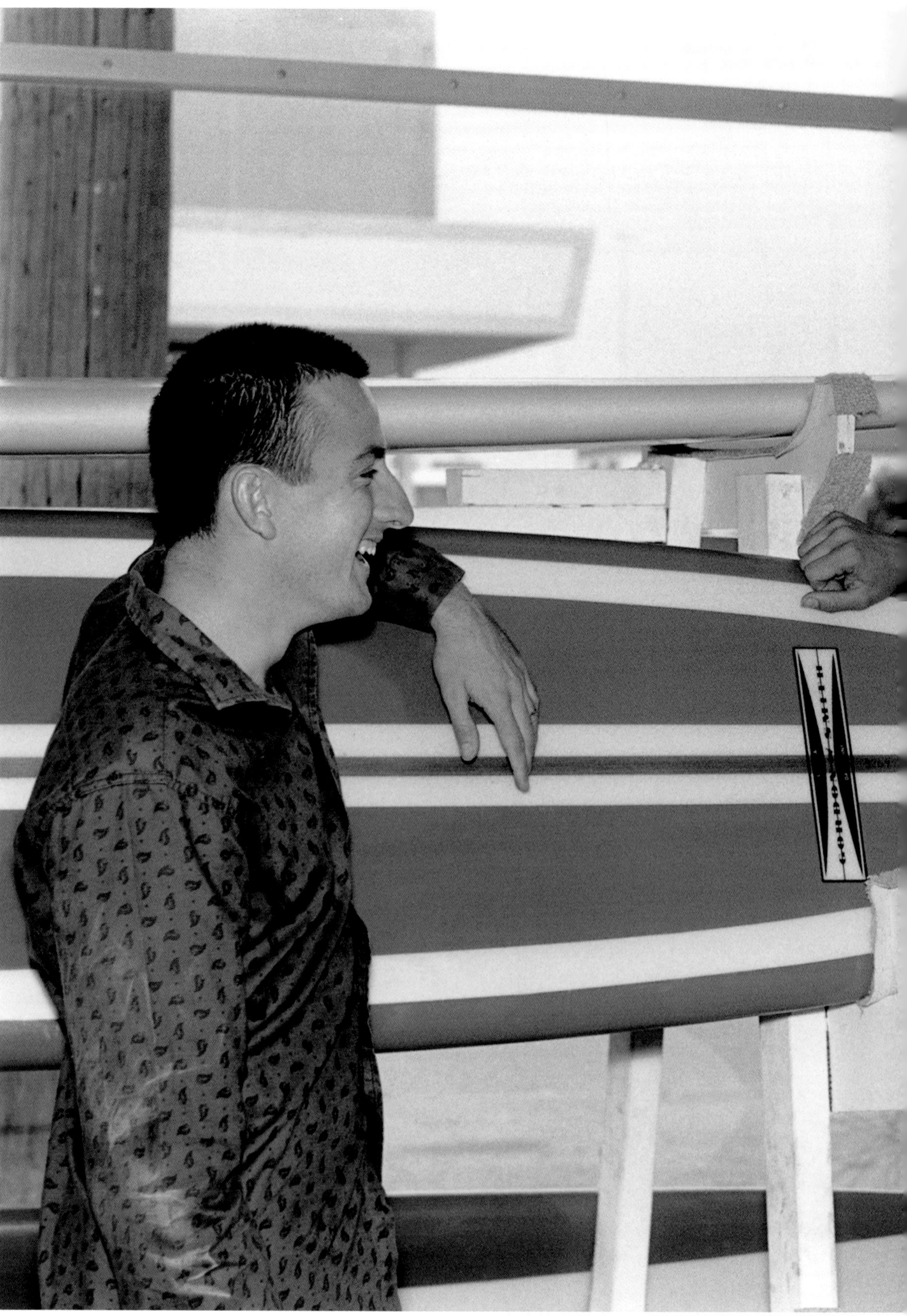

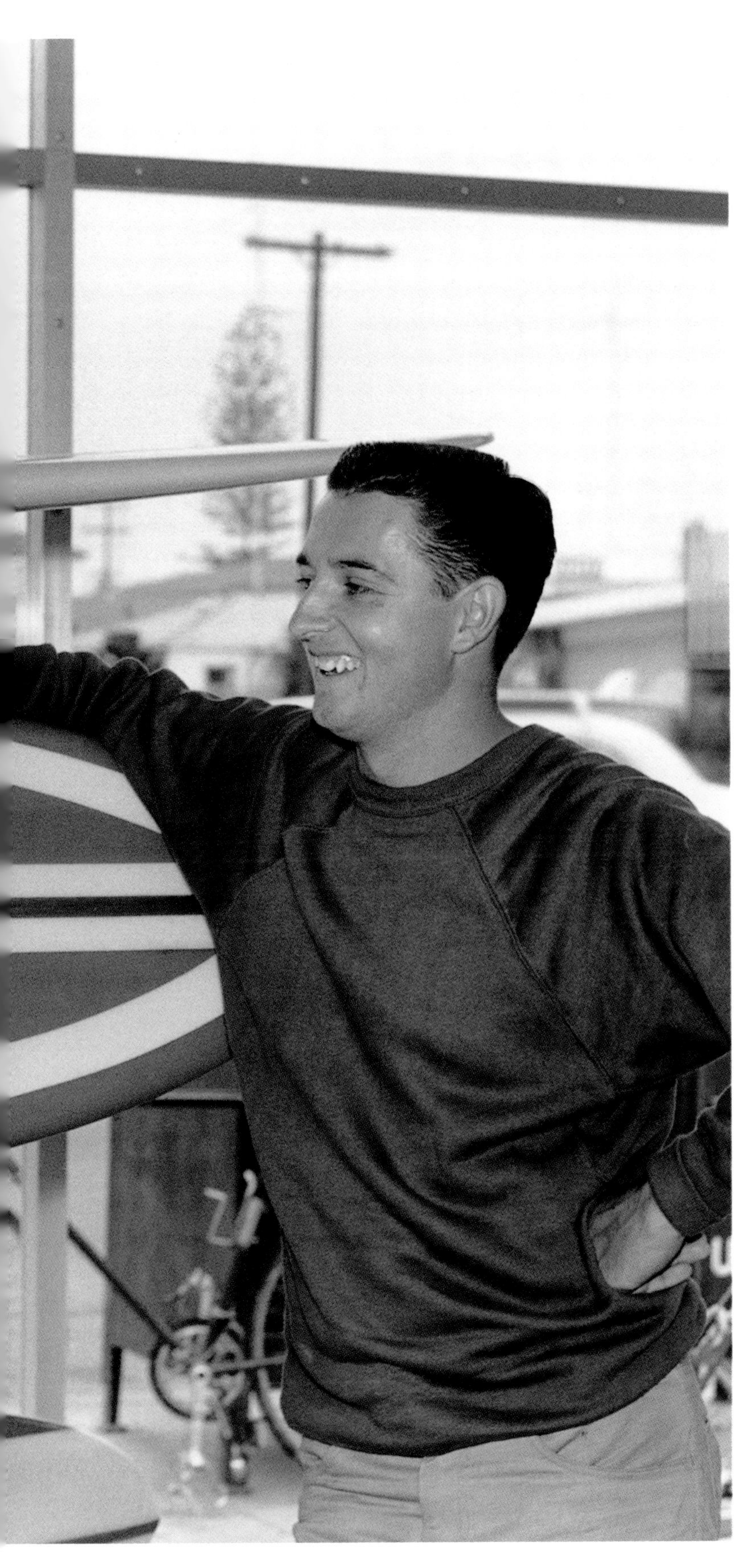

**Larry Gordon, Floyd Smith, Pacific Beach, San Diego, 1963**

Gordon and Smith, or "G&S," have employed the elite of surfboard shapers over their forty-six-year history.

Bei Gordon und Smith, oder „G&S", arbeiteten im Verlauf der sechsundvierzigjährigen Firmengeschichte alle führenden Surfbrett-Shaper.

Gordon and Smith (G&S) peut compter sur le talent de l'élite des shapers depuis plus de 46 ans.

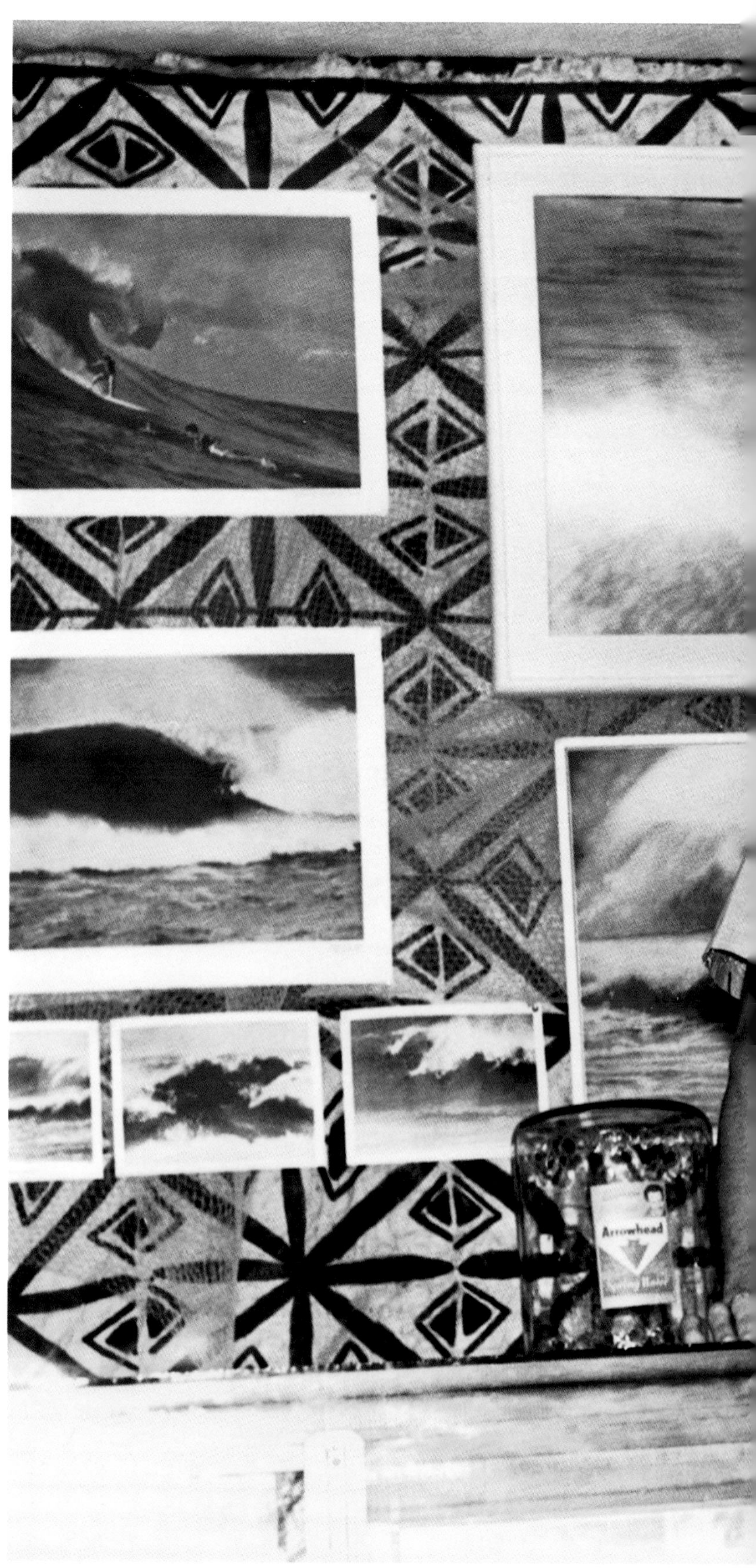

**Jack Haley Shop, Seal Beach, 1963**

Nicknamed "Mr. Excitement" for his charismatic style, Haley later opened a popular restaurant called Captain Jack's in nearby Sunset Beach.

Für seinen charismatischen Stil erhielt Haley den Spitznamen „Mr. Excitement". Später eröffnete er ein beliebtes Restaurant mit dem Namen „Captain Jack's" am nahe gelegenen Sunset Beach.

Surnommé « Mister Excitement » en raison de son style charismatique, Jack Haley ouvrira plus tard non loin de sa boutique, à Sunset Beach, un restaurant très en vogue auquel il donnera le nom de Captain Jack's.

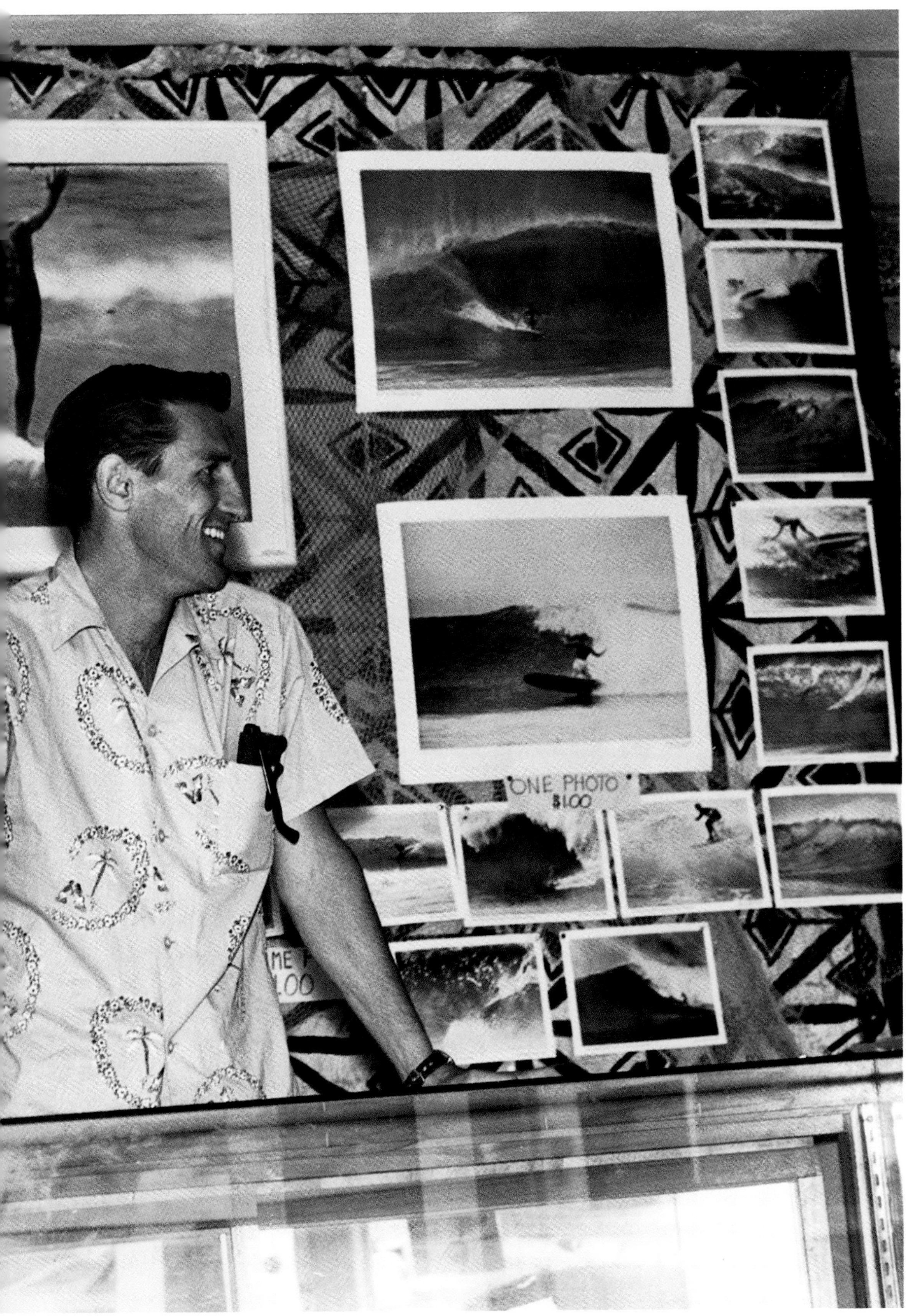
ONE PHOTO
$1.00
ME
$1.00

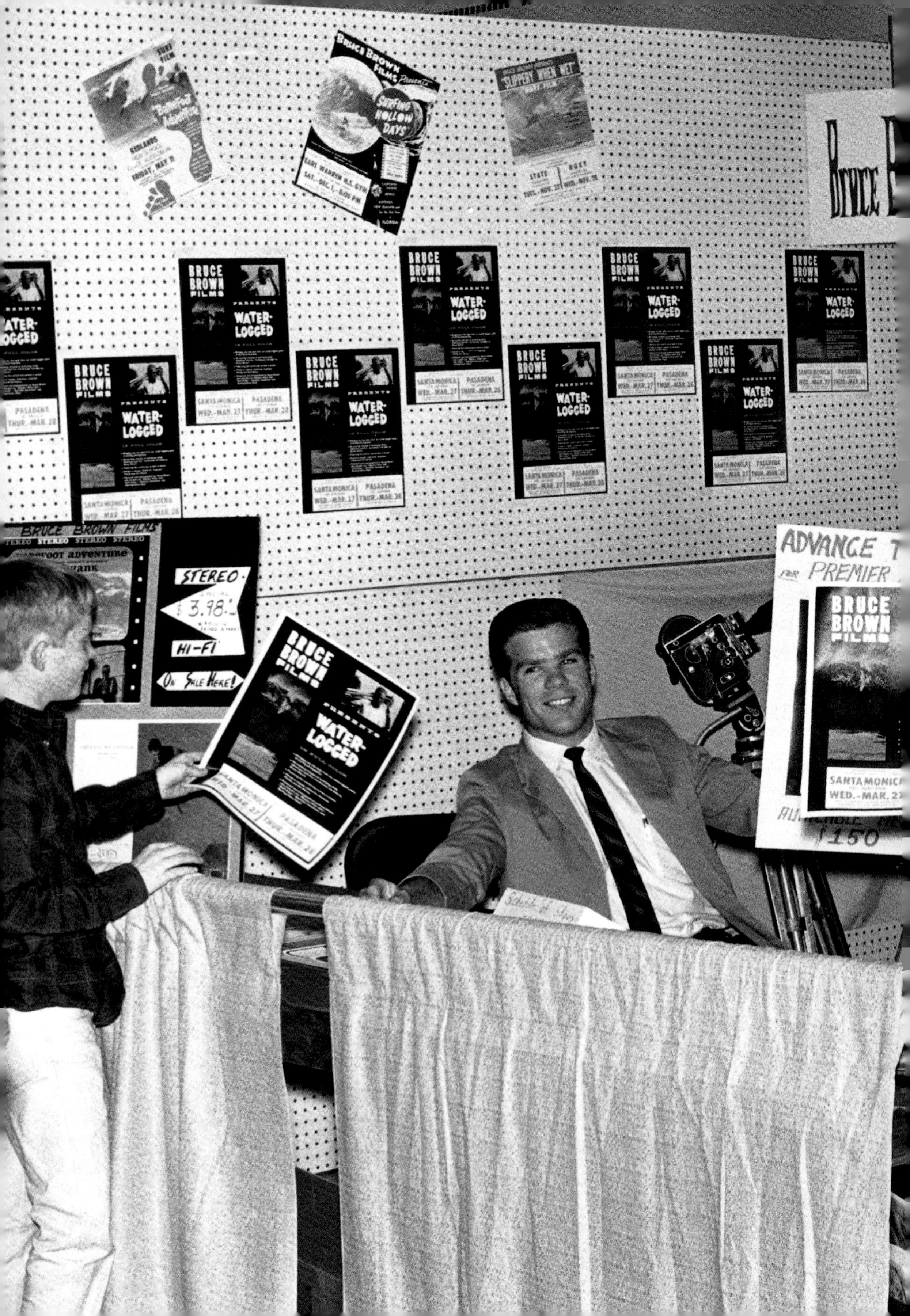

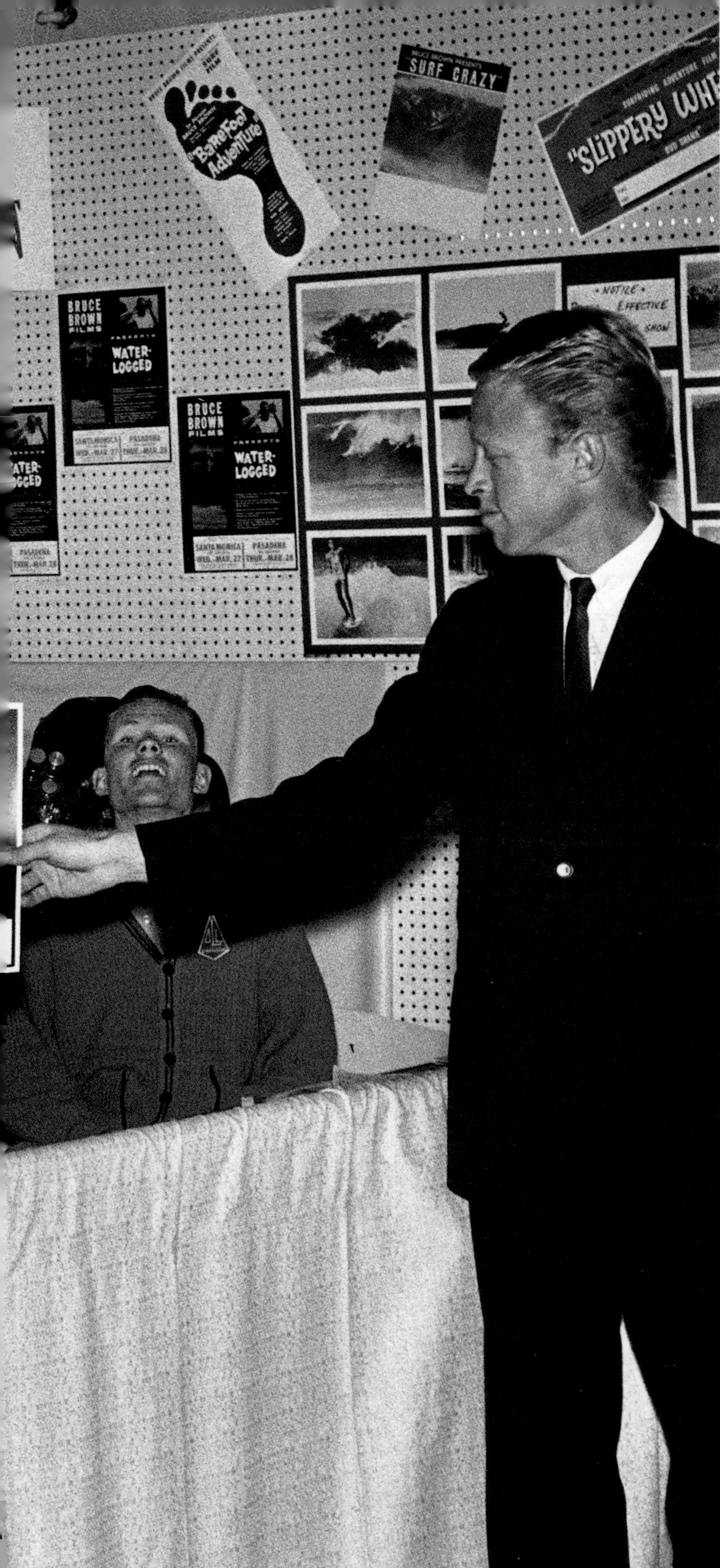




**Santa Monica, 1963**

"Bergman of the Boards" Bruce Brown made five full-length surf films from 1957 to 1963 before embarking on his masterpiece, *The Endless Summer*.

Der „Bergman der Boards" Bruce Brown drehte zwischen 1957 und 1963 fünf Surffilme, bevor er sein Meisterwerk *The Endless Summer* vorlegte.

Bruce Brown, dit le « Bergman de la planche de surf », a réalisé cinq longs métrages consacrés au surf entre 1957 et 1963 avant de se lancer dans son œuvre maîtresse, *The Endless Summer*.

Pages 234–235
**Hermosa Beach, 1965**

At a "Dana Point Mafia" party thrown by Greg Noll at his Hermosa Beach factory. Left to right: Mickey Muñoz, Jeff Logan, Ronald Patterson.

Auf einer von Greg Noll in seiner Hermosa Beach Factory veranstalteten „Dana Point Mafia"-Party. Von links nach rechts: Mickey Muñoz, Jeff Logan, Ronald Patterson.

Au cours d'une soirée du club « Dana Point Mafia » organisée par Greg Noll dans sa boutique sur la plage de Hermosa. De gauche à droite : Mickey Muñoz, Jeff Logan et Ronald Patterson.

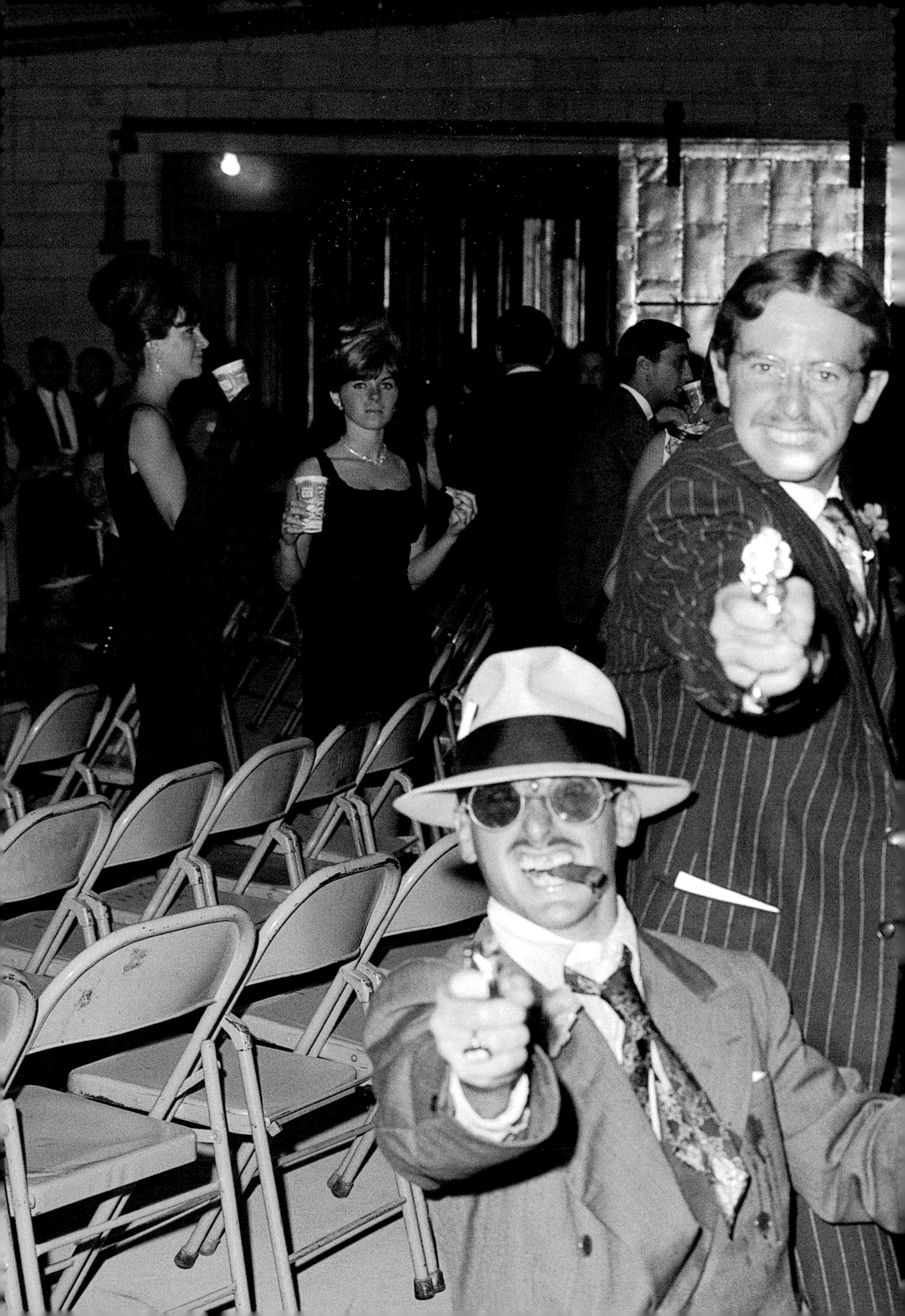

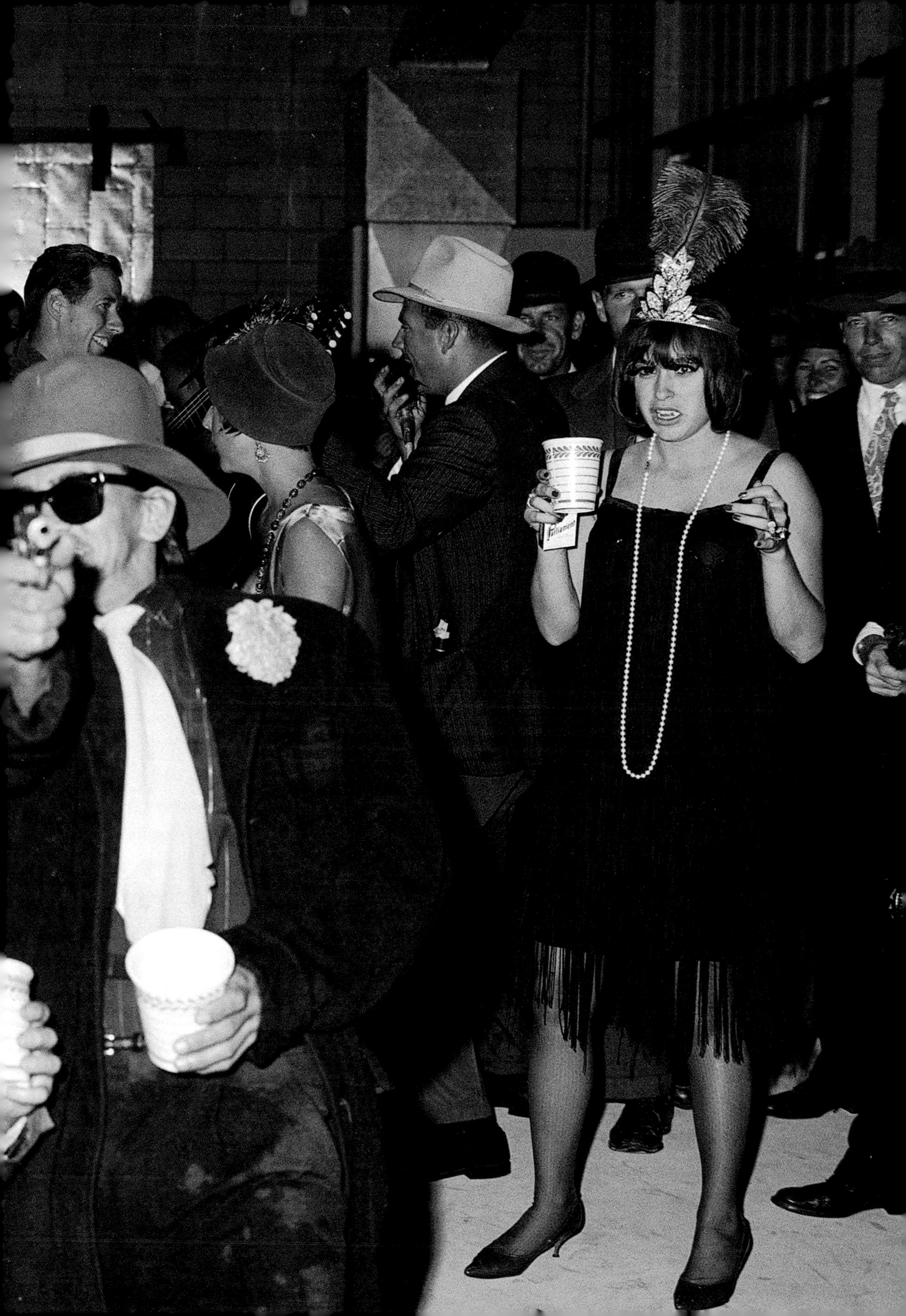

**Malibu, 1967**

Beach haircut.

Haare schneiden am Strand.

Séance de coiffure
sur la plage.

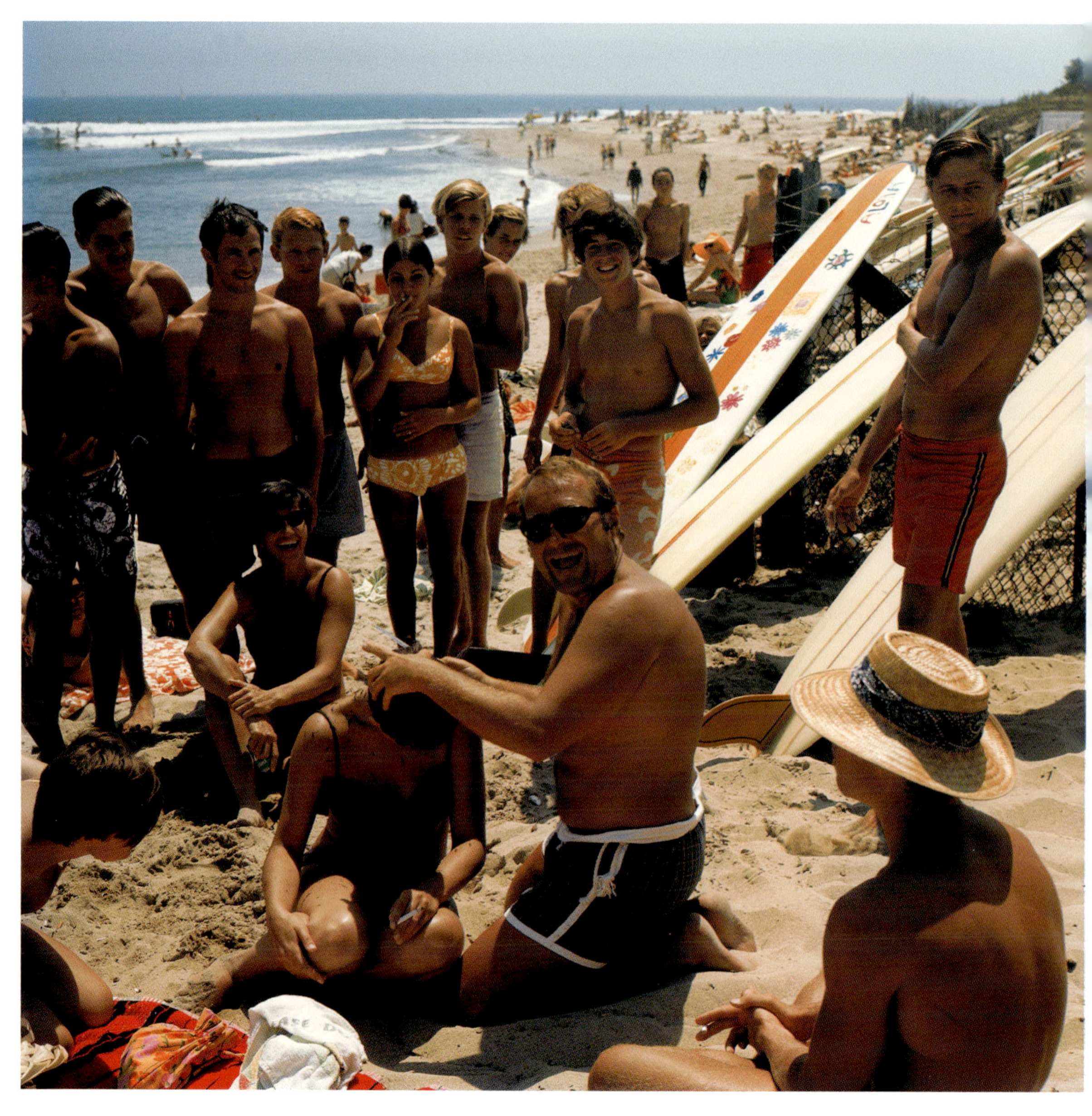

## Hermosa Beach, 1967

It seemed that every other girl on Hermosa Beach, located just five miles from Los Angeles International Airport, was an off-duty stewardess.

Man hatte den Eindruck, dass jedes zweite Mädchen in Hermosa Beach, nur acht Kilometer vom Los Angeles International Airport entfernt, eine Stewardess außer Dienst war.

Les filles de Hermosa Beach étaient si belles qu'on pouvait penser que la moitié d'entre elles étaient des hôtesses de l'air en escale (la plage n'est qu'à huit kilomètres de l'aéroport international de Los Angeles).

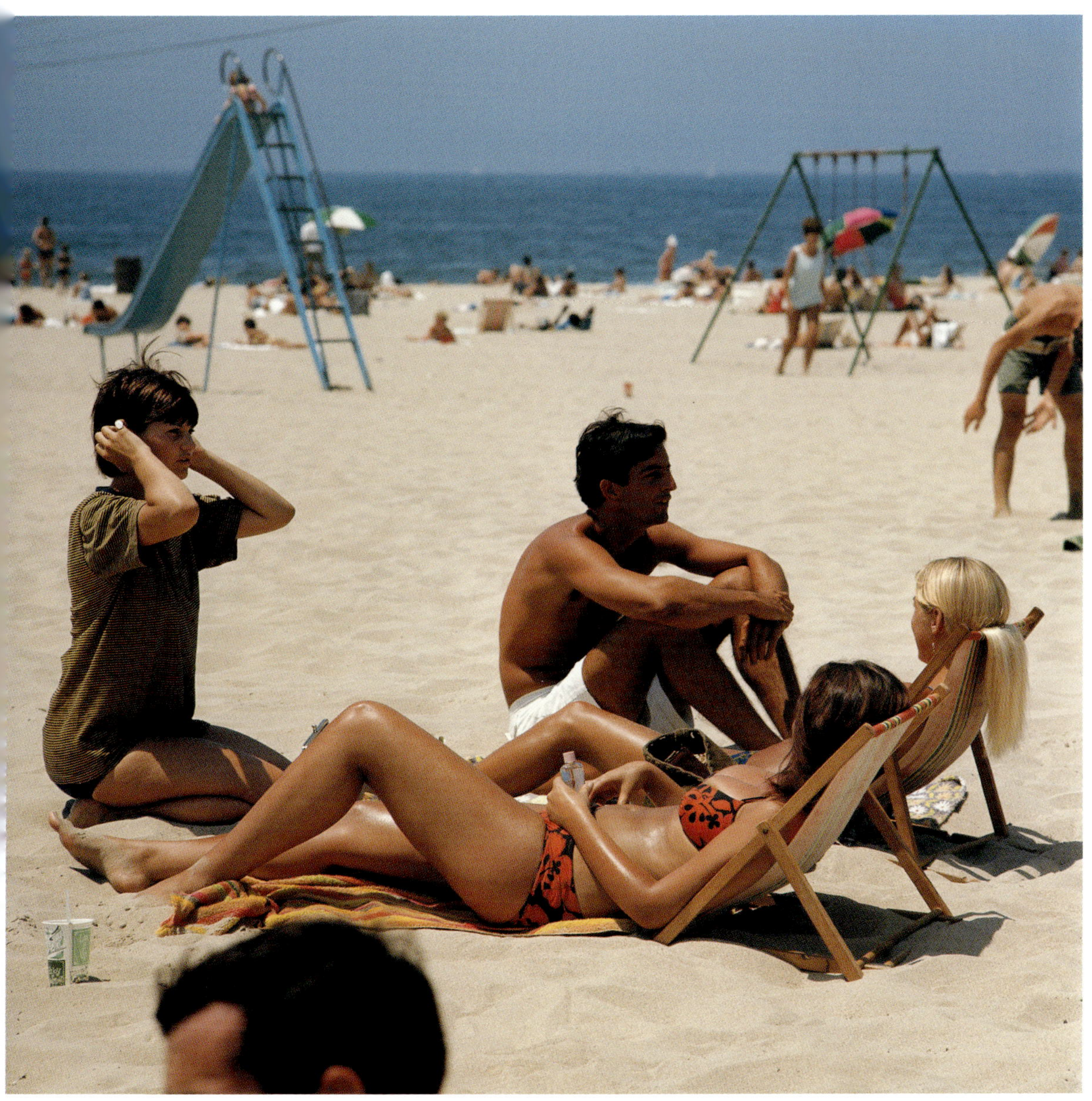

## Malibu, 1965

Sixties surfing, while not misogynis-
tic, was definitely sexist. A perfect
"surfer girl" was expected to wait
hours for her surf hero to come in.

Die Surfszene in den Sechzigern
war zwar nicht frauenfeindlich,
aber definitiv sexistisch. Von einem
perfekten „Surfer Girl" wurde
erwartet, dass es stundenlang
wartete, bis ihr Held vom Surfen
zurückkam.

Sans être misogynes, les surfeurs
des années 1960 cultivaient
néanmoins un sexisme à toute
épreuve. Même les « surfeuses de
rêve » devaient attendre des heures
entières le retour de leurs héros,
trop occupés qu'ils étaient à danser
avec les vagues.

## Hermosa Beach, 1967

It took eons of westward global
migration to create this iconic
California beach scene.

Generationen mussten westwärts
ziehen, bis diese typisch kalifornische Strandszene entstehen konnte.

Cette scène de plage idyllique
de Californie est l'aboutissement
d'un long processus de migration
humaine et de conquête de l'Ouest.

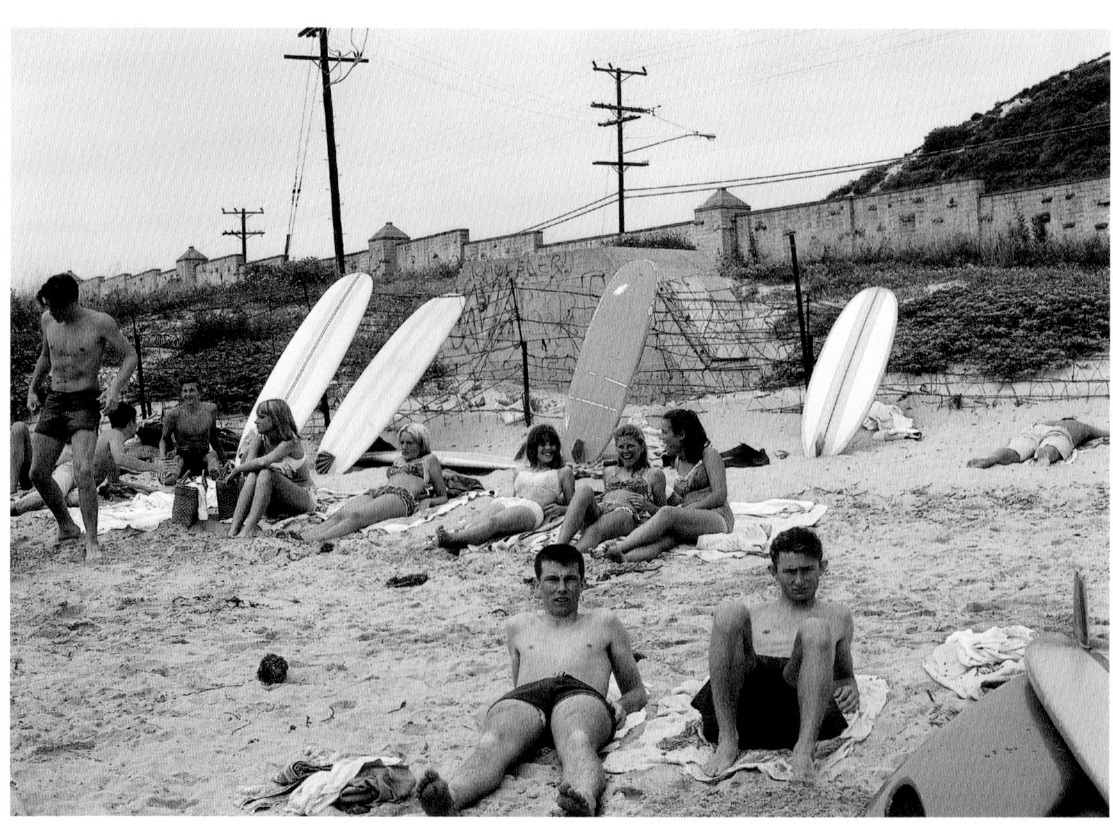

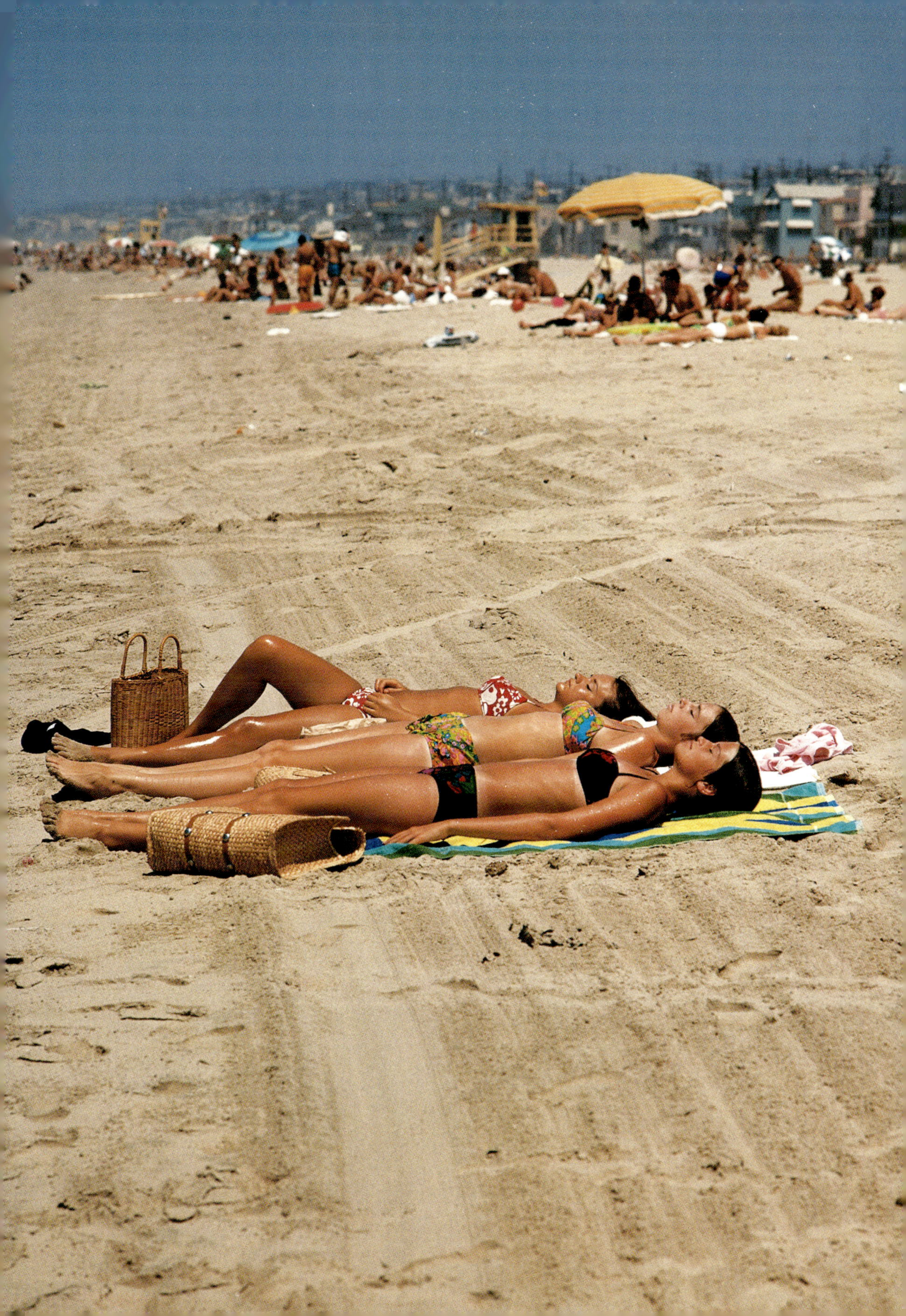

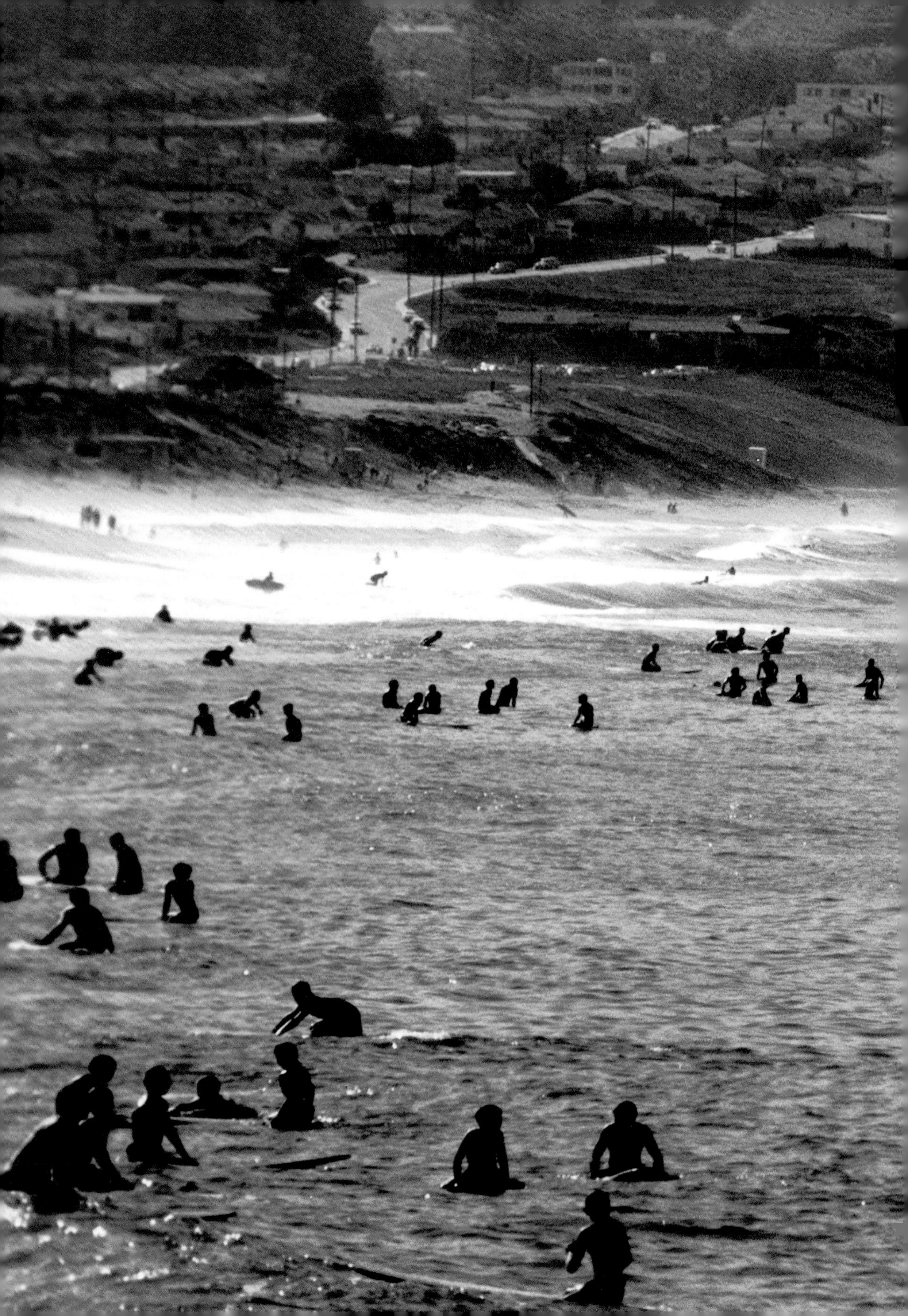

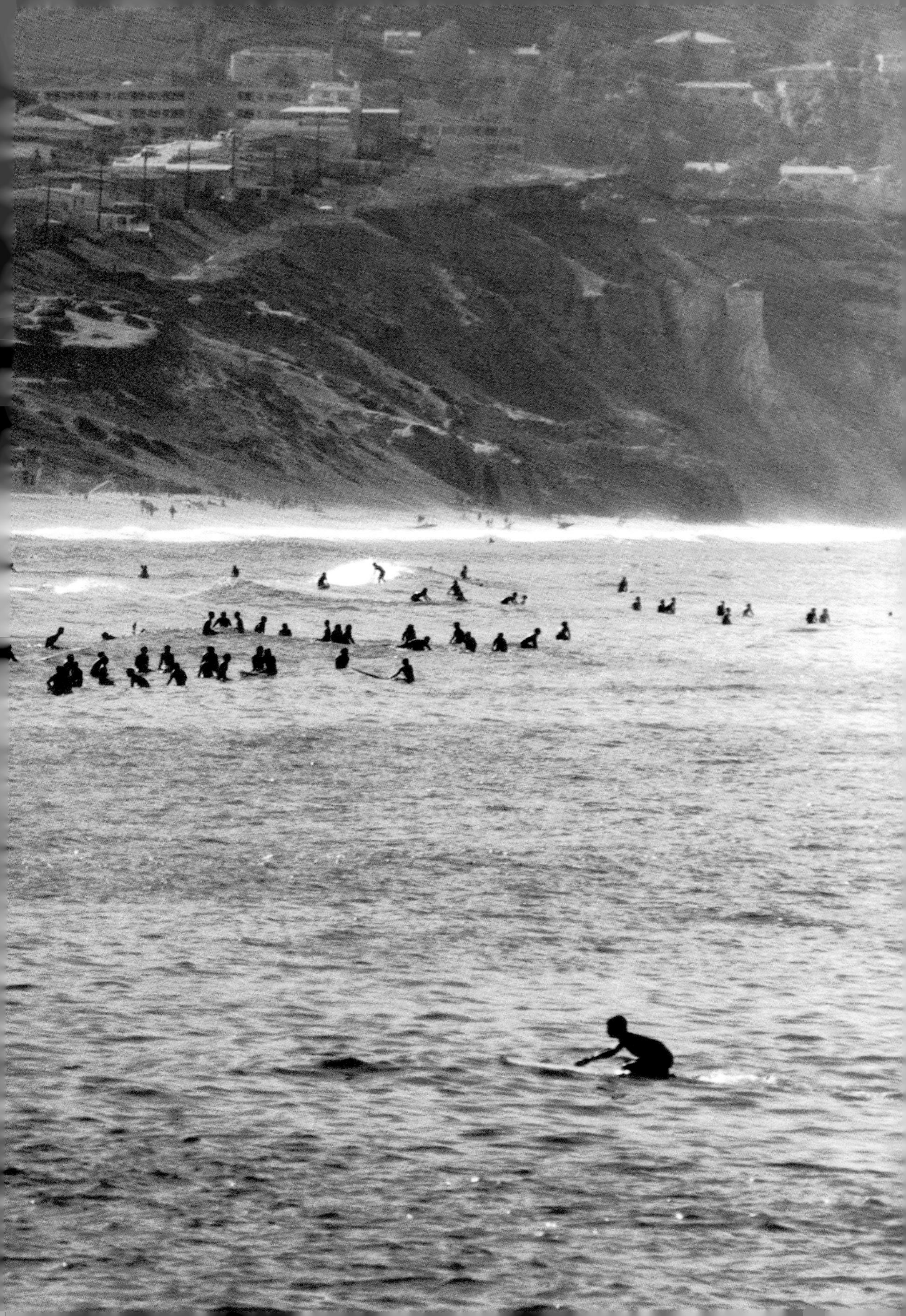

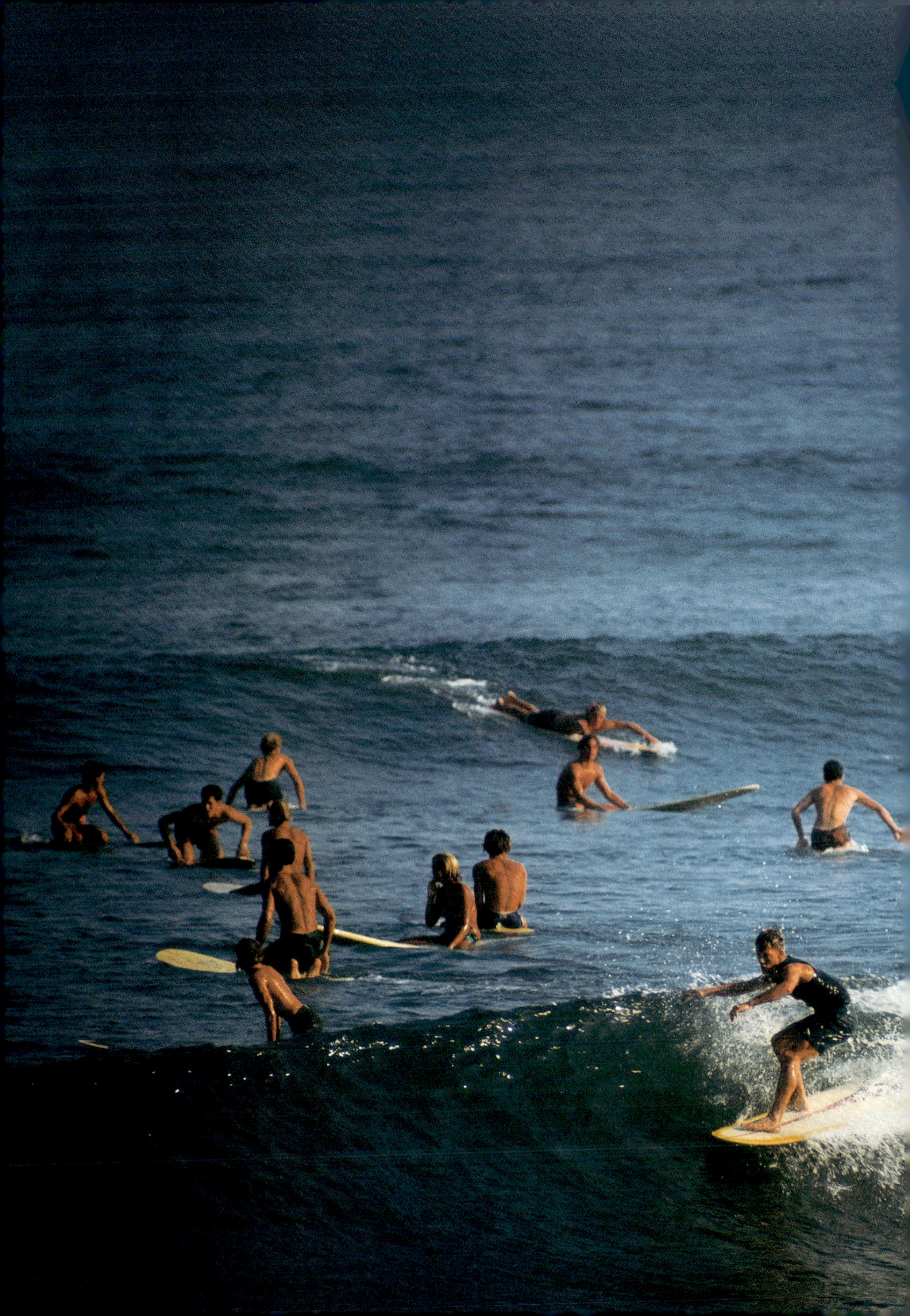

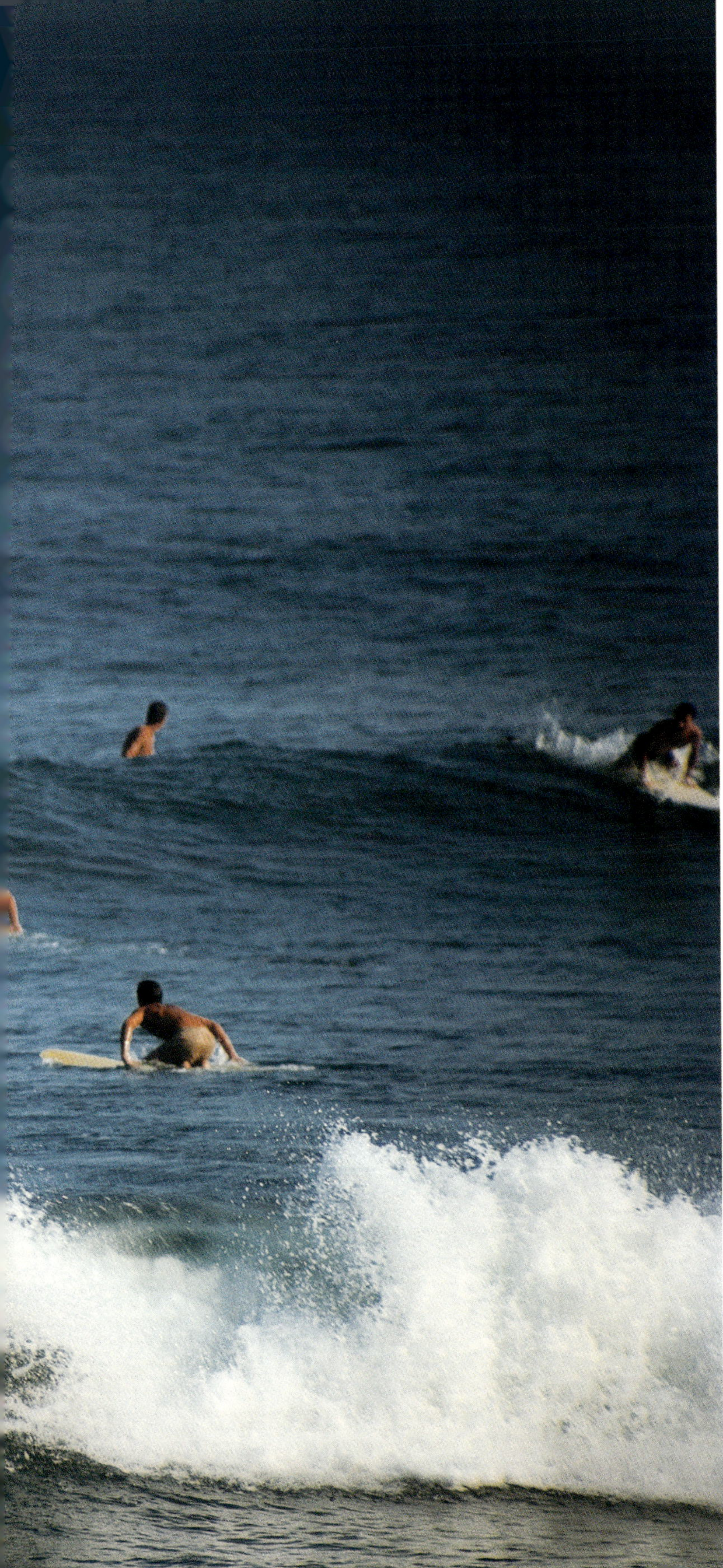



**Torrance Beach, 1964**

A weekend logjam at Rat's Beach.
The Palos Verdes peninsula is in
the background.

Ein Wochenendstau am Rat's
Beach. Im Hintergrund sieht man
die Halbinsel von Palos Verdes.

Affluence de week-end à Rat's
Beach. À l'arrière-plan, la
péninsule de Palos Verdes.

**Malibu, 1967**

When Grannis returned with a
friend to Malibu shortly after World
War II, they found a crowd of
twelve people surfing. "That's it,"
he said. "This place is ruined."

Als Grannis kurz nach dem Zweiten
Weltkrieg mit einem Freund zurück
nach Malibu kam, sahen sie zwölf
Leute surfen. Er sagte: „Das war's.
Der Ort ist ruiniert."

Quand Grannis retourne à Malibu
avec un ami peu après la Seconde
Guerre mondiale, il y croise en
tout et pour tout une douzaine de
surfeurs. « Et voilà, soupire-t-il, il
n'y a plus rien à chercher par ici ! »

**Hermosa Beach, 1960**

**Johnny Fain, Miki Dora, Malibu, 1965**

The infamous Dora "tap." Fain later
said, "When I felt those icy fingers
along the seat of my pants, I knew
it was all over."

Der berüchtigte „Klaps" von Dora.
Fain sagte später: „Als ich diese
eisigen Finger an meiner Hose
spürte, wusste ich, dass es aus ist."

La fameuse « fessée de Miki Dora »
a inspiré un jour à Johnny Fain le
commentaire suivant : « Quand je
sentais ces horribles doigts glacés
sur mon postérieur, je savais que
la partie était perdue. »

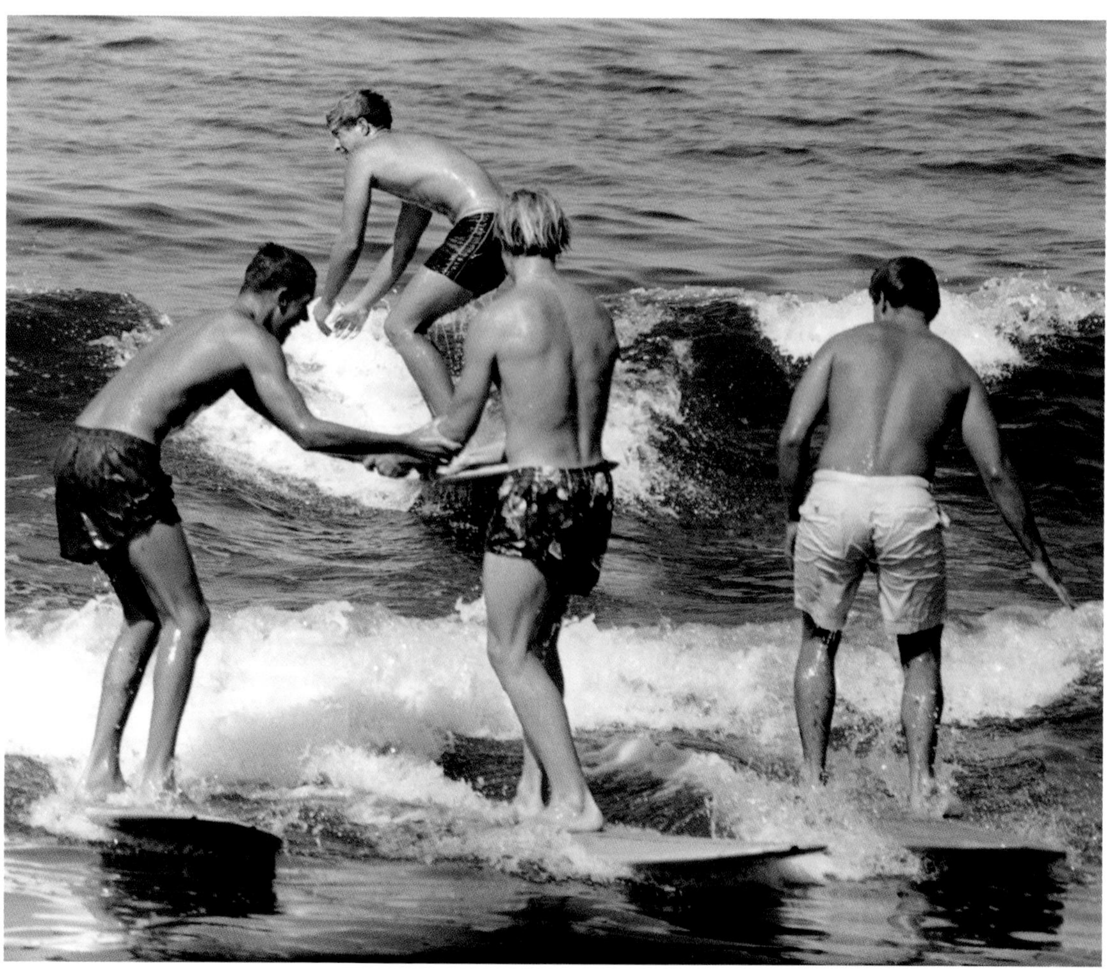

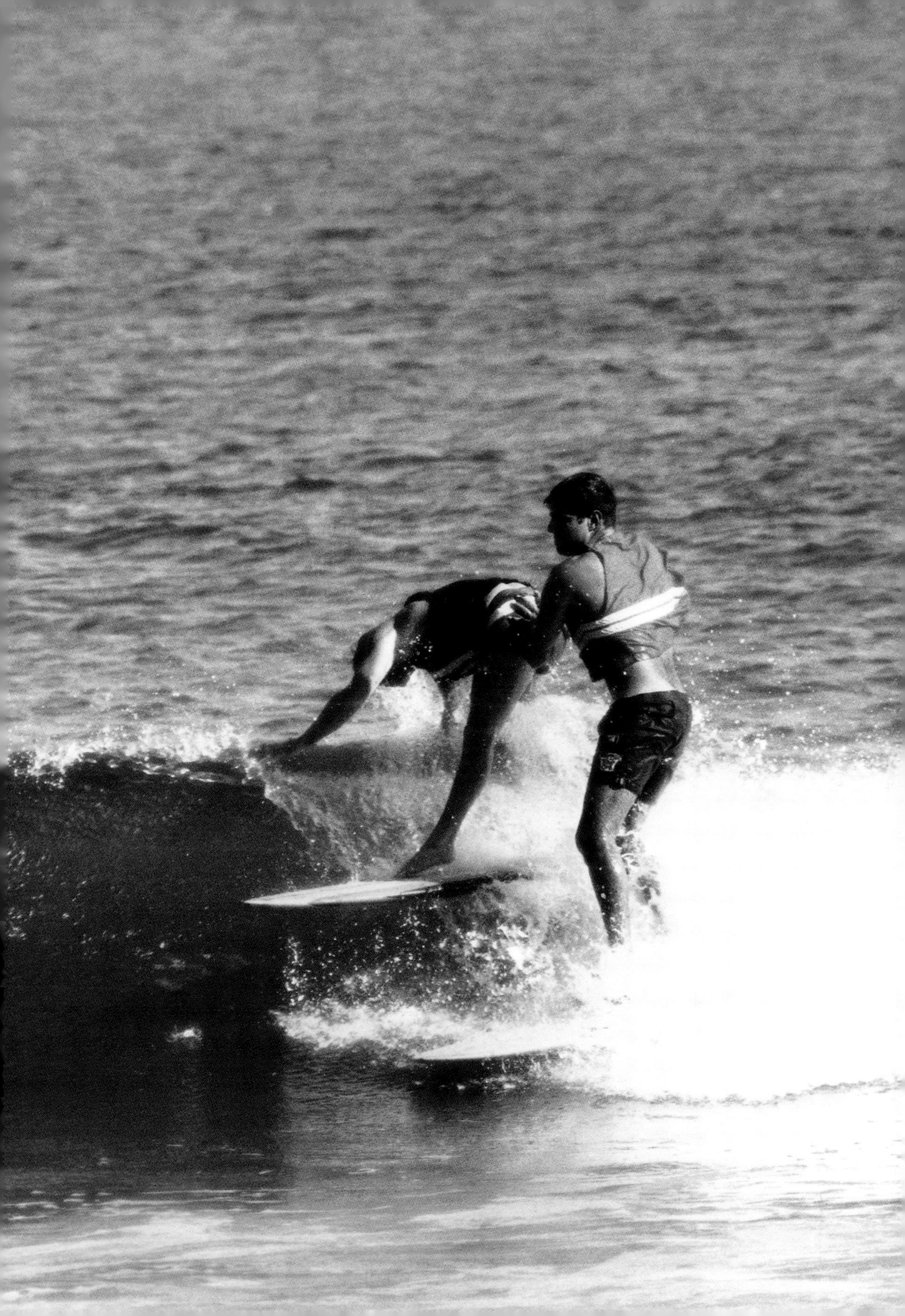

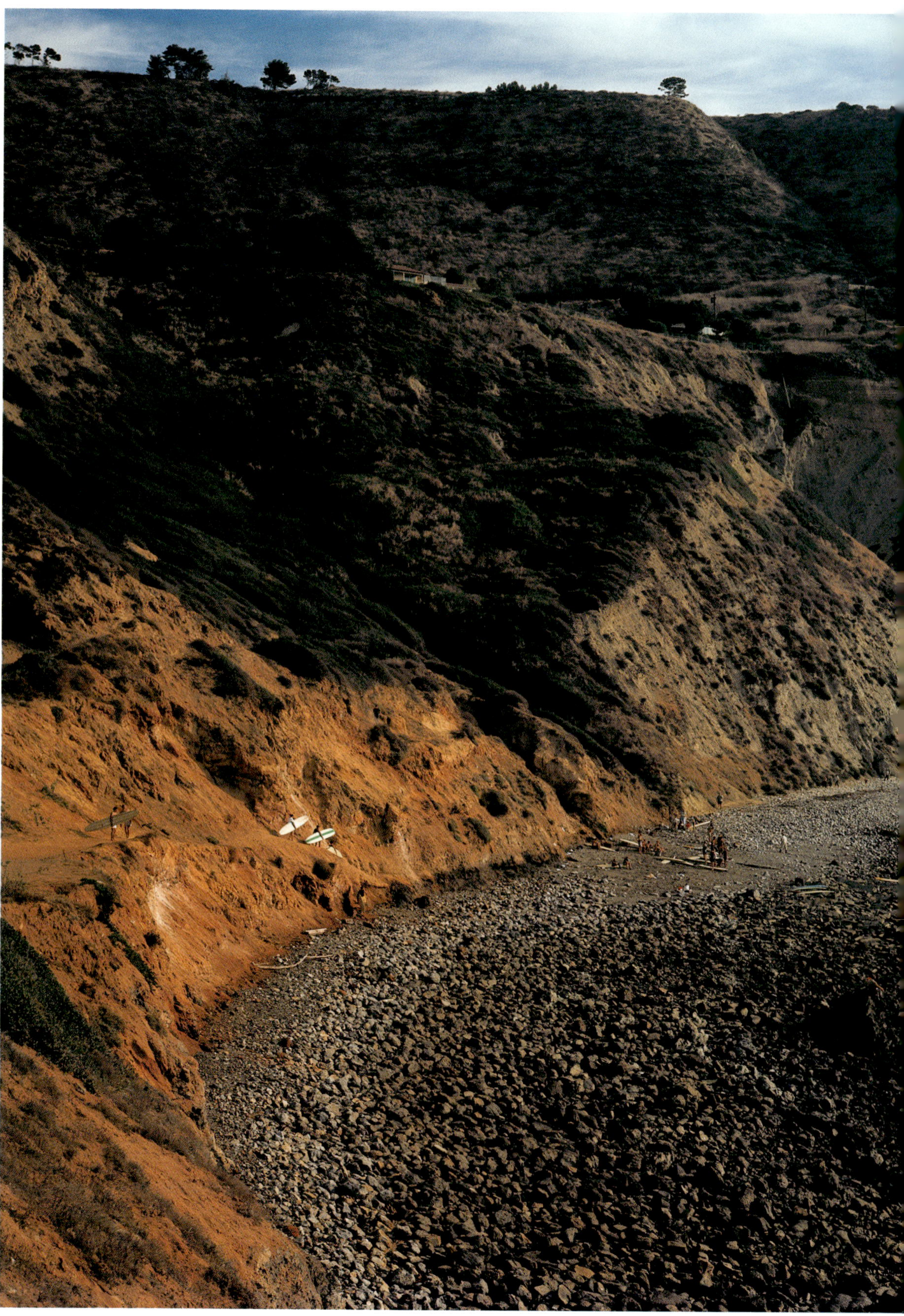

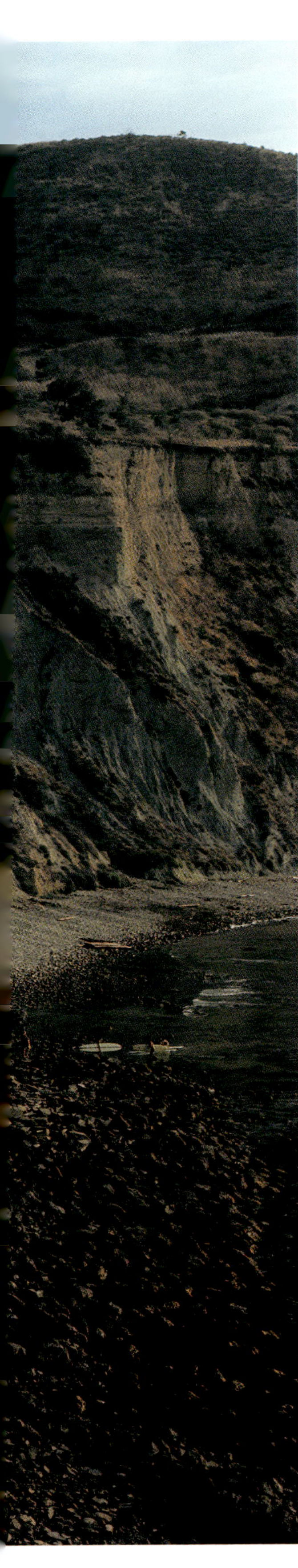

**Palos Verdes Cove, 1967**

On a big winter swell, waves of
twenty feet or larger march into
the cove.

Bei einer starken Winterdünung
stürzen über sechs Meter hohe
Wellen in die kleine Bucht.

Pendant les swells d'hiver, des
vagues de plus de six mètres de
haut se brisent dans la baie.

*Pages 248–249*
**Lunada Bay, 1970**

Los Angeles's premier big-wave
spot, notorious for sharks, nasty
currents, and even nastier locals.
In 1961, Greg Noll rode twenty-
foot waves there.

Der beste Big-Wave-Spot in Los
Angeles, berüchtigt für Haie,
schlimme Strömungen und noch
schlimmere ortsansässige Surfer.
1961 ritt Greg Noll hier sieben
Meter hohe Wellen.

Le meilleur spot de grosses vagues
de Los Angeles, réputé pour ses
requins, ses courants dangereux
et le caractère exécrable de ses
habitants. En 1961, Greg Noll y a
surfé des vagues de sept mètres.

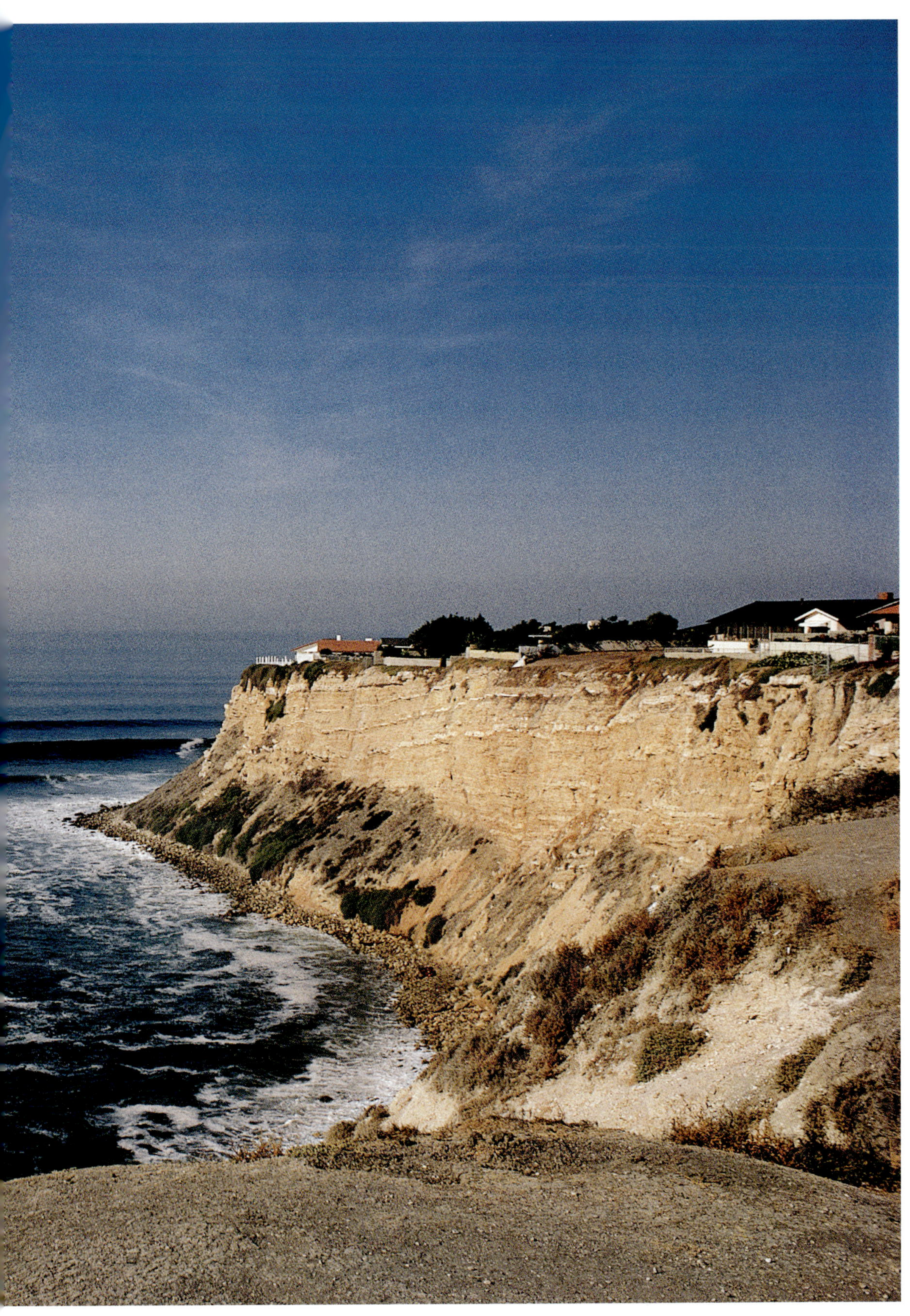

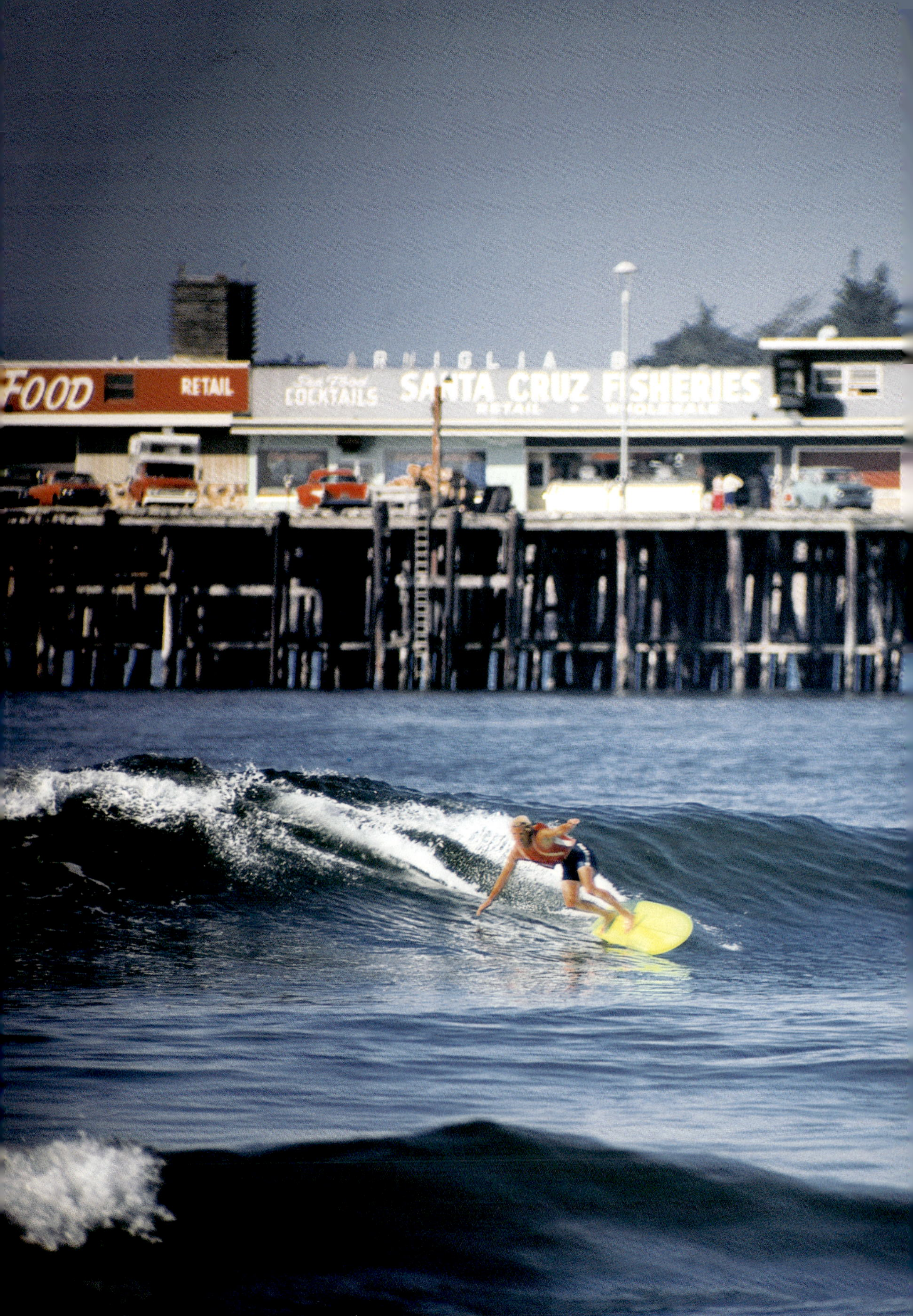
FOOD    RETAIL
COCKTAILS    SANTA CRUZ FISHERIES
RETAIL    WHOLESALE

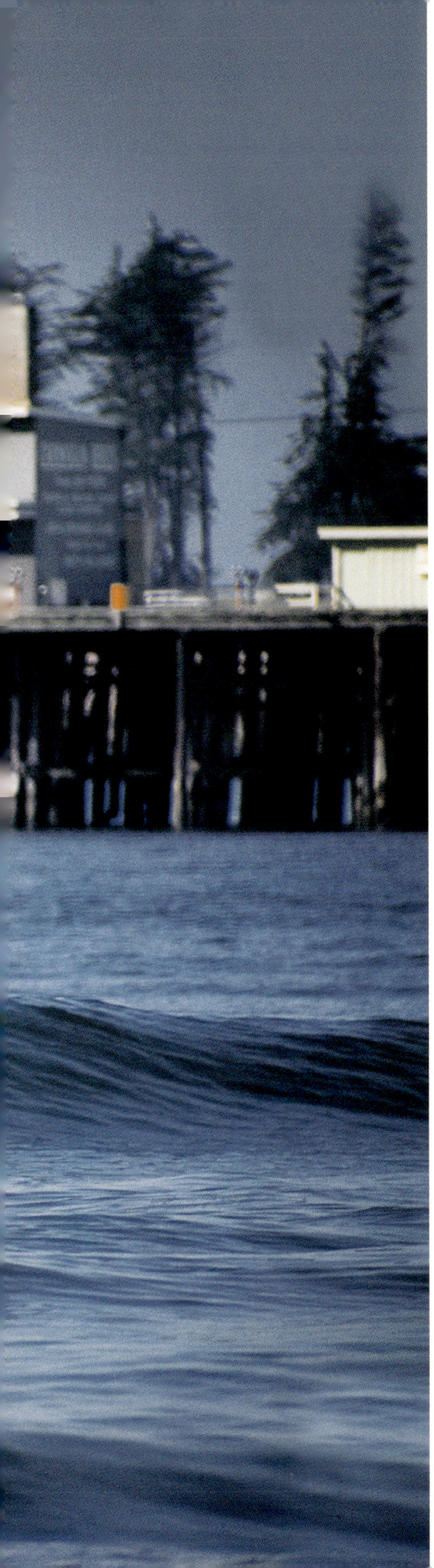

**Dale Dobson, Santa Cruz, 1967**

The "Rivermouth" is a sandbar break popular with Santa Cruz locals. Average year-round water temperature: 12°C.

„Rivermouth" ist eine bei den Surfern aus Santa Cruz beliebte Sandbank-Welle. Die Wassertemperatur beträgt das ganze Jahr über um die 12° C.

« Rivermouth » est un *break* à bancs de sable très apprécié par la population locale de Santa Cruz. L'eau y affiche une température moyenne de 12 °C été comme hiver.

*Pages 252–253*
**Jack O'Neill, Corky Carroll, Steamer Lane, Santa Cruz, 1969**

O'Neill, a pioneer Santa Cruz surfer, developed the first surfing wetsuits to brave Monterey Bay's excellent but chilly waves.

O'Neill, ein Wegbereiter der Surfszene von Santa Cruz, entwickelte die ersten Neopren-Anzüge für Surfer, die den fantastischen, aber eisigen Wellen der Monterey Bay trotzten.

Jack O'Neill, un des pionniers du surf de Santa Cruz, a mis au point les premières combinaisons en néoprène permettant d'affronter les vagues exceptionnelles – mais glaciales – de Monterey Bay.

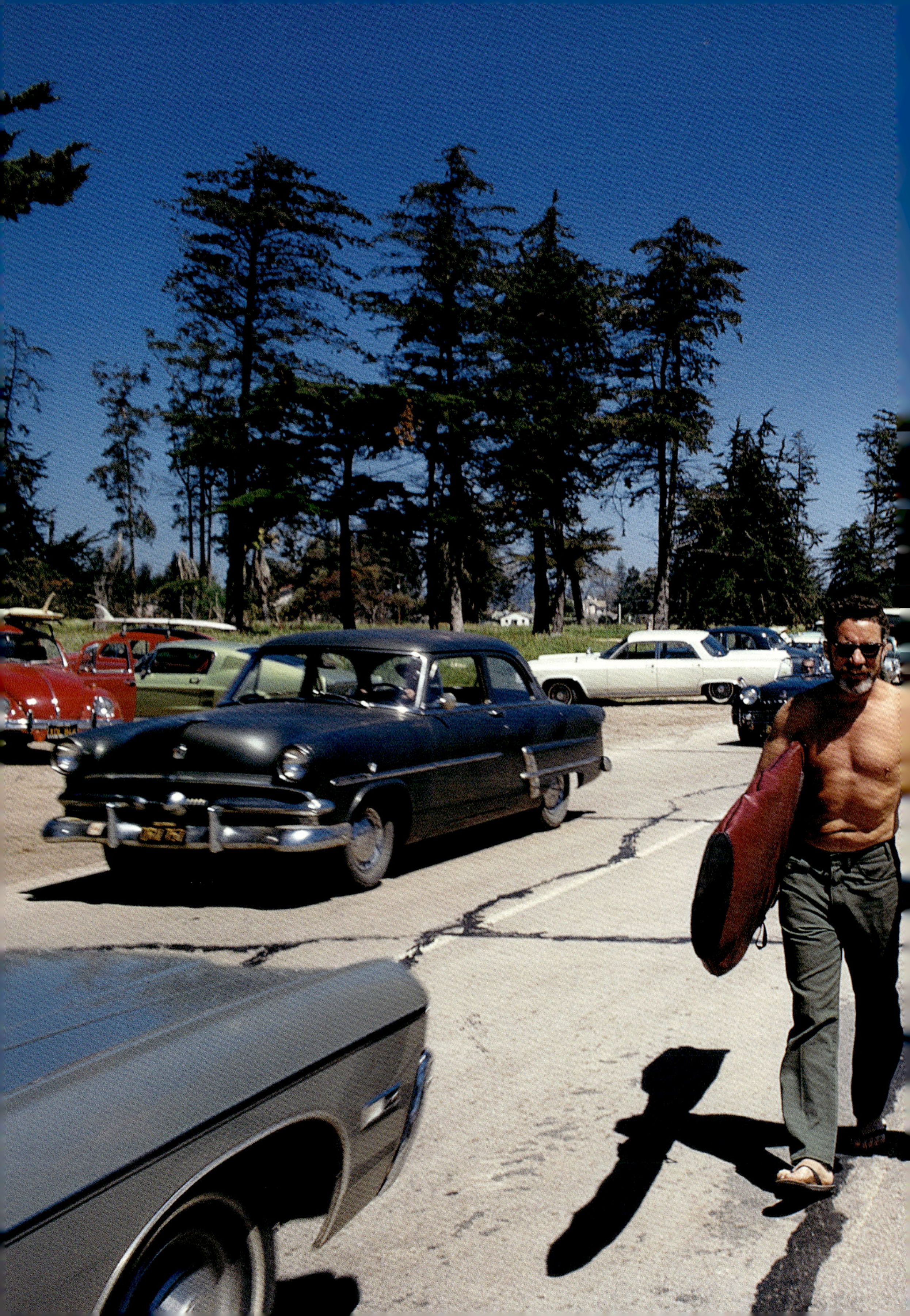

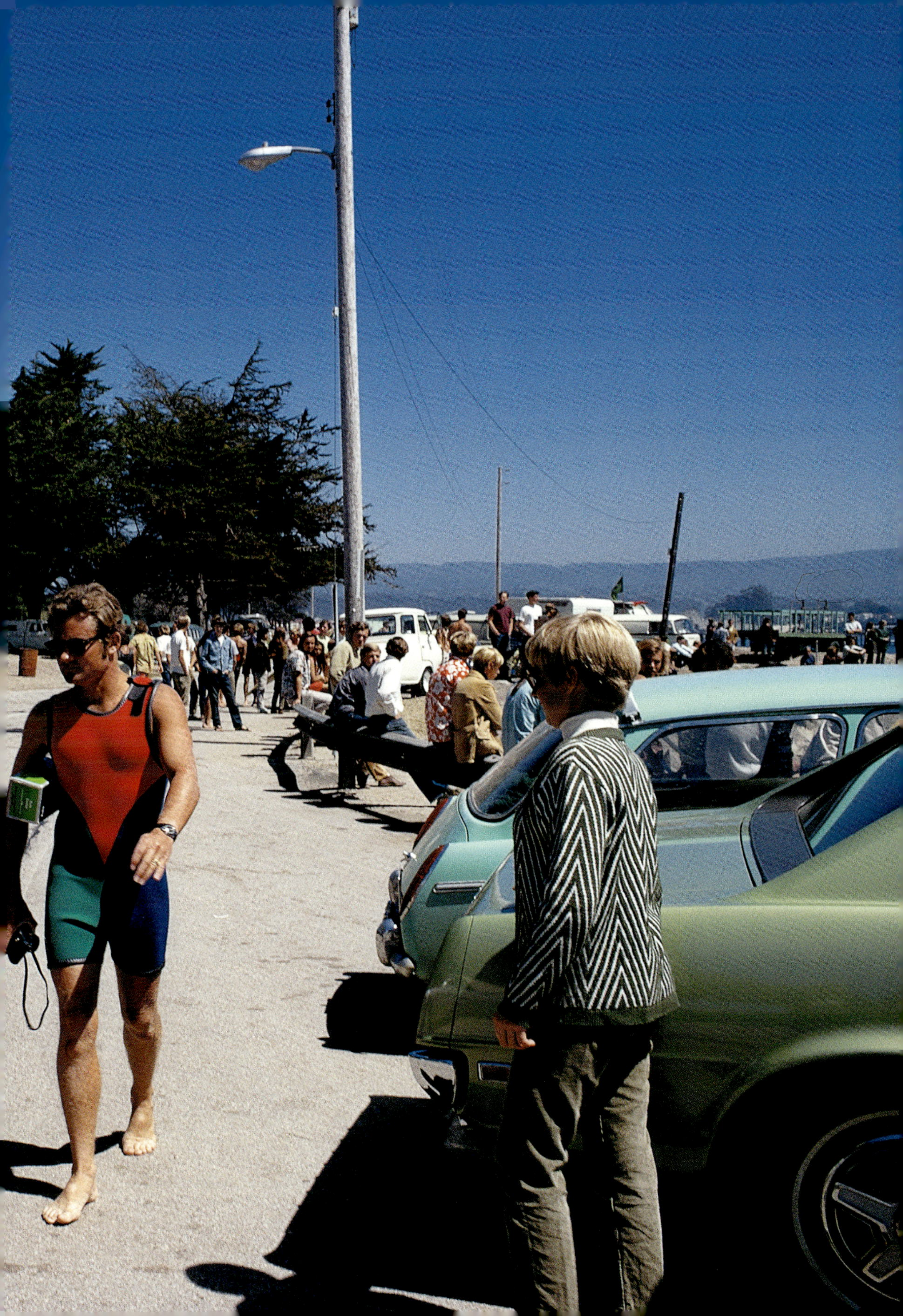

**Palos Verdes Cove, 1970**

The lineup at "Ski Jump," a
big-wave spot at the north end of
Palos Verdes Cove.

Unterwegs zum „Ski Jump", einem
Big-Wave-Spot am nördlichen Ende
von Palos Verdes Cove.

Descente vers « Ski Jump », un
spot de grosses vagues à l'extrémité
nord de Palos Verdes Cove.

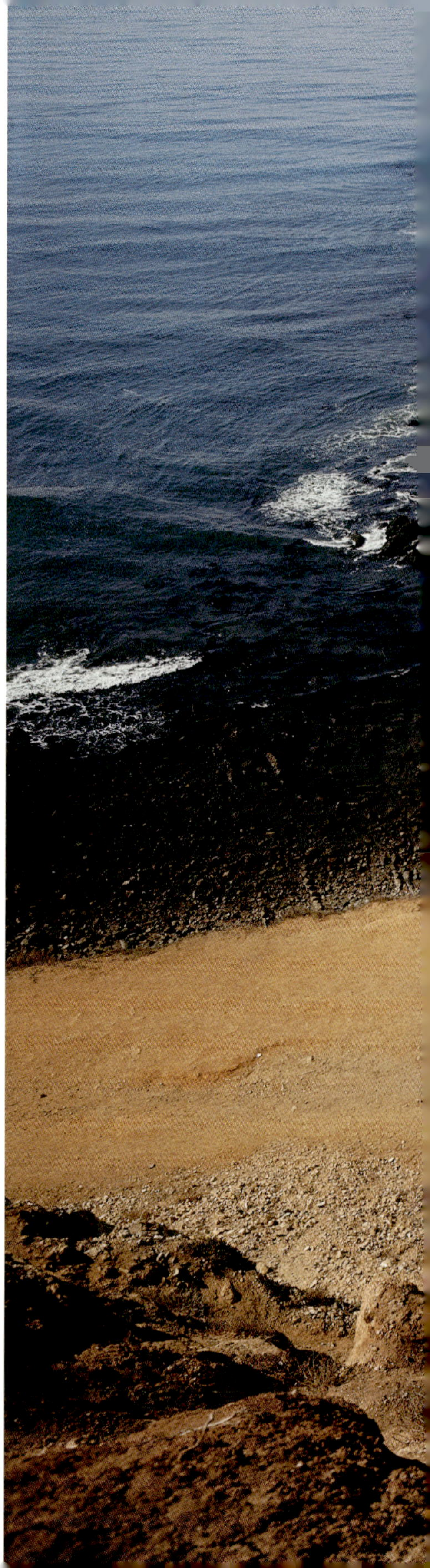

*Pages 256–257*
**Arroyo Sequit Beach, 1963**

Only twenty miles from Hollywood,
Arroyo Sequit beach is often used
as a location for films and TV. Look
for it in *Point Break, The Karate
Kid,* and *Baywatch.*

Der nur dreißig Kilometer von
Hollywood entfernte Strand von
Arroyo Sequit wird häufig als
Drehort für Film und Fernsehen
benutzt, so z. B. in *Point Break,
Karate Kid* und *Baywatch.*

À seulement 30 kilomètres de
Hollywood, la plage d'Arroyo Sequit
a servi de lieu de tournage pour
bon nombre de films et de séries.
On la reconnaît dans des longs
métrages comme *Point Break,
Karaté Kid* et dans la série
*Alerte à Malibu.*



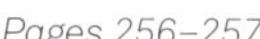

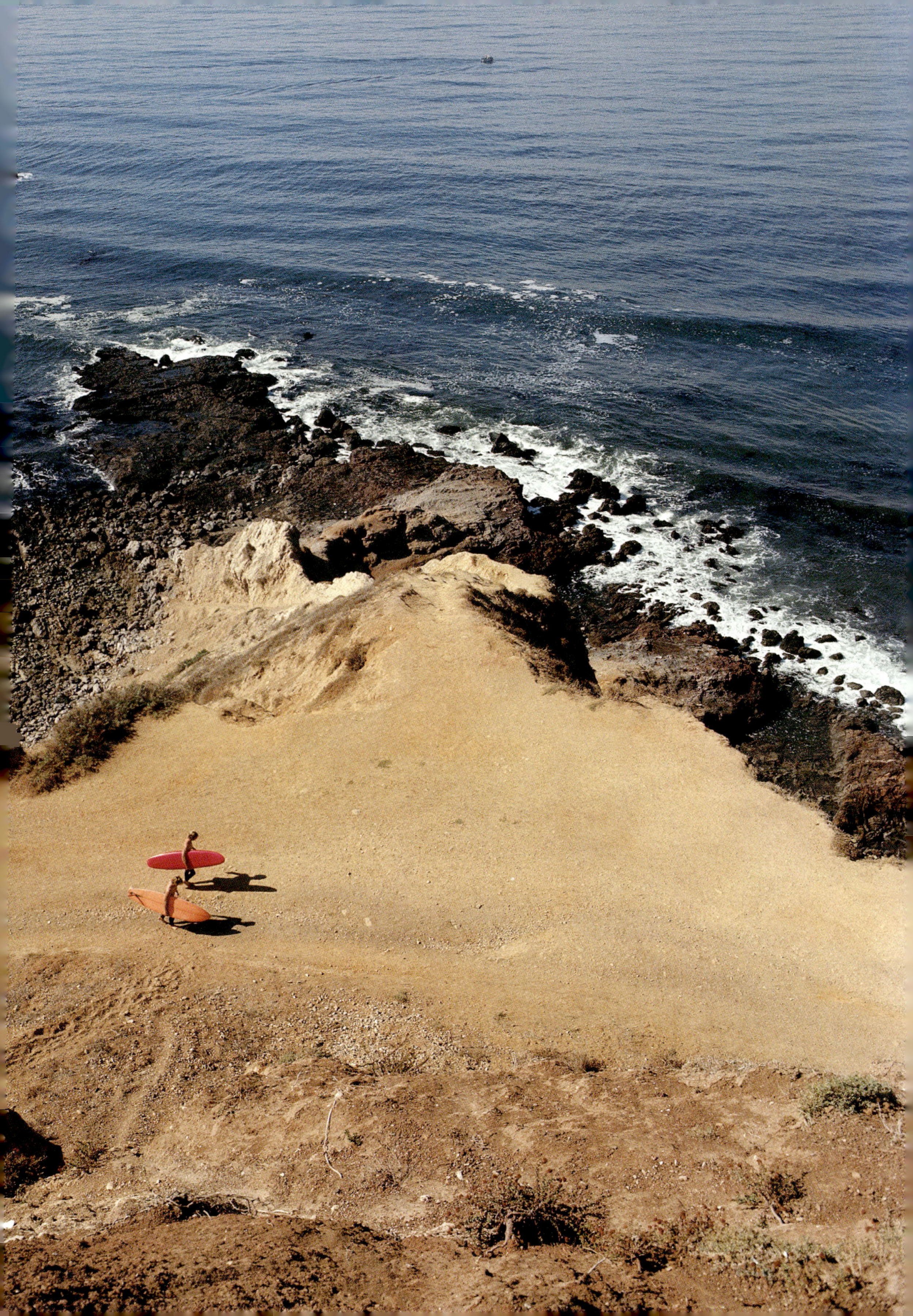

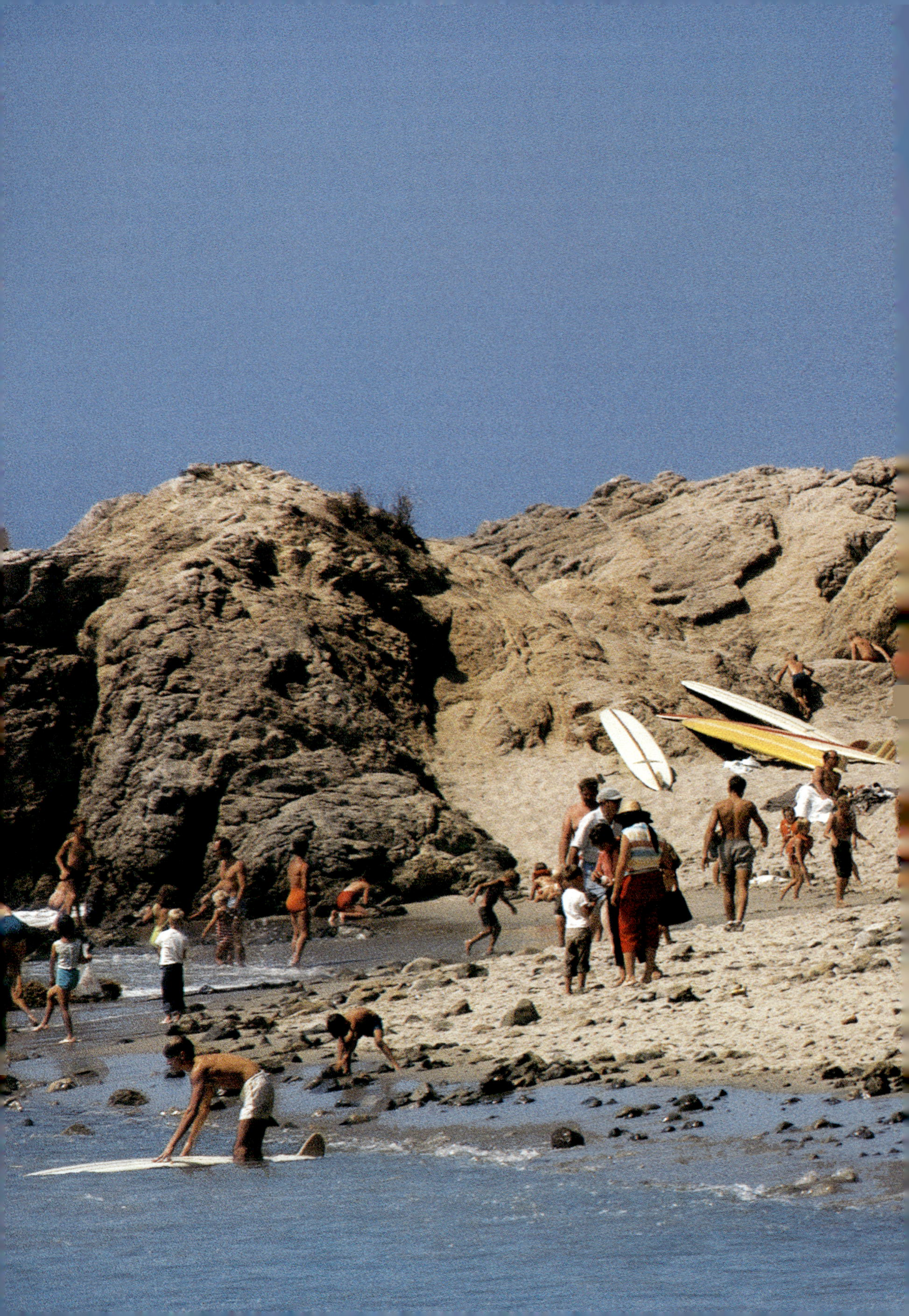

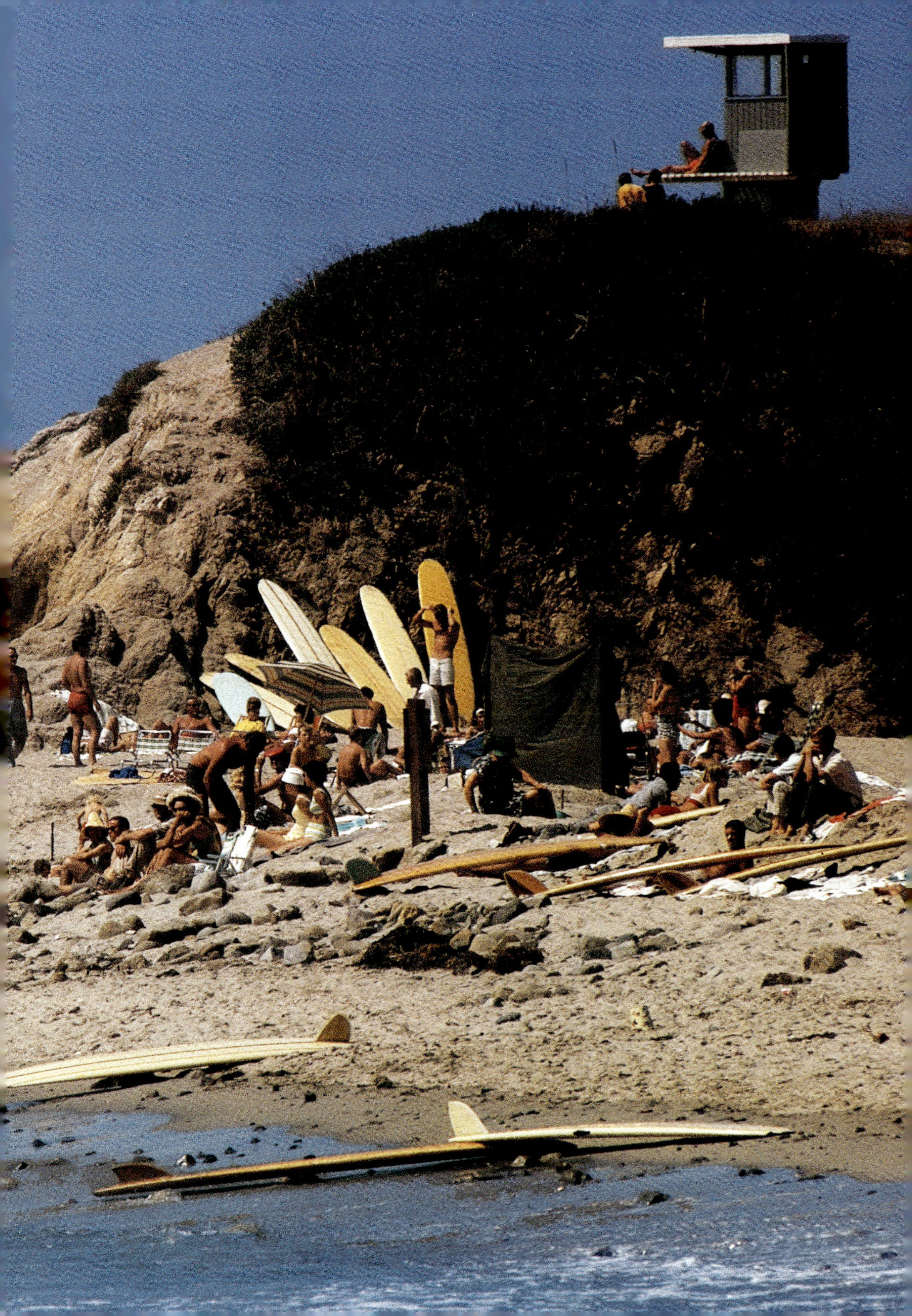

**Joey Cabell, Laguna Beach, 1964**

Cabell "the Gazelle" was a
transplanted Hawaiian who was
considered one of the sixties'
finest surfers. He later founded
the hugely successful Chart House
restaurants.

Cabell, „Die Gazelle", war ein
zugezogener Hawaiianer und galt
als einer der besten Surfer der
Sechziger. Später gründete er
die erfolgreichen Chart-House-
Restaurants.

Joey Cabell, dit « La Gazelle »,
un natif de Hawaï, fut considéré
comme l'un des meilleurs surfeurs
des années 1960. Il fonda plus
tard la chaîne de restaurants à
succès Chart House.

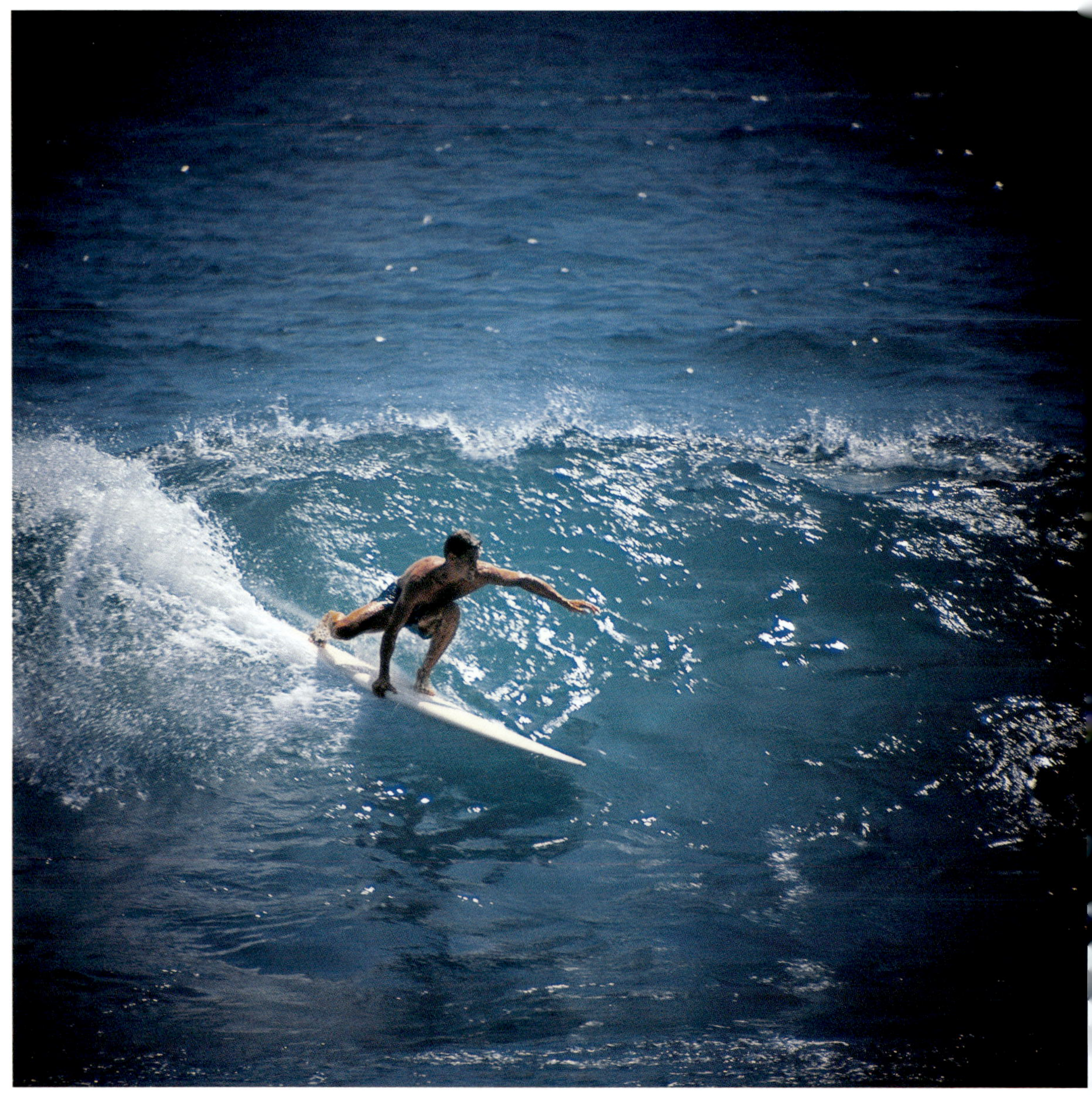

**Dru Harrison, Huntington Beach, 1969**

Harrison, raised in Hermosa Beach as a classic longboard stylist, made the radical transition to shortboards in the late sixties.

Der in Hermosa Beach aufgewachsene Harrison war ein klassischer Longboard-Surfer, bevor er Ende der Sechziger den radikalen Wechsel zum Shortboard vollzog.

Dru Harrison, qui a grandi sur les plages de Hermosa, fut d'abord un virtuose du longboard avant de passer au shortboard à la fin des années 1960.

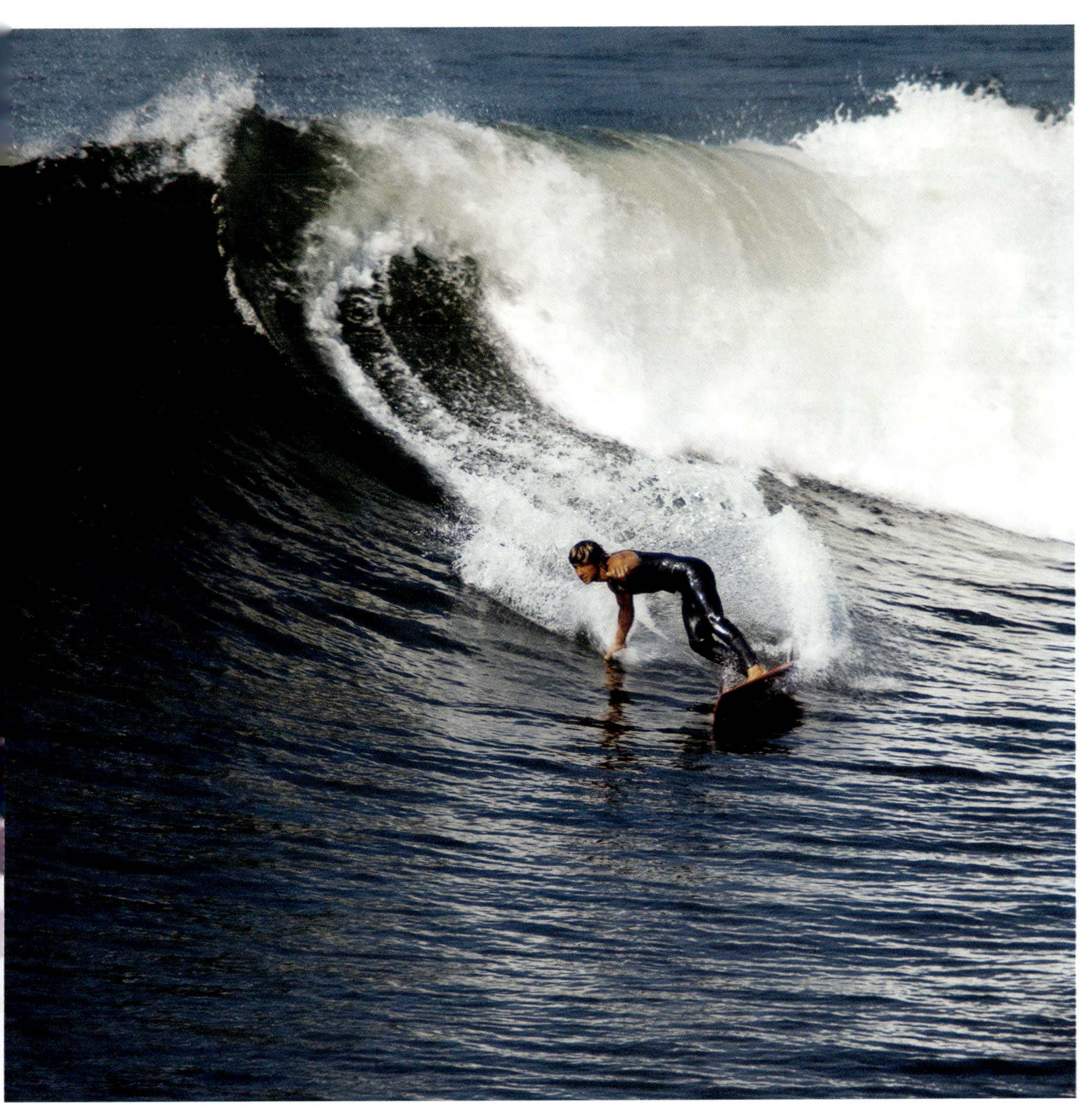

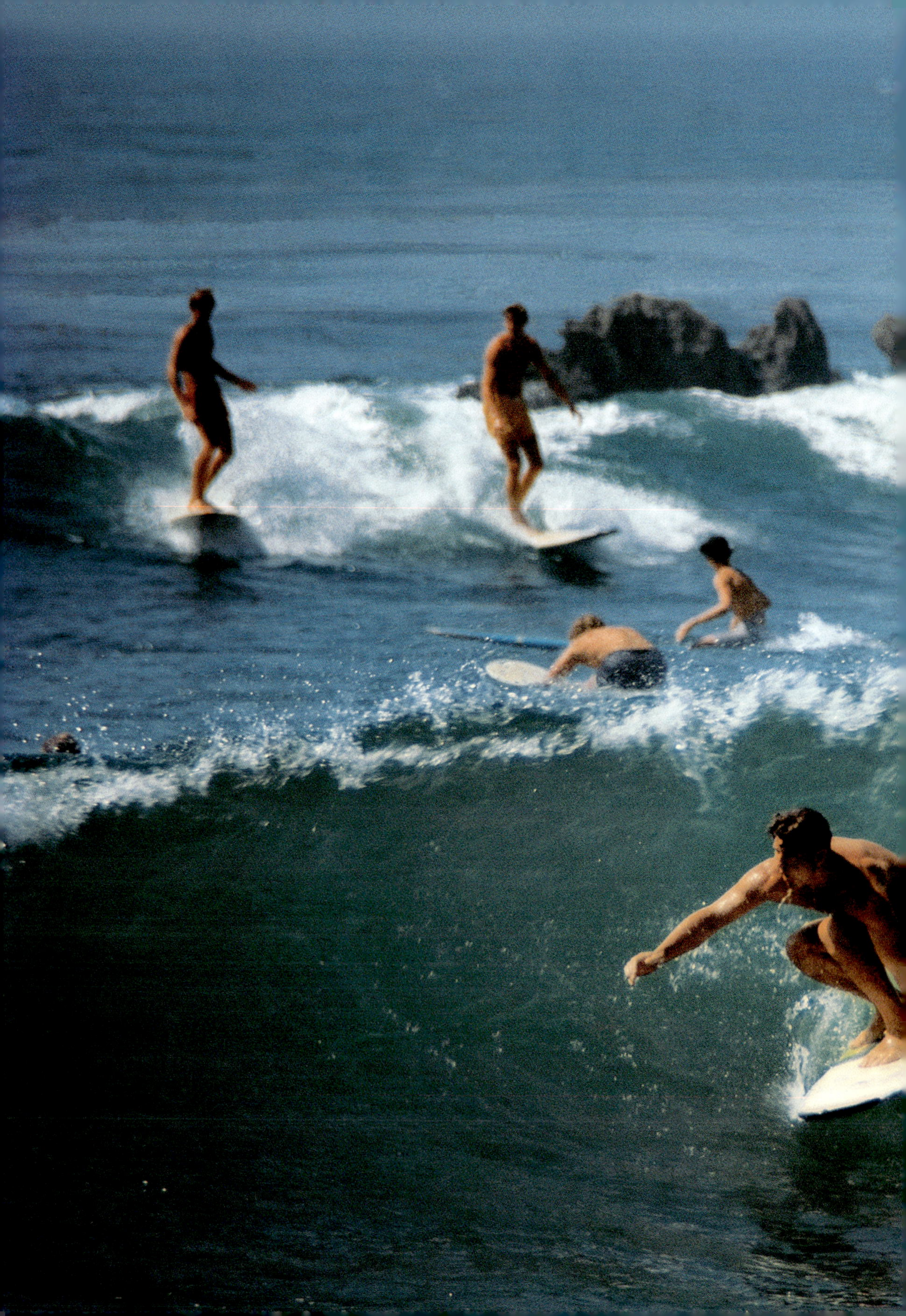

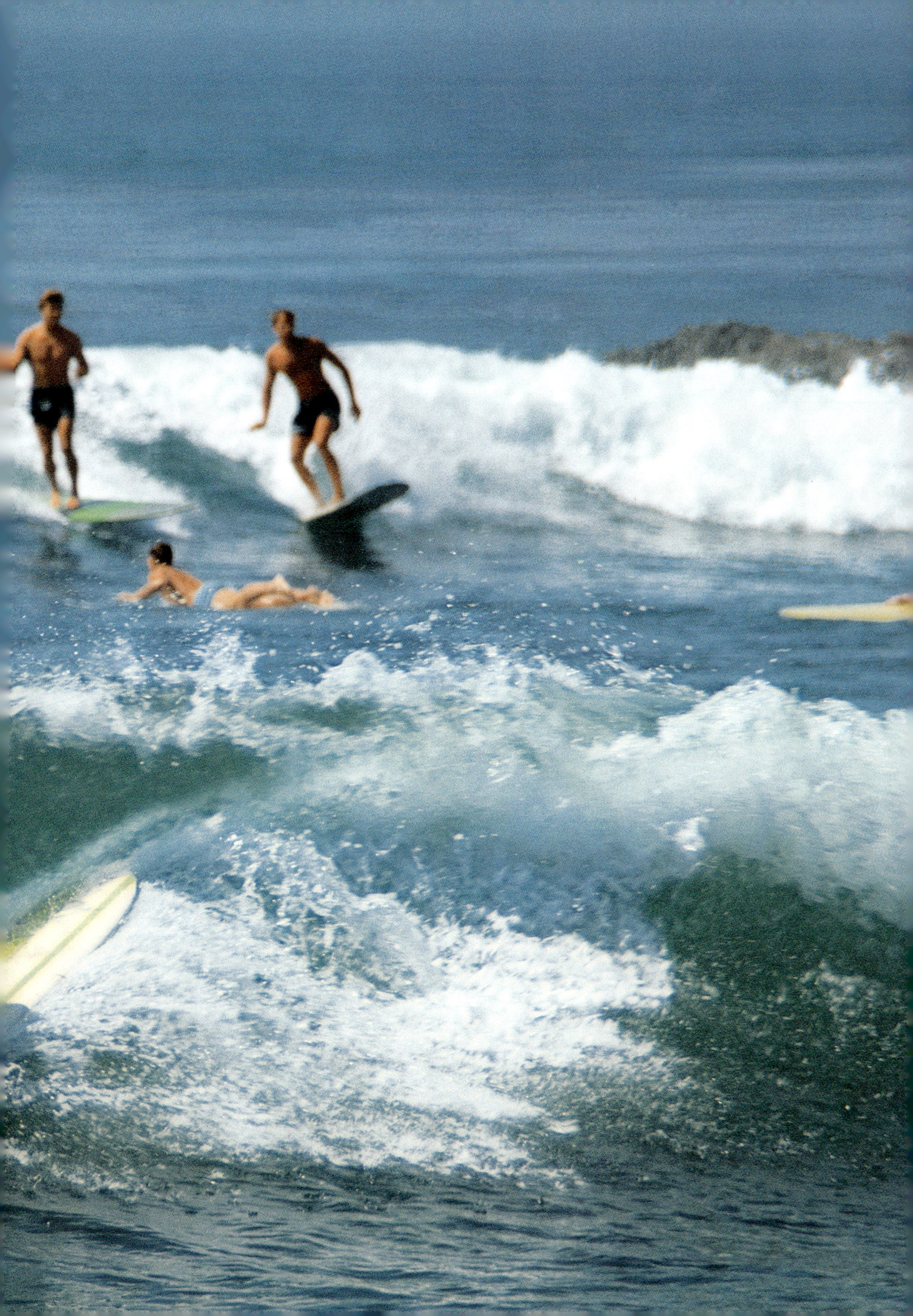

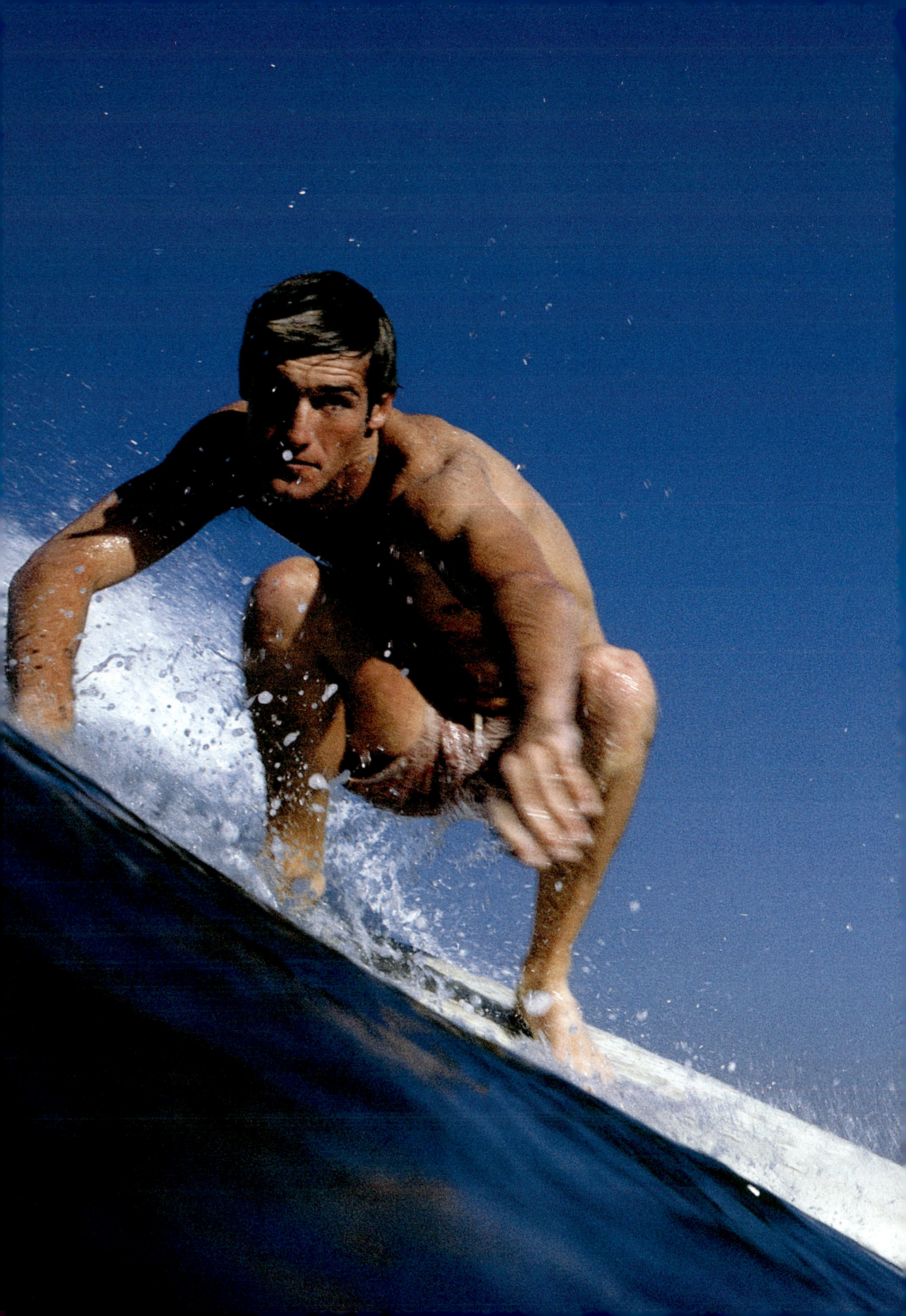

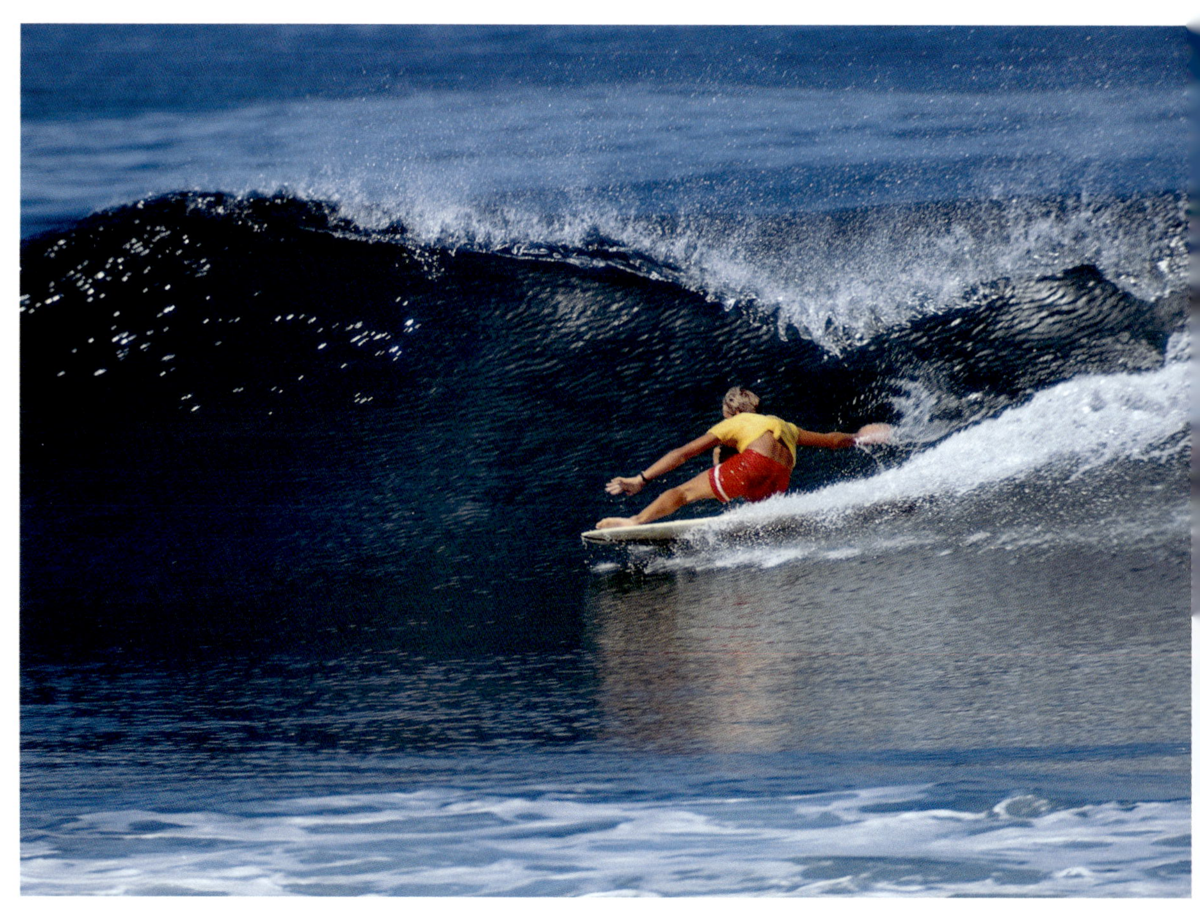

**Skip Frye, Rincón, Puerto Rico, 1968**

Californian Frye, who gracefully bridged the longboard and shortboard eras, performs a flawless "stretch five" during the World Championships.

Der Kalifornier Frye, der elegant den Übergang von der Longboard- zur Shortboard-Ära meisterte, zeigt bei der Weltmeisterschaft einen fehlerlosen „Stretch Five".

Le Californien Skip Frye, qui a su gérer avec brio la rupture entre le longboard et le shortboard, exécute un impeccable « stretch five » lors d'une épreuve des championnats du monde.

**Angie Reno, Rincón, Puerto Rico, 1968**

The evidence left from an all-night beach party held during the trouble-plagued and controversial 1968 World Championships.

Überbleibsel einer nächtlichen Strandparty während der problembeladenen und kontroversen Weltmeisterschaft von 1968.

Traces d'une interminable beach-party nocturne pendant les championnats du monde controversés et agités de 1968.

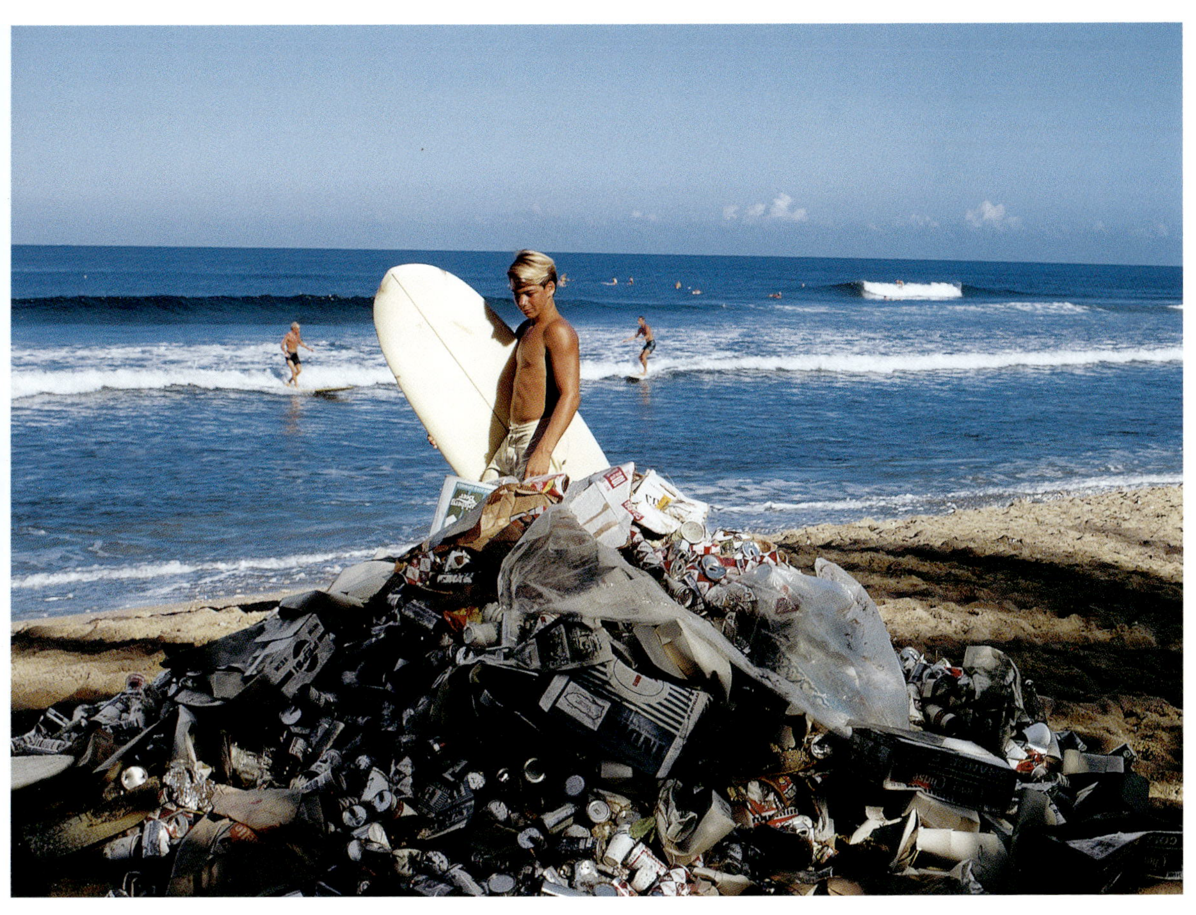

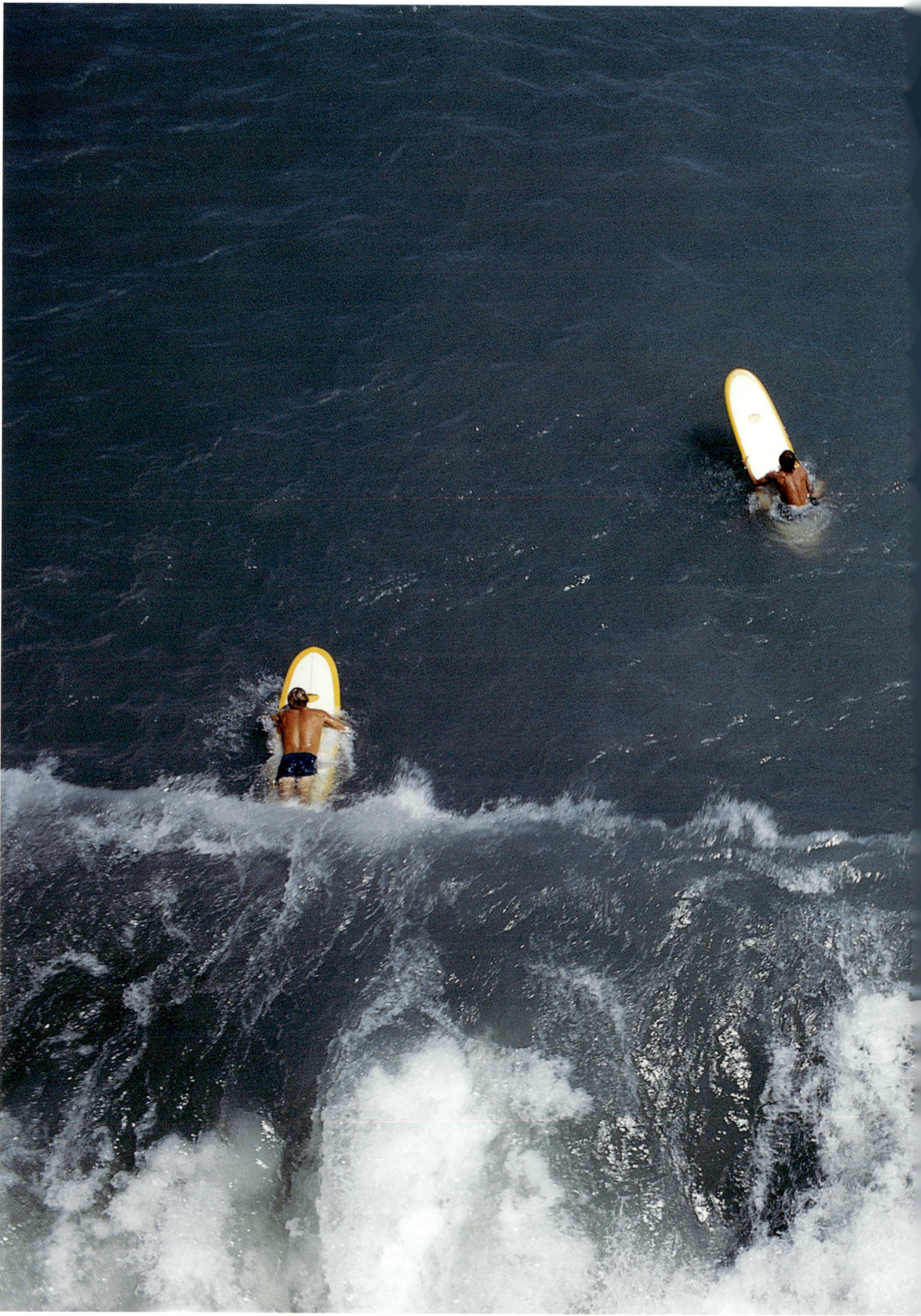

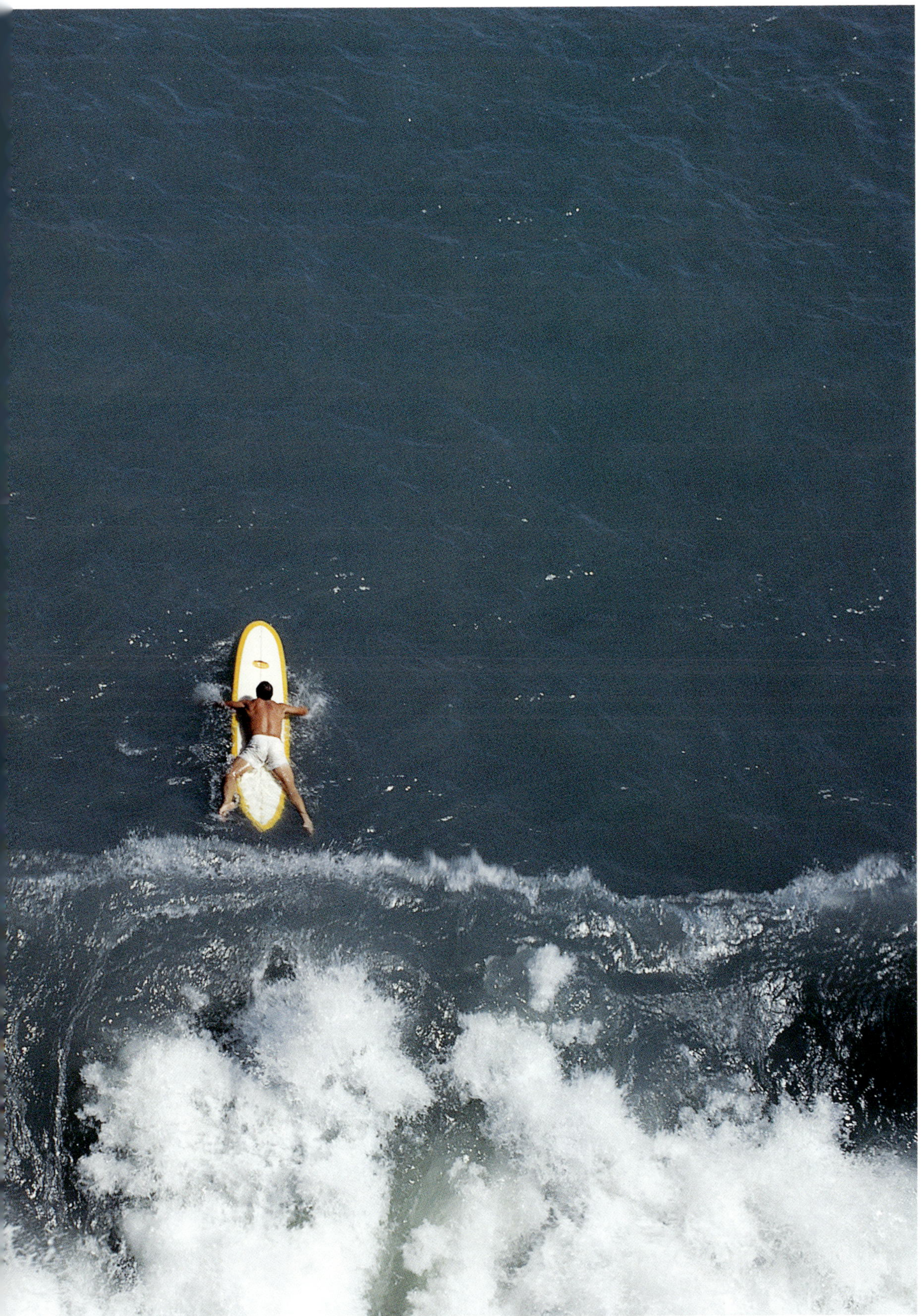

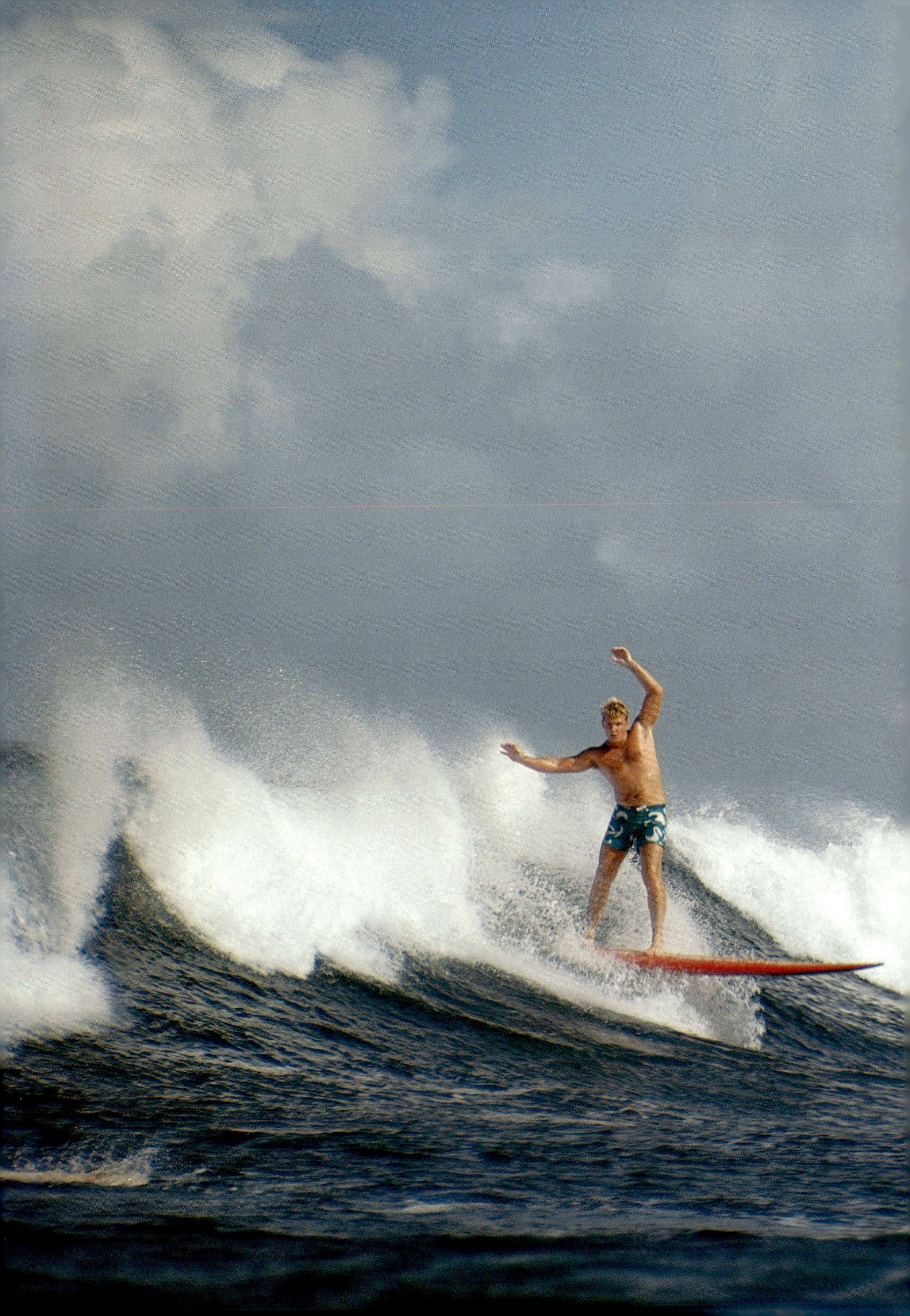

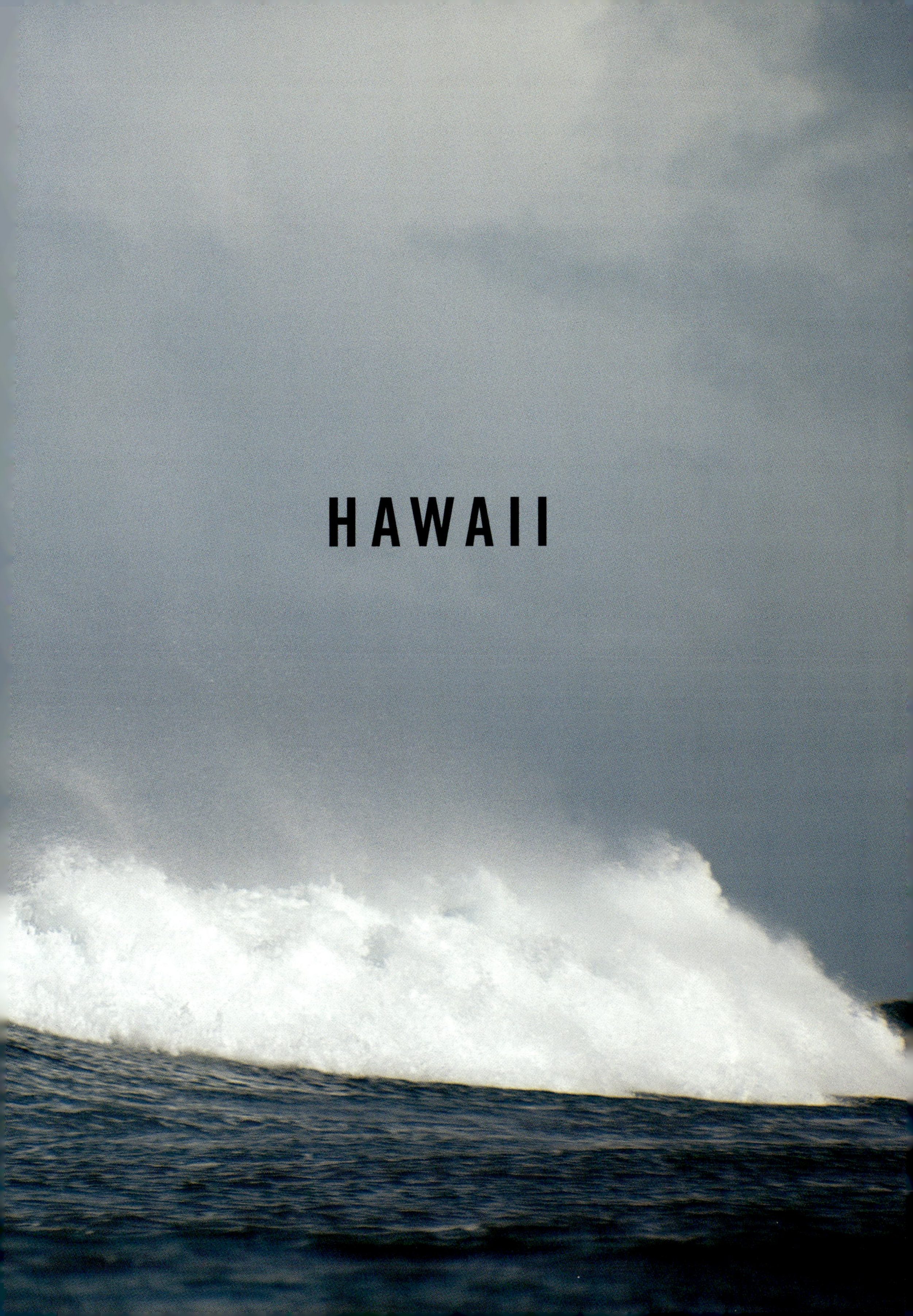
HAWAII

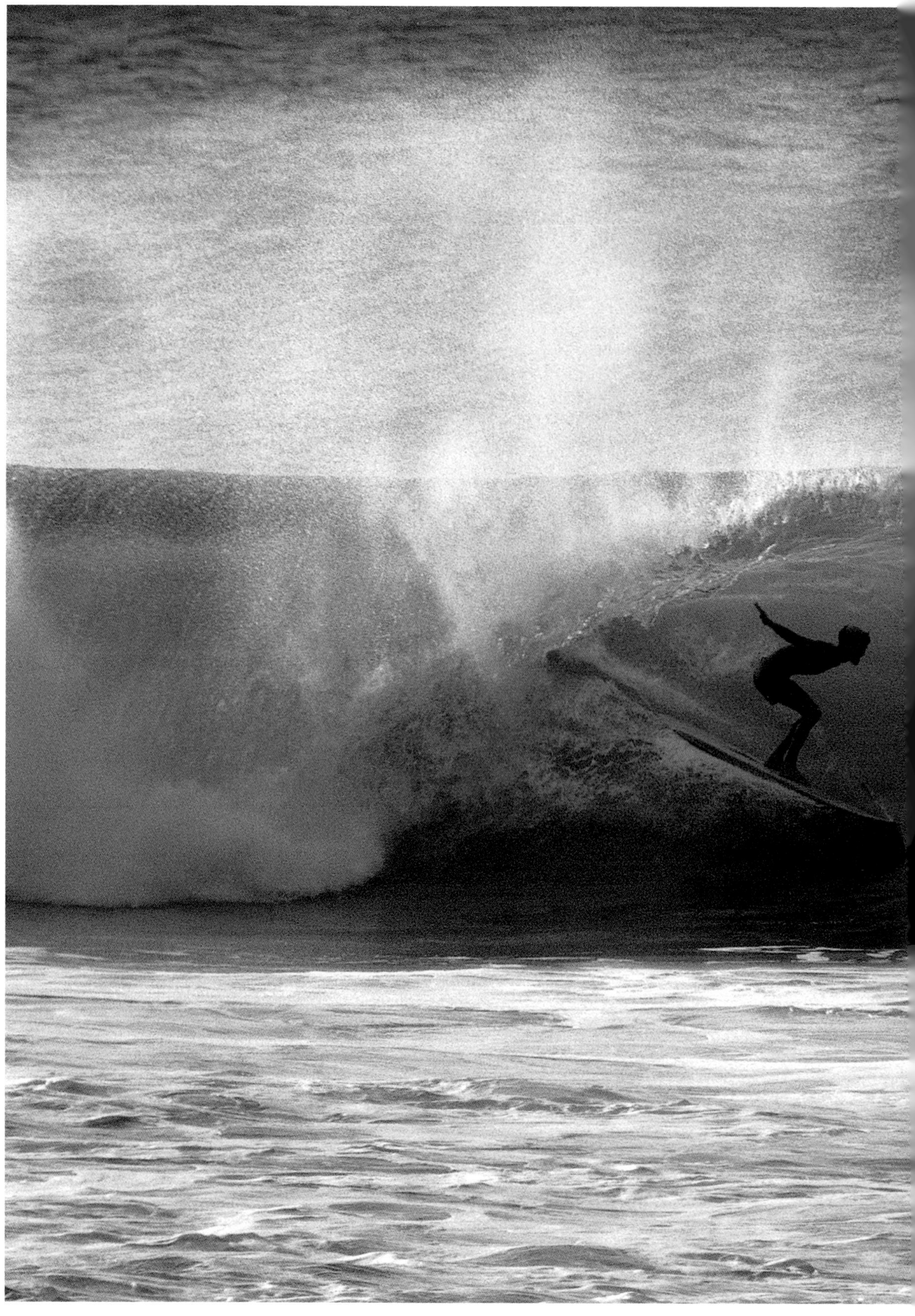

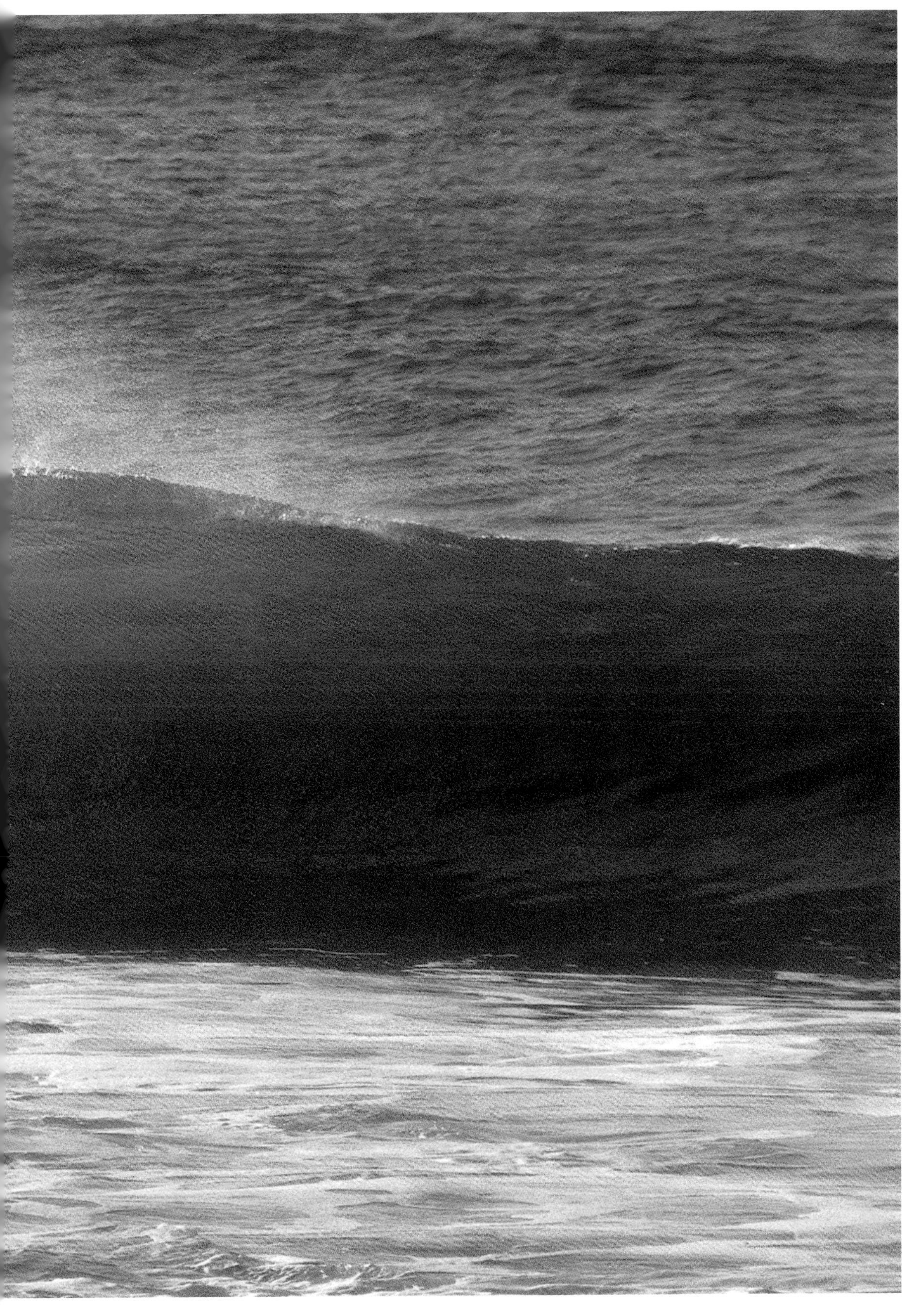

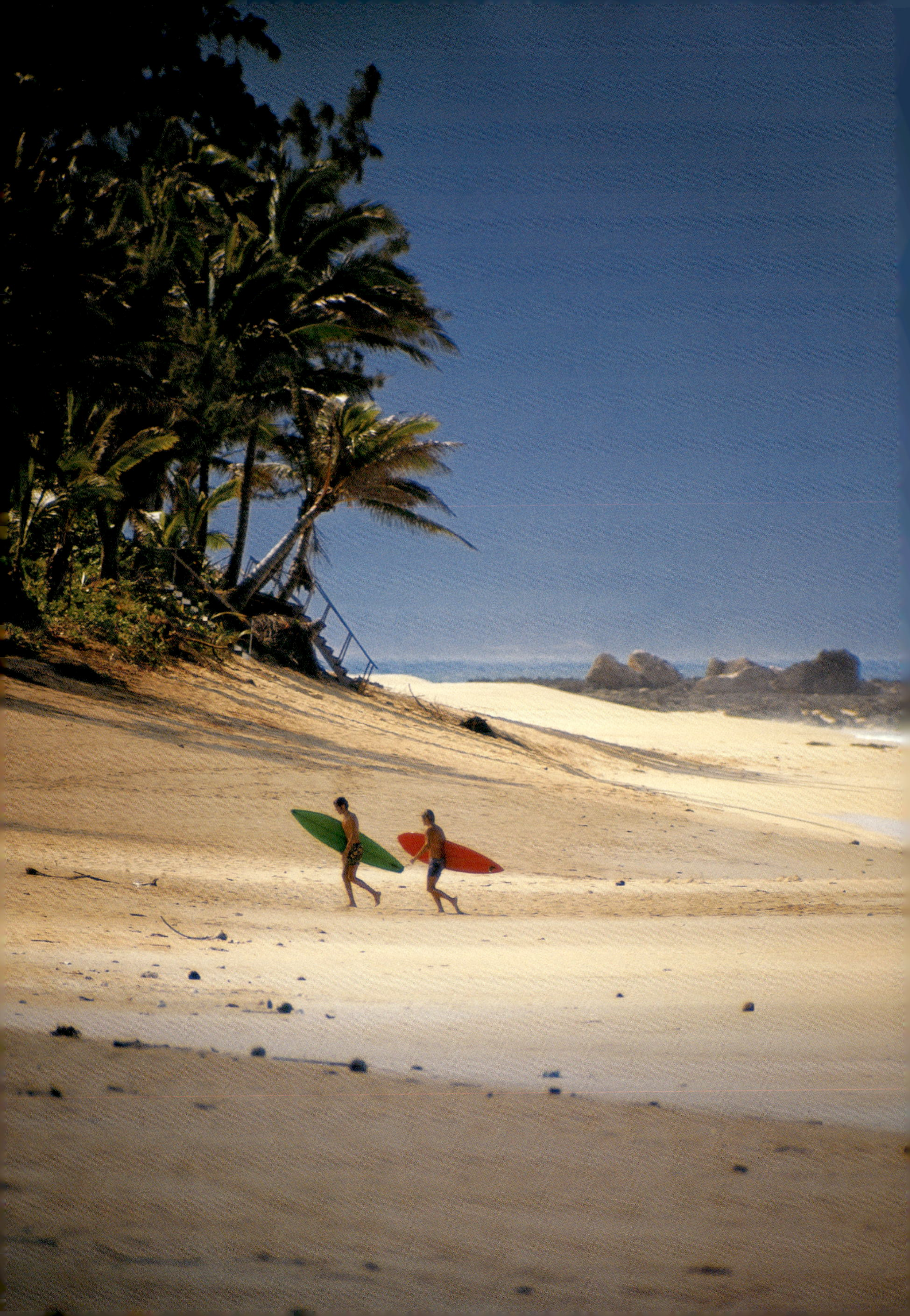

**Shark's Cove, North Shore, 1974**

The view from Ehukai Beach
toward the razor-sharp lava rocks
of Ke Iki Beach.

Aussicht von Ehukai Beach auf die
rasiermesserscharfen Lavafelsen
von Ke Iki Beach.

Vue sur les rochers de lave acérés
de Ke Iki Beach depuis Ehukai
Beach.

Pages 268–269
**Chun's Reef, 1965**

One of the North Shore's gentler
breaks, Chun's is favored by
longboarders, kids, and older
surfers.

Als einer der sanfteren Breaks
am North Shore wird Chun's von
Longboardern, Kindern und älteren
Surfern bevorzugt.

Relativement peu exigeant, le
*break* de Chun, sur le North Shore,
est particulièrement prisé par les
longboarders, les enfants et les
vétérans.

Pages 270–271
**Jock Sutherland, Pipeline, Hawaii,
1966**

The Hawaiian-born Sutherland
pioneered tuberiding in the early
sixties on Oahu's North Shore.

Der auf Hawaii geborene
Sutherland war Anfang der
Sechziger der erste Tuberider
am North Shore von Oahu.

Au début des années 1960, le
Hawaïen Jock Sutherland se
distingue comme le pionnier du
*tube riding* sur le North Shore,
la côte nord de l'île d'Oahu.

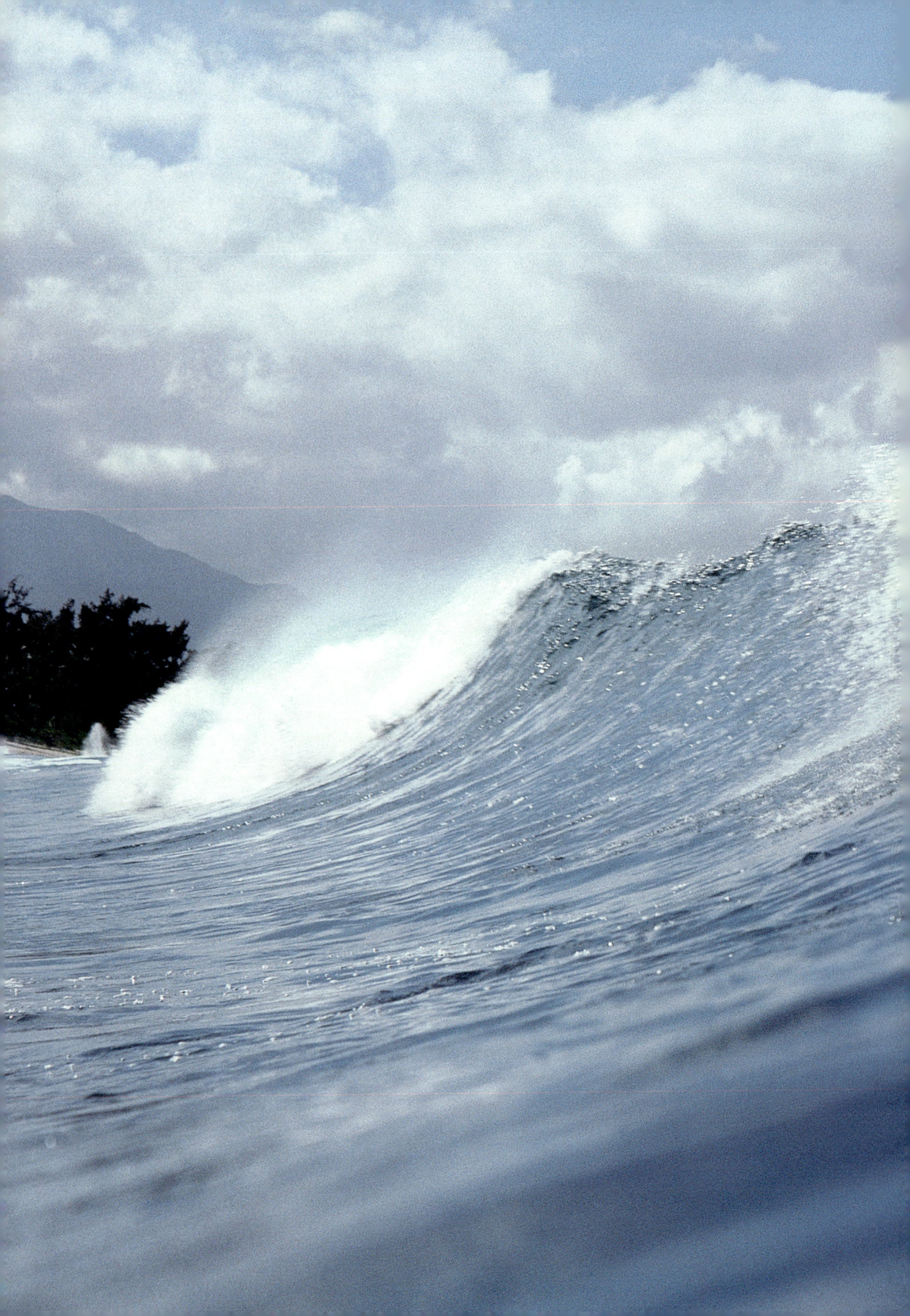

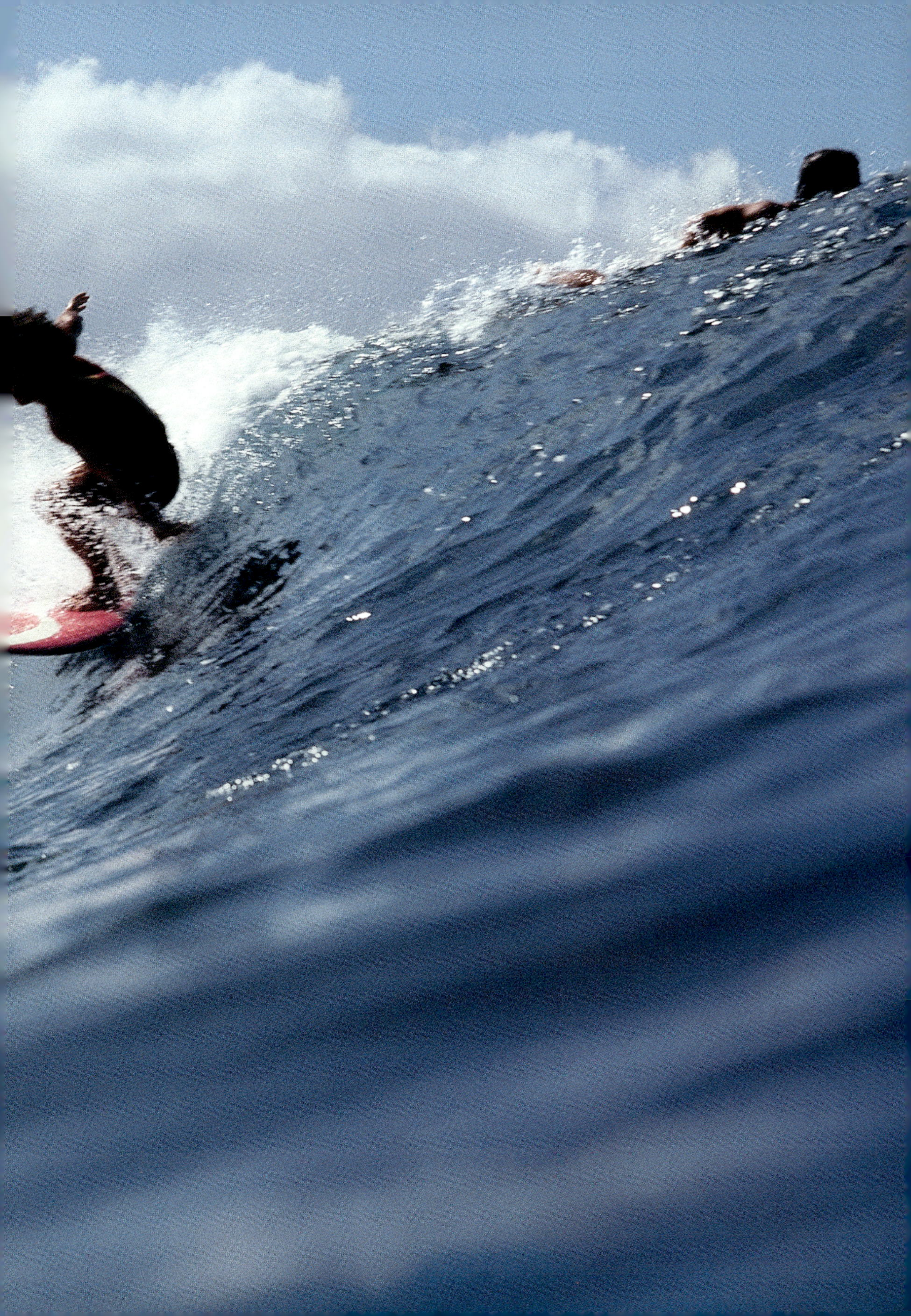

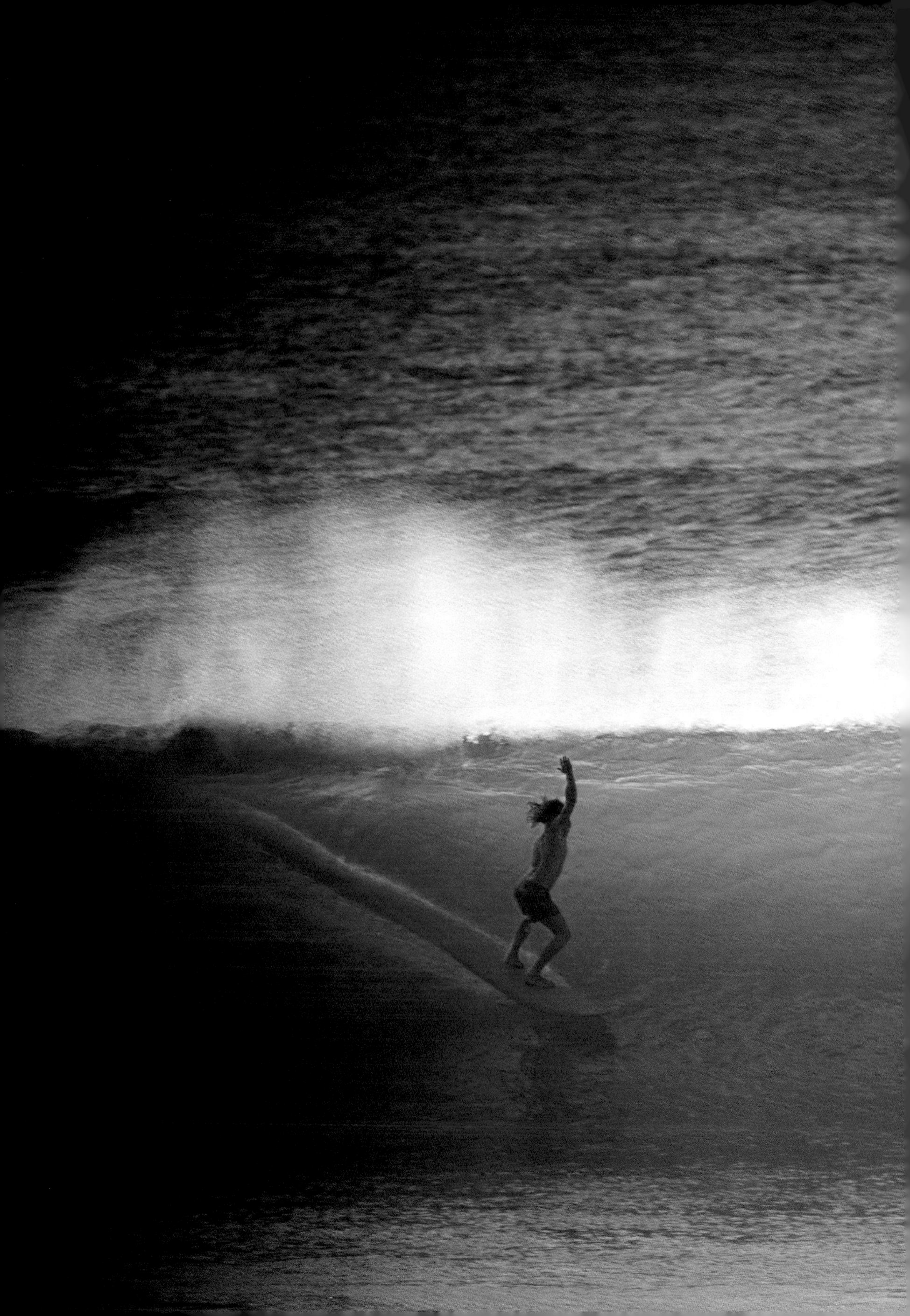

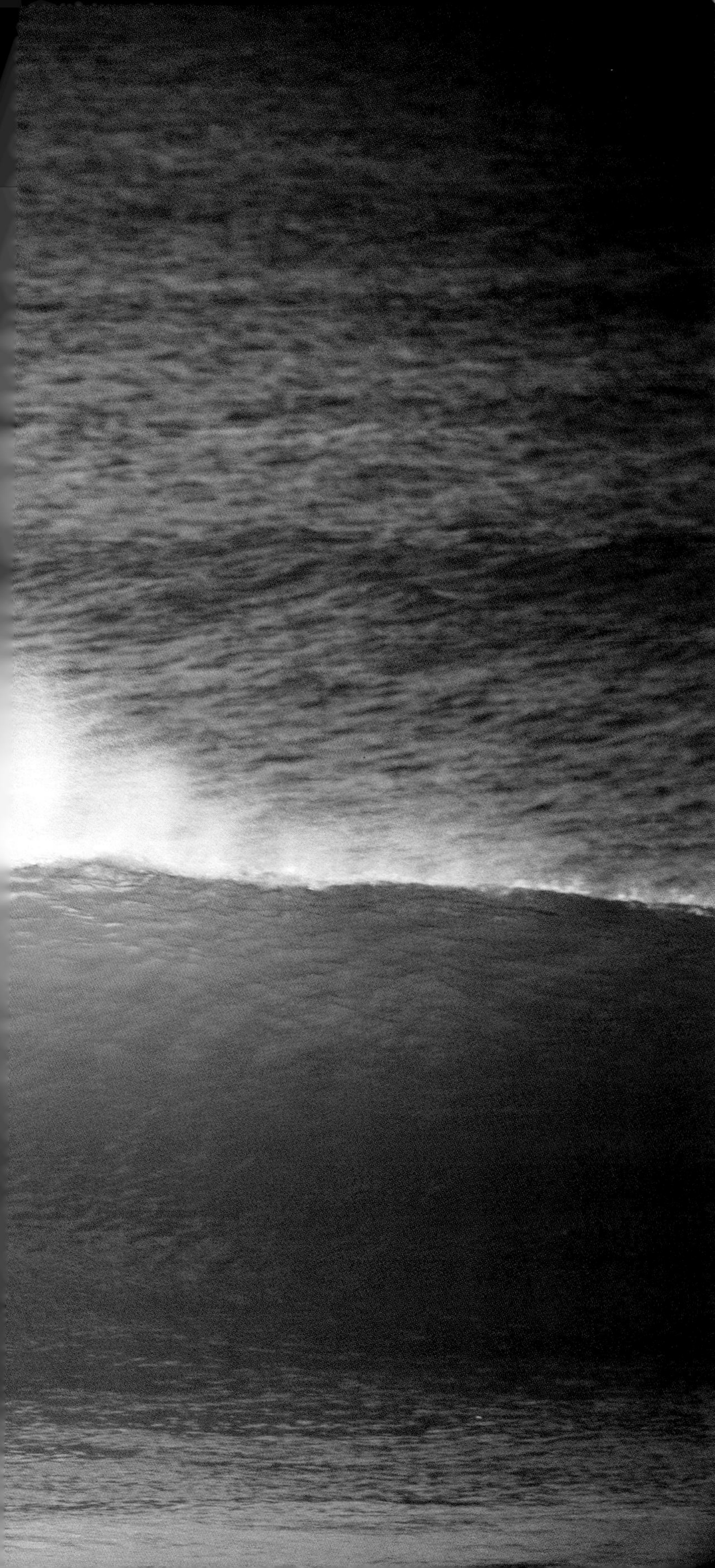



**John Boozer, Pipeline, 1966**

**Rusty Miller, Waimea Bay, 1966**

Miller, a Californian, had gotten off
the jet only an hour before tackling
this twenty-foot Waimea wall.

Der Kalifornier Miller bezwang diese
Sechs-Meter-Welle in Waimea,
nachdem er nur eine Stunde zuvor
dem Flugzeug entstiegen war.

Le Californien Rusty Miller affronte
un mur d'eau de six mètres de haut
à Waimea une heure seulement
après sa descente d'avion.

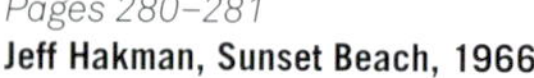

*Pages 280–281*
**Jeff Hakman, Sunset Beach, 1966**

Fickle, incredibly powerful, and
often crowded, Sunset is still the
ultimate litmus test of a complete
surfer. Foreground, Don James
with his "waterbox" camera.

Launisch, unglaublich gewaltig
und häufig überfüllt: Sunset
ist noch immer die ultimative
Bewährungsprobe für jeden
richtigen Surfer. Im Vordergrund:
Don James mit seiner „Waterbox"-
Kamera.

Imprévisible, d'une puissance
inouïe et souvent bondé, le spot
de Sunset est un laboratoire idéal
pour révéler les nouveaux talents.
Au premier plan : Don James avec
son appareil photo à « boîtier
étanche ».

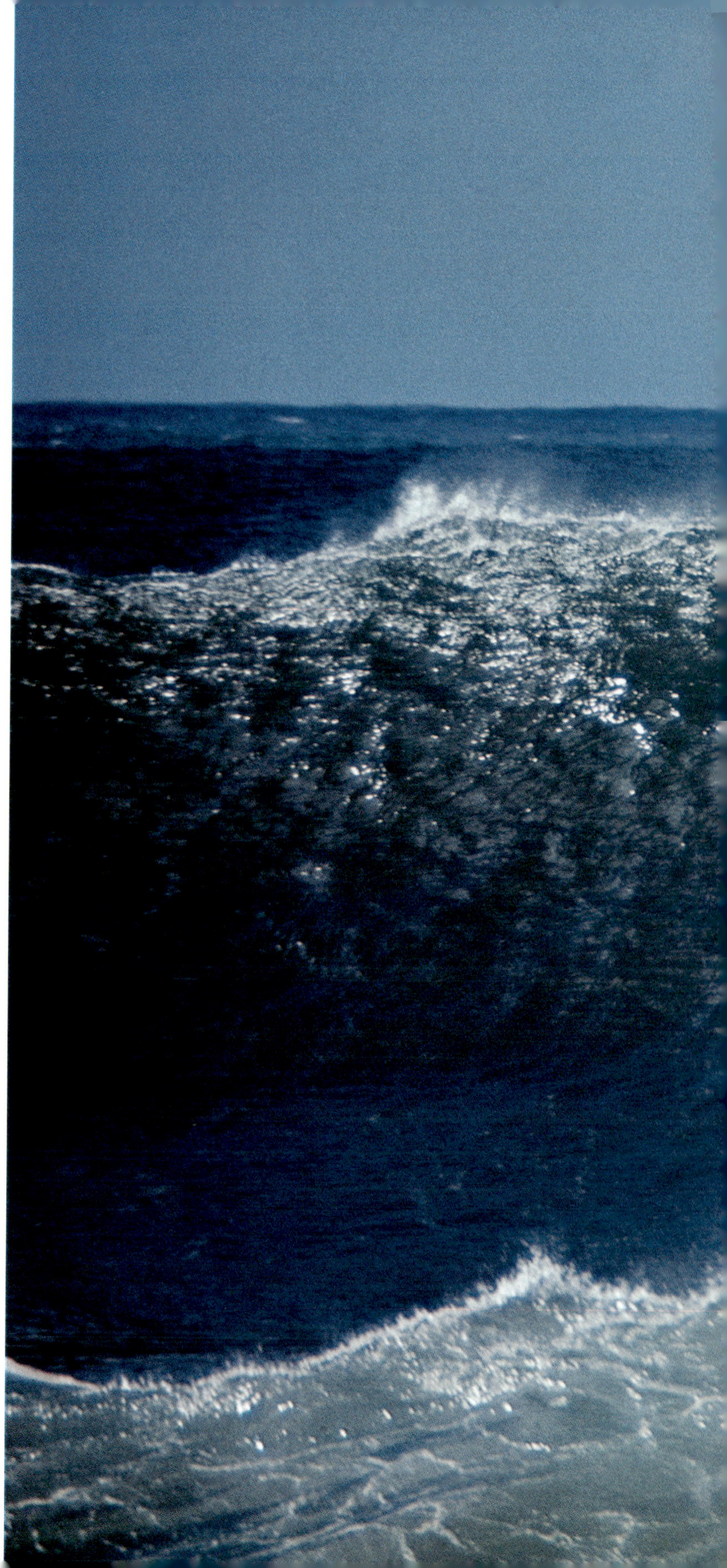

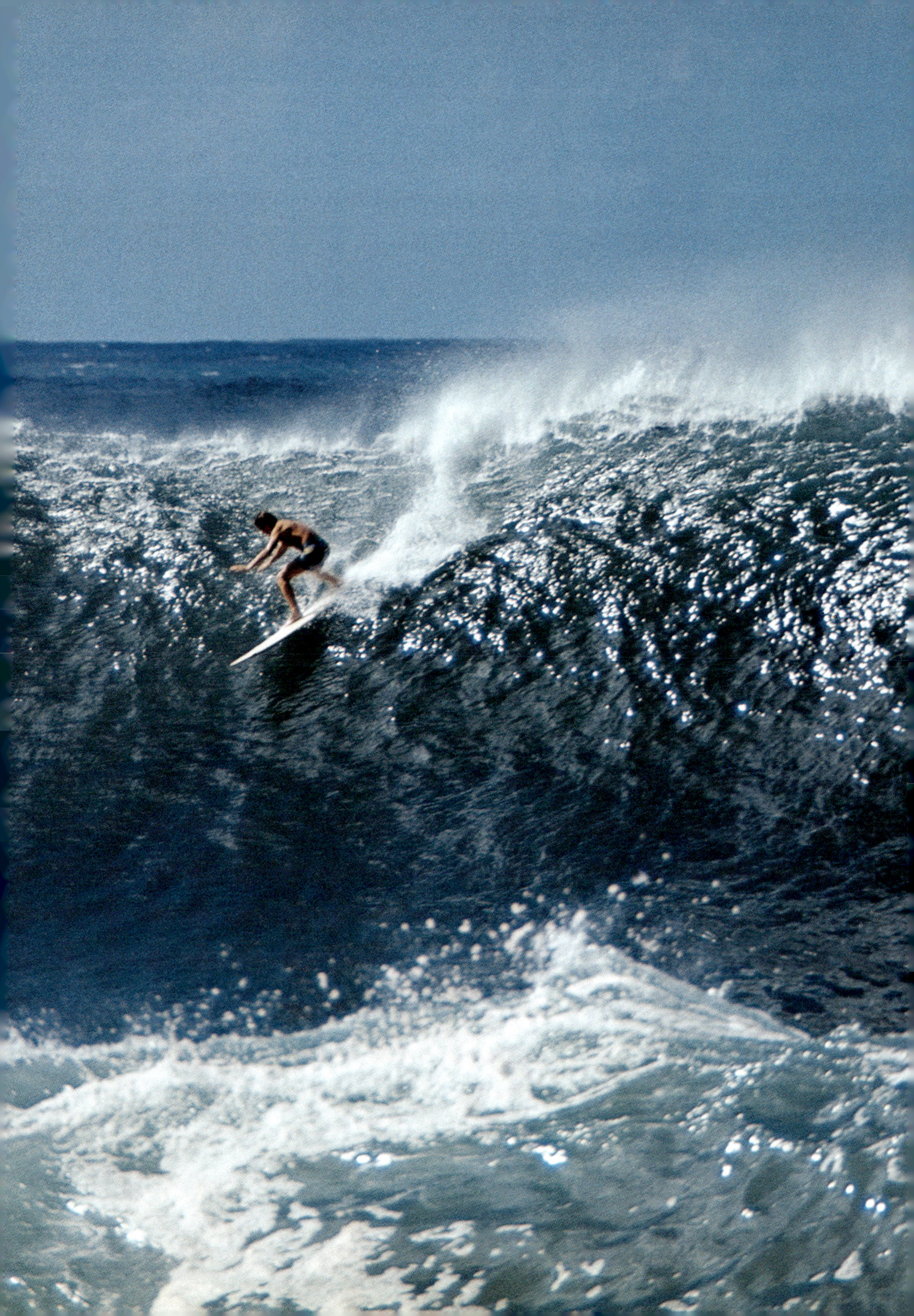

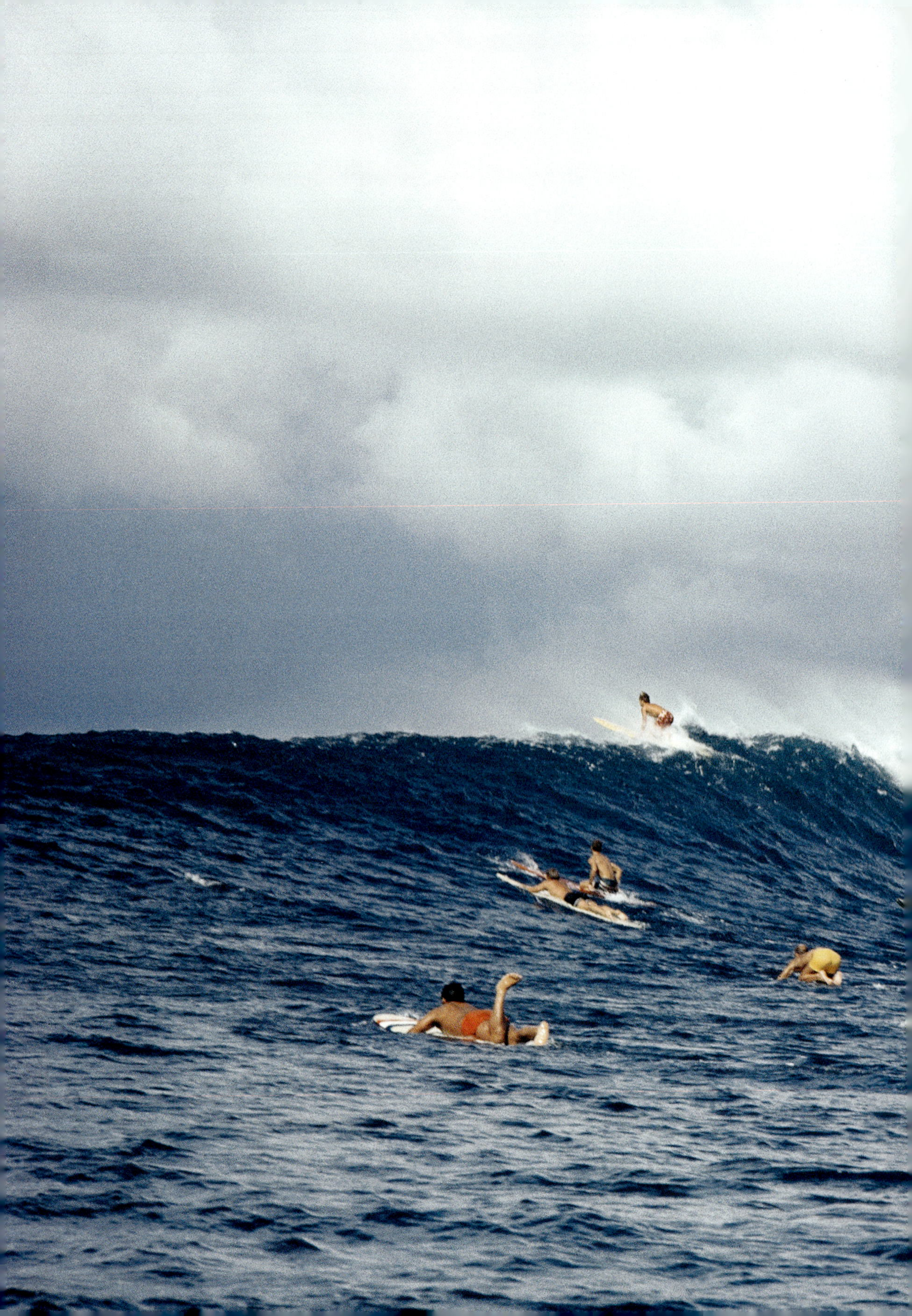

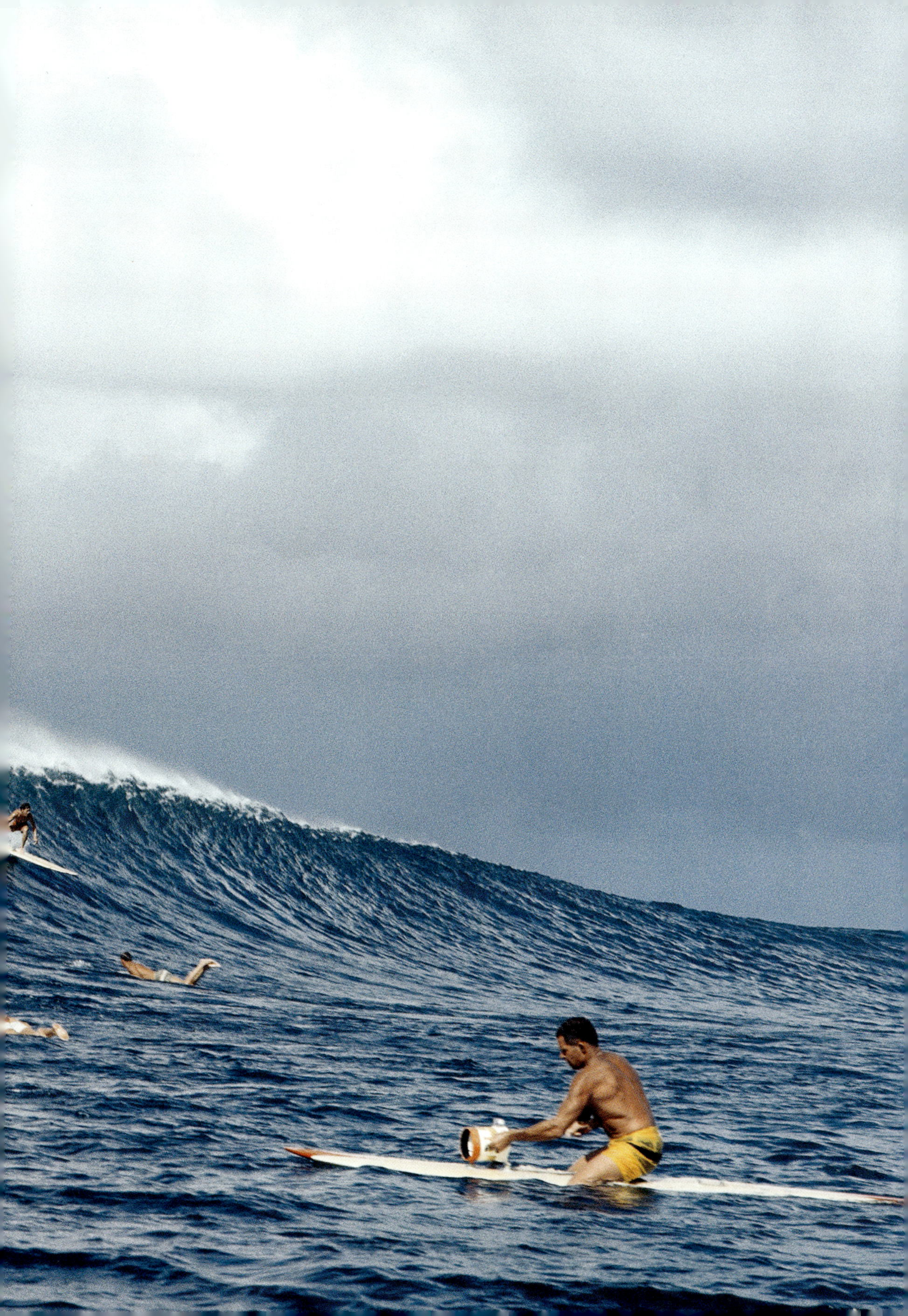

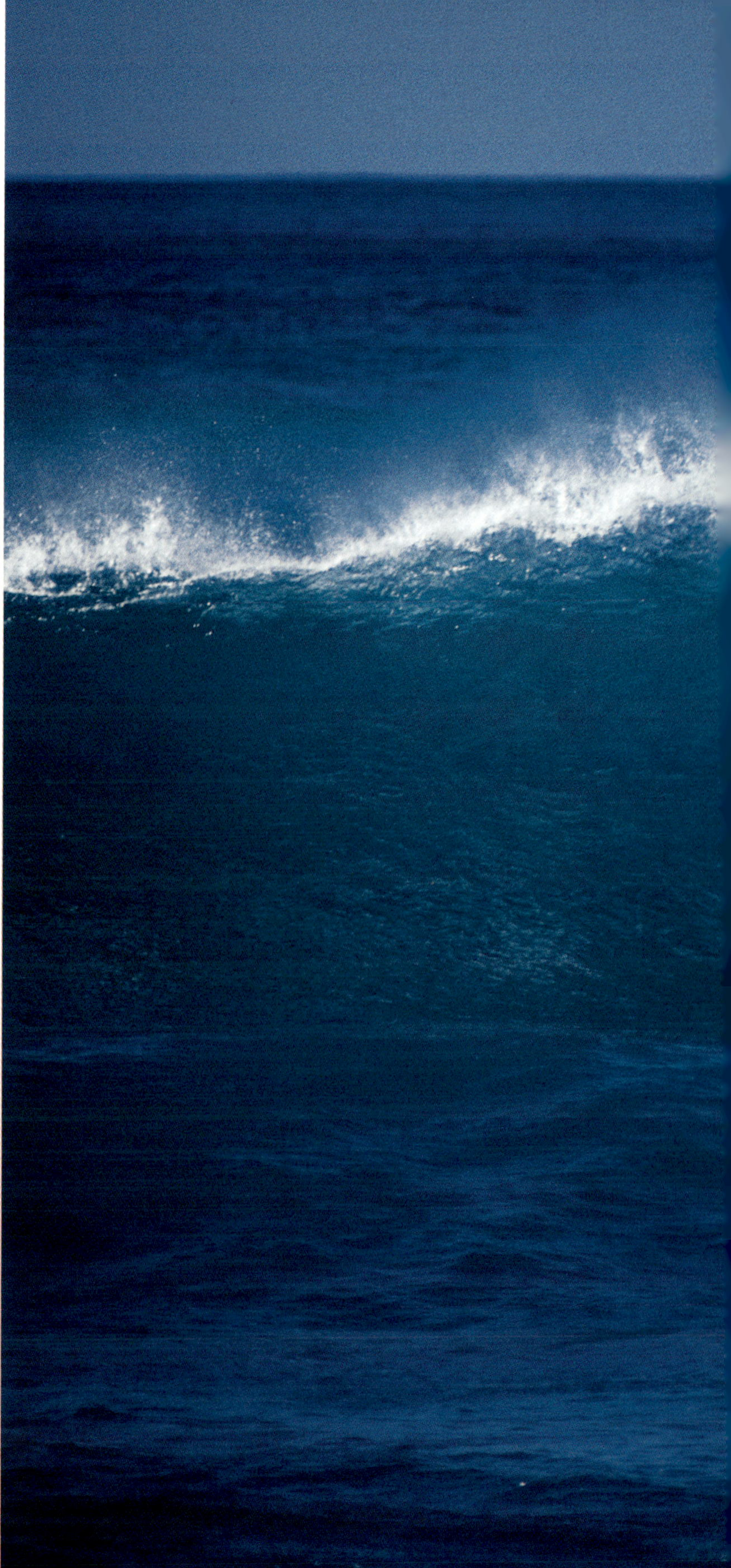

Maile Point, Oahu, 1964

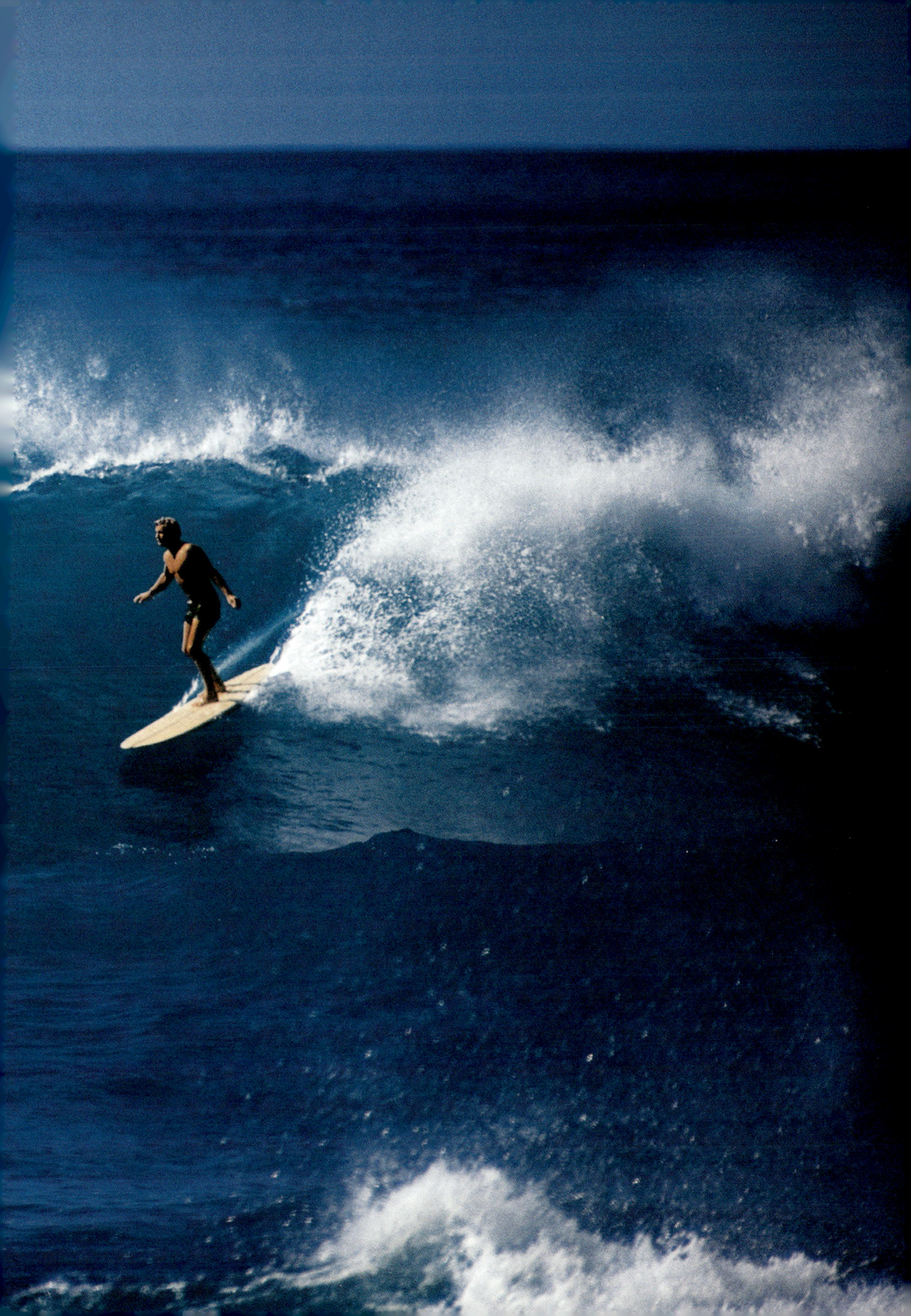

**Buffalo Keaulana, Sunset Beach,
1965**

Keaulana, known for his shaggy red
hair, is the unofficial "Mayor of
Makaha." His sons Brian and Rusty
are world-class surfers and
watermen.

Keaulana, berühmt für seine
zotteligen roten Haare, ist der
inoffizielle „Bürgermeister von
Makaha". Seine Söhne Brian und
Rusty sind Weltklassesurfer und
-wassersportler.

Buffalo Keaulana, réputé pour sa
chevelure rousse hirsute, était
officieusement considéré comme
le « maire de Makaha ». Ses fils
Brian et Rusty jouissent d'une
renommée mondiale dans le milieu
des sports aquatiques … et du surf.


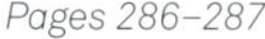


*Pages 286–287*
**Waimea Bay, 1966**

Left to right, Ron Newman, un-
identifiied, and Ponce Rosa (wiping
out). On days this big, surfers have
reported seeing huge boulders
rolling beneath the waves.

Von links nach rechts: Ron
Newman, ein Unbekannter und
Ponce Rosa (beim Hechtsprung).
Bei solchem Wellengang haben
Surfer schon riesige Felsblöcke
unter den Wellen herumrollen
sehen.

De gauche à droite: Ron Newman,
non identifié et Ponce Rosa
(en train de plonger). Certains
jours de swell comme celui-ci,
des surfeurs ont affirmé avoir vu
d'énormes galets rochers sous
les vagues.

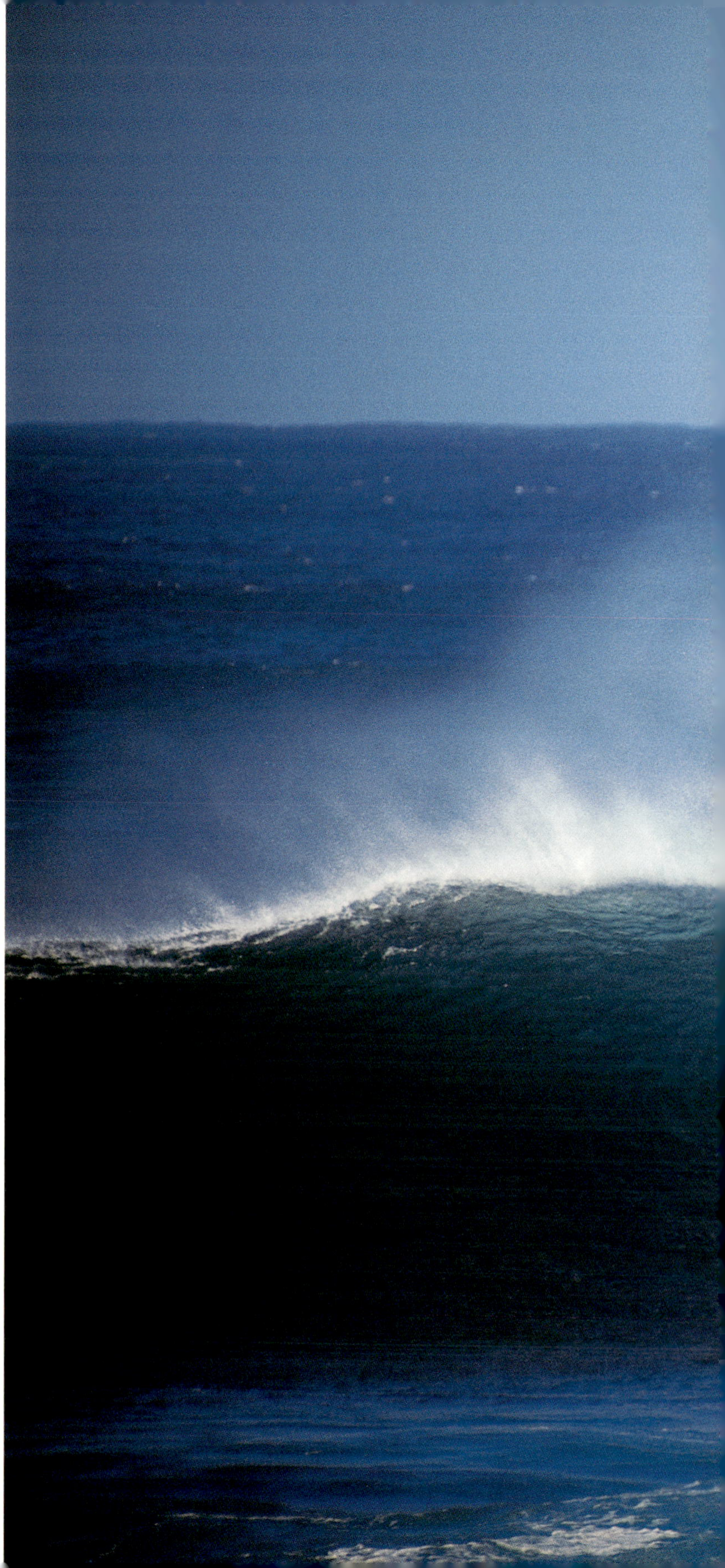

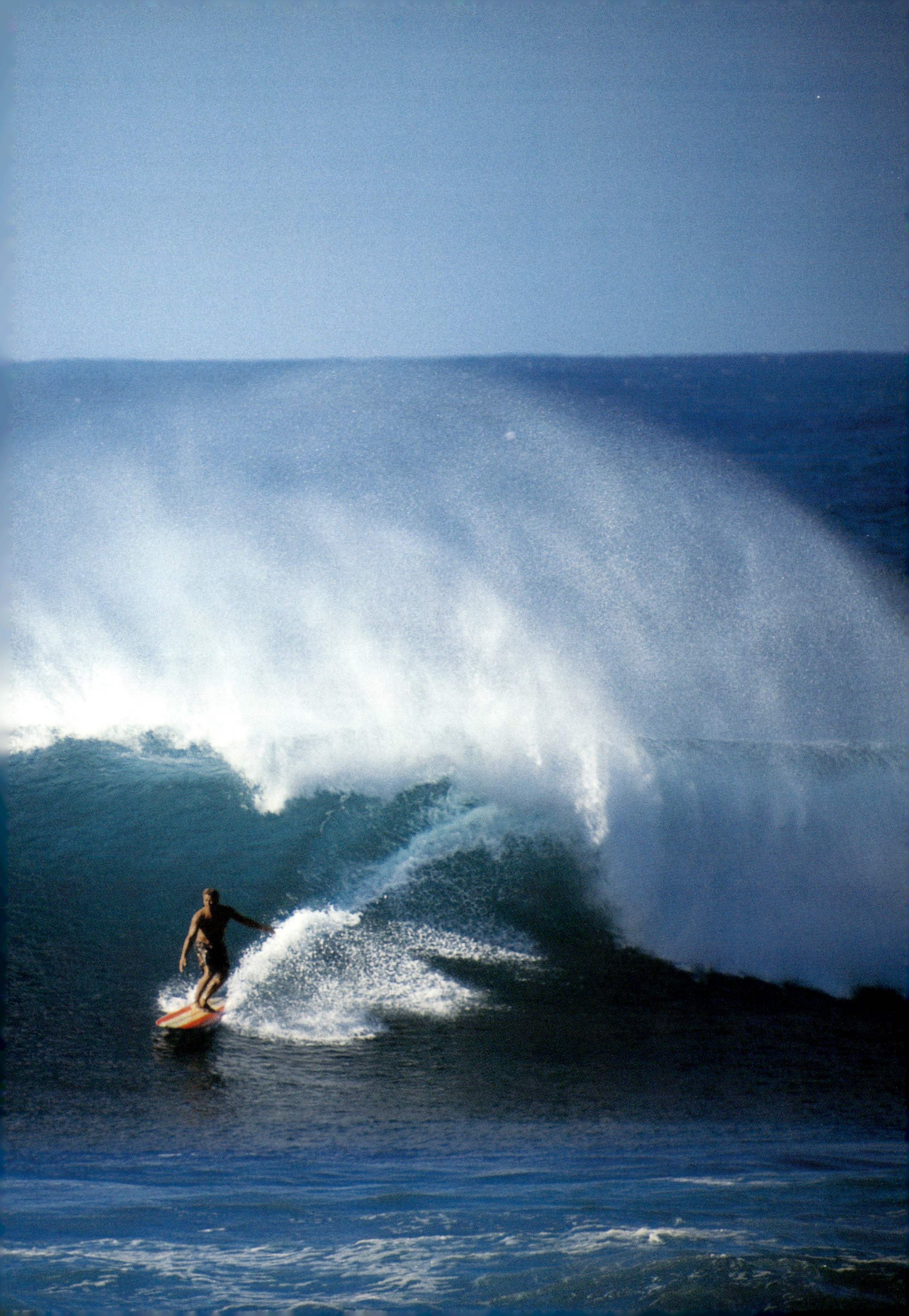

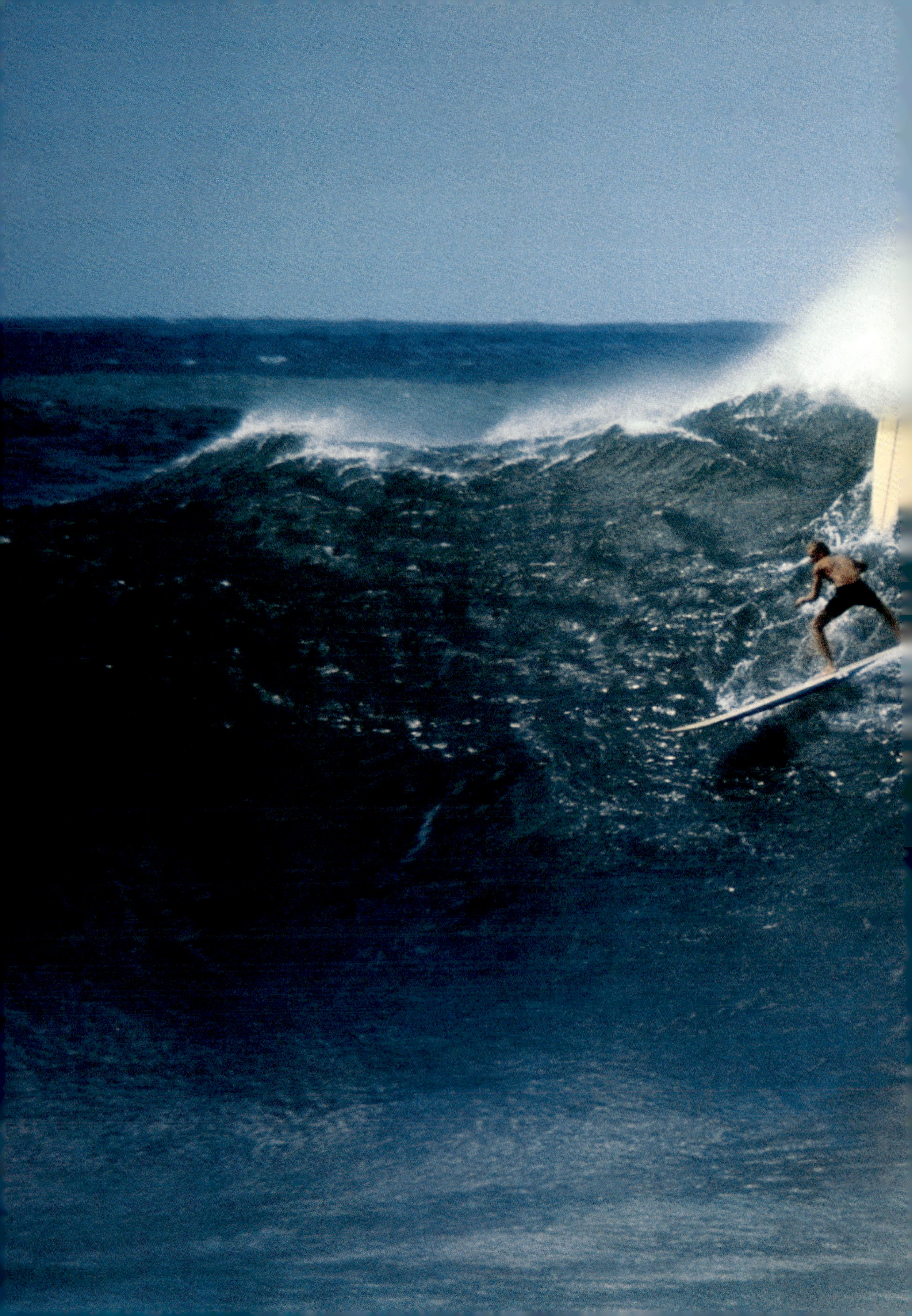

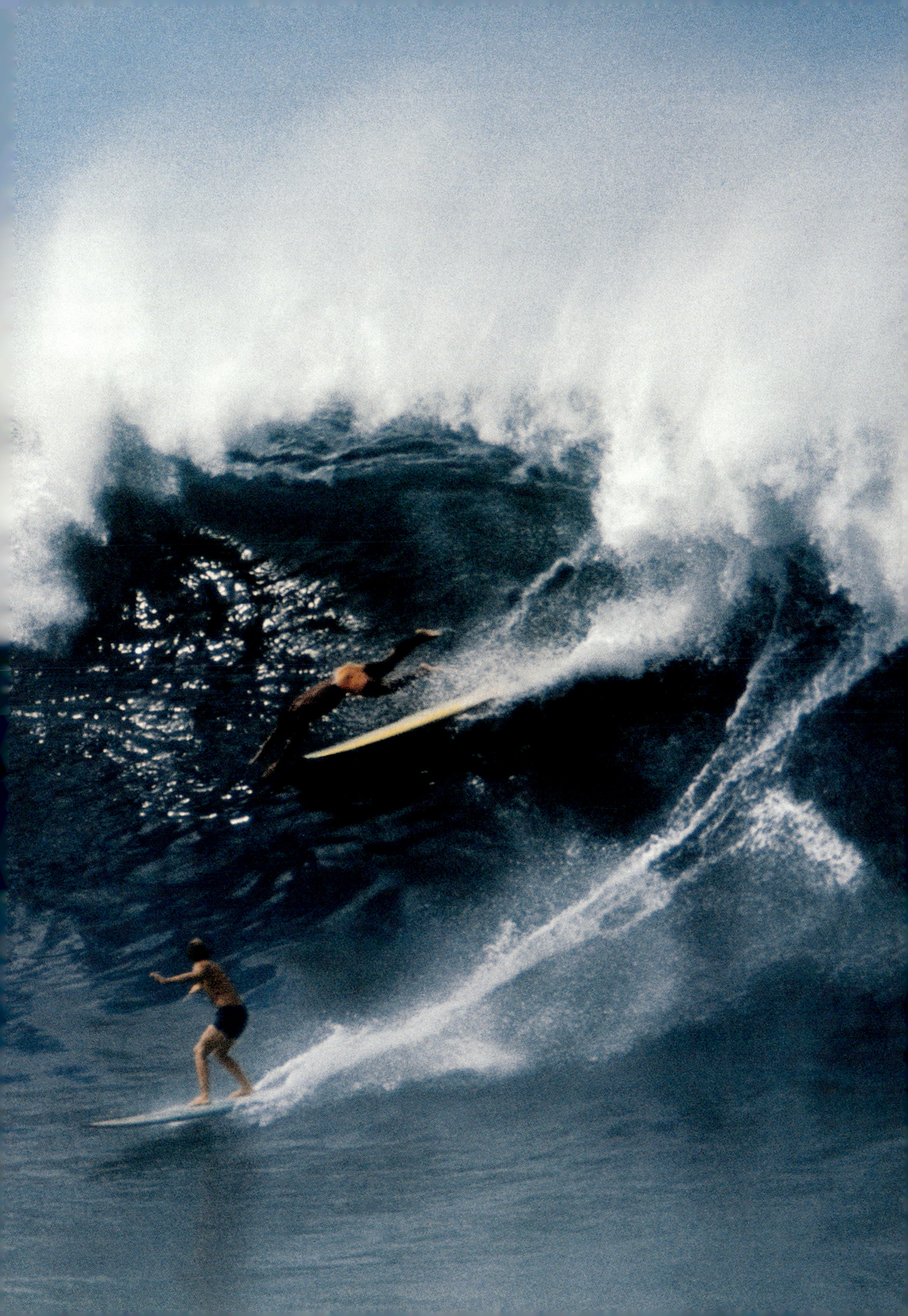

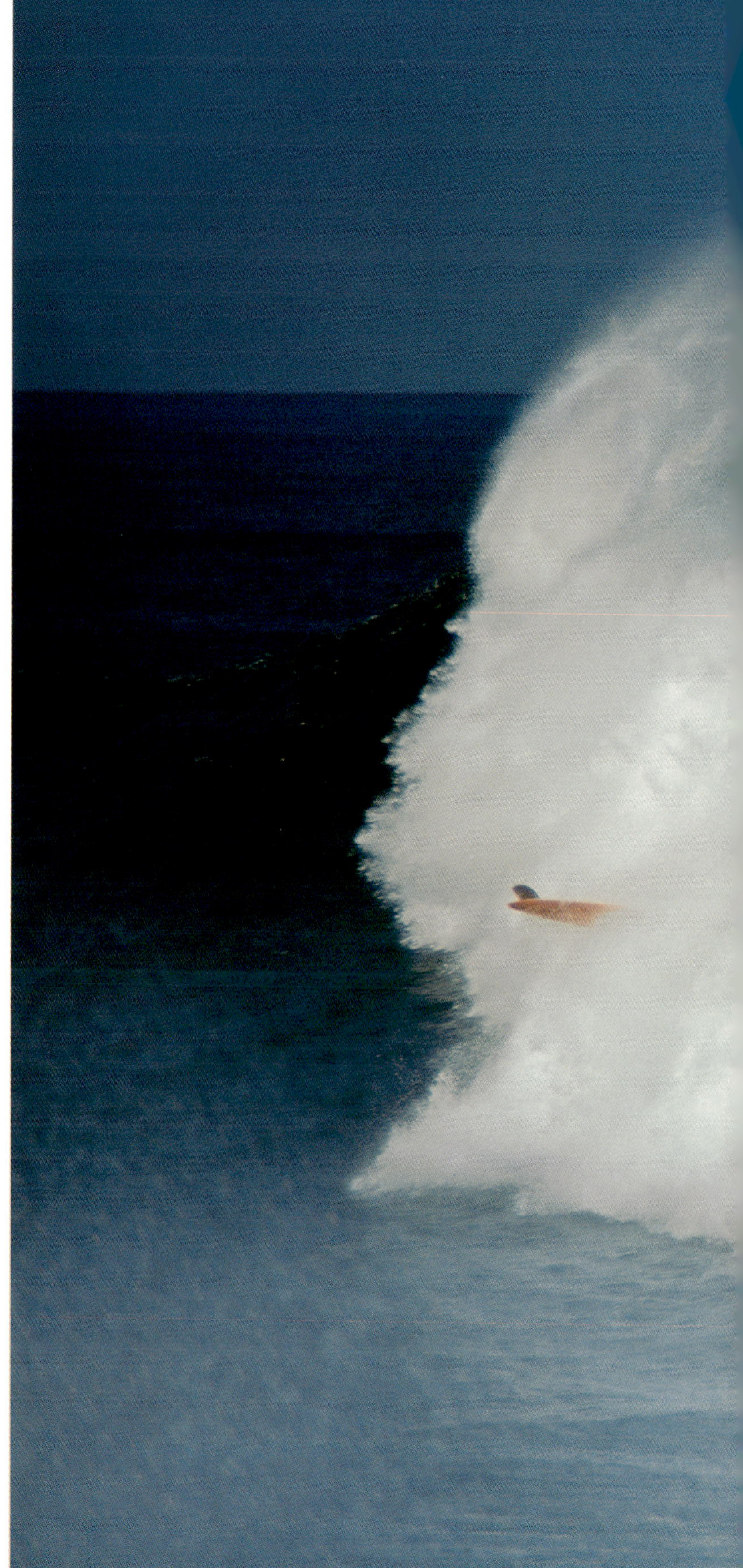

**Greg Noll, Waimea Bay, 1966**

"The Bull" about to be buried by
a Waimea avalanche.

„The Bull", kurz bevor er von einer
Waimea-Lawine begraben wird.

« The Bull » sur le point de se faire
avaler par un monstre à Waimea.

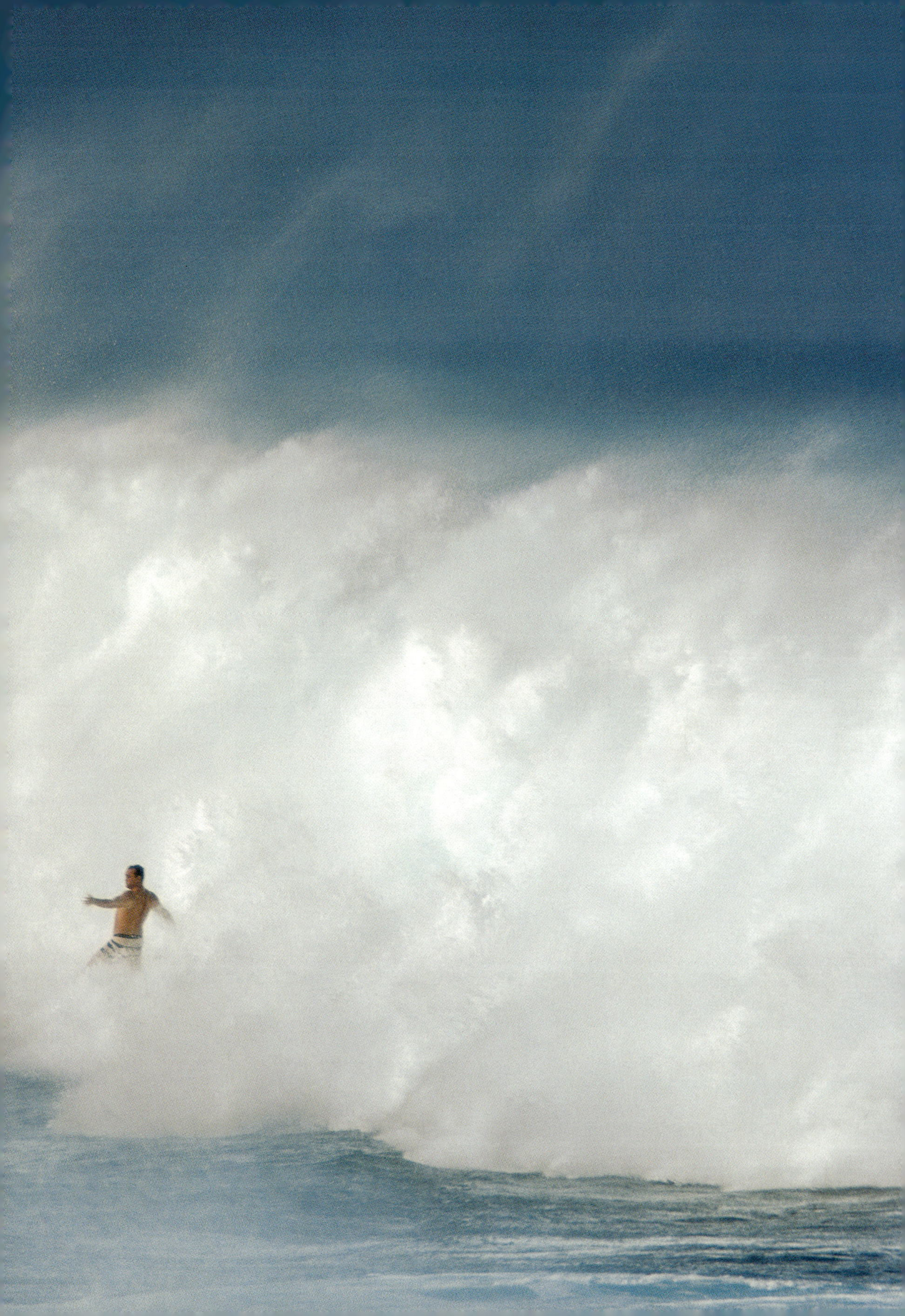

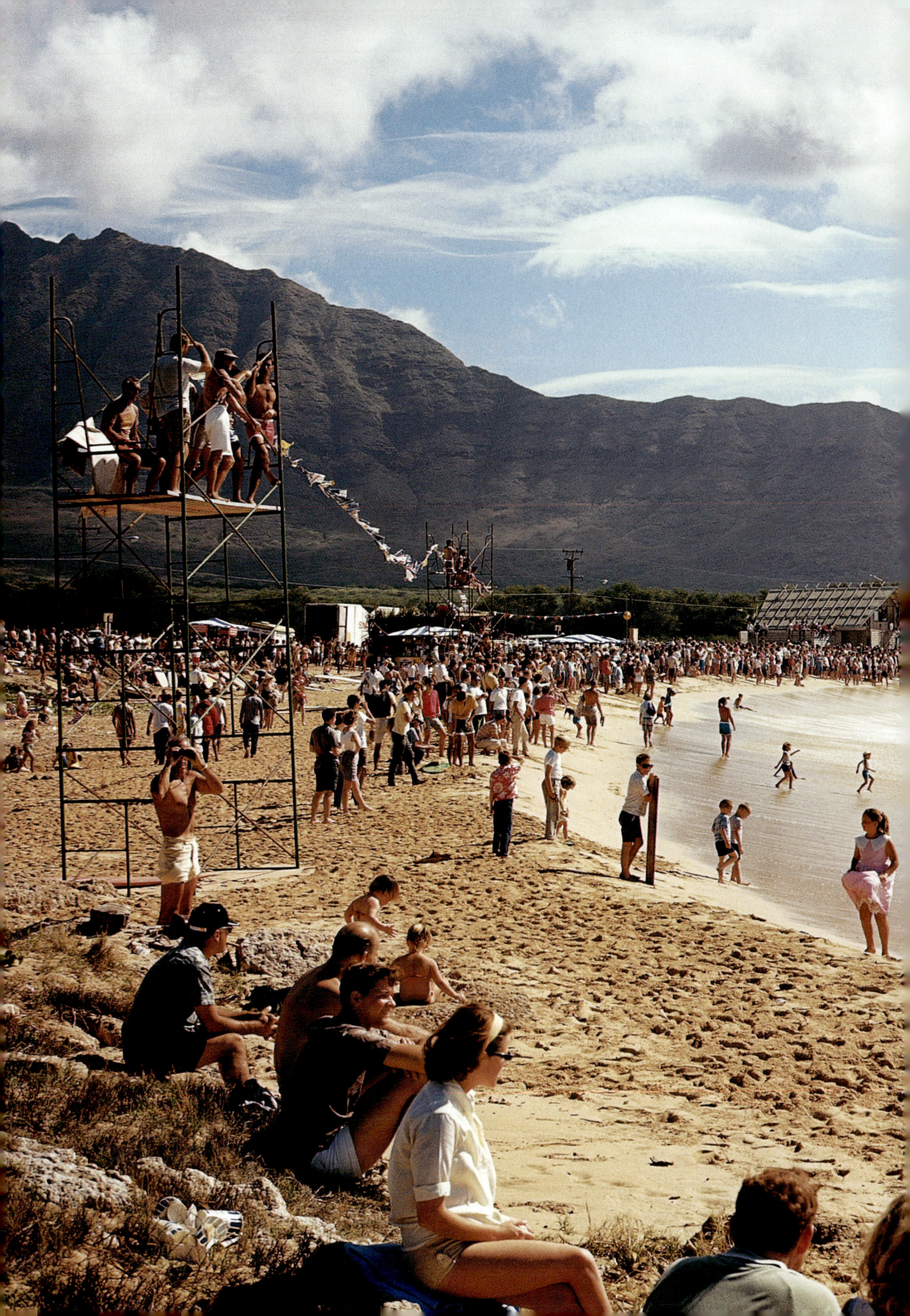

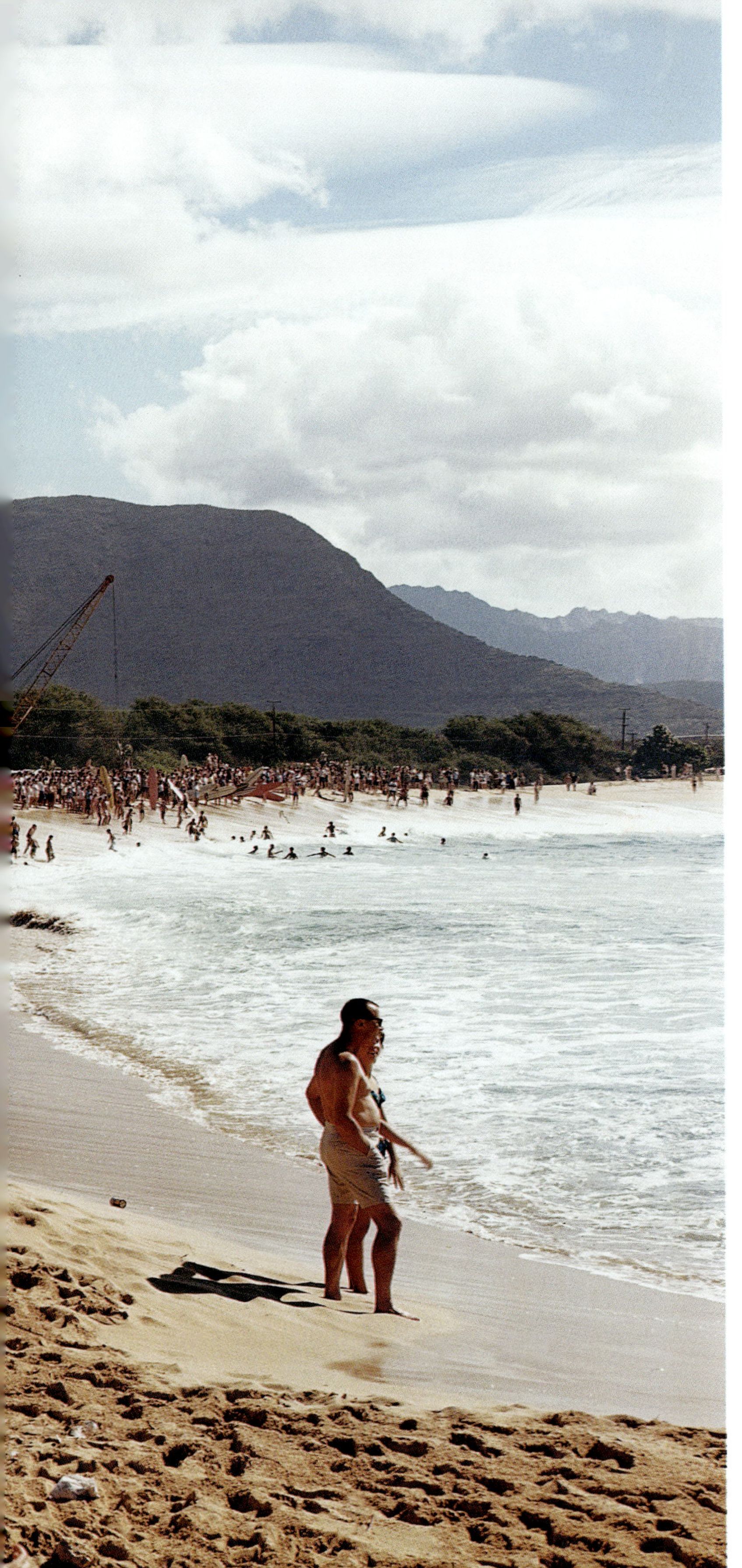

Makaha Championships, 1963

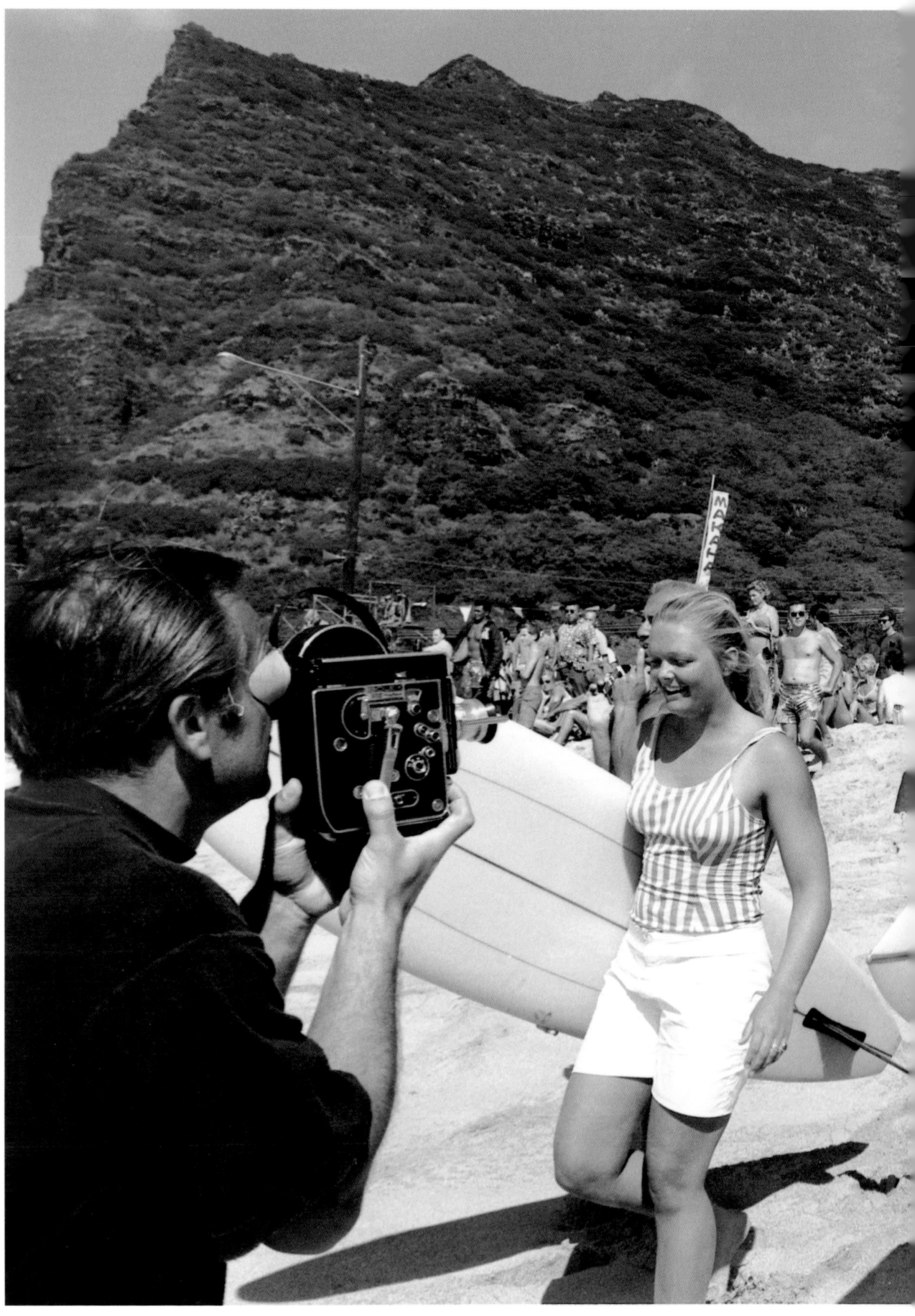

MAKAHA

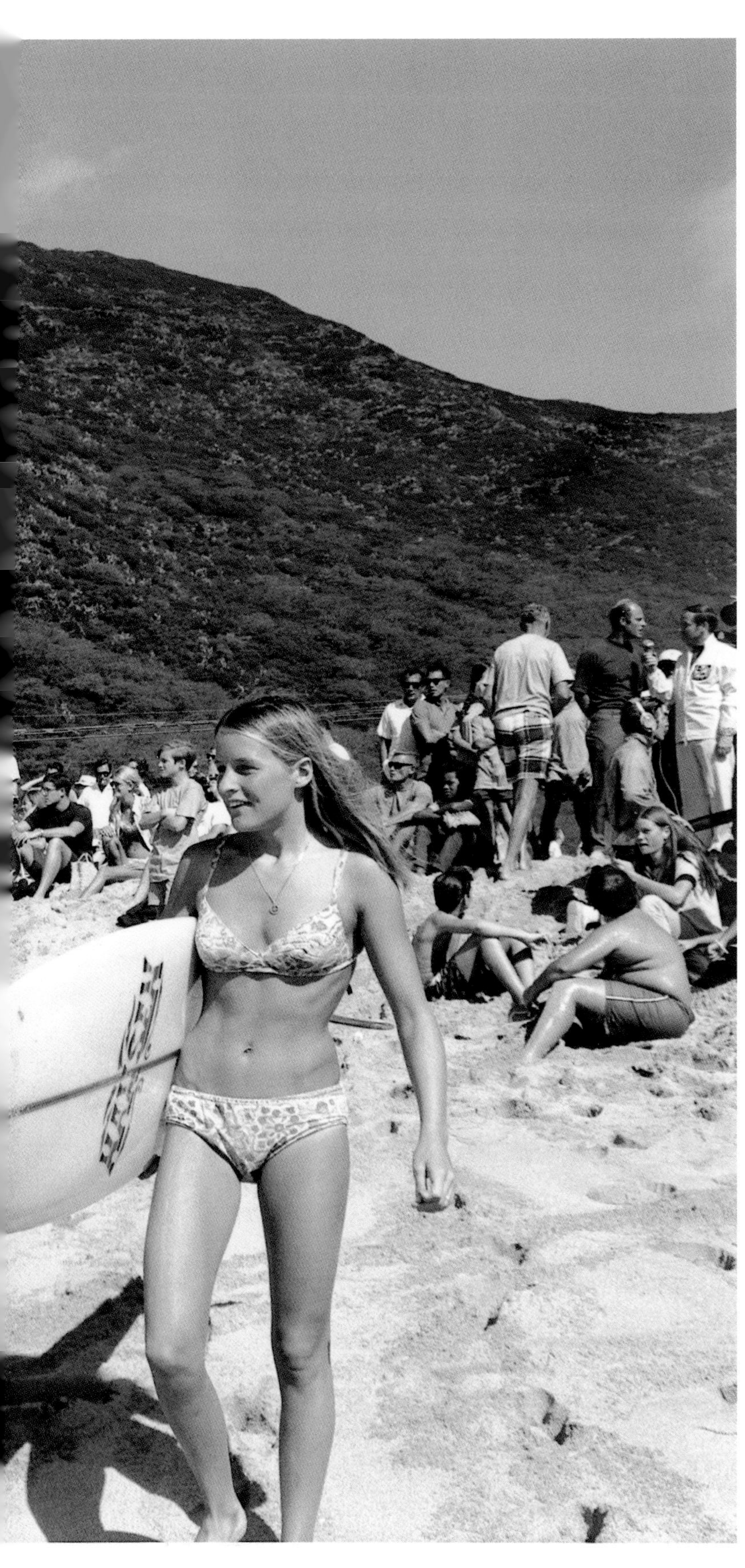

**Joyce Hoffman, Margo Godfrey, Makaha, 1968**

Just prior to the Makaha contest's women's finals. La Jolla's Godfrey (later Oberg) would eventually win the championship.

Unmittelbar vor dem Finale der Frauen beim Wettbewerb von Makaha. Godfrey (später Oberg) aus La Jolla gewann den Wettbewerb.

Quelques minutes avant la finale féminine du championnat de Makaha. L'épreuve fut remportée par Margo Godfrey (plus tard Oberg) du club de La Jolla.

**The Calhouns, Makaha, 1962**

Real women have curves and
surfboards. A famous shot of the
Calhoun women. Left to right:
Robin, Marge, and Candy.

Wahre Frauen haben Kurven
und Surfbretter. Eine berühmte
Aufnahme der Calhoun-Frauen.
Von links nach rechts: Robin,
Marge und Candy.

Les « vraies femmes » ont des
courbes … et une planche de surf.
Un fameux cliché des « sœurs
Calhoun ». De gauche à droite :
Robin, Marge et Candy.

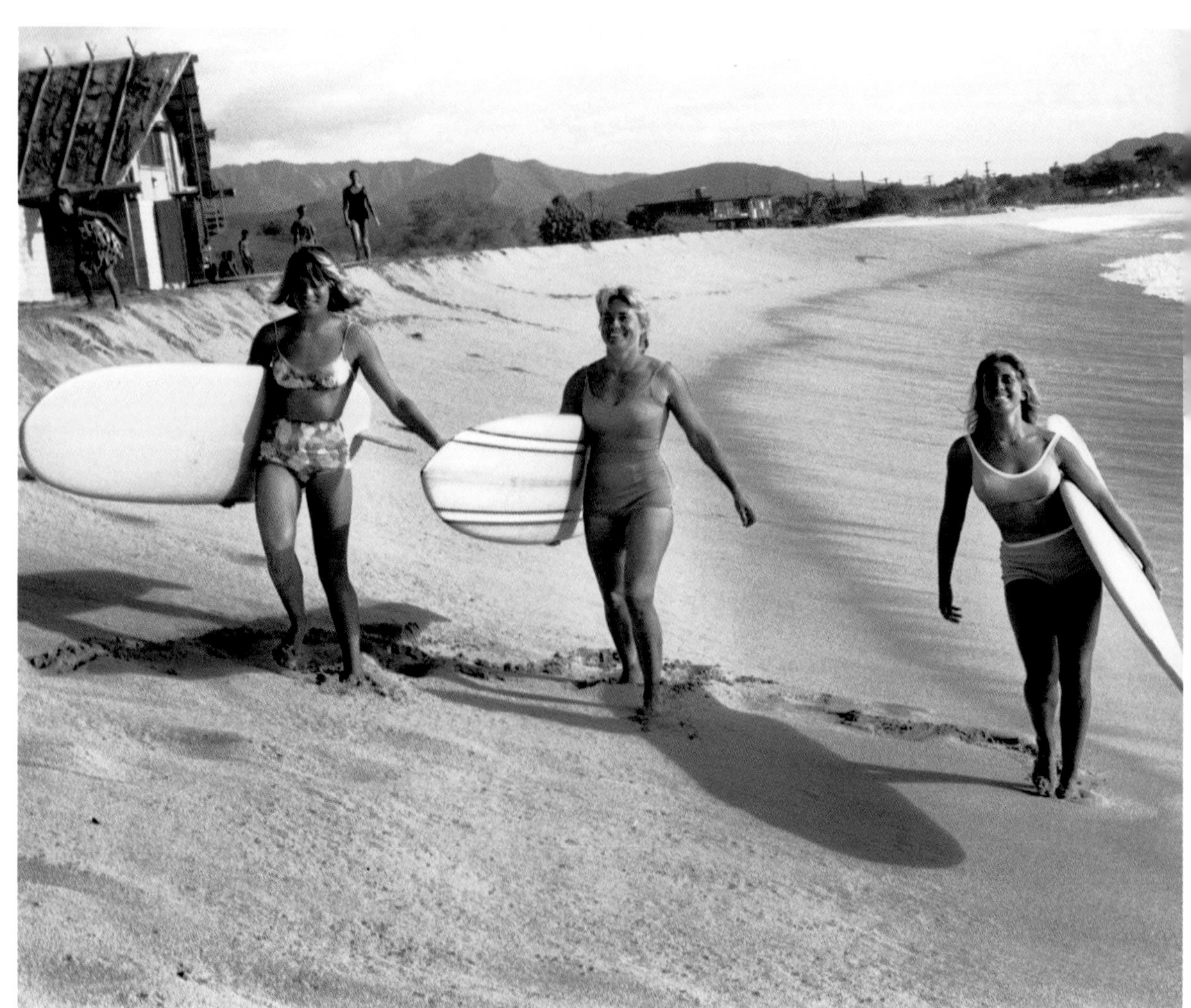

**Don James, Makaha, 1962**

Dr. Don James was Grannis's
good friend and surf photography
associate for decades.

Dr. Don James war für Grannis
jahrzehntelang ein guter Freund
und Partner bei der Surffotografie.

Le photographe de surf Don James
fut l'associé et le fidèle ami
de Grannis pendant de longues
années.

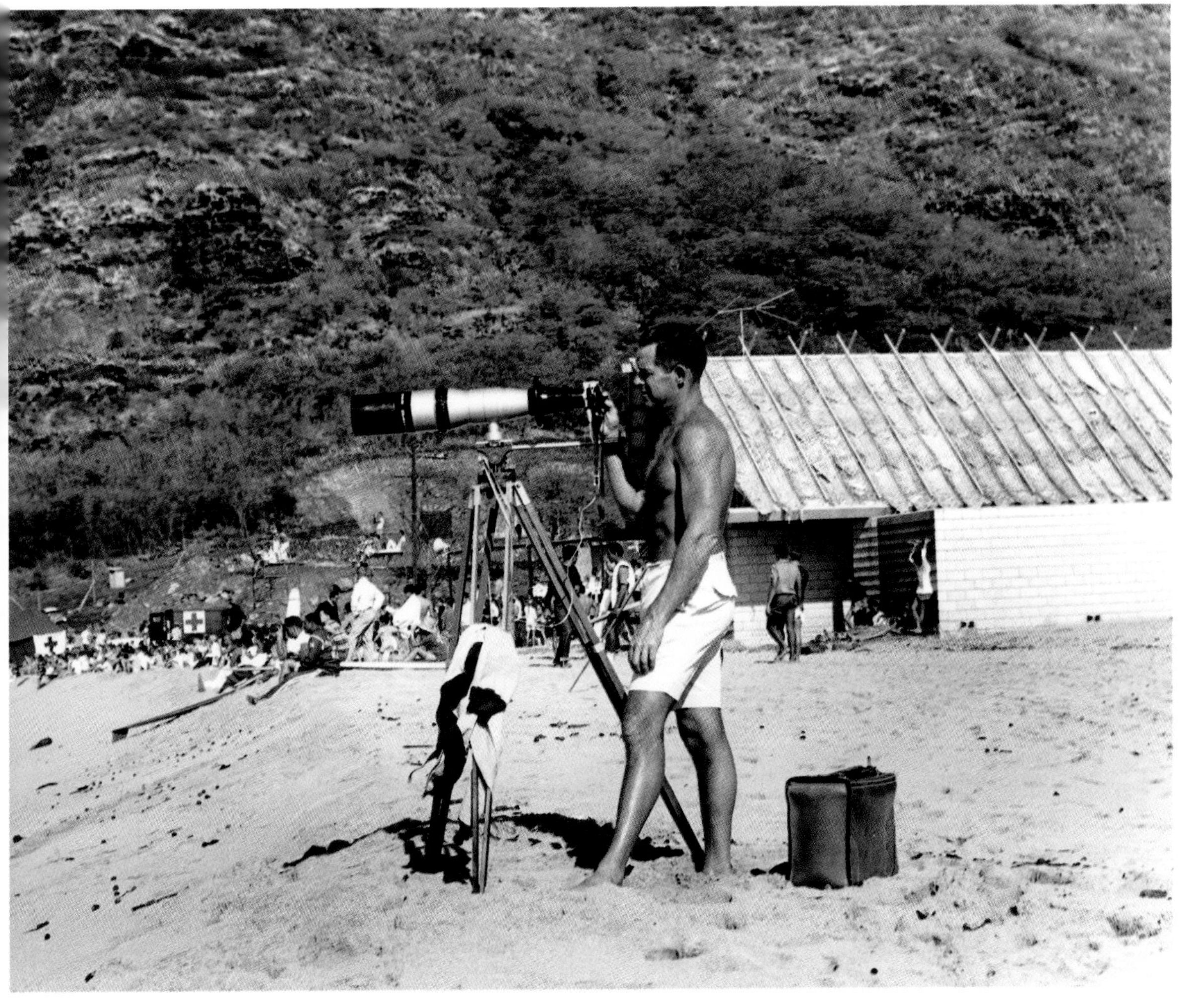

**Buzzy Trent, Sunset Beach, 1968**

Trent, a holdover from the fifties, was an ace waterman well into the eighties. Shown catching a ride in between lifeguarding duties for the Duke Classic.

Trent, ein Überbleibsel aus den Fünfzigern, war bis in die Achzigerjahre ein großartiger Wassersportler. Hier surft er zwischen seinen Schichten als Rettungsschwimmer beim Duke Classic.

« Rescapé » des années 1950, Buzzy Trent resta un virtuose de la planche jusque dans les années 1980. Sauveteur pendant les épreuves de la Duke Classic, on le voit ici en train de dévaler une vague juste avant de reprendre son service.

**Jock Sutherland (right), Waimea Bay, 1966**

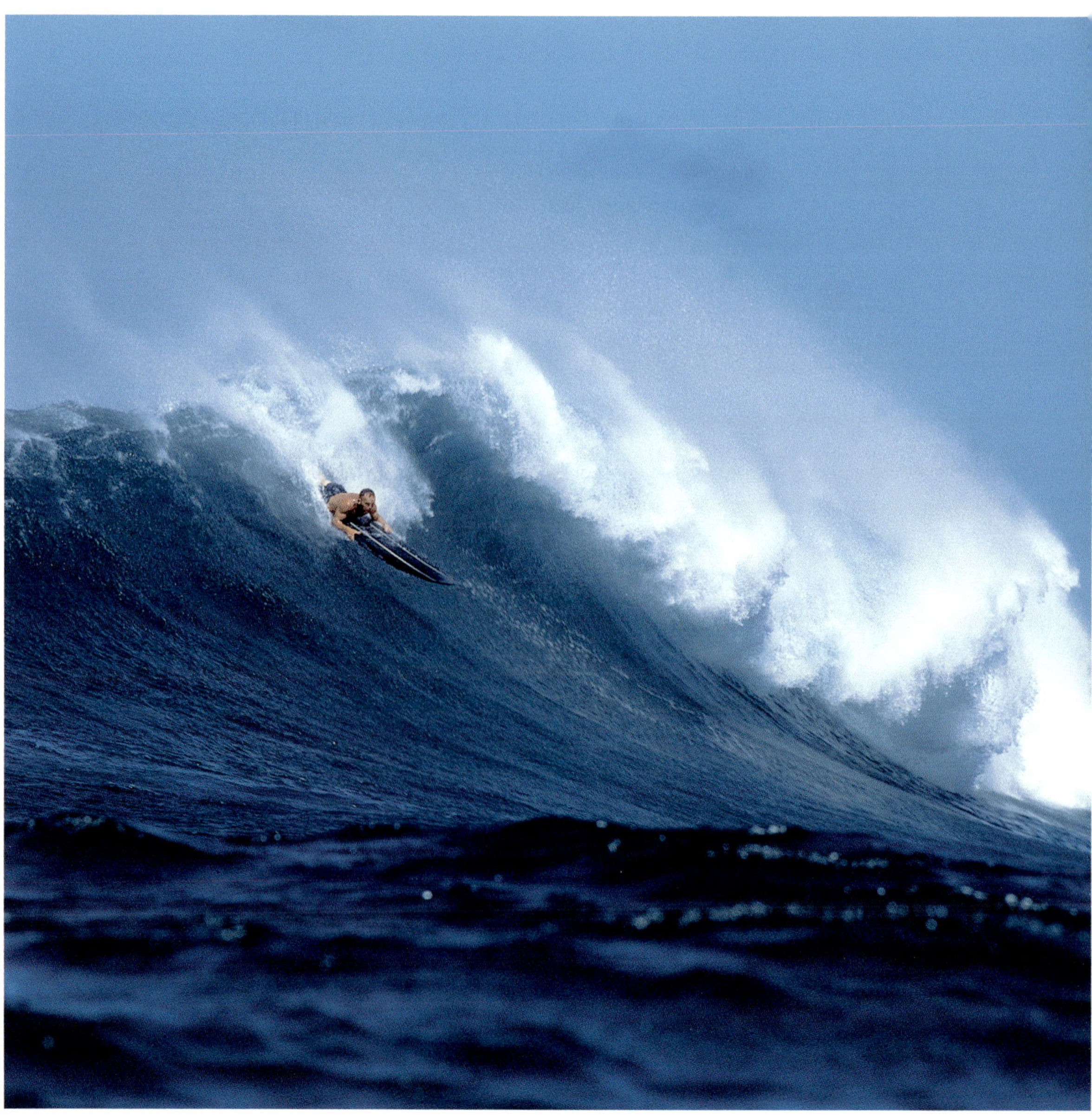

**Windansea Surf Club, Makaha, 1964**

La Jolla's Windansea Surf Club bought this old junker for $65 in Honolulu and made it their official team car for the Makaha Championships. Left to right: Eric Hauser, George Rotgans, Dickie Moon, John Sandera, Rodney Sumpter.

Der La Jolla Windansea Surf Club kaufte die alte Klapperkiste für 65 Dollar in Honolulu und benutzte sie als offiziellen Team-Wagen für die Makaha Championships. Von links nach rechts: Eric Hauser, George Rotgans, Dickie Moon, John Sandera, Rodney Sumpter.

Le Windansea Surf Club de La Jolla acheta cette épave à Honolulu pour 65 dollars et en fit sa voiture d'équipe pour le championnat de Makaha. De gauche à droite : Eric Hauser, George Rotgans, Dickie Moon, John Sandera et Rodney Sumpter.

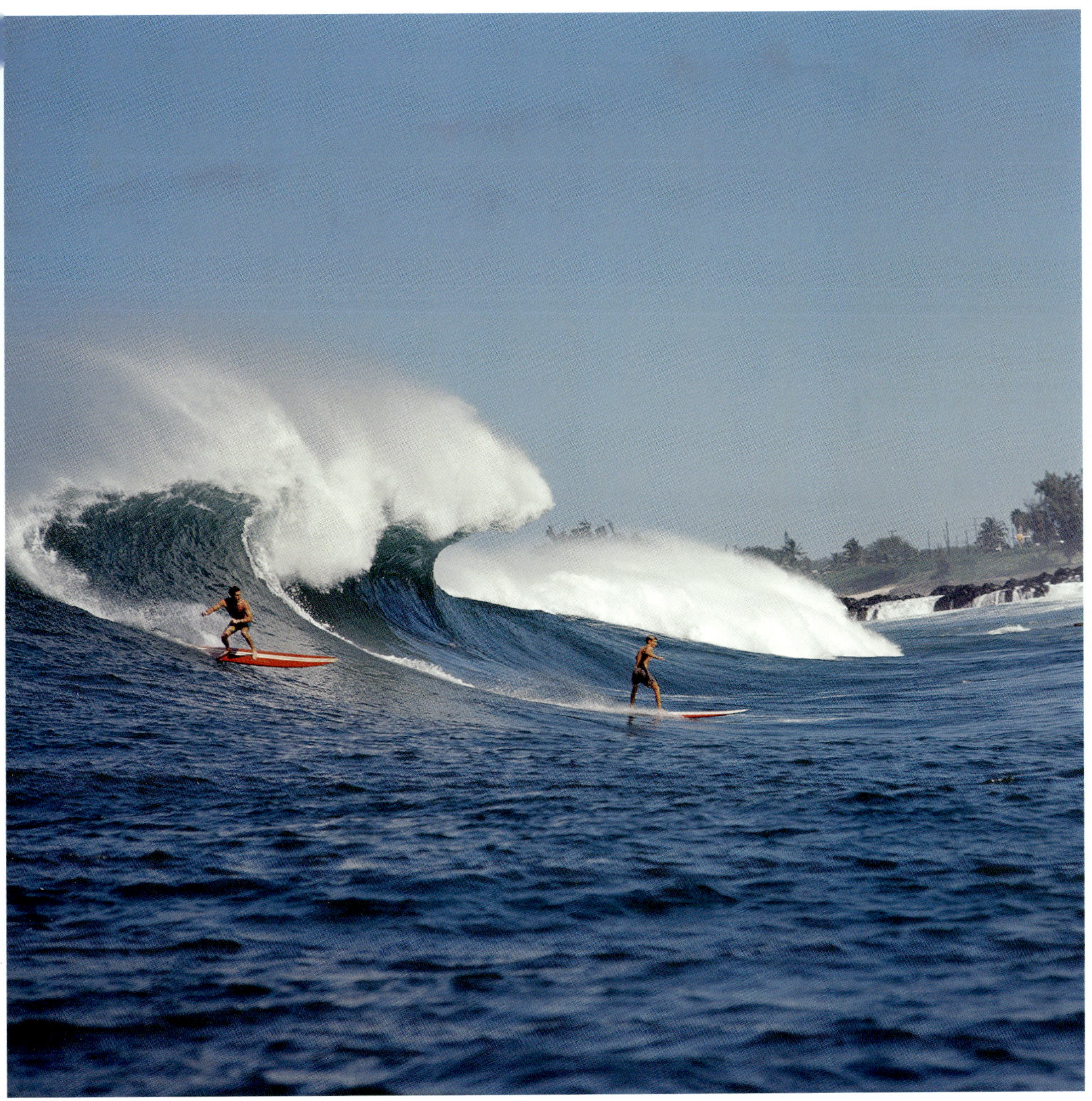

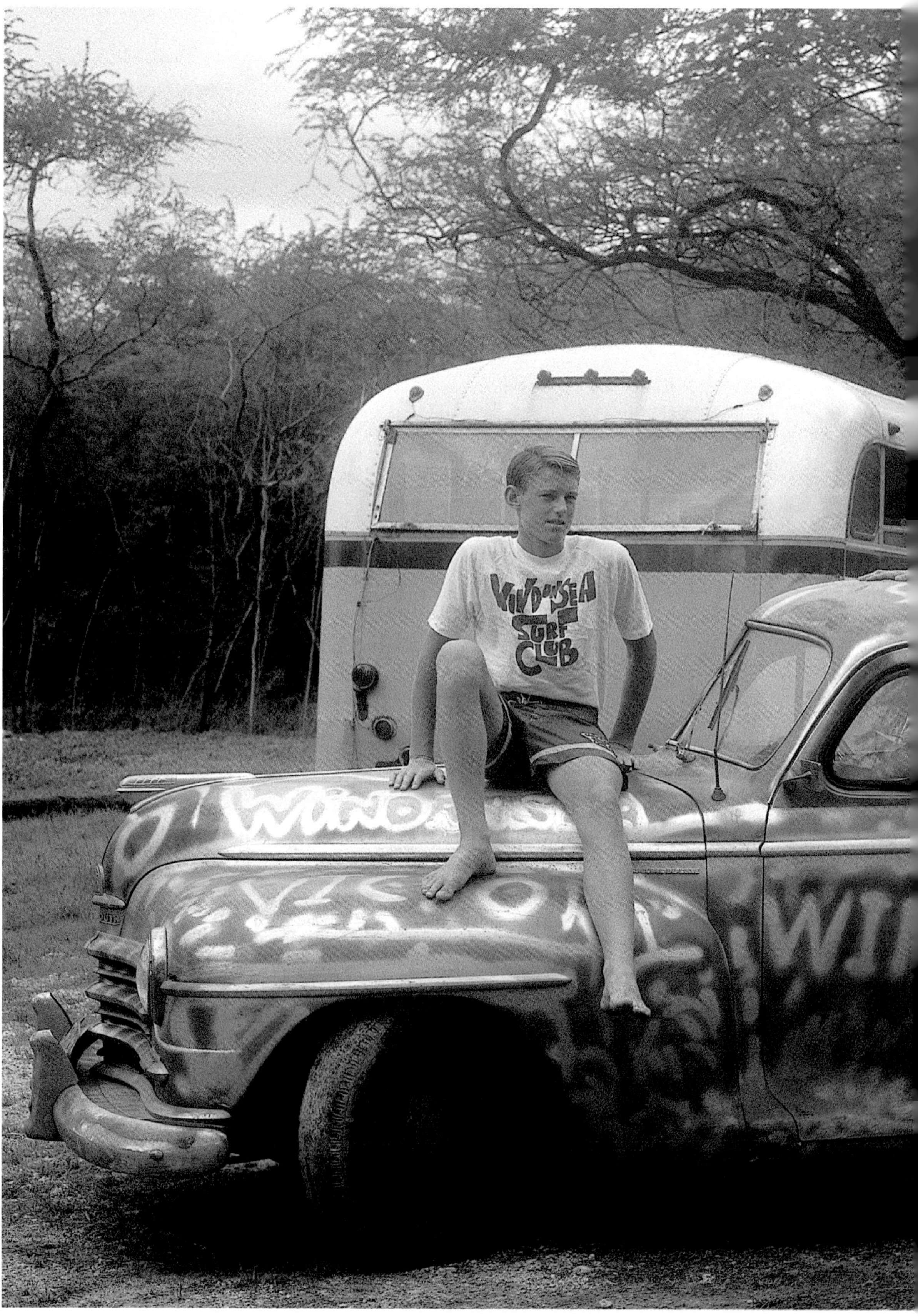

WINDANSEA SURF CLUB
WINDANSEA

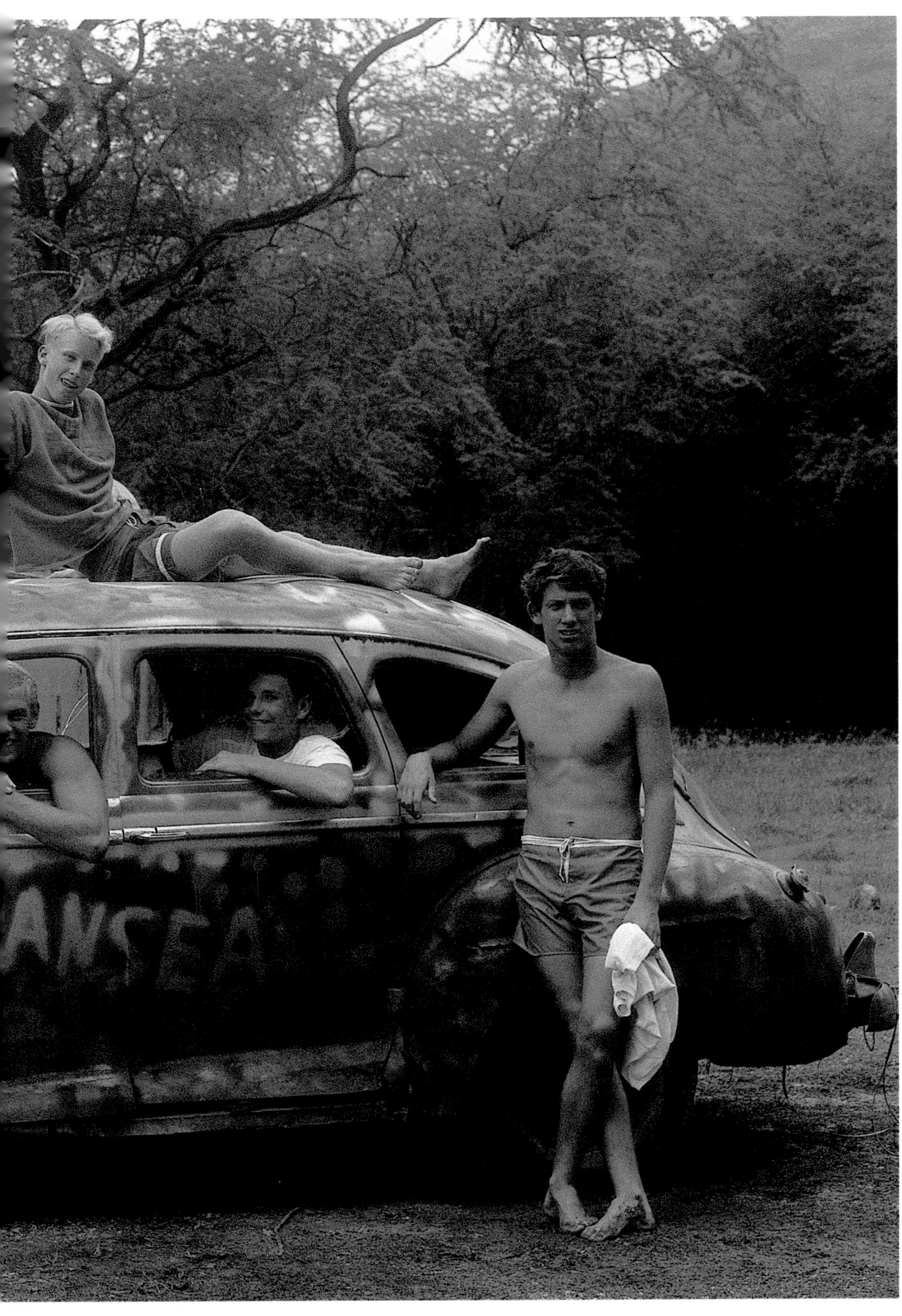

**Makaha, 1965**

Semifinalists, men's division, Makaha Championships. Left to right: Fred Hemmings Jr., Buffalo Keaulana, Steve Bigler, Dewey Weber, George Downing, Paul Strauch Jr., Joey Cabell, Rick Steere, Kiki Spangler, Ken Rocky, Ben Aipa, Aka Hemmings, Mike Doyle. Downing won the contest.

Teilnehmer am Halbfinale der Männer, Makaha Championships. Von links nach rechts: Fred Hemmings Jr., Buffalo Keaulana, Steve Bigler, Dewey Weber, George Downing, Paul Strauch Jr., Joey Cabell, Rick Steere, Kiki Spangler, Ken Rocky, Ben Aipa, Aka Hemmings, Mike Doyle. Downing gewann den Wettbewerb.

Semi-finalistes des épreuves masculines du championnat de Makaha. De gauche à droite: Fred Hemmings Jr., Buffalo Keaulana, Steve Bigler, Dewey Weber, George Downing (vainqueur), Paul Strauch Jr., Joey Cabell, Rick Steere, Kiki Spangler, Ken Rocky, Ben Aipa, Aka Hemmings et Mike Doyle.

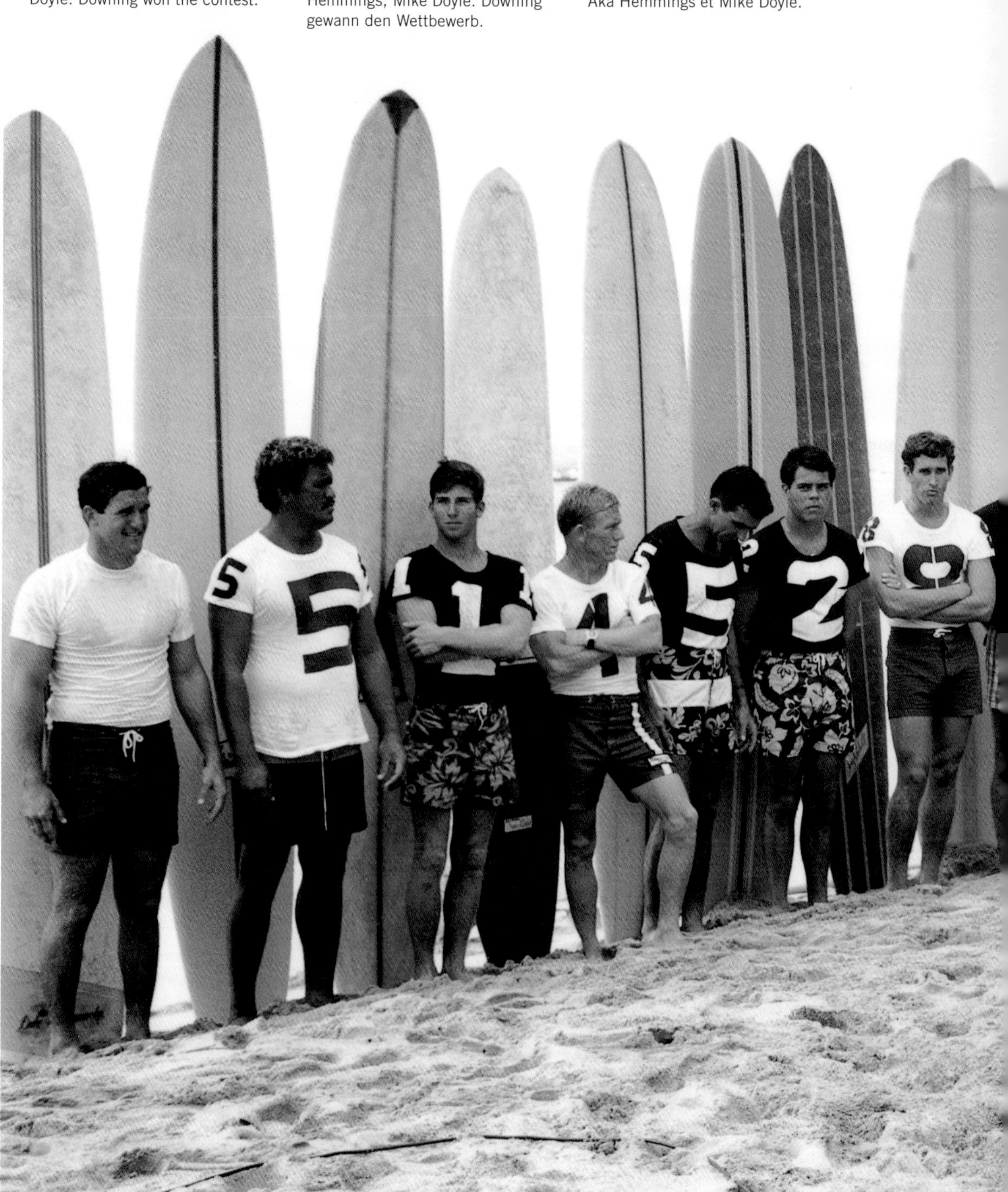

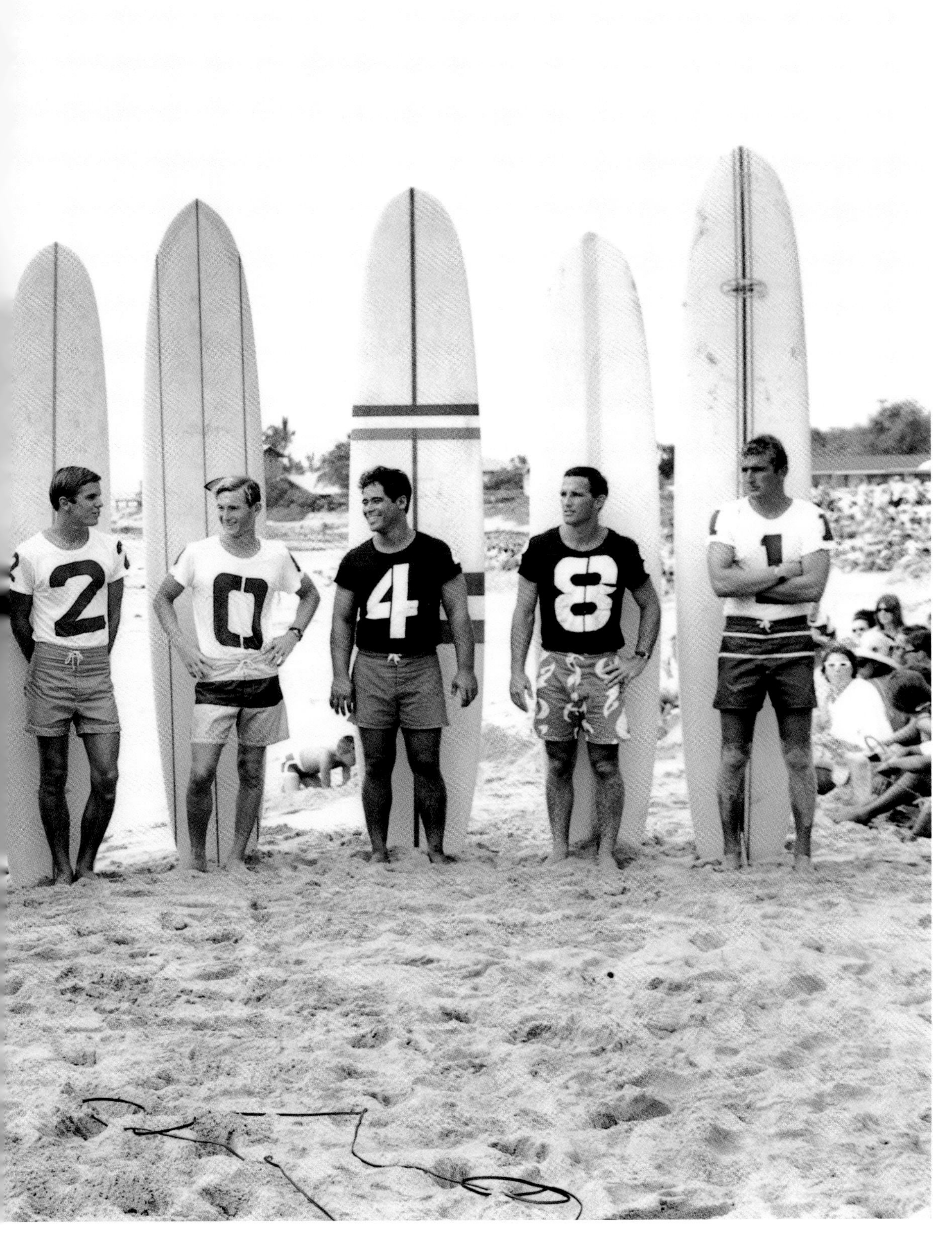

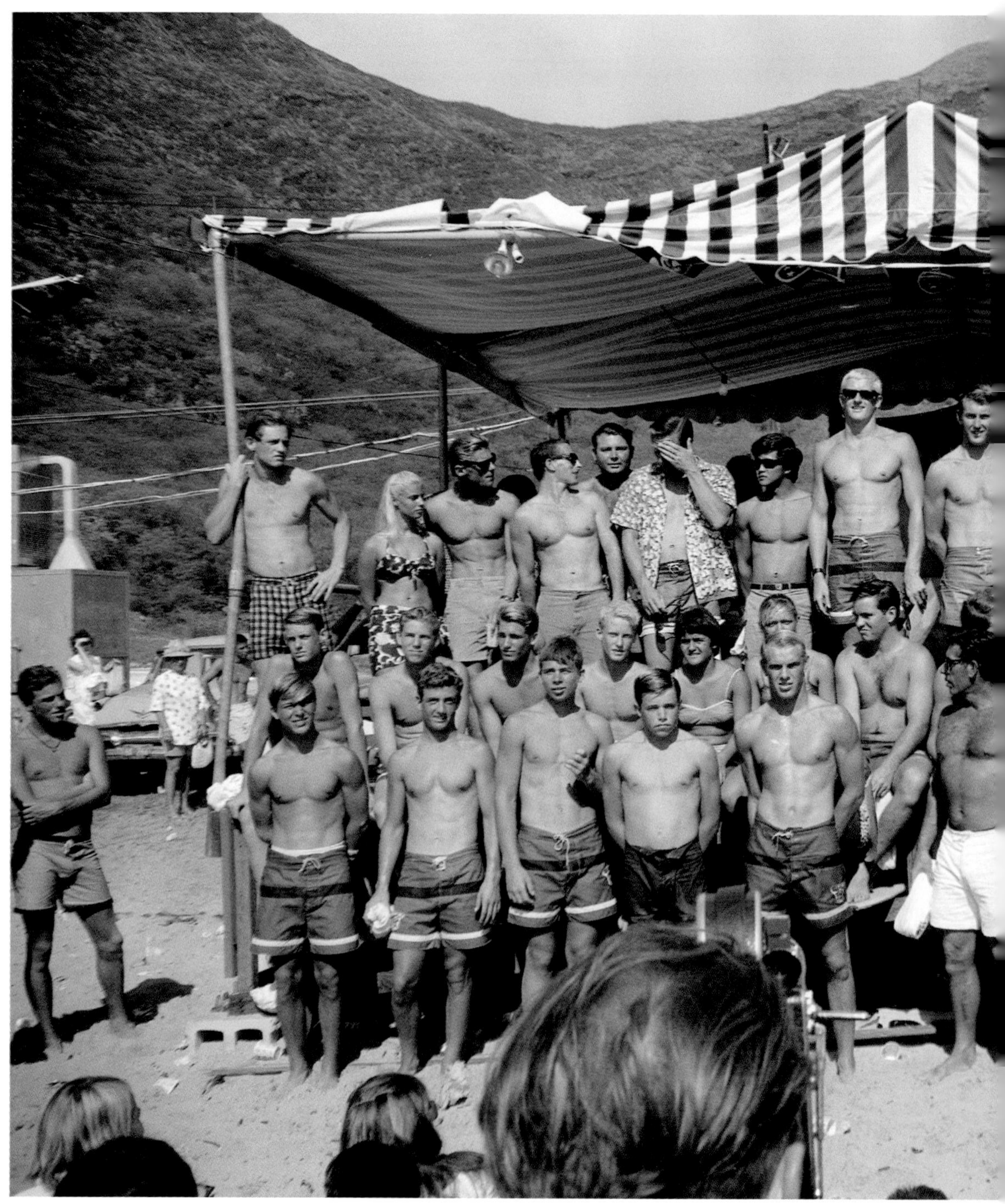

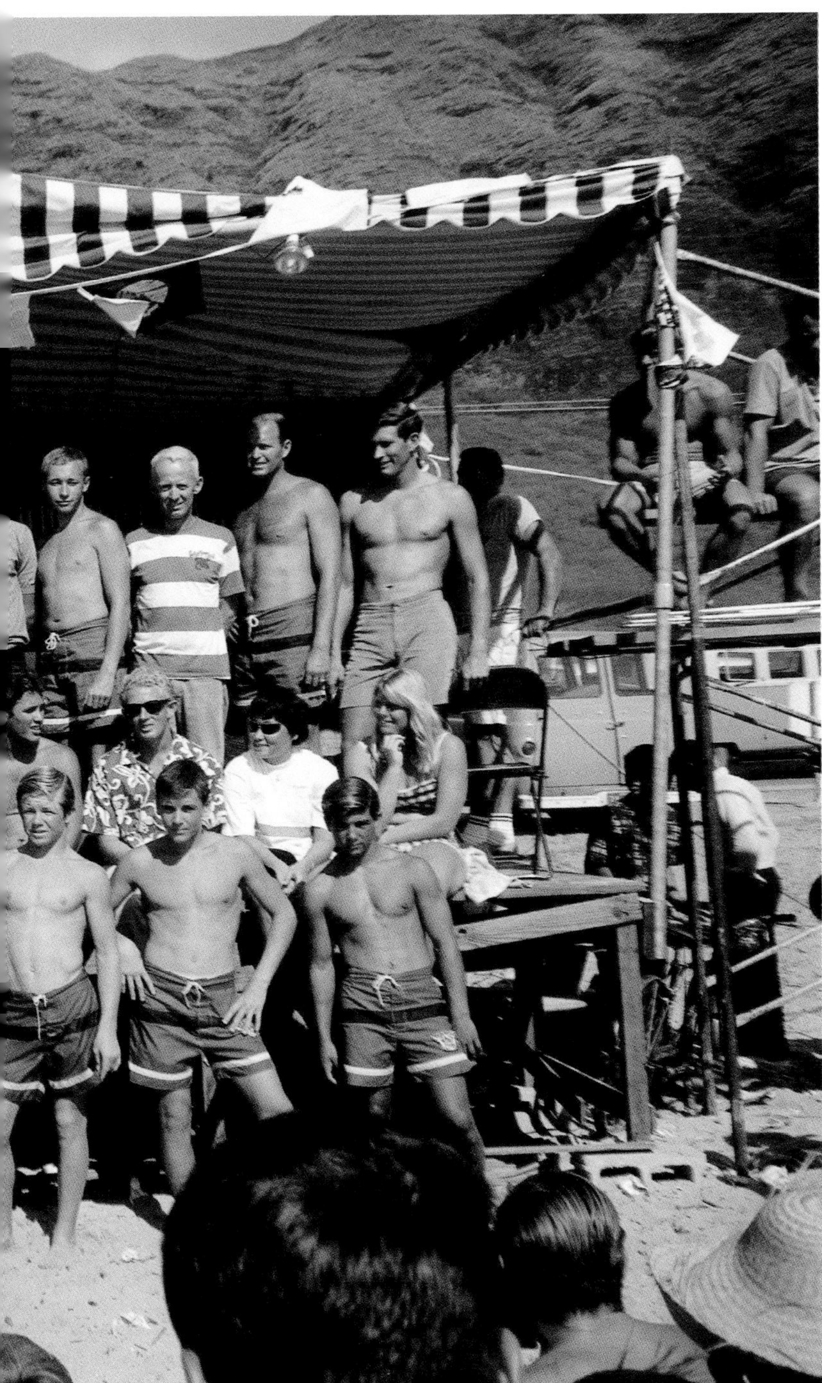

**Windansea Surf Club, Makaha, 1964**

The star-studded Windansea Club at the height of the amateur contest era. Top row, left to right: Lee Kiefer, Diane Bolton, Mike Hynson, Mickey Muñoz, J. J. Moon, Hobie Alter, Donald Takayama, Ken Adler, Robert Keneally, Rodney Sumpter, Lee Lewis, Thor Svenson, Chuck Hasley, Joey Cabell. Middle row, left to right: Eric Hauser, Chris Prowse, Don Schmidt, Dickie Moon, Dede Arevalos, Joyce Hoffman, Howard Chapleau, Billy Hamilton, Barry Kanaiaupuni, Skip Frye, Joey Hamasaki, Judy Dibble. Bottom row, left to right: David Adams, Steve Jenner, Steve Broda, Petey Johnson, George Rotgans, Bob Moore, Mike Purpus, John Sandera, Dru Harrison.

Der von Stars wimmelnde Windansea Club auf dem Höhepunkt der Ära der Amateur-Wettbewerbe. Obere Reihe, von links nach rechts: Lee Kiefer, Diane Bolton, Mike Hynson, Mickey Muñoz, J. J. Moon, Hobie Alter, Donald Takayama, Ken Adler, Robert Keneally, Rodney Sumpter, Lee Lewis, Thor Svenson, Chuck Hasley, Joey Cabell. Mittlere Reihe, von links nach rechts: Eric Hauser, Chris Prowse, Don Schmidt, Dickie Moon, Dede Arevalos, Joyce Hoffman, Howard Chapleau, Billy Hamilton, Barry Kanaiaupuni, Skip Frye, Joey Hamasaki, Judy Dibble. Untere Reihe, von links nach rechts: David Adams, Steve Jenner, Steve Broda, Petey Johnson, George Rotgans, Bob Moore, Mike Purpus, John Sandera, Dru Harrison.

La piste aux étoiles du Windansea Club à l'époque glorieuse des compétitions d'amateurs. Rangée du haut, de gauche à droite : Lee Kiefer, Diane Bolton, Mike Hynson, Mickey Muñoz, J. J. Moon, Hobie Alter, Donald Takayama, Ken Adler, Robert Keneally, Rodney Sumpter, Lee Lewis, Thor Svenson, Chuck Hasley et Joey Cabell ; rangée du milieu, de gauche à droite : Eric Hauser, Chris Prowse, Don Schmidt, Dickie Moon, Dede Arevalos, Joyce Hoffman, Howard Chapleau, Billy Hamilton, Barry Kanaiaupuni, Skip Frye, Joey Hamasaki et Judy Dibble ; rangée du bas, de gauche à droite : David Adams, Steve Jenner, Steve Broda, Petey Johnson, George Rotgans, Bob Moore, Mike Purpus, John Sandera et Dru Harrison.

**Makaha, 1965**

The Makaha Championships
queen. The annual contest, started
in 1954, was the unofficial world
championship until the early sixties.

Die Königin der Makaha
Championships. Der seit 1954
jährlich stattfindende Wettbewerb
war bis in die frühen Sechziger
die inoffizielle Weltmeisterschaft.

L'héroïne du championnat de
Makaha. La prestigieuse compétition annuelle dont la première
édition remonte à 1954, conserva
jusqu'au début des années 1960
le statut de championnat du monde
non officiel.

*Pages 306–307*
**Sunset Beach, 1967**

Sunset Point on the North Shore
is a powerful magnet for waves
as well as surfers.

Der Sunset Point am North Shore
ist ein besonderer Anziehungspunkt
für Wellen und Surfer.

Sunset Point, sur le North Shore,
exerce une attraction littéralement
magnétique tant sur les vagues
que sur les surfeurs.



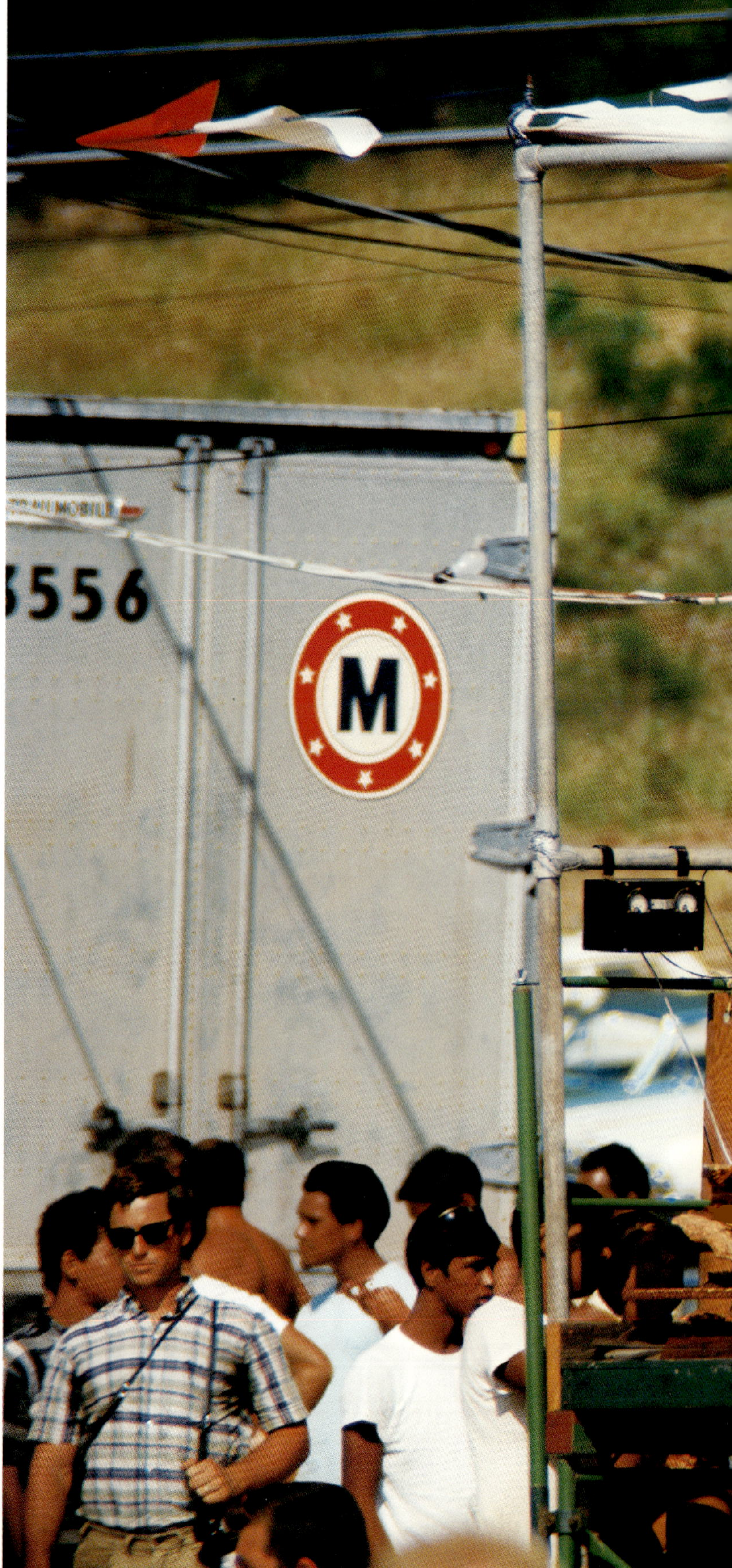

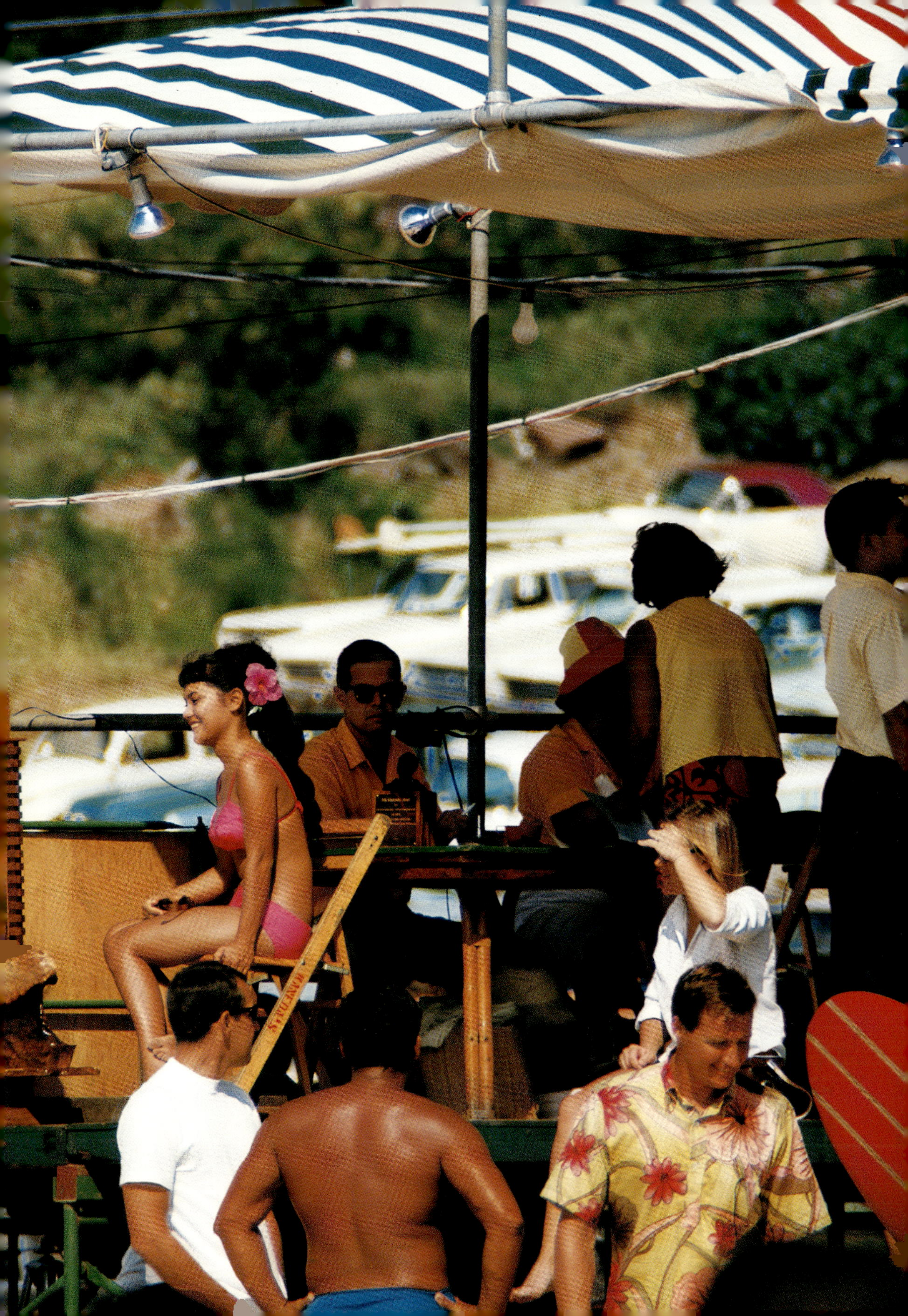

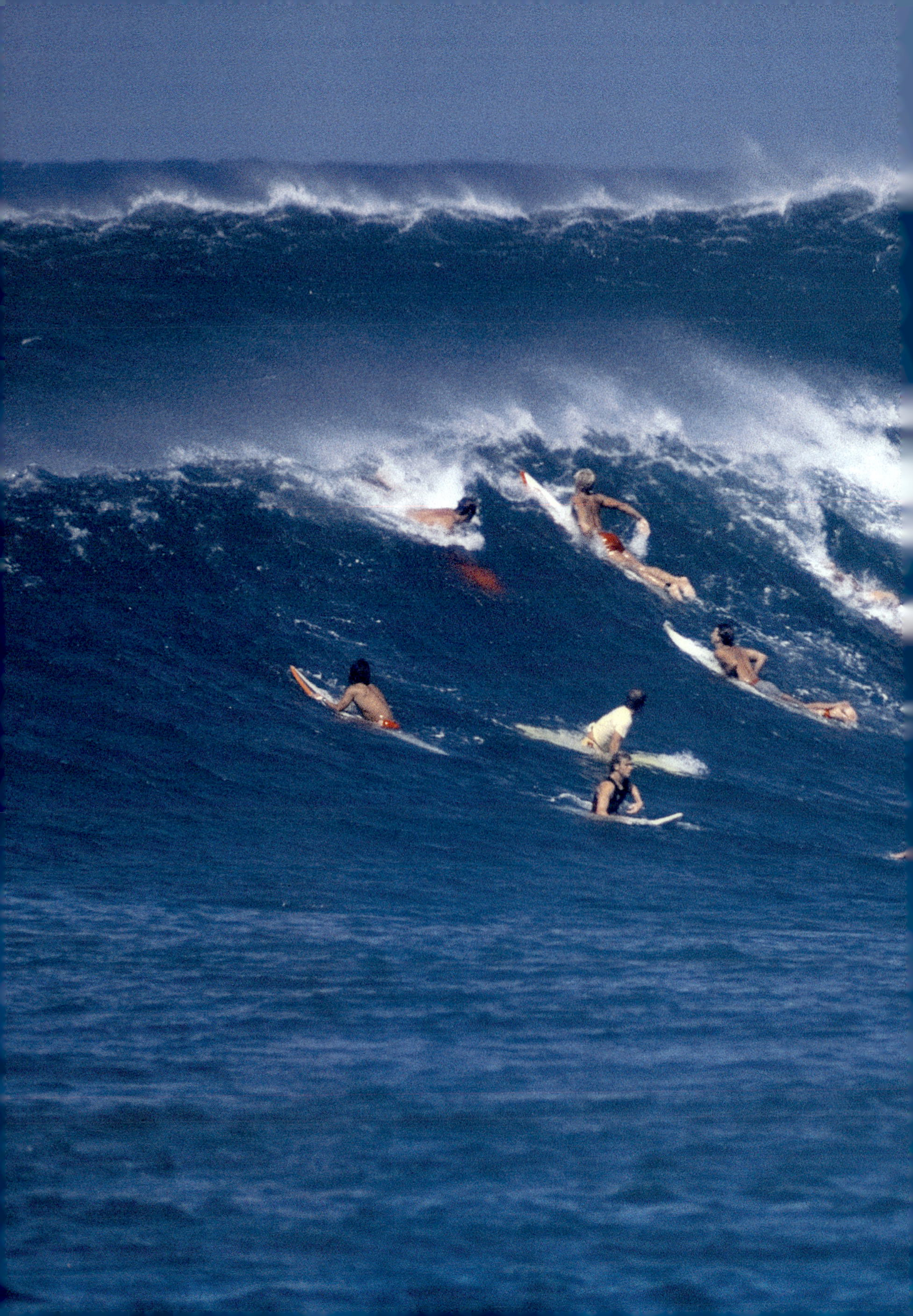

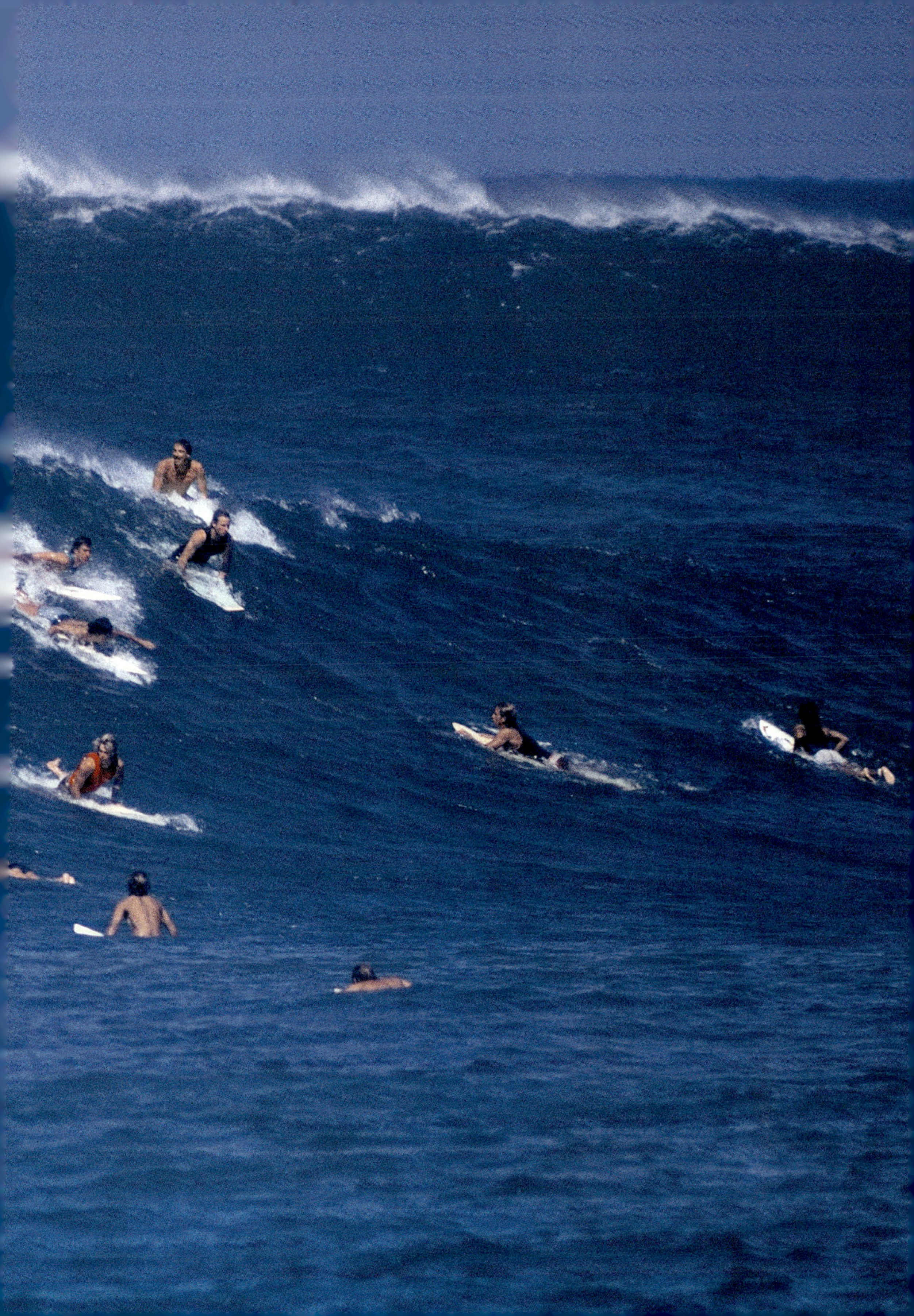

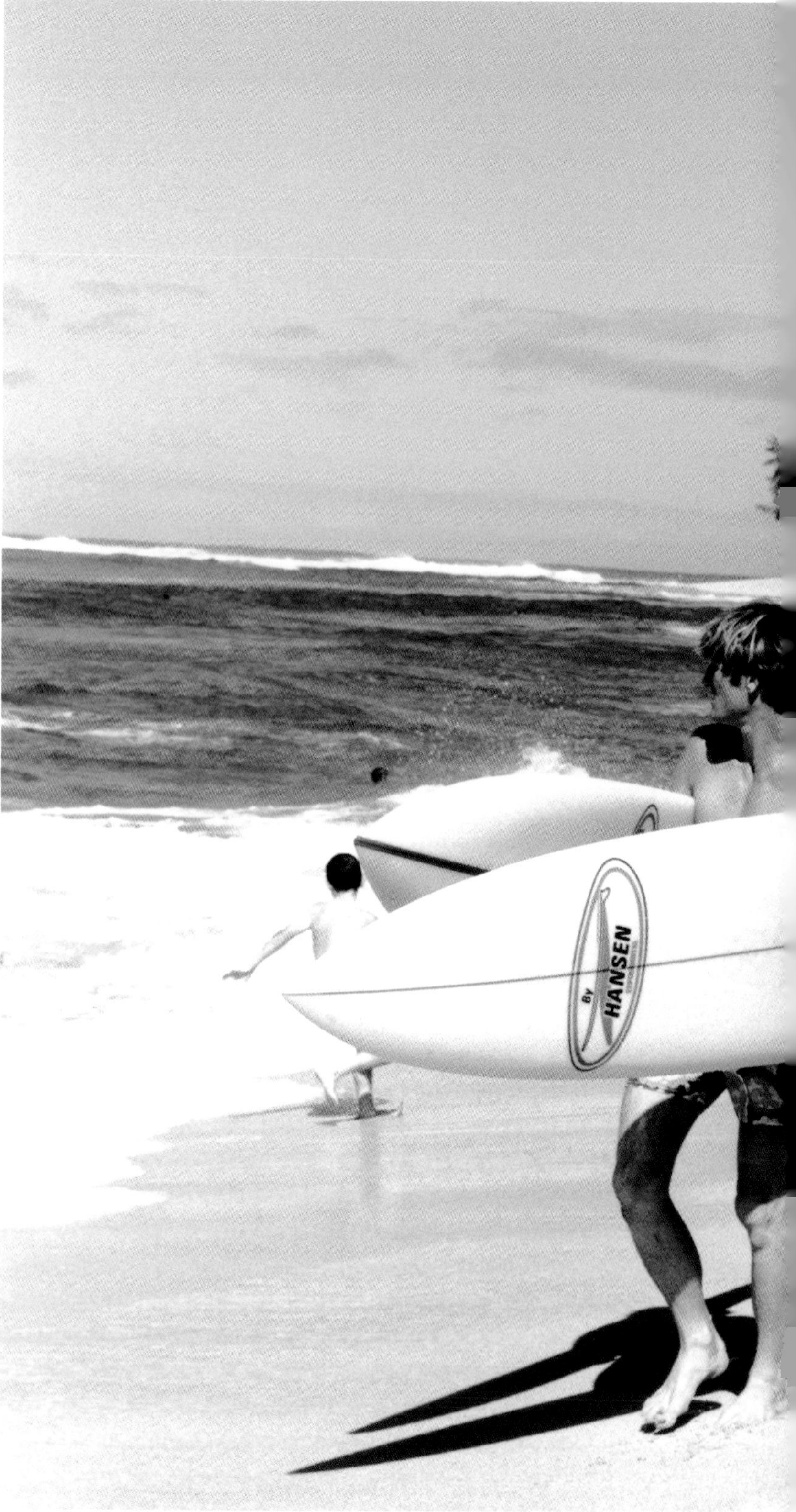
BY HANSEN

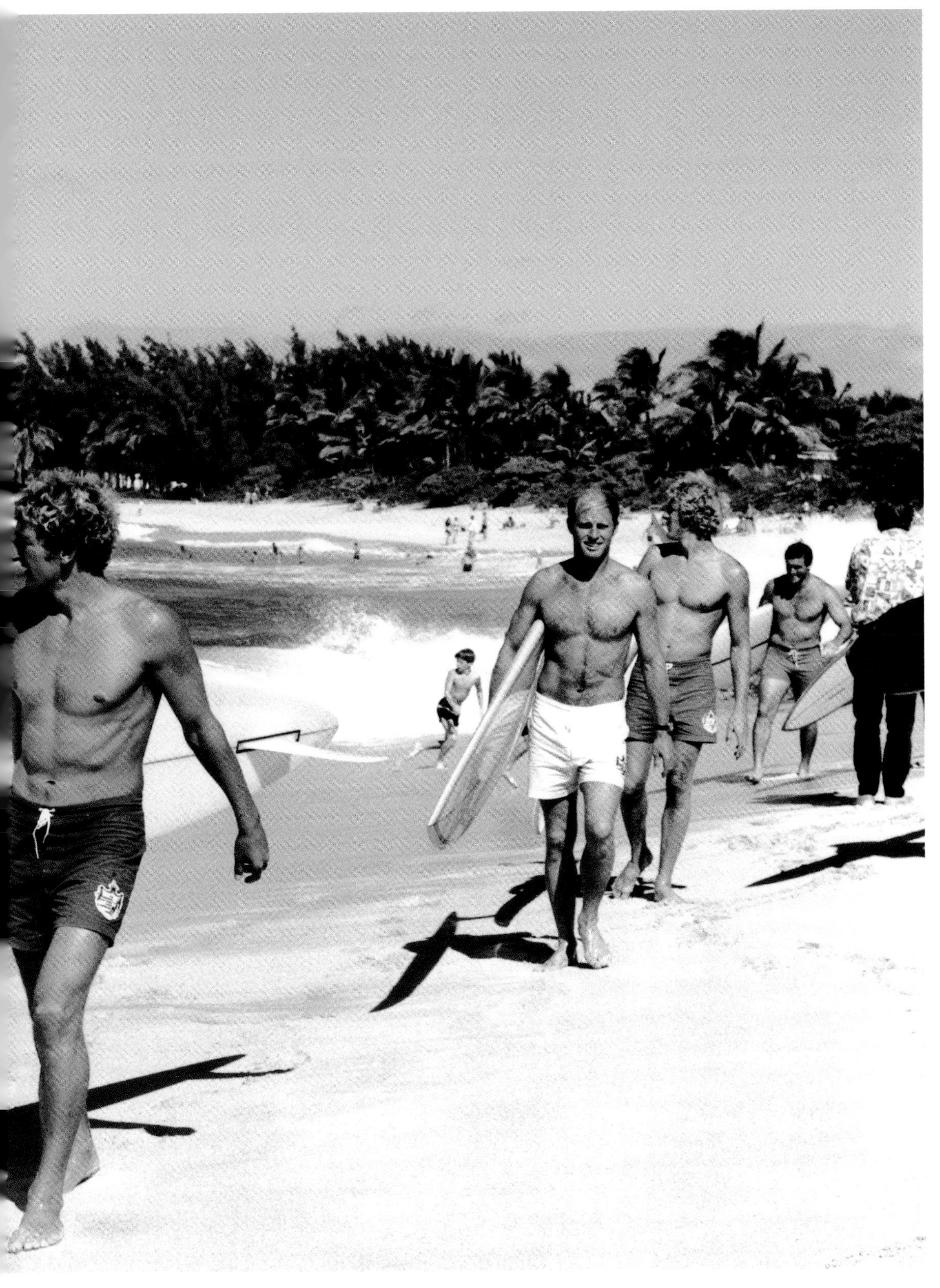

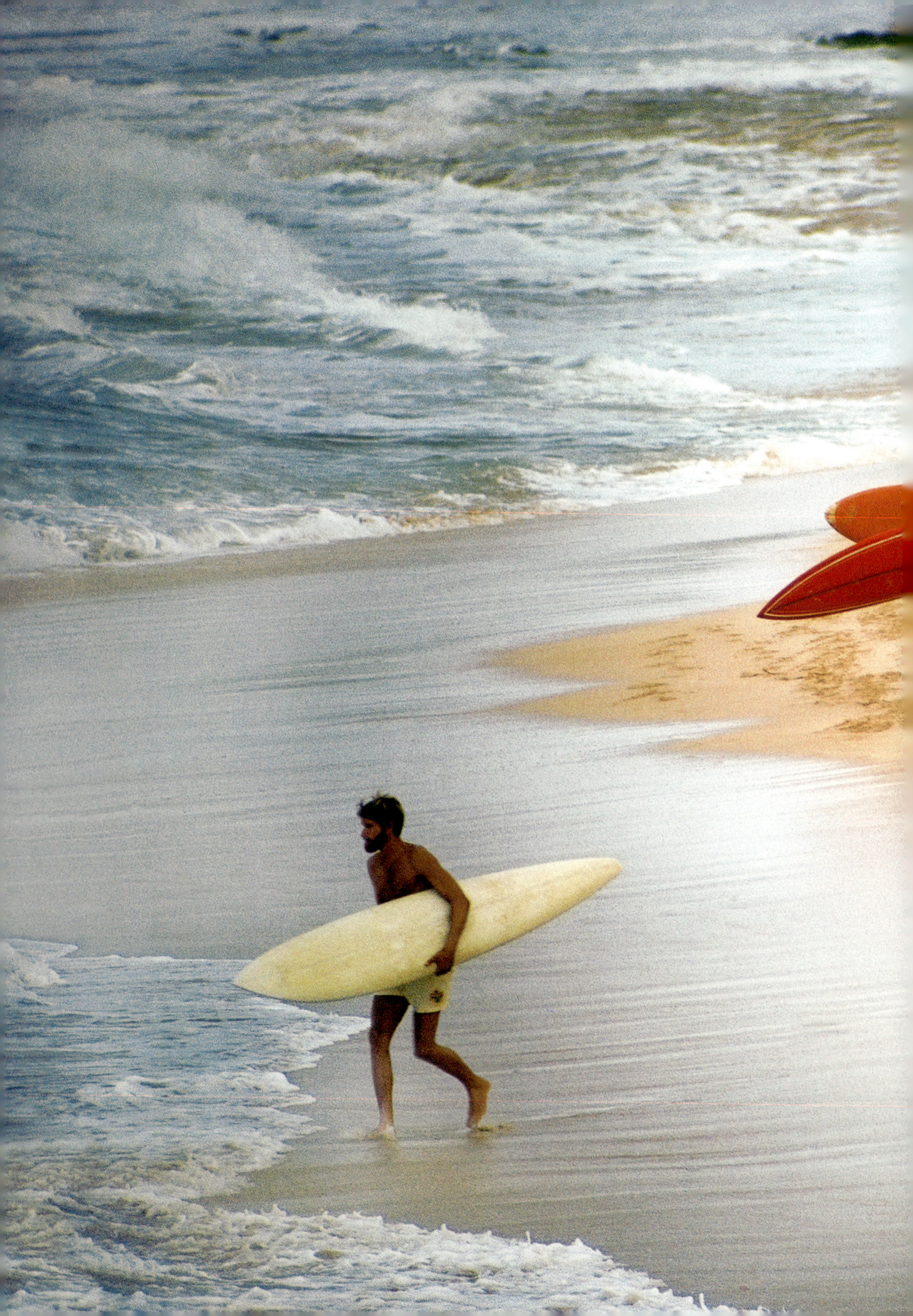

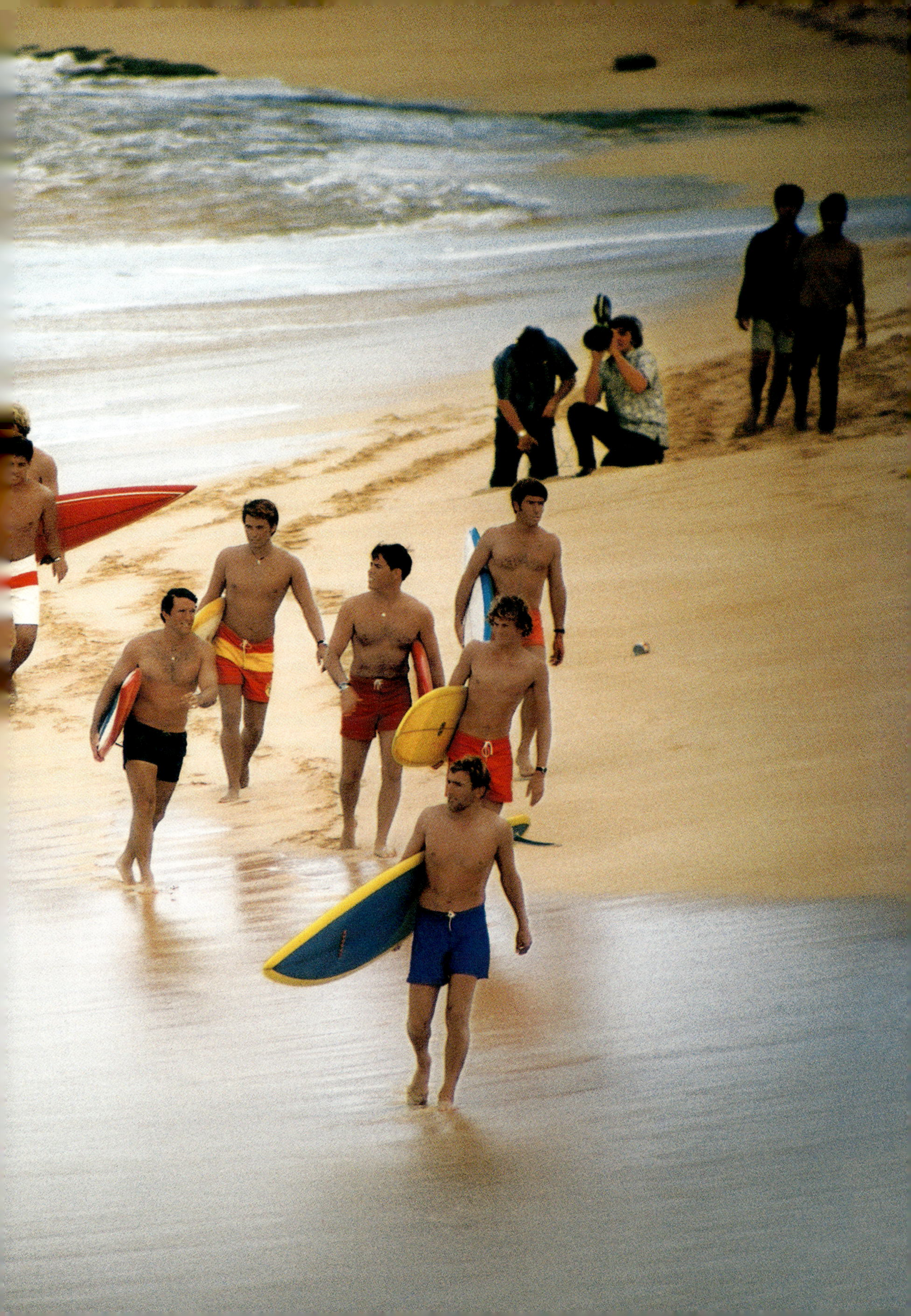

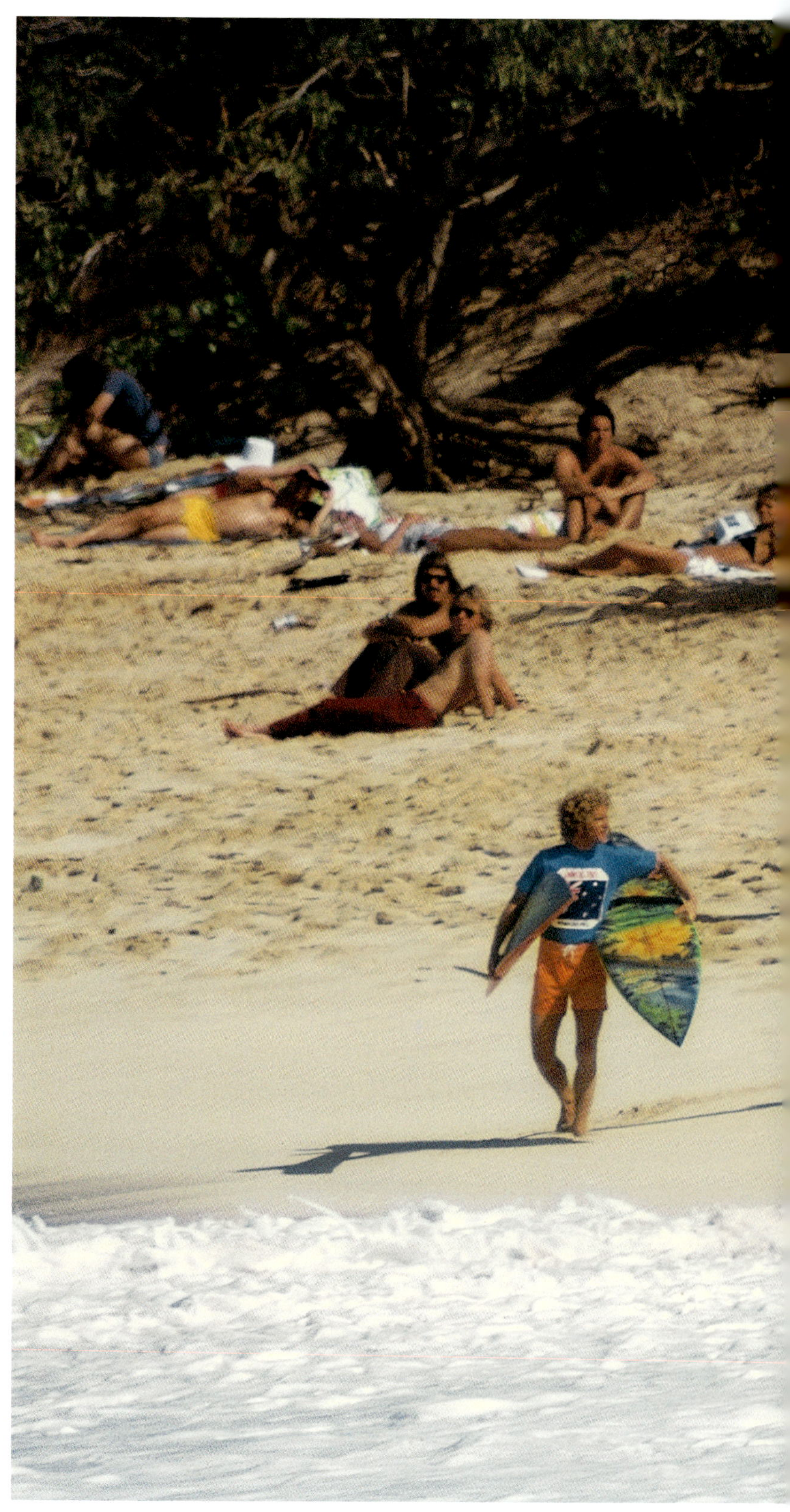

**Duke Classic Contestants,
Sunset Beach, 1972**

Terry "Speed Sultan" Fitzgerald
and Leroy Dennis just prior to their
contest heat. Fitzgerald was famed
for his beautiful boards, decorated
by Martin Worthington.

Terry „Speed Sultan" Fitzgerald
und Leroy Dennis direkt vor ihrem
Wettbewerbs-Heat. Fitzgerald war
für seine schönen, von Martin
Worthington gestalteten Bretter
bekannt.

Terry « Speed Sultan » Fitzgerald
et Leroy Dennis juste avant leur
*heat*. Fitzgerald était réputé pour
ses planches magnifiquement
décorées par Martin Worthington.

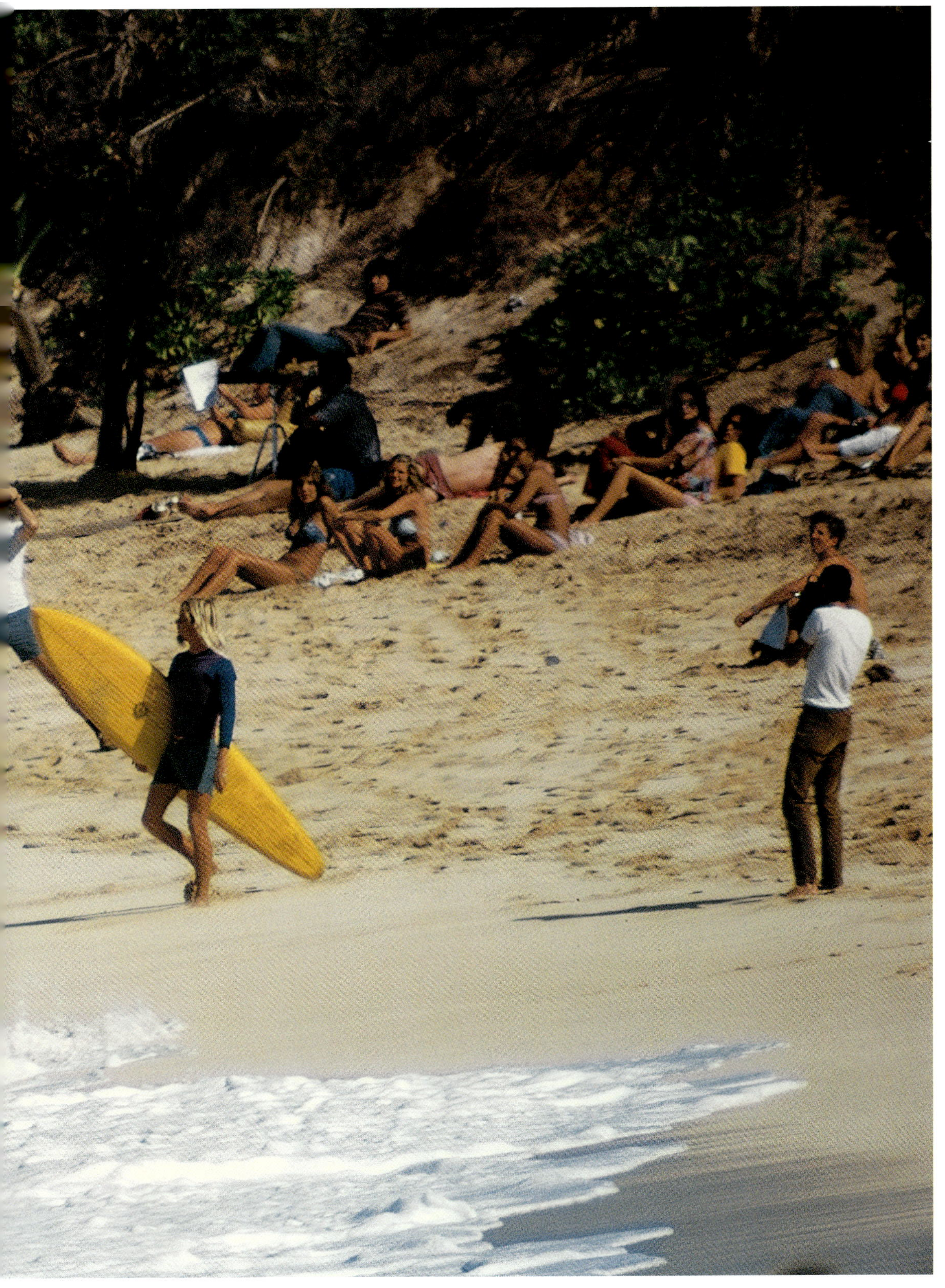

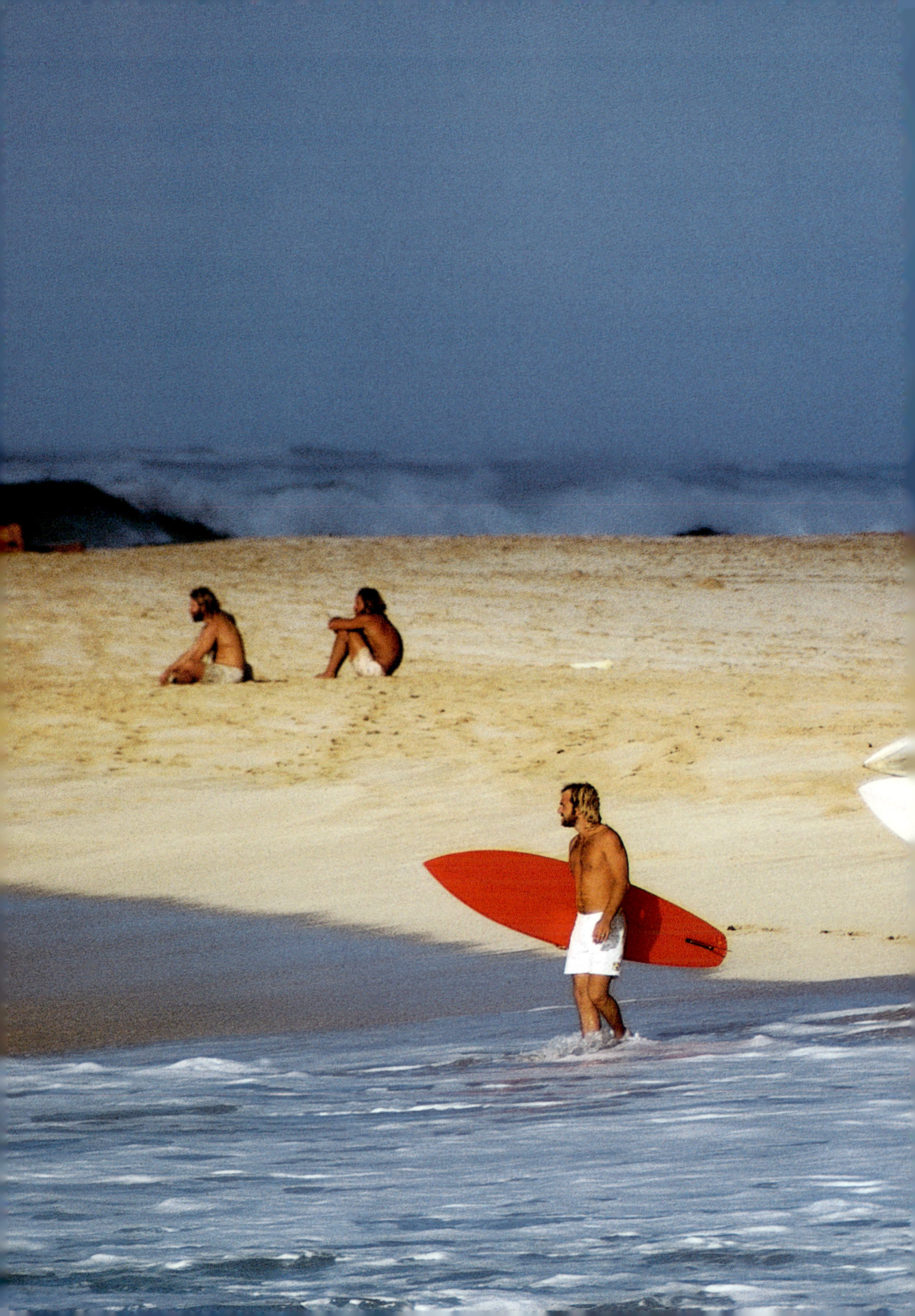

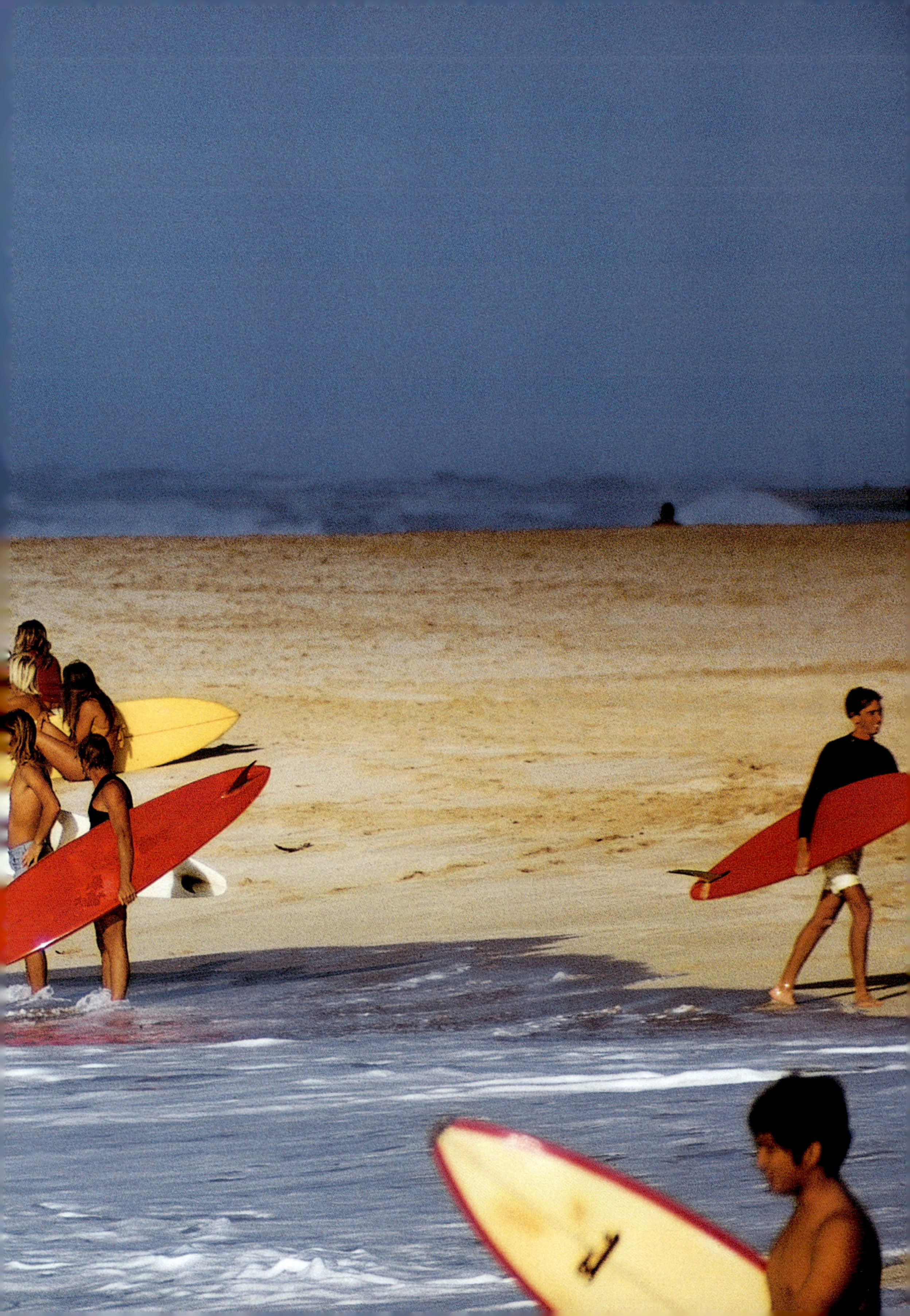

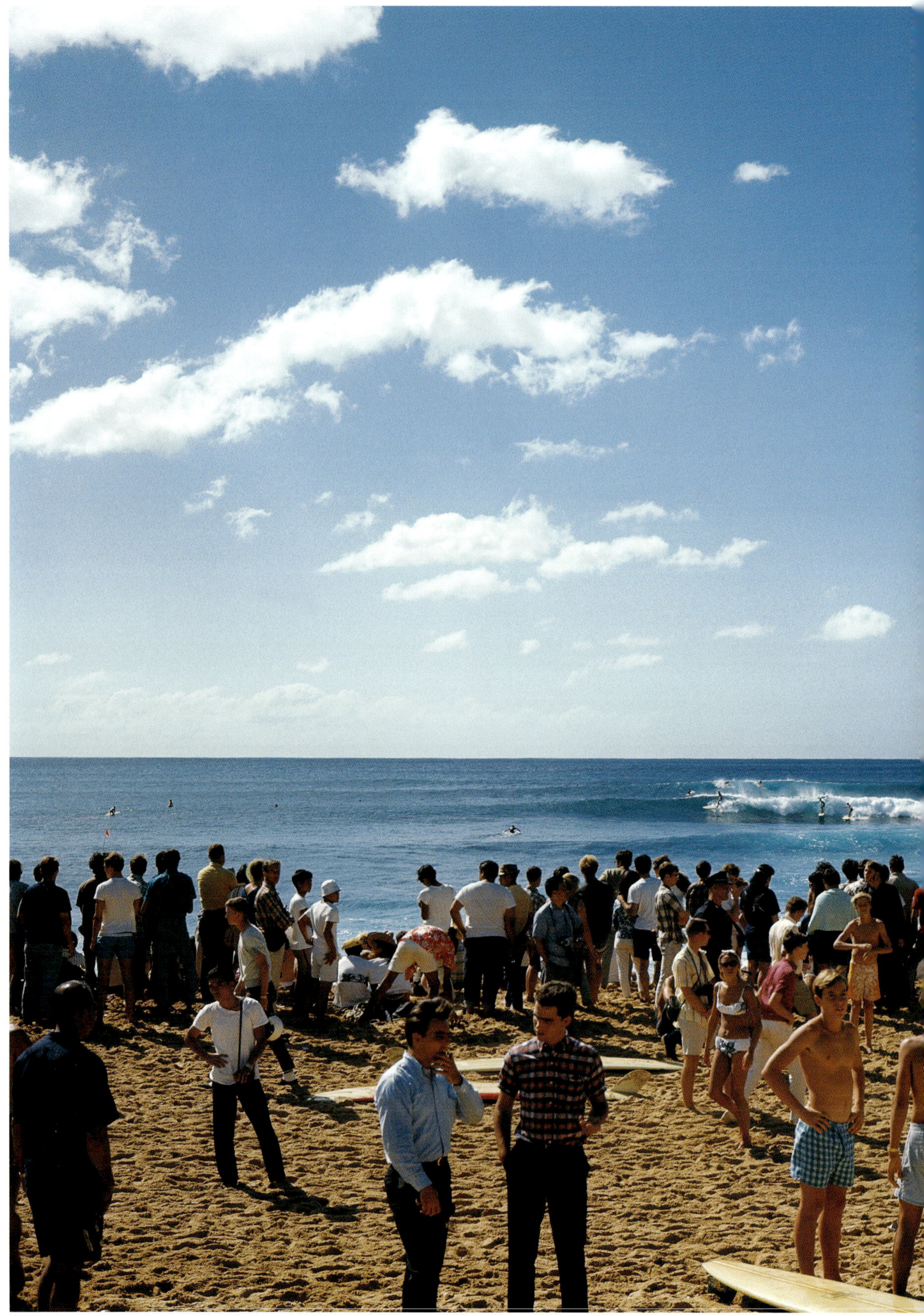

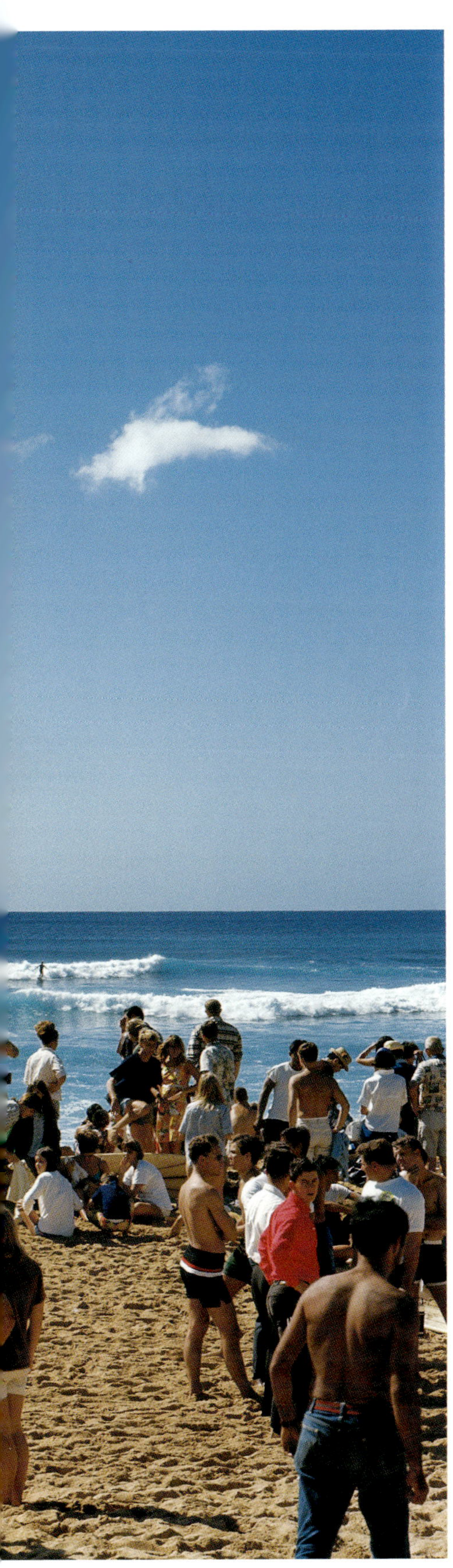



Pages 314–315
**Pupukea, North Shore, 1971**

Waiting for a lull between
big waves.

Warten auf eine Lücke
zwischen den großen Wellen.

En attendant un creux entre
deux grosses vagues.

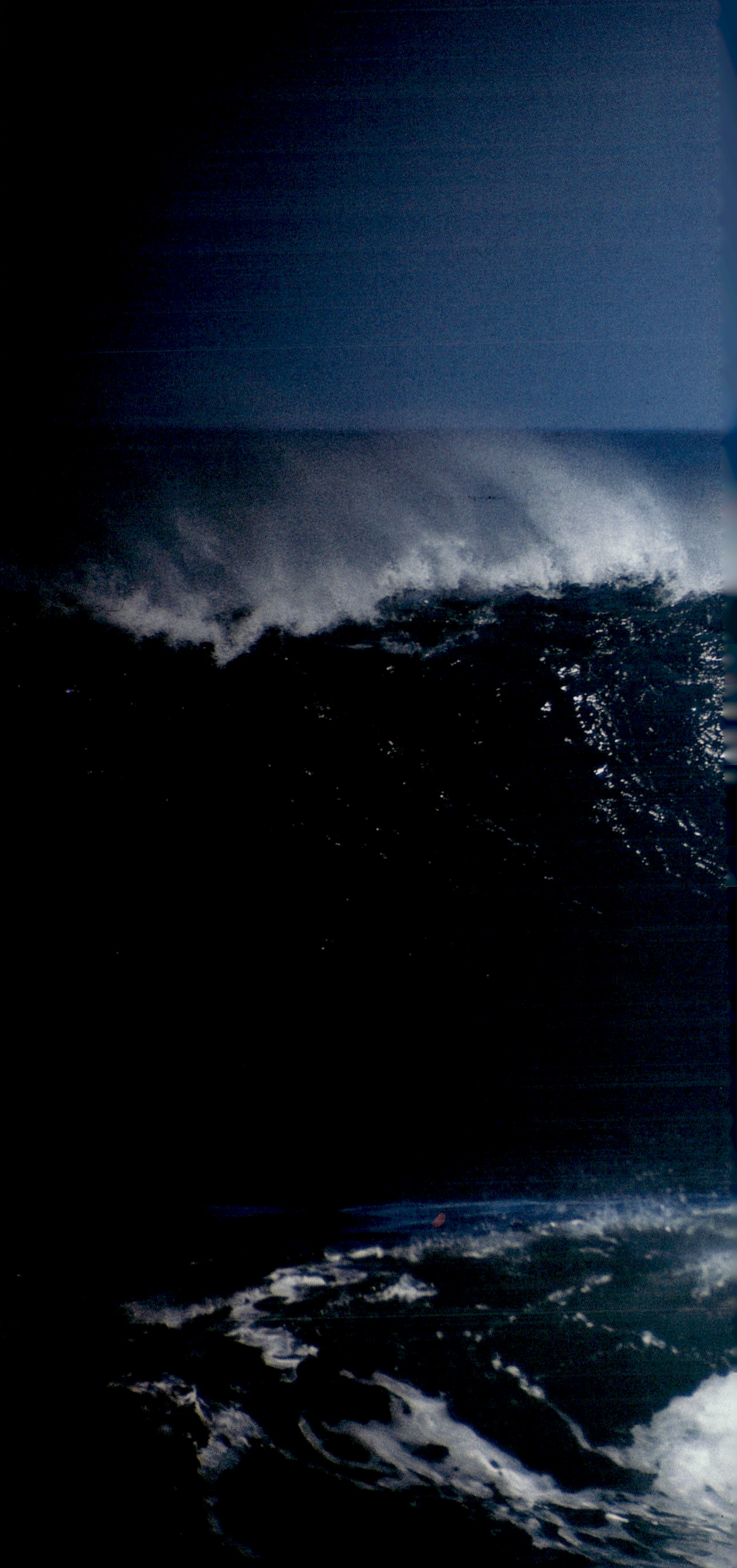

**Eddie Aikau, Haleiwa, circa 1972**

A kingly big-wave surfer and the North Shore's first professional lifeguard, Aikau later lost his life in 1978 while attempting to paddle twelve miles at night for help after the sailing canoe *Hokule'a* overturned in the Molokai Channel.

Aikau, der großartige Big-Wave-Surfer und erste professionelle Rettungsschwimmer am North Shore, kam 1978 ums Leben, als er versuchte, bei Nacht zwanzig Kilometer zu paddeln, um Hilfe für das Segelkanu *Hokule'a* zu holen, das im Molokai-Kanal gekentert war.

Le roi du *big-wave riding* Eddie Aikau, qui fut aussi le premier sauveteur professionnel du North Shore, est mort en 1978 alors qu'il tentait de parcourir, en pleine nuit et à la seule force de ses bras, les vingt kilomètres qui le séparaient de la côte pour chercher du secours après le dessalage du catamaran *Hokule'a* dans le canal de Molokai.

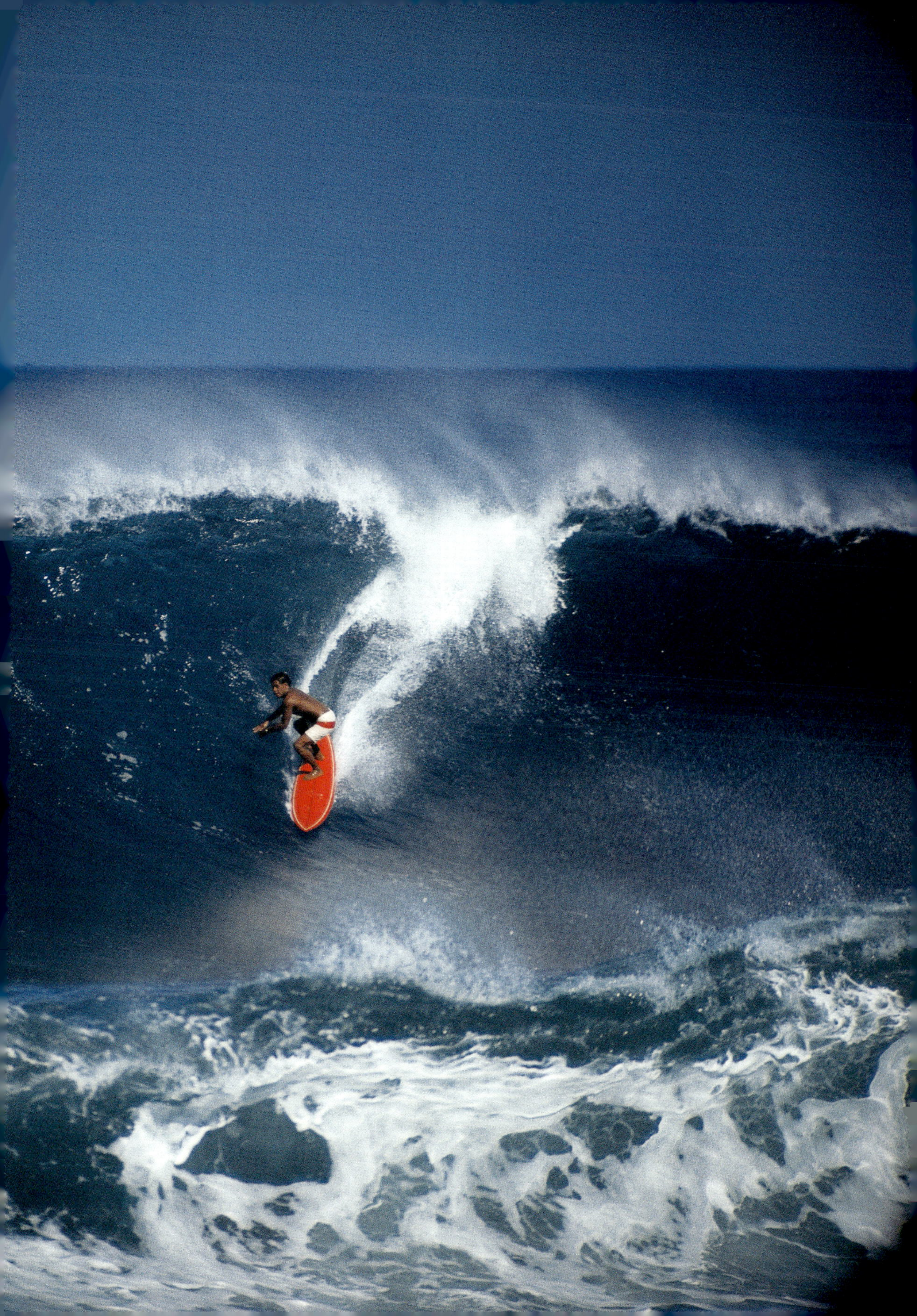

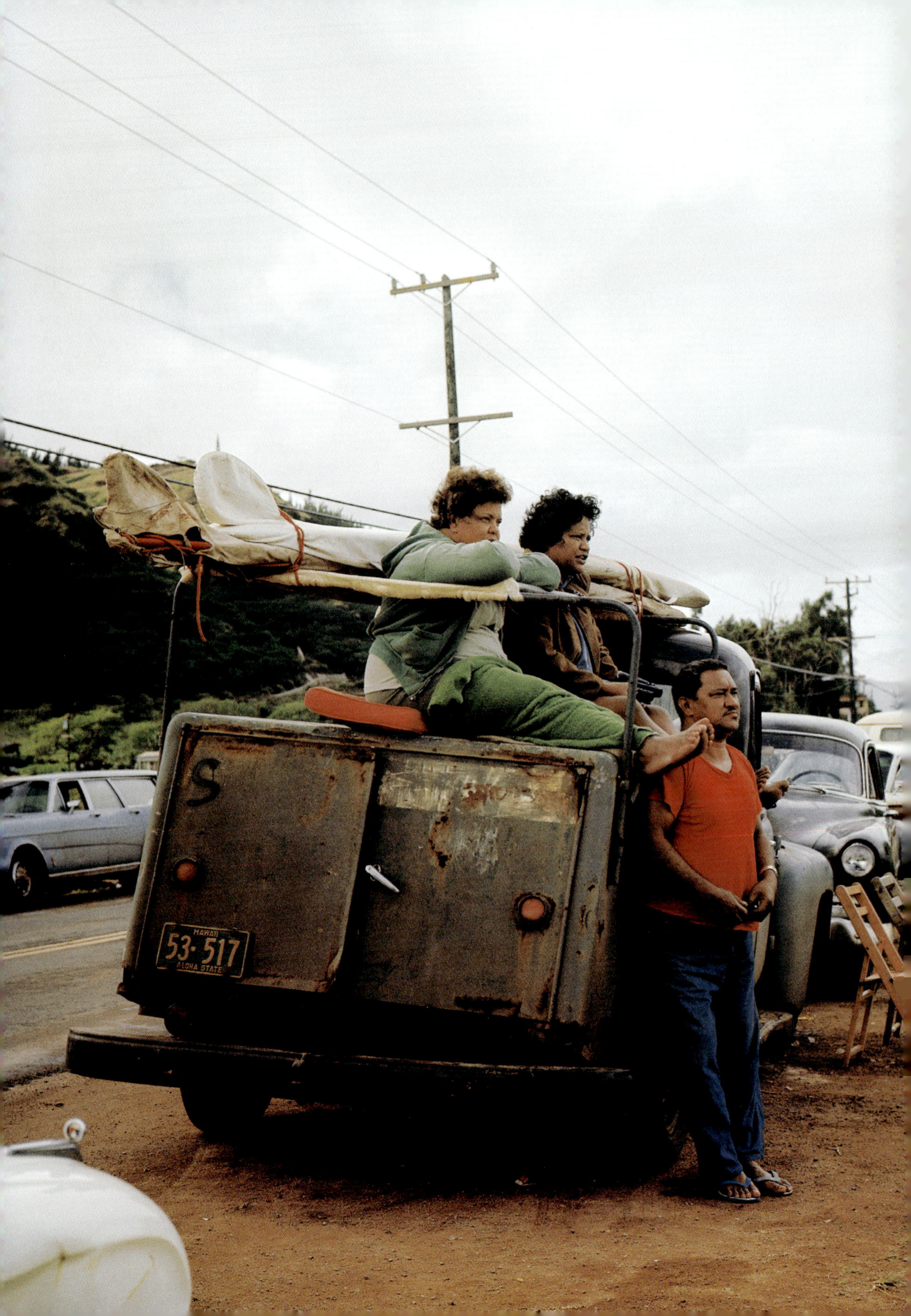

S
HAWAII
53·517
ALOHA STATE

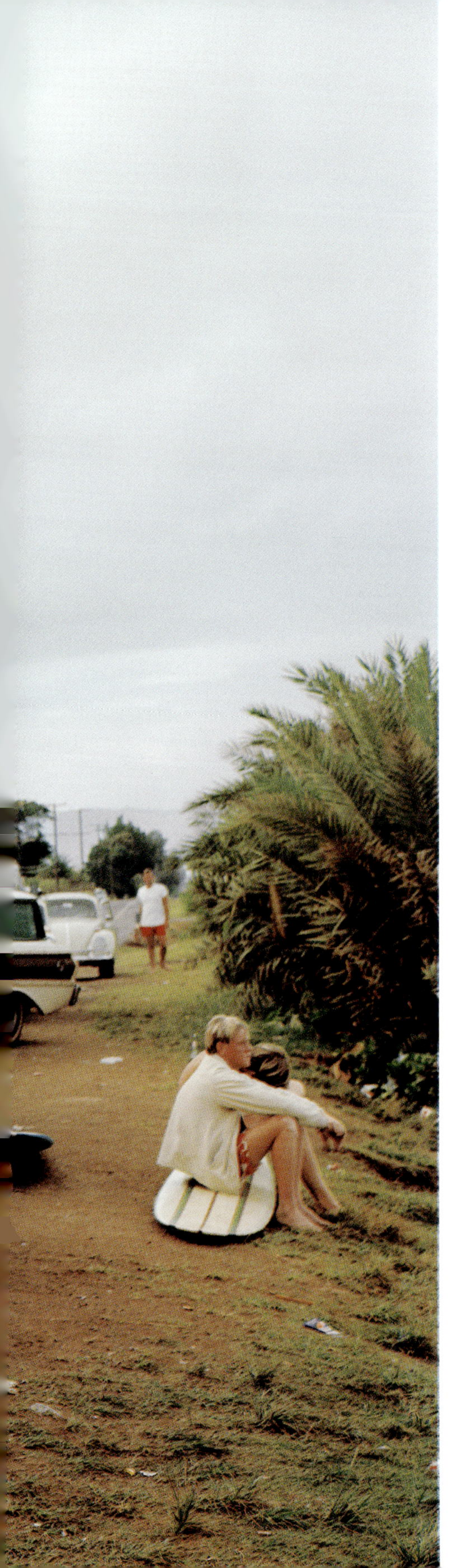

**Aikau Family, Sunset Beach, 1967**

Myra, Mama, and Sol Aikau watching Eddie compete in the third Duke Classic. Eddie won the contest in 1977, and died three months later.

Myra, Mama und Sol Aikau sehen Eddie beim dritten Duke Classic zu. Eddie gewann den Wettbewerb 1977 und starb drei Monate später.

Myra, Mama et Sol Aikau suivent les exploits d'Eddie lors de la troisième édition de la Duke Classic. Dix ans plus tard, Eddie Aikau remportera la compétition trois mois avant de mourir dans des circonstances tragiques.

Pages 322–323
**Eddie Aikau, Sunset Beach, 1967**

Aikau taking the big drop during the Duke Classic. Note the vignette effect from the Century 1000 lens used by surf photographers of the time.

Aikau nimmt einen steilen Drop beim Duke Classic. Hier sieht man die Abdunklung an den Ecken des Fotos, verursacht vom Century-1000-Objektiv, das damalige Surffotografen verwendeten.

Eddie Aikau exécutant un *big drop* pendant les épreuves de la Duke Classic. On remarquera l'effet « vignette » dû à l'objectif Century 1000 utilisé par les photographes de surf de l'époque.

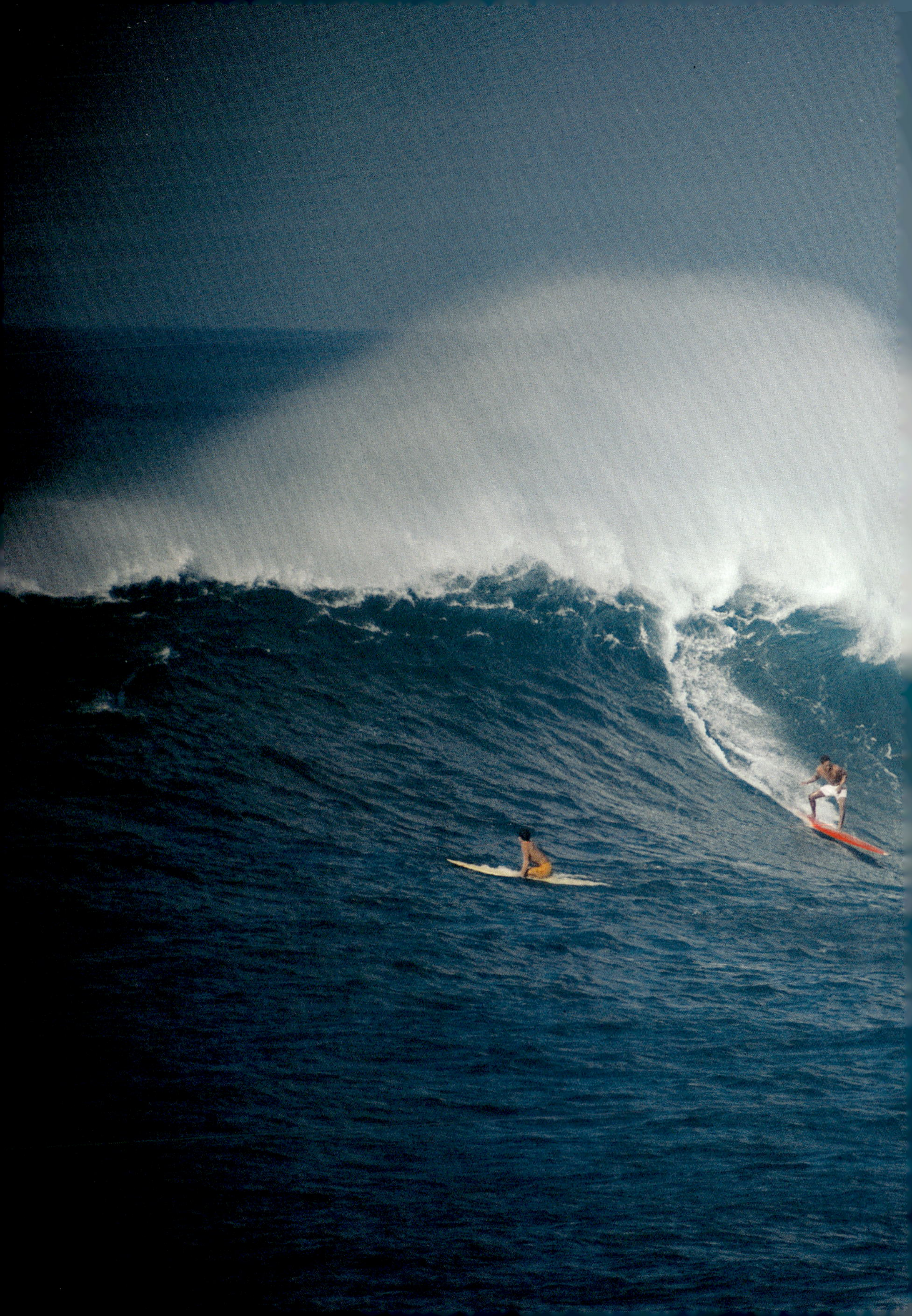

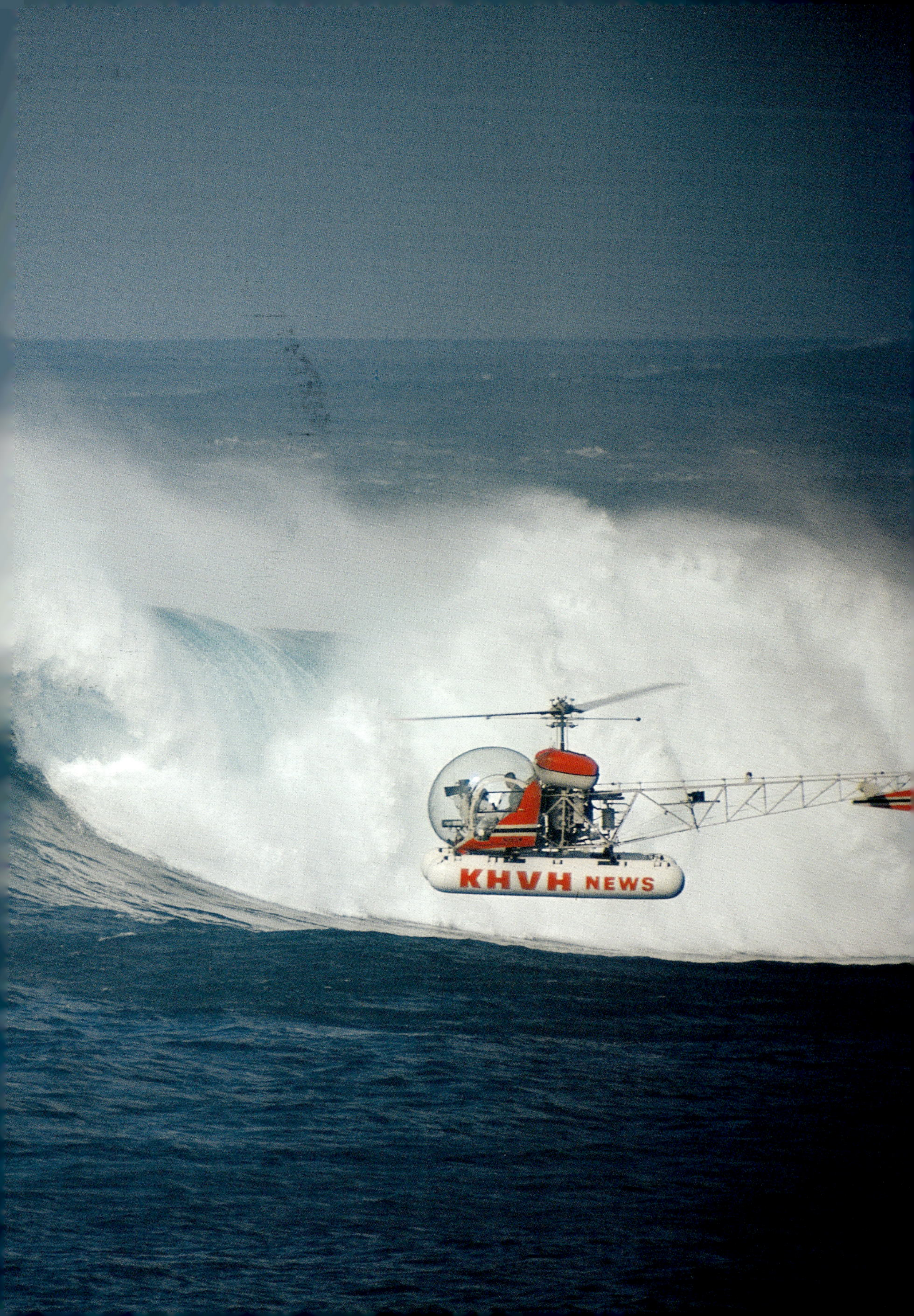

KHVH NEWS

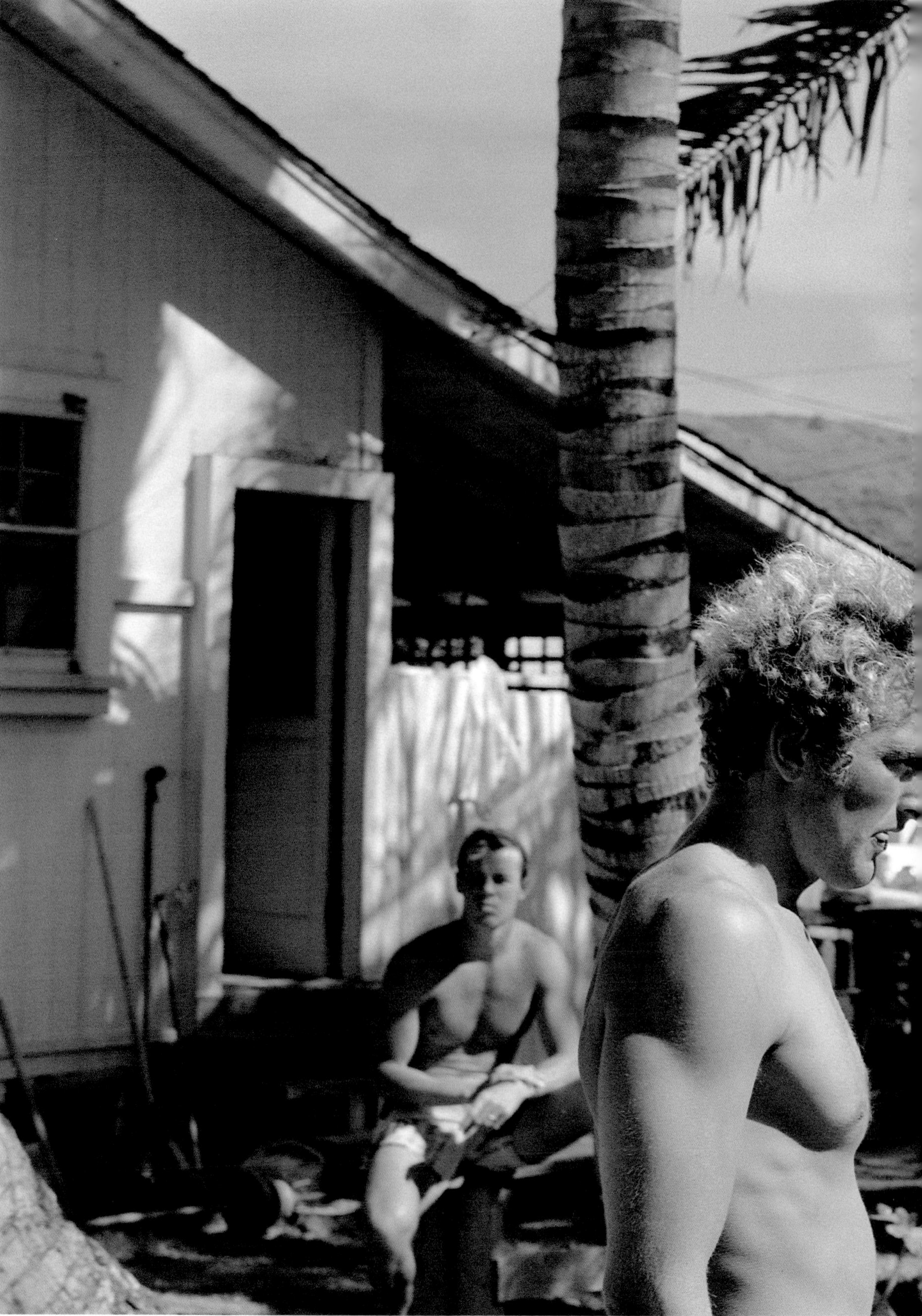

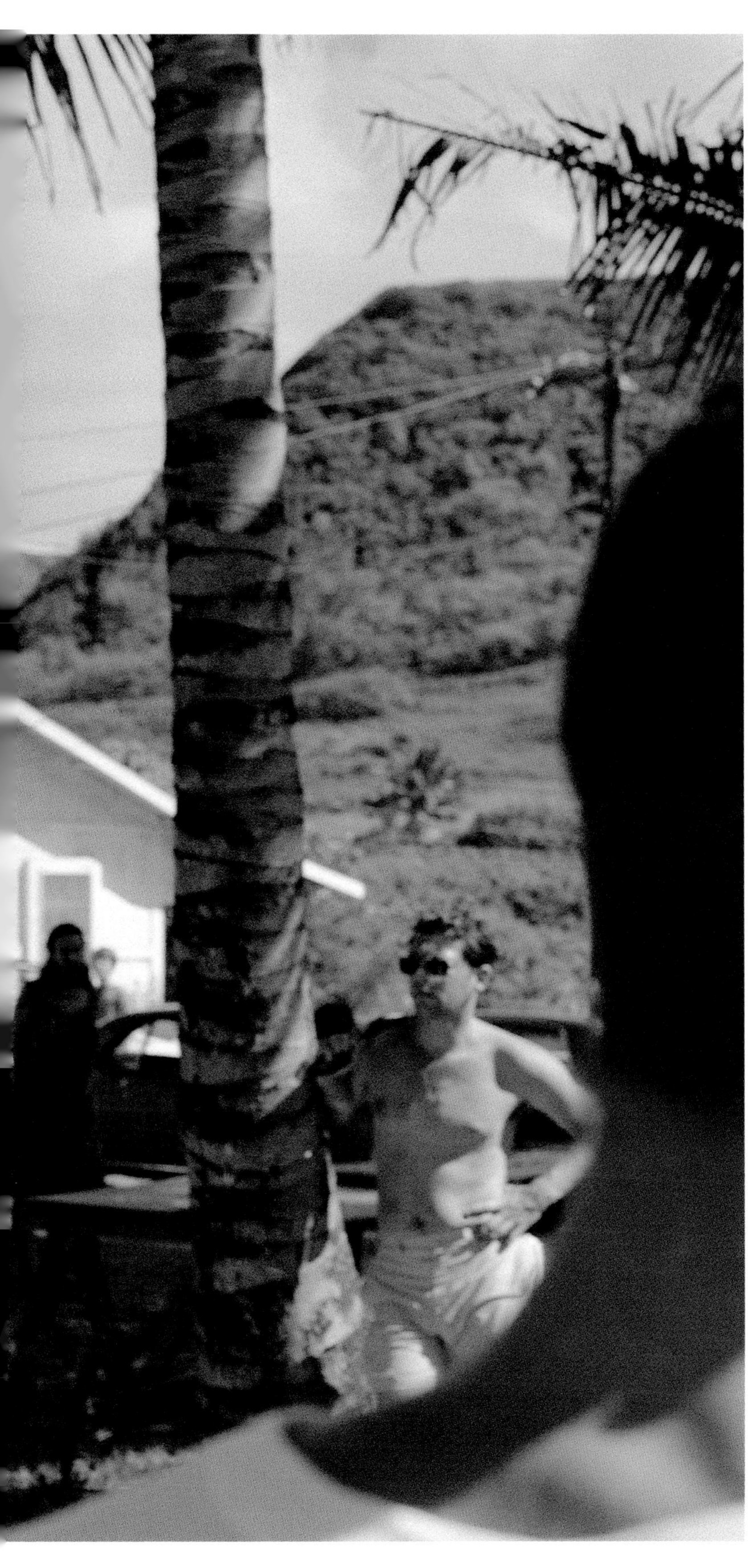

**Mike Doyle, Sunset Beach, 1968**

Doyle shortly before the Duke
Classic at surf filmmaker Val
Valentine's Sunset Point house,
the unofficial contest headquarters.
"Val's Reef" is named after
Valentine.

Doyle kurz vor dem Duke Classic
beim Haus des Surfregisseurs
Val Valentine in Sunset Point, dem
inoffiziellen Wettkampfzentrum.
Das „Val's Reef" ist nach Valentine
benannt.

Mike Doyle peu avant les épreuves
de la Duke Classic devant la maison
du réalisateur de films de surf Val
Valentine à Sunset Point, Q. G.
officieux de la compétition.
Valentine a donné son nom au
spot de « Val's Reef ».

**Charlie Galento, North Shore, 1966**

Galento was one of the unsung
surfers who kept riding Waimea
when big-wave popularity dipped
in the seventies. He's shown with
his "speed paddleboard."

Galento war einer der vielen Surfer,
die weiter in Waimea surften,
als die Popularität des Big-Wave-
Surfing in den Siebzigern zurück-
ging. Hier sieht man ihn mit
seinem „Speed Paddleboard".

Charlie Galento faisait partie de
ces surfeurs de l'ombre qui ont
continué à surfer les grosses vagues
de Waimea jusque dans les années
1970 malgré la baisse de popularité
du *big-wave riding*. On le voit ici
avec son « speed paddleboard ».

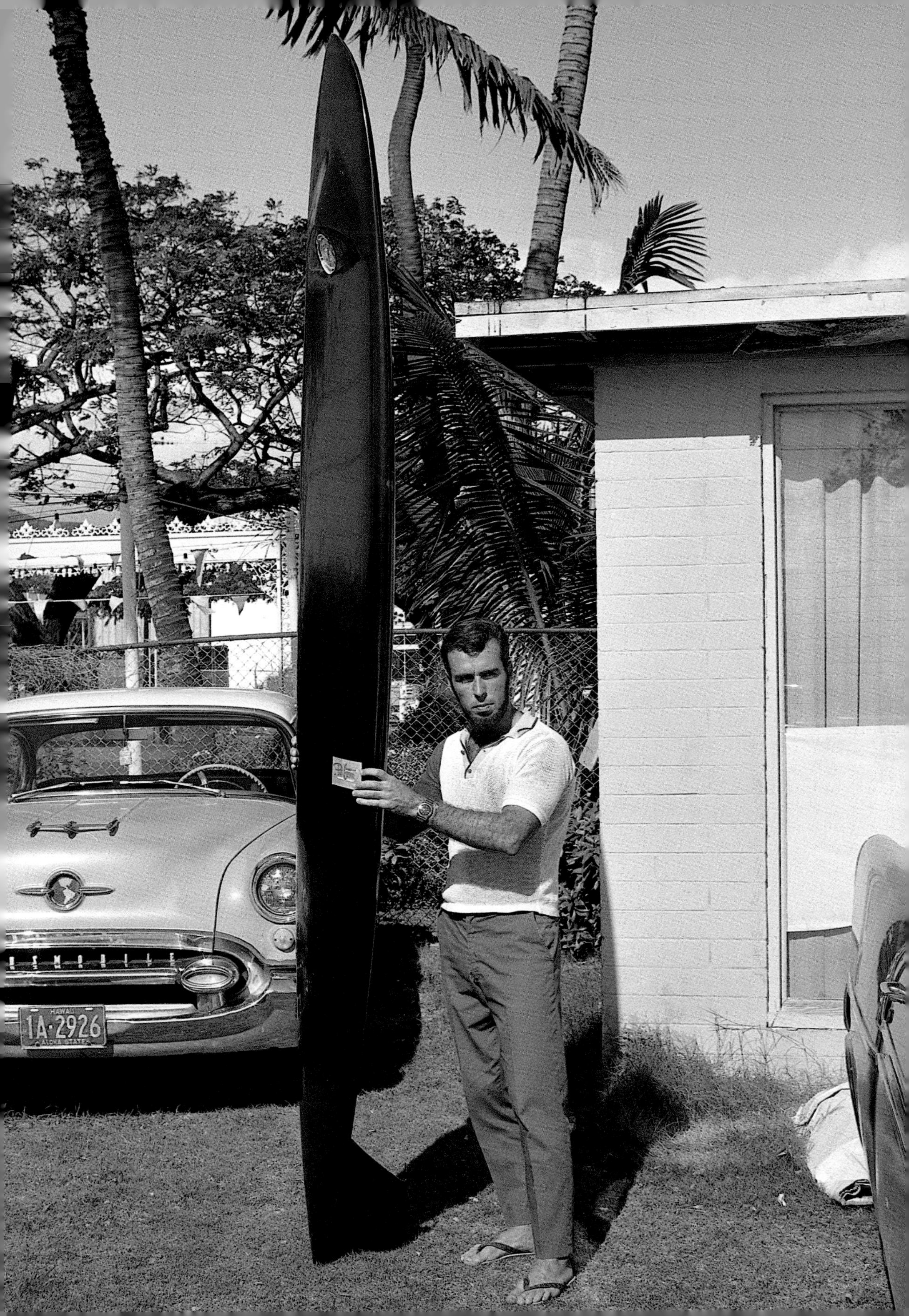

**Jock Sutherland, North Shore, 1968**

Nicknamed "the Extraterrestrial"
for his brilliant LSD-fueled style,
Sutherland surfed Waimea alone, at
night, in 1969. He called Pipeline
"the Pope's living room."

Für seinen genialen, LSD-inspirier-
ten Stil wurde Sutherland „the
Extraterrestrial" genannt. 1969
surfte er Waimea allein bei Nacht.
Er nannte die Pipeline das „Wohn-
zimmer des Papstes".

Surnommé « L'Extraterrestre » en
raison de son style génial et
psychédélique – inspiré par le
LSD –, Jock Sutherland a surfé
Waimea seul et de nuit en 1969. Il
a surnommé le spot de Pipeline
« Le Salon du pape ».

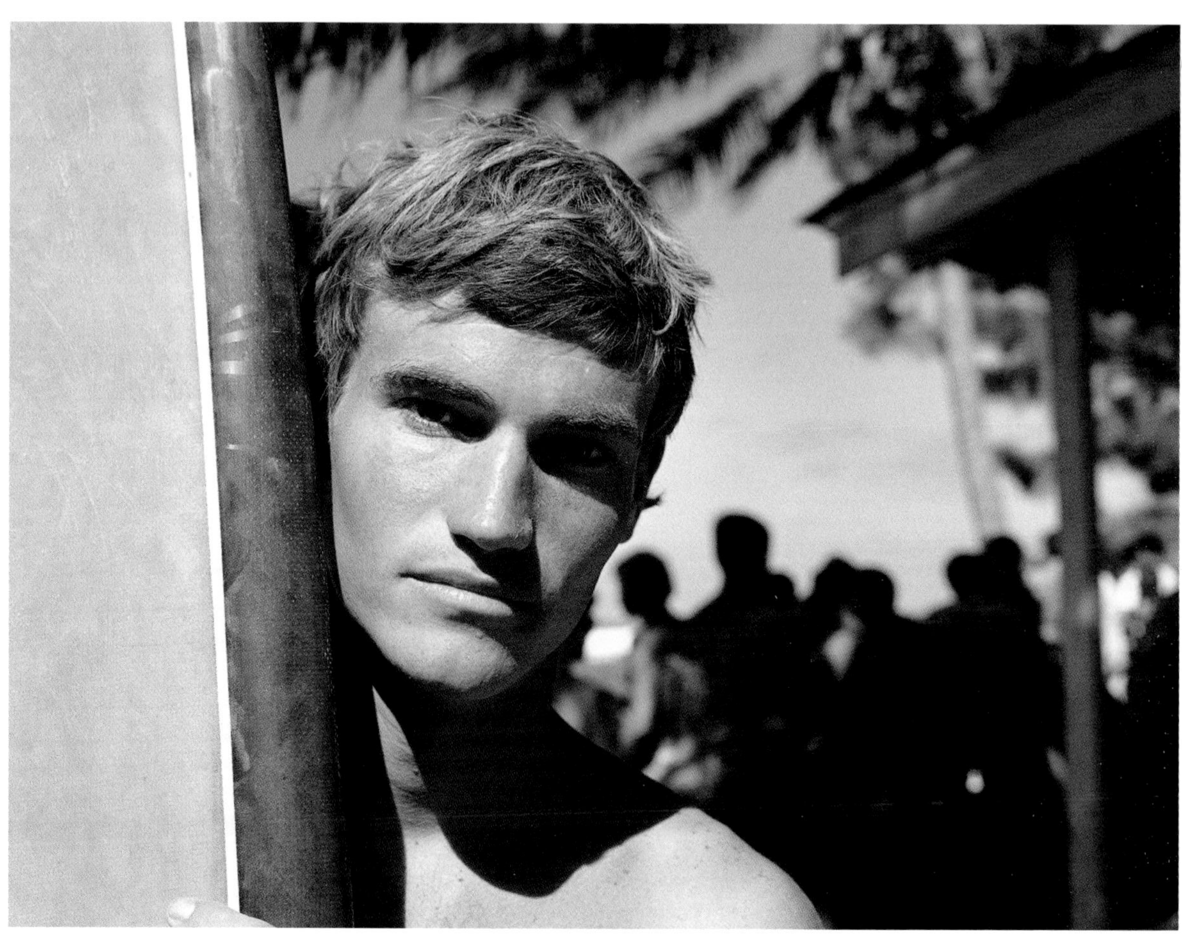

**Margo Godfrey, Makaha, 1968**

Shown here at fifteen, shortly before she won the first of four world championships.

Im Alter von fünfzehn Jahren, kurz bevor sie den ersten ihrer vier Weltmeistertitel gewann.

Margo Godfrey à l'âge de quinze ans, peu avant le premier de ses quatre titres de championne du monde.

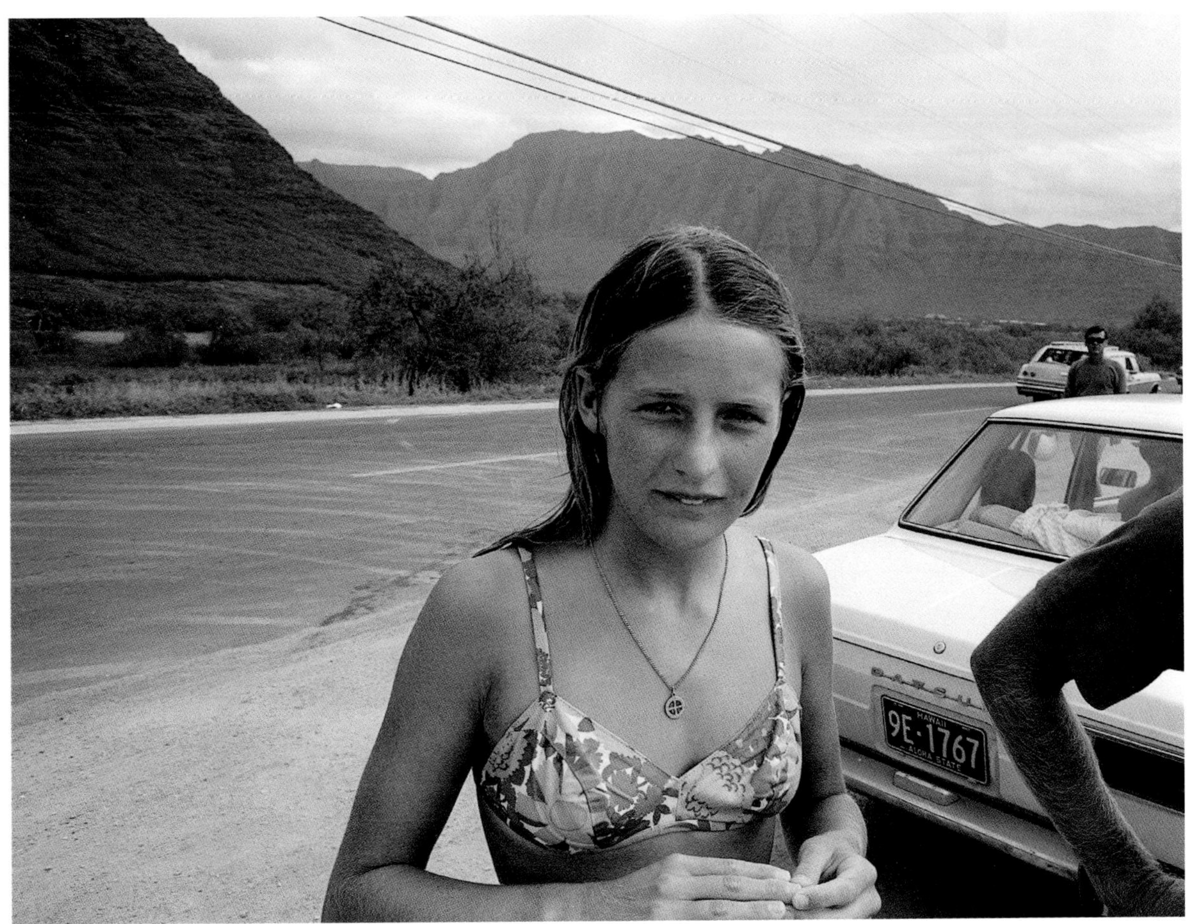

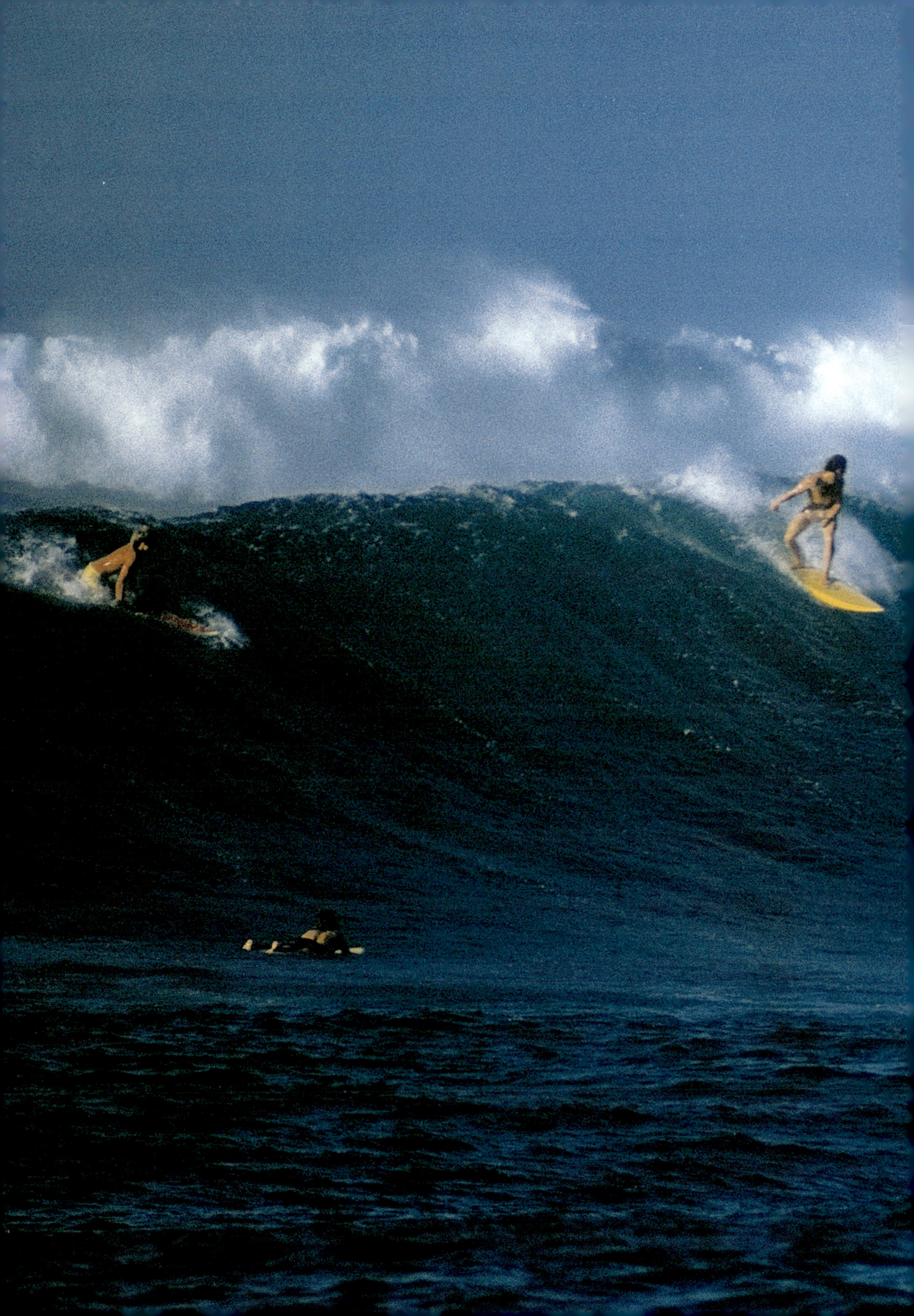

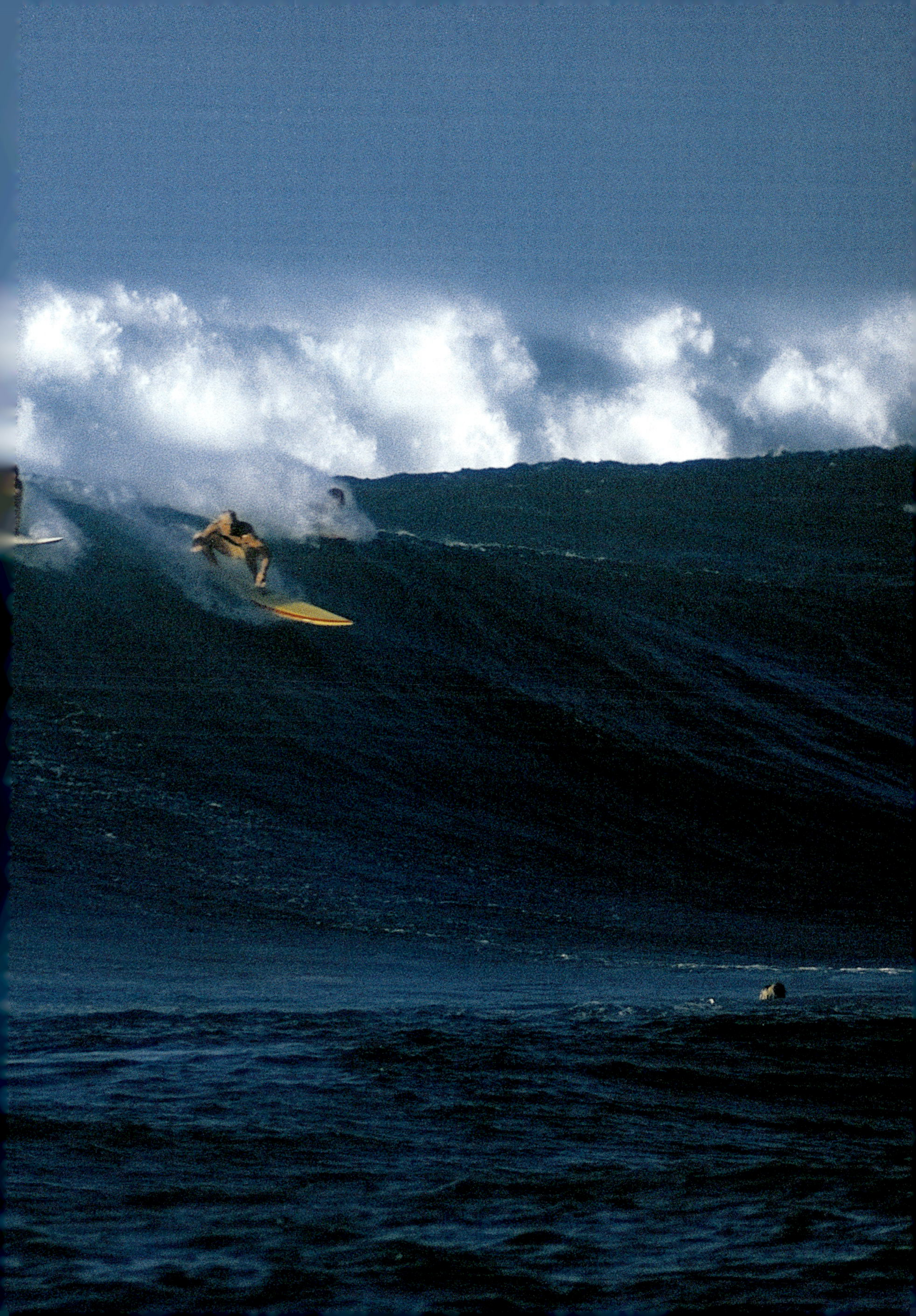

**Jackie Eberle, Waimea Bay, 1964**

Two-time Duke Classic winner
Eberle talked softly but surfed big.
He was one of the best of the first
generation of surfers to tackle
Pipeline.

Der zweimalige Duke-Classic-Sieger
Eberle sprach leise, surfte aber
aufsehenerregend. Er gehörte zu
den Besten der ersten Surfergene-
ration, die sich an die Pipeline
wagten.

La nature débonnaire du double
vainqueur de la Duke Classic Jackie
Eberle tranchait avec sa témérité à
toute épreuve. Il fut l'un des plus
brillants surfeurs de la première
génération à dompter les swells
de Pipeline.

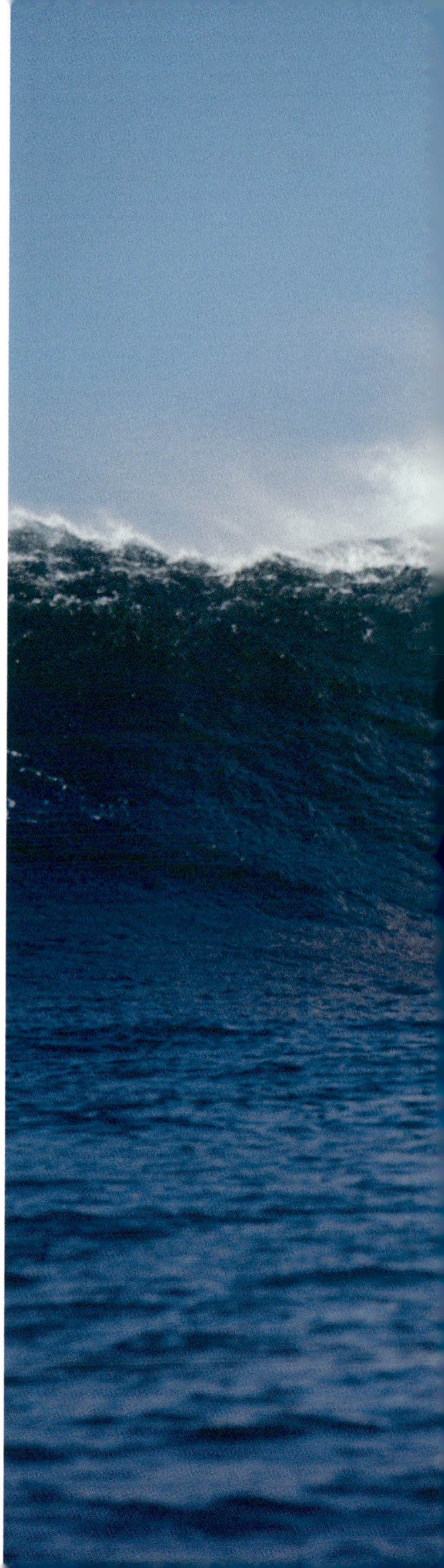

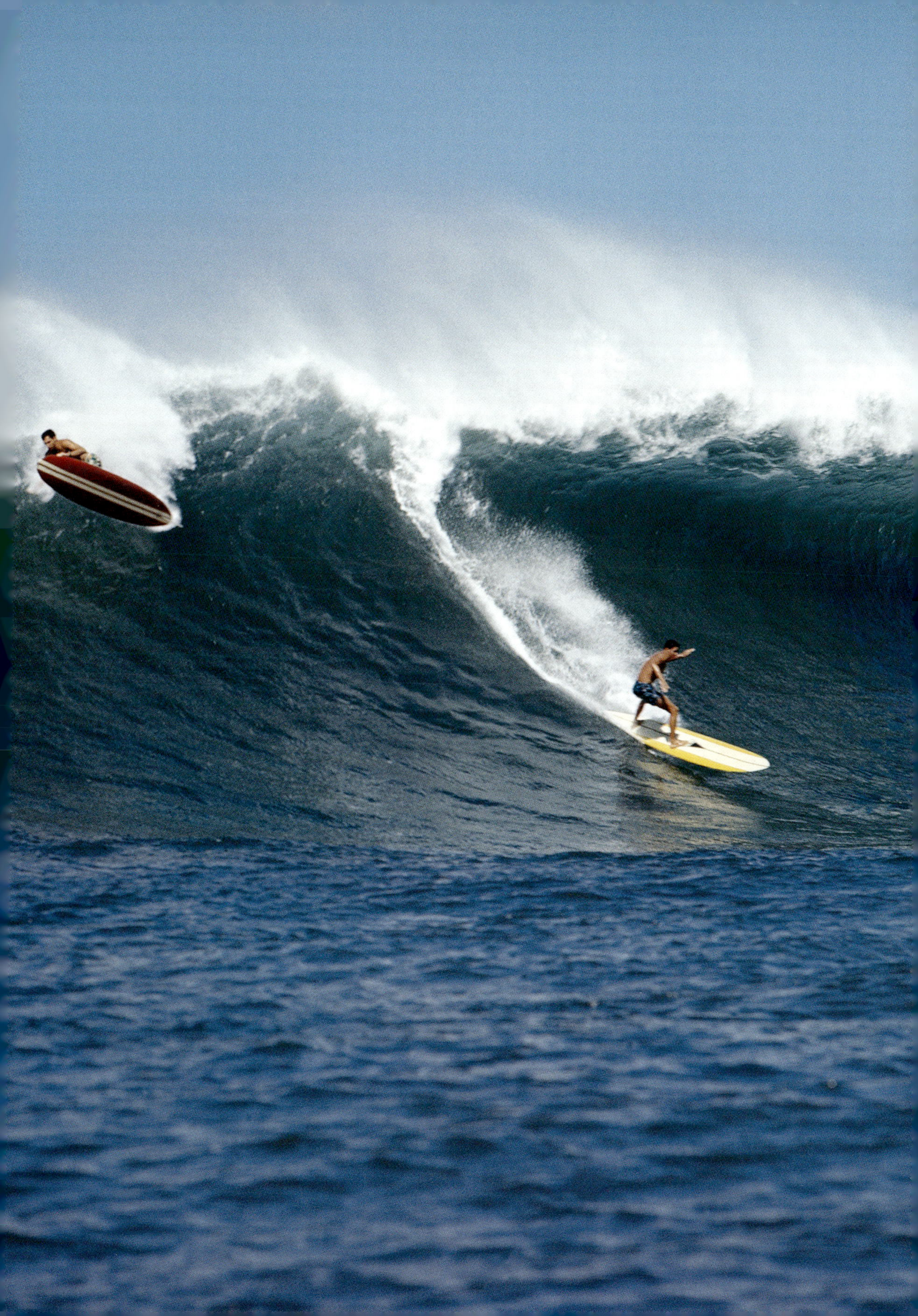

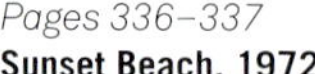

**Makaha, 1966**

The infamous Makaha shore break launches another victim. This classic shot has been used in many advertisements.

Der berüchtigte Shorebreak von Makaha findet ein weiteres Opfer. Diese klassische Aufnahme wurde in vielen Werbeanzeigen verwendet.

Le surfeur malchanceux est terrassé par l'impitoyable *shore break* de Makaha. Ce cliché devenu célèbre fut utilisé dans de nombreuses publicités.

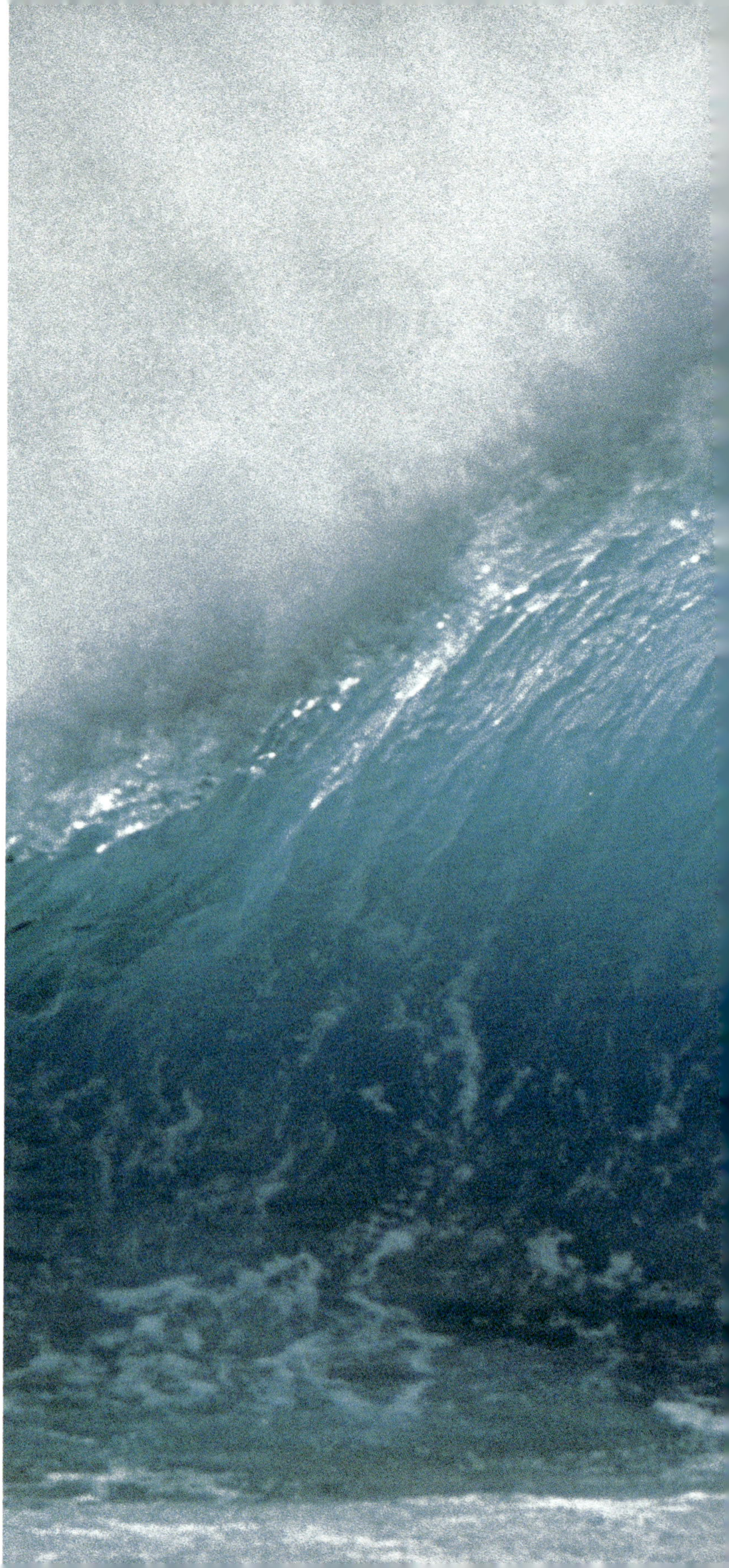

*Pages 336–337*
**Sunset Beach, 1972**

A quick exit out the back of a nonnegotiable Sunset wave.

Eine schnelle Flucht nach hinten aus einer nicht zu bewältigenden Sunset-Welle.

Face à ce monstre indomptable de Sunset Beach, une seule échappatoire : passer par derrière.

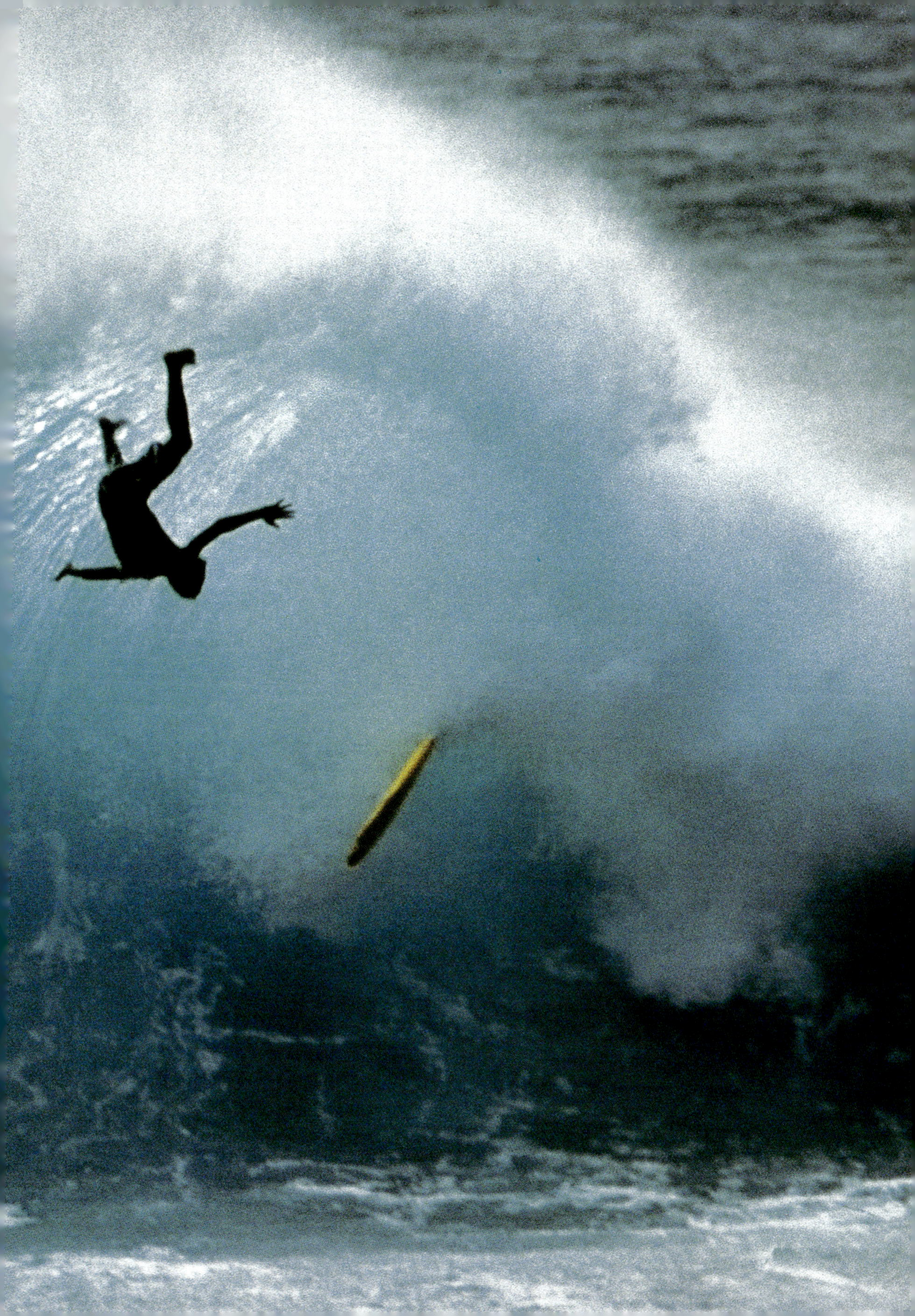

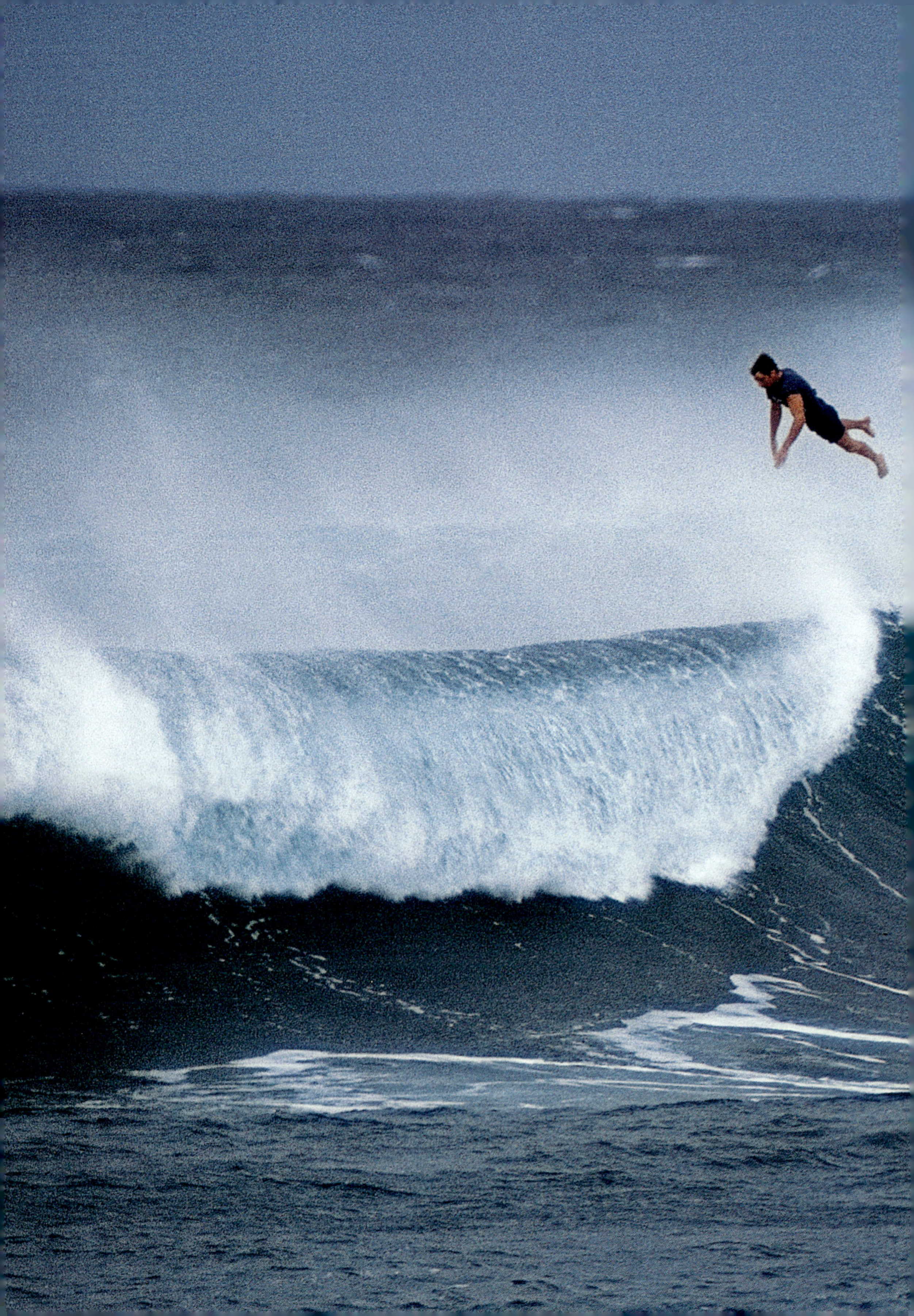

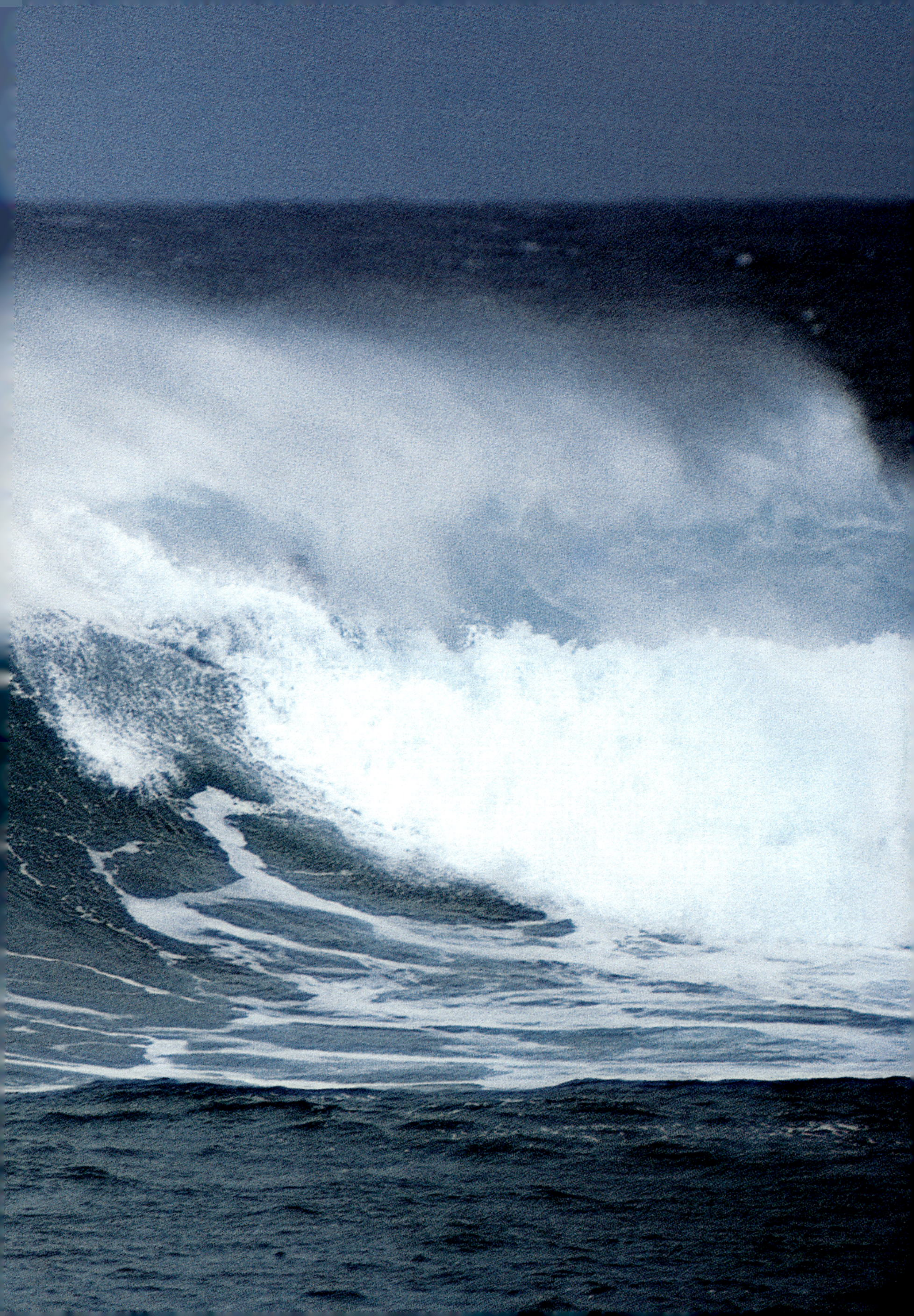

**Fred Hemmings, Pipeline, 1964**

Often the first sound you hear on
the North Shore during a big swell
is an ambulance siren's howl.

Oft ist das erste Geräusch, das
man bei einem großen Swell am
North Shore hört, die heulende
Sirene eines Krankenwagens.

Les premiers sons que vous
entendez les jours de gros swell sur
les plages du North Shore sont
souvent les hurlements des sirènes
d'ambulances.

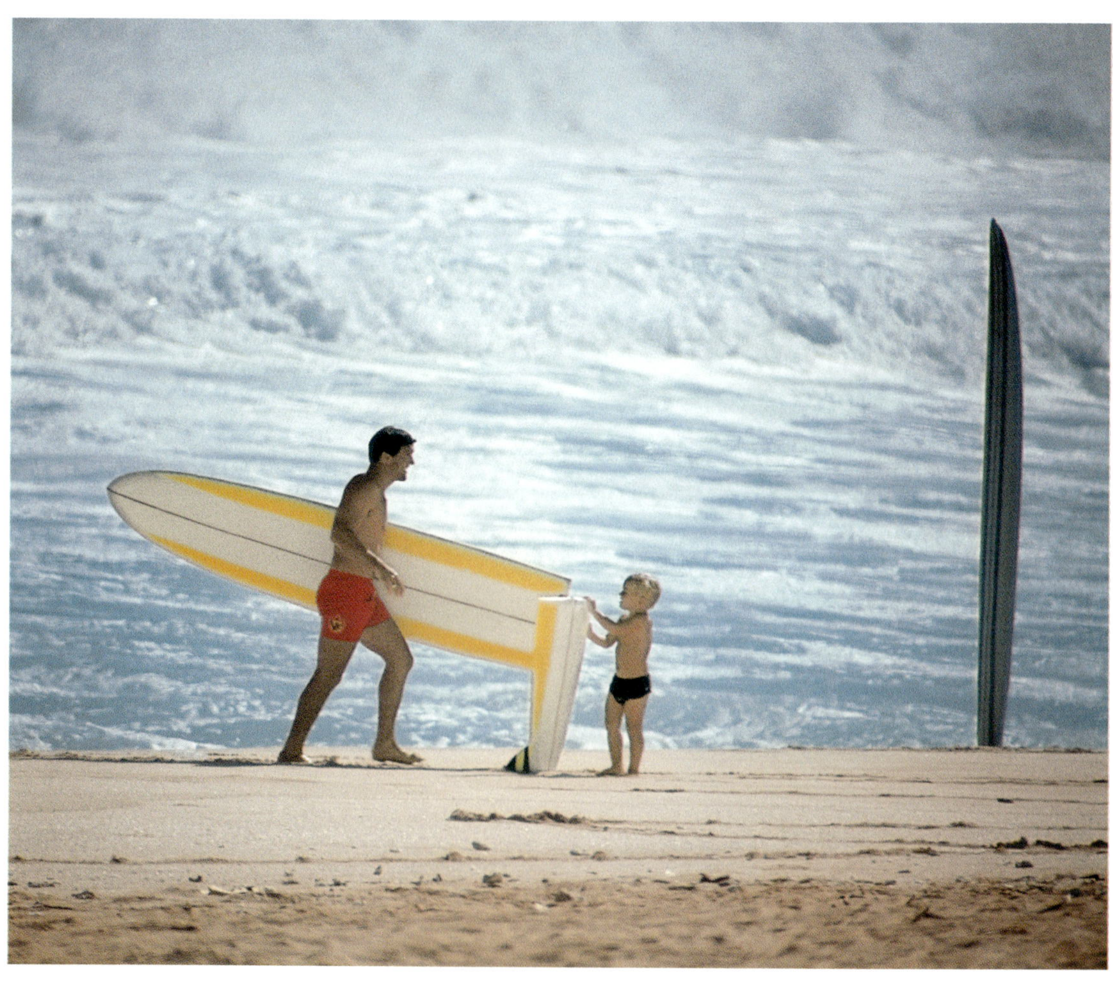

**Pipeline, circa 1965**

Until Dick Brewer and a handful of other shapers designed special shortboards for Hawaiian wave power, surfers took their chances, and often failed, at Pipeline.

Bevor Dick Brewer und eine Handvoll weiterer Shaper spezielle Shortboards für die gewaltigen hawaiianischen Wellen entwarfen, versuchten zwar viele Surfer ihr Glück in der Pipeline, scheiterten aber häufig.

Dick Brewer et une poignée d'autres shapers ont conçu des shortboards spéciales pour venir à bout des monstres de Hawaï. Avant eux, la plupart des tentatives se soldaient par l'échec.


**Billy Hamilton, James Jones, Eddie Aikau, Waimea Bay, 1973**

"The Bay" in its day was the Mt. Everest of surfing. Now surfers use jet skis to tow into waves three times this size.

„The Bay" war einst der Mt. Everest des Surfens. Heute benutzen Surfer Jet-Skis, um sich in dreimal so hohe Wellen ziehen zu lassen.

« The Bay » était considéré en son temps comme l'Everest du surf. Aujourd'hui, les surfeurs utilisent des jets-skis pour grimper au sommet de vagues trois fois plus hautes que celle-ci.

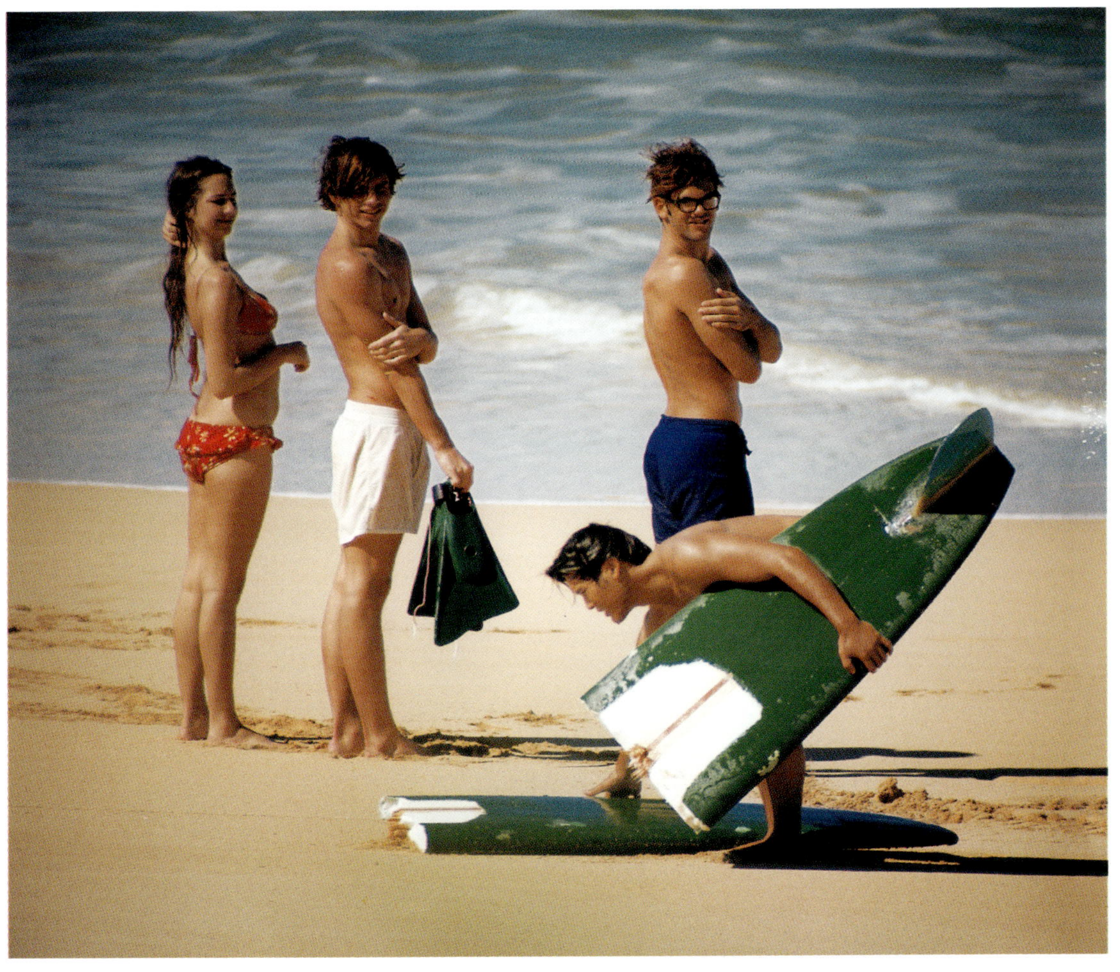

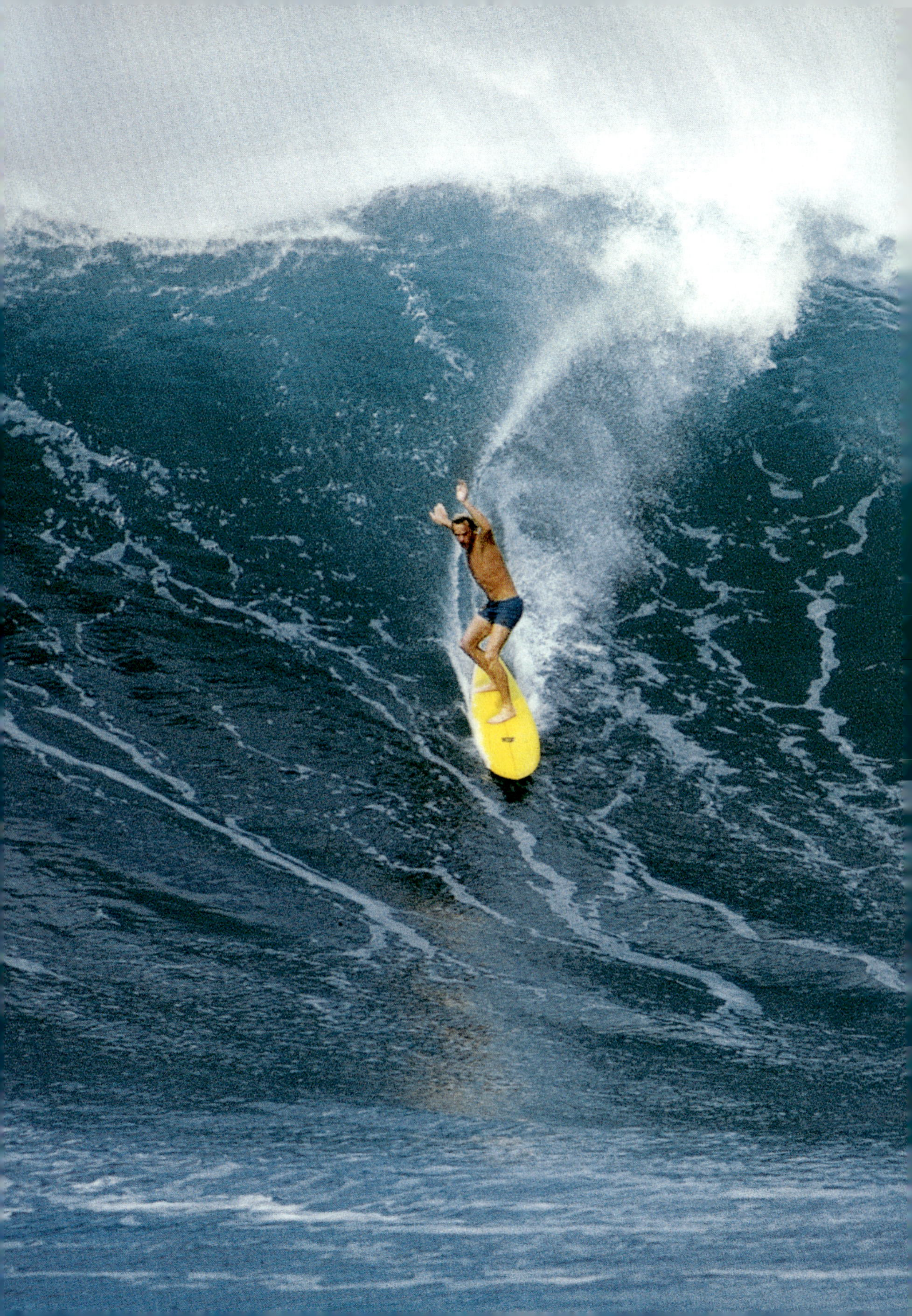

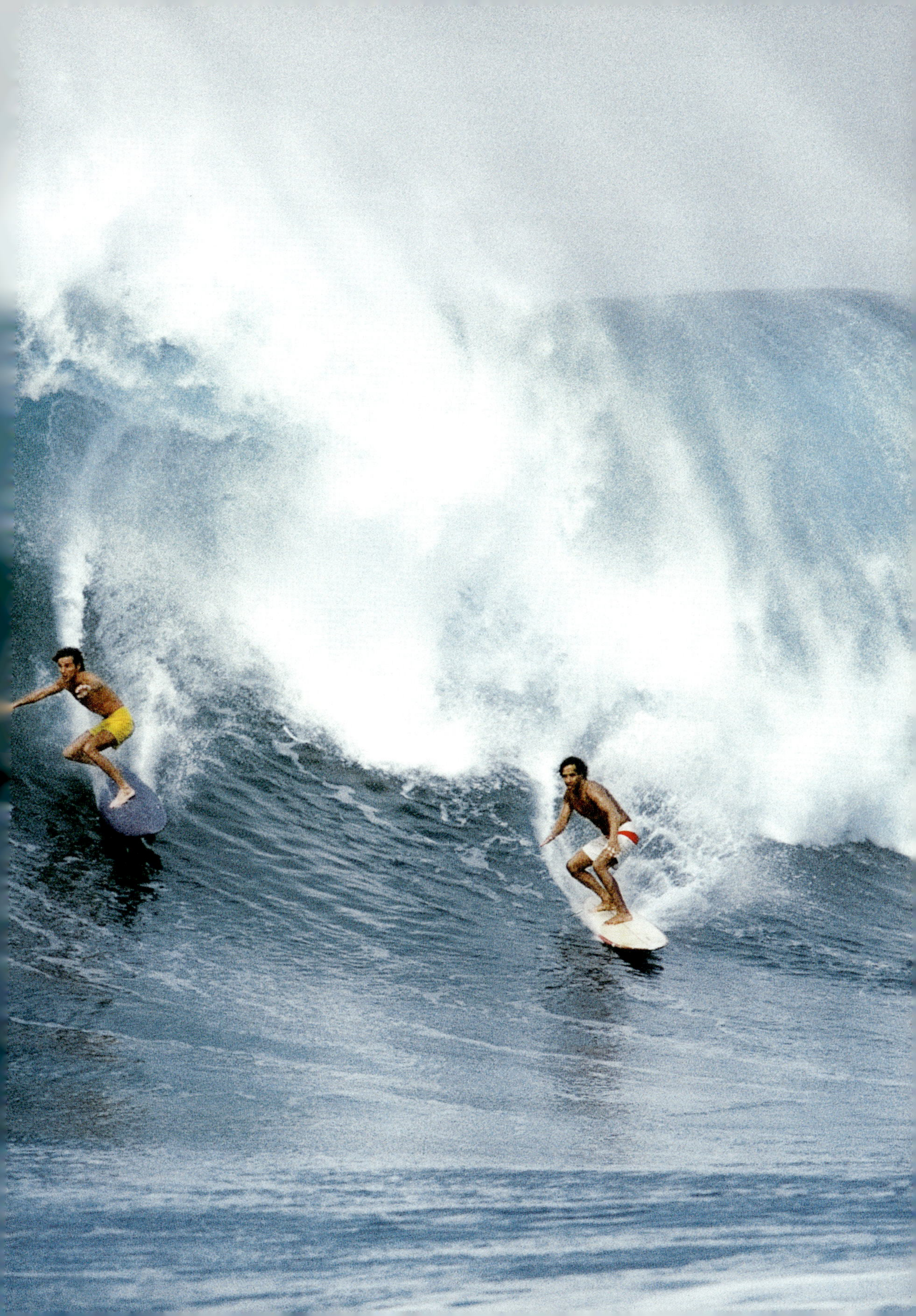

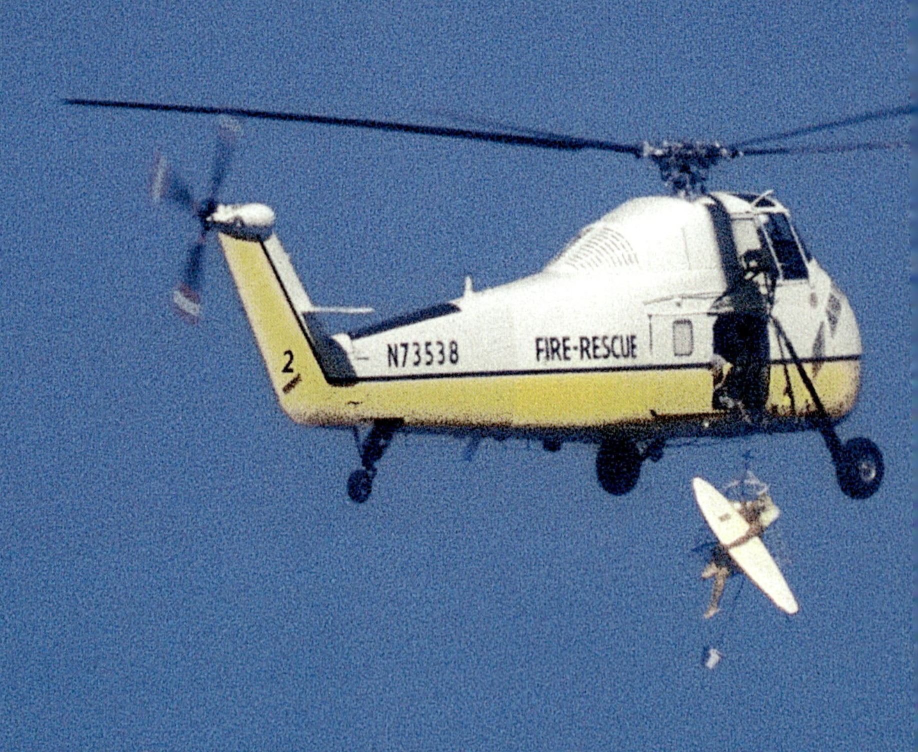
N73538
FIRE-RESCUE
2

*Pages 342–343*
**Pipeline, circa 1972**

There are huge days when there is
no exit from Pipeline except up.

Es gibt Tage mit so hohen Wellen,
dass der einzige Ausweg aus der
Pipeline durch die Luft führt.

Certains jours de gros swell, la
seule issue pour échapper aux
monstres de Pipeline passe par
les airs.

*Pages 346–347*
**Ehukai Beach, 1977**

A small beach crowd watching
the Pipeline Masters contest.
These days, there are thousands
of viewers and hundreds of
telephotos on the beach.

Eine kleine Zuschauermenge
beobachtet den Pipeline Masters
Wettbewerb. Heute gibt es
Tausende von Zuschauern und
Hunderte von Teleobjektiven am
Strand.

Attroupement de curieux sur la
plage pendant les épreuves des
Pipeline Masters. Aujourd'hui,
l'événement sportif attire des
milliers de spectateurs et des
centaines de photographes
équipés de téléobjectifs.

**Waimea Bay, circa 1968**

Left to right: unidentified,
Mike Doyle, Eddie Aikau.

Von links nach rechts: unbekannt,
Mike Doyle, Eddie Aikau.

De gauche à droite : non identifié, Mike Doyle et Eddie Aikau.

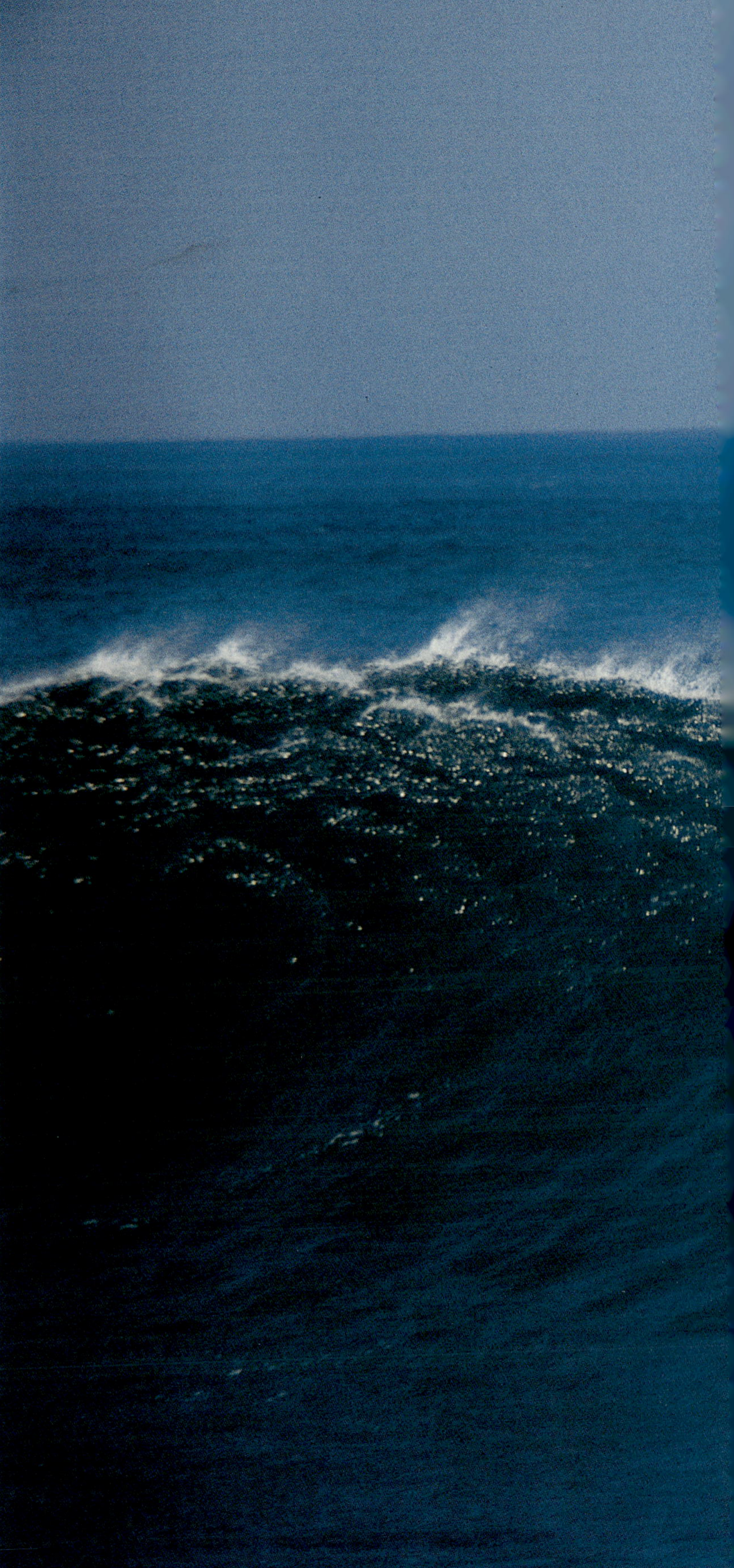

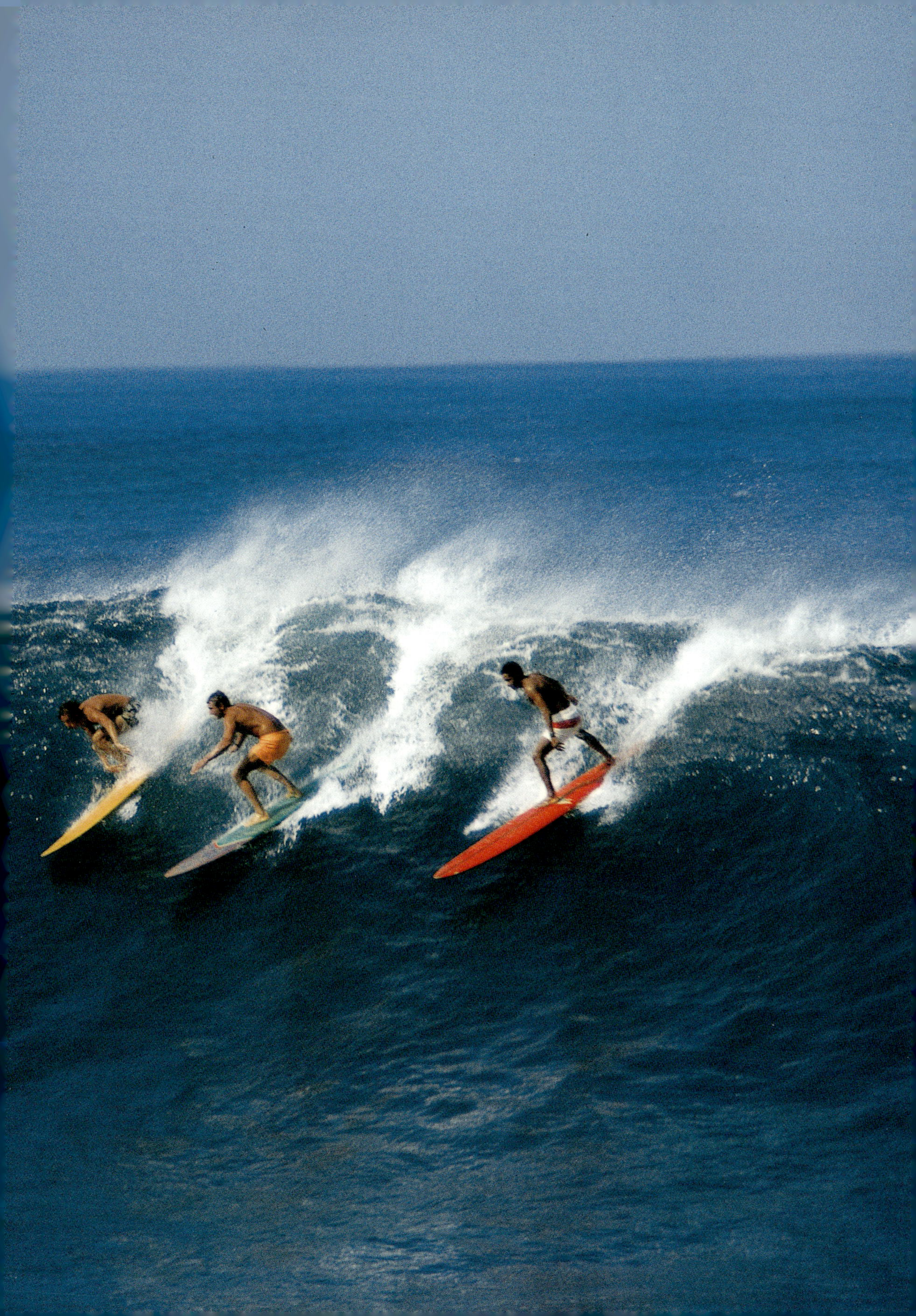

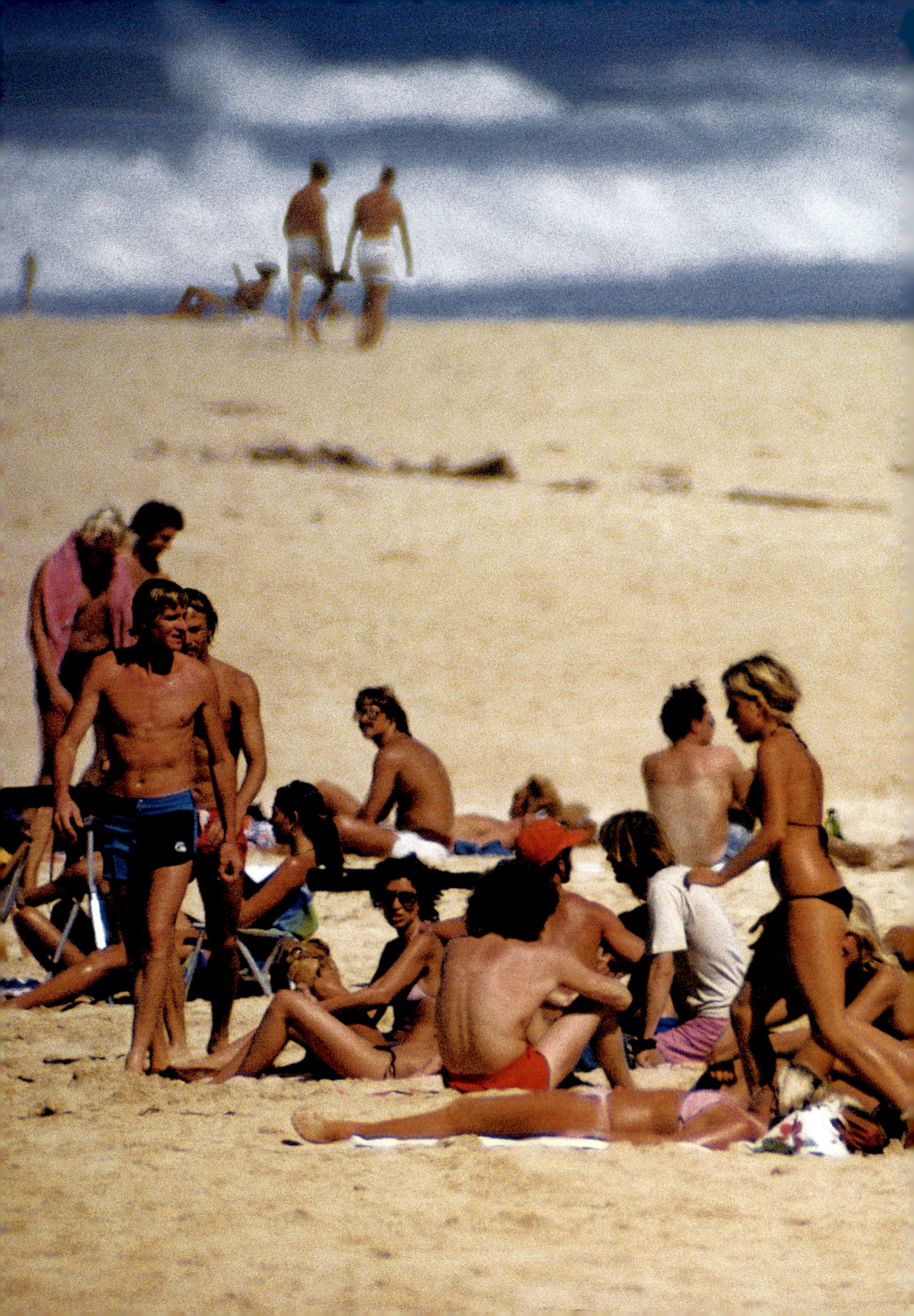

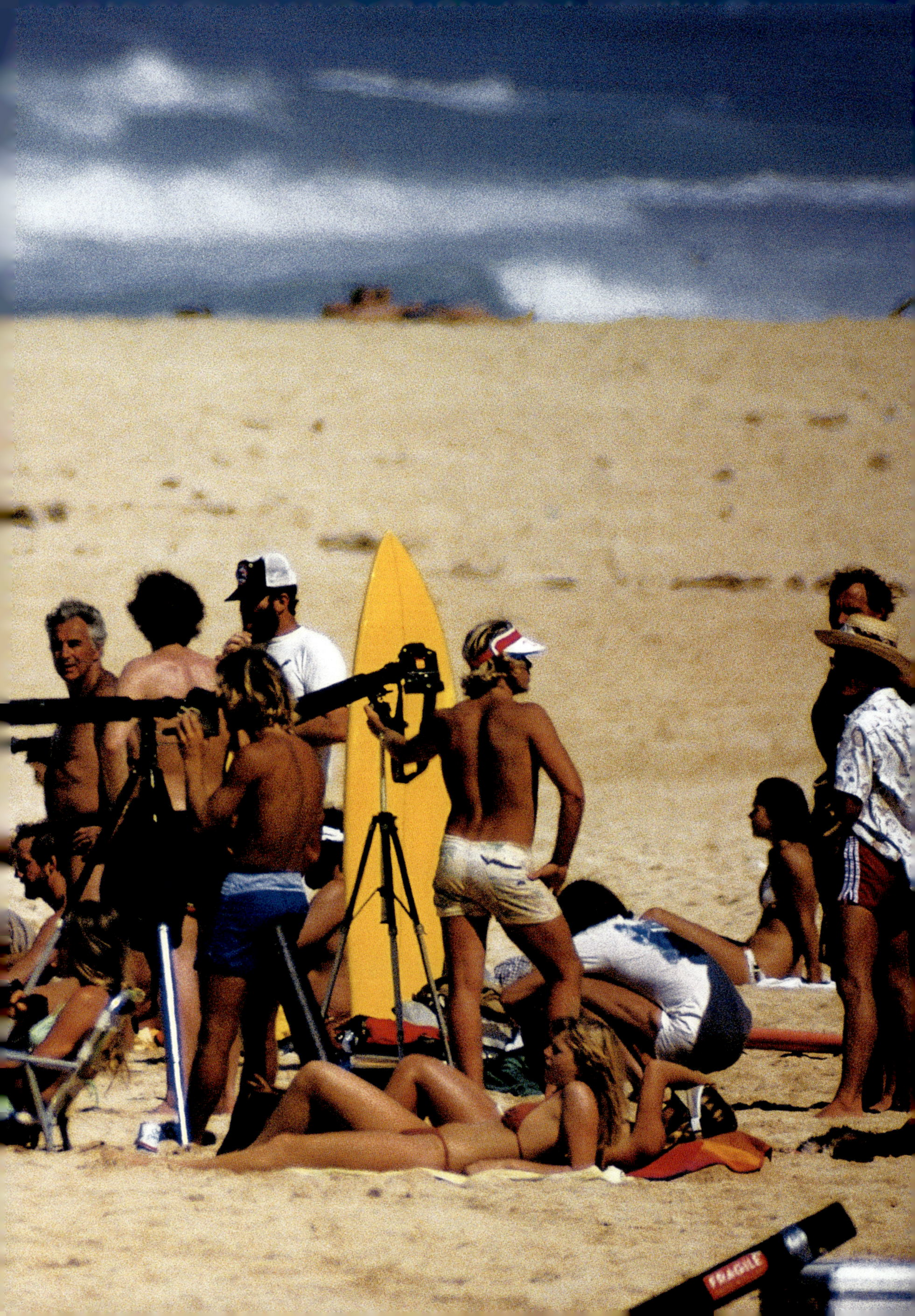
FRAGILE

**Sunset Beach, 1968**

Duke Classic contestants just prior
to their heats. Left to right: Mike
Doyle, Rick Grigg, Fred Hemmings,
Felipe Pomar.

Teilnehmer des Duke Classic
direkt vor ihren Heats. Von
links nach rechts: Mike Doyle,
Rick Grigg, Fred Hemmings,
Felipe Pomar.

Concurrents de la Duke Classic
quelques instants avant leurs
*heats*. De gauche à droite : Mike
Doyle, Rick Grigg, Fred Hemmings
et Felipe Pomar.

**Sunset Beach, 1968**

Greg Noll surf team all-stars, left to
right: Rick Grigg, Fred Hemmings,
Felipe Pomar, Greg Noll.

Die Stars des Greg-Noll-Surfteams,
von links nach rechts: Rick Grigg,
Fred Hemmings, Felipe Pomar,
Greg Noll.

Le plateau de stars de l'équipe
de Greg Noll. De gauche à droite :
Rick Grigg, Fred Hemmings,
Felipe Pomar et Greg Noll.

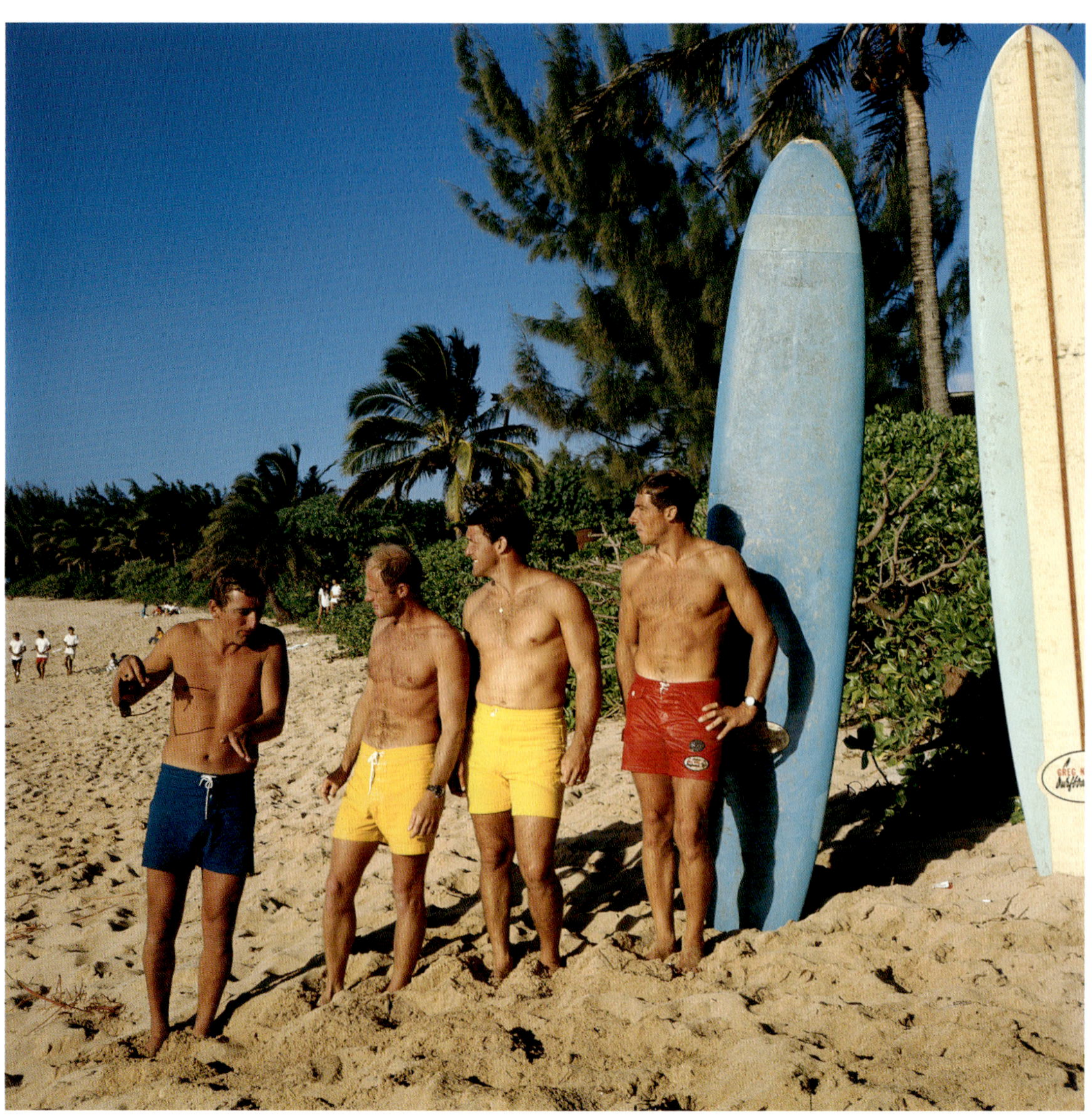

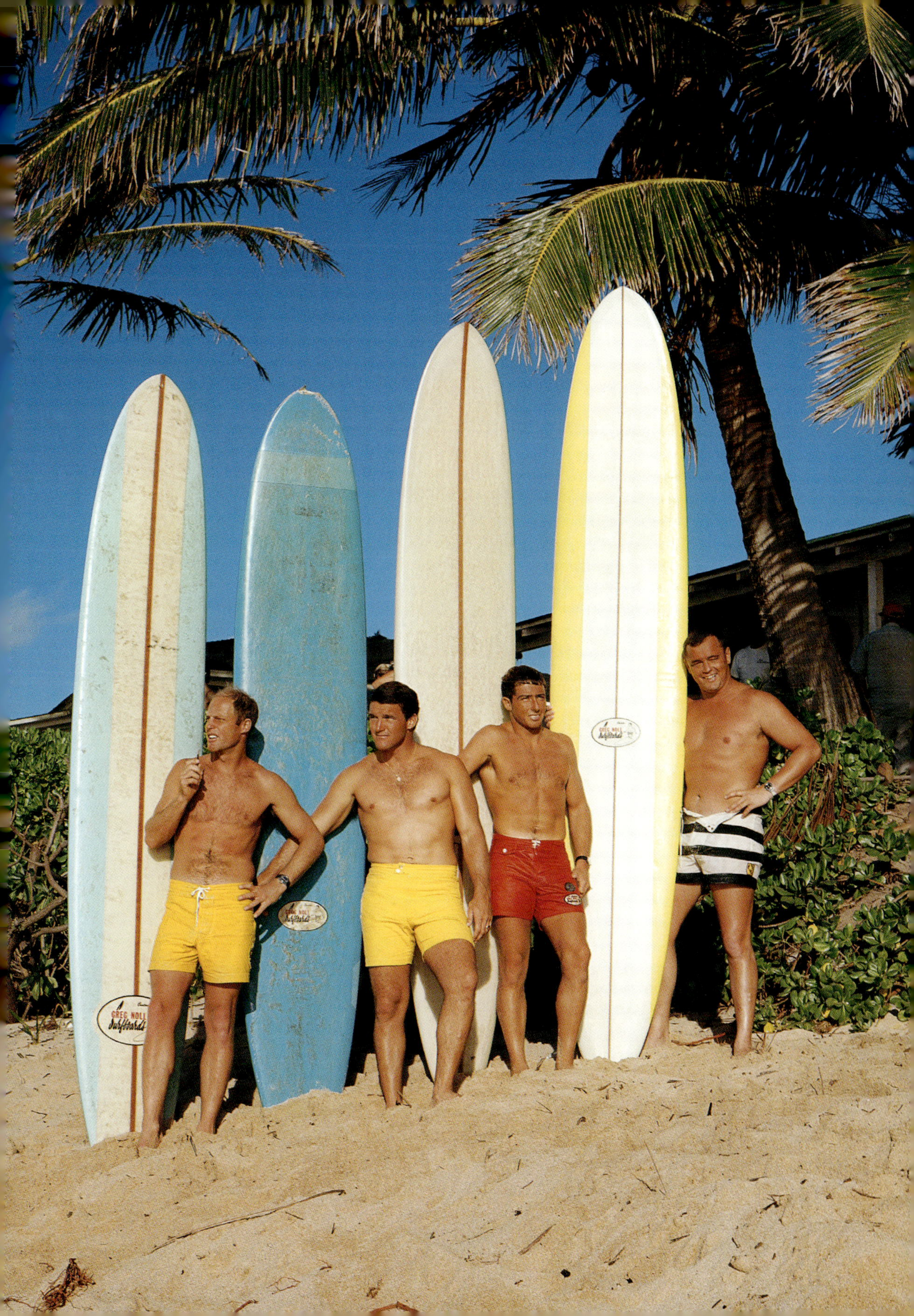

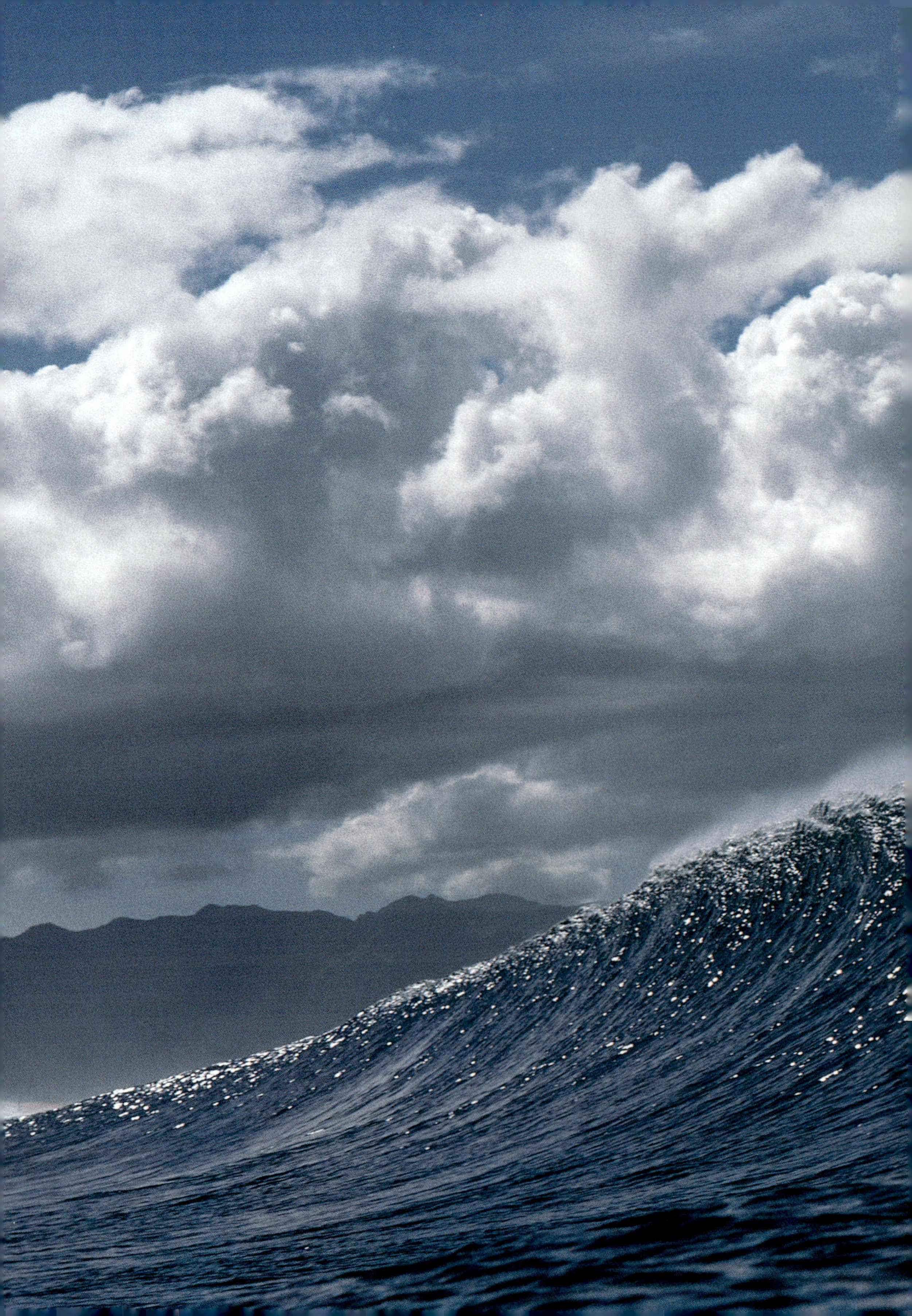

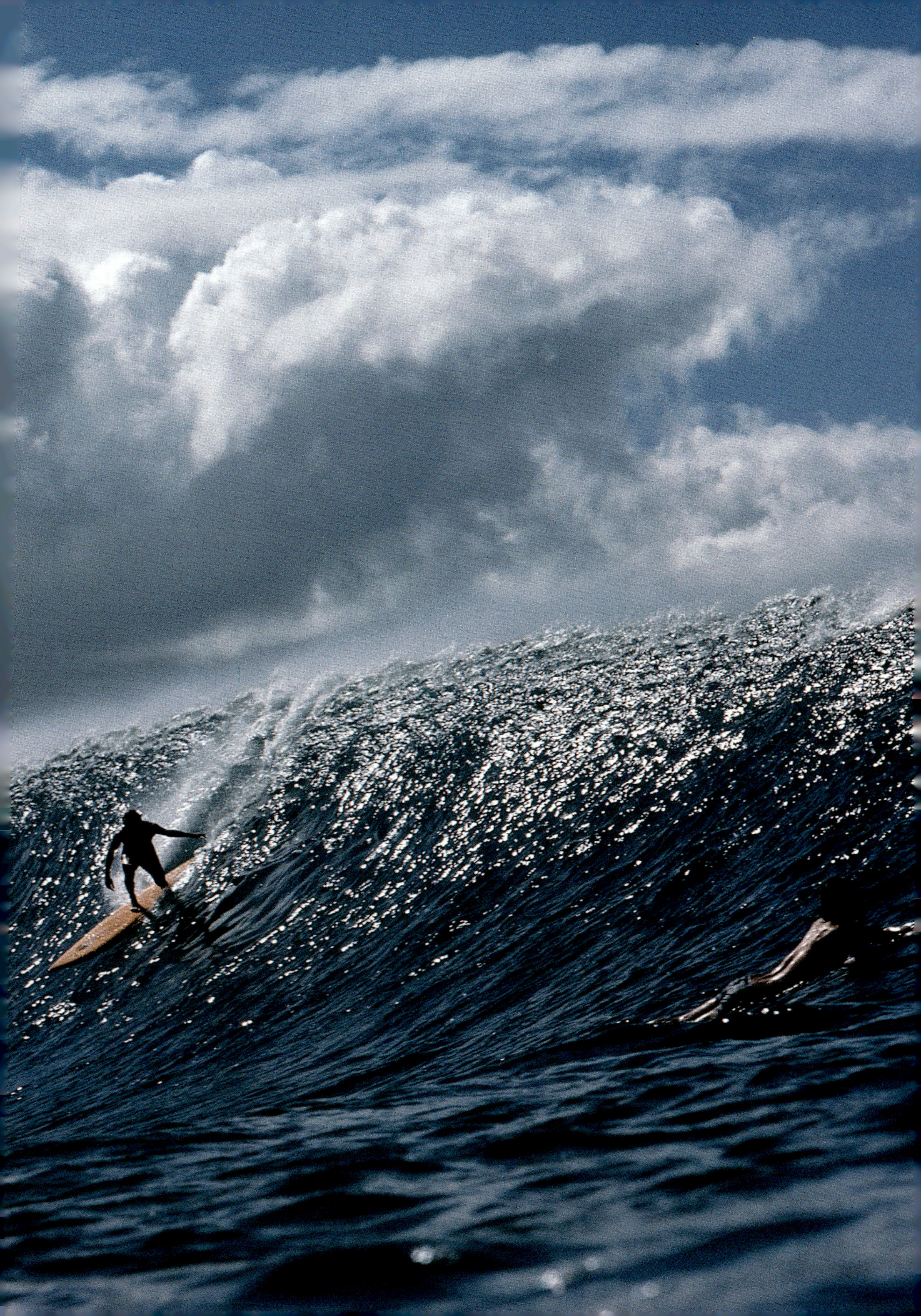

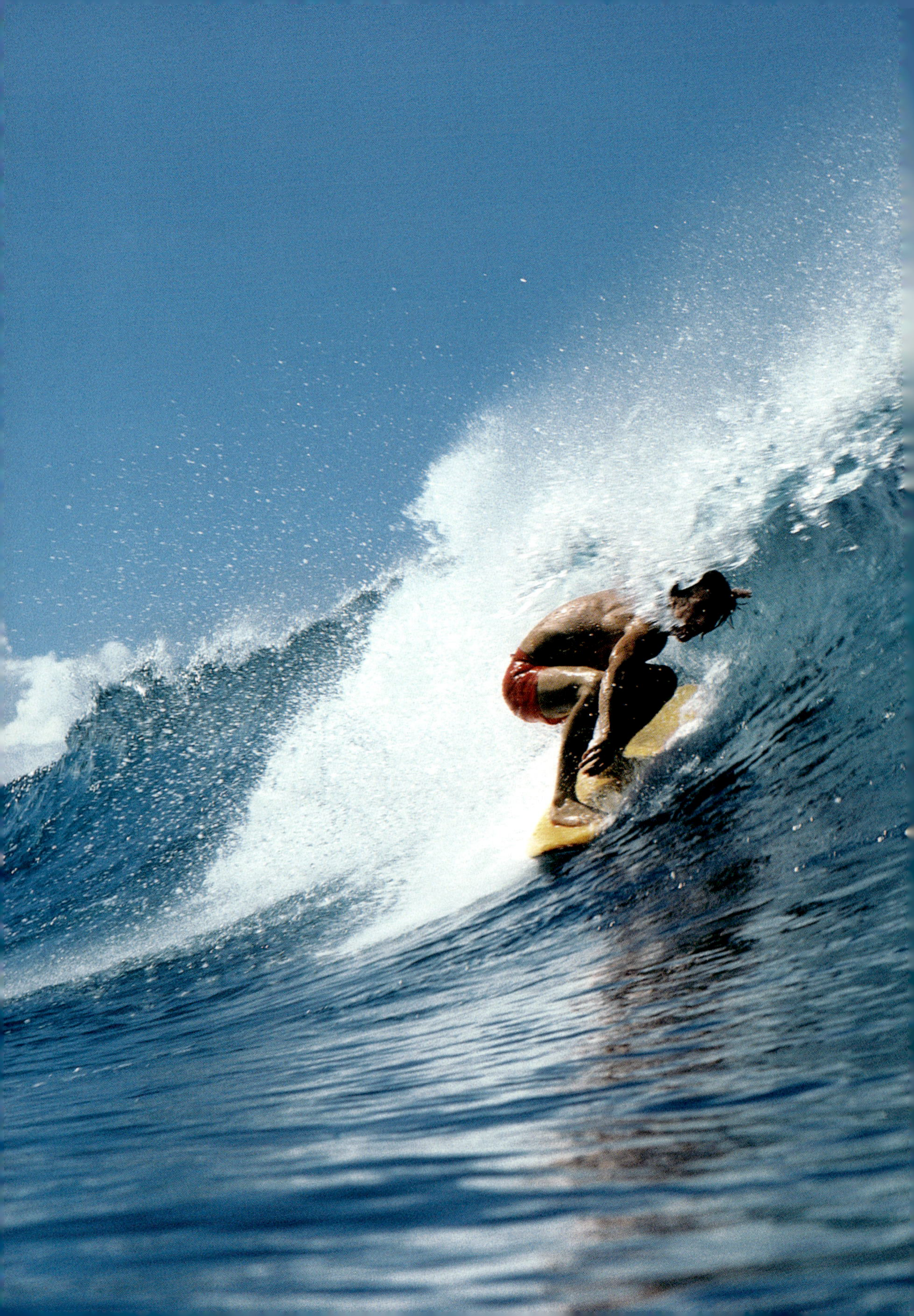

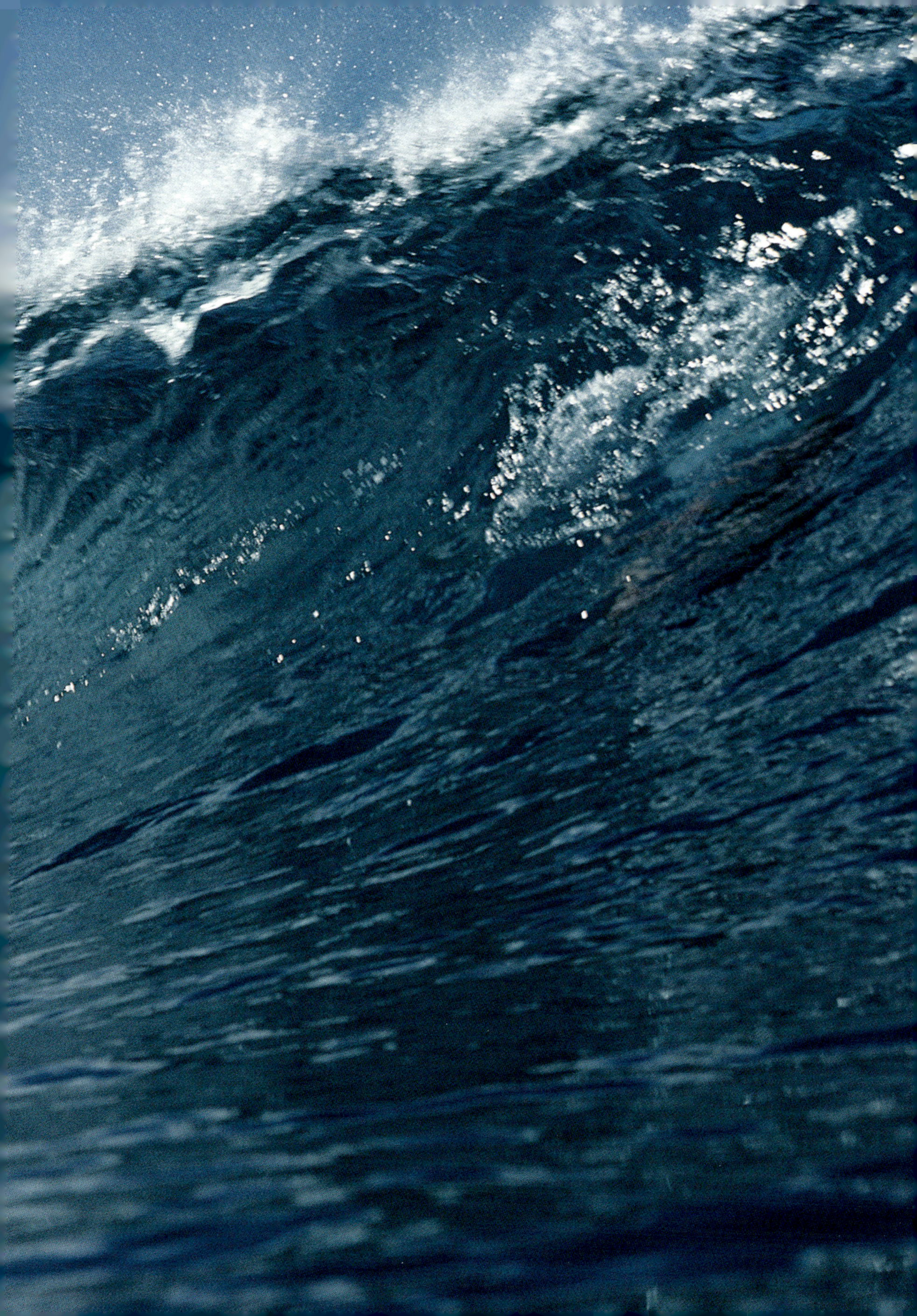

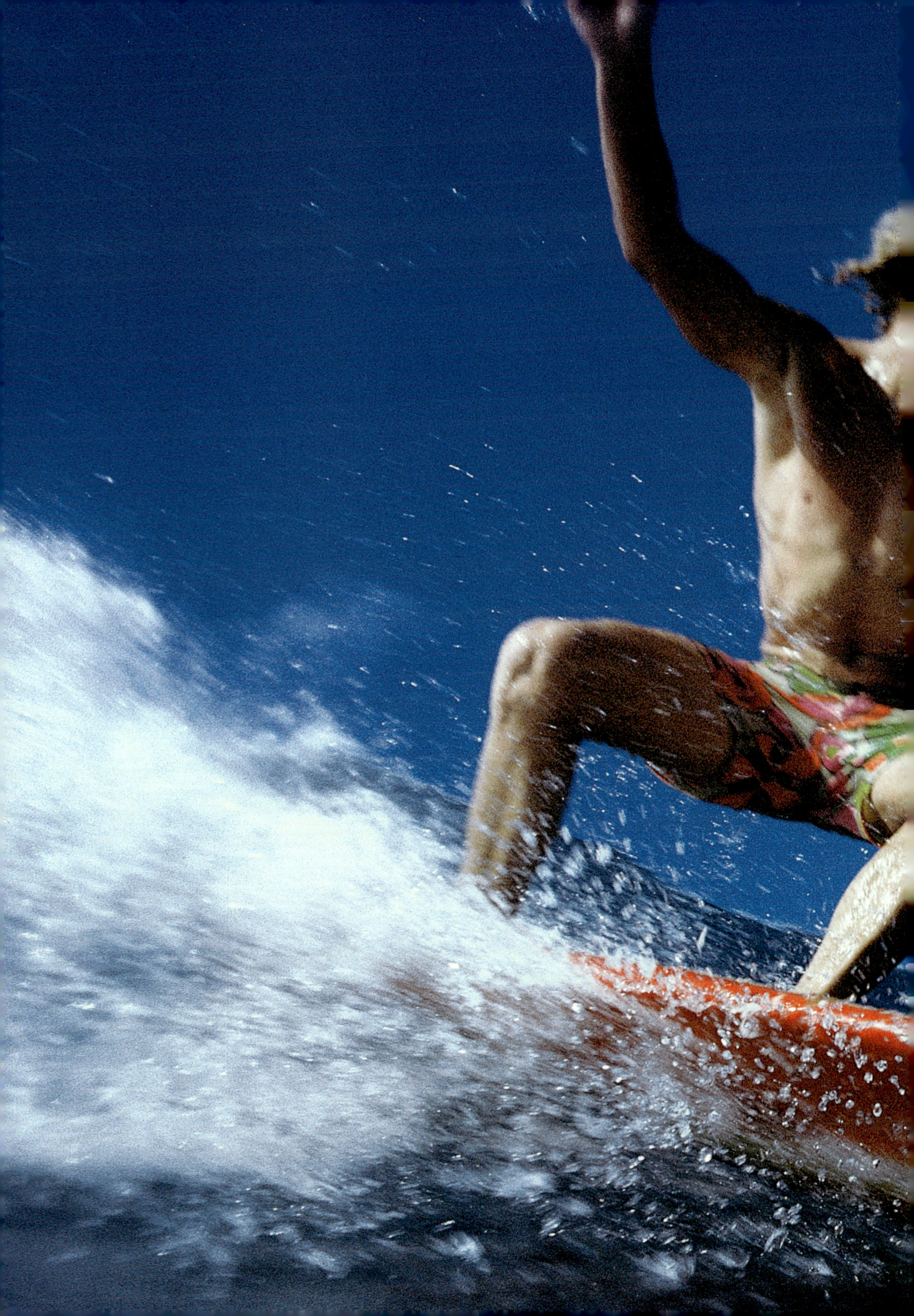

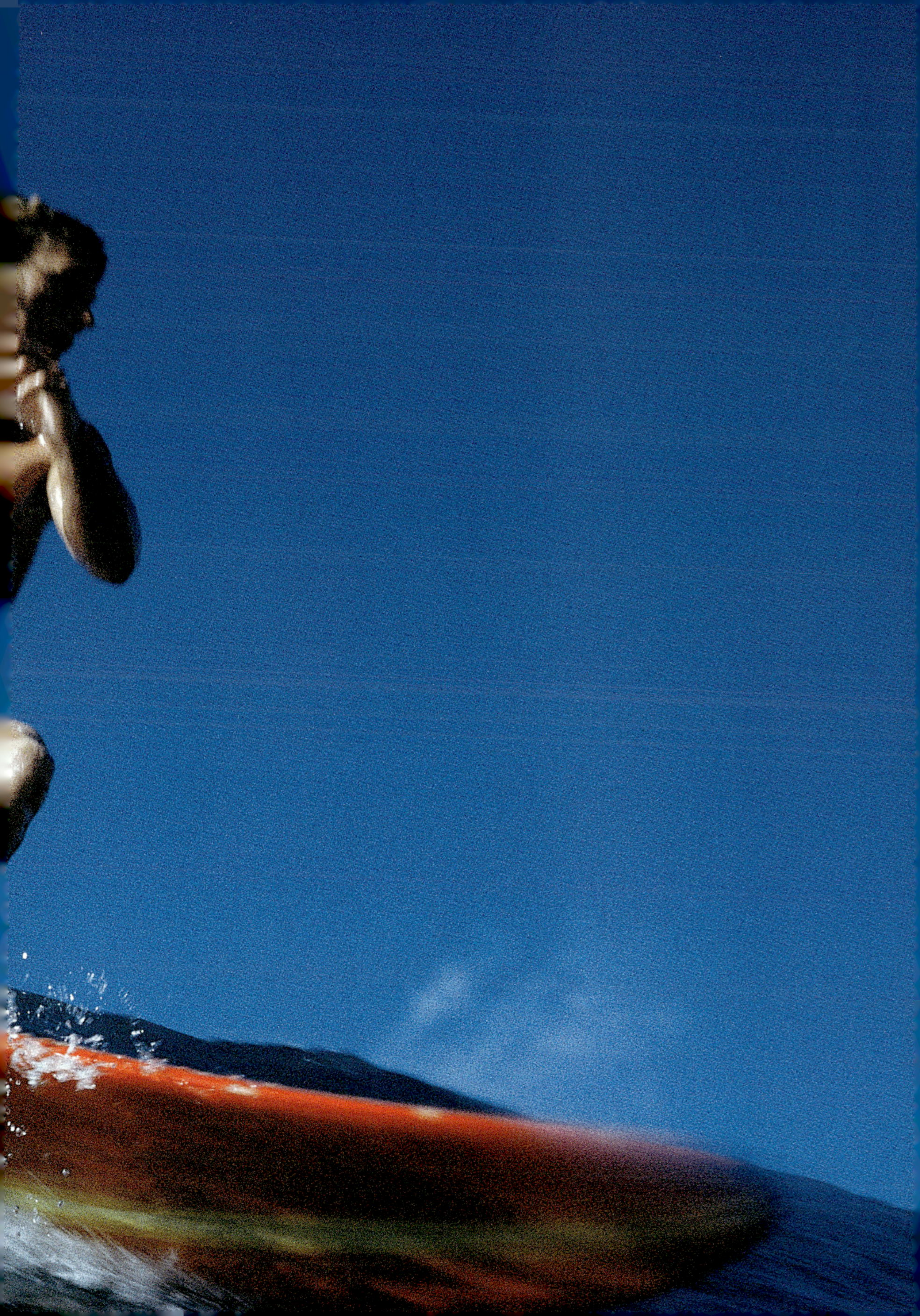

**Pipeline, 1975**

One water photographer compared
the narrow Pipeline channel to
being on the sidelines of the Super
Bowl—and then having the Super
Bowl fall on you.

Ein Wasserfotograf verglich den
schmalen Tunnel der Pipeline mit
dem Gefühl, das ein Spieler beim
Super Bowl nahe der Seitenlinie
haben müsse – als ob einem das
Stadion über dem Kopf zusammen-
bräche.

Un photographe aquatique a décrit
un jour en ces termes la passe
étroite de Pipeline: «C'est un peu
comme si vous vous promeniez sur
la ligne de touche pendant le Super
Bowl et que tout à coup le stade
s'effondrait sur votre tête!»


**Pipeline, 1977**

Small, fun Pipeline. This surfer
sets up for a "head dip."

Kleine, amüsante Pipeline. Dieser
Surfer setzt zum „Head Dip" an.

Petit pipeline plutôt amusant.
Ce surfeur s'apprête à exécuter
un «head dip».


**Midget Farrelly, Pupukea, 1970**

Bernard "Midget" Farrelly,
inaugural world champ in 1964,
timelessly bridging the eras.

Bernard „Midget" Farrelly, dem
ersten Weltmeister von 1964,
gelang es mühelos, die großen
Epochen des Surfens durch seinen
zeitlosen Stil zu überbrücken.

Bernard « Midget » Farrelly, qui
remporta le premier titre officiel
de champion du monde en 1964,
a traversé les grandes époques du
surf avec une constance impressionnante.

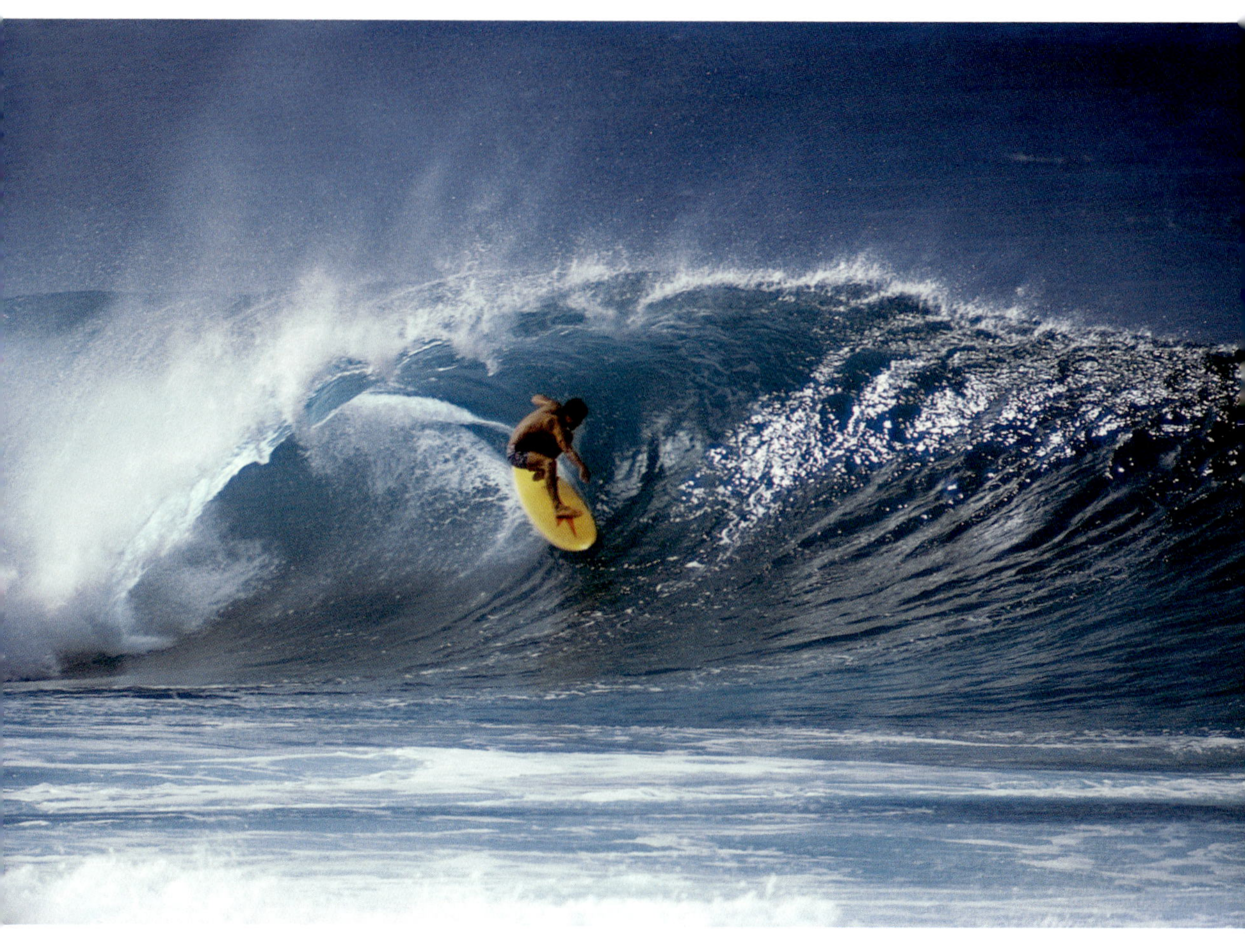

Pages 356–359
**Gerry Lopez, Pipeline, 1972**

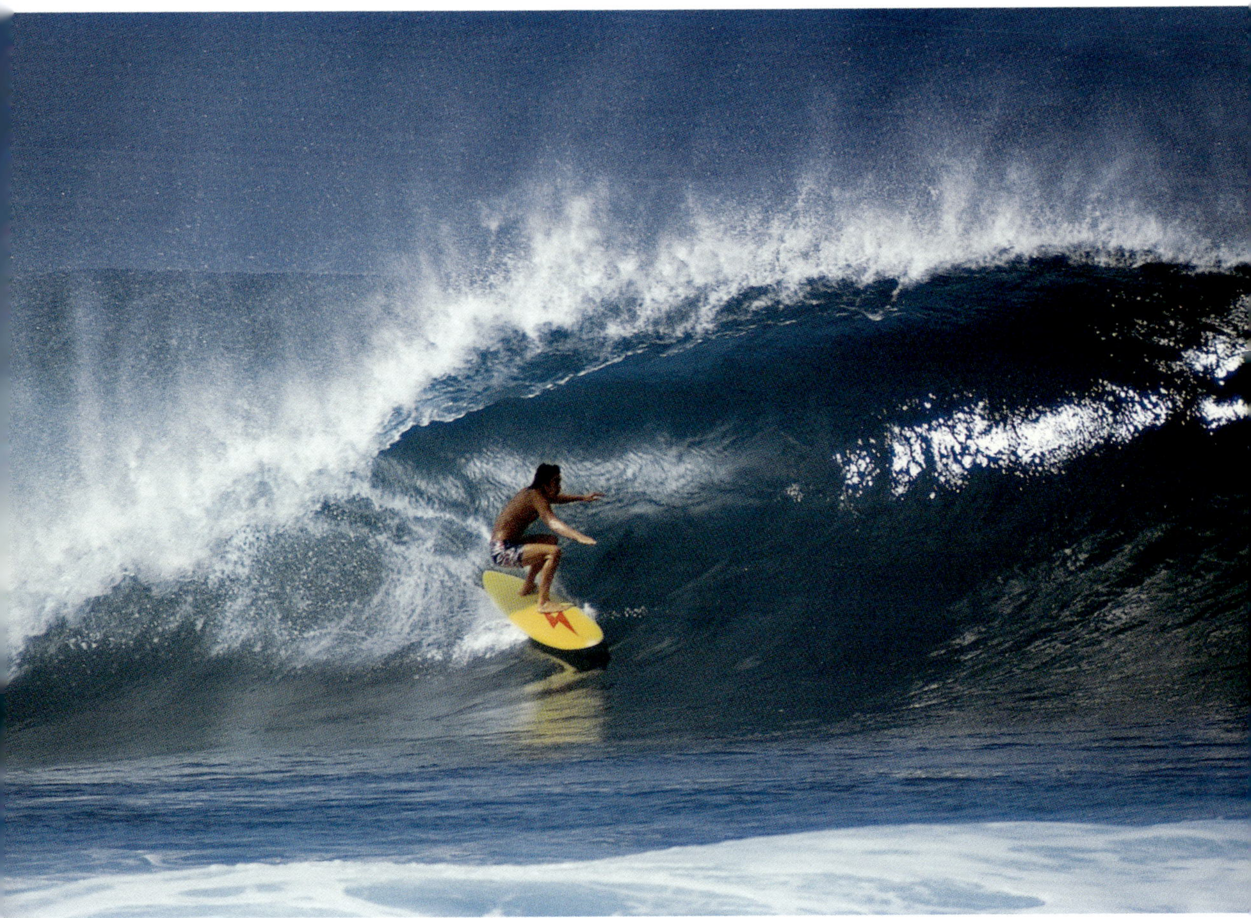

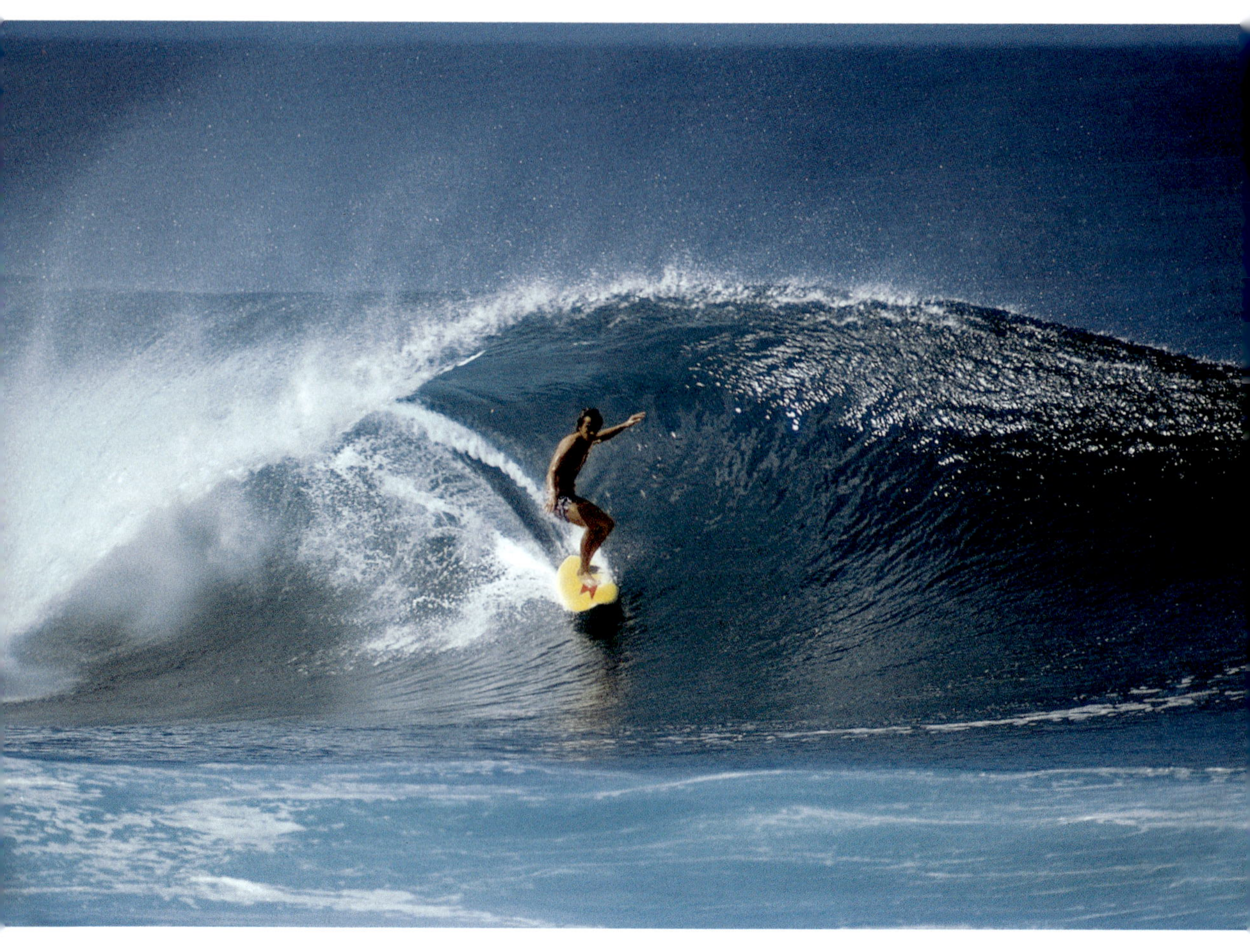

Pages 360–361
**Gerry Lopez, Pipeline, 1974**

Lopez was the reigning "Mr. Pipeline" in the early seventies. He once described riding the thundering tubes as a "cakewalk."

Lopez war in den frühen Siebzigern der amtierende „Mr. Pipeline". Er beschrieb den Ritt durch den donnernden Tunnel einmal als „Kinderspiel".

Au début des années 1970, Gerry Lopez – « Mister Pipeline » – régnait en maître sur ce redoutable spot. Surfer ses tubes vrombissants était pour lui une « promenade de santé ».

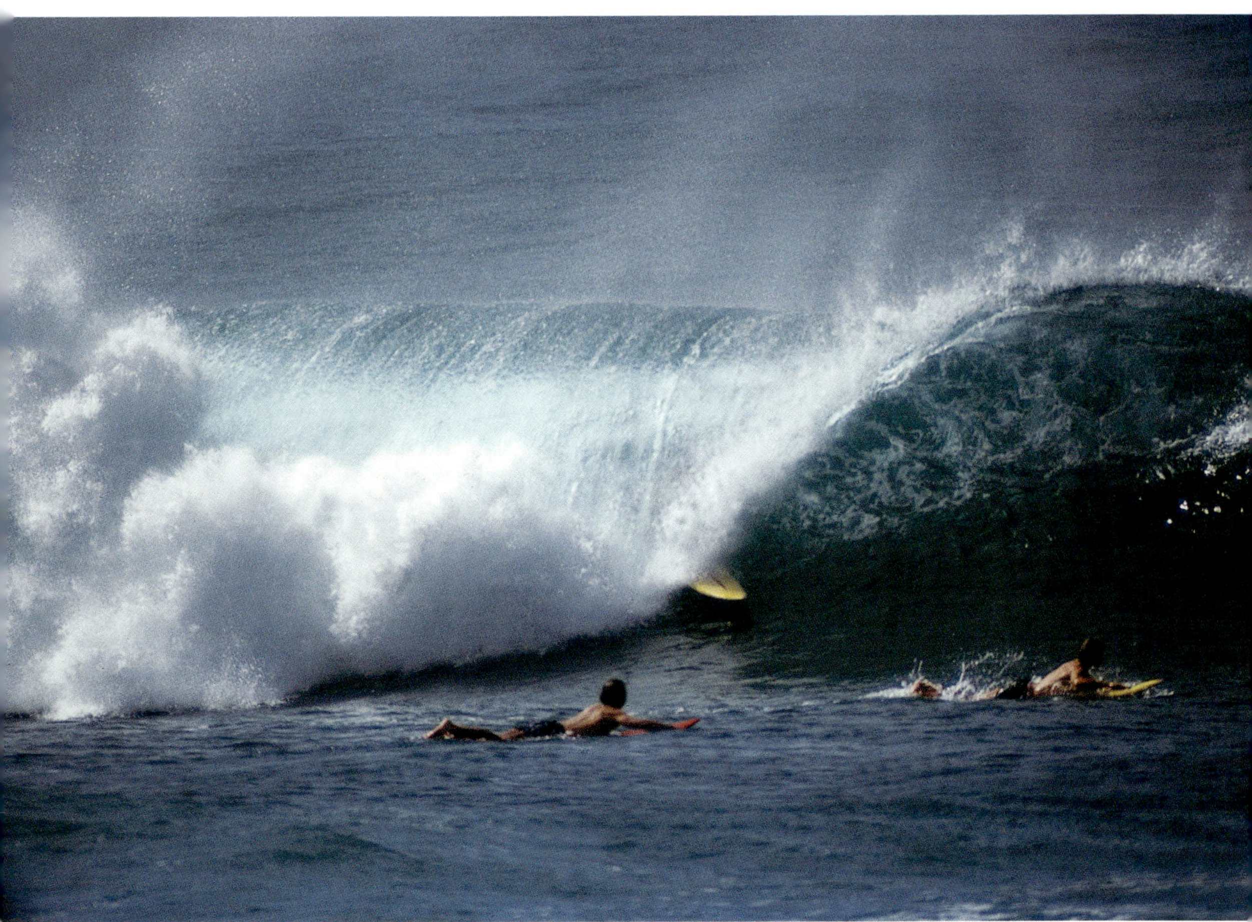

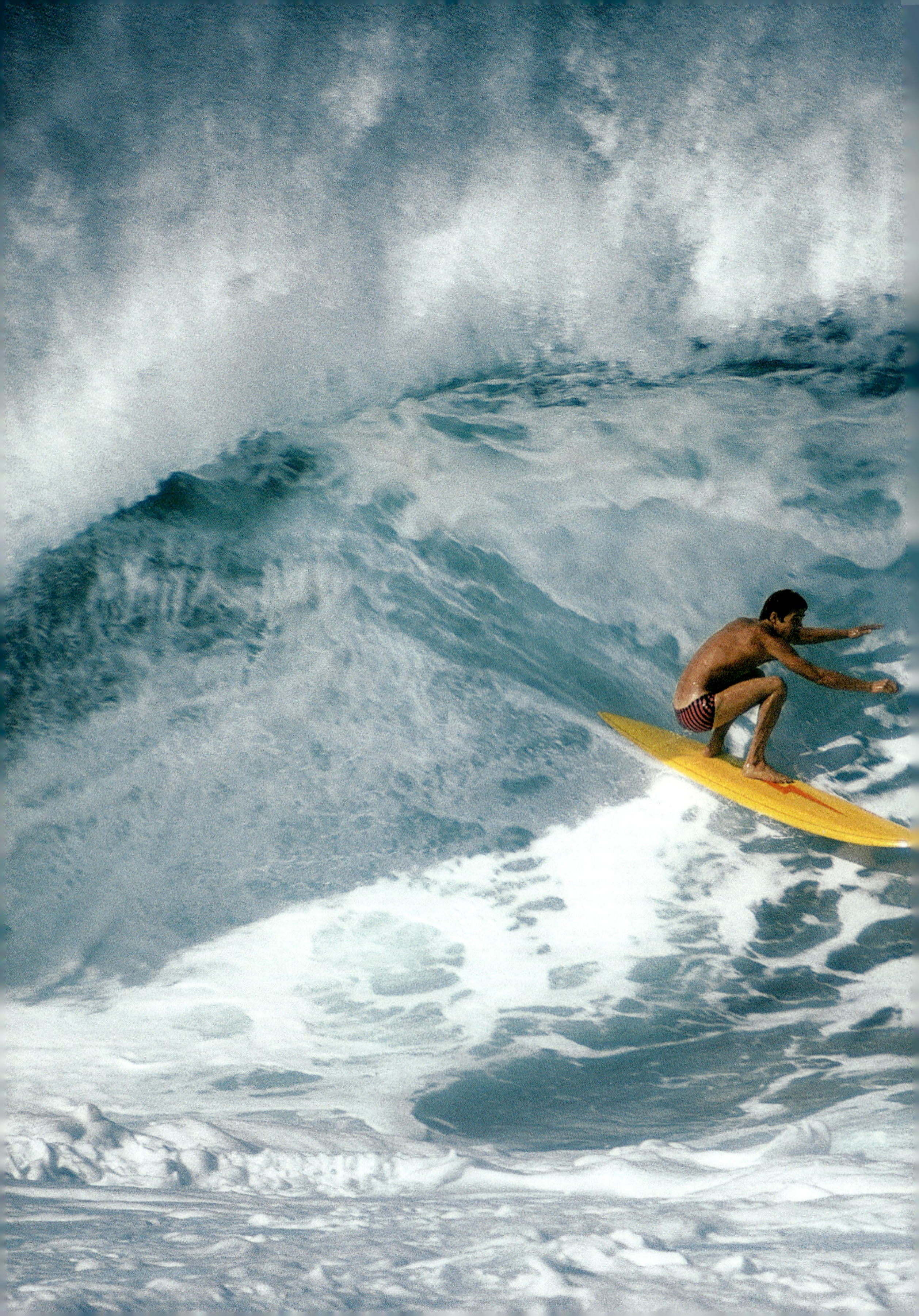

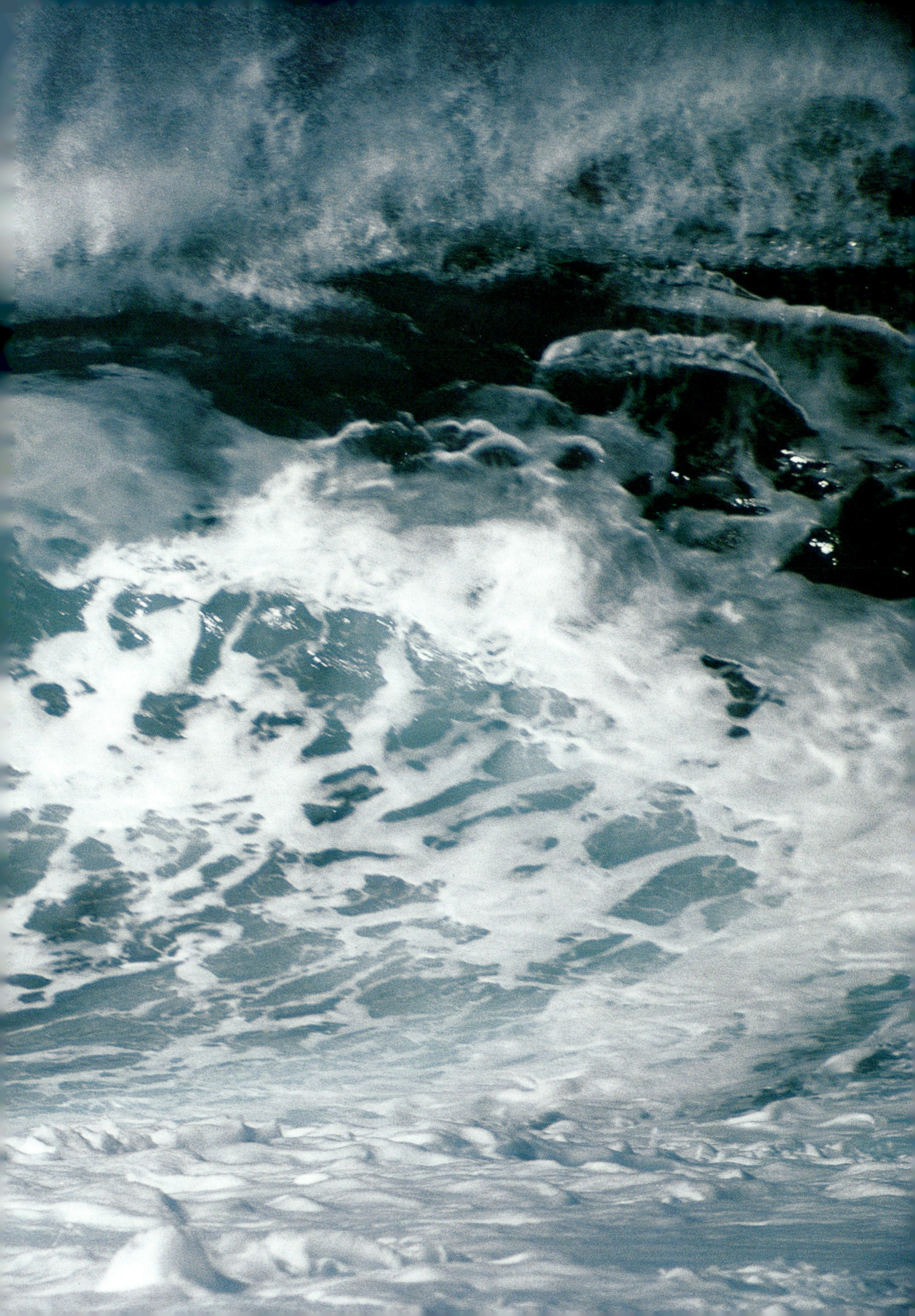

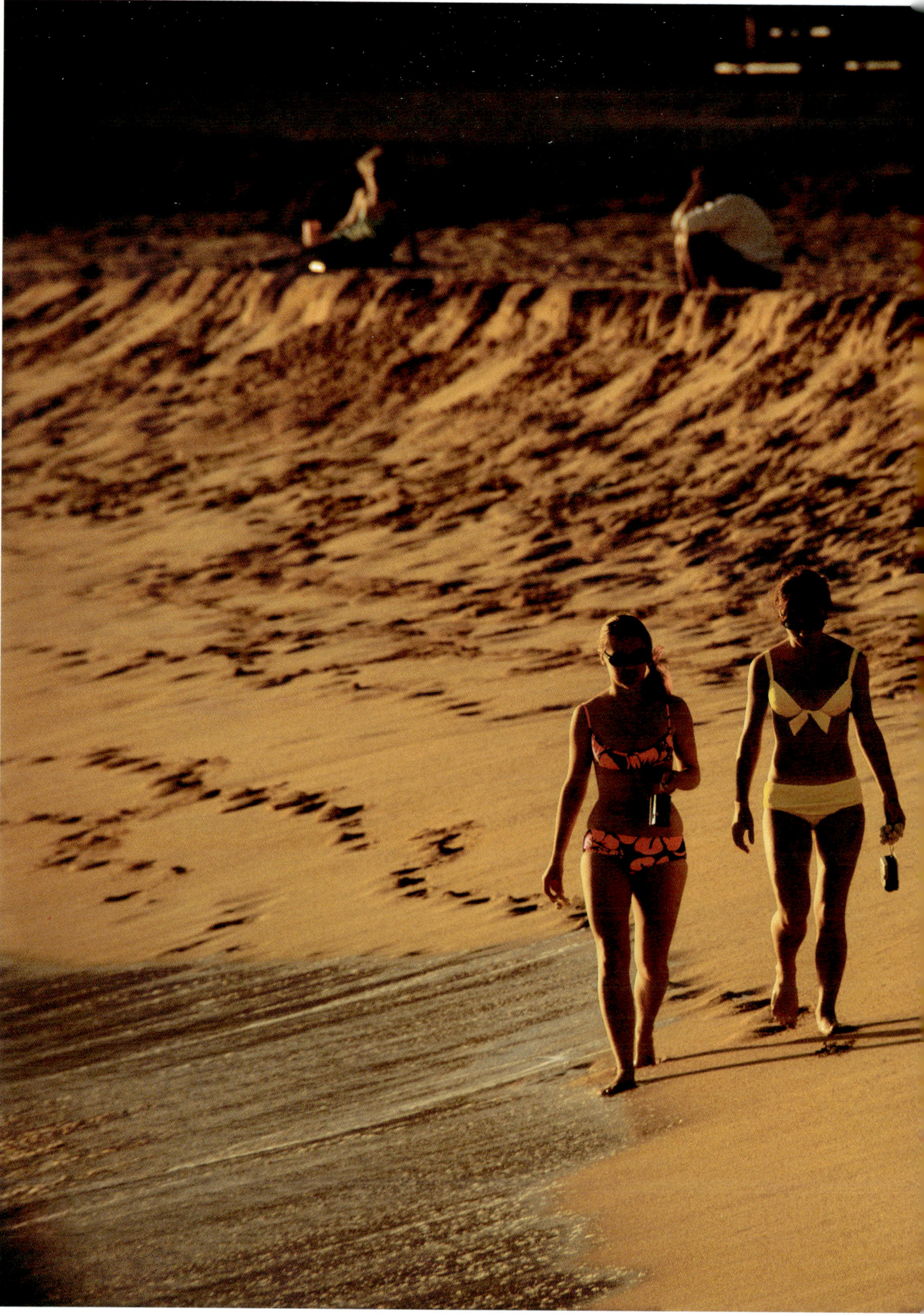

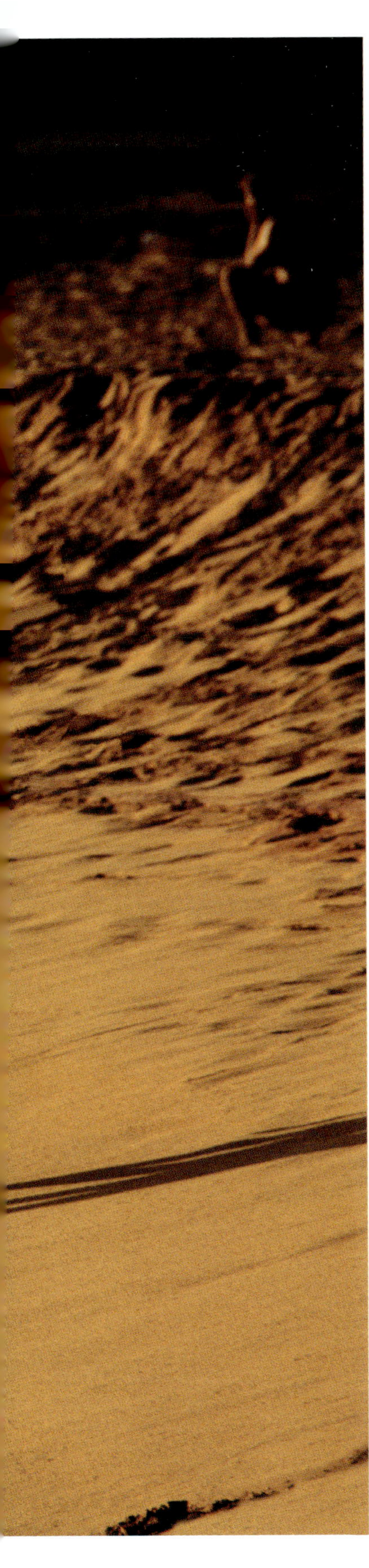

Makaha, circa 1968

Makaha, circa 1968

*Pages 364–365*
**Jackie Dunn, Pipeline, 1972**

Dunn, an underground but vastly
respected seventies Pipeline
master.

Dunn, ein wenig angepasster,
aber in den Siebzigerjahren sehr
angesehener Meister der Pipeline.

Jackie Dunn, un surfeur de Pipeline
extrêmement respecté pour ses
exploits dans les années 1970,
était aussi un anticonformiste.

*Pages 366–367*
**Waimea Bay, circa 1972**

Left to right: Larry Bertleman,
Reno Abellira, Clyde Aikau.

Von links nach rechts: Larry
Bertleman, Reno Abellira,
Clyde Aikau.

De gauche à droite : Larry
Bertleman, Reno Abellira,
Clyde Aikau.

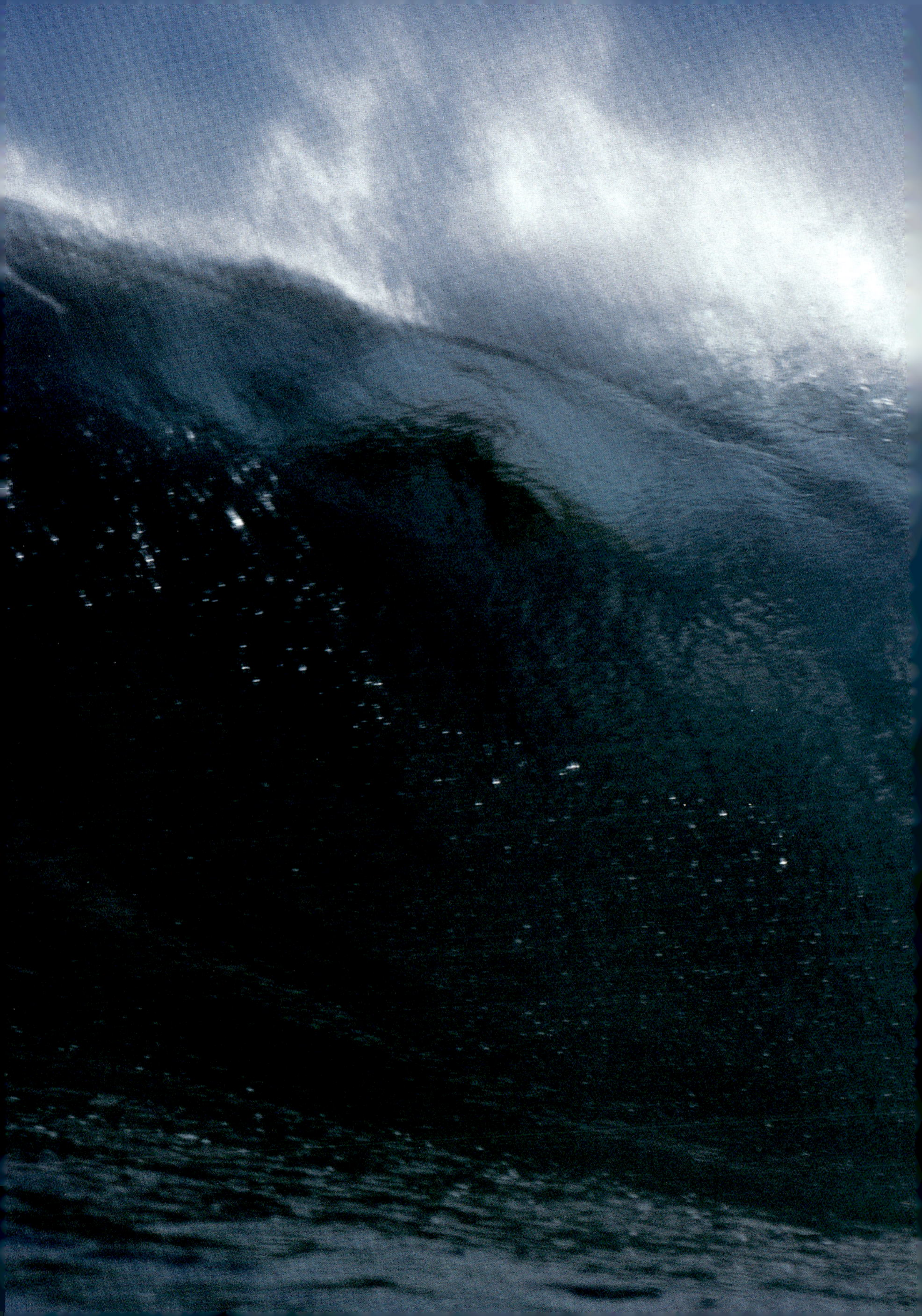

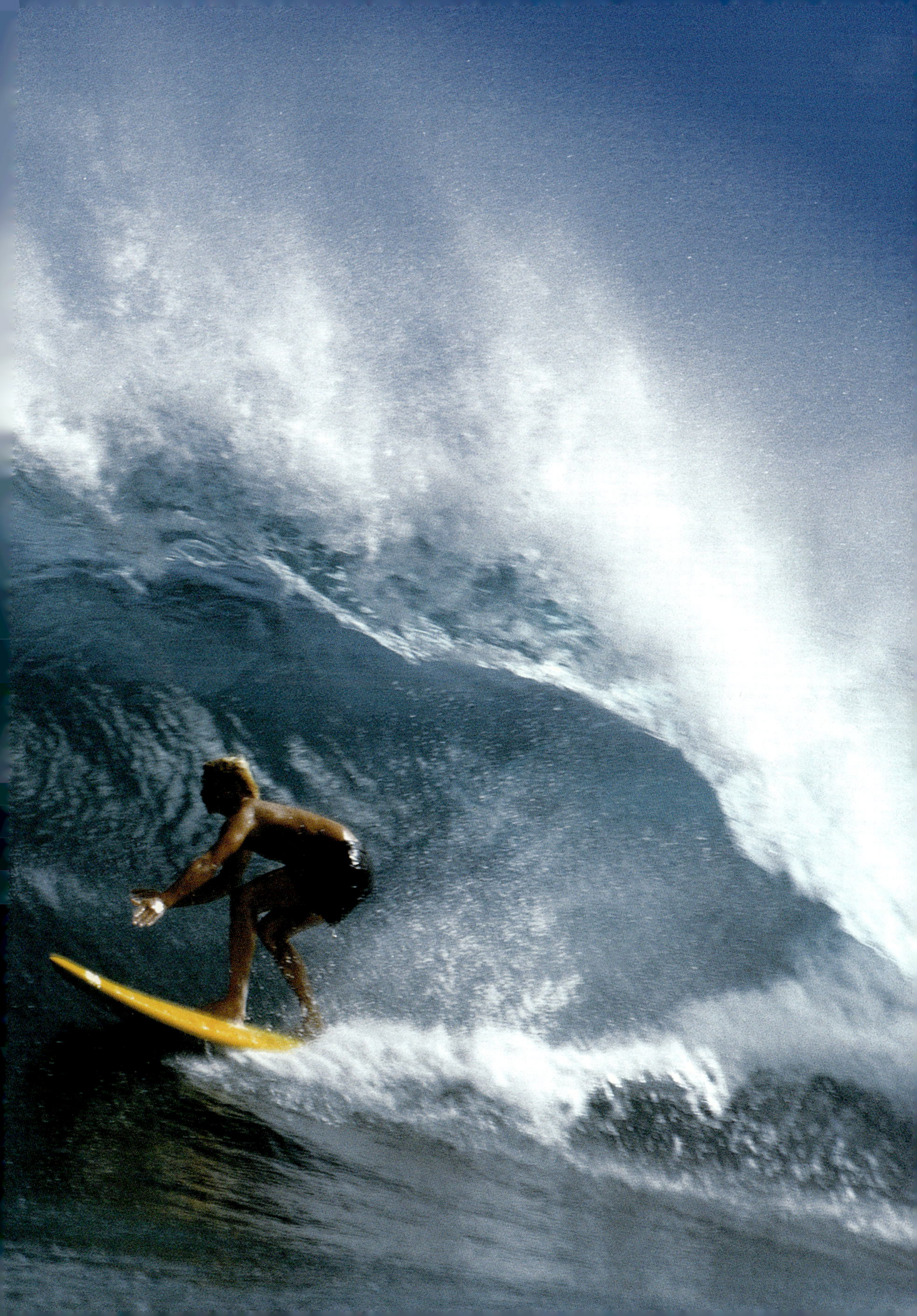

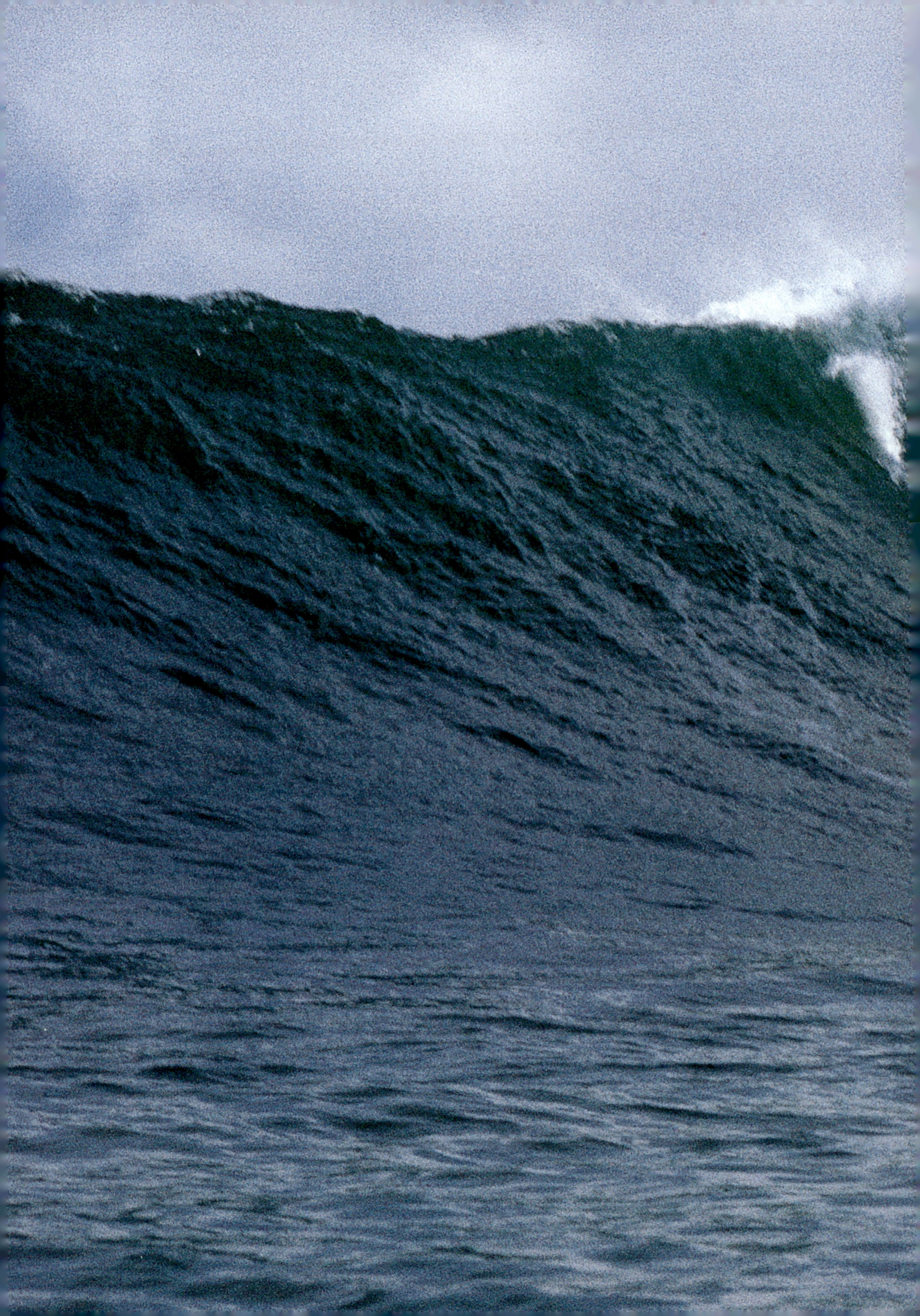

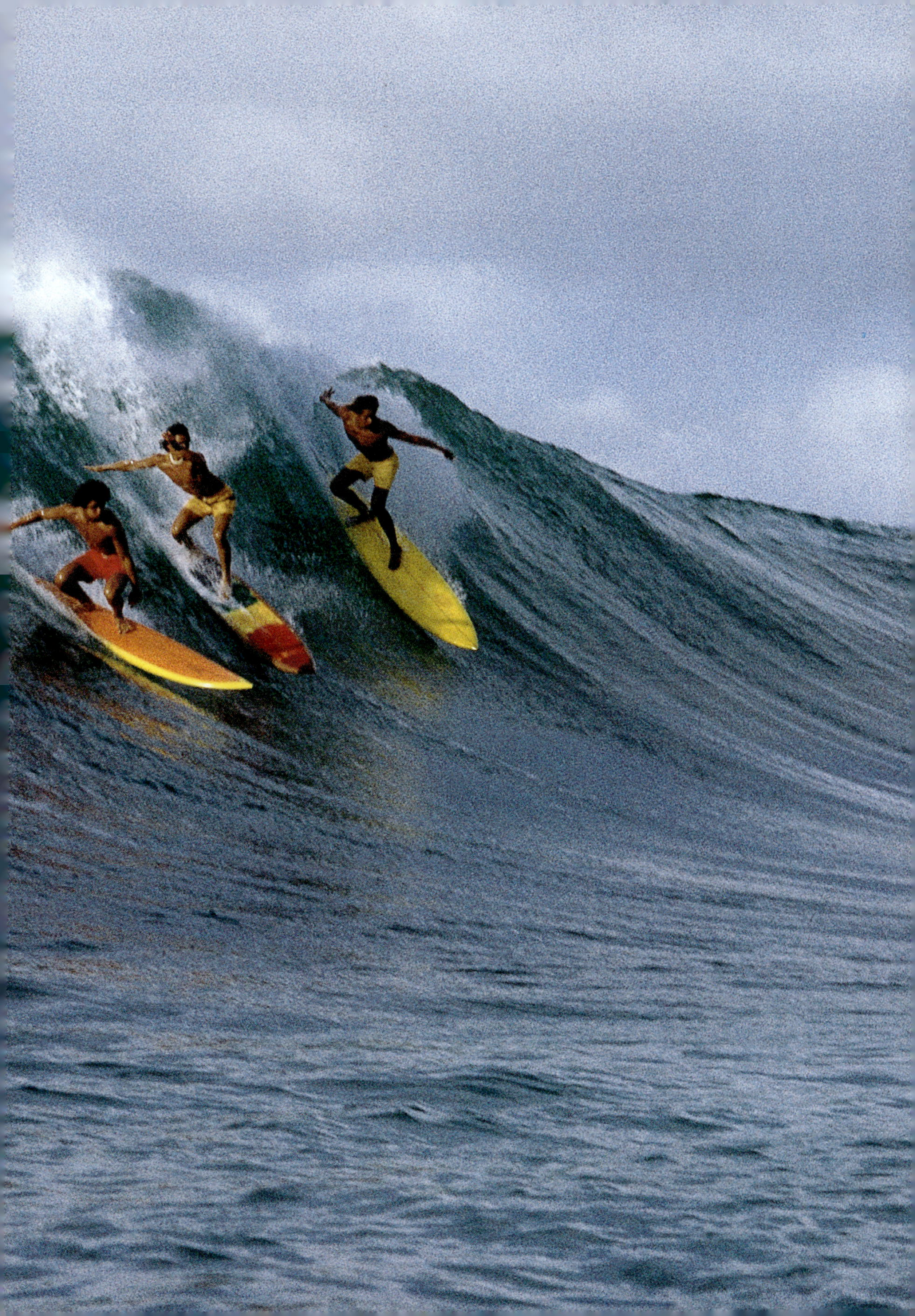

Margo Godfrey-Oberg, Makaha, 1968

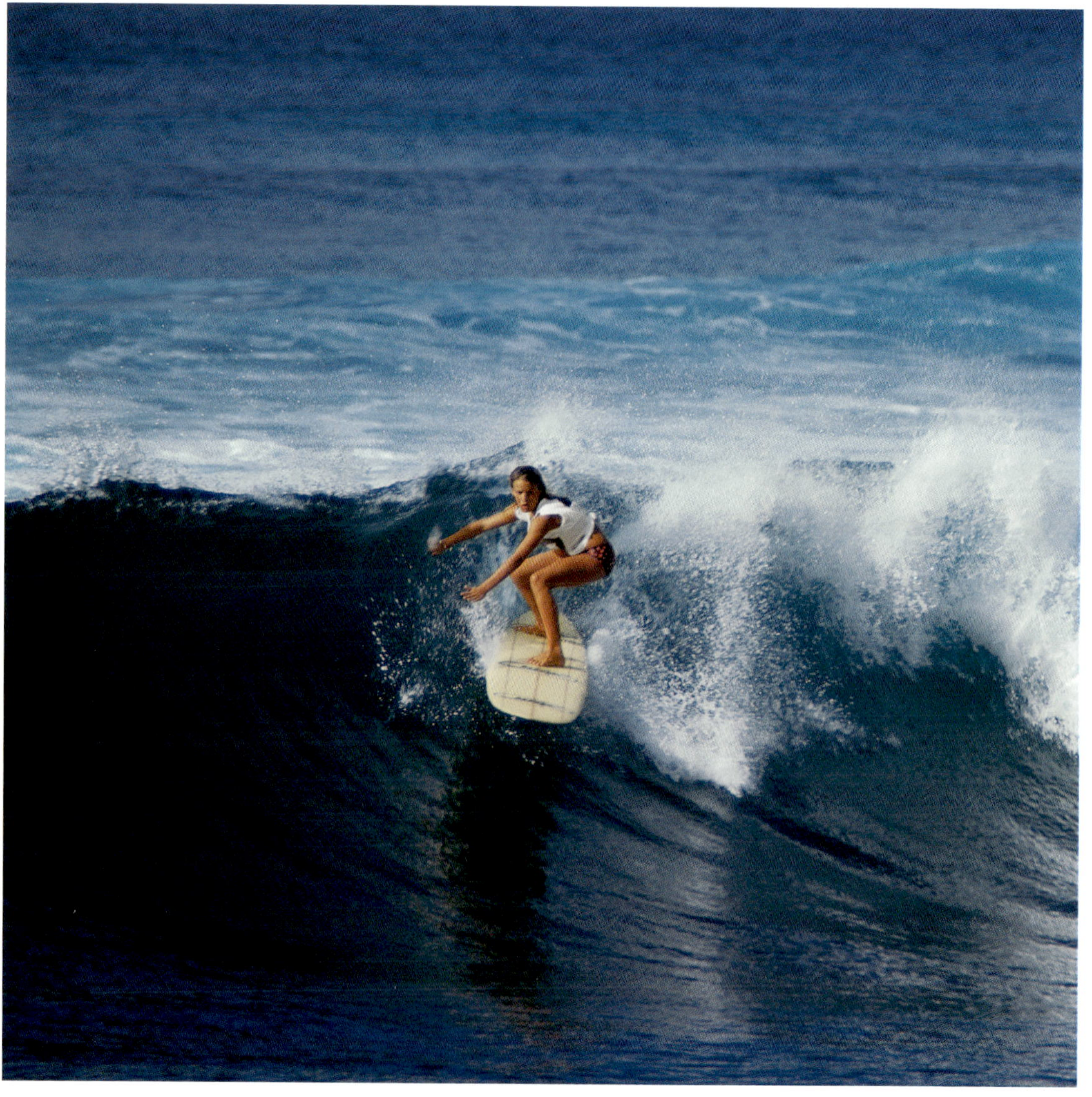

**Dale Dahlin, Haleiwa, 1977**

Dahlin, one of the North Shore's
best female surfers, was known as
"Mrs. Haleiwa." Her son Kanoa is
a world-class longboarder.

Dahlin, eine der besten Surferinnen
des North Shore, war als „Mrs.
Haleiwa" bekannt. Ihr Sohn Kanoa
ist ein Weltklasse-Longboarder.

Dale Dahlin, qui fut l'une des
meilleures surfeuses du North
Shore, était surnommée « Mrs.
Haleiwa ». Son fils Kanoa est un
longboarder de renommée
mondiale.

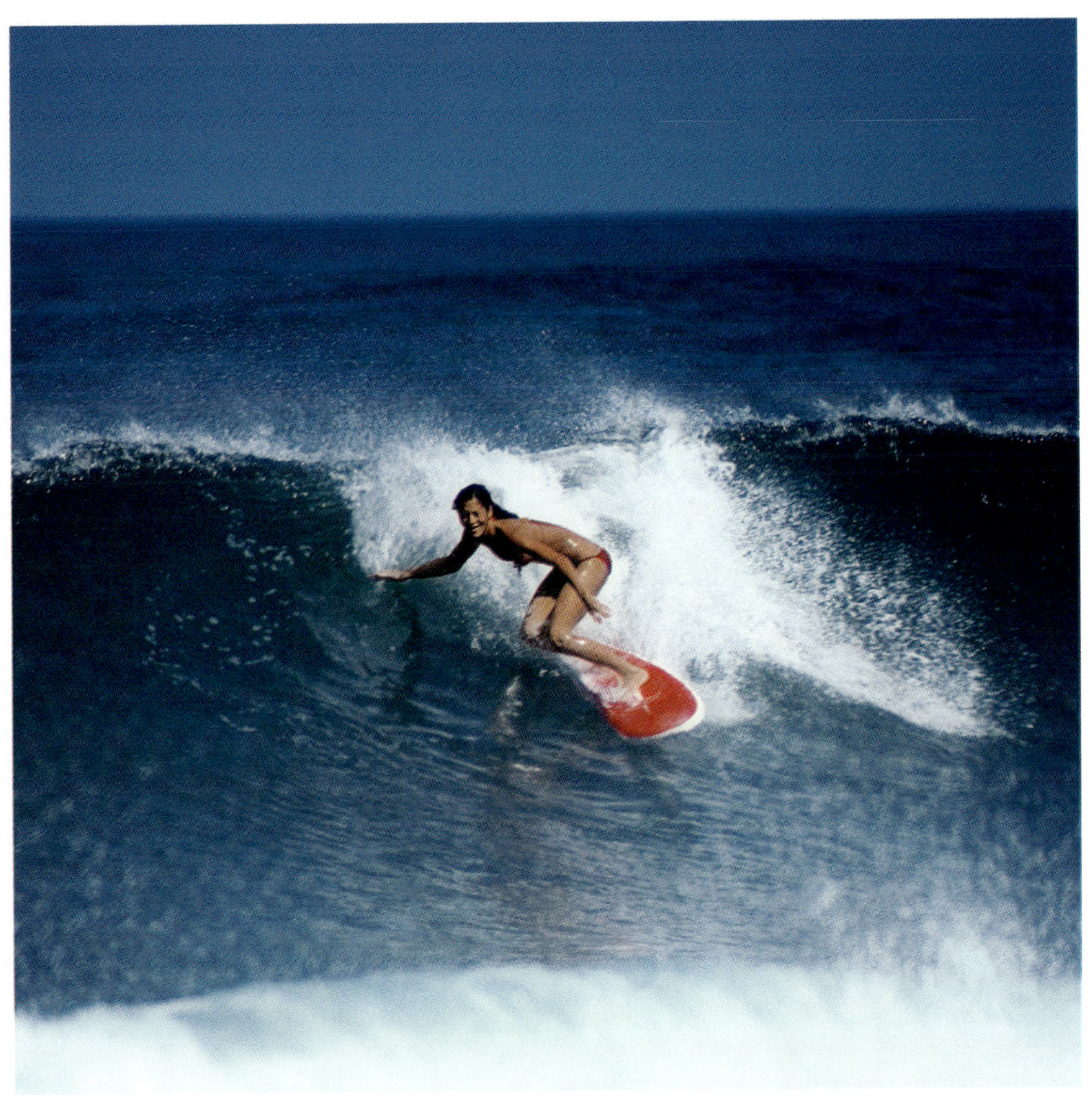

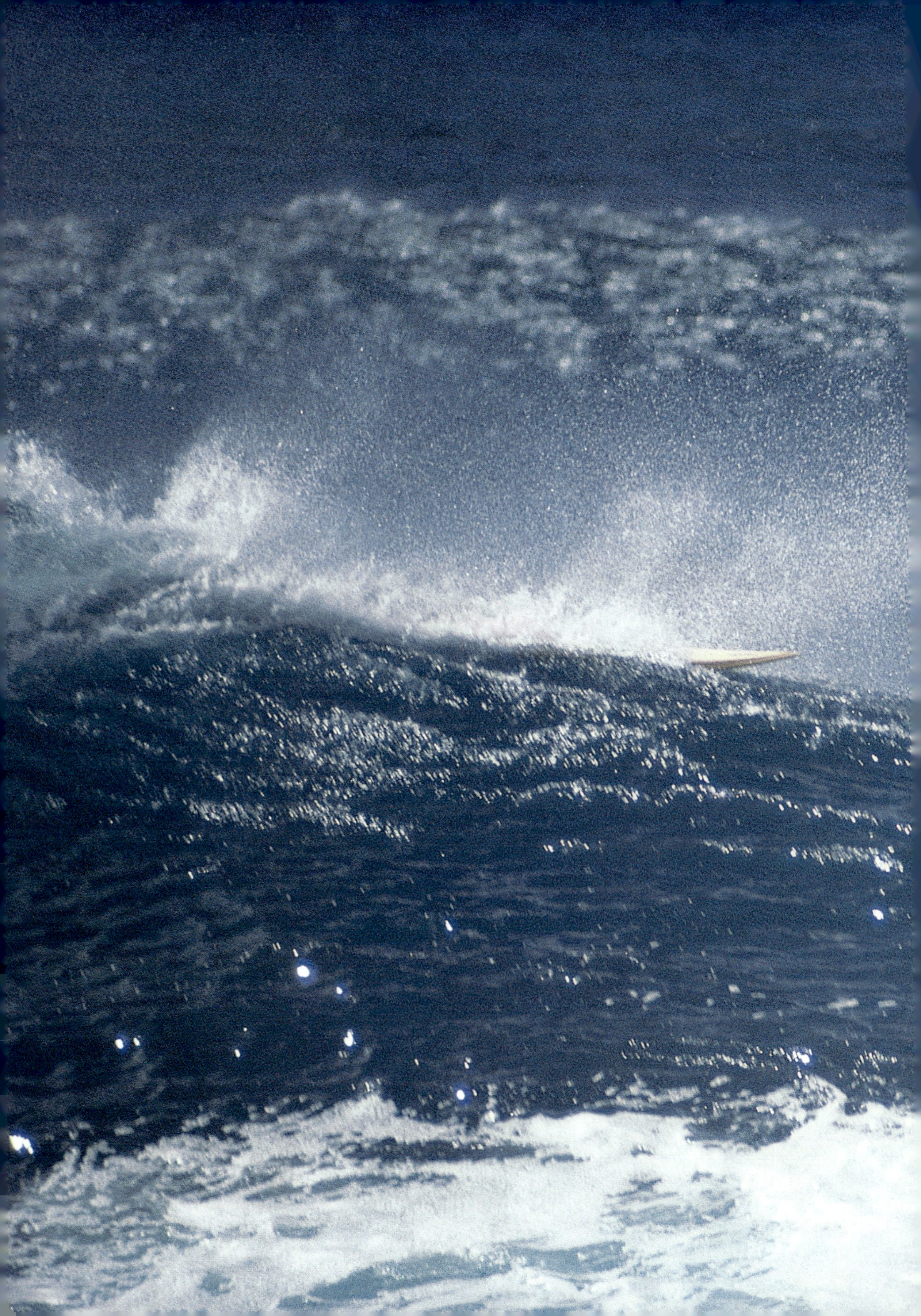

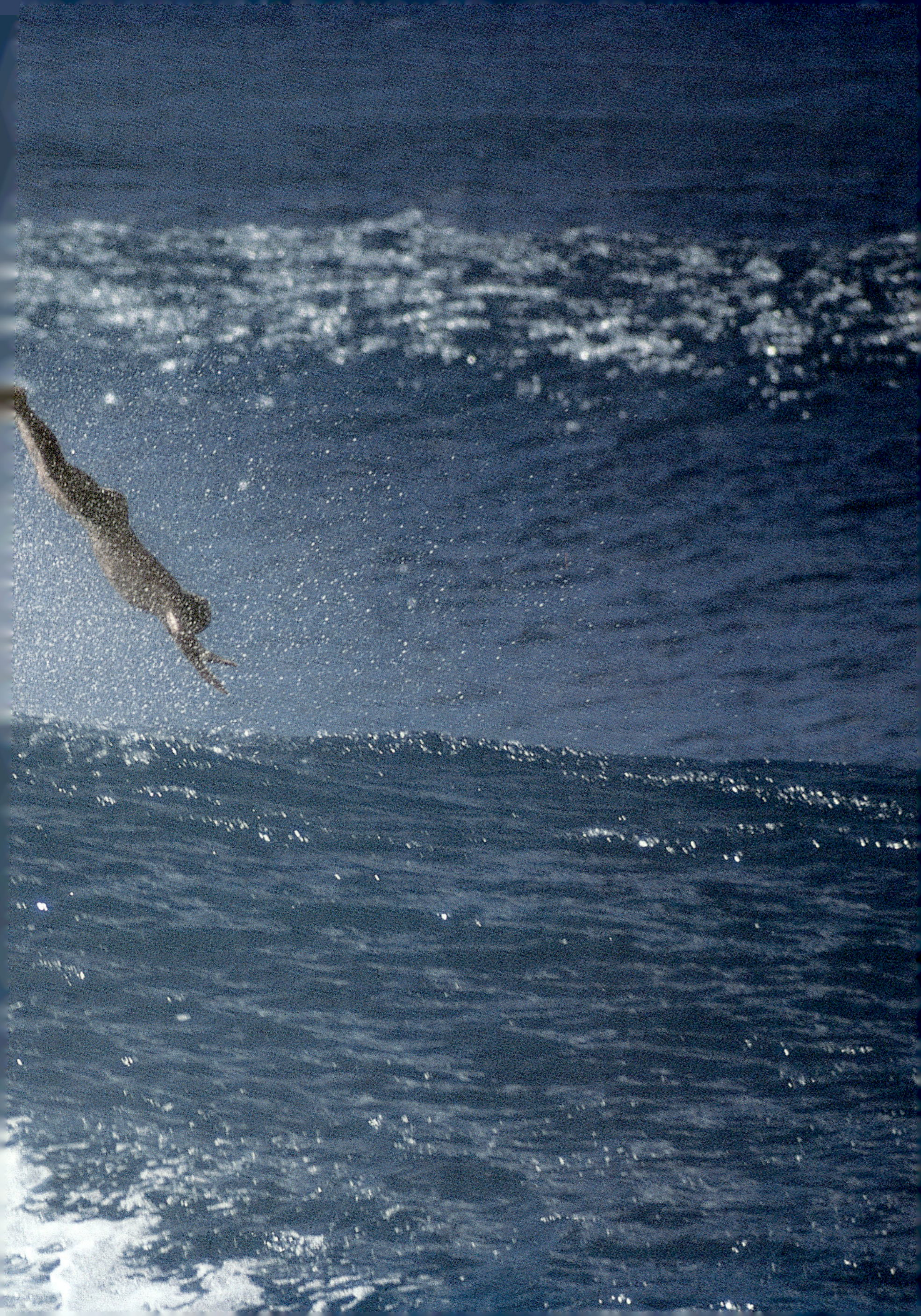

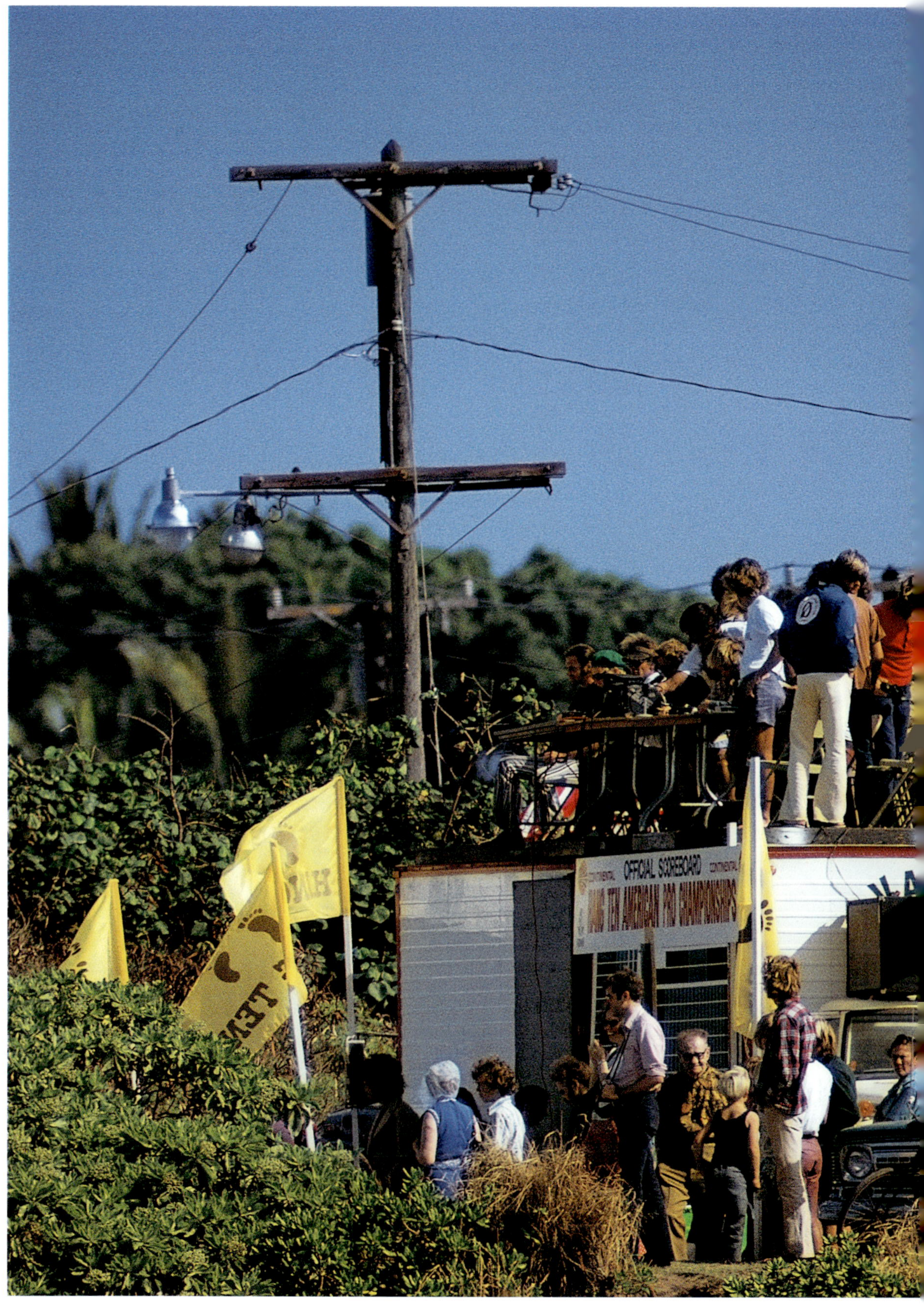
OFFICIAL SCOREBOARD    CONTINENTAL
BIG TEN AMERICAN PRO CHAMPIONSHIPS

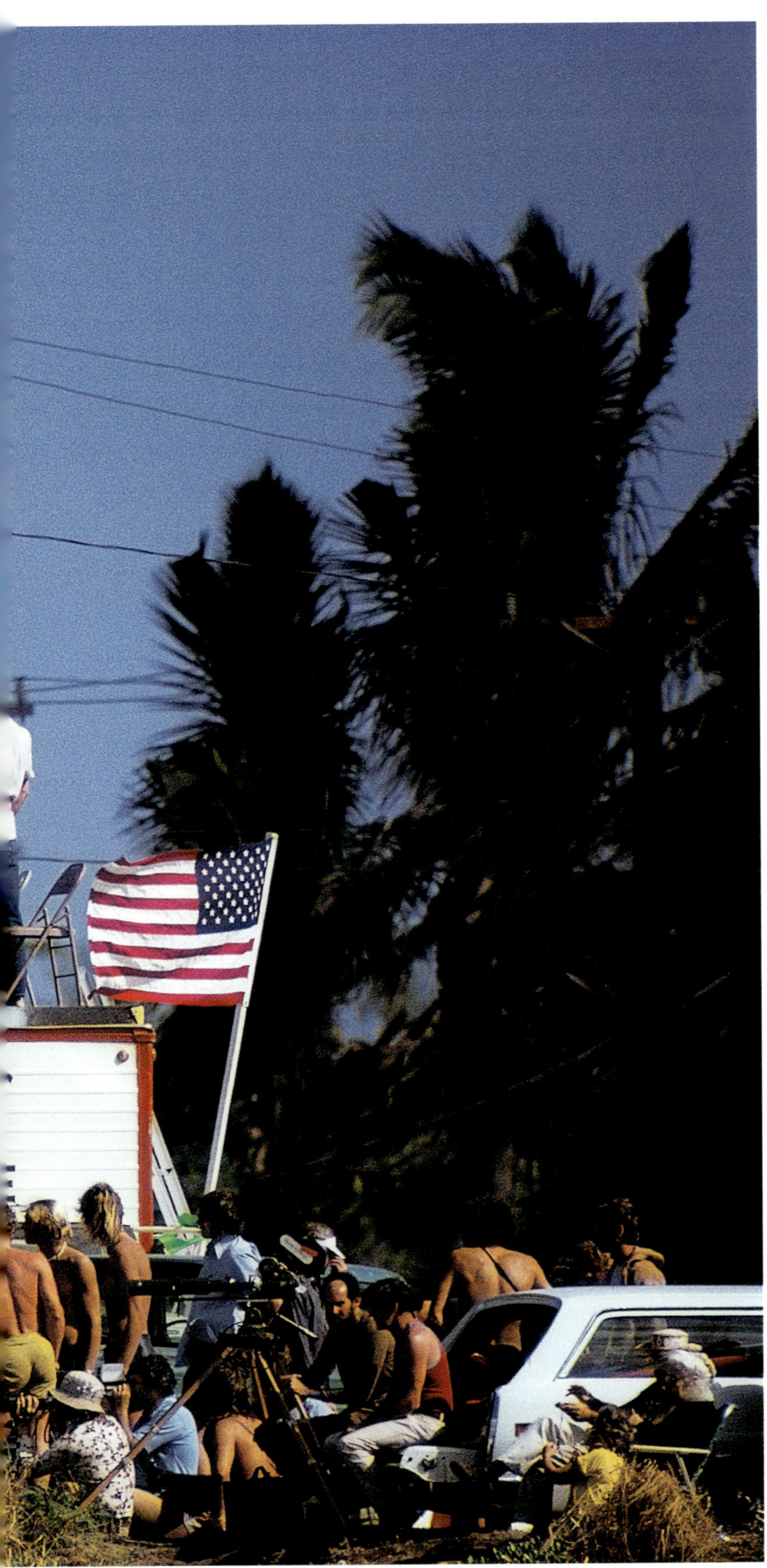

Pages 370–371
**Pipeline, 1980**

Pre-leash Pipeline ejection.

Sturz aus der Pipeline ohne Leash.

Un surfeur sans leash se fait
éjecter par une vague de Pipeline.

**Sunset Beach, 1972**

Judges' stand at the Duke Classic.
Big-wave specialist James "Booby"
Jones won this year.

Punktrichterstand beim Duke
Classic. In diesem Jahr gewann
der Big-Wave-Spezialist James
„Booby" Jones.

Podium du jury de la Duke Classic.
Cette année-là, la victoire est
remportée par le spécialiste du
*big-wave riding* James « Booby »
Jones.

**Makaha, 1965**

Founded in 1954, the annual
Makaha event was the unofficial
world championship until the early
sixties.

Der seit 1954 jährlich stattfindende Wettbewerb in Makaha
war bis in die frühen Sechziger
die inoffizielle Weltmeisterschaft.

Lancée en 1954, la rencontre
annuelle de Makaha a conservé le
statut de championnat du monde
non officiel jusqu'au début des
années 1960.

*Pages 376–377*
**Haleiwa, 1972**



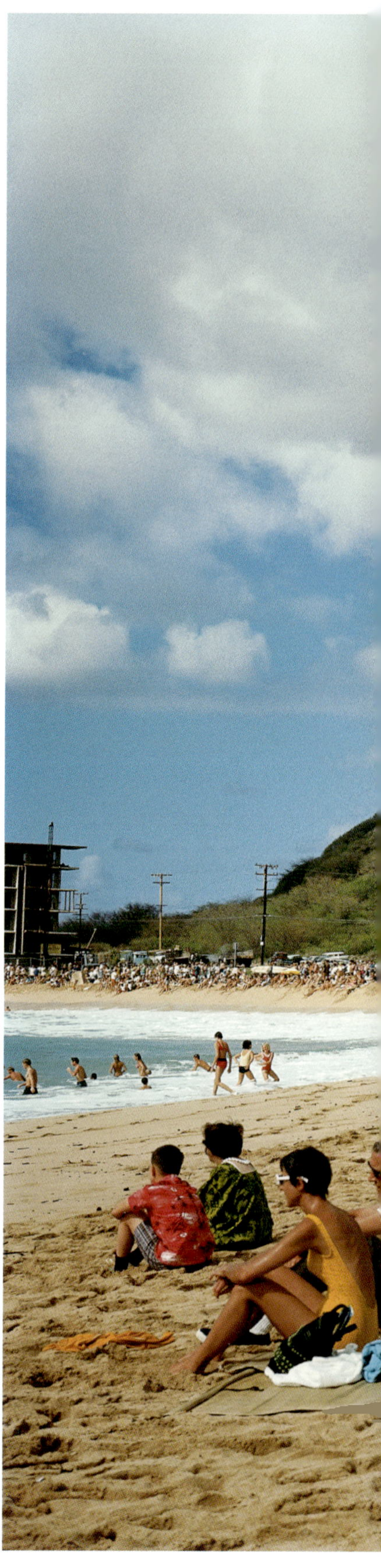

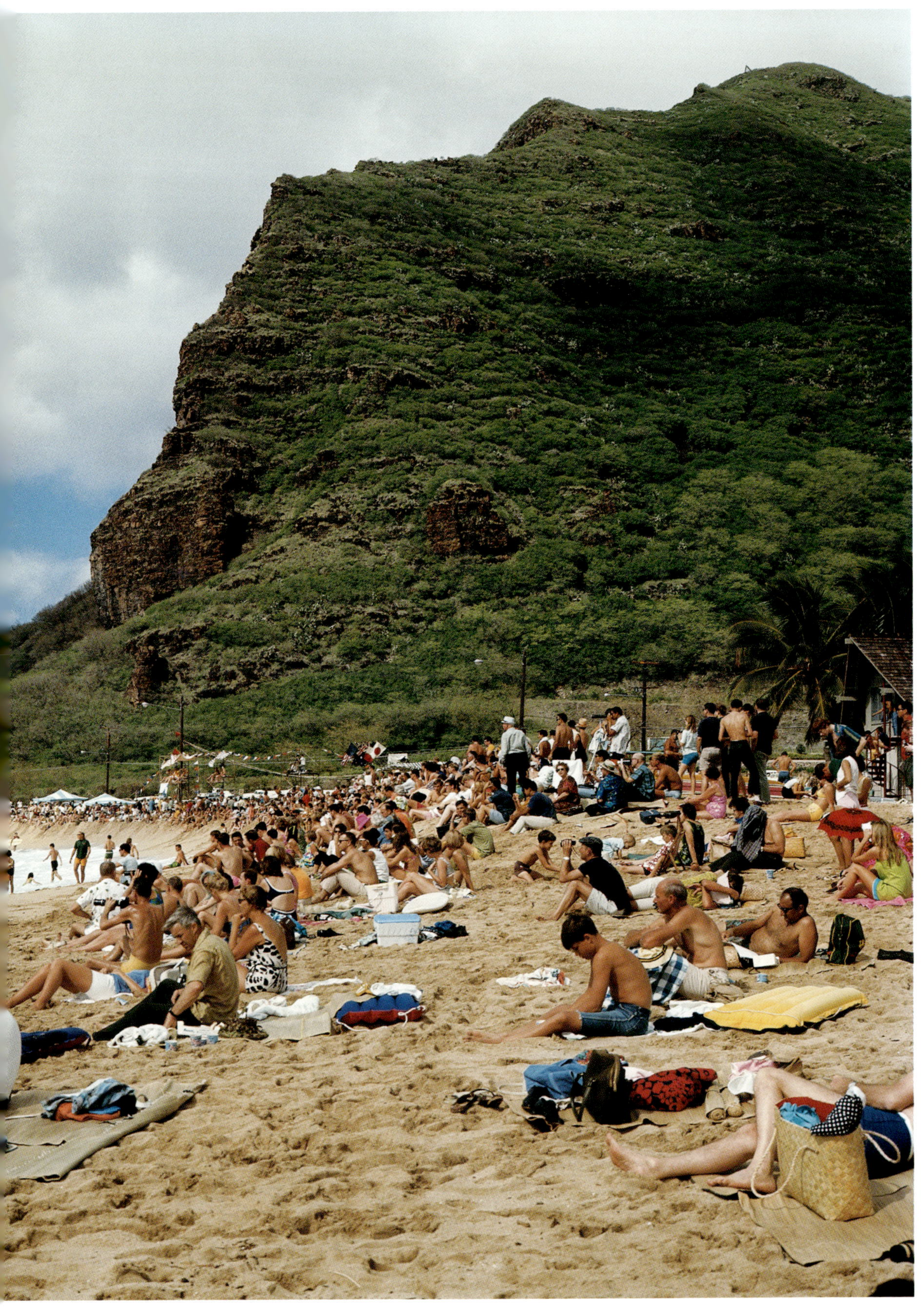

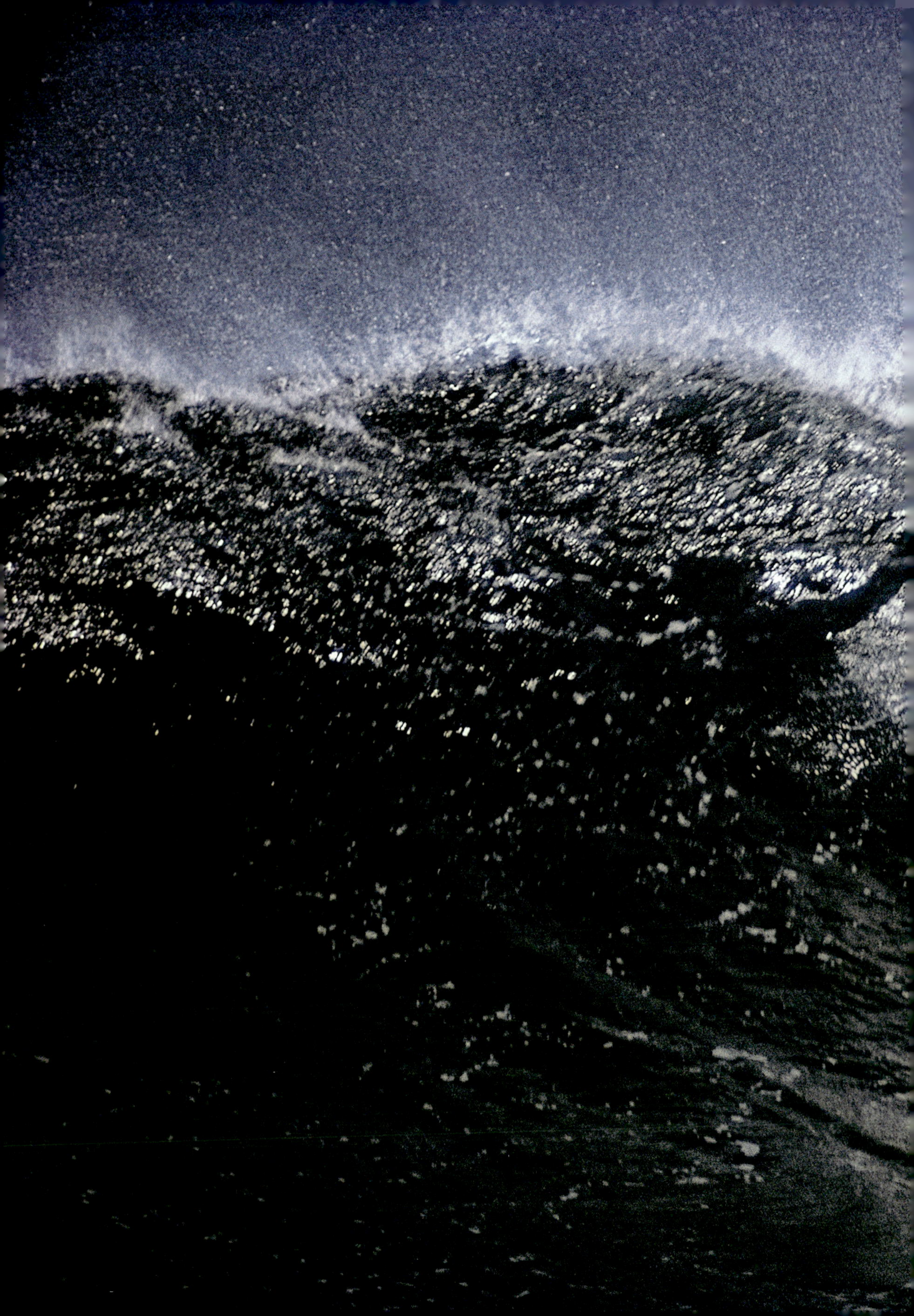

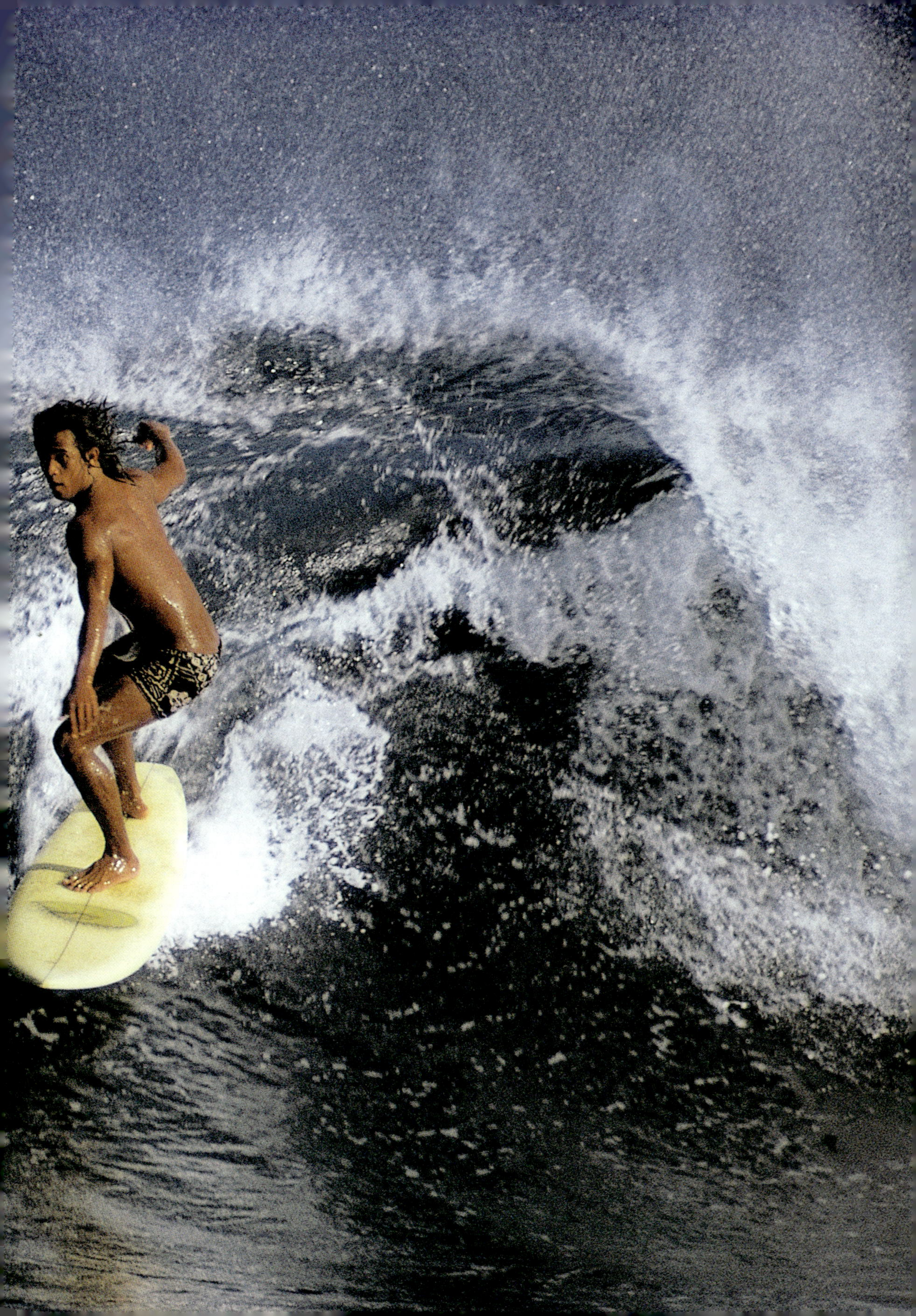

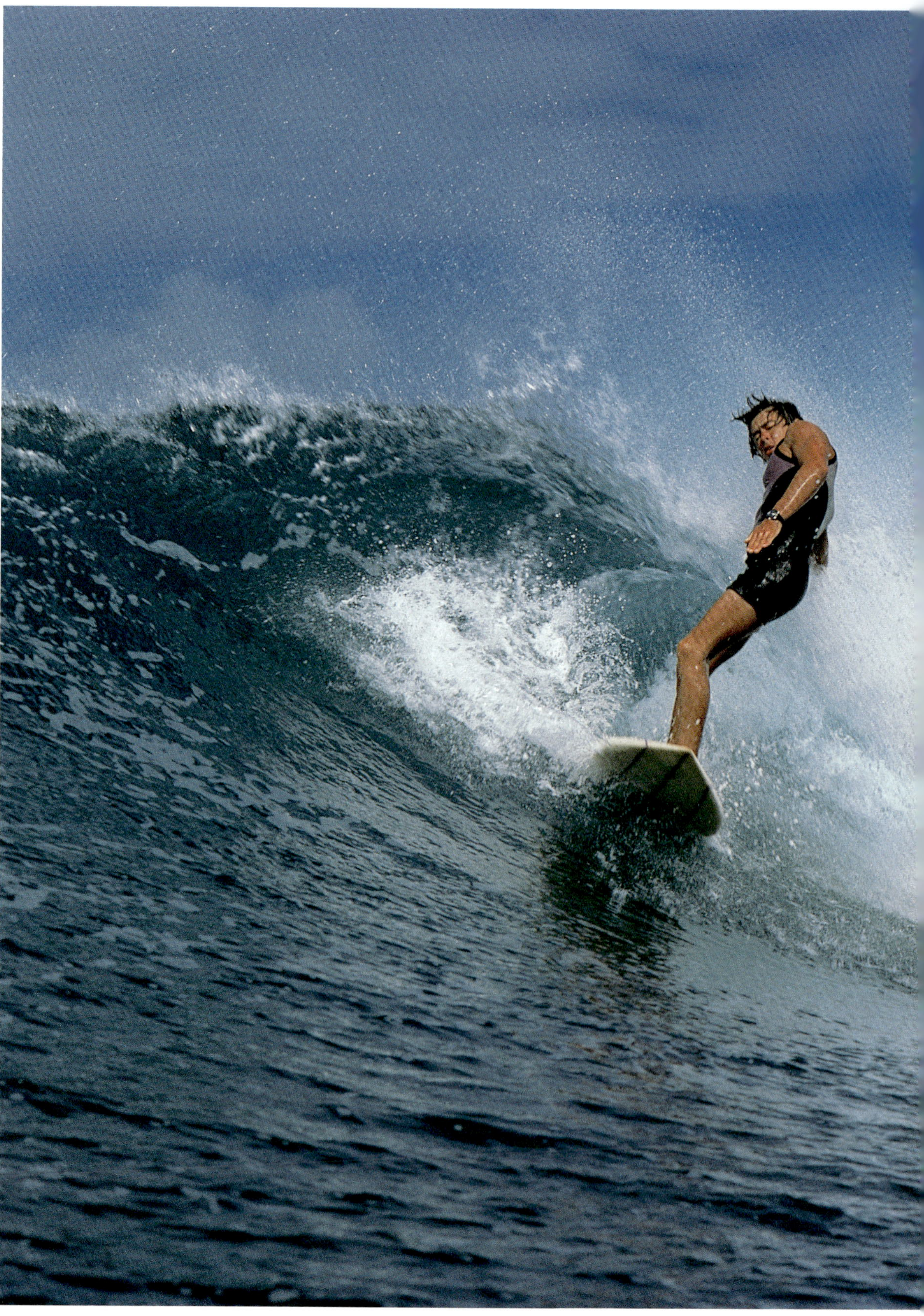

**James Jones, Velzyland,
North Shore, 1974**

Filmmaker Bruce Brown named
Velzyland in honor of boardmaker
Dale Velzy, who sponsored his first
movie, *Slippery When Wet,* in
1958.

Der Filmemacher Bruce Brown
benannte Velzyland nach dem
Board-Hersteller Dale Velzy, der
1958 seinen ersten Film *Slippery
When Wet* sponserte.

Le réalisateur Bruce Brown fut
baptisé « Velzyland » en l'honneur
du shaper Dale Velzy qui sponsorisa
son premier film, *Slippery When
Wet,* en 1958.

*Pages 380–381*
**Pipeline, 1970**

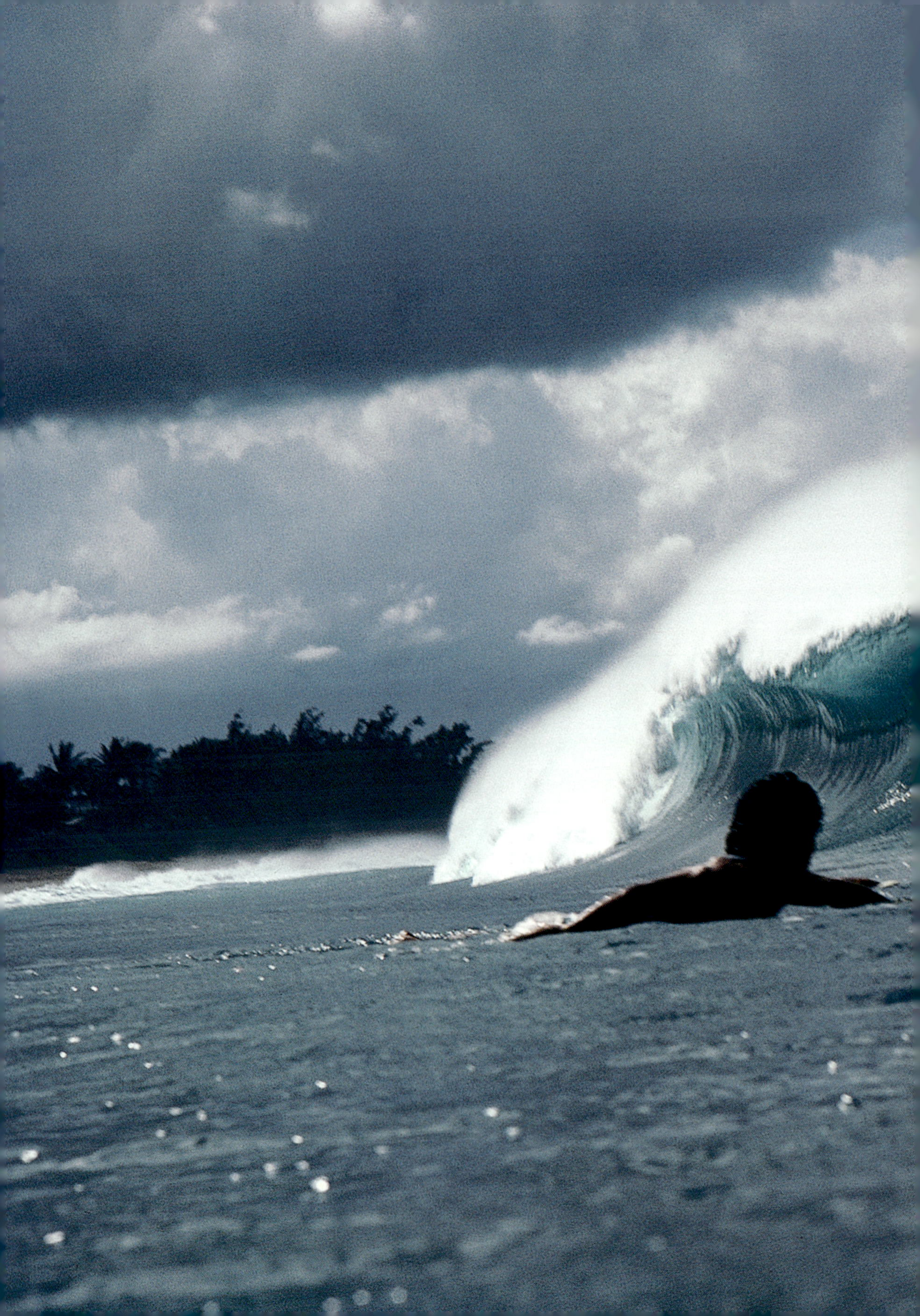

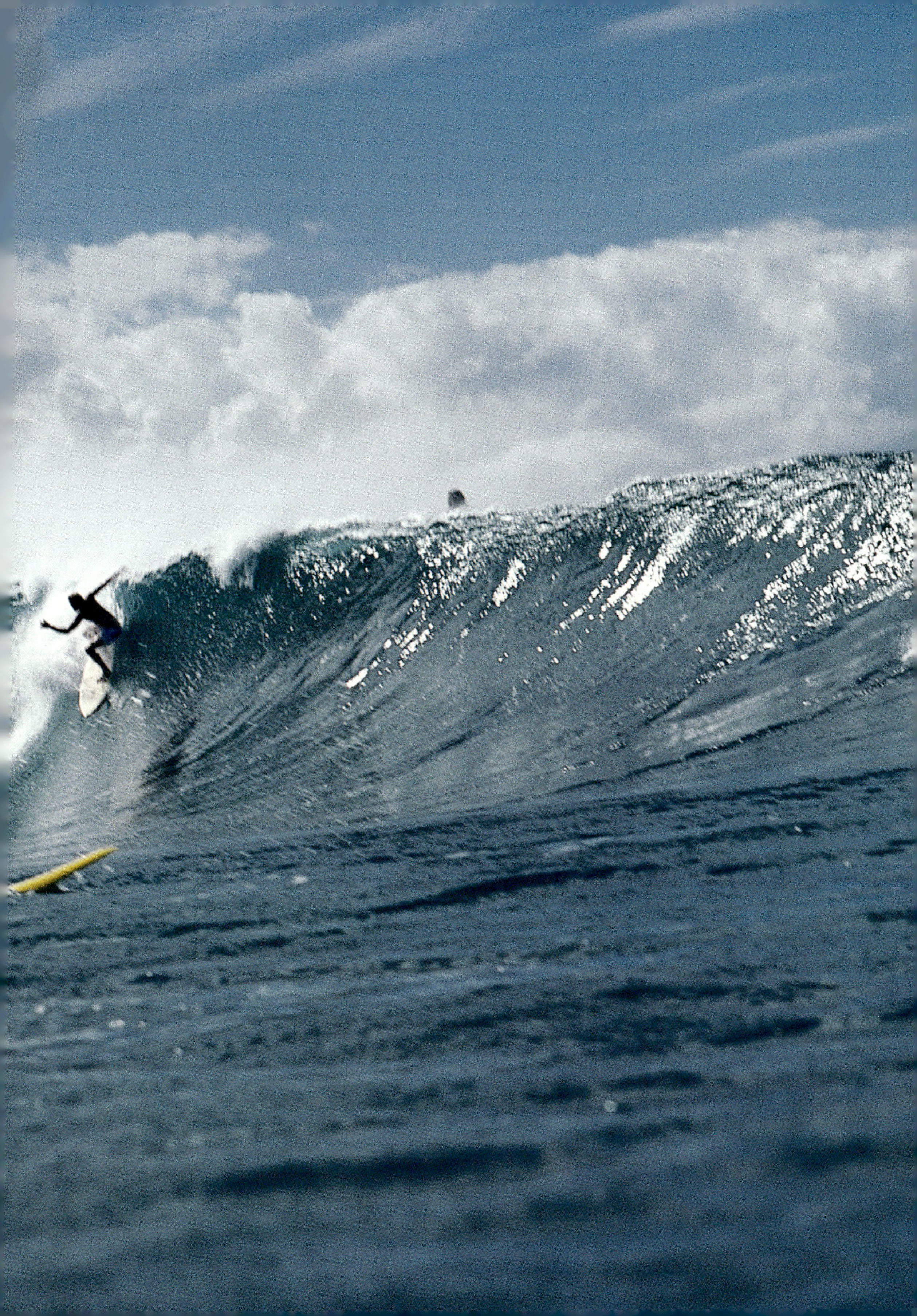

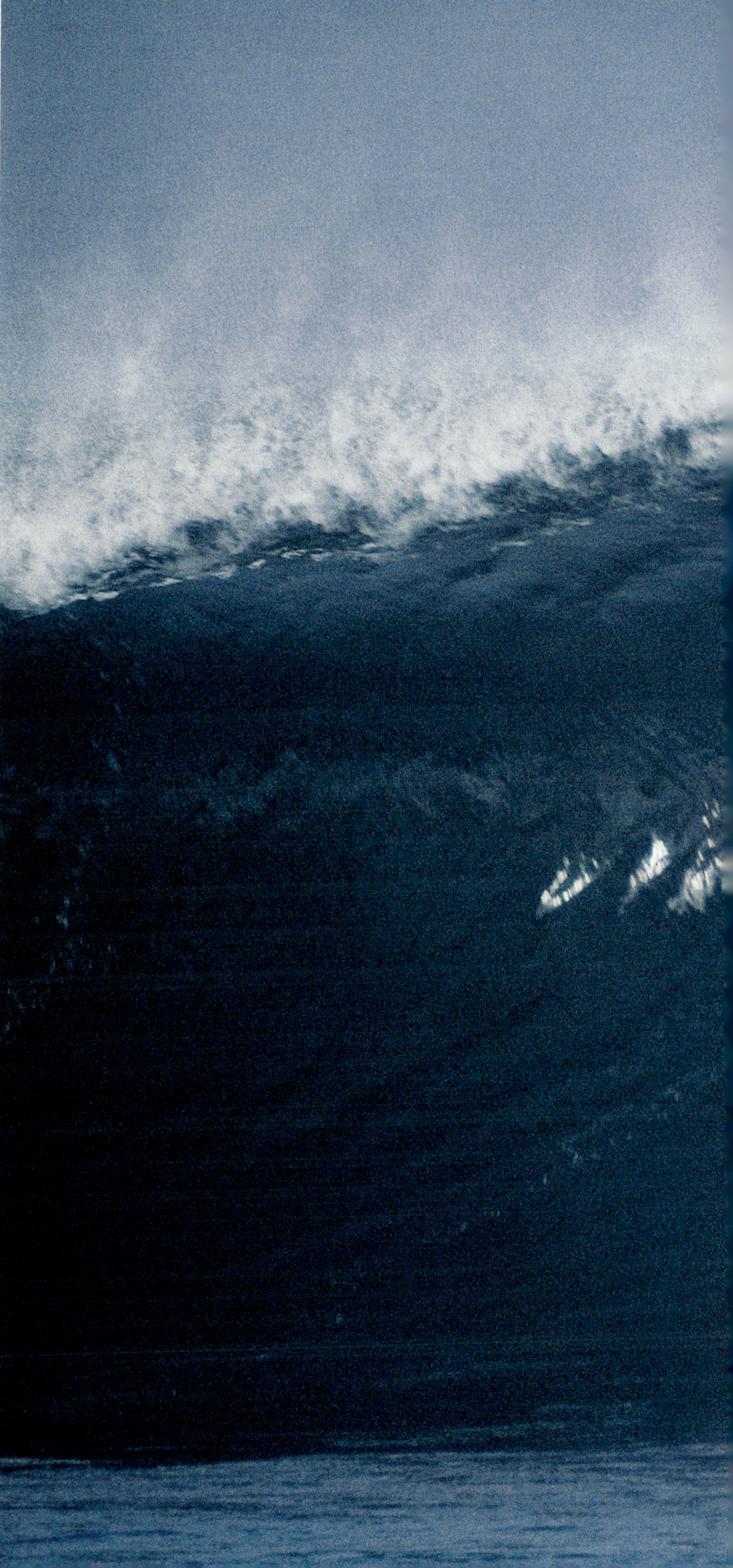

**Mark Richards, Pipeline, 1982**

Although a four-time world champion and a 1980 Pipeline Masters winner, the Australian Richards said he never liked surfing Pipeline.

Obwohl er vierfacher Weltmeister und Sieger bei den 1980er-Pipeline-Masters war, sagte der Australier Richards, dass er die Pipeline nicht gern surfe.

Malgré ses quatre titres de champion du monde et sa victoire aux Pipeline Masters en 1980, l'Australien Mark Richards a affirmé qu'il n'avait jamais aimé surfer Pipeline.

*Pages 384–385*
**Pipeline, 1970**

This surfer has successfully made the drop and is setting up for the tube.

Dieser Surfer hat den Start gemeistert und wappnet sich für den Kanal.

Drop réussi pour ce surfeur qui s'apprête à enchaîner sur un tube.

*Pages 386–387*
**Pipeline, circa 1972**

*Pages 388–389*
**Rocky Point, 1972**

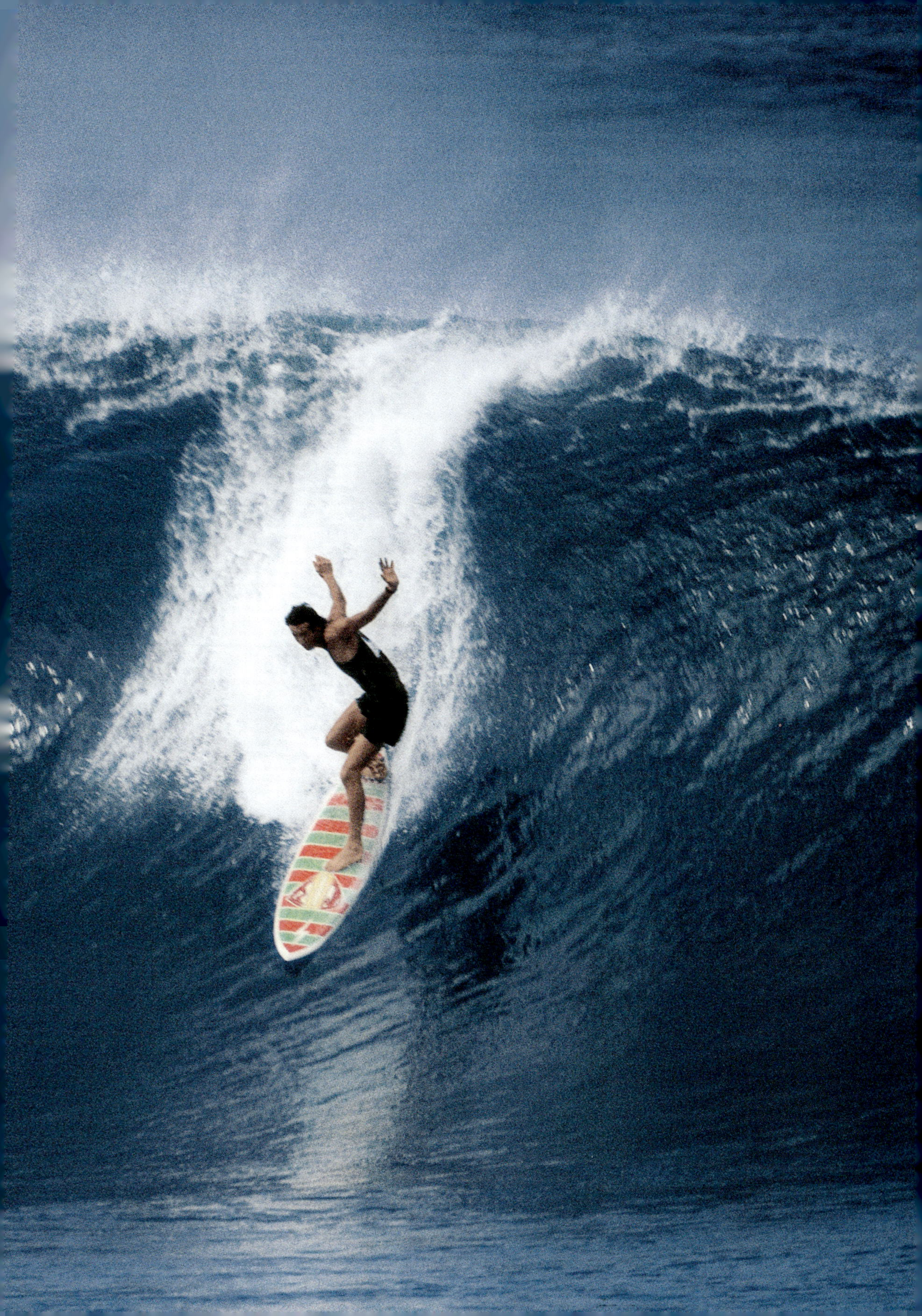

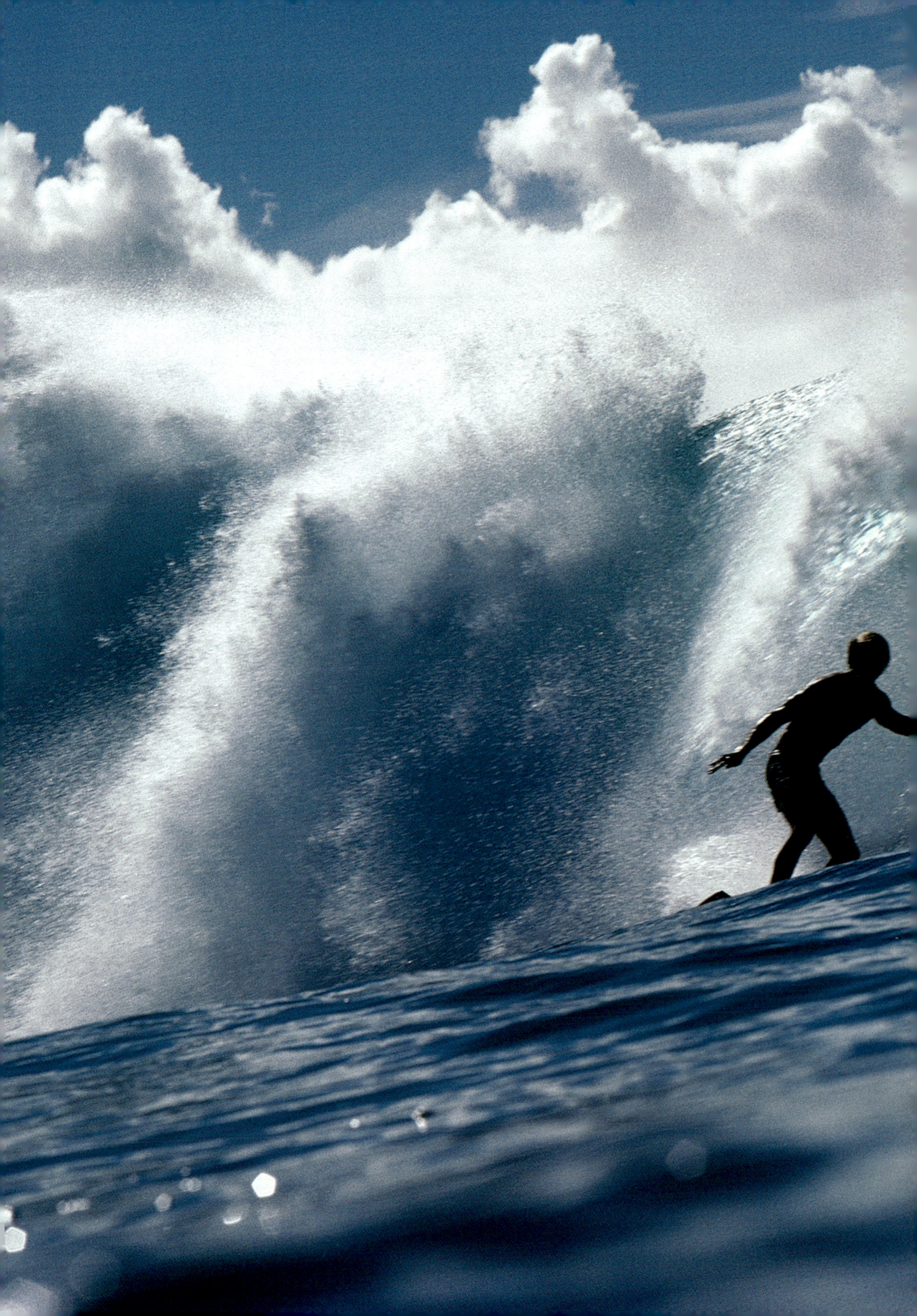

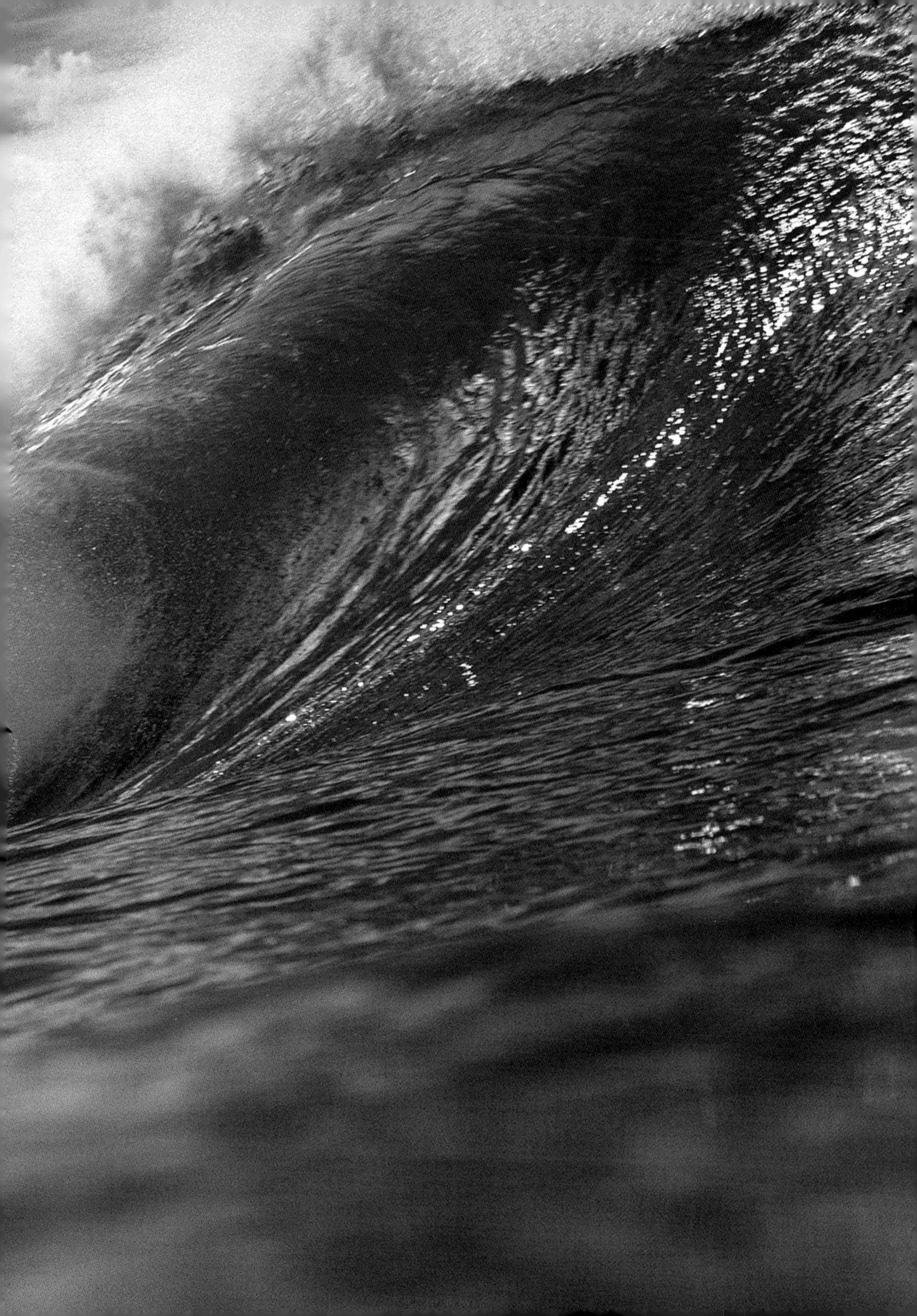

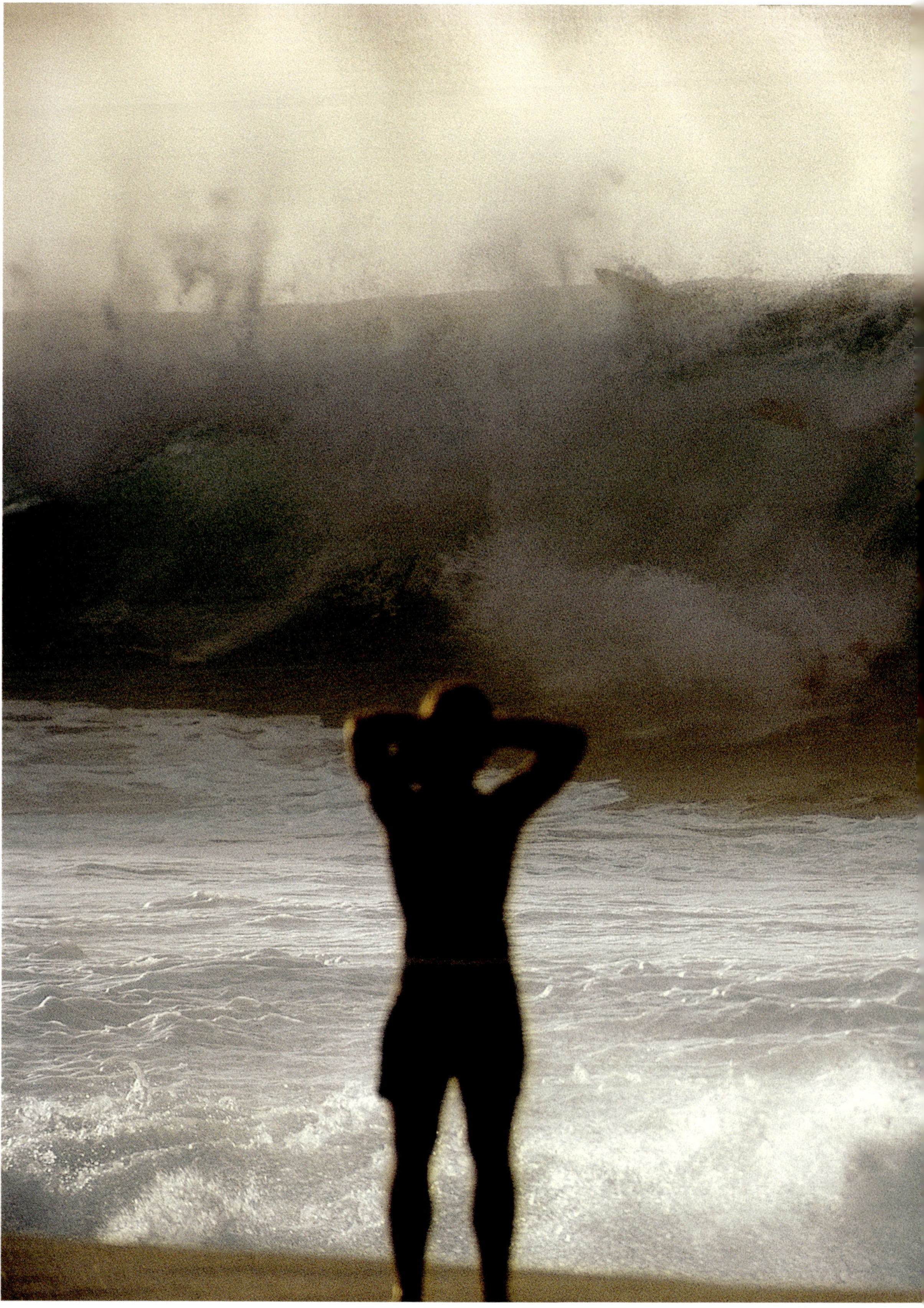

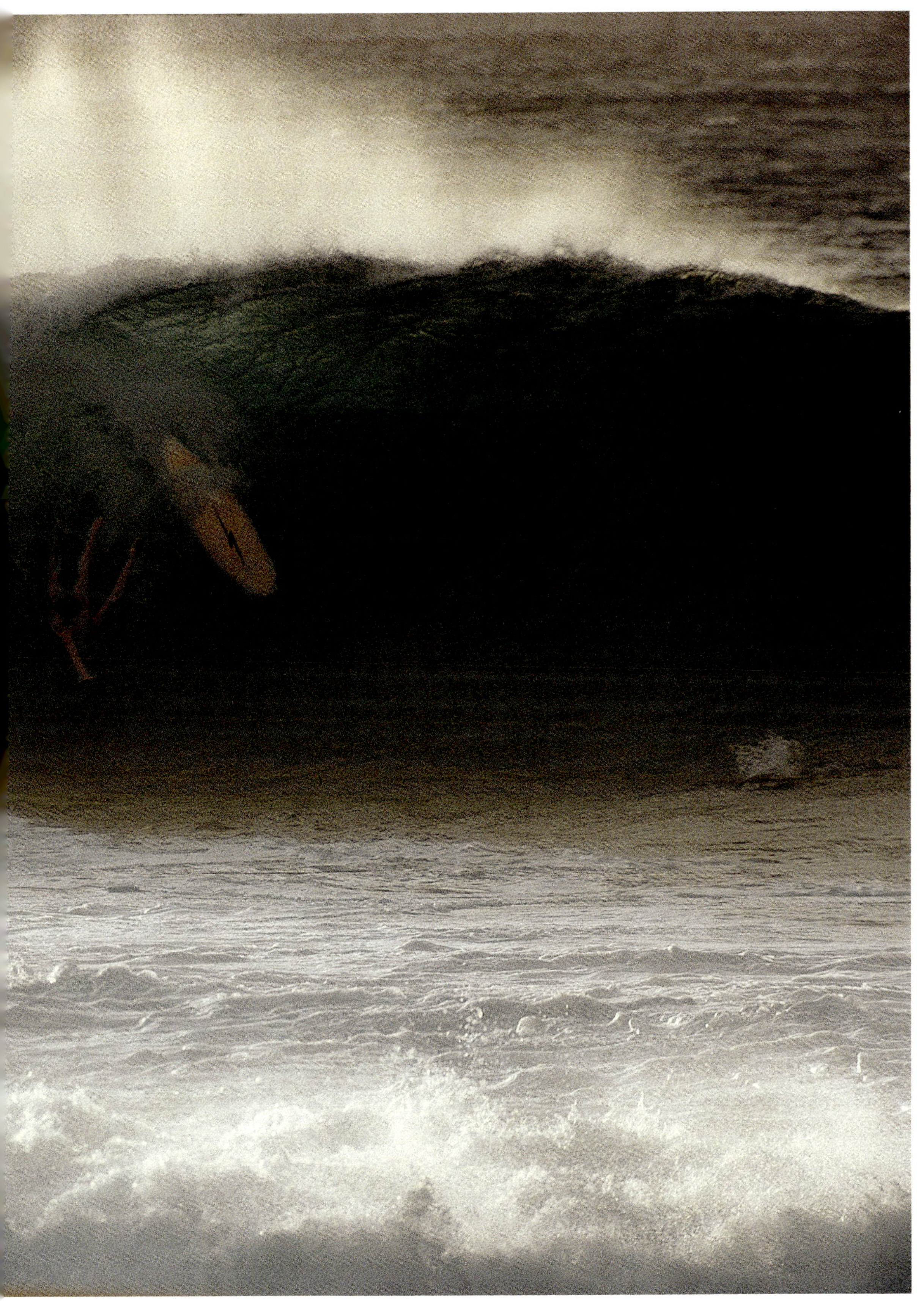

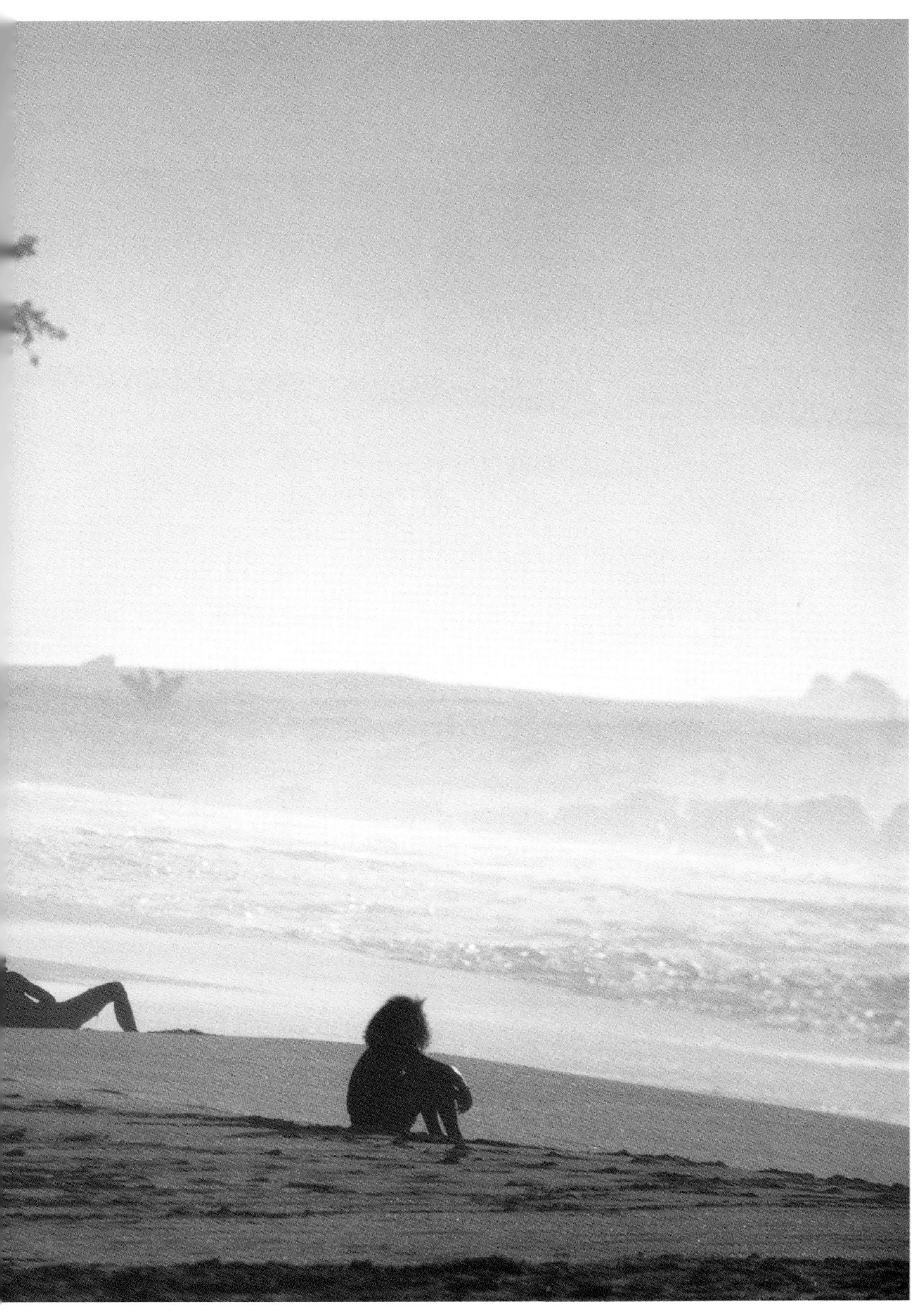

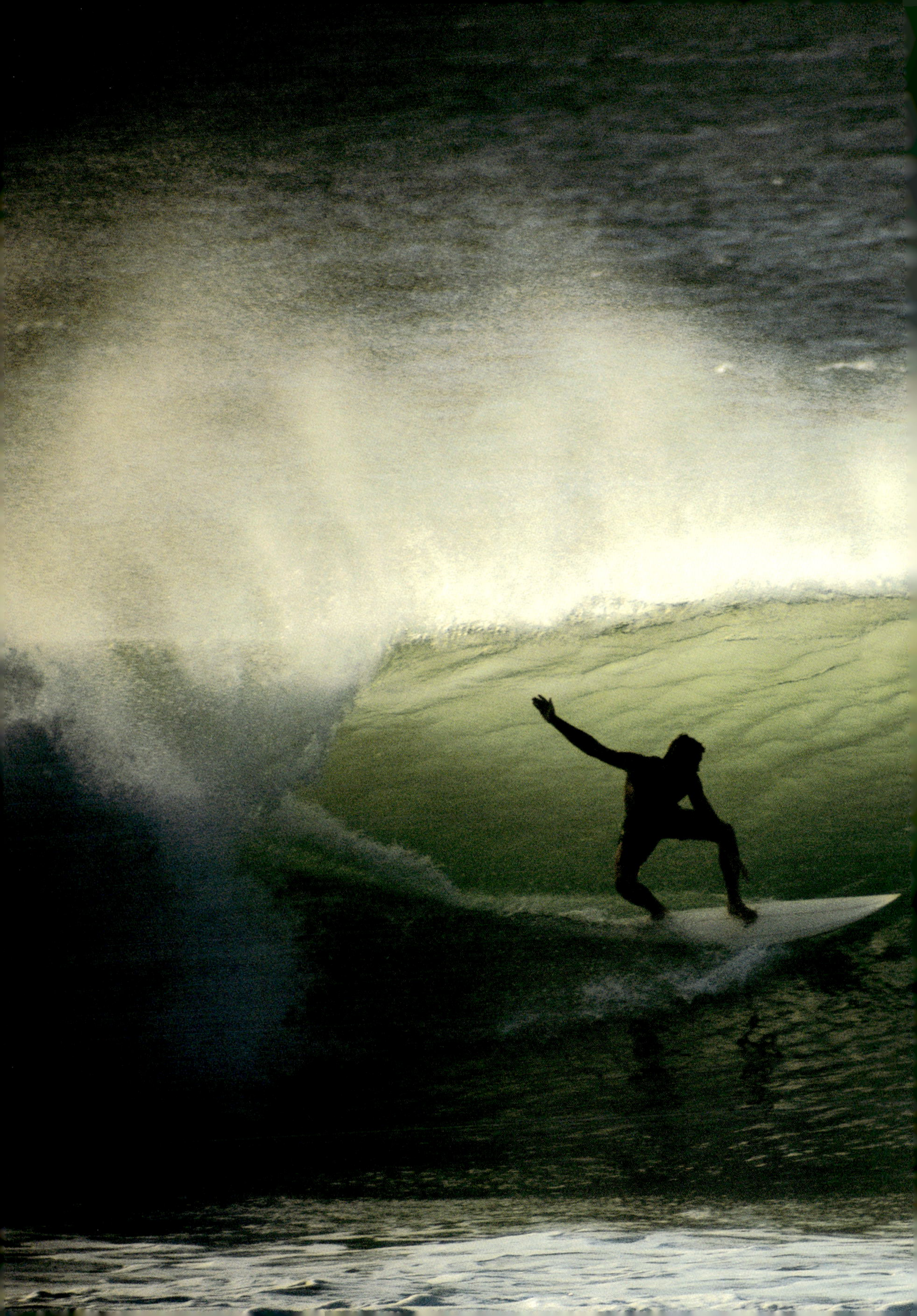

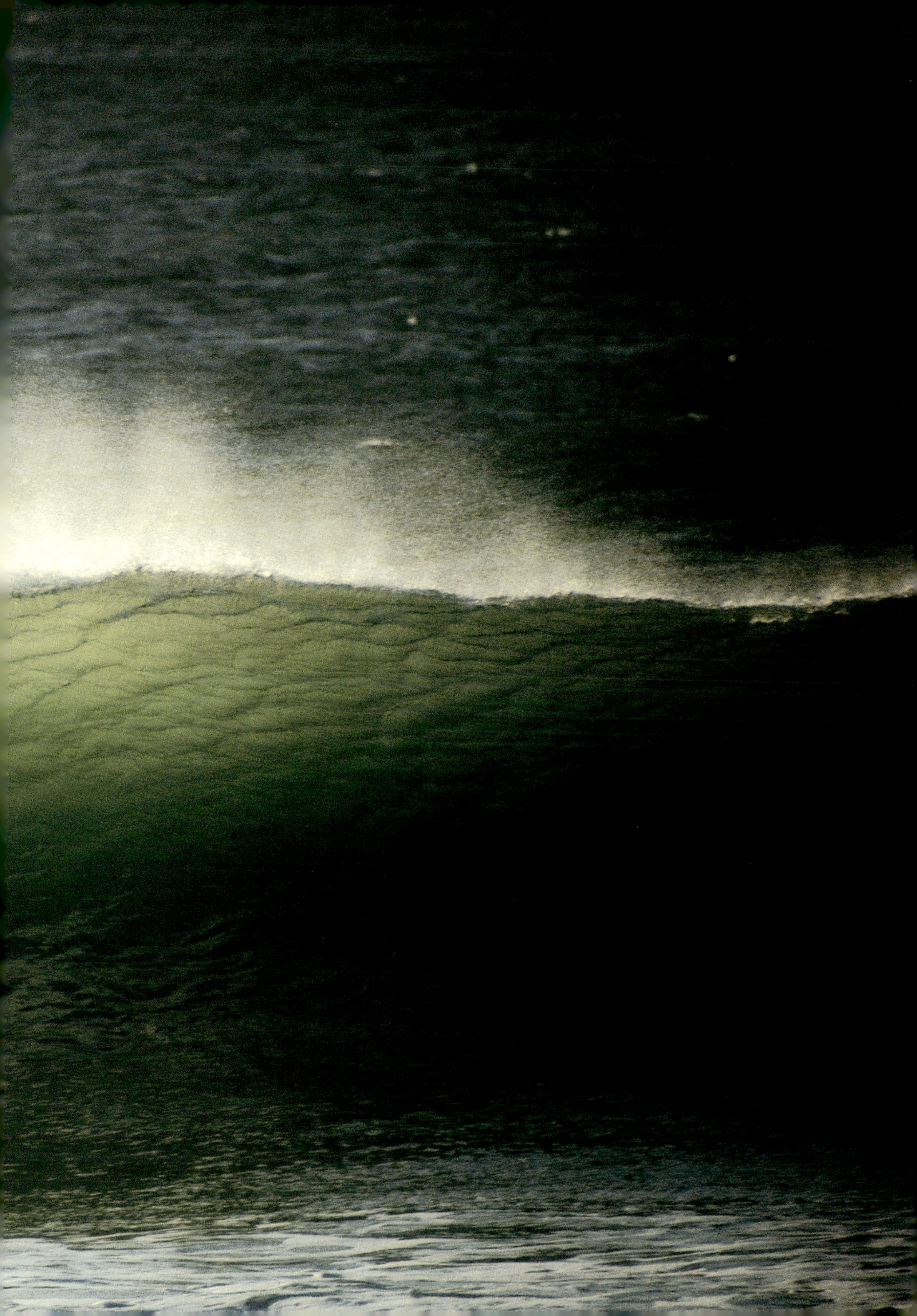

*Pages 390–391*
**Pipeline, circa 1972**

*Pages 394–395*
**Ehukai Beach, 1969**

The "Swell of '69" was considered the swell of the century, with monster waves of up to sixty feet slamming the Hawaiian Islands and causing millions of dollars in damage.

Der „Swell von 69" galt als Swell des Jahrhunderts. Gigantische, bis zu zwanzig Meter hohe Wellen peitschten auf die hawaiianischen Inseln ein und verursachten Schäden in Millionenhöhe.

Le « Swell de 1969 » restera dans les annales comme la houle du siècle. Cette année-là, des vagues géantes de plus de vingt mètres balayèrent l'archipel hawaïen et provoquèrent plusieurs millions de dollars de dégâts.

**Midget Farrelly, Makaha, Hawaii, 1968**

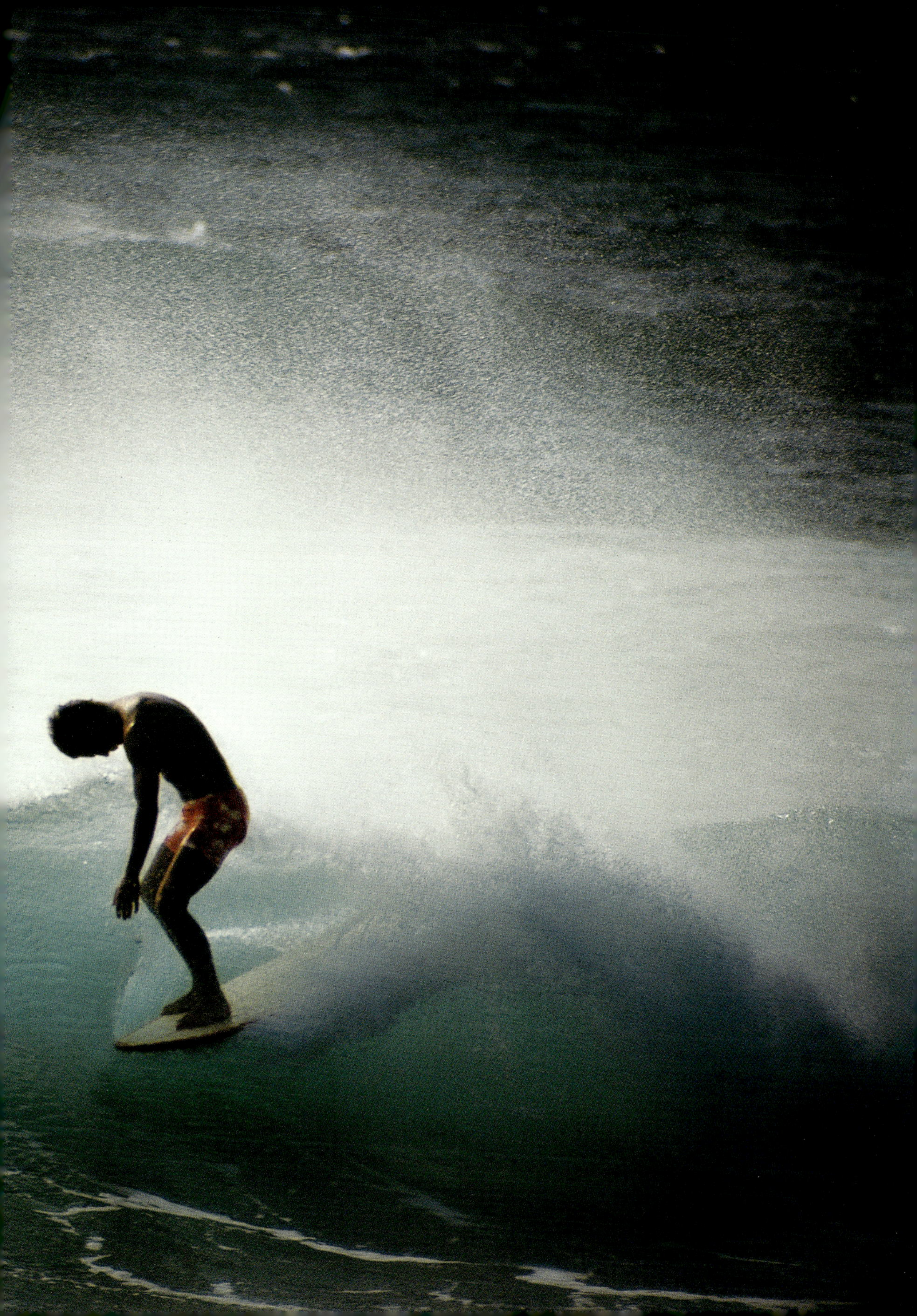

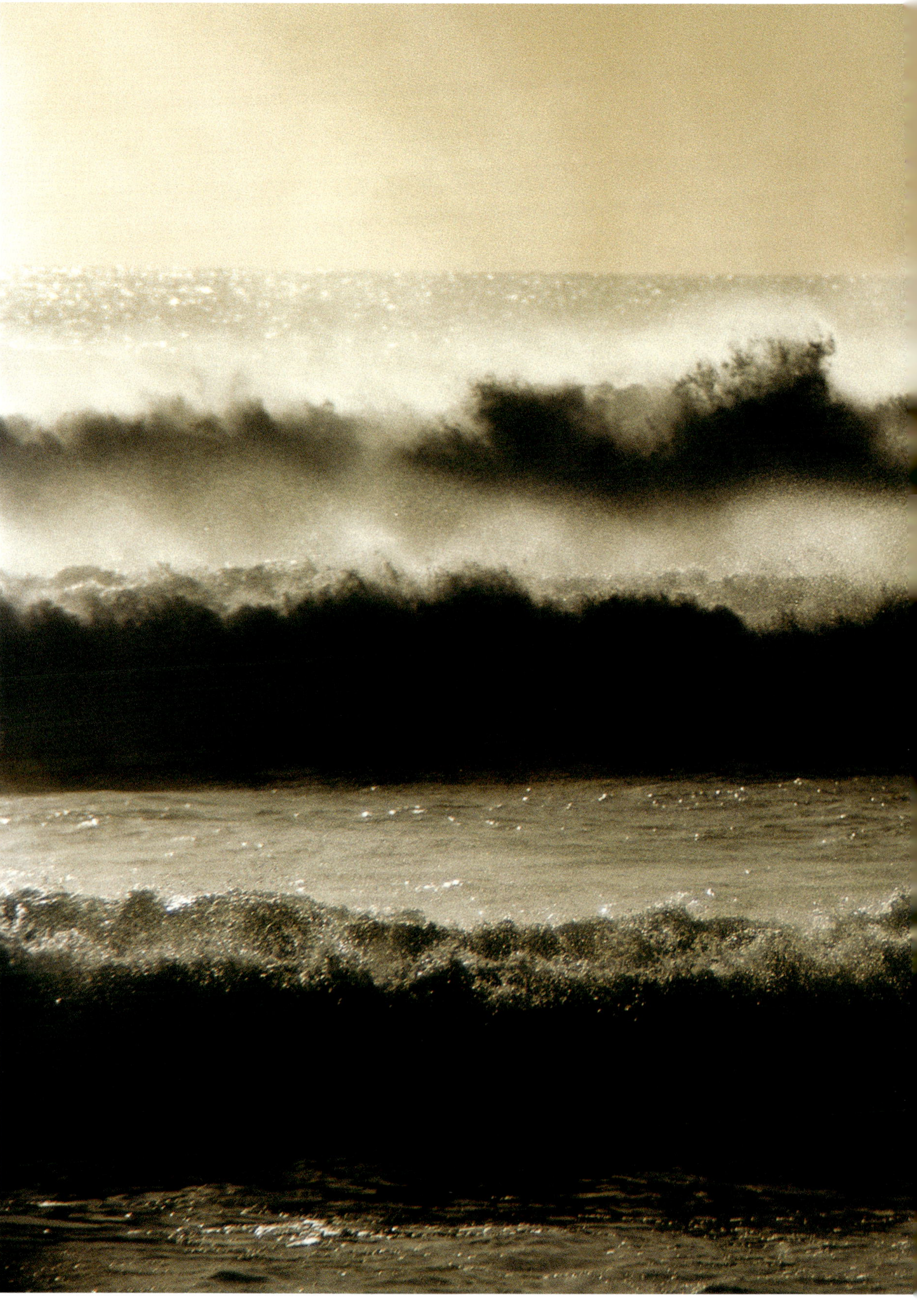

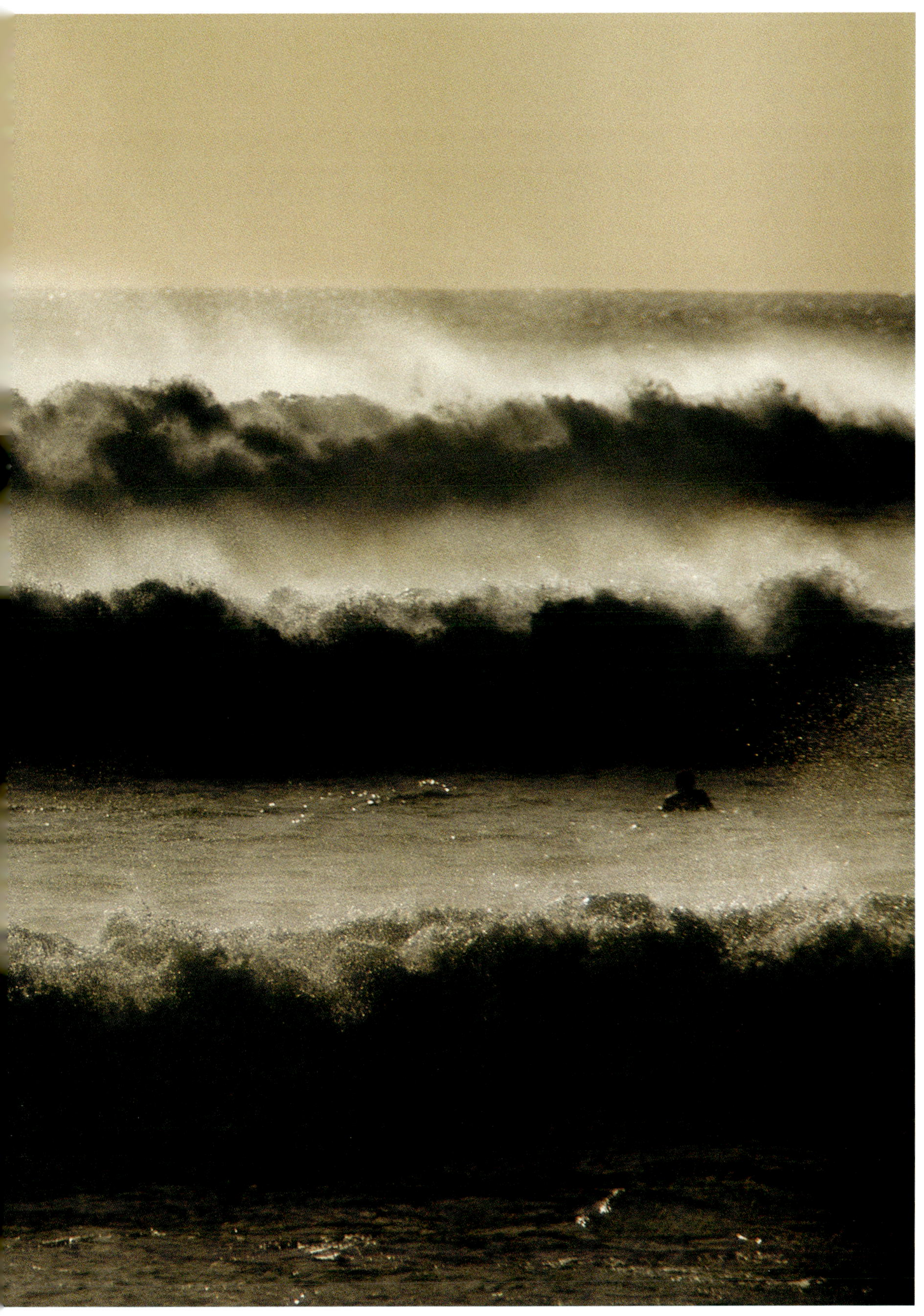

# Captions: Opening Sequence

*Page 1*
**Surf Photos by Grannis Sticker, 1963**
"Granny's" famous stickers, designed by Stuart Lough, are now collectors' items. Grannis gave one out to everyone he met.

Die berühmten Aufkleber von „Granny", entworfen von Stuart Lough, sind heute Sammlerstücke. Grannis verteilte sie an jeden, den er traf.

Les fameux stickers de « Granny » réalisés par Stuart Lough sont devenus des collectors. Grannis continuait de les distribuer généreusement autour de lui.

*Page 2*
**Palos Verdes Cove, California, 1967**
Backlit late afternoon on the trail down to Palos Verdes Cove.

Der Weg hinunter in die Bucht von Palos Verdes im spätnachmittäglichen Gegenlicht.

Soleil aveuglant de fin d'après-midi sur le chemin côtier qui mène à la plage de Palos Verdes Cove.

*Pages 4–5*
**Malibu, California, 1967**
At Malibu's infamous "Pit" during the Summer of Love, an impromptu hair-cutting session draws a crowd.

Im berüchtigten „Pit" von Malibu im Sommer der Liebe: Eine Menschenmenge versammelt sich bei einer spontanen Haarschneideaktion.

Pendant le « Summer of Love », un salon de coiffure improvisé attire les curieux sur la plage de Malibu, près du « Puits de l'enfer ».

*Pages 6–7*
**Malibu, California, 1965**
"The 'Bu" in full Sunday glory during a late spring swell. Today, on a good day, there might be more than 150 surfers out jockeying for an empty wave at Malibu.

Malibu, auch „The 'Bu" genannt, an einem herrlichen Sonntag mit einem Spätfrühlings-Swell. Heute kann man in Malibu an einem guten Tag über 150 Surfer beobachten, die im Wasser auf eine freie Welle warten.

Swell idéal à « The 'Bu » par un beau dimanche de fin de printemps. Aujourd'hui, à Malibu, les « jours de gros » peuvent attirer plus de 150 surfeurs prêts à en découdre pour être les premiers sur les vagues « libres ».

*Pages 8–9*
**Phil Edwards, Haleiwa, Hawaii, 1962**
Edwards, "the Guayule Kid" from Oceanside, California, was a visionary surfer once voted the best in the world for his radical power and grace.

Edwards, „the Guayule Kid" aus Oceanside in Kalifornien, war ein bahnbrechender Wellenreiter, der für seine Energie und Anmut zum besten Surfer der Welt gewählt wurde.

Phil Edwards, surnommé « The Guayule Kid » d'après la localité dont il est originaire, près d'Oceanside en Californie, était un surfeur visionnaire. Sa puissance et sa grâce hors pair lui ont valu le titre de meilleur surfeur du monde.

*Pages 10–11*
**22nd Street, Hermosa Beach, California, 1963**

*Pages 12–13*
**Fred Hemmings, Waimea, 1967**
Hemmings was part of the conservative North Shore old guard that was left behind by the pwsychedelic vanguard. "They were rock 'n' rollers," he said, "while I tried to waltz with waves."

Hemmings gehörte zur konservativen alten Schule des North Shore, die von der psychedelischen Avantgarde überholt wurde. „Das waren Rock'n'Roller", sagte er. „Ich wollte mit den Wellen Walzer tanzen."

Fred Hemmings faisait partie de la vieille école du surf du North Shore qui fut balayée par la vague de l'avant-garde psychédélique. « La mode était au rock 'n' roll, tandis que moi, je m'exerçais encore à danser la valse avec les vagues », confia-t-il un jour.

*Pages 14–15*
**San Onofre, California, 1963**
With its wide beaches, grass shacks, and long, rolling waves, San Onofre is called "California's Waikiki."

Die breiten Strände, strohgedeckten Hütten und langen, gleitenden Wellen trugen San Onofre den Titel „Waikiki von Kalifornien" ein.

Avec ses vastes plages, ses cabanons à toit de paille et ses longues vagues déferlantes, San Onofre est surnommé le « Waikiki californien ».

*Pages 16–17*
**Makaha, Hawaii, 1962**
A classic forties-era woody flanked by a crew of young surfers between heats at the Makaha Championships. Left to right: unidentified, Ivan Vanetta, Frank Grannis, Paul Strauch, Candy Calhoun, Robin Calhoun.

Ein toller alter Ford Woody aus den Vierzigerjahren mit einer Gruppe junger Surfer zwischen den Heats bei den Makaha Championships. Von links nach rechts: unbekannt, Ivan Vanetta, Frank Grannis, Paul Strauch, Candy Calhoun, Robin Calhoun.

Une équipe de jeunes surfeurs pose devant un Ford Woody typique des années 1940 entre deux heats de la prestigieuse compétition de Makaha. De gauche à droite : Ivan Vanetta, Frank Grannis, Paul Strauch, Candy Calhoun et Robin Calhoun.

*Pages 18–19*
**Waimea Bay, Hawaii, 1967**
Greg Noll, Eddie Aikau (red board), Bobby Cloutier (diving). This photo won third place in a 1970 *LIFE* magazine photo contest.

Greg Noll, Eddie Aikau (rotes Brett), Bobby Cloutier (beim Sprung). Dieses Foto erhielt 1970 den dritten Platz bei einem Fotowettbewerb der Zeitschrift *LIFE*.

Greg Noll, Eddie Aikau (planche rouge) et Bobby Cloutier (en train de plonger). Ce cliché remportera le troisième prix d'un concours photographique organisé en 1970 par le magazine *LIFE*.

*Pages 398–399*
**Pupukea, 1970**
Sunset over Kaena Point. The ancient Hawaiians believed that Kaena is where dead souls walked over the Rainbow Bridge to the afterlife.

Sonnenuntergang über Kaena Point. Früher glaubten die Hawaiianer, dass in Kaena die Seelen der Verstorbenen über die Regenbogenbrücke ins Jenseits gingen.

Coucher de soleil sur Kaena Point. Dans la croyance des anciens Hawaïens, Kaena est le lieu où les âmes défuntes traversent le Pont Arc-en-Ciel pour rejoindre l'au-delà.

*Page 400*
**LeRoy Grannis, Carlsbad, California, 2001**
Photo: James Cassimus.

# Bibliography

Barrett, Bradley Wayne. *Grannis: Surfing's Golden Age, 1960–1969.* San Clemente: Surfer's Journal, 1998.

Doyle, Mike and Steve Sorenson. *Morning Glass: The Adventures of Legendary Waterman Mike Doyle.* Three Rivers: Manzanita Press, 1993.

George, Sam. *The Perfect Day: 40 Years of Surfer Magazine.* San Francisco: Chronicle Books, 2001.

Lueras, Leonard. *Surfing, the Ultimate Pleasure.* New York: Workman Publishing, 1984.

Jenkins, Bruce. *North Shore Chronicles: Big-Wave Surfing in Hawaii.* Berkeley: North Atlantic Books, 1990.

Kampion, Drew. *Stoked: A History of Surf Culture.* Santa Monica: General Publishing Group, 1997.

Noll, Greg, and Andrea Gabbard. *Da Bull: Life Over the Edge.* Berkeley: North Atlantic Books, 1989.

Stecyk, Craig, and David Carson. *Surf Culture: The Art History of Surfing.* Laguna Beach: Ginko Press, 2002.

Stecyk, Craig, Drew Kampion, and Steve Pezman. *Dora Lives: The Authorized Story of Miki Dora.* New York: D.A.P./T. Adler Books, 2005.

Warshaw, Matt. *The Encyclopedia of Surfing.* Orlando: Harcourt, Inc., 2003.

Wright, Bank. *Surfing California; A Complete Guide to the California Coast.* Redondo Beach: Mañana Publishing, 1973.

# Acknowledgments

The author would like to thank: Steve Pezman, Brad Barrett, Matt Warshaw, Art Brewer, Randy Rarick, Gerry Lopez, Drew Kampion, Bernie Baker, Jon Close, Robert Lindkvist, Greg MacGillivray, Mickey Muñoz, Mike Doyle, Bruce Gabrielson, Huntington Beach Surf Club, Janet Duckworth, Marilyn Barilotti, Nina Wiener, Kate Soto, Jim Heimann, and LeRoy Grannis.
—Steve Barilotti, San Diego

From the editor: My sincere thanks go to all who contributed to creating this book. First and foremost to Granny, who was on board with the project from the beginning and was gracious and trusting in the handling of his original material. It was a wonderful experience to work with a legend, who transported me back in time with his tales and images. It was also a pleasure to get to know his wife, Katie, who provided Granny with companionship, support, and a fruitful life amid the waves.

My gratitude also goes to designer and surfer Paul Mussa, who created a clean and cool masterpiece; writer Steve Barilotti, who deftly put into words what I was thinking; Janet Duckworth; Tom Adler; Steve Pezman; Craig Stecyk; Benjamin Trigano; Matt Warshaw; and Mr. Taschen, who was as captivated as I was with Granny's work and gave the green light to a winner of a project. Gut gemacht, Blödmann!
—Jim Heimann, Los Angeles

# Imprint



**EACH AND EVERY TASCHEN BOOK PLANTS A SEED!**
Each year, we offset our annual carbon emissions with carbon credits at the Instituto Terra, a reforestation program in Minas Gerais, Brazil, founded by Lélia and Sebastião Salgado. To find out more about this ecological partnership, please check: taschen.com/institutoterra.
**Inspiration: unlimited.**
**Carbon footprint: (almost) zero.**

Want to see more? Visit taschen.com to view our current publications, browse our latest magazine, and subscribe to our newsletter.

© 2026 TASCHEN GmbH
Hohenzollernring 53, D-50672 Köln
**taschen.com**

Original edition: © 2006 TASCHEN GmbH

Printed in Bosnia-Herzegovina
ISBN 978–3–8365–6679–7

# The Photographer

LeRoy Grannis's initial foray into surfing began at age 14, but it wasn't until the age of 42 that he picked up a camera and made a career out of it. Under doctor's orders to take up a hobby, Grannis built a darkroom in his garage and began shooting surfers at Hermosa Beach, and "Photo: Grannis" quickly became a hallmark of the California surf scene of the 1960s. Grannis is considered one of the most important documentarians of the sport, and was inducted into the Surfing Hall of Fame in 1966. He died on February 3, 2011.

LeRoy Grannis machte seine ersten Surf-Erfahrungen mit 14. Doch erst mit 42 Jahren begann er zu fotografieren und damit berühmt zu werden. Weil ihm sein Arzt nahe legte, sich ein Hobby zu suchen, richtete er in seiner Garage eine Dunkelkammer ein und fotografierte die Surfer am Hermosa Beach. Bald wurden seine Motive in großen Surf-Magazinen veröffentlicht und Grannis wurde zu einer der bedeutendsten Persönlichkeiten der kalifornischen Surf-Szene der sechziger Jahre. Er gilt noch heute als einer der wichtigsten Dokumentatoren dieses Sports und wurde 1966 in die Surfing Hall of Fame aufgenommen. Er starb am 3. Februar 2011.

Si LeRoy Grannis s'est lancé dans le surf à 14 ans, ce n'est qu'à 42 ans qu'il s'est jeté à l'eau avec son appareil photo pour en faire son métier. Les médecins lui ayant recommandé de se trouver un hobby, Grannis s'est construit une chambre noire dans son garage et a commencé à photographier des surfeurs à Hermosa Beach. Ses photos n'ont pas tardé à se retrouver dans les magazines de surf émergents, et « Photo : Grannis » s'est vite imposé comme marque incontournable du monde du surf californien des années 1960. Grannis, qui fait partie des plus grands documentaristes de ce sport, a fait son entrée au Surfing Hall of Fame en 1966. Il est mort le 3 fevrier 2011.

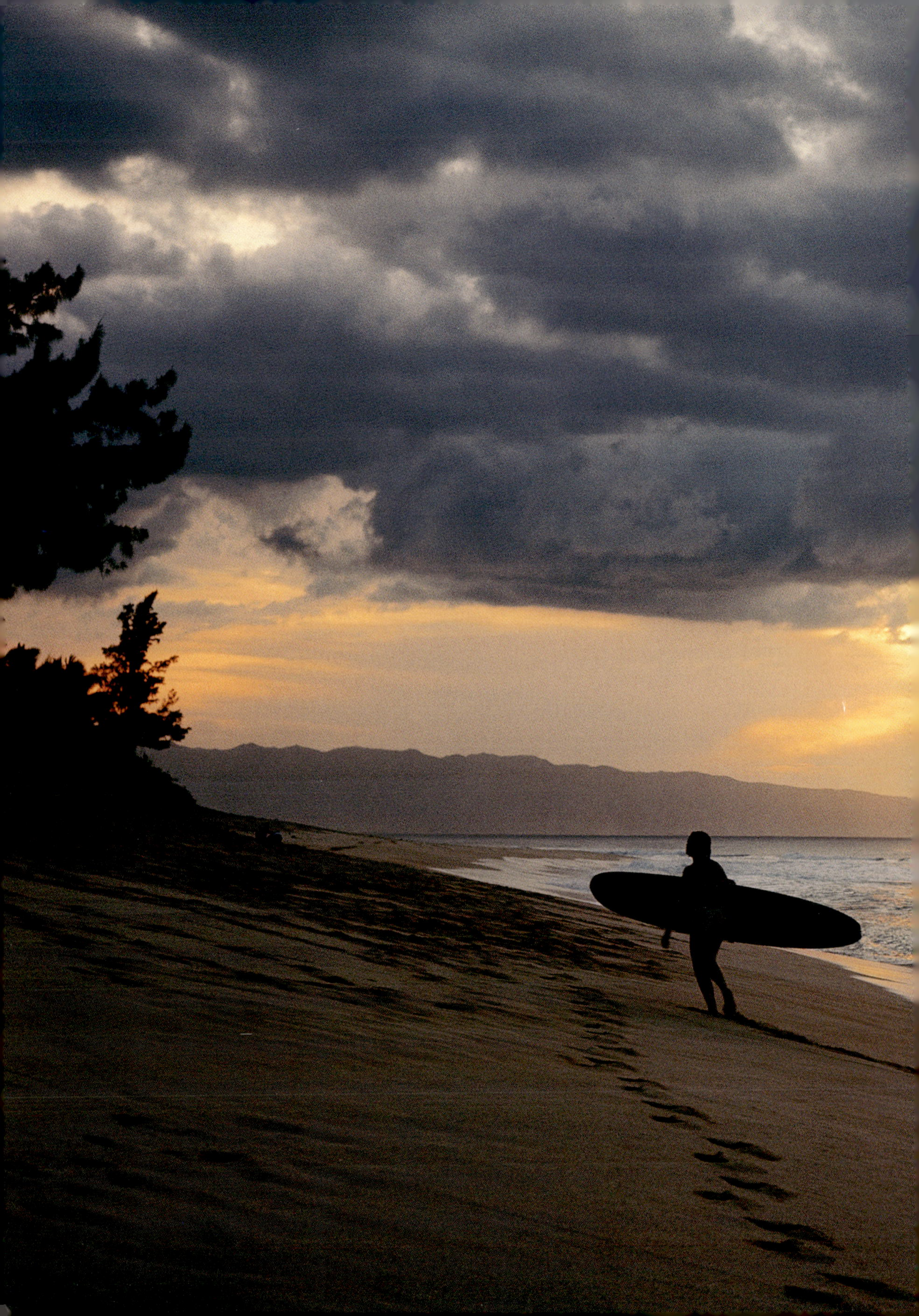

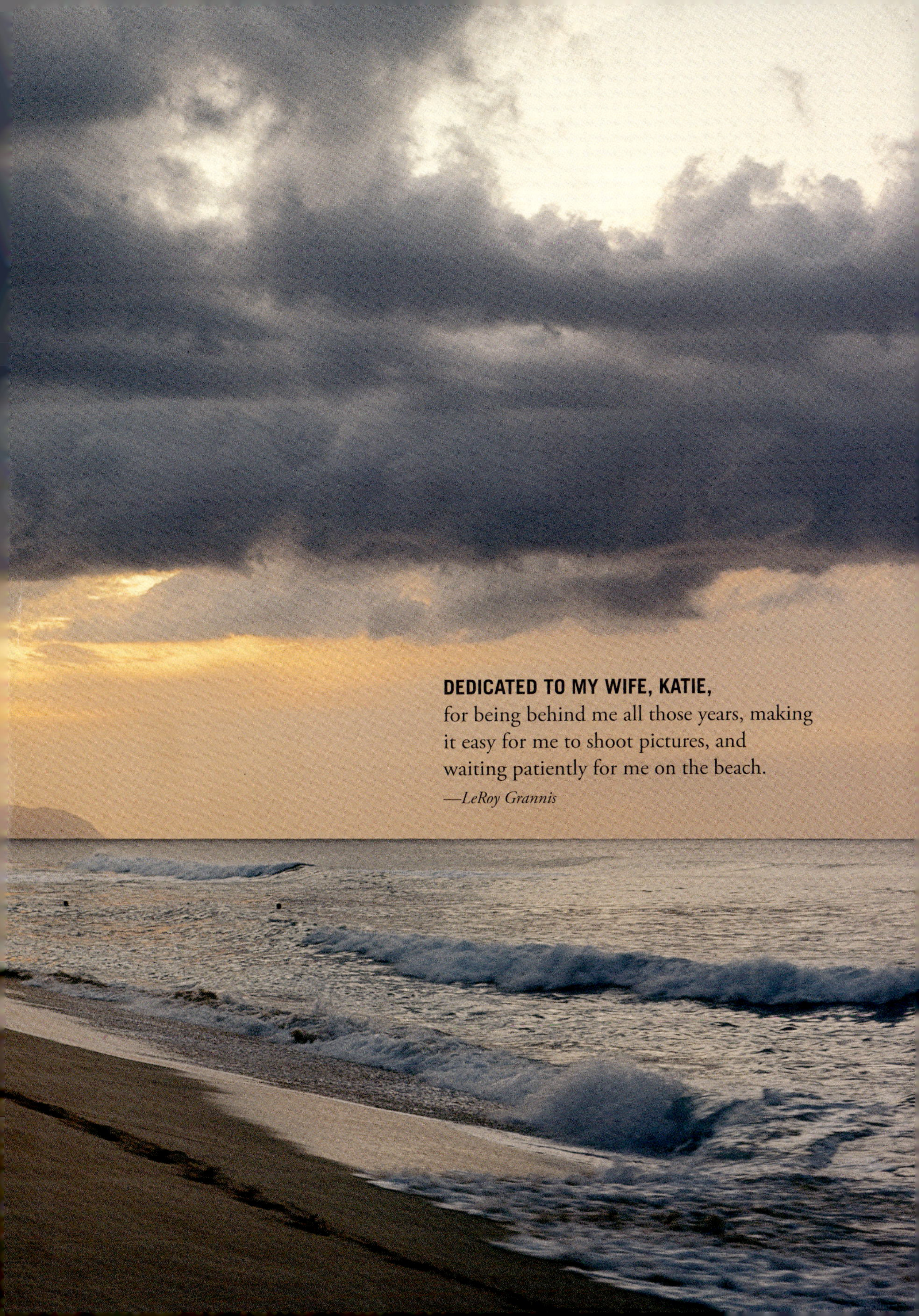

DEDICATED TO MY WIFE, KATIE,
for being behind me all those years, making
it easy for me to shoot pictures, and
waiting patiently for me on the beach.
—LeRoy Grannis

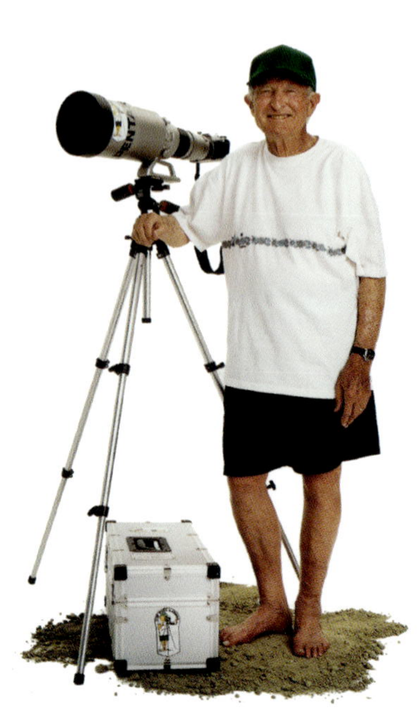

**"LeRoy Grannis had an eye for the perfect wave... The secret of his photographs lies in the tranquility despite the excitement, the sublime aspect of the risk involved."**
*Surfers*

The editor:
**Jim Heimann** is the Executive Editor for TASCHEN. A cultural anthropologist, historian, and an avid collector, he has authored numerous titles on architecture, pop culture, and the history of Los Angeles and Hollywood, including TASCHEN's *Surfing, Los Angeles. Portrait of a City, California Crazy*, and the *All-American Ads* series.

The author:
Working as *SURFER* magazine's editor at large for over a decade, photojournalist **Steve Barilotti** has made it his business to document the sport, art, and lore of surfing. He has also contributed to *The Perfect Day* and written the texts for books by renowned surf photographers Art Brewer and Ted Grambeau.

**ALSO AVAILABLE**

### Surfing. 1778–Today
Jim Heimann

"The undisputed bible of surf culture."
*Vogue*

### Los Angeles. Portrait of a City
Kevin Starr, David L. Ulin, Jim Heimann

"A photographic celebration of L.A."
*Los Angeles Times*

### California Crazy. American Pop Architecture
Jim Heimann

"Heimann's bible of oddball buildings has opened many eyes to the fascinating catalysts behind an architectural subculture that is widely ignored by traditional academics."
*AnOther Magazine*